After the Civil Wars

Pearson
Education

After the Civil Wars

English Politics and Government in the Reign of Charles II

John Miller

An imprint of Pearson Education

Harlow, England · London · New York · Reading, Massachusetts · San Francisco · Toronto · Don Mills, Ontario · Sydney
Tokyo · Singapore · Hong Kong · Seoul · Taipei · Cape Town · Madrid · Mexico City · Amsterdam · Munich · Paris · Milan

In memory of Ken Haley and John Kenyon

Pearson Education Limited
Edinburgh Gate
Harlow
Essex CM20 2JE
England

and Associated Companies throughout the world

Visit us on the World Wide Web at:
www.pearsoneduc.com

First published 2000

ISBN 0-582-29898-9 PPR
ISBN 0-582-29899-7 CSD

British Library Cataloguing-in-Publication Data

A catalogue record for this book is available from the British Library

Library of Congress Cataloging-in-Publication Data

Miller, John, 1946–
After the Civil Wars : government in the reign of Charles II / John Miller.
p. cm.
Includes bibliographical references (p.) and index.
ISBN 0–582–29898–9 (PPR) — ISBN 0–582–29899–7 (CSD)
1. Great Britain—Politics and government—1660–1688. 2. Great Britain—History—Charles II, 1660–1685. I. Title.

DA445.M44 2000
941.06′6—dc21 00–042426

Set in 35 in 11/12pt Adobe Garamond
Produced by Pearson Education Asia Pte Ltd.
Printed in Singapore

Contents

Preface *page vii*
Prologue *1*

Part one: The working of politics

1 Rulers and ruled **7**
A self-governing people 7
The law 10

2 Centre and localities **19**
Policy- and decision-making 19
Local government 23
The means of coercion 26

3 Favour and reward **35**
The mechanisms of patronage 35
The nature of rewards 41

4 News **53**
The demand for news 53
Print 55
Handwritten news 58
Word of mouth 63

5 Popular politics **72**
The nature of popular politics 72
Riot 76
Elections 83

6 Parliament **99**
Representatives and represented 99
The business of Parliament 101
King and Parliament 105

Part two: Political division and conflict

7 The issues: I. Popery and arbitrary government **111**
The ancient constitution 111
Anti-popery 115
Popery and arbitrary government 118

8 The issues: II. Church and Dissent **126**
Before the Restoration 126
The Restoration settlement 132
Church and people 135
The nature of Dissent: Presbyterians 141
The nature of Dissent: Independents, Baptists and Quakers 144
Persecution 147

9 The frustrations of the Cavaliers, 1660–64 **161**
The liquidation of the past 161
The resentments of the Cavaliers 164
The machinery of coercion 169
The Corporation Act 171
The church settlement 174
The Cavaliers' revenge? 181

10 Politics in flux, 1664–73 **195**
The second Dutch war and its aftermath 195
The Cabal 198
Church and Dissent 202

11 The rebirth of party, 1673–78 **217**
Danby and the direction of policy 217
Danby and the patronage system 222
Partisan divisions: Parliament 226
Partisan divisions: the localities 227
The politicization of the legal system 235

12 'Guelphs and Ghibellines', 1679–81 **245**
A county divided 245
The political issues: an exclusion crisis? 249
Church and Dissent 254
The process of political division 256
Elections 257
Petitions and addresses 261
The law 263

13 The triumph of the Tories, 1681–85 **272**
Tory and Whig 272
Royal policy 277
Church and Dissent 279
The law 283
The towns 285
The general election of 1685 288

Abbreviations *296*
Select bibliography *301*
Glossary *307*
Index *312*

Preface

This book has been a long time in gestation. Although I have spent much of the last thirty years working on the politics of Restoration England, my focus has mostly been on 'high' politics: royal policy-making, the workings of the royal court, the relationship of king and Parliament. Although I have been aware of the local reactions – real and perceived – to what happened at the centre, these have usually played only a minor, peripheral part in my published work. I have, however, become more and more aware that this left an imbalance in my understanding, a large void that needed to be filled. That awareness was fuelled in part by the work of other scholars of early modern England: 'political' historians who are learning to place 'politics' in a much wider social and cultural context and 'social' historians who are placing increasing stress on the 'politics' of social interaction. It also owes much to experience, not only of research in an ever-widening range of archives, but also of teaching – organizing ideas and trying to explain them, as well as learning from students' awkward questions and different perspectives. Since the early 1980s I have been accumulating material on towns, elections, riots and other topics, in the hope that some day I would be able to write a full-scale study of how Restoration politics worked. When in 1994–95 I enjoyed my first ever year of sabbatical leave, I began to reorder my material and to assess what else I needed to read. I originally intended to include several 'case study' chapters, but having written the first (a substantial piece on Norfolk) I decided instead to integrate the material into the main body of the work. In addition, having intended the book to be essentially thematic, partly to avoid the risk of going again over familiar ground, I came to appreciate the crucial importance of change over time. As a result, the chronological chapters are now much more substantial than I originally planned, but I have been careful to focus on the local dimension – and especially the theme of political and religious division – sketching in only as much of the 'high' political background as is necessary to understand what is going on. At the same time, the many years I spent studying the course of political events have proved invaluable in picking up nuances, making connections and (not least) knowing who people are. Without that experience, I could not have written this book.

Two final points. First, this is unshamedly a work on English (and Welsh) history. The political and social structures of Scotland and Ireland were very different from those of England, and their relationship with England added further complexities. Had I extended my focus to embrace all of the British Isles, this book would have been much longer and much less coherent. Secondly, I decided at an early stage not to carry the story through to 1688. It seems to me that there is a certain coherence, a symmetry about Charles II's reign. For much of the time the issues and divisions of the civil wars remained relevant and at the beginning and end of the reign they were crucial; the Exclusion Crisis seemed to many a re-run of 1640–42. By contrast, James II radically altered political alignments and the context and content of political debate. His reign undoubtedly deserves further study, but not here.

In the course of my researches I have incurred many debts of thanks. I am most grateful to the Duke of Beaufort, the Duke of Norfolk, the Marquess Townshend, the Arundell family and John Montagu for permission to read manuscripts in their possession and to the Master and Fellows of Magdalene College, Cambridge, for access to the Pepys Library. Having worked in many libraries and archives, I have been struck by the courtesy and kindness shown by their staff in what for many are difficult times, but I should like to single out the staff of Duke Humfrey's Library at the Bodleian, the British Library Manuscripts Department Students' Room, Durham University Library, Norfolk Record Office, QMW Library and (last, but not least) the Institute of Historical Research, which is in many ways in a league of its own as a scholarly resource and a centre of historical excellence. I am very grateful to the many historians, young and older, who attend the Institute's Seminar in Seventeenth-Century British History. The seminar papers and the discussions afterwards, formal and informal, are a constant source of stimulation and information. The seminar makes it much easier to keep in touch with the work being done on the period by a number of impressive younger historians on both sides of the Atlantic, whose influence on this book is very apparent: Perry Gauci, Mark Goldie, Paul Halliday, Mark Knights, Steve Pincus and Jonathan Scott, to name but a few. The seminar also benefits greatly from the contribution of members of the staff of the History of Parliament. If I have tended to stress the importance of conviviality in this book, that too may owe something to the seminar. I should also like to remark that, while there is plenty of lively historical debate among historians of the Restoration period, it is almost invariably courteous and good humoured. On a more individual level, I am most grateful to James Jones for reading and commenting on my draft chapter on Norfolk. Many years ago, shortly after he examined my Ph.D., I mentioned that I thought I might try to investigate the continuities, or otherwise, between the two sides in the civil wars and the parties in the Exclusion Crisis. He dissuaded me and I can see now that he was right. I have also learned a lot – often much more than they realise – from many of my students and especially Beverly Adams and Bob Birmingham, to whom many thanks. As usual, my family and particularly my wife have had to put up with my absence on research trips and my reluctance (when present) to be distracted from writing; I am most grateful for their patience and forbearance. My final debt of thanks is recorded in the dedication, to two fine scholars, alas no longer with us, who worked on this period when it was less fashionable than it is now and who gave me every assistance and encouragement over many years. Whatever qualities I may possess as a historian, I owe in considerable part to them.

John Miller
London, September 1999.

A note on spellings and dates

All spellings have been modernized and punctuation has been added, where necessary. Dates in the text are 'old style', as before the calendar revision of 1752. The year is taken as starting on 1 January and not, as in the seventeenth century, 25 March. Foreign ambassadors followed the 'new style' calendar used on the continent in dating their dispatches, so when these have been cited by date NS (new style) has been added.

Prologue

On 3 May 1660 a group of Somerset gentlemen met at Hinton St George, the home of Lord Poulett, a leading local Royalist. At one o'clock letters arrived from London, containing news of the meeting of the Commons and Lords on 1 May, at which the king's Declaration of Breda had been read. The Lords had declared that, by the fundamental laws of the kingdom, the government should be by king, Lords and Commons and the Commons had agreed.[1] The gentlemen read the letters joyfully, kissed the royal coat of arms and went into the cellar to drink the king's health. Lord Poulett sent out couriers with printed papers giving the news and summoned the parish and his near neighbours to meet him at the old warren, whither he sent 'two cartloads of faggots, a hogshead of March ale, six dozen of bottles of claret wine, neats' tongues, pies &c without number'. Around seven the neighbours appeared, bringing not only faggots but 'substantial belly timber'. 'Well the linen was spread upon a fair green carpet and upon that the dishes and upon them fell we first one round and then another.' At that stage 'the people thought it was now a time they might storm in and that they could not be merry enough for this news without being mad.' They threw 'fire into the faggots, wine and ale into themselves' and their hats into the air. As darkness fell 'so many bonfires appeared about us far and near that if we had not known the true cause of it we should have apprehended a general rising of the fanatics', who, if they had chosen to rise, would 'have catched their sturdiest opponents not napping but soundly asleep'.[2]

This account, by the spendidly named Amyas Poulett, is one of many describing the celebrations of the proclamation of Charles II and his triumphal return to his kingdom. The news was greeted with bonfires and bells, eating and drinking, maypoles and morris dancing.[3] When he entered London on 29 May, the road thirty miles and more from the capital was lined with people; over a hundred thousand waited on Blackheath. In London, the streets were strewn with flowers and the fountains ran with wine.[4] It is easy to dismiss such enthusiasm as a transient spasm, enhanced by strong drink. Time would show that Charles could not possibly fulfil the many, often conflicting, hopes of those who hailed his return. Time would also show that the initial impression he created of dignity, responsibility and even piety was misleading. Disillusionment set in, exacerbated by humiliating defeat in the Dutch War of 1665–67. Within twenty years there were widespread fears of another civil war and his relationship with Parliament had deteriorated to a point where he refused to summon it in the last four years of his reign.

There are several ways of explaining this disillusionment. One would be that Charles inherited the malevolent intentions (and/or incompetence) of his father. Another would be that Parliament, having tasted power in the civil wars, was determined to impose its will on a feckless king. Yet another would be that the divisions of civil war were too deep to allow a return to the old ways. Even in Poulett's Somerset Eden there were serpents, 'the poor malcontent fanatics', who skulked indoors listening to the shouts of celebration.[5] There is a vigorous historiographical tradition that the upheavals of 1640–60 were so profound that nothing could be the same again: the ideas then unleashed, and the execution of the king, fatally damaged the ideological foundations of the old regime.[6] It has always struck me as odd that historians of France argue that the mid-century upheavals strengthened the monarchy by creating a yearning for stability, while historians of England often argue the exact opposite. It is one thing to say that the new ideas of the Interregnum had the **potential** to undermine the traditional order; it is quite another to show that they did so. How one views the Restoration regime depends very much on one's vantage point. Seen from 1688, it could appear flimsy. Looking from 1685, Charles II has defeated the Whigs and imposed his will on London; James II's control over the electoral system secures him the most compliant Parliament of the century. We are often warned against teleology, the assumption that because something happened it was bound to happen. No scheme of historical inevitability could possibly accommodate James II.

The assumption that the civil wars irrevocably changed England is often linked to the claim that they were the products of long-term structural weaknesses in English society. In recent years, historians such as John Morrill and Conrad Russell have argued that civil war was much less likely in the mid seventeenth century than it had been a century before, when England faced the destabilizing forces of rapid and contentious agrarian change, dynastic uncertainty and conflict between Protestant and Catholic. Under the early Stuarts there were riots in the countryside rather than rebellions, the dynasty was secure and Protestantism had triumphed. In addition, the military power of the nobility had withered away in England – although not in Scotland. Looking for destabilizing forces in early Stuart England, historians now focus on the fraught interrelationship of England, Scotland and Ireland; the tensions within English Protestantism; the financial problems of the English crown; and above all, 'the man Charles Stuart'.[7]

The perception that civil war was profoundly unlikely in seventeenth-century England can be supported by recent studies of social relationships and of the workings of English government and law. While giving due weight to tensions and conflicts, social and legal historians have emphasized the ways in which these could be contained and resolved. Neighbours and superiors pressed contending parties to resolve disputes by agreement rather than by prosecution and punishment. Mediation, arbitration and a preference for restitution rather than revenge were all part of what one historian has called a 'culture of reconciliation'.[8] Grafted onto an older awareness of the extent of popular participation in government and an emphasis on consensus and cooperation in politics, these new insights suggest a society which was rather good at avoiding deep and lasting divisions.

And yet such divisions opened up with a vengeance in the civil wars, which had an immense impact on the English people and created an unprecedented level of popular political consciousness. Another recent body of historical work examines the impact of the ideological divisions of the civil wars on the reign of Charles II. One unfortunate side-effect of decades of searching for the holy grail of 'the causes of the civil war' in the century before 1640, and the assumption that nothing could be the same afterwards, has been to create an almost impermeable barrier between the periods before and after 1660 – for historians of politics at least. This in turn has led to the practice, started (as far as I know) by Betty Kemp, of treating the period 1660–1832 as 'the long eighteenth century'.[9] While this concept appears to be widely accepted by historians of the eighteenth century proper, the same cannot be said of scholars of the Restoration. Jonathan Scott has argued forcefully that it is impossible to understand Restoration politics without understanding the civil wars. Not only did the wars scar the English psyche, but the issues which they raised – the nature of the English monarchy, the divisions within Protestantism – were to be raised again under Charles II and indeed well after 1688.[10] This is a viewpoint which I broadly share: one purpose of this book is to reconnect the Restoration period to what had gone before and to see the continuities as well as the discontinuities of seventeenth-century England.

My aim in writing this book is much wider than that, however. I also wish to investigate how politics **worked**. I use the term 'politics' in a wider sense than most political historians, a sense closer to that employed by social historians interested in power relationships and dispute resolution, often within small communities.[11] I also wish to consider how individuals and groups pursued material as well as ideological objectives. This view of politics would seem natural to historians of France, where much of the bargaining and brokerage which are an inescapable part of 'politics' occurred within the royal administration and involved interminable appeals and counter-appeals and the creation of complex clientage networks.[12] It requires an investigation of patronage, lobbying and the practicalities of getting things done. It also involves a consideration of the workings of local government and the legal system, of the role of Parliament and the activities of MPs. Much of the picture that emerges comes from the patient accumulation of small details but at times – as with discussion of the criminal law or political ideas – I have been able to draw on a rich existing literature.

The organizing principle behind the book is the tension between 'consensus' and 'contention'. On one hand, there was an administrative and legal system and a political culture which encouraged and facilitated the peaceful resolution of disputes and tended to contain divisions of interest and ideology. On the other, the political and religious divisions bequeathed by civil war tended to divide communities, Parliament and the nation itself. One central argument is that it was far from a foregone conclusion that contention would triumph over consensus – indeed, it was only in the last years of the reign that it did so. This organizing principle has dictated the structure of the book. Part I deals with the working of politics, Part II with the major issues and with the extent to which they dictated the direction of politics during the reign.

Notes

1 *LJ*, XI.8–9; *CJ*, VIII.8.
2 BRO, AC/C64/81.
3 Pepys, I.121–2; H. Newcome, *Autobiography*, ed. R. Parkinson, 2 vols, Chetham Soc., 1852, I.121; D. Underdown, *Revel, Riot and Rebellion: Popular Politics and Culture in England, 1603–60*, Oxford, 1985, pp. 271–5.
4 *HMC 5th Report*, p. 167; Evelyn, III.246.
5 BRO, AC/C64/81.
6 L. Stone, *The Causes of the English Revolution, 1529–1642*, London, 1972, pp. 146–7. The same assumption permeates Mark Kishlanksy's *Parliamentary Selection*, discussed at length in chapter 5.
7 See for instance C. Russell, *The Causes of the English Civil War*, Oxford, 1990; Morrill, *Nature*, pp. 1–6.
8 C. Muldrew, 'The Culture of Reconciliation and the Settlement of Economic Disputes in early modern England', *HJ*, XXXIX, 1996, pp. 915–42.
9 B. Kemp, *King and Commons, 1660–1832*, London, 1957. J.C.D. Clark further developed the idea in *English Society, 1688–1832*, Cambridge, 1985 and *Revolution and Rebellion*, Cambridge, 1986.
10 J. Scott, 'Radicalism and Restoration: The Shape of the Stuart Experience', *HJ*, XXXI, 1988, pp. 453–67; J. Scott, *Algernon Sidney and the Restoration Crisis, 1677–83*, Cambridge, 1991, chs 1–4.
11 See, for example, K. Wrightson, 'The Politics of the Parish in Early Modern England' in P. Griffiths, A. Fox and S. Hindle (eds), *The Experience of Authority in Early Modern England*, London, 1996, ch. 1.
12 See R. Bonney, *Political Change in France under Richelieu and Mazarin*, Oxford, 1978; A.L. Moote, *The Revolt of the Judges: The Parlement of Paris and the Fronde*, Princeton, 1971; S. Kettering, *Patrons, Brokers and Clients in Seventeenth-Century France*, New York, 1986; C. Giry-Deloison and R. Mettam (eds), *Patronages et Clientelismes 1550–1750*, Lille, 1995.

Part one

THE WORKING OF POLITICS

Chapter one

Rulers and ruled

A self-governing people

Long before the Restoration, in December 1596, as the effects of a third consecutive bad harvest began to bite, a self-constituted group of 'chief inhabitants' met in Swallowfield. Swallowfield was neither a village nor (strictly speaking) a parish, and although it was located in Berkshire, part of it belonged jurisdictionally to Wiltshire. Concerned at the 'disorderly' conduct of the poor, whether expressed in 'backbiting' or hedge-breaking, drunkenness or promiscuity, the 'chief inhabitants' drew up what was in effect a village constitution. Noting that the Wiltshire JPs 'are far off', they set down a series of articles for the government of the community, 'to the end we may the better and more quietly live together in good love and amity to the praise of God and for the better serving of her majesty'. The articles dealt with a range of matters, including the relief of the 'honest' poor and the proper observance of the sabbath. Despite the rhetoric of harmony and unity, the articles called for stern action against 'disorderly' elements within the community: habitual drunkards were to be set in the stocks and 'inmates' who could not support themselves were, if possible, to be prevented from marrying.[1]

The Swallowfield articles offer an extraordinary illustration of the capacity of English villagers to organize themselves into a 'body politic' and to order their own affairs. As far as they can be identified, these 'chief inhabitants' were drawn from the 'middling' elements in the village, who served as churchwardens and jurymen, but were well below gentry status.[2] Their experience of office and other responsibilities within the community will have given them an insight into the practicalities and problems of government. Their perception of themselves as the 'chief' inhabitants, the 'better sort' in economic and moral terms, provided the imperative and the justification to order the lives of their humbler and less self-disciplined neighbours. Their concerns were by no means unique: a similar concern with moral order and the avoidance of division could be found in other villages, where it often found organizational expression in the vestry – a 'parish council', which might be elected by the parishioners, but which was increasingly likely to be self-selecting as the seventeenth century wore on.[3] In corporate towns there was no need to create or adapt a body dedicated to the maintenance of order and good governance. Empowered by their charters to form themselves into a body politic, borough corporations dispensed justice, managed charitable funds and oversaw the enforcement of the poor laws and so exercised considerable control over the lives of the townspeople. In many towns they deployed their authority in a struggle to create a more truly Christian community – sober, industrious, morally upright and above all God-fearing.[4] Nor did such efforts cease after 1660. The Norwich mayor's court continued to battle against disorderly alehouses, scolds and quarrellers, fought to keep the sabbath holy and tried to ban smoking in the streets.[5]

Norwich was (by the standards of the time) a large city, with a sophisticated polity and virtually complete jurisdictional autonomy from the surrounding county. The rulers of smaller towns had less extensive powers, those of rural parishes fewer still. And yet they used what powers they possessed and invoked outside authorities where necessary. In many towns and villages in the first half of the seventeenth century, those who controlled the raising and spending of the poor rate denied relief to the 'undeserving' – the idle, drunken and promiscuous. In the Vale of Gloucester in the 1590s, churchwardens repeatedly cited parishioners before the local church courts on charges of absence from church, failure to take communion or sexual misconduct. Their proceedings emphasized the integrity and unity of the parish, but 'unity' was maintained by the demonization and humiliation of deviants: the courts imposed 'shame' punishments, carried out in front of the congregation.[6] Ducking scolds and flogging vagrants served a similar function as warnings to the wayward and reaffirmations of the values upheld by the 'better sort' in the community.

This brief discussion of parish and urban government raises several points of considerable relevance for this study. First, there was a long tradition of local and communal self-government, exemplified in the corporations and the vestries, but also in manorial courts and the multifarious juries which identified problems and offered solutions. As at Swallowfield, many villagers held offices and served on juries. Not all offices were eagerly sought. The post of village constable was one which many tried to avoid: it was easy to be blamed for being too slack or too officious (or both). The post of sheriff in most counties and many boroughs involved a lot of expense and trouble and many were prepared to pay good money to avoid the honour. Public service was a duty, which to some extent was a function of one's standing in the community. Members of the leading county families could expect to serve as justices of the peace and deputy lieutenants (although there are signs after 1660 that some sought to avoid the former position). Leading merchants and businessmen saw service in civic office as their duty. Members of the 'better sort' in villages served as churchwardens. Given the miniscule state apparatus inherited by Charles II – apart from tax collectors there were virtually no paid officials in the provinces – it was vital to enlist the leading men of the localities in local government. They possessed the local knowledge, the local standing and (in the case of the gentry) the leisure needed for effective local government and they were ready to serve without pay. Such recompense as they received (apart from the satisfaction of a clear conscience or of a good job well done) was in the form of prestige, deference and respect, elaborate courtesy often reinforced by hospitality and sociability.

The extent of popular participation ensured a high level of knowledge and a sophisticated understanding of government among Charles II's subjects and very definite expectations about how it should be carried on, as Charles I had discovered to his cost in the 1630s. Given the king's dependence on his subjects in the localities this could pose problems, especially if their conception of good governance did not match his. With no police force other than the militia and town watches (both composed of ordinary citizens), together with the beleaguered village constable, the king's powers of coercion were limited. Indeed, had royal government depended on coercing a recalcitrant populace, England would quickly have crumbled into chaos. But, as at Swallowfield, the main concern of the 'better sort' in county, town and parish was to maintain **order**, under the crown. Moreover, they understood 'order' in a sense much broader than a lack of serious violence and the peaceful resolution of disputes. Their conception embraced an essentially Christian moral order which extended into the economic domain: the regulation of markets, weights and measures and quality control in cloth manufacture.[7] If Charles II proved able to rule England effectively, it was because on most issues for most of the time, he and the 'natural rulers' of the localities were pulling in the same direction. Despite their image of rebelliousness and disorder, transmitted across Europe as a result of the civil wars, the English were a very governable people, because they were prepared not only to be governed but also to participate constructively in the processes of government.

From the foregoing, it will be apparent that the relationships of 'rulers' and 'ruled' were complex. Parish and town officials were in a real sense answerable to their neighbours and fellow inhabitants, at least those of the 'better sort'. They lived in close proximity to those over whom they exercised authority, who shared their concern that property should be protected and 'good order' maintained. The 'better sort' (whether they held office or not) advised those who were considering litigation or criminal prosecutions and acted as arbiters in disputes, seeking to maintain communal harmony and avoid expensive recourse to the law. In so doing, they showed that alongside the formal structures of government were others which were informal. Although there were pressures to apply rules consistently, there were also pressures to apply them sensibly: a sense of natural justice, or fair play, could triumph over the letter of the law. The involvement of ordinary citizens in government made possible all sorts of bargaining and negotiation, in which personal contacts, patronage and clientage and the exchange of favours and courtesies could play their part (see Chapter 3). Often this worked to resolve conflicts more quickly and with less lasting rancour than if they had been taken to the courts. But it could also work against the marginal and the friendless, those perceived as undeserving, who were more likely to be prosecuted for theft and denied poor relief than their more respectable neighbours.

Given the extent of popular participation in government and the complex relationships which operated within and alongside formal structures of authority, many people were both 'rulers' and 'ruled'. Some relationships seem straightforward enough: parish overseers exercised considerable discretion in relieving the poor, but were answerable to county JPs. Others were not. Rotating chargeable offices meant that those wielding power over their neighbours could find the roles reversed the following year. Jury service inverted normal power relationships, as farmers decided the fate of gentlemen. Grand juries and hundred juries informed the JPs of the failings of the great as well as the humble. And, throughout, the workings of friendship, patronage and clientage bypassed normal procedures and the possibility of bargaining softened the impact of government on the people. It would therefore be a gross over-simplification to see government just as a 'top-down' process. It was partly that, and at times the burdens imposed by the state (especially taxes) provoked violent resistance. But the state and its law courts were also a **resource**, which people could **use** to achieve their ends.[8] They were encouraged to do so by a familiarity, born of participation, with government and law-enforcement. Moreover the state's varied elements made it a diverse resource: those who failed to receive satisfaction from the privy council could try the law courts, or petition Parliament. The fact that there were so many avenues available helped to reconcile opposing interests and contain conflict: disappointment in one area could be tempered by hope of success in another. This helps explain the apparent paradox, that a state with such minimal police resources saw little large-scale disorder.

The law

The extent of popular participation in government, and the ways in which informal or personal influences could shape seemingly impersonal processes, can be illustrated with reference to the law – by far the most widely used 'resource' provided by the Restoration state. The law provided the means for resolving disputes and obtaining redress for injuries suffered and in the seventeenth century the workings of the English criminal law reveal a strong concern with restitution as well as punishment.[9] The decision to prosecute in criminal cases was normally taken by the victim or their kin. They were responsible for gathering evidence and organizing witnesses and they had to bear the costs of even a successful prosecution. In deciding whether to prosecute they were influenced by the seriousness of the crime and the attitude of the perpetrator: compensation or an apology would often be enough to avert prosecution. They were also influenced by the attitude of the community towards the victim and the accused. Often neighbours or the parson or squire sought to reconcile the parties in the interests of communal harmony. Accused persons subject to the authority of a master, an employer or a husband were normally seen as best dealt with within the home. Those seen as tolerable or redeemable were often given the benefit of the doubt. John Aston of Myddle, Shropshire 'was a sort of a silly fellow, very idle and much given to stealing of poultry and small things. He was many times catched in the fact and sometimes well cudgelled by those that would trouble themselves no further with him. But at last he grew unsufferable and . . . was . . . imprisoned and indicted for stealing twenty-four cocks and hens.'[10]

This community input did not end with the decision to prosecute. More serious cases (felonies) were usually heard at the county assizes. First a grand jury heard the prosecution case and decided whether there was a case to answer. If it thought there was none, it returned a finding of *ignoramus* (we do not know). If it thought there was a plausible case, it found a true bill (*billa vera*) and the case went before a trial or petty jury. Trial juries supposedly consisted of freeholders but where there were many cases to be heard more or less any adult male could be pressed into service.[11] They decided whether the accused was guilty and of what offence (for example homicide or manslaughter) and valued the goods stolen. By valuing them below one shilling (twelve pence) they ensured that the accused would be found guilty not of felony, which potentially carried the death penalty, but of misdemeanour, which led to a lighter punishment such as branding. In the case of John Aston, following a broad hint from the judge, the jury valued the goods at eleven pence, 'at which the judge laughed heartily and said he was glad to hear that cocks and hens were so cheap in this country.'[12]

In the courtroom, as in the decision to prosecute, the perceived moral worth of the accused was a vital factor. Character witnesses considerably influenced proceedings. Members of the audience made clear their views of accuser and accused and in the eighteenth century – and perhaps earlier – jurors often reached their verdicts inside the courtroom, assisted by the audience.[13] Community perceptions of the convicted person's character were also taken into account in sentencing. Even after sentence, pleas for clemency or pardon often succeeded, especially if the convicted person was seen as young, misled and redeemable.

I have talked of 'community' opinion, by which I mean not the poor and marginal, but the 'better sort'. Trial juries, in theory, consisted of freeholders; grand juries included substantial yeomen, minor (and sometimes major) gentry. Historians' emphasis on community input in the criminal law in the seventeenth century may in part reflect a reaction against the very different view put forward by E.P. Thompson, Douglas Hay and other historians of the eighteenth century. These see the criminal law as an instrument of gentry hegemony, using a mixture of brutality, theatre and calculated shows of mercy. Just as the elite used Parliament to promote its material interests, through enclosure acts and the game laws, so it used the criminal law to deter assaults on its property, the definition of which was gradually extended, as customary perquisites such as gleaning were redefined as theft.[14] This thesis has been severely criticized by some historians of the eighteenth century[15] but it does raise the question of the role of members of the 'elite' in the workings of the criminal law.

The interpretation of the seventeenth-century criminal law outlined above depicts magistrates largely as facilitators. When approached by an aggrieved victim, they examined the accused; if they thought there was a case to answer, they either committed them to gaol until the assizes or bound them over to appear. Such discretion conferred power and this power could be even more apparent in misdemeanour cases, in which magistrates often possessed powers of summary conviction: the accused never came before a court or a jury. Under a statute of 1610 anybody deemed by a JP to be 'loose, idle and disorderly' could be sent to the house of correction for a whipping and a few days' hard labour. Those who suffered in this way were generally young, single and unemployed, without a husband or master to speak for them. Once labelled 'disorderly' they would find it hard to gain legitimate employment and in general the scales of the criminal law were weighted against the poorest, because they lacked legal knowledge and the money to seek legal advice or redress.[16]

This is not to suggest that the Thompson-Hay view of the criminal law is convincing after all. The dichotomy which it assumes between 'the gentry' and 'the plebs' is too crude to accommodate the complex social stratification and power relationships in seventeenth-century England. However, those identified by the 'better sort' or the magistrates as deviant or dangerous risked being treated unfairly under the criminal law. There was, moreover, one more 'elite' element: the judges who presided at the assizes. As the case from Myddle shows, judges could take in good part jurors' attempts to protect wrongdoers from the full wrath of the law. They could also, as outsiders, bring an element of neutrality to counteract local malice and ensure that justice was done, within the courtroom or by recommending clemency after conviction. But they could also try to influence – indeed bully – jurors whom they regarded as partial and their role as 'lions under the throne' could make their conduct in political trials particularly contentious. Even so, it is clear that popular participation in, and recourse to, the criminal law was far more widespread than in most other European countries. A similar pattern was apparent in civil cases, where the law was widely used in the process of dispute resolution. As the economy became more complex and trading over distance increased, there was greater use of written agreements which could be enforced in the courts: oral contracts might be appropriate to the face-to-face society of the village, but proved increasingly unreliable.[17] Not that litigation was normally undertaken lightly: it was expensive, divisive and often inconclusive. Parties often preferred arbitration, with each nominating one or two arbiters. If one party seemed reluctant to agree, the other might initiate legal proceedings, as a way of putting on pressure to agree to arbitration. They might also take the first steps towards a criminal prosecution (usually for misdemeanour) or have the other person bound over to keep the peace with a similar objective in mind.[18]

For much of England's population, the law was not something alien, imposed by a remote and impersonal state. However, it was a resource more easily available to some than to others. Married women were legally subordinate to their husbands. A married woman was unlikely to be punished for any offence committed in her husband's presence, but she had limited redress against her husband and poor, single women found access to the law extremely difficult. Similarly, wealth and power were very unequally distributed within villages, with perhaps the biggest divide between those who paid the poor rate and distributed poor relief and those who received it. Only the 'better sort' would have the knowledge and financial resources to consider having recourse to the law.[19]

Great landowners, of course, exercised more power still. Occasionally that power was expressed through violence. In around 1660, in Warwickshire, Sir William Underhill seriously wounded Walter Devereux and was ordered by the court to pay him £1,500 damages. He refused and some years later was ordered to hand over his house and lands, but he gathered together a band of armed men and made a forcible entry: several were wounded and one of Devereux's men was killed.[20] Such affrays, common a century or two earlier, seem to have been rare, except perhaps in the bandit country close to the Scottish border, where the judges needed an armed escort. In the same region, three of the Musgraves allegedly kept Sir John Ballantine out of his lands, none of the local JPs daring to oppose them.[21] In South Wales the Marquis of Worcester used the garrison of Chepstow virtually as a private army in pursuing his disputes in Wentwood Forest.[22]

Such calculated use of force was exceptional. Aristocratic violence was common, but was usually spontaneous and incited by drink. Still more common was the use of personal influence to deny justice to humbler people or to pursue vendettas against them.[23] Great men tried to influence judges and juries. The only case I can find of even an indirect attempt to bribe a judge, by offering money to his son, dates from 1683 and involved the Earl of Danby, who (after nearly four years' imprisonment) was desperate to get out of the Tower.[24] More common were attempts to determine which judge heard a particular case[25] or to arrange for a friend to have a quiet word with the judge beforehand or to send a small gift.[26] Sir Ralph Verney spoke to the judges who were to ride his circuit on such matters as the suppression of an alehouse and a settlement certificate granted to a widow.[27] Juries could be packed. John Skelton, who (he claimed) killed Francis Edgecumbe in self-defence, was tried (in his absence) by a jury containing several of Edgecumbe's father's servants and tenants. A Quaker whose son was killed by a member of Doncaster corporation complained that the jury (chosen by the magistrates) found it self-defence.[28] In civil disputes, those who possessed the right connections tried to influence the composition of the jury.[29] All those who embarked on litigation had also to reckon with the costs of counsel, the fees of court officials and treating the jurors afterwards.[30] After the Earl of Rutland won a case against the Duke of Buckingham, the jurors were given ten guineas each, on the grounds that 'they were of great quality and fortunes in their country and come on purpose to serve'.[31]

Those who suffered the worst injustices were those who were vulnerable because of their religious or political beliefs or simply unlucky. Treason trials were heavily weighted against the accused and served a didactic purpose; the judges felt obliged to secure a guilty verdict and often bullied the accused.[32] At times of crisis the government or the local authorities thought it necessary to execute a few people to serve as examples to others who might be tempted to rebel.[33] During such panics, the authorities might send people to gaol who subsequently found it hard to get out, because they refused to swear the oath of allegiance or could not find sureties for good behaviour.[34] Some seem to have been forgotten: in 1667 the son of former Secretary Nicholas enquired about Thomas Fletcher, whom Nicholas had committed to gaol in 1662 and whom none of the council seemed to know anything about; he was released.[35]

Such cases were very much the exception. Normally the king and his law officers were careful to operate within the law and encouraged the peaceful and equitable resolution of disputes.[36] Perhaps the least defensible use of royal power was the repeated pardoning of violent aristocrats for killing watchmen, linkboys or those who happened to get in their way.[37] As John Verney remarked, gentlemen who killed were always pardoned.[38] But gentlemen who sought to influence the processes of the law were not concerned only to advance their material interests, still less to get away with murder. Often they pleaded for clemency;[39] less often they protested against what they saw as undue leniency, as when Sir James Clavering claimed that 'the country' was alarmed by the reprieve for six weeks of a 'notorious rogue' convicted of burglary at York.[40]

If there is significant, if scattered, evidence that members of the elite tried to manipulate the legal system, there is also considerable evidence that they did not always get their way. A key factor here was the independence shown by juries. In principle, members of the landed elite subscribed to the belief that juries and Parliaments were the twin pillars of English liberties. In practice, they often criticized the performance of particular juries. Two criticisms stood out. First, they were 'insufficient': jurors were supposed to be freeholders, but many freeholders were poor – the property qualification was only £2 p.a. – or infirm or ignorant; others used all kinds of pretexts to avoid serving. Court officials accepted gifts from those who did not want to serve; Sir Ralph Verney said a small payment each year to the undersheriff was sufficient to gain exemption.[41] Those best fitted to serve, the gentry, avoided what Edmund Verney called the 'slavery' of jury service, which the Duke of Newcastle blamed on their 'tinsel pride'.[42] On special occasions, for example after the assault on Sir John Coventry or the Colchester weavers' riot, care was taken to have a 'substantial' or 'sufficient' jury,[43] but on other occasions peers and gentry complained that juries were biased against them.[44] The Commons tried to tackle these problems. In 1665 an Act decreed that all jurors had to have freehold land worth at least £20 p.a. (£8 p.a. in Wales). JPs were to go through the freeholders' books, striking out the names of those who were insufficient and adding the names of others who had been omitted. Sheriffs were not to take money to excuse attendance.[45] The Act was only temporary. The issue was raised again in 1668 and again in 1670, when it was suggested that substantial copyholders and leaseholders should also be made 'subject to serve'. Some argued that these would protect others with similar tenures against their landlords, others that their landlords might put pressure on them to behave unjustly; the bill did not pass.[46] In 1678 a bill similar to the Act of 1665 passed the Lords but was rejected by the Commons. It was noted that the court strongly favoured the bill, which explains why it was rejected and why the Act of 1665 (which, like the Five Mile Act, was passed amid security scares during the Dutch War) was only temporary. At a time of partisan division, the Commons had no wish to give the JPs – appointed by the crown – permanent and extensive powers over the composition of juries.[47]

The other great complaint against juries was that they were biased: against the gentry, against foreigners[48] but above all against the Church – too many jurors were 'fanatics'.[49] In 1667 a London jury acknowledged that a group of Quakers had been convicted twice before for attending conventicles and that they had been taken again at their usual meeting place, the Bull and Mouth, but claimed that they did not believe that it had been proved that they had met for a 'religious act', as the Conventicle Act required.[50] The Commons were perturbed by evidence of the misdeeds of juries, but were equally wary of allowing judges too much power to threaten or punish recalcitrant jurors. The Commons tacitly accepted Judge Kelyng's explanation for having fined and threatened jurors in this and other cases, but voted that fining and imprisoning jurors was illegal and resolved to bring in a bill against such practices.[51] The respected lawyer John Vaughan persuaded the House to omit the word 'menacing', on the grounds that a judge needed to be able to warn a corrupt jury against proceeding contrary to their oaths.[52] The bill did not pass, but the practice of imprisoning jurors was outlawed by the judges themselves, after the jury in the case of Penn and Meade had been fined, imprisoned and kept without food and drink for three days. Their ruling was delivered by the same John Vaughan, now a judge.[53] This did not stop judges from trying to influence – or intimidate – juries, sometimes successfully, sometimes not.[54] In February 1680, when belief in the Popish Plot remained intense, an aged Catholic, Sir Thomas Gascoigne, was tried before a Yorkshire jury, accused of complicity in the Plot. The judge, Pemberton, was very severe against the accused, but the foreman of the jury roundly told him that it was well known in Yorkshire that the two leading witnesses against him were rogues. When the judge criticized one of the jurors, Mr Tancred, for being too favourable to the accused, twenty of the gentry, headed by Lord Fairfax, waited on the judge and told him of Tancred's standing in the shire. The judge apologised to Tancred in open court; Gascoigne was acquitted.[55]

The Gascoigne case showed that the English legal system was still capable of delivering what we would call justice in the most improbable circumstances. It undoubtedly treated some more favourably than others – the wealthy were better able to afford litigation and the best counsel and more likely to be able to have a quiet word with the judge. But they could not, by and large, control the selection of jurors, which was in the hands of lesser officials who sought to turn their power over the selection process into cash. The king might have been able to establish greater control over jury selection had he selected sheriffs on political lines and had sheriffs been expected to select partisan juries. For much of the reign, however, they were not. The office of sheriff remained burdensome and unpopular (except in Lancashire and Yorkshire, where it was profitable) and those unfortunate enough to be chosen were concerned primarily to limit their financial losses. Until the mid 1670s the various influences which might distort the fair running of the system – gentry influence, jury partiality, the whims and ill-temper of judges – worked randomly and may have cancelled one another out. The victims of injustice were not negligible in terms of numbers, but they tended to be scattered individuals, poor and powerless. From about 1676, however, the nation became politically divided and the law became a weapon which each party tried to use against the other. Jury selection and the whole legal process came to be politicized, leaving the losers, the Whigs, complaining that the whole system had been perverted for party ends. But they criticized the perversion, not the system.

Notes

1 S. Hindle, 'Hierarchy and community in the Elizabethan parish: the Swallowfield articles of 1596', *HJ*, XLII, 1999, pp. 835–51 (quotations from p. 848). See also P. Collinson, 'The Monarchical Republic of Elizabeth I' in J. Guy (ed.), *The Tudor Monarchy*, London, 1997, pp. 111–12.
2 *Ibid.*, pp. 841–4.
3 *Ibid.*, pp. 843–4; J.R. Kent, 'The Centre and the Localities: State Formation and Parish Government in England c. 1640–1740', *HJ*, XXXVIII, 1995, pp. 391–4.
4 See, for example, D. Underdown, *Fire from Heaven: Life in an English Town in the Seventeenth Century*, London, 1993.
5 See NRO, MCB 23–5, *passim*.
6 D.C. Beaver, *Parish communities and religious conflict in the Vale of Gloucester, 1590–1690*, Cambridge, Mass. 1998, pp. 117–31.
7 See J. Miller, 'Town governments and Protestant Strangers, 1560–1690', *Proceedings of the Huguenot Society*, XXVI, 1997, pp. 577, 585–6.
8 My only major criticism of Kent, 'Centre and Localities', is that she insists on seeing 'the state' as the driving force behind change in the localities – when all too often she in fact means Parliament, which in turn was often responding to pressures from the localities: pp. 364–7, 373, 390. Yet she also appreciates that the state could be a resource: pp. 395, 403.
9 My account of the criminal law is based in particular on J.A. Sharpe, *Crime in Seventeenth-century England: A County Study*, Cambridge, 1983; J.A. Sharpe, *Crime in early modern England*, London, 1984; C. Herrup, *The Common Peace; Participation and the Criminal Law in Seventeenth-century England*, Cambridge, 1987; J.M. Beattie, *Crime and the Courts in England, 1660–1800*, Oxford, 1986.
10 R. Gough, *The History of Myddle*, ed. D. Hey, Harmondsworth, 1981, p. 145.
11 J.S. Cockburn, *A History of English Assizes, 1558–1714*, Cambridge, 1972, ch. 6; Beattie, *Crime*, pp. 378–406.
12 Gough, *Myddle*, p. 146.
13 Beattie, *Crime*, pp. 396–9.
14 D. Hay, 'Property, Authority and the Criminal Law' in D. Hay *et al.* (eds), *Albion's Fatal Tree: Crime and Society in Eighteenth Century England*, London, 1975, pp. 17–63; E.P. Thompson, *Whigs and Hunters: The Origins of the Black Act*, London, 1975.
15 J.H. Langbein, '*Albion's* Fatal Flaws', *P & P*, no. 98, 1983, pp. 96–120 and (more temperately) J. Broad, 'Whigs, Deer-stealers and the Origins of the Black Act', *P & P*, no. 119, 1988, pp. 56–72.

16 R.B. Shoemaker, *Prosecution and Punishment: Petty Crime and the Law in London and Rural Middlesex, c. 1660–1720*, Cambridge, 1991, pp. 35–40, 49, 61, 67–71, 166–97.
17 Muldrew, 'Culture', *passim.*
18 Muldrew, 'Culture'; Shoemaker, *Prosecution*, pp. 6–8, 23–5; S. Hindle 'The Keeping of the Public Peace' in Griffiths, Fox and Hindle (eds), *Experience*, ch. 7; J. Aubrey, *Brief Lives*, ed. O. Lawson Dick, Harmondsworth, 1962, p. 274.
19 Wrightson, 'Politics' and Hindle, 'Keeping' in Griffiths, Fox and Hindle (eds), *Experience.*
20 *CSPD 1666–7*, p. 53.
21 *Norths* I.179–80; *CSPD 1670*, pp. 611–2.
22 M. McClain, 'The Wentwood Forest Riot' in S.D. Amussen and M. Kishlansky (eds), *Political Culture and Cultural Politics in early modern England: Essays presented to David Underdown*, Manchester, 1995, ch. 5.
23 See the cases of Sir Philip Monckton (*CSPD 1670*, pp. 214–5, 308) and Lord Fanshawe, *HMC Verulam*, pp. 63, 72.
24 Egerton MS 3338, fo. 171. On at least two other occasions, Danby or his sons gave more general assurances of future 'favour' in return for present help: *ibid.*, fos 147–8; BL, Add. MS 34079, fos 44–5.
25 Arundel Castle, Autograph Letters 1632–1723, no. 412.
26 Bradfer, Lord to Lady Yarmouth, 24 March 1679; BL, Add 34079, fos 44–5 (in which Danby promises in general terms to repay any favours received); *CSPD 1675–76*, p. 276.
27 M636/29, Sir Ralph to Edmund Verney, 8 and 15 June 1676, M636/33, Sir Ralph to John Verney, 12 and 28 July, William Fall to Sir Ralph, 18 July 1679. (Fall, who worked in the lord chancellor's office, was a useful contact.)
28 *CSPD 1668–9*, p. 154, *1664–5*, pp. 206–7.
29 M636/18, Sir Richard Temple to Sir Ralph Verney, 12 October 1662.
30 M636/26, Sir Ralph to Edmund Verney, 29 May 1673; *HMC 7th Report*, p. 493; BL, Add MS 29571, fo. 295. After the successful prosecution of Sir Patience Ward for perjury, the jury was treated at the king's expense: *HMC Kenyon*, p. 160.
31 *HMC Rutland*, II.82.
32 BL, Add MS 63057B, fo. 60; J.P. Kenyon, *The Popish Plot*, London, 1972, pp. 115–31, 157–67.
33 Carte MS 46, fo. 20; BT 110, Battailler to Louis, 30 November 1662 NS; T. Harris, 'The Bawdy-house Riots of 1668'*HJ*, XXIX, 1986, pp. 548–52; *CSPD 1675–76*, pp. 513–4; BL, Add MS 25124, fos. 42–3, 50–1.
34 See, for example, *HMC Kenyon*, p. 86; *CSPD 1665–66*, p. 373, *1671–72*, p. 597, *1674*, pp. 179, 206.
35 Egerton MS 2539, fos 112, 119. See also PC 2/59, pp. 609–11, PC 2/60, p. 81.
36 See for example *CSPD 1670*, pp. 236–7, *1673–75*, p. 406.
37 BL, Add MS 29571, fos 311, 312; Pforz, Coleman to Bulstrode 22 May 1676; *HMC 7th Report*, p. 470; *CSPD 1661–62*, pp. 352, 359.
38 M636/37, John to Edmund Verney, 11 December 1682.
39 *CSPD 1668–69*, pp. 339–40, *1673–75*, pp. 209, 229; M636/25, Sir Ralph Verney to Sir Roger Burgoyne, 22 Feb., same to Edmund Verney, 2 May 1672.
40 *CSPD 1671–72*, p. 286.
41 *CJ*, IX.99–100; Grey, I.230–1; *SR*, V.553–4; *HMC 9th Report, Part II*, p. 122; Carte MS 228, fo. 143; M636/36, Sir Ralph to John Verney, 19 June 1682.

42 M636/36, Edmund to John Verney, 29 June 1682; Strong, pp. 198–9.
43 *CSPD 1671*, p. 129, *1675–76*, pp. 513–4.
44 BL, Add MS 32679, fo. 12; Hodgson, p. 215; Grey, I.230.
45 *SR*, V.553–4.
46 *CJ*, IX.70, 99–100; Grey, I.226, 230–1.
47 *CJ*, IX.510; *HMC 9th Report, Part II*, p. 122; Carte MS 228, fo. 143.
48 *CSPD 1670*, p. 56.
49 Hodgson, p. 215; *CSPD 1664–65*, p. 39, *1668–69*, p. 159; M636/31, John to Edmund Verney, 23 May 1678
50 Grey, I.67; Milward, pp. 159, 166–7.
51 Milward, pp. 159–60, 162–3, 166–70; Grey, I.62–3, 67; *CJ*, IX.4, 35–6, 53, 74.
52 Grey, I.84; Milward, pp. 190–1.
53 Marvell, II.318; *Cosin*, II.252; Browning, *Docts*, pp. 86–9.
54 *CSPD 1673–75*, pp. 209, 229; BL, Add. MS 25124, fo. 80; Althorp MS C5, Weymouth to Halifax, 20 August 1683.
55 BL, Add MS 29572, fo. 206; Carte MS 39, fo. 113; Reresby, p. 198. See also *State Trials*, VII.959–1044.

Chapter two

Centre and localities

Policy- and decision-making

Having established the extent of popular participation in local administration and law enforcement, we now turn to the influence of central government on the localities. The framework within which county and parish officials operated was laid down by parliamentary statutes. Few of these had been passed as 'government' measures. Whereas now most legislation in the British Parliament is promoted by the government and pushed through by the party whips, using weight of numbers, the Tudors and Stuarts rarely had any measures that they wished to pass, other than money bills. The initiative for most legislation came from ordinary MPs, promoting local interests, but often 'local' problems were sufficiently widespread to produce 'national' measures (such as the Poor Laws of 1598 and 1601) which drew on local experience of tackling practical problems and of trying to enforce earlier Acts. In the absence of anything resembling modern political parties, there was no simple way of pushing bills through: indeed, there was a preference for avoiding votes and for the Houses to debate their way to a consensus, before presenting the bill to the king for his assent.

Legislation was not the only function of Parliament. The Commons brought the nation's grievances before the monarch and the fact that the king needed the House's consent for taxation and (less often) other legislation gave them some leverage: he might be induced to assent to bills he disliked as 'the price of money'.[1] Under Charles II, the Commons were initially coy about explicitly demanding 'redress before supply', preferring to suggest that in return for their grants of money the king should see fit to redress the people's grievances. From about 1673, however, the connection was made more openly.[2] If financial need forced Charles II to call Parliament more frequently than his predecessors had done, it still met irregularly and he was reluctant to take it into his confidence. In April 1678, urged to make a firm statement on foreign policy, Charles recoiled: 'Then they'll be able to see all that has been done and what we are doing'.[3] Charles saw Parliament as a nuisance, a possible nemesis or a regrettable necessity, but after the legislation of 1660–63 re-established effective monarchical government, he never saw Parliament or parliamentary legislation, other than fiscal legislation, as contributing to the task of governing the country.

What then, in Charles's eyes, were the purposes of government? Put at their most basic, they were the effective conduct of foreign policy (at best, colonial and commercial expansion, at worst, defence of the realm against attack) and the maintenance of order at home. Insofar as his government concerned itself with social and religious policy, it did so because it feared that excessive hardship or religious friction could trigger serious disorder.[4] After the early 1660s, the privy council showed little inclination to intervene in the marketing of grain, in order to ensure adequate supplies for the poor. Instead, the perception grew that there was too much grain on the market, depressing prices, which led the Commons to introduce the first corn bounty, to encourage exports, in 1673.[5] Charles I had had his own distinctive (and unpopular) vision of the Church of England and made at least a show of concern for the poor in his Books of Orders; Charles II did neither. His was a government with little discernible spiritual or moral vision. If there was a vision of any kind, it was of empire and naval greatness,[6] but Charles was concerned mainly with survival and having a good time. Similarly, whereas Charles I had tried to bring the churches of Scotland and Ireland into line with that of England, his son's main concern was to keep his two outlying kingdoms quiet and to build up a potential reserve of military force there in case of upheaval in England.[7]

However, although the ambitions of Charles II's government were limited, policies and decisions had to be made – about appointments in the church, armed forces and local government, about the administration of the navy and army, about gathering and spending money. In making policies and decisions, the traditional source of advice was the privy council, consisting of the monarch's leading ministers – such as the lord chancellor, lord treasurer and the two secretaries of state – and a selection of leading peers (including the Archbishop of Canterbury); the ministers provided administrative expertise, the peers could help ensure that the council's commands were obeyed in the localities. Charles II re-established the privy council on traditional lines, but showed little enthusiasm for it. On one hand, it was too large to preserve secrecy; on the other, he felt constrained by its formality and wished to reserve the power to change his mind after taking more private advice.[8] In 1640–42, faced with the impossibility of preventing Charles I from being swayed by 'evil counsellors', there had been moves to make the king more subject to his councillors and the councillors more accountable to Parliament, culminating in the demand that all matters of importance should be discussed in the council and that councillors should set their hands to what they advised. Charles II had no intention of being bound in this way. The privy council became a forum for routine discussion, hearing petitions and resolving disputes; but the real decisions were made elsewhere. In 1663, the king established the Committee for Foreign Affairs, comprising the lord chancellor, Clarendon, the lord treasurer, Southampton, and other leading ministers.[9] This committee, also known as the cabinet council, continued for most of the reign. In 1668, after Clarendon's fall, the king established other committees to handle military and naval affairs, petitions and trade and the plantations. The council was to reach no decision on any matter until it had been discussed by the appropriate committee. The committee for foreign affairs, meanwhile, was to supervise local government, traditionally a key responsibility of the council as a whole.[10] The creation of these committees reduced the privy council still further to a routinely administrative role. Of the new committees, that for trade became something of a pressure group for advocates of religious toleration, arguing that this was a necessary precondition for commercial success.[11] The committee for foreign affairs, in keeping with the king's preferences, was very informal. Whereas the registers of the privy council were neatly written and carefully indexed, self-consciously 'public' records, the minutes of the committee of foreign affairs (where they survive) consist of scrappy notes, written by under-secretary Joseph Williamson for his own use.[12] That was how the king wanted it: the fewer records that survived, the better.

In the spring of 1679, faced with a major political crisis, Charles reconstituted his privy council. The new one was half the size, numbering about thirty, equally composed of office-holders and leading peers and commoners: the fact that it included two from each rank of the peerage reminded cynics of Noah's ark. Shaftesbury, the king's most conspicuous critic, was made lord president and the committee of foreign affairs was abolished. The lord chancellor told the new council that the secrecy of the committee and the king's practice of taking advice from only a few had bred distrust. The king had decided that greater transparency was necessary and was determined to follow wise, steady counsels in the future.[13] Whereas in 1640–42 his father had stubbornly resisted being made subject to his council, Charles II apparently did so voluntarily, in a gesture designed to rebuild trust. Appearances proved deceptive. Charles allegedly exclaimed 'they have put a set of men about me, but they shall know nothing!'[14] It became clear that he was not prepared to follow unpalatable advice, evading pressure to remove 'loyalists' from local offices and refusing to ask his councillors' opinion about proroguing or dissolving Parliament, saying if they had said nothing they could not be called to account.[15] The fact that details of the council's supposedly secret discussions soon became public cannot have added to his willingness to trust it.[16] The new councillors gradually realized that they were incurring the odium for unpopular royal policies but exercising little real influence, so they resigned or were dismissed and by April 1681 the king again had a council of his own choosing. Meanwhile, the council's committee of intelligence was quietly converted into a new committee for foreign affairs. The term was being used again by the end of 1680 and the king's Catholic brother, the Duke of York, was readmitted after the plot against their lives in 1683.[17]

Charles II was not the sort of man to allow himself to be bound by any routine or to tie himself to follow the advice of any committee, even one hand-picked by himself. Years of exile and betrayal had convinced him that he could trust nobody: even the most outwardly devoted ministers would put their own interests before his. To avoid being misled, he therefore sought to play one off against another: the Marquis of Halifax referred to his 'humour of hearing everybody against anybody'.[18] He did little to restrain the rivalries of his ministers and courtiers, to a point where they seemed far more concerned to ruin one another than to carry on his business.[19] To make matters worse, despite his cynicism, Charles was easily influenced, especially by those who amused him, his mistresses and those (like the Duke of Buckingham) with personalities stronger than his own. It was difficult, especially in the 1660s, to get and hold his attention; when letters were read in the cabinet council, he could be distracted by others talking.[20] Once he had made a decision there was every chance that he could be made to reverse it. Ideally, he would sign an order there and then,[21] but often there were delays while the necessary documents were drawn up, which allowed time to change his mind. Those who had to make a case from a distance found themselves outmanoeuvred by those on the spot. The Earl of Essex, as lord lieutenant of Ireland, repeatedly tried to expose the misdeeds of Lord Ranelagh, the vice-treasurer, whose slowness in paying the Irish army was matched only by his reluctance to produce accounts. Essex complained that his letters had less effect than Ranelagh's whispers in the king's ear.[22] When Ormond was lord lieutenant he always kept one of his sons at court, to guard his interests and counter his detractors.[23]

Although Charles assured his sister that he was fully in control of his government,[24] few shared this view. Instead, the overwhelming impression was of vacillation and deceit. Pepys complained that the king's 'satisfaction is nothing worth, it being easily got and easily removed'.[25] In 1674 the king was said to have changed his mind six times in six hours. Sir William Temple wrote of 1678: 'Our counsels and conduct were like those of a floating island, driven one way or t'other according to the winds or tides'. He added that such inconsistency led observers to see hidden designs which were not there.[26] Pepys, driven to distraction by the incompetence all around him, found little solace in the thought that the king and his brother lacked the brains or foresight to establish a military absolutist regime.[27] There were repeated rumours of such plans but there is rarely any solid evidence that the king seriously entertained them.[28] Nevertheless, the free access which he allowed to successive French ambassadors and the all too visible influence of Catholic mistresses, like Castlemaine and Portsmouth (the latter was also French) encouraged observers to think the worst. Even without such suspicions, the court projected an image of debauchery, incompetence and corruption, which was not wholly accurate. In 1667 Charles appointed a treasury commission to monitor spending and to save him from his own generosity: he urged them to be 'rough and ill-natured', not easily moved by importunities.[29] More significant, if less theatrical, was Charles's insistence on ruling according to law. Whereas Charles I had repeatedly bent and stretched the law, mainly to raise money, Charles II and his advisers were cautious. Doubtless they feared arousing the wrath of Parliament, but Charles habitually referred proposals and projects to his law officers. Again and again, those who took their disputes to the privy council found themselves being 'left to the law'.[30] In 1668 Ormond remarked that no court had ever governed with so little care or had ever been regarded with such contempt. Its distribution of 'favours, recompenses and employments' was anything but fair. But he conceded that justice was fairly administered in the courts.[31] In its dealings with local government, Charles

II's regime made modest demands and generally adhered to the law. How did local governors respond to those demands?

Local government

If members of the gentry were generally willing to serve as JPs, they were far less willing to serve as sheriffs. The sheriff was responsible for serving writs and collecting fines, for which he had to account in detail in the Exchequer. He (or his undersheriffs) chose panels of jurors – and jury-service was far from popular.[32] He was also expected to entertain the assize judges and to provide an escort for them. To offset these chores and expenses, the sheriff had few sources of profit, except in Yorkshire and (some said) Lancashire and Somerset.[33] Sir John Reresby was very disappointed to make only £300 from his year as sheriff of Yorkshire and sought to be retained for a second year. At the other extreme, it was alleged that a conscientious sheriff of Wiltshire could find himself £1,000 worse off at the end of the year.[34] Those who feared being chosen as sheriffs mobilized their friends and beseeched courtiers to get them off. The arguments they used offer an insight into contemporary views of the qualities which made a man fit for county office. Some pleaded poverty or ill-health, others losses incurred in the civil wars or loyalty to the Royalist cause. Sir Robert Vyner claimed that his brother-in-law was trebly inappropriate as a 'bumpkin', a 'rank Anabaptist' and worth no more than £150 a year.[35] It was claimed that service as a militia officer was sufficient to merit exemption, while some saw the shrievalty as a punishment.[36] The Commons considered ways of reducing the cost of the shrievalty and in 1675 the gentry of several counties launched subscriptions to spread it: it was estimated that the Lincolnshire subscription reduced the cost by at least £500.[37] How long the subscriptions lasted is uncertain. In Buckinghamshire it was still operating at the end of 1680, but doubts were expressed whether it would last much longer. In Gloucestershire, where the idea originated, the subscription was still functioning in 1690.[38] In 1681–85, the shrievalty assumed a new importance: with law enforcement distorted by partisanship, it became imperative for the king to choose sheriffs who would empanel Tory jurors.

The office of JP was more prized, albeit less than before the civil wars. Removal from commission was a blow to a man's honour and an indication that his friends and kinsmen lacked favour 'above'.[39] In appointing members of the gentry as JPs, the king's government made use of their local knowledge and standing, which gave them a degree of bargaining power when dealing with the centre and a degree of leeway in implementing legislation. As far as law and order were concerned, the privy council had little choice but to trust in the JPs' integrity and good sense; it could reasonably be assumed that it was in their interest to prevent disorder and to secure property. Some JPs proved loath to suppress Nonconformist meetings, but it was a moot point whether the king really wanted them to. More problematic were those areas where the interests of the centre could conflict with those of the locality and the most important and contentious of these was tax collection.

England's fiscal system had been revolutionized in the 1640s. Much of Charles I's revenue came from the exploitation of his property, feudal and prerogative rights, in ways which were widely seen as unfair. The only regular tax consisted of customs duties, mostly on imports, which were also contentious because Charles, unlike his predecessors, had not been granted them by Parliament. Most of the king's personal or domanial revenues were swept away in 1641. With the outbreak of the civil war, most of the customs were collected by Parliament, which added the assessment and the excise. The former was a substantial land tax, much more efficiently assessed and collected than the old subsidy. The latter taxed goods produced and sold within the realm: the fact that it fell on beer, among other commodities, meant that it brought even the poorest within the tax system. For the moment, the bulk of the cost of the war effort was met by the assessment, but the excise was to prove the more important innovation as it could be extended to more and more commodities. The impact of these changes was enormous. Mike Braddick has suggested that between the 1620s and 1650s the amount of 'national' tax paid in Norfolk and Cheshire increased ten or even twentyfold.[40] And yet the new taxes seem to have been collected with relatively little opposition. How can this be explained?

As far as the assessment is concerned, the involvement of the local gentry in both assessment and collection was important. Although each county had a fixed weekly or monthly quota there was some scope for negotiation to soften the burden of national demands on the localities. In addition, the English were conditioned to obey the law and to submit to government: there had been few open refusals to pay ship money until the Scottish troubles of 1640 raised the prospect that Charles I would be forced to call Parliament. The assessment, unlike ship money, had the full weight of Parliamentary authority behind it. Despite quibbles over rating, most people paid and there was little open resistance.[41] After 1660, it continued in all but name, but it was now occasional rather than permanent, voted only when Parliament judged it necessary. Members of the gentry were eager to serve on the commissions who oversaw assessment and collection. Edmund Verney remarked that this was the only county office which he sought; those who were left out could be very annoyed. The collection of these land taxes was uncontentious, provoking little opposition.[42]

Although the excise initially brought in less than the assessment, it attracted far more opposition. This was partly because it was at first collected at the point of sale, so that excisemen had to contend with angry butchers and tipplers and sometimes faced serious riots. The meat excise was soon abandoned and the beer excise began to be collected from the brewer rather than in the alehouse, but hostility continued. One reason was its novelty; another was that it fell more heavily on the poor than on the rich and so was seen as unfair in a way that the assessment was not. The introduction of farming (contracting out collection) in the 1650s offered scope for negotiation and compounding: collectors might find it easier to accept less than the statutes strictly required in return for prompt payment. In the 1650s and again under

Charles II there were attempts to persuade locals to become involved in excise farms, but they were soon superseded by London businessmen.[43] In addition, there were attempts to involve county JPs in excise collection, both before and after 1660. Parliament granted them jurisdiction over the excise in 1663, hoping to curb what were seen as the misdeeds of the excisemen, but the privy council also expected the JPs to dampen down opposition and increase yields.[44] Some JPs, however, were more concerned to restrain the 'arbitrary' conduct of the excisemen, arguing that it did the king's service no good. It was stressed that the mayor of Leeds and one of his aldermen, who had tried to rectify the 'insolences' of the excise officers, were very loyal men.[45]

Although there were a few riots against the excise, and rather more assaults on excisemen, this was as nothing compared to the opposition provoked by the hearth tax. On the face of it, this was equitable: someone with a large house with many hearths could afford to pay far more than someone with one or two. Moreover, the legislation exempted those who were not liable to pay the poor rate or whose houses were worth less than £1 a year in rent. Even so, the tax proved bitterly unpopular, because it was seen as intrusive – taxmen could demand to enter people's homes – and as falling most heavily on the poor. Local officials sided with taxpayers rather than collectors, not least because JPs had no jurisdiction over the tax. JPs, churchwardens and overseers of the poor freely issued certificates that people were too poor to pay.[46] When the hearth tax officers distrained goods from those refusing to pay, JPs ordered the goods to be returned.[47] A bill was brought into the Commons in 1668 to curb the excesses of collectors and to give JPs jurisdiction over them.[48] In the 1670s there were complaints that the collectors, as outsiders, were more severe than locals would have been: collection was increasingly put into the hands of professionals who had a vested interest in maximizing yields.[49] Despite this professionalization, local opinion still mattered: in 1683 it was remarked that those accused of obstructing the hearth tax in Buckinghamshire were likely to get off, as their reputations were far superior to those of the 'roguish' collectors.[50] Given the obvious sympathies of many JPs and MPs, and the expectation that local juries would show similar sympathies, recalcitrant taxpayers were encouraged to respond violently. Many collectors were insulted or assaulted and several were killed.[51]

Faced with obstruction or defiance from JPs, the council and treasury trod carefully. A few JPs were dismissed,[52] but the central government generally relied on reprimands (or threats), together with exhortations from the circuit judges.[53] The extent of opposition should not be exaggerated. Many JPs made it clear that they would cooperate with the hearth tax collectors, whose powers (after all) rested on an Act of Parliament.[54] Often disputes centred on ambiguities. Kilns were exempt; logic suggested that smiths' hearths or bakers' ovens should be exempt as well, but the Act did not explicitly say so. In 1676 Sir John Reresby told the Sheffield cutlers that they were not liable to pay the tax and ordered that goods distrained from them should be returned. The collectors complained to Lord Treasurer Danby, who declared that he had consulted counsel, who confirmed that the cutlers were obliged to pay; he advised Reresby not to obstruct the king's revenue. At the next assizes, the JPs read Danby's letter and unanimously confirmed Reresby's order; a later meeting of JPs reiterated this decision, despite an attempt by two judges to dissuade them. In 1677 Reresby persuaded Danby to order the collectors not to distrain for 'industrial' hearths until Parliament had clarified the law. As a mark of the cutlers' gratitude, he was invited to their feast.[55] This cosy relationship survived into the 1680s, despite Reresby's annoyance at their failure to support his preferred candidate in a parliamentary election. By now, however, he was beholden to the treasury for his salary as governor of Bridlington and York. He was also angered by the cutlers' seeking the patronage of other JPs, notably his arch-enemy Jessopp. He continued to argue the cutlers' case, but less publicly than before.[56]

Reresby's experience illustrates the tensions created by involving local notables in county government and the problems faced by one conscientious JP in trying to serve both court and country. At first he was content that 'whatever I lost there [at court] I gained in my country'. He refused to become involved in the excise farm because 'no man was beloved in his country' who did so.[57] In 1682 he remarked that some of his neighbours thought him too inclined to the court, while some at court suspected him of putting local interests first, especially in revenue matters. 'I resolved first to keep the honour of my employment [as governor of York] and the good opinion of my master and friends above . . . as long as I justly and honestly could; and at the same time to do country business, but only defensively, and as it was brought to me, according to my conscience.'[58] Conscious of his role as a broker between locality and centre, he still tried to serve both as far as he could. He was able to do so because, on one hand, both the theory and the practice of English government assumed a congruence rather than a conflict of interests between locality and centre. On the other, Reresby (like many of his fellows) was imbued with a deep respect for the rule of law: before being sworn as a JP, he was careful to study the statutes that he would apply. This led him to use the powers conferred on him by the king disinterestedly rather than for his own advantage.[59] In general, English local government worked well because of, not despite, its largely amateur personnel. The widespread dispersal of discretion, exercised by jurors and magistrates, ensured that law enforcement and administration were carried on in a manner broadly acceptable to local opinion; where it did not, it was usually possible to appeal 'above' for redress – at least for the 'better sort'. Only the marginal, in a moral, economic or religious sense, were likely to be treated arbitrarily.[60] Not until the early 1680s was the definition of 'marginal' extended to embrace a substantial proportion of the nation – Dissenters and Whigs – whereupon the law became an instrument of partisan vengeance.

The means of coercion

Charles II's government used persuasion wherever possible, but persuasion was not always enough. He was the first Stuart king to possess a standing army, but it was not large, never exceeding 10,000 men in peacetime, although substantial additional forces were raised for war.[61] Many of his subjects feared that he wished to use the army to establish absolute monarchy. These fears were most acute in wartime – in 1666–67, 1672–73 and 1678. In peacetime, the army was scattered in garrisons at home and abroad, including as many as 3,000 in Tangier, with the result that it would be difficult to gather more than a few hundred soldiers together in an emergency. The king tried in 1661–62 to persuade the Commons to agree to his having a larger army, but the Commons refused to provide the money, urging him to rely on the militia; Charles did not press the point.[62] He remained conscious of the weakness of his military resources, but, aware of his subjects' anxieties, he promptly disbanded the regiments raised in wartime and was careful not to provoke Parliament. He was also cautious about military discipline. The common law did not recognize the existence of the army, so mutiny and desertion were not criminal offences. Discipline was established through specially issued articles of war, enforced by courts martial. Under the Petition of Right it was illegal for any such court to impose the death penalty and Charles's government stressed that the only penalties they could impose were loss of place and pay. A bill was brought into Parliament in 1666 to lay down a code of discipline for the army, but it failed to pass.[63] At the start of the Dutch War, in 1672, the committee for foreign affairs discussed a new set of articles of war and considered whether mutiny and desertion could be punished with death. Lord Keeper Bridgeman declared that this would be illegal, so other lawyers were consulted to see if they could 'find it lawful'. In the end, the articles included no mention of the death penalty and stressed that all civil matters should be handled by the civilian authorities, to whom the military should defer.[64] The articles still went too far for Bridgeman, who refused to affix the great seal.[65] A proclamation of 4 December 1672 tried to regulate the relations between soldiers and civilians: it ordered officers to respond to complaints from civilians; if they failed to do so, the matter would be dealt with by the civil magistrate. Edmund Verney thought that the proclamation set up two distinct and equal systems of government, with no way of judging between them. The Commons claimed that it exempted soldiers 'in a manner' from the normal course of justice.[66] In the summer of 1673 fears of martial law were widespread, as a substantial army was gathered for a planned invasion of the Dutch Republic. Indiscipline was rife, but senior officers did not dare punish the malefactors in life or limb, for fear of Parliament, and had to rely on threats to secure obedience.[67] In the years that followed, unruly soldiers were generally prosecuted in the civil courts.[68] At least twice, in 1678 and 1684, soldiers were condemned to death for desertion, although some thought the judges had stretched the law.[69]

Fears of martial law were exaggerated because Charles and his advisers were careful to keep within the law: Clifford's suggestion that Charles could dispense with the Petition of Right was not taken up.[70] Similarly, the government dealt sensitively with disputes between soldiers and civilians. Despite the fear of standing armies, civilian attitudes towards the military were not invariably hostile. A garrison brought money into a town and offered protection against attack.[71] Many officers took care to establish good relations with the town authorities.[72] Troops who behaved well and paid their bills were generally welcomed.[73] Nevertheless, friction could arise. It was difficult to find recruits for the army; many were 'gaol-birds, thieves and rogues'.[74] Even the king admitted that discipline was poor and many officers were too drunk or lax to keep their men in order;[75] Scottish regiments were particularly unruly.[76] Some officers regarded civilian authority as inferior to their own, while soldiers rescued their fellows from custody.[77] At times the soldiers faced aggression and provocation: the townspeople of Dartmouth called them papists and 'scum of Goring': memories of the civil war still rankled.[78] On the other hand, when Captain Stradling's troop plundered the people of Huntingdon (Cromwell's birthplace) and berated them as rebels, the king ordered that Stradling should be cashiered and prosecuted and that his men should make full restitution. Significantly, he ordered that details of the punishment should be printed in the official *Gazette*.[79] This was not an isolated incident: Charles was generally concerned to show that the military were not above the law.[80]

Popular suspicion of the abuse of military power necessarily limited the army's usefulness as a means of coercion. Soldiers were used for some police duties, escorting bullion shipments and searching for highwaymen. They destroyed illegally grown tobacco in Gloucestershire and (occasionally) assisted the militia in suppressing conventicles; it should be noted, however, that when Lord Hawley took regular troops to Yorkshire early in 1664, in the aftermath of the 'Northern rising', he was to be under the command of the lord lieutenant and on a par with his deputies.[81] References to 'soldiers' breaking up conventicles could apply to the militia as well as the army, especially in the City of London, which jealously guarded its right to keep the peace. For most normal purposes, the main means of coercion available to the government was the militia, supplemented for much of the 1660s by volunteer troops of horse raised by Royalist gentlemen. For many, the militia was little more than a joke: once or twice a year bumbling rustics would be put through their paces by gentlemen whose martial pretensions far exceeded their abilities, before going off to get drunk ('the business of the day') and then departing, leaving the town barren of provisions and local maidens pregnant.[82] It took several years to get the militia going again at the Restoration, after two decades of neglect. The lists of those who were to pay the militia rate and to serve were hopelessly out of date and it was not until 1663 that the full legislative basis of the militia was in place. Nevertheless, there is ample evidence that lords lieutenant and their deputies worked hard during the 1660s to organize musters, provide colours and trophies, replenish magazines and chase up those who failed to meet their obligations. Their diligence owed much to fear of rebellion and they watched vigilantly for suspicious travellers and clandestine meetings 'upon pretence of religion'. Faced with invasion scares in 1666 and 1667, the militia was even more active and several Dutch raiding parties were driven off.[83]

After 1667, the council gave a greater priority to coastal defences than to the militia, which in many counties was allowed to decay.[84] In Norfolk, which had a conscientious lord lieutenant and deputies, regular musters continued into the 1670s and beyond. In Hampshire after a lull in the 1670s, the militia was again fully operational by 1682.[85] By contrast, the Earl of Dorset, who became lord lieutenant of Sussex in 1670, found himself beset with refractory deputies, sick or absent officers and uncooperative constables. Sir John Pelham told him that the office of deputy was unpopular as it involved doing things 'ungrateful to the country'. He agreed to serve, but only after checking that the other deputies were personally acceptable to him. Dorset was driven to complain to the king that some of the gentry were refusing to accept commissions.[86] The prospect that service in the militia might secure exemption from the shrievalty made it somewhat more attractive, but officers still quibbled about precedence, the precise form of their commissions and the colours they were to wear.[87] Dorset realized that only by holding regular musters could the muster rolls be kept up to date. With great difficulty, he organized one in 1672 but was unable to hold another until 1676.[88] Similarly, no muster was held in Westmorland between 1676 and 1679.[89] In Lancashire the militia mustered increasingly irregularly and no muster is recorded after 1679.[90] Meanwhile, much money due in the 1660s had still not been collected. Sussex was not the only county facing this problem: in Dorset the deputies tried manfully in 1671 to extract the arrears from 1662 and 1663, but with little success.[91]

Apart from keeping the militia in a state of preparedness, lords lieutenant and their deputies were assigned police functions. Again and again, between 1660 and 1667, they were ordered to secure suspicious persons, tender the oath of allegiance to them and make them find sureties for their good behaviour. Their legal authority to act in this way was not entirely certain: it was remarked that the government would be unwise to allow it to be tested in the courts.[92] In addition, the lord lieutenant maintained a general oversight over county government, recommending changes in the lieutenancy and commission of the peace. Charles II, unlike his father, reserved the final say in the appointment of deputies, but in practice he generally followed the advice of his lords lieutenant. Victor Stater has suggested that, whereas early Stuart deputies often defended local interests against the central government, acting as mediators or brokers, their successors under Charles II were much more the agents of the centre. Similarly, deputies were no longer chosen only because of their local standing: political allegiance mattered as well.[93] It is clearly true that the role of the militia became more partisan under Charles II, especially in the early 1660s and early 1680s. It is less clear that the deputies became the agents of central government, not least because in the early 1660s Charles failed to give the old Cavaliers the lead or the licence they expected. We have seen that deputies could be awkward and refractory: at times Dorset's, and those of the Duke of Richmond, effectively told them what to do rather than the other way round.[94] When the Earl of Yarmouth, whose health was poor and militia experience limited, became lord lieutenant of Norfolk, he repeatedly deferred to his deputies' better judgment.[95] Equally, lords lieutenant and deputies were adept at fending off unacceptable demands from the king. In June 1667 the council wrote to the lords lieutenant stressing the danger from the Dutch and claiming that the militia was obliged to appear, even if it had already served for the month which the statutes required and for which pay was provided. The council rather vaguely suggested that the money might be found from the funds for ammunition and from fines on defaulters.[96] The Lincolnshire deputies urged their lord lieutenant, the Earl of Lindsey, to ask that he might have the power to grant commissions to volunteers, who would be paid by the king. Soon after, the council told Lindsey that the king was now raising an army for the war, which would relieve the burden on the militia, but also leave him without money to pay it. He was ordered to summon the JPs and deputies to consider the most painless way of paying for the militia. The few who appeared declared that the county was too exhausted to raise any more money. The council then asked Lindsey to persuade people to lend money on the security of the tax recently voted by Parliament. He replied that the gentry were very loyal and willing, but were unable to raise anything: the county was drained of cash, tenants could not pay their rents.[97]

Beneath the language of deference and loyalty – the responses from the West Riding and Norfolk were similar[98] – there was a clear hint that the council's demands were unreasonable (and probably illegal): if the king wanted money, he should call Parliament, and the fact that the attorney and solicitor general had been asked to examine the militia statutes suggests that the council was less than sure of itself.[99] It was also tactless to suggest that, if the deputies had allowed any militiamen to serve beyond the statutory month, that was their fault and the king would not pay them. It was remarked in several counties that the prospect of serving without pay had reduced the militia's zeal.[100] Parliament preferred the militia to a standing army because, although the king chose the deputies, they determined how effectively it would function. When they actively obeyed commands from the centre, they did so because they accepted that those commands were necessary. Doubts were often expressed about the reliability of the militia soldiers, particularly when dealing with political or religious dissidents.[101] In practice they seem generally to have obeyed their officers, which meant that when the deputies and officers were determined to suppress conventicles or search the 'disaffected' for arms, they did so effectively. The militia might not be a match for fully-trained professionals, but it was more than a match for unarmed civilians, a point emphasized by the volleys and shouts at musters and other exercises.[102] At the Restoration the crown tried hard to re-establish a monopoly of firearms and the searches after the Rye House Plot of 1683 reinforced that monopoly.[103] The fact that Charles II ruled a largely unarmed population meant that, despite his anxieties, rebellion was unlikely, at least in England: Scotland was another matter. On the other hand, his reliance on the gentry, in the commissions of the peace and the militia, meant that there was little prospect of his imposing measures which the gentry generally disliked. Given the king's limited political ambitions, it was unlikely that he would try to do so.

Notes

1 Marvell, II.315.
2 J. Miller, 'Charles II and his Parliaments', *TRHS* 5th series, XXXII, 1982, pp. 15–16.
3 SP 104/180, fo. 179.
4 A.M. Coleby, *Central Government and the Localities: Hampshire 1649–89*, Cambridge, 1987, pp. 125–7.
5 *CJ*, VIII.350–1; PC 2/56, fos. 123, 163; *CSPD 1667*, p. 456; Marvell, II.135–6; R.B. Outhwaite, 'Dearth and Government Intervention in English Grain Markets, 1590–1700', *EconHR*, XXXIV, 1981, pp. 389–406.
6 See J. Miller, *Charles II*, London, 1991, especially ch. 7.
7 T. Barnard, 'Scotland and Ireland in the later Stewart Monarchy' in S.G. Ellis and S. Barber (eds), *Conquest and Union: Fashioning a British State 1485–1725*, London, 1995, pp. 270–3.
8 Clarendon, II.327, 455–6, III.18, 103.
9 CPA 79, Cominges to Lionne, 14 June 1663 NS; Clarendon, I.369–70. The lists of members of the committee in these two sources are very different.
10 Egerton MS 2543, fo. 205 (summary in *CSPD 1667–68*, p. 261).
11 Egerton MS 2539, fos 281, 365. See also K.H.D. Haley, *The First Earl of Shaftesbury*, Oxford, 1968, ch. 12.
12 SP 104/176–80.
13 Sir W. Temple, *Works*, 2 vols, London, 1731, I.333–4; *HMC Ormond*, NS V.55–6; PC 2/68, pp. 1–2.
14 Ailesbury, I.35.
15 R. North, *Examen*, London, 1740, pp. 75–8; BT 143, Barrillon to Louis, 19 June 1679 NS; Temple, *Works*, I.338, 346; *HMC Ormond*, NS IV.521, 545.
16 Morrice, p. 207; *Hatton*, I.211–13; *HMC Ormond*, NS V.454, 459; BT 146, Barrillon to Louis, 28 October 1680 NS.
17 G. Davies, 'Council and Cabinet, 1679–88', *EHR*, XXXVII, 1922, pp. 55–60; Clarke, I.738; BT 155, Barrillon to Louis, 8 July 1683 NS.
18 G. Savile, Marquis of Halifax, *Complete Works*, (ed.) J.P. Kenyon, Harmondsworth, 1969, p. 256.
19 BT 111, Cominges to Louis, 30 April 1663 NS; BT 129, Croissy to Louis, 6 and 9 November 1673 NS; BT 131, Ruvigny to Louis, 16 April 1674 NS; Carte MSS 217, fo. 433, 70, fo. 558; BL, Add MS 63057B, fo. 20.
20 *HMC Heathcote*, p. 48; *Lauderdale*, I.149–50; Stowe MS 211, fo. 216.
21 Stowe MS 201, fo. 162.
22 Stowe MS 216, fos 118–19. For the Irish army, see Stowe MSS 210, fos 402–4, 216, fos 93, 106, 221.
23 See Miller, *Charles II*, pp. 32–7 and *passim*.
24 C.H. Hartmann, *Charles II and Madame*, London, 1934, pp. 204, 217.
25 Pepys, IX.447. See also Pepys, VIII.573.
26 *Essex*, I.140; Temple, *Works*, I.470. See also BL, Add MSS 29571, fo. 394, 29577, fo. 409.

27 Pepys, VIII.332.
28 Perhaps the strongest evidence comes from 1672: see Miller, *Charles II*, p. 177. See also J. Miller, 'The Potential for "Absolutism" in later Stuart England', *History*, LXIX, 1984, pp. 187–207.
29 Clarendon, III.243–5; H. Roseveare, *The Treasury 1660–1870: The Foundations of Control*, London, 1973, ch. 1.
30 P. Halliday, *Dismembering the Body Politic: Partisan Politics in England's Towns, 1650–1730*, Cambridge, 1998, pp. 132–43 and *passim*. For Charles I, see W.J. Jones, *Politics and the Bench: the Judges and the English Civil War*, London, 1971.
31 Carte MS 48, fo. 290.
32 M636/30, Edmund Verney to Sir Ralph, 25 July 1677, M636/31, same to same, 8 July 1678; Henry, p. 257.
33 Egerton MS 2542, fo. 511. For Lancashire see Finch MS P.P. 57(ii), p. 42; for Somerset, BRO, AC/C74/29.
34 Reresby, p. 73; *CSPD 1667*, p. 489, *1670*, p. 3.
35 *CSPD 1670*, p. 524.
36 CKS, U269/C36/6; *CSPD 1672–73*, pp. 121–2, *1676–77*, p. 327.
37 Grey, II.440–1; *HMC 7th Report*, p. 493; *CSPD 1676–77*, p. 406. See also below, pp. 236–7.
38 M636/34, William Denton to Sir Ralph Verney, 11 November 1680; Stowe MS 180, fos. 108–9.
39 M636/31, Edmund Verney to Sir Ralph, 24 and 27 June, 1 and 8 July 1678; *HMC Finch*, II.282.
40 M.J. Braddick, *Parliamentary Taxation in Seventeenth-Century England*, Woodbridge, 1994, pp. 274–5.
41 Braddick, *Taxation*, pp. 132–5, 142–58, 283–4, 295–6.
42 M636/27, Edmund to Sir Ralph, 1 January 1674; M636/27, Sir Ralph Verney to Sir Richard Temple and Sir William Smith, 1 May, Smith to Verney, 5 May 1673; Braddick, *Taxation*, pp. 158–67; C.D. Chandaman, *The English Public Revenue 1660–88*, Oxford, 1975, ch. 5.
43 Braddick, *Taxation*, pp. 168–211.
44 *CSPD 1661–62*, p. 420; Braddick, *Taxation*, pp. 192–3, 211–13.
45 *CSPD 1668–69*, pp. 119, 232.
46 *CSPD 1663–64*, p. 433, *1667*, p. 3.
47 *CSPD 1667*, pp. 3, 142, *1667–68*, p. 52.
48 Grey, I.98; Braddick, *Taxation*, pp. 258–60.
49 *CSPD 1675–76*, p. 369; Braddick, *Taxation*, pp. 261–5, 270.
50 M636/37, Edmund Verney to Sir Ralph, 19 April 1683. See also *CSPD 1667*, p. 77.
51 Braddick, *Taxation*, pp. 253–8, 266, 270.
52 PC 2/66, p. 78; Braddick, *Taxation*, p. 256.
53 Braddick, *Taxation*, pp. 260, 288.
54 *CSPD 1667*, p. 77; Coleby, *Hampshire*, pp. 118–25, 191, 196. P.J. Norrey, 'The Restoration regime in action: the relationship between central and local government in Dorset, Somerset and Wiltshire', *HJ*, XXXI, 1988, pp. 798–803 suggests that in these counties the JPs were less cooperative.
55 Reresby, pp. 104–5, 119, 125, 127.
56 *Ibid.*, pp. 187, 199, 270, 272–3, 376, 278–9.
57 *Ibid.*, pp. 105, 125.

58 *Ibid.*, pp. 278–9.
59 *Ibid.*, pp. 69–70; M.J. Braddick, 'State formation and social change in early modern England', *Social History*, XVI, 1991, pp. 14–15. For 'brokerage' see *ibid.*, pp. 2–10.
60 Tanner MS 47, fo. 47; Braddick, 'State formation', p. 14.
61 J. Miller, 'Catholic Officers in the later Stuart Army', *EHR*, LXXXVIII, 1973, pp. 42–3.
62 *CJ*, VIII.167, 339–40; *HMC Beaufort*, pp. 51–2; Egerton MS 2043, fo. 37; Bodl, MS Eng Letters c. 210, p. 82; *LJ*, XI.359.
63 *CSPD 1663–64*, p. 77; *CJ*, VIII.628.
64 SP 104/177, fos 59, 91–2.
65 BL, Add MS 28040, fo. 7; *Norths*, I.115.
66 *CSPD 1672–73*, pp. 243–4; M636/25, Edmund Verney to Sir Ralph, 11 December 1672; *CJ*, IX.276.
67 *Williamson*, I.88, 94, 116, 158; *Hatton*, I.111; *CSPD 1673*, p. 455; Miller, *Charles II*, pp. 197–8.
68 PC 2/64, pp. 191, 194; *CSPD 1673–75*, pp. 265–6; Rochester, J. Wilmot, Earl of, *Letters*, (ed.) J. Treglown, Oxford, 1980, p. 199.
69 BL, Add MS 29572, fo. 16; *CSPD 1684–85*, pp. 103–4.
70 SP 104/177, fo. 91.
71 *CSPD 1660–61*, p. 582, *1663–64*, p. 439; WYAL, MX/R 12/44; Coleby, *Hampshire*, pp. 107–8, 217.
72 NRO, MCB 23, fo. 249; W. Rye (ed.), *Depositions before the Mayor and Aldermen of Norwich and Extracts from the Court Books*, Norfolk and Norwich Archaeological Soc., 1905, p. 148; *CSPD 1672*, p. 682; A. Coleby, 'Military-Civilian Relations on the Solent, 1651–89', *HJ*, XXIX, 1986, pp. 949–61.
73 *CSPD 1672–73*, pp. 32, 141.
74 *Williamson*, I.24, 58; M636/31, Edmund Verney to Sir Ralph, 25 March 1678.
75 BT 128, Croissy to Louis, 24 July 1673 NS; *CSPD 1673*, p. 455; *Williamson*, I.88.
76 Pepys, VIII.309; *CSPD 1667*, p. 522, *1672*, pp. 509, 555, 567; Bodl, Rawl Letters 104, fo. 116.
77 *CSPD 1666–67*, p. 210, *1679–80*, pp. 124, 144, 145; *CCSP*, V.330; M636/26, Sir Ralph to Edmund Verney, 21 November, M636/27, same to same, 24 November 1673.
78 *CSPD 1667*, pp. 363–4; M636/31, Edmund to John Verney, 15 April 1678; *CSPD 1672*, p. 265.
79 *CSPD 1672*, pp. 415–16, 449–50, 478, 550; PC 2/63, pp. 294–5.
80 *CSPD 1660–61*, p. 511, *1665–66*, p. 350, *1680–81*, pp. 182–3, *July–September 1683*, p. 6; Marvell, II.94. For an order to protect soldiers from prosecution, see *CSPD 1667–68*, pp. 137–8.
81 *CSPD 1663–64*, p. 468; J. Childs, *The Army of Charles II*, London, 1976, pp. 68–71.
82 Browning, *Docts.*, p. 796; BRO, AC/C64/80.
83 *CSPD 1667*, pp. 223–6, 242, 249, 263, 266; Stater, *Noble*, pp. 115–20; Fletcher, *Reform*, pp. 319–29.
84 Norrey, 'Regime', p. 795; Coleby, *Hampshire*, pp. 111–3.
85 R.M. Dunn, *Norfolk Lieutenancy Journal 1660–76*, NRS, XLV, 1977, *passim*; B. Cozens-Hardy (ed.), *Norfolk Lieutenancy Journal 1676–1701*, NRS XXX, 1961, *passim*; Coleby, *Hampshire*, pp. 181–2.

86 CKS, U269/C40/2, C48/8, 9.
87 CKS, U269/C36/6, C43/2, C48/4, 7.
88 CKS, U269/C40/2, 6, 42/1, C48/1, 5, 13–18.
89 *HMC le Fleming*, p. 159.
90 D.P. Carter, 'The Lancashire Militia 1660–88', THSLC CXXXII, 1982, pp. 164–6.
91 CKS, U269/C44/1; BL, Add MS 29148, fos 78, 116, 120, 147.
92 *CSPD 1664–65*, p. 565, *1665–66*, pp. 36–7; BL, Add MS 25124, fos 87–90, 101–2.
93 Stater, *Noble*, pp. 18–21, 26–31, 71–86 and *passim*.
94 For Richmond, see BL, Add MS 21947, fos 167, 191, 298.
95 BL, Add MS 27447, fos 444, 453, 470.
96 PC 2/59, pp. 442, 443, 447.
97 CUL, MS Dd IX 43, pp. 129, 134–7, 139–41.
98 Althorp MS B6, Reresby and others to Burlington, 31 July 1667; Dunn, *Journal*, p. 104.
99 PC 2/59, p. 438.
100 Carte MS 35, fo. 534; *CSPD 1667*, pp. 244, 523.
101 *CSPD 1667*, p. 261, *1671*, pp. 141–2.
102 Carter, 'Lancashire', pp. 166, 169–70.
103 J.L. Malcolm, 'Charles II and the Reconstruction of Royal Power', *HJ*, XXXV, 1992, pp. 319–22; Coleby, *Hampshire*, p. 182; PRO, WO 55/1761: 'An accompt of arms, armour and ammunition seized and taken from persons disaffected to the government'. (I am very grateful to Peter Le Fevre for this reference.)

Chapter three

Favour and reward

The mechanisms of patronage

The rudimentary formal structures of government were supplemented by more informal structures and mechanisms. Often these involved the exchange of favours, courtesies and rewards. Municipal corporations were bound together by ceremony and conviviality and the later seventeenth century saw a proliferation of clubs, often based at a tavern or a coffee-house. The relationships of landlord and tenant, or parliamentary candidate and voters, were smoothed by hospitality, ranging from harvest suppers and Christmas dinners to free beer on election days. Reciprocity did not imply equality – far from it – but it did imply a recognition of obligations on both sides: each had something to gain from the relationship – respect, self-esteem, material reward. At a time of falling rents, landlords needed good tenants and elections gave voters real power, especially in small boroughs. Landowners were expected to be generous and hospitable; social and political relationships were facilitated by courtesies and gifts. When a great lord came to town, civic dignitaries put on their gowns and provided a feast in the town hall (with music); he would respond with money for the poor, a piece of plate, a buck for a special occasion and favours for the town or townsmen.

The seeking and giving of rewards was an essential feature of what one might call a culture of reciprocity. It helped to lubricate the mechanisms of government and to bind society together. Networks of patronage and clientage often centred on people who held major government offices and so had access to the patronage resources of the state, but in many cases they did not, partly because patrons had resources of their own and partly because many who were not major office-holders influenced the distribution of 'government' patronage. Henry Howard, who succeeded his mad brother as sixth Duke of Norfolk in 1677, held no major office (other than that of Earl Marshal) because he was a Catholic. This did not prevent him from wielding very considerable power in Norfolk, based on his massive wealth – he spent £30,000 rebuilding the Duke's Palace at Norwich[1] – and the favour he enjoyed at court. At the Restoration, Norwich corporation looked to him to secure the king's favour, consulted him about the renewal of their charter and meekly accepted his nomination of Thomas Corie, one of his men of business, as town clerk.[2] He was also an important electoral patron: in 1661 he disposed of both seats at

Castle Rising and had substantial interests at Aldeburgh, Arundel and Thetford.[3] His patronage took little account of political or religious affiliations. Despite a stated dislike of 'Presbyterians', he visited Lord Delamere (formerly Sir George Booth) in 1663, found a seat for the old Parliamentarian Sir John Holland in 1661 and was on friendly terms with Edward Reynolds who, before becoming bishop of Norwich, was widely seen as a Presbyterian.[4]

While Howard's personal patronage resources were considerable, they paled into insignificance compared with those of the crown: indeed the effectiveness of such men as patrons depended substantially on their ability to beg favours from the king. **The** source of rewards was the king's court. Before discussing the mechanisms and content of patronage, however, it is worth asking whom the king chose to reward and why. There was an element of personal favour. Charles's mistresses and illegitimate children, together with close friends (like Charles Berkeley, Earl of Falmouth) enjoyed more than their fair share of his bounty. Others were rewarded for services: past, present and future. Throughout the reign – and particularly in the 1660s – petitions stressed sufferings and services in the civil wars. Others claimed rewards for current services: in local government and in Parliament, as ambassadors, as office-holders whose outdated salaries barely met their costs. And others could expect reward because of who they were and the services they could perform in future. Lords lieutenant acted as the king's eyes and ears in the provinces and imposed his will in times of crisis. While the richest rewards went to the most powerful and well-connected, many smaller items went to lesser fry: by securing places as postmasters or customs officers for their clients, or benefices in the church for their chaplains, substantial provincial figures bolstered their local standing. Moreover, important figures in the administration and the court also profited from securing favours for others. Although in an ideal world such men would have been happy to serve the king for nothing, the culture of reciprocity was deeply engrained. As one MP wrote in 1673: 'it is an ill omen of the fall of a state where such as serve the public out of a good conscience have no other reward for so doing but the satisfaction of their good conscience.'[5]

Let us consider how favours were secured. In a personal monarchy, those who did not personally enjoy the king's favour had to enlist the help of others who did. Access to the king was crucial. Intelligent and quick-witted though he was, Charles was easily influenced – by those who amused him, by those with stronger personalities than his own and by those who nagged with sufficient brazenness and determination.[6] Often he consented to requests to free himself from importunity or to avoid upsetting people – only to change his mind later.[7] The ability to speak to the king – having 'the king's ear' – was a valuable asset.[8] In February 1667, at a time of severe financial stringency, two gentlemen of the bedchamber were exempted from the general order to suspend the payment of pensions[9] and, in general, well placed and importunate courtiers enjoyed a substantial share of the royal bounty.

It should not be assumed that all those seeking favours were greedy or cynical. Royalists who had suffered heavy losses felt that they had a claim on the king's gratitude, but many were reluctant to ask. Daniel Fleming's father had lost his life and estate; he himself served diligently as a JP and in the militia but told Williamson that he would become a beggar before he became good at begging favours (which he proceeded to do).[10] Others were driven by a sense that others, less deserving than themselves, had been rewarded.[11] Others were made desperate by debt.[12]

The Earl of Winchilsea served as ambassador at Constantinople partly in the hope of living more cheaply there, but his debts continued to mount when he returned home, his health deteriorated and the king failed to reimburse what he had spent.[13] Philip Fetherstonhaugh, whose father had been killed at Worcester, was given a horse and arms and a place in Lord Oxford's regiment in 1662, but the horse died, he lost his place and petitioned the king for a new horse; it is not recorded that the petition was granted.[14]

Those with no access to the king needed a patron at court: Winchilsea remarked that since the death of the Earl of Southampton he had had no friend to remember him.[15] One reason for the Earl of Arlington's success as a patron was that he was approachable, loyal and considerate: Evelyn told Pepys that Arlington did far more for his clients than Clarendon, who would do nothing except for money.[16] The Earl of Bristol advised the Duke of Richmond that Arlington was much more likely than his beautiful duchess (a favourite of the king's) to secure the favour he asked, because Arlington knew the right time to press for it. The chancellor of Cambridge University told the Master of Pembroke Hall that Arlington could be relied upon to repay the respects shown him with civility and kindness.[17] In return for securing favours, patrons expected to be treated with tact and respect. In 1673, when Sir Edward Dering's search for a place or pension was failing, he let Arlington know that he still looked upon him as his patron and had made no approach to anyone else.[18] Arlington was less than pleased that his client, Clifford, was appointed lord treasurer, and Williamson turned against him.[19] Clarendon was still more prickly: he was offended in 1667 that Ossory (Ormond's son) had received three honours, none of them from him, but (as Ossory remarked) it was not unreasonable that Arlington – his brother-in-law – should do him favours.[20]

Among those influencing the distribution of patronage, women played a significant role. Charles's love of women is well known, but he claimed that they did not influence his government. There are few recorded instances of his mistresses influencing high policy, although early in 1678 Charles discussed Louis XIV's latest peace proposals with Portsmouth.[21] However, those seeking favours were quick to approach them and they were quick to cash in on their influence. As Clarendon wrote, Charles 'did not in his nature love a busy woman and had an aversion to speaking with any woman, or hearing them speak, of any business, but to that purpose he thought them all made for; however, they broke in afterwards upon him to all other purposes.'[22] Clarendon blamed his fall in large part on Lady Castlemaine. Later Portsmouth established an ascendancy which seemed to be based more on friendship than passion: in 1682 Reresby remarked that she dominated the distribution of patronage, although it was generally believed that he had not slept with her for months.[23]

The king's leading mistresses profited enormously from his generosity. Marvell claimed in 1671 that Castlemaine was receiving nearly £10,000 a year from the excise, £10,000 from the customs farmers and £5,000 from the Post Office, together with a plethora of one-off grants: for example, Charles granted her Phoenix Park in Dublin, without bothering to consult the lord lieutenant first.[24] In 1682, having found it impossible (for legal reasons) to assign Portsmouth £5,000 a year on the Post Office, Charles granted her £100,000 over two and a half years for a 'project' to secure her in her old age.[25] She also accumulated offices and other rewards for her son. Early in 1682 it was reported that she wished to combine his existing post of Master of the Horse with that of Master of the Wardrobe, which would create the richest office at the court.[26] The influence of Castlemaine and Portsmouth made it essential for those in power, and those seeking favours, to cultivate their goodwill. Castlemaine's £10,000 a year on the customs was a reward for her assistance in securing the new customs farm.[27] Portsmouth, for her part, was careful to establish a mutually advantageous rapport with successive lord treasurers: she used her influence with the king on their behalf while they looked after her interests at the treasury. Others courted her even if they disapproved of her as a Frenchwoman, a Catholic and a mistress. The city fathers of York disapproved of stage-plays: in the words of one (far from impartial) observer, 'I believe there is not such a fanatic bench of aldermen in all the king's dominions.' Nevertheless they thought it politic in 1683 to appoint her son as their high steward in the hope that she would ward off the threat of the loss of their charter.[28]

It was not only the leading mistresses who acted as patrons or solicited for patronage. Like the Duke of Richmond, Winchilsea and Robert Paston, Earl of Yarmouth sent their wives to press for favours. Winchilsea was also promised the help of the Duchess of Somerset and Lady Southampton (wife of the lord treasurer), but to little avail.[29] Paston's experiences were, if anything, more dispiriting. The spectre of debt preyed on his mind and impaired his health. The debts he inherited from his father were compounded by his own extravagance: he had a passion for collecting and insisted on entertaining the king and queen at vast expense when they came to Norfolk in 1671; he also had a large family.[30] His correspondence with his wife is filled with the tribulations of seeking favour. After he became lord lieutenant of Norfolk in 1676, he had to spend more time in the county, so that the main burden of lobbying devolved on his wife. It was a role which she embraced enthusiastically, but with limited success: her son was later told that she was regarded at court as indiscreet and mischievous.[31] Among those she sought to use were a number of women. In their correspondence, she and her husband used symbols for Portsmouth, Lady Danby (widely believed to take bribes in return for influencing her husband[32]), the Countesses of Peterborough and Bath, Lady Shannon, Mrs Knight and Mrs Progers (presumably the wife of Edward Progers of the bedchamber). She was also advised by a certain Lady Baker to enlist the support of Nell Gwynn, on the grounds that she had more wit than the rest.[33]

The difficulty of securing favour owed much to the fact that the demand for rewards far outstripped the supply. The Royalists' losses greatly increased the number of people with a claim on the king's gratitude, while fear of parliamentary censure and the advent of treasury control reduced the range of possible items of patronage. The pivotal role of the king and his susceptibility to influence added to the uncertainties facing those seeking reward. Quite apart from his habit of making promises that he did not intend to keep, or fending off suitors with fair words, there was the problem that grants might be stopped by one of his great officers or that he might be persuaded to change his mind at some stage before the grant could be completed.[34] This made the securing of any favour a frustrating, time-consuming and perilous endeavour, in which apparent success could turn into failure at any point. Ormond told his son to attend the *levées* of the king and his brother, in case Irish affairs were mentioned: 'sloth and too nice a modesty can be of no use'.[35] If a matter went before the council, it was necessary to brief friends and canvass others.[36] If the approval of more than one official or courtier was required, it needed luck and skill to ensure all were present at one time.[37] The tortuousness of the process gave considerable power to those involved in every stage: not only the secretaries of state, lord treasurer and those who controlled the great and privy seals (lord chancellor, or lord keeper, and lord privy seal) but also the under-secretaries, clerks and doormen, who controlled access to their masters and produced the documents. These men were usually paid derisory salaries, but were compensated by the fees they exacted and by the payments which they expected – or demanded – in return for their services.[38] What would now seem gross corruption was generally viewed as a natural part of an administrative system that was rudimentary, underfunded and dependent for its effective operation on exchanges of services and favours. It rested on a view of office as property. Some offices passed from father to son; others were bought and sold. Although the latter practice was nothing like as extensive as in France, it was common for outgoing office-holders to be bought out by their successors, sometimes with the assistance of the king.[39] This posed some problems for the crown. In France, the systematic sale of offices left the king legally and politically unable to dismiss a very wide range of officials. Charles had to contend with a similar problem, albeit on a far smaller scale, but this arose because of the practice of granting some offices for life, rather than the practice of purchase, which operated between individuals, not between office-seekers and the crown. Thus one of the king's most forthright critics in the Commons, Colonel John Birch, auditor of the excise, continued in office (at a salary of £500 a year) until his death. Similarly Buckingham, in disgrace with both king and Commons in 1674, was compensated for the loss of the mastership of the horse, which he had purchased for life – with the king's help.[40] In addition, granting reversions (promising the succession of a place on the death or retirement of the current incumbent) enabled the king to stretch his meagre patronage resources further, but at the cost of further reducing his control over his servants in the future.[41]

Given the nature of office, and the culture of reciprocity, it was natural that patrons, courtiers and officials expected due recognition for their services. The papers of Sir Joseph Williamson, under-secretary and later secretary of state, are full of requests for favours, often accompanied by promises of payment. William Sheridan, bishop of Clogher, offered £6 for a letter to the lord lieutenant saying that he was too ill to travel to his diocese.[42] Lady Mary Graves, whose late husband had sustained great losses in the civil war, offered Williamson and his superior, Arlington, as much as £500 (plus the necessary fees) if they could ensure success in any of a series of projects.[43] Similarly, he was offered money for procuring revenue farms,[44] offices in the revenue or local government (Reresby offered 'one hundred pieces' in return for a second year as sheriff of Yorkshire),[45] patents for new inventions,[46] payment of moneys owed by the crown[47] and even (despite the risk of simony) preferments in the church.[48] Similarly, his underlings and those of other senior officials routinely expected douceurs from those with dealings with their masters, as a 'remembrance', 'to be the welcomer when we come next'.[49] A failure to match up to expectations could cause offence.[50] These habits and attitudes ran through all aspects of government. The Earl of Sandwich was told that to keep the friendship of courtiers required 'the continual warmth of mutual offices' or at least the expectation thereof.[51] When Arlington took over the Post Office, postmasters offered up to £20 to keep their places; some London merchants received overseas letters sooner than others because they gave wine or money to the clerks.[52]

These practices were well established in Elizabeth's reign and continued under the first two Stuarts,[53] but some forms of payment were regarded as more acceptable than others. Pepys was in many ways a new breed of civil servant: conscientious, methodical and imbued with a sense of service to the state. But he was also concerned to make his way in the world. Offered £200 a year out of a naval contractor's profits, he wrote:

> . . . as I would not by anything be bribed to be unjust in my dealings, so I was not so squeamish as not to take people's acknowledgement where I have the good fortune by my pains to do them good and just offices. And so I would not come to be at an agreement with him, but I would labour to do him this service and to expect his consideration thereof afterward, as he thought fit.[54]

He would never take money to the detriment of the king's service, but he would be happy to receive due acknowledgement once he had done his best for the king; he would never ask payment in advance: that was bribery.[55] Others were less scrupulous. Lord John Berkeley allegedly boasted in 1663 that he had made £50,000 in douceurs since the Restoration; the lord chamberlain's secretary told Pepys that his horse, boots, wine and almost everything he had were bribes.[56] As for Williamson, his correspondence does not reveal how many of the proffers he accepted, but when offered money by Croissy, the French ambassador, he said that he could not accept a present until the treaty between England and France had been concluded. He added that he had no influence over Arlington in matters of state, but would let Croissy know if he heard anything of relevance.[57] It is possible that Williamson was more scrupulous about taking money from foreign powers than from English suitors. Clarendon refused a gift from Nicolas Fouquet (on which the king told him he was a fool), but had no qualms about demanding or accepting gifts from Englishmen.[58] Others who were even less scrupulous still drew a line between bribes and legitimate payments. John Ashburnham was expelled from the Commons in 1667 for taking bribes from French wine merchants. Some MPs were not convinced that he had agreed a price beforehand for doing their business in Parliament, but others claimed that he had accepted the 'bribe' not as an MP but as a courtier, which apparently made everything all right.[59] The Commons did not condemn members who had received unsolicited gifts of wine from the merchants or the House's clerk and sergeant, who had been paid their fees in wine.[60]

The nature of rewards

In an ideal world, the king's bounty would have been just that: granting away only what was his – money, lands, offices. A lucky few received gifts of cash or lucrative offices; rather more were granted pensions, but pensions needed to be assigned on secure branches of the revenue and often fell into arrears.[61] In periods of retrenchment pensions, like the 'board wages' and free meals of courtiers, were among the first expenditures to be axed. It made far better financial sense to annoy aged or impoverished Royalists and courtiers[62] than the City bankers on whose credit the government depended: the one occasion when the government broke this rule, in the Stop of the Exchequer of 1672, it took years to repair the damage. Moreover, however generous the king might be, he had to contend with lord treasurers who sought to curb his generosity. In 1667 the treasury commission was set up to monitor spending and so laid the foundations of treasury control.[63] This did not stop him from trying to divert money from the Exchequer to the privy purse – he always liked to have a fund under his own control, which made it even more vital to have the king's ear.[64] As for lands and offices, the crown lands had been severely depleted by sales under the Tudors and early Stuarts. The lion's share of what remained was granted to the queen and queen mother as their jointures; the remainder was mostly either sold off or let on long leases, so that little was left for use as patronage.[65] As for offices, the number of genuinely lucrative places, in terms of salary, fees or the prospect of additional earnings on the side, was relatively small – certainly far too small to meet the demand. It could be expanded somewhat by granting reversions, but an office in reversion was obviously a less valuable commodity than present enjoyment of the office. For this reason Charles occasionally announced that he would grant no more reversions, but soon did so: he was always inclined to break his own rules.[66]

As the king had far too few rewards of his own to satisfy the hordes of aspirants, he fell back on forms of patronage which cost him nothing, fell outside the regular revenue or could be granted at the expense of others. Of those which cost nothing, honours were among the most sought after – and so needed to be managed with care. There was a flurry of peerage creations and promotions at the Restoration, which included old Parliamentarians like

Albemarle, Ashley (later Shaftesbury), Holles, Anglesey and Crew as well as Royalists like Clarendon, Bath and Newcastle (promoted from marquis to duke). In 1665, however, Charles told Clarendon that he thought the peerage had become too large and that he had decided to create no more peers: there was a danger that the lustre of the peerage would be diminished and with it the peers' influence.[67] He did not entirely keep to his resolution, but his creations thereafter were sparing – especially when compared to the 'inflation of honours' in which James I and Charles I indulged under the influence of the first Duke of Buckingham.[68] Between 1660 and 1680 there were twenty-eight creations and fourteen promotions. Of these twelve went to royal bastards, their spouses and their mothers, but the remaining thirty went to men who came of ancient families or who held high public office or had rendered significant services to the Stuarts. There was a new surge of twenty-five creations and promotions in 1681–85, the majority going to Tory magnates (such as Beaufort and the Earl of Plymouth) in the vanguard in the fight against Whiggery and Dissent in the provinces. These creations were offset by extinctions with the result that the peerage was little larger in 1685 than it had been in 1646.[69]

As far as other honours were concerned, the most exclusive was the Garter: Charles was embarrassed when the youthful but ambitious Ralph Montagu persuaded Louis XIV to press for his admission to the Order.[70] Knighthoods and baronetcies were, by contrast, relatively easy to come by, to a point where some thought the honour had been devalued. Daniel Fleming decided that he did not really want to be a knight: there were enough in his county already. Baronetcies had been created for sale (by James I) at £1,000 each, but in 1660 the market was so glutted that the going rate was £400 or less.[71] Serjeant Newdigate was disappointed to be made a baronet: he had hoped to be made a judge or an Irish viscount.[72] The dignity was further reduced by the fact that the right to nominate a baronet was often given as a reward and then sold by the recipient.[73] Moreover, while the warrants to create the new baronets usually spoke of their ancient lineage, substantial estates and loyalty, the veracity of such statements was open to question: few Royalists would see the old Cromwellians Sir Samuel and Sir Thomas Barnardiston as men of 'irreproachable loyalty'.[74]

Moving on from grants of honours, which harmed no-one and were undoubtedly in the king's gift, we come to a greyer area, much of it concerned with what one might call the private enterprise aspects of administration and law enforcement. One aspect of the relative underfunding of the English monarchy (at least before 1688) was the inadequacy of officials' salaries and their consequent reliance on fees and other payments from the public. Another was the granting of what would normally be seen as 'public' functions to private individuals who were rewarded for their services out of moneys paid by the public. Those seeking favours from the crown therefore needed to identify 'something to beg' – an economic privilege, a task that needed performing, a law that needed to be enforced (involving the collection of fines) or moneys due to the crown that needed to be collected. Of these, the economic privileges had perhaps been the most resented in the half-century before 1640. Before the 1624 Monopolies Act, the crown had the legal right to grant monopolies on particular overseas trades or home-produced manufactured products (usually with the pretence that the latter were a new invention). Equally it could legally grant letters patent empowering individuals to perform particular tasks for the public good – for example, to build a harbour or render a river navigable – and to recoup their costs from those who benefited. Used responsibly, such powers could protect bona fide inventions, encourage trade and industry and facilitate public works projects. Between the late 1580s and the 1630s, the crown's powers were often misused to 'legitimize' scams or protection rackets, allowing favoured individuals to make extortionate profits at the expense of particular groups of people – alehousekeepers, gold and silver thread makers, religious refugees – or the general public. The 1624 Monopolies Act outlawed most grants of this kind, but contained loopholes, which were closed by a second Monopolies Act in 1641. Charles II never tried to create any monopoly of the sort misused by his predecessors. His secretary to the treasury advised him to be wary of projects and monopolies, which were tempting to a king short of money, but ruinous to the state.[75] He issued patents granting the sole use of a new invention, but always with a proviso that the patent would be withdrawn if it were found not to be really new, or proved prejudicial to the public.[76] In at least one case the sole right to a manufacture was endorsed by Act of Parliament.[77] When Sir Sackville Crow suggested setting up a corporation to encourage the manufacture of tapestry, he was advised to prepare a parliamentary bill to vest the necessary power in the king.[78]

More problematical were patents to perform services seen as beneficial to the public, which might be open to abuse. Pedlars and petty chapmen were viewed with suspicion by market towns (who saw them as taking away business), by county magistrates (who saw them as little better than vagabonds) and by the government (who worried that they might disperse seditious literature). There was thus a strong case for licensing them – it was claimed that the more respectable pedlars wanted this – and in 1665 a patent was granted to set up a licensing office; they would charge a fee for each licence and pay the king an annual rent of £666 13s 4d. They claimed that they would issue licences only on receipt of a certificate from a JP and a recognizance for good behaviour and asked the king to issue a proclamation to publicize the office. No proclamation appears to have been issued. Seven years later they claimed that they had lost money seeking legal confirmation and publication of their grant. The king wrote to the Lord Keeper on their behalf, but in 1676 they had still failed to put their patent into effect.[79] Meanwhile the Commons in 1675 brought in a bill to suppress (rather than regulate) pedlars and petty chapmen. It failed, but another passed into law in March 1678; it stated that any patent or charter to license them was null and void.[80]

The failure to establish by patent a system for licensing pedlars in part reflected the practical problems of regulating such mobile and solitary people, who clearly met an economic need. It also probably reflected the hesitancy of the crown's law officers, especially in the face of the Commons' deep suspicion of patentees. In the first years of the reign the Commons denounced patents for ballasting ships and for the discovery of lands gained from the sea in Sussex and other counties. The House condemned the actions of those executing the patents rather than the patents themselves, but ordered the impeachment of the patentees. The king apologized for the misuse of the lands patent and assured the House that he always sought legal advice on such projects and heard objections.[81] After 1663 he does not seem to have issued any patents which offered scope for extortion, but the possibility of contention remained, notably concerning lighthouses. It was generally agreed that it was reasonable to expect merchants and shipmasters to contribute to the cost of lighthouses, from which they benefited, but the Commons were very sensitive to any levy of moneys other than by Act of Parliament. For this reason, in 1660, the promoter of a plan to build a lighthouse on Spurn Head stressed that he would try to secure an Act.[82] However, from 1661 the king granted licences to levy a charge on ships passing certain lighthouses, with a flurry of grants in 1665.[83] In at least two cases it was stated that the patent would be confirmed by Act of Parliament[84] but the bills did not pass. In November 1667, with the Commons in angry mood, the patent for a lighthouse at Milford Haven was attacked, with claims that the patentees had levied substantial sums. Some months later the patent was voted a grievance and the king withdrew it.[85] The following year Sir Robert Paston was told that if he wished to seek such a grant he would need the written agreement of a substantial number of shipmasters to pay for the upkeep.[86] In 1671, following complaints of masters and owners from Chester and Liverpool, a patent to establish lighthouses on the coasts of Ireland was voted a grievance, although the House stopped short of declaring it 'illegal', because they did not wish to impinge on the king's prerogative.[87] In 1676 a licence to build lighthouses stressed that any payment for their maintenance had to be voluntary.[88]

There had long been a private enterprise element in the enforcement of penal statutes (those imposing penalties). Many provided for informers to receive a share of the fines in case of a successful prosecution; this continued under Charles II (for example, in the 1670 Conventicle Act). Informers were often unpopular and sometimes roughly treated, but their activities were rarely politically contentious – they were helping to enforce Acts of Parliament – and they were not dependent on patrons or patronage for their profits. More dubious were threats of legal proceedings (or legislation) in order to extort money. Those who feared exclusion from the Act of Indemnity bought off those who threatened them.[89] In 1664 the Earl of Berkshire (who had extorted £500 from Bulstrode Whitelocke in 1660) claimed that he had a verbal order from the king to prosecute the Jews for being in England contrary to law; he added that he would desist if they came to a financial arrangement with him. The Jews petitioned the king and were told he had issued no such order.[90] According to Clarendon Berkshire's 'interest and reputation were less than anything but his understanding',[91] but he was adept at finding favours to beg and, as a gentleman of the bedchamber, he was well placed to beg them. He was especially interested in collecting fines. In theory fines imposed by the courts and moneys from forfeited recognizances were due to the king, but they often proved difficult to collect. There was thus a case for turning the collection of fines over to private individuals, giving them the power to compound – to accept less than the full sum was a lesser evil than receiving nothing at all or waiting for payment.[92] The practice of compounding was well established and was used in the beer excise, where the precise amount of leakage and spillage was impossible to prove. Those granted the right to collect fines would either pay a rent to the crown and keep all they collected, or receive a proportion of the moneys they collected: perhaps as much as half, usually much less.[93]

Grants of this type were quite frequent, especially in the early 1660s. Apart from collecting the fines imposed by the criminal courts (granted mostly to a syndicate which included Berkshire), there were similar grants to recover fines for breaches of the Navigation Acts, the Acts concerning sewers, against new building in London and against forestalling and regrating corn, wool and cattle.[94] Other grants involving the legal system included some of the profits of the central courts, leased out to courtiers (such as the Earls of Berkshire and Suffolk): these included the fees for sealing writs in King's Bench and Common Pleas, the Greenwax fines in the Exchequer and the 'post fines' of Common Pleas.[95] Similar grants were given to discover concealed royal lands (cases where royal ownership had simply been forgotten) or other royal property[96] and to recover a wide range of moneys collected during the civil wars and Interregnum and not yet accounted for: mostly taxes, but also money for the Committee for the Propagation of the Gospel in Wales.[97]

In some respects these could be seen as sensible measures, which enabled the king to reward his servants and compensated for the inadequacies of the regular administration. There was scope for negotiation: the auditors of the arrears of the monthly assessment remarked that it was easier and less contentious to recover the money by compounding than by recourse to the law.[98] But there were snags. Seeking out concealed lands called men's titles into question; chasing up moneys collected in the 1640s and 1650s went against the spirit of the Act of Indemnity. In 1662 it was declared that 'the king will grant no more discoveries': he did not fully adhere to his resolution, but they were granted less often and had more or less disappeared by the end of the decade.[99] In 1665 Clarendon and Southampton warned the king of the dangers of Berkshire's patent to collect fines. The judges had complained that he and his agents compounded even with those convicted of great misdemeanours, which obstructed justice. JPs set smaller fines if they saw fines going to private individuals. Charles was later to order that all fines should be paid initially into the Exchequer. Now he resolved to call in Berkshire's patent and to make no more such grants; the lease of the Greenwax and post fines to Berkshire and Sir Robert Howard may well have been the compensation which Charles had promised if Berkshire surrendered his patent.[100] The surrender of Berkshire's patent seems to have marked the end of the farming of fines within the criminal law. In 1679 a syndicate (including Lords

Peterborough and Yarmouth) was empowered to collect details of fines, forfeited recognizances and the like, but not to collect the money.[101] The king retained the right to grant away, as a pure favour, fines on individuals or forfeitures of property. These included the estates of some of the regicides and of Lord Grey of Wark, condemned for treason in 1684.[102] But the king also granted away the forfeitures of lesser fry, such as Pope Danvers, who had killed a man and whose estate had been begged by the Earl of Peterborough, or a certain Combes, charged with manslaughter, whose estate (if convicted) was promised to Lord Hawley, one of the less fortunate old Cavaliers. (In the event Combes was pardoned.)[103] More odious still was the practice of begging a number of convicts to be transported (for the grantee's profit) to the plantations. This reached its apogee in the disposal of the captured rebels after Sedgemoor in 1685. Lord Chief Justice Jeffreys informed James II that they were worth £10 to £15 a head and urged that they should be granted to deserving people or else 'persons that have not suffered in your service will run away with the booty'.[104]

If such practices as the granting of the property or persons of convicted felons continued throughout the reign, some forms of patronage used in the early 1660s fell into disuse thereafter, because they harmed the revenue, were grievous to the subject, interfered with the course of justice or provoked the wrath of Parliament.[105] Tougher control of expenditure by the treasury commissioners and lord treasurers from 1667 further restricted the scope of patronage, leaving suitors to look elsewhere. In the 1660s prize goods allowed some scope. In about 1663 Monmouth was granted all moneys due from prizes since 1642, but Ashburnham complained that anyone who had prize goods seized was allowed to compound and then found a courtier to beg the money he had paid and split the proceeds with him.[106] In the Dutch War of 1665–67 all those who could helped themselves to Dutch and French prizes. The fact that the king intended prize moneys to go into a special fund which he could control without the lord treasurer's supervision added to the chaos. Sandwich was made scapegoat for the general plunder, having distributed the cargo of a Dutch prize to his flag officers, with the king's permission. Pepys believed that others had taken far more, but Sandwich received all the blame. The king also granted away so many prizes that he received little income from them.[107]

The golden shower of prize goods dried up before the war ended and was not repeated in the Third Dutch War of 1672–74, when the proceeds from their sale were paid into the Exchequer.[108] Suitors had to cast their eyes elsewhere. After the attack on the Milford Haven lighthouse patent, Charles made no further grants in England and Wales, but he continued to do so for Ireland, where the Restoration land settlement had offered rich pickings to well-placed Englishmen in the 1660s.[109] Although the powers of the treasury commision extended to Ireland, there are signs that a more relaxed attitude prevailed under Clifford and Danby,[110] the latter using Irish patronage to compensate for the dearth of resources in England. This led experienced predators like Castlemaine to beg favours such as Phoenix Park. The Earl of

Essex, a diligent and honest lord lieutenant, repeatedly found himself hamstrung by patents, grants and other encumbrances. Any money not assigned for a particular purpose would be begged by an English courtier. Small wonder that Essex compared Ireland to the corpse of a stag, torn to pieces by hounds.[111]

Thus far I have tended to stress the inadequacies of the administrative system, which left scope for granting out tasks which it found difficult. In one area, the revenue, Charles II inherited an administration far more sophisticated and efficient than that of his father. By the end of the reign the customs, excise and hearth money were all being collected directly, by a salaried service with clear rules of procedure, promotion and discipline: personal favour in tax collection had been replaced by routine.[112] The 'Downing proviso' of 1665 attempted to establish a similar regularity and predictability in the payment of moneys owed by the crown.[113] Such a professional revenue system would not seem likely to provide much scope for patronage, but two points are worth making. First, even after professionalization had been taken even further, the revenue system played a vital part in the Whig patronage machine under the first two Georges. Secondly, direct collection started in the customs in 1671, but in the excise and hearth money only in 1683–84. The latter two branches were farmed, in one way or another, for most of the reign and even after 1671 a number of small customs duties continued to be farmed by private individuals.[114] Policy towards the customs, and its use as patronage, was notably more *ad hoc* than policy towards the excise. Apart from the perennial flow of those seeking places in the customs, including Williamson's brother George,[115] there were also farms, but these carried risks. After earning the king's gratitude by proposing the figure of £2,500,000 for a grant of taxation in December 1664, Sir Robert Paston cast around for a suitable reward. He offered £2,700 a year (or whatever the king thought fit) for the farm of the duties on a wood, glass, earthen and stone wear, oranges, lemons and pomegranates, which were said to be worth £3,300 a year, although others put the value at over £4,700. He was granted the farm in February 1666, but the huge increase in timber imports following the Great Fire led the king's ministers to renegotiate the contract and he was forced to agree to a new annual payment of £6,500.[116] Thereafter, what had seemed the solution to his financial problems became a millstone around his neck and by 1671 he was, he said, staring ruin in the face.[117] His friend (and later foe) Lord Townshend suffered badly when the depredations of the Dutch on the coaling trade drastically reduced the profits of his coal farm.[118]

The excise was less likely than the customs to be disrupted by war, which made excise farms a safer proposition. Parliament encouraged the gentry to invest in farms by laying down in 1660 that the first lessees should be nominated by the JPs in quarter sessions, a means of compensating old Cavaliers for their losses in the civil wars. In some counties there was considerable interest. George Williamson was ready to offer as much as £2,000 for the excise for Cumberland and Westmorland (plus £100 for his brother) but desisted when two of the major county gentry entered the bidding. In the majority of counties the farm was awarded to the nominees of quarter sessions, 'the country gentlemen'.[119] When a new farm was launched in 1665, the gentry were more wary. Fleming doubted if anyone could compete with the existing farmers, who knew exactly what it was worth but were also prepared to 'rack' the county more than the gentry were willing or able to do.[120] The gentry had found that it was hard to make a profit without imposing an undue burden on the 'country' and risking widespread unpopularity. Some, indeed, made a loss.[121] Financial and commercial interests, most of them London-based, moved into excise collection. They proved more efficient (and had greater financial resources), but their more ruthless methods also provoked greater popular resistance.[122] By the early 1670s, the usefulness of excise farms as an instrument of patronage seemed to have been exhausted.

The patronage system of Charles II's England seems in many ways corrupt and unfair: overfed gentlemen of the bedchamber profited vastly while old Cavaliers went hungry. Recipients of royal favour exploited the vulnerable and unfortunate. And yet it is difficult to find any very coherent challenge to the system. Particular complaints of injustice and general denunciations of the rapacity of courtiers[123] did not build into sweeping proposals for reform: a proposal in 1668 to substitute salaries for fees in the Exchequer came to nothing.[124] Often complaints reflected the resentment of the 'outs' against the 'ins'. Reresby was shocked when he was told in 1677 how many 'Country' leaders had solicited rewards from the king.[125] By that time, there were signs of party divisions, which were far less apparent in the 1660s, when court and council contained a mixture of old Cavaliers and old Parliamentarians, supporters of unbending Anglicanism and of comprehension and indulgence (not to mention Catholics). As Henry Howard showed in Norfolk, the patronage system was broadly non-partisan: few were excluded wholly from its benefits, apart from rigid Dissenters and irreconcilable republicans. If many were disappointed, those who failed could always try again, borne up by the eternal optimism of suitors and a comforting awareness of the element of luck. Even the slowness of the system was not altogether a disadvantage: it delayed satisfaction but it sustained hope.[126] Only when the crown's patronage began to be distributed on systematically partisan lines in the 1670s did the system itself begin to fall into disrepute.

Notes

1 *HMC Portland*, II.269–70.

2 NRO, FAB6, fos 213, 218, 219; F. Blomefield, *An Essay towards a Topographical History of Norfolk*, 11 vols, London, 1805–10, III.404; T. Corie, *Correspondence*, (ed.) R.H. Hill, NRS, 1956, pp. 10, 29.

3 *HP*, I.323, 332–3, 394–5, 418.

4 H. Newcome, *Diary*, (ed.) T. Heywood, Chetham Soc. 1849, p. 210; C. Robbins, 'Election Correspondence of Sir John Holland of Quidenham, 1661', *Norf Arch*, XXX, 1947–52, pp. 130–9; *HP*, I.323; Tanner MS 46, fo. 51. For Howard's attitude towards Presbyterians, see BL, Add MS 18744, fo. 33.

5 *Williamson*, II.78.

6 See Miller, *Charles II*, pp. 30–7.
7 Clarendon, III.3; North, *Examen*, pp. 657–8.
8 *HMC 5th Report*, p. 154; Ailesbury, I.88; Stowe MS 216, fo. 139.
9 *CSPD 1666–67*, p. 515.
10 *CSPD 1673–75*, p. 521 (summary *HMC le Fleming*, p. 115).
11 CKS, U269/C319, Lord Hawley to Lord Fitzharding, 8 January 1664.
12 *CSPD 1666–67*, pp. 401, 402, *1667–68*, p. 54, *1670*, p. 280, *1673–75*, p. 355.
13 *HMC Finch*, I.293, 459, 470–1; *CSPD 1675–76*, pp. 446–7, *1680–81*, p. 361.
14 *CSPD 1665–66*, p. 146.
15 *CSPD 1675–76*, p. 447.
16 Pepys, VIII.185–6. For Arlington, see BT 110, Cominges to Louis, 15 January 1663 NS; Burnet, *Suppl*, p. 66; Pepys, VIII.289. For Clarendon, *HMC Heathcote*, pp. 54–5; Egerton MS 2537, fos 279–80.
17 BL, Add MS 21947, fo. 239; *CSPD 1671*, p. 68.
18 CKS, U1713/C1, no. 20.
19 CPA 104, Croissy to Pomponne, 8 December 1672 NS; Evelyn, IV.119.
20 Carte MS 220, fos 257–8.
21 BT 138, Barrillon to Louis, 31 January 1678 NS.
22 Clarendon, III.61.
23 Reresby, pp. 247–8.
24 Marvell, II.325–6; Stowe MSS 201, fos 389, 391, 202, fo. 34; *Essex*, I.58, 73.
25 BT 150, Barrillon to Louis, 18 December 1681 NS; Clarke, *James II*, I.724–5, 729–30.
26 CPA 149, Barrillon to Louis, 4 March 1682 NS.
27 Chandaman, *Revenue*, p. 27n.
28 WYAL, MX/R 18/93 (quoted), 18/87a, 21/26, 23/2, 24/7. For the hostility to plays, see *ibid.*, 21/27.
29 *HMC Finch*, I.459, 287, 290–1.
30 R.W. Ketton-Cremer, *Norfolk Portraits*, London, 1944, pp. 31–7, 43; *CSPD 1671*, p. 516; Bradfer, Lord to Lady Yarmouth, 22 October 1677, 14 April 1678; NRO, MC 107/4, Charles Cornwallis to Mary Heveningham, 10 October 1671.
31 Morrice, p. 361; BL, Add MS 36988, fo. 233.
32 Reresby, p. 172. Note similar allegations against the Duchess of Albemarle: Clarendon, I.366.
33 BL, Add. MS 27447, fo. 447. For the ciphers, see *ibid.*, fos 303–5.
34 North, *Examen*, pp. 657–8; Ailesbury, I.96; Burnet, *Hist*, I.466; Clarendon, III.3.
35 *HMC Ormond*, NS IV.93.
36 BL, Add MSS 29560, fo. 334, 29571, fos 196–7, 346.
37 Stowe MS 201, fo. 162; BRO, Common Council Proceedings 1670–87, fos 192–5.
38 See Sandwich's comment in Pepys, I.223.
39 *CSPD 1672–73*, p. 510 (Buckingham); CPA 92, Croissy to Lionne, 11 October 1668 NS (Trevor); BT131, Ruvigny to Pomponne, 21 June 1674 NS (Williamson); Temple, *Works*, I.448 (offer to help pay half of the cost of the secretaryship if Temple would pay the other half).
40 *HP*, I.654–5; BL, Add. MSS 18979, fos 285–6, 25123, fo. 34; Stowe MS 204, fos 174, 281, 283; *CSPD 1672–73*, p. 510 (for the king's assisting the purchase).
41 For a full discussion of appointments, reversions and tenure at an earlier period, see G.E. Aylmer, *The King's Servants: the Civil Service of Charles I*, London, 1961, pp. 69–125.

42 *CSPD 1668–69*, pp. 517–8, 522.
43 *CSPD 1660*, pp. 36, 256, 376, 395, 440–1, *1663–64*, pp. 48, 368, 672.
44 *CSPD 1663–64*, p. 577.
45 *CSPD 1667*, p. 489. For other examples, see *CSPD 1660–61*, pp. 480–1, 490, *1667–68*, pp. 386, 573, *1668–69*, p. 184, *1677–78*, pp. 638–9.
46 *CSPD 1663–64*, p. 435.
47 *CSPD 1665–66*, p. 594.
48 *CSPD 1667*, pp. 491–2, *1667–68*, pp. 581–2, *1671*, p. 200.
49 *HMC Kenyon*, p. 69; Newdigate, p. 28. For other examples, see *Cosin*, II.29; H. Stocks and W.H. Stevenson (eds), *Records of the Borough of Leicester IV 1603–88*, Cambridge, 1923, p. 473; *CCSP*, V.21; *CSPD 1671–72*, p. 568.
50 *CSPD 1667–68*, p. 303.
51 Mapperton, Letters from Ministers etc, II, fos 110–1.
52 *CSPD 1667*, pp. 8, 28, 44, 52, *1667–68*, p. 429, *1666–67*, p. 502.
53 See J.E. Neale, *The Age of Catherine de Medici*, London, 1963, pp. 145–70.
54 Pepys, IV.415–6.
55 *Ibid.*, IV.436, 439–40, V.5.
56 *Ibid.*, IV.331, VIII.369.
57 BT 120, Croissy to Louis, 19 November 1668 NS.
58 Clarendon, I.522–3; Burnet, *Suppl*, p. 55; BT 108, Bartet to Mazarin, 23 November 1660 NS; Whitelocke, pp. 608, 661–2; *CSPV 1661–64*, pp. 97, 198, 206; Pepys, II.213, VIII.185–6; BL, Add. MS 40713, fo. 32.
59 Milward, pp. 132, 134–5; Egerton MS 2539, fo. 145; BRO, AC/C74/33; *HP*, I.552–3.
60 Milward, p. 137
61 *CSPD 1665–66*, p. 594, *1666–67*, p. 402, *1667–68*, p. 54.
62 See Pepys, V.73; Carte MS 33, fo. 170.
63 See Roseveare, *Control*. Even Southampton, the feeblest of his lord treasurers, tried to curb the king's generosity: Pepys, V.40, 50; Clarendon, III.3.
64 Clarendon, II.341; Burnet, *Hist.* II.100. Pensions assigned on the privy purse were more likely to be paid than those assigned on the Exchequer: *CSPD 1665–66*, p. 594.
65 Egerton MS 2542, fo. 408; Chandaman, *Revenue*, pp. 110–15.
66 *Williamson*, II.14. The treasury commissioners denounced reversions in 1679: Dering, *Papers*, p. 115.
67 Clarendon, II.314.
68 Stone, *Crisis*, ch. 3.
69 Miller in Moore and Smith, (eds), *Lords*, pp. 70–1, 76–7.
70 CPA 103, Croissy to Pomponne, 7 and 11 April 1672 NS. For the dashing of Winchilsea's hopes of a Garter, see *HMC Finch*, I.287, 291.
71 *CSPD 1673–75*, p.521; *HMC 5th Report*, p. 205.
72 Newdigate, pp. 25, 32
73 *CSPD 1660–61*, pp. 438–42, *1663–64*, pp. 96, 368.
74 *CSPD 1663–64*, pp. 79, 93, 96, 359; *HP*, I.595–8.
75 Dorset RO, D124, box 292, 'Analyses and comparisons of state of royal revenue . . . 1618–67'. fos 1–2.
76 See for example, *CSPD 1663–64*, pp. 186–7, *1664–65*, p. 405, *1667–68*, p. 398, *1668–69*, p. 422; Marvell, II.267.
77 *LJ*, XII.443, 446.

78 *CSPD 1661–62*, p. 277.
79 *CSPD 1664–65*, p. 400, *1672*, p. 350, *1676–77*, p. 34; PC 2/65, p. 162. There is no proclamation on this topic from 1665–67 in R. Steele, *Tudor and Stuart Proclamations: I England and Wales*, Bibliotheca Lindesiana, Oxford, 1910.
80 *CJ*, IX.332, 367, 373, 399, 456; *HMC 9th Report, Part II*, p. 110.
81 For the ballast patent, see *CJ*, VIII.272, 279–80; Marvell, II.28–9, 33; *HMC 7th Report*, p. 145. For the lands patent, see *CJ*, VIII.507, 511; *CSPD 1663–64*, p. 177. For similar earlier grants concerning coastal lands, see *CSPD 1661–62*, pp. 238–9, 582.
82 *CSPD 1660–61*, pp. 135, 386.
83 *CSPD, 1661–62*, pp. 52, 446, *1664–65*, pp. 226, 457.
84 *CSPD 1661–62*, p. 446, *1664–65*, p. 226.
85 Milward, p. 109, 247–8; Grey, I.126; Marvell, II.131.
86 *HMC 6th Report*, p. 366.
87 *CJ*, IX.199, 202; Marvell, II.130–1; Grey, I.383–7; Dering, *Diary*, p. 74.
88 *CSPD 1676–77*, pp. 33–4.
89 Whitelocke, pp. 600–1, 608; Evelyn, III.245.
90 Whitelocke, pp. 600–1; *CSPD 1663–64*, p. 672.
91 Pepys, X.199.
92 Egerton MS 2549, fos 44, 46; *CSPD 1661–62*, pp. 73–4, 280.
93 *CSPD 1660–61*, p. 369, *1661–62*, p. 74, *1663–64*, p. 354, 357; *1664–65*, p. 95. See Braddick, *Taxation*, pp. 205–6.
94 *CSPD 1660–61*, p. 524, 47, *1663–64*, pp. 401–2, 372, 642.
95 *CSPD 1660–61*, pp. 209, 577.
96 *CSPD 1663–64*, pp. 354, 357, *1666–67*, pp. 544, 551, *1667–68*, p. 309, *1670*, pp. 356–7.
97 *CSPD 1660–61*, pp. 260 (Welsh CPG), 369, 564, *1663–64*, p. 354, *1664–65*, p. 68, *1666–67*, p. 551.
98 *CSPD 1660–61*, p. 564.
99 *CSPD 1661–62*, p. 451, *1664–65*, p. 68, *1667–68*, p. 309.
100 *CSPD 1665–66*, pp. 71, 412–3, *Jan–June 1683*, p. 265; BL, Add MS 28051, fo. 12.
101 Morrice, p. 187: see also *ibid.*, p. 353 for the failure of a bid to farm the Greenwax fines.
102 *CSPD 1660–61*, pp. 558–9, *1661–62*, p. 72; BT 159, Barrillon to Louis, 21 August 1684 NS; *HMC Ormond*, NS IV.595–6.
103 *CSPD 1678*, p. 401, *1663–64*, pp. 264, 270, 272, 336, 343. For Hawley, see CKS, U269/C319, Hawley to Fitzharding, 8 January 1664; *HP*, II.515–6.
104 *CSPD 1665–66*, p. 138, *1685*, no. 1644.
105 See the arguments in Egerton MS 2549, fos 44, 46; *CSPD 1665–66*, p. 71.
106 *CSPD 1663–64*, p. 400–1; CKS, U269/C315, Ashburnham to Charles Berkeley, 4 May 1663.
107 Clarendon, II.341; BL, Add MS 4182, fo. 49; Mapperton, Letters from Ministers etc, I, fo. 67; Pepys, VI.314, 342; Carte MS 34, fo. 453.
108 Chandaman, *Revenue*, p. 132.
109 Carte MS 32, fos 56–7; *Hatton.*, I.34; CPA 86, Courtin to Lionne 23 July 1665 NS.
110 Roseveare, *Control*, pp. 35, 42–3.
111 Stowe MSS 214, fo. 111, 201, fos 107, 393, 215, fo. 167.

112 Chandaman, *Revenue*, pp. 27–36, 72–6, 104–9.
113 H. Roseveare, *The Financial Revolution, 1660–1760*, London, 1991, pp. 14–15. For the damage done to this system by the Stop of the Exchequer, see *ibid.*, pp. 21–3.
114 Chandaman, *Revenue*, pp. 30–1.
115 *CSPD 1660–61*, pp. 187, 469, *1670*, p. 24. He also became a hearth tax collector, *CSPD 1664–65*, p. 343.
116 *CSPD 1665–66*, pp. 104, 228; *HMC 6th Report*, p. 365; *HP*, III.211–2.
117 *HMC 6th Report*, pp. 365, 370; *CSPD 1671*, p. 516.
118 Coventry MS 4, fo. 67.
119 Chandaman, *Revenue*, pp. 42–3, 54; *CSPD 1660–61*, pp. 364, 401, 529, *1661–62*, p. 444.
120 *HMC le Fleming*, p. 36. It should be added that the previous year Fleming had considered farming the even more unpopular hearth tax: *CSPD 1663–64*, p. 618. He had also showed an interest in farming the Lancashire excise: *CSPD 1664–65*, pp. 24, 211.
121 *CSPD 1670*, p. 612.
122 Chandaman, *Revenue*, pp. 55–6; Braddick, *Taxation*, pp. 207–11; P. Halliday. 'A Clashing of Jurisdictions: Commissions of Association and Restoration Corporations', *HJ*, XLI, 1998, pp. 443–5.
123 For example BL, Add MS 10116, fo. 237; *HMC 5th Report*, p. 205; Burnet, *Suppl*, p. 44; M636/25, Edmund Verney to Sir Ralph, 19 February 1672.
124 Egerton 2539, fo. 281.
125 Reresby, p. 123.
126 See the constant optimism shown by Sir William Smith in his 'tin business': BL, Add. MS 28077, fos 41–3, 93, 107 (covering the period February 1674 to March 1675); M636/28, Edmund Verney to Sir Ralph, 21 December 1674; M636/29 same to same, 8 May 1676; *HMC 7th Report*, p. 468; M636/30, John Verney to Sir Ralph, 26 March 1677, M636/33, Sir Ralph to John Verney, 21 July, 20 and 27 October 1679; M636/37, same to same, 13 November 1682.

Chapter four

News

The demand for news

The civil wars had divided the English people ideologically to an unprecedented extent and had greatly heightened popular awareness of political events. Both Parliament and king soon accepted that this was a war for hearts and minds as well as one fought with arms. Through the press, the pulpit and the marching armies the issues were carried to most parts of the land. Members of rural and urban elites were quickly forced to declare their allegiance, but humbler people too developed their own opinions, from soldiers talking politics in winter quarters to Cornish women who attacked Roundhead soldiers as they retreated from the county.[1] After the first civil war the issues were never to seem as clear-cut, but there was still much to preoccupy the reading public, from reports of victories in Ireland and Scotland to prurient accounts of Ranters and Quakers. People in the 1640s and 1650s had been exposed to a volume of news and political information vastly greater than had ever been seen in England before. Was this exposure to continue under Charles II? And would his subjects' thirst for news breed divisions and threaten the stability of his regime?

It was generally agreed that Restoration Englishmen were addicted to news. 'News is as necessary an ingredient for a letter as straw is for brick'; it 'is grown as constant an ingredient of a London letter as the picture is of the almanac'.[2] In 1678 Sir Ralph Verney wrote to his son John: 'your news supplies us all with chat for a week after, till the carrier comes again and then we are as greedy of more as you can imagine.'[3] For Sir Edward Dering in 1671 'to enjoy the peace and quiet of the country and yet know what part is acting upon the great theatre of the world is surely one of the most pleasant conditions we are capable of.'[4] London was the source of news, the 'fountain head'.[5] Sir Roger Burgoyne remarked that those who stayed in the country lived in the dark and that events in town were riddles that needed to be explained.[6] Edmund Verney wrote to his father that sending news to London was like sending coals to Newcastle. Nevertheless, those who lived 'hermit like' in the country 'are as high conceited of our abilities to judge, rule and govern any affairs whatsoever . . . as any of you all'. The Marquis of Newcastle's plea that gentlemen should talk only of hunting and hawking was hopelessly anachronistic.[7]

Nor was it only the gentry who were interested in news. The Marchioness of Worcester urged her husband to forbid his servants to send news to their colleagues in the country.[8] In 1680 one writer complained that the shouts of the London news-sellers kept him awake.[9] In 1665 a French diplomatic delegation commented that in England everyone thought himself competent to discuss politics. Boatmen ferrying peers to the Lords expected them to discuss the day's business, while what was said in the king's closet soon became public knowledge.[10] In 1673 a future Whig MP, Sir Thomas Player, complained that 'every carman and porter is now a statesman'; Newcastle made a similar comment more than a decade earlier.[11]

This thirst for news antedated 1640. The first regular manuscript newsletters appeared in the 1590s. They became more numerous in the 1620s and were supplemented by printed 'corantos' (dealing with foreign news) and manuscript 'separates': parliamentary proceedings and speeches and other items of interest.[12] The 'corantos' were cautious and bland, but the newsletters mixed information with comment, often partisan or scurrilous. Letter-writers focused on conflict, privy councillors 'leaked' details of divisions in the council. Between 1621 and 1628 there were five general elections, in which MPs campaigned on their records in the House. The net result was a more informed public, presented with a largely oppositionist view of national politics.[13] The boldness of the newsletters made the government's ability to censor the printed word less significant than it might seem. Nevertheless, the collapse of censorship in 1640 led to an explosion of news in print, as publishers exploited public curiosity about the dramatic events that were unfolding and both sides in the civil war appealed for support. Parliament became convinced that liberty of the press was degenerating into licence, but not until the Protectorate was an effective censorship reimposed.[14] By then, the reading public had become accustomed to a regular diet of news. The early Stuarts had made little attempt to exploit the media, except through proclamations and the occasional printed treatise. In 1621 the council rejected a suggestion that it should produce a 'gazette of weekly occurrants'.[15] Charles II, too, disliked public discussion of politics[16] but realized that the media had to be used as well as controlled, that the public's hunger for news had to be fed with a healthy diet of 'accurate' information.

This chapter discusses the dissemination and control of information under Charles II. There were three major differences between his regime and Charles I's. First, it provided its own news service, supplementing the proclamations and other approved documents (such as the king's speeches to Parliament) which were sent into the provinces, to be posted up or read aloud in market squares or at quarter sessions; both king and Parliament at times ordered that documents be read in parish churches.[17] It did so through the printed *Gazette* and officially approved newsletters. These were more informative than the *Gazette* and went some way to meet the demand for news: whereas commercially-produced newsletters flourished in the 1620s,[18] I have found only limited evidence of them under Charles II before 1675. Secondly, the dissemination of news was linked to the gathering of intelligence, at home and abroad. Thirdly, the government used the Post Office to intercept private correspondence and to give approved newsletters a price advantage over possible commercial rivals by allowing them to be sent post free. I shall look in turn at the main modes of dissemination: print, handwritten materials and word of mouth, although it is artificial to distinguish sharply between them. News was gathered by word of mouth in London, transmitted in handwritten letters or in print into the provinces, where it became the object of 'chat'. Reading newsletters or newspapers aloud made written news available to the semi-literate or the illiterate, as did ballads, prints, playing cards and other visual representations.[19] Nevertheless, it is easier to deal in turn with each mode of transmission – and government attempts to control it.

Print

For much of the reign print was probably the least important means of dissemination. As the most 'public' medium, it was the most open to government control and the least suited to confidential items: Newcastle thought manuscript newsletters did more harm, because they were bolder.[20] The Licensing Act of 1662 was the first to provide a statutory basis for pre-publication censorship. It set up a system of licensing and laid down punishments for the authors, publishers and printers of unlicensed works. It also aimed to reduce the number of presses, by providing that the number of master printers should be reduced to twenty. It was intended to be only temporary, but was extended in 1665 until the end of the next Parliament (which turned out not to be until May 1679). It then lapsed until it was re-enacted under James II.[21] For the greater part of the reign the crown had in place an unquestionably legal censorship system, but it proved difficult to make it effective. The surveyor of the press, Roger L'Estrange, was diligent to the point of fanaticism, but he met with little support and witnesses against clandestine printers were hard to find.[22] Moreover, his view of what constituted 'seditious' material might not coincide with that of the king's ministers and he claimed that his powers of search lapsed when Arlington ceased to be secretary of state.[23]

Other methods of control were therefore needed. It was hoped that the Stationers' Company, in return for their monopoly of certain lucrative works (the 'English stock'), would police the trade, but they were more concerned with infringements of their monopoly than with works unacceptable to the government. Neither threats to the Company's charter in 1670, nor the promise of the fines for illicit printing proved sufficient to jolt the Stationers out of their lethargy.[24] Other weapons at the government's disposal could be used only after the offending item had been published. In extreme cases it invoked the law of treason, on the grounds that seditious publications were designed to bring about the king's removal or death. In 1664 John Twyn was executed for treason. Two prominent publishers, Francis Smith and Giles Calvert, were held on treason charges in 1661; Smith was imprisoned on the same charge in 1681.[25] Charges of treason were hard to prove however. In 1676 Freake and

Radford were accused of producing a libel which included the line 'Let's seize the king and outdo Blood.' (Colonel Thomas Blood had tried to kidnap Ormond – and to steal the crown jewels.) The council could find only one witness against Freake, who was acquitted, as was Radford, though only after a grand jury had found a true bill against him.[26] There were a few prosecutions for seditious libel, but this was never easy to prove and tended to be used as a substitute for the Licensing Act (after it expired) rather than as a supplement to it.[27] The government also insisted that those who licensed hawkers and pedlars should forbid them to carry seditious pamphlets.[28]

Whatever the Act's defects, although many unlicensed religious tracts were published, few politically 'seditious' works appeared before 1679. Quaker publications accounted for nearly 6 per cent of all titles between 1674 and 1684, but the Quaker leadership took care to ensure that they were politically innocuous.[29] Some politically contentious works were printed abroad, such as Peter Du Moulin's *England's Appeal* (1673) or the memorials and other documents dispersed by the Dutch and Spanish ambassadors. Copies of the Amsterdam and Haarlem *Gazettes* circulated in London.[30] Disgruntled army officers printed an account of their mistreatment in the French service with 400 copies for MPs. In the 1670s a number of polemical oppositionist works, such as *A Relation of the Most Material Matters handled in Parliament* (1673), Shaftesbury's *A Letter from a Person of Quality* (1675) and Marvell's *An Account of the Growth of Popery and Arbitrary Government* (1678) were printed in England (although Marvell's title page claimed that it had been published in Amsterdam).[31] After the Licensing Act expired, far more politically contentious works were published. L'Estrange proposed that the king should incorporate the printers as a company separate from the stationers as a means of controlling the trade, but the scheme failed.[32] The council instructed L'Estrange to seize libels and prosecute their printers according to law, but it was unclear what the law was. In October the council ordered Lord Chief Justice North and the attorney general to decide whether two particularly objectionable pamphlets warranted prosecution.[33] On the basis of their report, the king issued a proclamation against seditious and scandalous books that were libels against any person or the government; those responsible for producing them were to be prosecuted according to law.[34] In effect, the government was reduced to using the law of seditious libel (which required evidence of seditious or malicious intent) or encouraging peers to bring actions of *scandalum magnatum* (which required evidence that a statement defaming a peer was untrue). It also persuaded the Lord Mayor to hamper the distribution of pamphlets by clamping down on hawkers.[35]

Such methods did little to stem the flow pouring from London's presses, although most newspapers suspended production. The crown secured one or two verdicts under the law of seditious libel, with Lord Chief Justice Scroggs arguing that the fact of publication was evidence of seditious intent, but the recent Habeas Corpus Act made it harder to keep printers in gaol pending trial.[36] In May 1680, the judges stated that the king could prohibit the publication of unlicensed pamphlets and newsbooks, as tending to a breach of the peace. This, in effect, reverted to censorship based on the prerogative. It marks a change from the judges' position the previous October and an important step in the politicization of the judiciary.[37] The government secured one conviction under this proclamation, that of Henry Care, but the election of two strongly Whig sheriffs ensured that all jurors empanelled for London and Middlesex would now be Whigs and that charges against Whig printers and booksellers would be thrown out. Meanwhile, the Commons' hostility drove Scroggs and Sir George Jeffreys (recorder of London) to resign their posts.[38] In 1682, however, two Tory sheriffs were declared to have been elected: henceforth, with Tory juries, the government could suppress unlicensed pamphlets despite the lapsing of the Act. The flood of Whig printed news dried to a trickle.[39] In 1684 an action of *quo warranto* against the Stationers' Company led to the installation of assistants who would do the government's bidding. A few unlicensed works still appeared, but mainly (like Lord Russell's speech on the scaffold) in manuscript; the press was dominated by Tory or pro-government works.[40]

Charles II's regime never believed that censorship alone was enough. He might not like people discussing his government – 'why should we make all the world wise of what we do?' – but he knew that, to counter rumour and innuendo, something had to be said to the people.[41] When he returned in 1660 the two weekly printed newsbooks were quickly taken over by the crown and all others were suppressed. Henry Muddiman produced the newsbooks until 1663, when they were assigned to L'Estrange in payment for his duties as surveyor of the press.[42] L'Estrange expressed little enthusiasm for his task, remarking that in an ideal world the people would be kept ignorant of matters of state and that his task was to 'redeem the public from their former mistakes.'[43] He proved an ineffective journalist so in 1665 the printed newsbooks were taken out of his hands and assigned to the office of Joseph Williamson, undersecretary (and later secretary) of state.[44] The *London Gazette*, as it became known, the only newspaper officially authorized between 1666 and 1688, was initially praised for the quality of its news.[45] Later, however, it contained mainly foreign news, proclamations and other official pronouncements – and advertisements, for which the clerks who wrote the copy received the money. When an address from the Commons was printed in the *Gazette* in 1678, there were complaints that the House had been reduced to the level of runaway servants and lost dogs.[46] Whereas the earlier newsbooks had included domestic news (including proceedings in Parliament) there was virtually none in the *Gazette*, although proclamations or accounts of executions for treason referred obliquely to events at home. In general, however, the tone was authoritative, impersonal and reassuring.[47] Occasionally it was accused of being too pessimistic or premature,[48] but in general its official status led shrewd observers to view its contents with scepticism.[49] Nevertheless, it provided a basic minimum of authoritative information, while its limited content enhanced the value of manuscript newsletters, which contained more news.

The government complemented the *Gazette* with other printed items, ranging from royal proclamations and speeches to *God and the King*, reprinted in

1662, which set out the subject's duty of allegiance and was supposed to form the basis of the instruction given by the clergy and heads of households. By the 1670s, the government was coming to appreciate the need to counter oppositionist propaganda. L'Estrange circumvented the licensing machinery in order to publish Marchamont Nedham's *Pacquet of advices . . . to the men of Shaftesbury* (1676).[50] L'Estrange also showed his own talents as a polemicist, in pamphlets (such as *Account of the Growth of Knavery* and the *History of the Plot*) and in the journal *The Observator*, in the first issue of which he stated: 'Tis the press that has made 'em mad and the press must set 'em right again'.[51] Although it was not an 'official' publication, L'Estrange had the text of each issue approved by a secretary of state. It was hugely successful, thanks to its wit and approachable, robust style: he was later described as one of the 'great masters of the English tongue'. It was claimed in 1681 that the *Observator* and another Tory publication *Heraclitus Ridens* had done more for the service of church and crown than all the nation's divines and lawyers put together. Having initially condemned their opponents for their 'popular' use of the press, the Tories matched them and the reimposition of censorship gave them an added advantage. In November 1682 a news-writer noted that all printed 'intelligences, courants and mercuries' had been suppressed, leaving only the *Observator*.[52]

Handwritten news

This can be divided into three categories: private correspondence, in which news was mingled with business and family matters; 'separates' (for example, parliamentary proceedings); and newsletters. Of these, the first survive in the largest quantities and were presumably the most numerous at the time. The correspondence of the Verneys of Claydon, for example, contains a wealth of news and political comment together with estate and family matters. Often letters were copied or passed on. In 1665 an account of a sea battle, sent by a chaplain with the fleet to a friend at Oxford, was transcribed by another person and sent to Richard Newdigate in Warwickshire. In 1660, Dr Thomas Smith of Cockermouth received news from various correspondents in London, which he sent to Daniel Fleming at Rydal, who in turn passed it on to William Ambrose at Lowick. Smith also received letters sent from George Johnson in Carlisle to Lady Fletcher, who also received letters from Anne Tolson.[53] In 1678 the Marquis of Worcester scoured Newbury for the latest news, eventually locating a man who was allowed to peruse the letters of a nearby parson, who showed him two newsletters, one from Muddiman, the other from a private correspondent.[54]

In 1653 the council of state had decreed that the carriage of letters within the kingdom should be a state monopoly, because 'a post office is the best means to maintain trade, convey dispatches and discover dangerous designs'. From the outset, the Post Office was intended to facilitate the interception of 'dangerous' correspondence; the methods – and some of the personnel – were taken over by the restored monarchy.[55] In theory, no letter could be opened without a warrant from a secretary of state and only letters of ambassadors, or those regarded as politically suspect, could be tampered with. In practice, 'politically suspect' was interpreted very widely. Letters from the Duke of Ormond were intercepted in 1669 (just after his dismissal from the lord lieutenancy of Ireland) and in 1684 (when he was again under threat). On both occasions, the intercepts were obtained by Ormond's political enemies.[56] The Earls of Orrery and Essex made similar complaints and others – even the king – feared that the same could happen to them.[57] Letter-writers often remarked that some news was not safe to commit to paper,[58] and their fears were not groundless. In 1663 Dick Lane was turned out of his post and banished to Jersey for reflecting on Lady Castlemaine, and the king's recent declaration in favour of toleration, in a private letter; his fate was still remembered fifteen years later.[59] Five individuals were made to enter into bonds totalling £1,000 to deliver the author of a 'seditious' letter sent to New England.[60] In 1676 Sir Philip Monckton was sent to the Tower for writing scandalous letters into the country. In 1684 Sir Samuel Barnardiston – arrested in 1667 on a charge of sending false news – was fined £10,000 for seditious libel for remarks in private letters.[61] Occasionally, letters were intercepted en bloc – for example, letters out of London after the Presbyterians' victory in the City parliamentary election in 1661.[62] Post Office officials intercepted some of Muddiman's newsletters, extracting news to use in those emanating from Williamson's office.[63]

Given the risks inherent in using the post, letter-writers used other methods. The safest was to send letters by a reliable bearer, but this was often not possible. Others included the use of carriers or stagecoaches. These could prove quicker than the post,[64] but sometimes letters went astray.[65] The Verneys were driven to distraction by the drunken son of the Brackley carrier, who had a habit of losing letters.[66] Once letters had been left at the nearest town some way had to be found of getting them to their destination: the Verneys usually relied on someone at Buckingham or Aylesbury market delivering them to Claydon.[67] Despite the drawbacks of carriers and coaches, many used them. In 1663 the postmaster general, Daniel O'Neale, fearing for his profits, asked the secretaries to forbid the transmission of letters by such means; in 1667 a proclamation forbade anyone not licensed by the postmaster general to carry letters and in 1683 another forbade carriers and coaches to carry letters unless they were enclosed in parcels.[68] From 1680, people in the London area had the option of the penny post, which delivered as far as Isleworth or Croydon; in 1683 it was incorporated into the Post Office.[69]

One contentious type of news related to Parliament, whose proceedings were supposedly confidential, until parliamentary reporting was legalized in 1771.[70] The Long Parliament had repeatedly published resolutions, manifestos and other documents, but in June 1660 the Commons ordered that no-one should presume to publish its proceedings without leave. The order was renewed in 1661 and again (on the Speaker's casting vote) in 1673. Not until 1680 did the House resolve to print its 'votes', once they had been perused by the Speaker. The Commons now authorized the publication of other material

– resolutions of the House, Plot narratives, Coleman's letters.[71] For most of the reign, however, it was more secretive – at least in theory. MPs were forbidden to take notes, but many did and there were complaints that they made public the deliberations of committees.[72] Manuscript copies of the 'votes' – summaries of proceedings, as recorded in the journals – could be obtained from the clerks of the two Houses, providing a valuable supplement to their earnings. These 'votes' circulated in letters and appeared in print in Dutch and French gazettes (and the early printed newsbooks).[73] Other, more confidential documents also found their way into the public domain. In Cheshire a draft of the bill to continue ministers circulated in 1661 and the Commons' petition against popish recusants in 1663.[74] In 1679 Thomas Comber received a manuscript copy of one of Danby's speeches, in Yorkshire, a fortnight before it appeared in print. A favoured few gained access to still more sensitive material. In 1678, Danby's incriminating letters to Ralph Montagu were read to a select group of ten or twelve in the Speaker's chamber; Lord Herbert wrote down the gist and sent it to his father. Sir Cyril Wyche went one better and secured copies from the clerks, which he sent to Ormond.[75] By 1679 it was also possible to obtain manuscript summaries of debates (the French ambassador enclosed translations in his dispatches) and more general accounts of the Commons' proceedings (and individual speeches) appeared in print.[76] Often their accuracy and authenticity were questionable, but a member of the 1681 Parliament thought that the printed account of its debates, though 'lame', was basically accurate.[77]

In October 1678 the Commons debated the dissemination of their 'votes'. All agreed that the journals were in the public domain and that MPs had a right to take copies. (Others who were not MPs took copies as well.)[78] Some members, however, argued (as their forebears had in 1641) that to publish debates was 'criminal' and an appeal to the people. The House resolved that its 'votes' should not be disseminated or published in coffee-houses.[79] However, it was widely accepted that MPs should keep their constituents informed of matters which affected them. In 1678 Danby's son, Lord Latimer, told the corporation of Corfe Castle that he believed that to be his duty. Sir Peter Tyrrell (unlike his predecessors) sent all kinds of material to the thirteen electors of Buckingham; Sir Ralph Verney followed suit during the brief Parliament of 1681.[80] Few were more assiduous than the MPs for Hull. William Ramsden assured the corporation that his accounts of the Commons' proceedings were fuller than those supplied by the clerks. Andrew Marvell sent detailed accounts of proposals for taxation as well as more general parliamentary news (for example the report of the commission of accounts in 1669: he had been able to obtain only one copy, so asked the corporation to send it back).[81] Nevertheless, Marvell doubted the propriety of revealing such information: he repeatedly asked that members of the corporation should keep it to themselves.[82] However, it is questionable whether – before 1675 or even 1678 – the public was better informed about events in Parliament than it had been earlier in the century. Not only do far more parliamentary diaries survive from the 1620s or early 1640s than from the 1660s, but an impressionistic survey of major archives suggests that information survives in much greater quantities on the Parliament of 1628 than on those of the 1660s (with the possible exception of the proceedings against Clarendon in 1667). This is not to suggest that there was little public interest in what happened in Parliament, but rather that events there in the 1660s were seen as less crucially important than in 1628. There was a lively interest, perhaps, but not deep anxiety or commitment.

Parliamentary 'votes' also had a place in the newsletters produced in the secretaries' offices. These had two great advantages: they were transmitted post free and used the information, domestic and foreign, gathered by the secretaries and so had a fuller factual basis than those of any private newswriter. Such information was too valuable to be made available in the *Gazette* at a penny a copy. It was sent to paying customers and to those who either needed it or could offer information in exchange: English ambassadors and consuls abroad, officials in the provinces, the publishers of leading continental gazettes. The letters formed part of an international barter economy: material from Muddiman's newsletters appeared in Casteleyn's Haarlem gazette.[83]

In the late 1660s Williamson had some 120 correspondents. The majority received their letters gratis; for him, at least, newsletters were not a commercial proposition and did little more than cover their production costs, notably the wages of the clerks. One senior clerk (in the 1670s Robert Yard) wrote the letters from the materials in the office and his junior colleagues copied them out.[84] Often the secretaries and their staffs were overwhelmed with other business and there were many complaints that the promised letters (or *Gazettes*) had not arrived (although this may at times have been the fault of the postal service). Williamson's letters did not have the field to themselves. After losing the printed newsbooks to L'Estrange in 1663, Muddiman had turned to producing newsletters. Encouraged by Secretary Nicholas, he had already built up a network of correspondents. Sir Henry Bennet (later Lord Arlington) succeeded Nicholas as secretary and ordered Muddiman to pass on relevant information to undersecretary Williamson, from whom he would receive foreign news in return. In 1666 Arlington dismissed Muddiman, allegedly for keeping the best news for himself, which Muddiman denied.[85] He moved into the office of the other secretary, Sir William Morrice, and remained there under his successors. At first there was an unscrupulous competition for custom. Muddiman tried to entice away Williamson's correspondents and gave out that Morrice's office dealt with all important business[86] and that his newsletters were much superior to Williamson's.[87] Williamson's ally James Hickes, of the Post Office, for a while refused to allow Muddiman to send his letters post-free and frequently intercepted them, partly to discover what Muddiman was saying about Williamson (and Hickes), partly to filch his news. Ill-feeling between Muddiman and Hickes continued well into the 1670s.[88] From 1666, therefore, rival newsletter services operated from the secretaries' offices. As the *Gazette* became anodyne, the newsletters became the lineal descendants of the earlier newsbooks, with domestic (including Parliamentary)[89] as well as foreign news. Paying customers (for either newsletter) were usually charged £5 a year: Muddiman demanded £10 from Hull corporation, which decided that the sum was better spent on its existing supplier, Robert Stockdale. A few privileged individuals (like Williamson's friend Daniel Fleming), paid less; others clubbed together to subscribe to Muddiman's letter. Muddiman's profits were sufficiently large to enable him to buy a country house, near Earl's Court. (One of his predecessors in the 1650s had allegedly made £500 a year.)[90]

If each secretary's office produced not much more than 100 newsletters each week, and some received letters from both,[91] these would not seem to qualify as 'mass media'. However, some recipients were peers and other powerful figures, with extensive clienteles and contacts.[92] Others were in a position both to gather information and to pass news on, either orally or by letter. Some noted that they had seen several copies.[93] For the Norwich tavern-keeper Robert Scrivener or the Yarmouth coffee-seller Richard Bower, up-to-date news was essential for their business. (Scrivener paid for his newsletters, though sometimes below the going rate; Bower provided intelligence.)[94] Postmasters and customs officers spoke to many people – especially if they also kept a tavern.[95] Williamson's correspondent in Coventry was a baker.[96] At times they were expected to pass on reassurance as well as news, for example, to allay public fears when the king fell ill.[97] After the Great Fire correspondents countered rumours and false news with the accurate material in the *Gazette* (better regarded then than it was to be later) and Williamson's letters. In 1678 Speaker Seymour asked Williamson for some 'intelligence, that I may barter with my neighbours, who are well furnished from the coffee-houses'.[98] On the other hand, when Williamson was informed in 1667 that the letters from his office were 'reflected on' in Nottingham as in a London coffee-house, the newsmonger was 'suppressed'.[99]

The letters from the secretaries' offices, while well informed, were politically 'safe'. There were exceptions: in 1677 Muddiman wrote that Spain was planning to declare war on England.[100] In 1676 Williamson was acutely embarrassed by a report, originating in his office, that the king intended to attack Algiers.[101] In general, however, the letters from the secretaries' offices seem to have been regarded as both authoritative and credible: Muddiman ostentatiously headed his 'Whitehall'. There are few signs of attempts to establish rival newsletter services before about 1675.[102] Some 'separates' – such as Lord Lucas's supposed speech of 1671 – and letters – like that from a French captain complaining, in 1673, that the French fleet had failed to fight – achieved wide circulation;[103] and there were always lampoons and satires.[104] A letter of 1672 referred to 'the newsmongers' implying that some made their living from news, but the first regular independent news service which I can identify was that of Edward Coleman, whose first letter to Sir Richard Bulstrode, ambassador at Brussels, dates from April 1675. By 1678, a writer could distinguish between Coleman's 'intelligence' and his 'public paper'.[105] Coleman, a busy man who eventually paid for his busyness with his life, was never afraid of stating his opinions. His forthright comments made his letters very different from those of Muddiman or Williamson's clerks, from whom he presumably obtained much of his news: he had spread the report about the projected attack on Algiers.[106] He was followed by others.[107] Giles Hancock, who began by copying newsletters he found in a coffee-house to make a little money, was only one of many. In 1683 an informant named twelve newsletter writers in London – and the list was not exhaustive.[108] What Whig newswriters lacked in reliable information, they made up in rumour, invention or polemic. Their unofficial status was now an asset: some cost £10 a year. Like the secretaries, they exchanged news with the publishers of foreign gazettes.[109] By now there are references to 'Bristol' and 'Oxford' newsletters, although it is unclear whether they were produced or merely distributed there.[110] By the end of 1681 the government was trying to prevent the sending of newsletters into the provinces,[111] but handwritten material proved more difficult to suppress than print.[112]

Word of mouth

Of all the means of news dissemination, word of mouth leaves the fewest traces in written records. It was, however, important in both the gathering and distribution of news. London was a hotbed of political gossip and little remained secret for long. In 1661 the privy council was sworn to secrecy when it discussed the king's proposed marriage, but Edward Gower soon obtained the gist of the discussion from the Duke of Buckingham. The diarist Roger Morrice quickly obtained details of a highly confidential council debate in 1679 and of the king's last illness and death (from one who was present almost the whole time).[113] When the Earl of Bristol presented his charges against Clarendon in 1663, the news was all over town within two hours.[114] Although news could be obtained at any venue for sociability, perhaps the most important were the royal court[115] and the Royal Exchange.[116] The Exchange offered opportunities to acquire commercial information and influence business opinion. Foreign ambassadors and agents tried to win support among the merchants, hoping to damage the king's credit and subject him to financial pressure.[117] The government countered by sending emissaries such as Pepys, Alderman Backwell (the banker) and Secretary Henry Coventry to reassure the merchants.[118]

Much news gathered by word of mouth was then transmitted in writing. Handwritten letters and print had their limitations as means of transmitting information: as Sir Ralph Verney remarked, Sir John Busby could give him more news in a quarter of an hour than could be written on a quire of paper.[119] Where face-to-face contact was not possible, the written word had to suffice. Once received, written news again became the subject of 'chat'. This could take place anywhere: after church, at quarter sessions or assizes, in the street or the tavern; travellers exchanged news on the road.[120] Before the Fire, newsmongering had centred on the Exchange and St Paul's Walk, the heart of the book trade.[121] After the Fire, while the Exchange retained its importance, the book trade became more dispersed. A memorandum of about 1675 spoke of the bookshops of John Starkey (who had sent out newsletters as early as 1667) and Thomas Collen. Both were said to receive all manner of news, printed and manuscript, which they entered into 'great books', where it could be read and copied by customers and sent around the City by 'conversation' and around the country, by letter.[122]

By the 1670s booksellers' were less important as centres of political gossip than coffee-houses or clubs. According to Aubrey, the first coffee-house in London opened in 1652 and their numbers soon increased rapidly. Of all centres of gossip, they most concerned those in authority: it was alleged that coffee left men dangerously sober and inclined to plot against the state. (In fact, as Alan Marshall has emphasized, many plots were hatched in taverns.)[123] Charles II's government first considered how to regulate or suppress coffee-houses in 1666–67. In 1672, at the beginning of the Third Dutch War the judges were asked how best to do so; there followed a proclamation against false news and licentious talk, especially in coffee-houses.[124] In December 1675 there were proclamations to suppress coffee-houses and to forbid the spreading of false and seditious reports: the two were clearly linked.[125] The coffee-sellers protested that they were holding large stocks of coffee (and tea) on which they had paid excise duty. Some had taken out long leases, fitted their houses out for coffee-selling and taken on apprentices. Their licences had often been granted for a fixed period and were linked to the payment of excise duties over the same period: suppression would have both legal and revenue implications. Besides, as Sir Ralph Verney remarked, 'no Englishman will long endure to be forbid meeting together, so long as they do nothing contrary to law.' If they were forbidden to drink coffee, they might change to herbal drinks, which paid no duty.[126] The judges agreed that they should be allowed to continue to trade for six months, provided they entered into recognizances to have no seditious papers on the premises and promised to report anyone who spoke of state affairs.[127]

Having failed to establish the legality, or equity, of suppressing coffee-houses, this attempt at regulation was unsuccessful. Complaints of seditious talk continued, but in January 1677 the coffee-sellers were allowed to trade for another six months.[128] In September thirty were summoned before the council for allowing written news to be brought onto their premises. The king, furious that state affairs should be 'prostituted' in this way, warned that their licences would not be renewed. The coffee-sellers said little or nothing in mitigation; one later remarked that as news was not available in his coffee-house his customers had gone elsewhere.[129] It should be emphasized that the government's main concern was London's coffee-houses,[130] but they were equally popular – and full of news – in Norwich, Bristol, Cambridge and Oxford.[131] After 1678 the government seems to have given up trying to suppress them. Only when the Tory reaction gathered momentum were there locally inspired attempts to do so.[132]

Faced with this flood of gossip, there was little that the government could do. Its police and espionage resources were very limited[133] and the jury system made it difficult to prosecute any but the most egregious offenders – at least before the Tory reaction, when the courts were more willing to convict those accused of speaking 'dangerous words' and to impose punitive fines. In general convictions for 'seditious words' were few: Buchanan Sharp found 241 cases from 17 counties between 1660 and 1685 (the records are incomplete). Of these more than half date from 1679–85 and one-third from 1684–85.[134] This relative mildness might be a matter of political calculation. In 1675 Secretary Coventry remarked that it was wiser not to prosecute persons of humble status, as it gave their news and views unnecessary publicity.[135]

Often those reported for seditious words were arrested, interrogated, frightened and released.[136] Meanwhile, the government distributed its own news using the media over which it had some control and backed it up with opinion and indoctrination. Two of the most important of these were the law courts (especially the charges at quarter sessions and assizes) and the church. Their importance was recognized by the Commons' decision that the exclusion bill should be read twice a year at every assizes and in every church.[137]

It is impossible to quantify the impact of news in Restoration England. It has been estimated that between five and ten million printed items were produced between 1679 and 1681, but how many of these were concerned with public affairs is impossible to tell. Nor is it possible to quantify the reading public – assuming one can satisfactorily define 'reading'. It has been estimated that between 30 and 40 per cent of men and between 15 and 25 per cent of women were able to sign their names in the second half of the seventeenth century. In addition, a significant (but unquantifiable) number of people learned to read without learning to write.[138] What can be said with confidence is that there was a huge appetite for news in Restoration England. A useful exemplar of the range of possible sources is the diary of young Thomas Isham of Lamport, Northamptonshire in the 1670s. It is peppered with references to the *Gazette*, but he occasionally notes that certain items were not included there.[139] Often he gives the source as letters[140] or reports brought back from London,[141] Northampton,[142] Leicester and Althorp.[143] Occasionally, news was brought by visitors.[144] Throughout the diary there is evidence of the interaction of print, manuscript and word of mouth, as in country houses, coffee-houses and taverns, at markets and fairs, people discussed the latest news.

But was the appetite for news as insatiable as so many contemporaries made out? Our evidence naturally comes from those who **were** interested in news. Over a century later, the radical journalist William Cobbett recalled his youth in rural Surrey in the 1760s, by which time literacy levels had risen and the range of reading matter had greatly increased:

> As to politics we were like the rest of the country people in England, that is to say that we neither knew nor thought anything about the matter. The shouts of victory and the murmur of defeat would now and then break in upon our tranquillity for the moment, but I do not remember ever having seen a newspaper in the house and most certainly that privation . . . did not render us less free, happy or industrious.[145]

There had always been some – like the king and L'Estrange – who regarded this hunger for news as unhealthy. By the early 1680s there were signs that appetites were sated. Sir Ralph Verney wrote that he could manage without the (printed) newsbooks and that he could find better uses for his time than transcribing manuscript newsletters. (He had apparently been receiving 14 newsbooks a week.)[146] Sir Edward Dering wrote in 1681 that there was a dearth of public news, adding 'possibly never the worse for that'.[147] For Verney, at least, the hunger soon returned, leaving the government little choice but to feed – or control – it as best it could. The means by which news was dispersed were too varied, the demand too great and the government's resources too limited for the flow of information to be stopped. It did not follow from this that Restoration England was bound to become ideologically divided, but if it did become so divided, the demand for news would grow, which would be more likely to widen divisions than to heal them.

Notes

1 M. Stoyle, *Loyalty and Locality: Popular allegiance in Devon in the English Civil War*, Exeter, 1994, p. 234.
2 Althorp MS C17, fo. 14; Marvell, II.310.
3 M636/32, Sir Ralph to John Verney, 9 December 1678.
4 CKS, U1713/C1, no. 11.
5 *HMC Ormond*, NS V.535–6; BL, Add. MS 17017, fo. 4; M636/33, Dr Denton to Sir Ralph Verney, 13 November 1679.
6 M636/19, Burgoyne to Sir Ralph, 22 and 28 June 1663. Bradfer, S Henshaw to Paston, 12 August 1671.
7 M636/31, Edmund Verney to Sir Ralph, 20 December 1677; M636/27, same to same, 29 June 1674; Strong, p. 220.
8 *HMC Beaufort*, p. 81.
9 Carte MS 39, fo. 107.
10 BT 115, Verneuil, Cominges and Courtin to Louis, 1 June 1665 NS; S. Sorbière, *Relation d'un voyage en Angleterre* (ed.) L. Roux, St Etienne, 1980, pp. 100–3.
11 *Williamson*, II.68; Strong, p. 220.
12 F.J. Levy, 'How information spread among the gentry', *JBS*, XXI, no. 2, 1982, pp. 20–3; R. Cust, 'News and politics in early seventeenth-century England', *P & P*, no. 112, pp. 60–90.
13 Cust, 'News', pp. 62–4, 71–84, 88–90; D. Hirst, *The Representative of the People? Voters and Voting under the Early Stuarts*, Cambridge, 1975.
14 Levy, 'Information', p. 23; F.S. Siebert, *Freedom of the Press in England, 1476–1776*, Urbana, 1952, chs 8–11, especially pp. 230–2.
15 Cust, 'News', p. 81 and n. 60.
16 Burnet, *Suppl.*, p. 49; Ailesbury, I.93.
17 *CSPD 1667*, pp. 419–20, 427, 450, 535; BL, Add MS 15643, fo. 48; Burnet, *Suppl.*, p. 106; Morrice, p. 275.
18 Cust, 'News', passim.
19 *Ibid.*, pp. 65–9; M. Spufford, *Small Books and Pleasant Histories*, London, 1981, pp. 22–37; A. Fox, 'Rumour, news and popular political opinion in Elizabethan and early Stuart England', *HJ*, XL, 1997, pp. 597–620; W. Ford, 'The problem of literacy in early modern England', *History*, LXXVIII, 1993, pp. 26–7.
20 Strong, p. 220. See also *CSPD 1661–62*, p. 283.
21 *SR*, V.428–33, 524, 556, 577.

22 DUL, Cosin Letter Book 5B, no. 122; *CSPD 1667–68*, pp. 353–4, 357–8, 360.
23 *HMC Finch*, II.9–11; *HMC 9th Report, appendix II*, p. 66.
24 T.J. Crist, 'Francis Smith and the Opposition Press in England, 1660–88', unpublished Ph.D. thesis, Cambridge, 1977, pp. 32–3, 55–6, 63–4, 77–9, 88–9; PC 2/62, pp. 267, 295, 2/65, p. 80; *HMC 7th Report*, p. 517; *CSPD 1666–67*, p. 430, *1673*, p. 413, *1675–76*, pp. 540–1.
25 Crist, 'Smith', pp. 107, 190–6.
26 PC 2/65, p. 227; *HMC le Fleming*, p. 127; Stowe MS 209, fo. 309; Pforz, Coleman to Bulstrode, 22 May, 30 June and 3 December 1676; *Essex*, II.64; Marvell, II.345, 349–50, 352–3.
27 Crist, 'Smith', pp. 90–2, 94, 107–8. But see P. Hamburger, 'The development of the law of Seditious Libel and the Control of the Press', *Stanford Law Review*, XXXVII, February 1985, passim.
28 Crist, 'Smith', pp. 94, 110–1; *CSPD 1660–61*, p. 447.
29 T. O'Malley, '"Defying the Powers and Tempering the Spirit": A Review of Quaker Control and their Publications, 1672–89', *JEH*, XXXIII,1982, p. 74 and *passim*.
30 K.H.D. Haley, *William of Orange and the English Opposition, 1672–74*, Oxford, 1953, pp. 98–100; *CSPD 1673–75*, p. 69; *Essex*, I.159; BL, Add. MS 25123, fos 1, 5; CPA 113, Ruvigny to Pomponne, 28 August 1674 NS; *HMC Ormond*, NS IV.412, 419–20; Grey, V.280–1; *Williamson*, II.82.
31 CPA 118, Ruvigny to Pomponne, 29 April 1675 NS. All four titles were printed in *State Tracts* (2 vols, 1689–92), vol. I.
32 PC 2/68, pp. 60, 94; Coventry MS 6, fos 64, 66, 71; Crist, 'Smith', pp. 100–1.
33 PC 2/68, pp. 203, 212, 229.
34 PC 2/68, pp. 256–7, 273.
35 Crist, 'Smith', pp. 110–13; *HMC 7th Report*, p. 474; Hamburger, 'Libel', pp. 668–9, 685–6.
36 Crist, 'Smith', pp. 118–23, 125–6, 130.
37 PC 2/68, pp. 369, 496, 512–13; *HMC 7th Report*, p. 478; Crist, 'Smith', pp. 136–9; Hamburger, 'Libel', pp. 687–8; A.F. Havighurst, 'The Judiciary and Politics in the Reign of Charles II', *Law Quarterly Review* LXVI, 1950, pp. 235–7.
38 BL, Add MS 29572, fo. 245; Morrice, p. 295; Burnet, *Hist*, II.268; Hamburger, 'Libel', pp. 688–90; Crist, 'Smith', pp. 141–52; *HMC 7th Report*, p. 405; L. Schwoerer, 'The attempted impeachment of Sir William Scroggs', *HJ*, XXXVIII, 1995, pp. 843–73.
39 Crist, 'Smith', pp. 190–6; 'Oates's Plot', newsletters dated 8 June, 30 October, 20 November, 11 December 1682; *HMC 7th Report*, pp. 406, 480; Morrice, p. 432; Miller, *Charles II*, ch. 13.
40 Crist, 'Smith', ch. 6. For Russell's speech, see Bodl, MS Eng Letters d 72, fo. 36; Warwicks. RO, CR136/B1307D; the only surviving printed edition was published in Scotland: Wing R2348G.
41 BL, Add MS 23136, fo. 130; Egerton MS 2538, fo. 186.
42 *CSPD 1663–64*, p. 240; P. Fraser, *The Intelligence of the Secretaries of State and their Monopoly of Licensed News*, Cambridge, 1956, p. 35; J.G. Muddiman, *The King's Journalist*, London, 1923, pp. 110–1, 124–30, 161–2.
42 *Lauderdale*, I.183–5; Fraser, *Intelligence*, p. 38; Muddiman, *Journalist*, pp. 163–4; C.J. Sommerville, *The News Revolution in England*, New York, 1996, pp. 60–3.
43 Fraser, *Intelligence*, p. 38.

44 Fraser, *Intelligence*, pp. 47–9; Muddiman, *Journalist*, pp. 172–93.
45 *CSPD 1665–66*, pp. 90, 201, *1666–67*, p. 129.
46 *CSPD 1667–68*, p. 466, *1671–72*, p. 436; Grey, III.442, VI.153; Carte MS 72, fo. 361.
47 For parliamentary news, see Staffs RO, D868/8, fos 9, 12. For the *Gazette*'s tone, see Sommerville, *News*, pp. 67–9, 91–4.
48 *CSPD 1672*, pp. 156, 171; *HMC le Fleming*, p. 94; BL, Add MS 22548, fo. 87.
49 Grey, III.122; M636/27, Sir Ralph to Edmund Verney, 25 June 1674; M636/29, same to same, 15 June 1676.
50 Fraser, *Intelligence*, p. 122n.; *CSPD 1661–62*, p. 583; *HMC 4th Report*, p. 231; M636/30, Sir Ralph to Edmund Verney, 15 February 1677; Pforz, Coleman to Bulstrode, 9 February 1677.
51 Crist, 'Smith', p. 184.
52 Muddiman, *Journalist*, p. 235; Tanner MS 36, fo. 106; 'Oates's Plot', newsletter of 20 November 1682; G.C. Gibbs, 'Abel Boyer: the making of a British subject, 1699–1706', *Proceedings of the Huguenot Society*, XXVI, 1994, p. 22 (quoted); M. Knights, *Politics and Opinion in Crisis 1678–81*, Cambridge, 1994, ch. 10 and *passim*.
53 Warwicks RO, CR 136/B534A; *HMC le Fleming*, pp. 24–6ff, 120.
54 *HMC Beaufort*, p. 77.
55 P. Aubrey, *Mr Secretary Thurloe*, London, 1990, pp. 33, 76; A. Marshall, *Intelligence and Espionage in Reign of Charles II*, Cambridge, 1994, pp. 23, 26, 79–82; *HMC Buccleuch (Montagu House)*, II(i) 49–50.
56 *CSPD 1663–64*, p. 149; Staffs RO, D1287/18/3/3 (copies of Ormond's letters in the Bridgeman MSS); *HMC Ormond*, NS VII.301–2.
57 *CSPI 1669–70*, p. 80; *Essex*, I.168; Stowe MS 217, fo. 142; Hartmann, *Madame*, p. 62. See also *HMC Beaufort*, p. 76; Carte MS 215, fo. 389; Mapperton, Appendix to the Earl of Sandwich's Papers, fo. 153.
58 E. Newton, *The House of Lyme*, London, 1917, p. 286; M636/23, Sir Ralph to Edmund Verney, 25 February 1669, M636/27, same to same, 15 January 1674; *CSPI 1669–70*, p. 80; Carte MS 35, fo. 682; Egerton MS 2539, fo. 276.
59 M636/18, Dr Denton to Sir Ralph and John Verney to Sir Ralph, 22 January 1663; Rochester, *Letters*, p. 186. See also NLI, MS 4728, fo. 3: 'many have suffered lately for being too free in their intelligences'. (I am very grateful to Alan Marshall for giving me a transcript of this document.)
60 *CSPD 1663–64*, pp. 63–5, 117.
61 *HMC 7th Report*, p. 368; Hants RO, 31M57/889; *CSPD 1667*, p. 246; PC 2/59, p. 484; *HMC le Fleming*, p. 128; *HP*, I.597.
62 *CSPD 1660–61*, pp. 535–43.
63 Marshall, *Intelligence*, p. 83: for examples, see *CSPD 1666–67*, p. 514, *1667*, p. 215, *1670*, pp. 392–3.
64 *Bax. Corr.*, II.173; M636/30, Sir Ralph to John Verney, 4 June 1677; *CSPD 1678*, p. 478.
65 M636/22, Edmund Verney to Sir Ralph, 4 November 1667, M636/30, Sir Ralph to John Verney, 18 October 1677.
66 M636/26, Sir Ralph to Edmund, 20 November 1673, M636/29, Edmund to Sir Ralph, 19 June 1676, M636/31, same to same, 11 March 1678. Bearers too could lose letters: M636/25, Sir Ralph to Edmund, 22 June 1672.
67 M636/25, Sir Ralph to Edmund, 24 June 1672, M636/30, same to same, 18 January, 15 February 1677, M636/30, same to same, 29 January 1680.

68 *CSPD 1663–64*, pp. 156–7, *1667*, p. 330; M636/38, John Verney to Sir Ralph, 17 September 1683.
69 *HMC 7th Report*, p. 480; Fraser, *Intelligence*, pp. 128–30.
70 Siebert, *Freedom of the Press*, ch. 17, especially pp. 356–63.
71 *CJ*, VIII.74, 249, IX.682; Bowman, fo. 22; Grey, II.175–7.
72 *HMC 5th Report*, p. 203; Staffs RO, D868/4, fo. 66; *HMC 3rd Report*, p. 95; Finch MS PP 57(ii), p. 53.
73 DCLD, Hunter MS 7, nos. 80, 91; DUL, Cosin Letter Book, 5B, no. 106; BL, Add MS 29571, fo. 471; Stowe MS 204, fo. 116; Badminton House, FmF 1/2/51; M636/31, Sir Ralph to Edmund Verney, 7 February 1678; Milward, p. 29; Staffs RO, D868/4, fos 9, 12.
74 Newcome, *Diary*, p. 39; Henry, p. 133.
75 T. Comber, *Autobiography and Letters*, (ed.) C.E. Whiting (2 vols. Surtees Soc., 1946–7) II.22; *HMC Beaufort*, p. 79; *HMC Ormond*, NS IV.286.
76 CPA 133, fos 280–3; Browne, I.299; Herts RO, D/ELw 28, Gorhambury XII, B44; *HMC Ormond*, NS IV.523.
77 M636/32, John Verney to Sir Ralph, 31 October 1678; *HMC 7th Report*, p. 469; *HMC le Fleming*, p. 106; JRL, Legh of Lyme Corr., Richard Sterne to Richard Legh, 30 April 1681.
78 DUL, Cosin Letter Book 5B, no. 106; M636/29, William Fall to Sir Ralph Verney, 22 November 1675.
79 Grey, VI.118–19, 149–51; *CJ*, IX.523.
80 Egerton MS 3338, fo. 149; *Savile*, p. 57; M636/32, Edmund Verney to Sir Ralph, 17 April 1679, M636/35, Sir Ralph to the Bailiff of Buckingham, 22 March 1681. See also Cust, 'News', p. 72.
81 Hull RO, BRL 945; Marvell, II.92 and *passim*.
82 Marvell, II.50, 113, 162, 164–6, 169, 175.
83 Fraser, *Intelligence*, pp. 1–2, 4, 28–30, 42–6; Marshall, *Intelligence*, pp. 59–61; *CSPD 1665–66*, p. 246.
84 Fraser, *Intelligence*, pp. 30–1, 33, 140–4; Marshall, *Intelligence*, pp. 45–6.
85 *CSPD 1665–66*, pp. 213, 246, 266–7, 280.
86 *CSPD 1665–66*, 266–7, 322, 342, 550, *1666–67*, pp. 30, 85, 129, 176, 282.
87 *CSPD 1666–67*, pp. 85, 214, 282, 555, *1667–68*, p. 102.
88 *CSPD 1665–66*, pp. 213, 246, 266–7, 281, 322, 342, 484, *1666–67*, pp. 79, 343–4, *1670*, pp. 165–6, 188–9, 300–1, *1672–73*, p. 585.
89 For secretaries' office letters, see those to Fleming in Bodl, MS Don c 37–8 (e.g., 38, fos 32, 35–6); for Muddiman, *CSPD 1666–67*, p. 214, *1670*, pp. 498–9, 531–2; Rawl MS A74, fos 37–46.
90 Fraser, *Intelligence*, p. 30; *CSPD 1665–66*, p. 465, *1670*, p. 189; Warwicks RO, CR136/B1307D; Hull RO, BRL 690, BRB 5, pp. 8, 275; *HMC le Fleming*, pp. 67–8, 123, 184; M636/28, Sir Ralph to Edmund Verney, 21 December 1674. In 1668 John Nicholas thought £10 p.a. the going rate: Egerton MS 2539, fo. 282. For profits, see Muddiman, *Journalist*, p. 166; Strong, p. 220.
91 Muddiman, *Journalist*, pp. 258–64; Fraser, *Intelligence*, pp. 140–4.
92 *CSPD 1665–66*, pp. 507, 515, *1667*, p. 321, *1667–68*, p. 550.
93 *CSPD 1675–76*, p. 379.
94 *CSPD 1665–66*, p. 497, *1666–67*, p. 20. When he lost his coffee-licence, Bower sold ale and 'mum': BL, Add MS 36988, fo. 119.
95 *CSPD 1666–67*, pp. 459, 485, *1675–76*, pp. 456–7; Fraser, *Intelligence*, pp. 140–4.

96 *CSPD 1670*, p. 52.
97 Tanner MS 37, fo. 28; *CSPD 1684–85*, p. 307–8.
98 *CSPD 1666–67*, pp. 196, 213, 236, 245, 260, 272, 296, *1678*, p. 304. For the warm reception initially given the *Gazette*, see *CSPD 1665–66*, pp. 90, 193.
99 *CSPD 1666–67*, pp. 333, 415.
100 BL, Add MS 32095, fo. 36.
101 *CSPD 1676–77*, pp. 356–7, 360, 368, 372; FSL, MS X d 529(2).
102 But see the newsletters from John Starkey, 1667–72, BL Add MS 36916.
103 *CSPD 1671*, p. 166; SP 104/176, fo. 289; *Williamson*, II.1–4, 11, 16.
104 Carte MS 77, fo. 256; DUL, Cosin Letter Book 5B, no. 119; *POAS*, I, 230–6, 248–51, 263–5, 277–82.
105 Hull RO, BRL 823; *Morrison*, 2nd series, II.246–7; *Bulstrode*, pp. 282–3 [Coleman expected letters from Flanders in return], 313 [for Coleman's authorship]; *CSPD 1678*, pp. 244–5.
106 *CSPD 1676–77*, pp. 360, 372; M636/32, Sir Ralph to Edmund Verney, 3 October 1678.
107 The letters from 'R.M.' to Francis Radcliffe are very different in style to those received earlier: *CSPD 1675–76*, pp. 252–3, 413, *1677–78*, pp. 94–5, *1678*, p. 453.
108 *CSPD 1677–78*, p. 339, *1683–84*, pp. 53–4. Champion and Cressett, who also sent newsletters, were not on the list: Althorp MS C2, Sir William Hickman to Halifax, 13 July 1681; *HMC Dartmouth*, I.47.
109 Fraser, *Intelligence*, pp. 120–30.
110 Coventry MS 7, fo. 158; Badminton, MS FmF 4/1/12; Warwicks RO, CR136/B1307A.
111 *CSPD 1680–81*, pp. 422, 466–7, 477, 535, *1682*, pp. 280, 327.
112 Warwicks RO, CR136/B1307D; Bodl, MS Eng Hist c. 711, fo. 13; *CSPD 1683–84*, pp. 150–1.
113 *HMC 5th Report*, pp. 151, 202; Morrice, pp. 207, 454–6. For other information about the council, see Coventry MS 11, fo. 443; *Hatton*, I.211–13; *HMC Ormond*, NS IV.454.
114 Carte MS 77, fo. 524.
115 Pepys, VIII.464; M636/31, Dr Denton to Sir Ralph Verney, 12 August 1678, M636/36, John Verney to Sir Ralph, 20 April 1682.
116 Pepys, VI.44–5, VII.242, VIII.317; M636/25, Dr Denton to Sir Ralph Verney, 10 October 1672; BL, Lansdowne MS 1236, fo. 205.
117 *CSPV 1671–72*, p. 328; BT 134, Courtin to Louis, 12 October 1676 NS; CPA 119, Courtin to Pomponne, 28 September 1676 NS; BT 137, Barrillon to Louis, 13 September 1677 NS; *CSPD 1676–77*, pp. 437, 440–1.
118 Pepys, V.194, VI.268, VIII.328–9; Carte MS 79, fo. 124; BT 137, Barrillon to Pomponne, 16 September 1677 NS.
119 M636/25, Sir Ralph to Edmund, 2 May 1672. See also M636/31, Edmund to Sir Ralph, 17 January 1678.
120 Henry, p. 90.
121 Cust, 'News', p. 70; Sorbière, *Relation*, p. 30.
122 Browning, *Danby*, III.2–3. For Starkey's newsletters, see BL, Add MS 36916.
123 Aubrey, *Lives*, p. 189; *Williamson*, II.68; Marshall, *Intelligence*, pp. 14–15; R.L. Greaves, *Secrets of the Kingdom: British Radicals from the Popish Plot to the Revolution of 1688–9*, Stanford, 1992, p. 171; S. Pincus, '"Coffee politicians

does create": Coffee-houses and Restoration Political Culture', *Journal of Modern History*, LXVII, 1995, pp. 805–34; Sommerville, *News*, ch. 6.

124 Seaward, pp. 257, 318; PC 2/63, pp. 173, 252, 259; *CSPD 1671*, p. 581, *1672*, p. 214; Isham, p. 85.

125 PC 2/65, pp. 79–81, 85–6; *CSPD 1675–76*, p. 465.

126 *CSPD 1675–76*, pp. 496–7, 500; M636/29, Sir Ralph to Edmund Verney, 3 January 1676.

127 PC 2/65, pp. 88, 93; M636/29, Sir Ralph to Edmund Verney, 10 January 1676.

128 BL, Add MS 29571, fo. 324; PC 2/65, p. 442.

129 PC 2/66, p. 108; *CSPD 1677–78*, p. 627; Morrice, p. 58; Carte MS 79, fo. 126; BL, Add MS 32095, fo. 38.

130 *CSPD 1677–78*, pp. 627–8. *CSPD 1676–77*, p. 368 implies that circulating news in London coffee houses was more heinous than sending news into the country.

131 Rye, *Depositions*, p. 157; *The Grand Juries Address and presentments to the mayor and aldermen of... Bristol*, n.d., c. April 1681; C.H. Cooper, *Annals of Cambridge* (4 vols, Cambridge, 1842–52) III.515, 569; M636/31, Edmund Verney to Sir Ralph, 11 February 1678.

132 Rye, *Depositions*, p. 157; *The Grand Juries Address*; 'Oates's Plot', letter dated 4 May 1682.

133 Marshall, *Intelligence, passim.*

134 B. Sharp, 'Popular political opinion in England, 1660–85', *HEI*, X, 1989, pp. 13–29.

135 BL, Add MS 21524, fo. 53.

136 Carte MS 222, fo. 32; *HMC le Fleming*, p. 128; *CSPD 1677–78*, p. 226. A Swede was whipped round the Exchange for spreading false news: Pepys, VI.43.

137 Sir P. Leicester, *Charges to the Grand Jury at Quarter Sessions, 1660–7*, (ed.) E.M. Halcrow, Chetham Soc., 1953, *passim*; *HMC Ormond*, NS V.342; *Norths*, I.206–8; Morrice, p. 275.

138 Knights, *Opinion*, pp. 168–72; D. Cressy, *Literacy and the social order: reading and writing in Tudor and Stuart England*, Cambridge, 1980, p. 177 and *passim*; Spufford, *Small Books*, ch. 2; K. Thomas, 'The meaning of Literacy in early modern England', in G. Baumann (ed.), *The Written Word: Literacy in Transition*, Oxford, 1986, ch. 4.

139 Isham, pp. 140, 150–1. See also Josselin, pp. 573, 609–10; *HMC le Fleming*, p. 94.

140 Isham, pp. 75, 163, 165, 179, etc.

141 Isham, pp. 147, 153, 173, 175 etc.

142 Isham, pp. 139, 143, 161, 195, 209.

143 Isham, pp. 15, 201.

144 Isham, pp. 207, 231.

145 Quoted in R. Porter, *English Society in the Eighteenth Century*, London, 1982, p. 241.

146 M636/37, Sir Ralph to John Verney, 23 and 30 November 1682, 26 March 1682[?83], John Stewkeley to Sir Ralph, 26 October 1682.

147 CKS, U1713/C2, no. 55.

Chapter five

Popular politics

The nature of popular politics

Just as political news was not the exclusive preserve of a narrow elite, but reached a wide public, and just as historians have become sceptical about the existence of a single 'popular culture', clearly distinct from 'elite culture',[1] so it is hard to see 'popular' and 'elite' politics as discrete entities. In the civil wars support for both king and Parliament permeated all social strata. Although **some** popular elements sought to turn the world upside-down, most did not: there was not a single popular agenda. Radical historians may feel that the masses should have been driven by class hatred and that they should have had no interest in the political and religious issues which preoccupied the elite; but the evidence suggests otherwise. Similarly, under Charles II, politics involved men (and often women) from all ranks of society. When humble people showed similar political concerns to the great, they were not being manipulated, tricked or bribed into participating in disputes which concerned only the elite. There is overwhelming evidence of people participating because these disputes seemed important to them.[2] Moreover, given the broad definition of 'politics' used in this book, we should be wary of defining popular political activity too narrowly: voting in elections was not the only way in which people participated in 'politics'. They used the law, civil or criminal: Paul Halliday is beginning to show how quite humble people applied to King's Bench for 'prerogative writs', such as *mandamus*, in order to secure what they claimed were their rights.[3] They petitioned their local mayor or magistrates, Parliament, the king and council, indeed anyone in authority. Such activities could be expressions of partisan difference, but very often they were not. Before 1679 petitions to king or Parliament rarely had a clearly partisan content and in general king and council heard both sides in any dispute and preferred to leave the disputants to the law.

That said, two manifestations of popular 'politics' could become vehicles for partisan rancour: the formation of clubs and popular celebrations. As far as the former are concerned, coffee-houses offered a new forum for sociability and political 'chat', but there were others: inns, taverns, alehouses, meeting-houses, booksellers. One phenomenon that was already established in London before the Restoration was the county feast. Gentlemen from a particular county or region would march to church to hear a sermon and then to a feast.

These feasts performed an obvious social function, helping newcomers make contacts and friends. They also offered the opportunity to pursue collective local interests; some established charitable funds (for example, to send poor boys to university).[4] The fact that they began in the 1650s suggests that they were designed to bring together former enemies and to rally the gentry and supporters of orthodox religion against the threat from the Quakers and Baptists.[5] The emphasis on collective action (reinforced by ritual) was designed to inculcate unity rather than division: the Norfolk feast was cancelled in 1679 because the political divisions in the county made it inappropriate.[6] Many informal 'clubs' were also concerned with sociability and harmony. A few might seem sinister to those in authority, such as the Nonsuch club (formerly the 'commonwealth club') in Bow Street, where John Wildman the Leveller was said to meet with Colonel Bishop (then postmaster general) and some of his clerks.[7] Other institutions, with a strong element of sociability, were dominated by ex-Royalists. The most important were the London Honourable Artillery Company (with its later offshoot in Bristol), whose martial functions were visible and significant. More shadowy was the Society of Archers, which met in the 1670s, and elected two stewards each year who received a 'cup, cap and arrow'.[8] Even as political divisions sharpened, from 1673, clubs might serve to heal divisions. One group, which included several MPs, met regularly, with a chairman. They dined and drank the health of absent friends, but also sought to rectify 'mistaken reports'. Sir Nicholas Armorer, a courtier, reported that his 'old friend', Henry Powle, was vigorously attacking 'popery' in the House, adding 'sometimes we scold, but always part good friends'.[9]

The first truly partisan club appeared in 1676 when it was noted that 'a certain sort of men', supporters of Shaftesbury, were wearing green ribbons to show that they were for a new Parliament.[10] By the end of 1678 this club had its headquarters at the King's Head tavern, near Temple Bar, and was buying the Commons' 'votes' and other political material. Membership was carefully controlled: applicants had to be vouched for by two existing members, unless they were MPs or peers or inhabitants of Taunton approved by the local panjandrum, John Trenchard. The following year it was decreed that only members of at least three years' standing could make nominations.[11] In 1679 the Club gave money for bonfires to celebrate the passage of the first exclusion bill and Monmouth's return to London; some members clubbed together to help the imprisoned journalist Henry Care.[12] The Green Ribbon was not the only exclusionist club. In late 1679 there were references to an informal club of peers;[13] a year later there were allegedly five or six 'great clubs' around London.[14] Clubs also formed in the provinces, at Bristol, York and (predictably) Taunton.[15] The opponents of exclusion were slower to organize, but in early 1682 a small 'royal club' was formed near Ludgate, which rapidly attracted members of both the nobility and the civic elite, until it numbered 300. Its purpose was to wrest control of the London common council and shrievalty from the Whigs. With county feasts also becoming increasingly Tory in tone, sociability was giving way to partisanship.[16]

In much the same way, popular celebrations could affirm communal harmony, but they could also be appropriated for partisan purposes. Whereas clubs tended to be private, and to some extent exclusive, popular celebrations were public and inclusive. Since the Reformation, the Catholic calendar of fasts and feasts had largely been swept away. In their place there developed celebrations which were either Protestant or secular and generally imposed by authority. Under Charles II, 30 January, the anniversary of his father's execution, was an official day of fasting and humiliation, while his accession day (29 May, also his birthday) was decreed by Parliament to be a day of celebration. In addition, the Prayer Book as revised in 1662 included a special service for Gunpowder Treason day, 5 November. On top of these, most towns had their own cycle of celebrations – for example, for a fair or for the election or installation of a new mayor. At Norwich, the corporation, besides 29 May and 5 November, celebrated the anniversary of the king's coronation (St George's day) and the city's 'guild day'. The bells were rung, bonfires were lit and guns were fired on the castle mound. Apart from offering noise and spectacle, these occasions were marked by feasting, drinking and general jollity. They were supplemented by 'one-off' celebrations, for royal weddings or for victories at sea or over rebellious Scots, or to mark the visit of the king or other great personages.[17] Some were spontaneous responses to national political events. The king's decision in 1673 to cancel his Declaration of Indulgence led to a rash of bonfires in London;[18] there were others in York, Ipswich, Nottingham and Manchester.[19]

Those celebrations which were officially sponsored, or commanded, should in theory have embraced the whole community; in practice, they could expose divisions. It was alleged that the 'fanatics' were unhappy about English naval 'victories' over the Dutch in 1665–66.[20] At Dover, the castle and the naval ships in the harbour celebrated, but the town did not.[21] Often reports of exuberant festivities came from towns where the government interest was strong, such as Portsmouth. Some of the secretaries' correspondents, like Edward Bodham at King's Lynn, referred most years to celebration of the king's birthday, while at times towns regarded as factious seem to have gone out of their way to show their loyalty.[22] Others showed little enthusiasm. Yarmouth celebrated the king's birthday with great solemnity in 1667, but in 1669 decided not to commemorate the coronation.[23] It was reported from Weymouth in 1665 that many insisted on opening their shops on 30 January.[24] Pepys noted in 1663 that there was little rejoicing in London for the king's birthday and it was generally marked far more exuberantly around Whitehall and Westminster than in the City.[25] By 1680, 29 May was marked by only one bonfire in central Oxford, where there had once been twenty, and there were so few in church at Deptford that the vicar did not preach.[26] Admittedly, the privy council had recently forbidden bonfires on 29 May (or any other unauthorized occasion), but that in itself was a tacit acknowledgement that such occasions were likely to show the strength of opposition to the government.[27]

Some celebrations were bound to be divisive, such as those commemorating the lifting of Royalist sieges. At Lyme Regis, it was claimed that the reports were exaggerated: a few 'inconsiderable' people put on their best clothes and ate roast meat.[28] At Taunton, however, it was reported that on 11 May people gathered in conventicles, celebrated with bonfires and bells and threatened to burn the houses of the town's few Cavaliers. Most shops were shut and people were summoned to their meetings by beat of drum.[29] At Gloucester, on the south gate, above the arms of the king and the Dukes of Gloucester and York, was a little figure with a sword and trowel and the legend, taken down only in 1671, 'a city assaulted by man and saved by God'. It was replaced by a Latin inscription referring to cruel and wicked rebels.[30]

Celebrations inspired by civil war could not but be divisive. The same could be true of anti-Catholic rituals. In theory, commemorating 5 November should have united Protestants. In practice, as political divisions came to be expressed in terms of anti-popery, it did not (see Chapter 7). High Churchmen and opponents of exclusion were accused of being 'favourers of popery'. They responded by accusing their opponents of using anti-popery as a smokescreen to cover their dastardly designs against monarchy and Church: on 5 November 1675 a preacher in Norwich cathedral told his hearers to beware of the Papists but not to forget the 'martyrdom' of Charles I.[31] In the 1660s 5 November was marked sporadically, with a few bonfires. London and Hull cancelled their celebrations in 1666 (in the aftermath of the Great Fire) and in 1670 the nonconformist Philip Henry claimed that the day had almost been forgotten.[32]

All that changed with the upsurge in alarm about 'popery' in 1673. On 5 November there were more bonfires between Charing Cross and Whitechapel than had been seen for thirty years. Youths made effigies of the pope, which they carried in procession and burned.[33] This was seen as a novelty, which one MP condemned as 'a barbarism which I thought no nation but the Hollander could have been guilty of', but it caught on. The night the Duke of York's Catholic bride arrived a pope worth £50 was burned at Southwark and country people who came to town asked where they could find a pope-maker.[34] Secretary Coventry was uneasy, but relieved that the pope-burnings passed off peacefully.[35] It is not clear that every 5 November was now marked in London with pope-burnings, but it was reported in 1677 that there were more than ever before; a large crowd gathered at the Monument, built to commemorate the Fire, which many believed had been started by the papists.[36] By now there were similar festivities on 17 November, Elizabeth's accession day, which had been celebrated under James I as an implicit criticism of Stuart kingship. There are references to bonfires on that day in the 1660s, but the first major pope-burning appears to have been in 1676, when the pope was carried shoulder-high from Leadenhall Street to Temple Bar, beaten with clubs and staves and burned. On 17 November 1677 a pope was burned with a string of oranges around his neck, a rare criticism of the marriage of York's daughter, Mary, to William of Orange. The effigy contained live cats 'which squalled most hideously as soon as they felt the fire'; claret was provided for the common people.[37]

In 1678, after the onset of the Popish Plot, the government awaited 5 November with trepidation lest 'the liberty belonging to the festival may give occasion to disorder'. It proved the most elaborate celebration yet, with the pope accompanied by the General of the Jesuits and other priests, but it passed off peacefully.[38] The processions of 17 November 1679 and 1680 were on a larger scale again. Funded partly by the Green Ribbon Club, they comprised a series of floats (as in the lord mayor's show) with figures from the Popish Plot and leading opponents of exclusion.The procession made its way across the City to Temple Bar, where the pope was burned in front of a statue of Elizabeth. The crowds were estimated at 100,000 in 1679 and more in 1680,[39] but both processions passed off peacefully, even though that of 1680 took place the day after the Lords rejected the exclusion bill. In 1679 the French ambassador was taken incognito to watch. He was shocked, but also astonished that at the end of it all, after much drinking, everybody went off quietly to bed. It would not have ended like that in Paris, he said.[40] The proponents of exclusion had appropriated the rituals of anti-popery, but had not succeeded in turning them into a major force against the government – indeed they probably had not intended to do so, assuming that a show of numbers would be enough. Besides, pope-burnings were ultimately affirmations of Protestantism. The more elaborate they became, the more entertaining they were. Contemporary partisan messages were added, but they never eclipsed the areas on which there was common ground among most English Protestants: the conviction that international Catholicism posed a threat to England and that there **had** been a popish plot – although many believed that it had been fully investigated by the autumn of 1679.

The exclusionists' appropriation of popular celebration did them little good; as with the formation of clubs, it provoked their opponents to respond in kind. From 1681, Tory crowds burned effigies of Jack Presbyter and Shaftesbury, the Covenant, the exclusion bill and green ribbons.[41] As the Tories gained the upper hand in the localities, their celebrations proclaimed their success. At Taunton the mayor marked the king's birthday in 1683 with bonfires, bells and a string of loyal toasts, accompanied by drums and trumpets.[42] Civic celebration, which should have united the townspeople, was now used to proclaim the triumph of one party over the other.

Riot

The absence of violence at pope-burnings is all the more striking when one considers its prevalence in Restoration society. While historians have stressed the decline of large-scale disorder and the erosion of the 'honour culture' under the Tudors, violence remained an everyday phenomenon. Duels and brawls were common and the career of the psychopathic seventh Earl of Pembroke showed that under Charles II, as under Elizabeth, aristocrats with friends at court could get away with murder.[43] But violence was not confined to aristocrats. Riot was a common mode of popular action, which (thanks to the nervousness of the authorities and the weakness of their means of coercion) often succeeded. But what were their objectives? Although they were clearly 'political' in the broadest sense of achieving material ends or righting perceived wrongs, how far were they 'political' in the narrower sense of perpetuating the ideological divisions of the civil wars?

Historians who have studied riots in the eighty years before the civil war stress the restraint, discipline and respect for the law which rioters usually displayed. They note that the legal definition of riot was very broad – any occasion on which three or more people joined to commit an illegal act. They show that riot was often a last resort, after appeals to the proper authorities had failed – a final stage in a process of bargaining. They note that people sometimes took legal advice before rioting or divided into groups of two so as not to fall foul of the law. With this awareness of legality went a strong sense of legitimation: the rioters felt that they were upholding the law, taking the law into their own hands. They marched in a quasi-military manner and concentrated their action on the immediate objects of their resentment. Food rioters tried to stop grain being transported to London or abroad in times of dearth, or demanded that dealers, farmers or millers sell off grain stored in their barns, echoing the explanation for dearth, and the remedy prescribed, by the central government, in the books of orders to JPs issued between 1552 and 1631. The rioters' sense of injustice that 'their' grain was being moved was often shared by the local magistrates, who needed little urging to turn back grain convoys or to order farmers and dealers to bring grain to market. Town and county JPs argued the rioters' case to the privy council and those participating in food riots – who often included a high proportion of women – were seldom severely punished. The execution of four rioters after the disorders at Maldon in 1629 was unique in the seventeenth century.[44]

A view of riot which minimizes the element of conflict is most appropriate to food riots. On one hand rioters were usually poor and rarely violent; on the other, those blamed for dearth were a small minority, widely seen as profiting from scarcity. Other agrarian disorders were more adversarial. Riots against the conversion of arable land to sheep pasture and the destruction of customary rights set farmers and labourers against landowners; as the latter might also be magistrates, there was little point in appealing to them for redress. Such riots usually involved violence against objects (especially fences) and animals (above all sheep). Still more contentious were systematic assaults on common rights in the fens of eastern England and the forests of the west. The prime movers in draining fens and clearing forests were often outsiders – City businessmen, courtiers (in some cases Catholics), foreigners. Their projects threatened to destroy both the livelihood and the way of life of the inhabitants, who depended heavily on common rights: grazing, fishing and wildfowling in the fens, grazing, mining and woodland crafts (not to mention free fuel) in the forests. To make matters worse, Charles I, eager for profit, misused the machinery of law on the projectors' behalf. Fenmen and forest-dwellers, convinced of the justice of their cause but denied legal redress, were thrown back on their own resources. Although some of their violence was symbolic, against effigies rather than people, much was very real, directed against the projectors' agents and (in the fens) against Flemish drainage workers who spoke no English and so were not susceptible to persuasion. Even so, only two people died during a century of rioting in the fens and in neither case is it clear that they died as a result of injuries inflicted by the rioters.[45]

We thus have a view of pre-civil war riots which emphasizes self-discipline, order within disorder, showing few signs of the savage violence so common in French riots.[46] But this is not the whole story. Keith Lindley has shown that there were frequent, and often violent, riots in early Stuart London. These were not, of course, agrarian in origin and were rarely concerned with food shortages: both the City fathers and the national government were careful to keep the metropolis well fed. Instead, some were associated with particular dates – especially Shrove Tuesday – while others were 'political' in the narrower sense, notably the lynching of the Duke of Buckingham's pet astrologer in 1628.[47] Rioting and violence remained endemic in later Stuart London. Often they involved conflict between particular groups, which could be sparked by a quarrel between individuals. A drunken altercation between an English cook and a Welsh noble on St David's day 1662 ended with the lord and his retinue being put to flight, not without risk of serious injury.[48] Londoners' dislike of foreigners had a long history; their violence tended to be more verbal than physical, but when there was a pitched battle between the servants of the French and Spanish ambassadors, the former ascribed the Spaniards' victory to the support they received from the citizens, who threw mud and insults at the French coach as it slunk home.[49] On at least two other occasions, crowds attacked the French ambassador's house.[50] Equally, riots could involve conflicts between different crafts, as when butchers and weavers battled it out in London in 1664, or between different branches of the armed forces: soldiers fought sailors at Deal in 1668.[51] In 1666 two people died as a result of a fight at Cowbridge fair, in Glamorgan, between people of two neighbouring parishes, for reasons which remained obscure to those living nearby.[52] Similar solidarity was shown by the gentlemen of the Inns of Court and London apprentices. In 1673 an attempt by some bailiffs to distrain goods in Fuller's Rents led to a pitched battle involving a hundred gentlemen of Gray's Inn and thirty 'lusty' bailiffs, which ended with one bailiff dead and twenty-one bailiffs and twelve gentlemen injured. The men of Gray's Inn were involved in another battle in 1684, this time with builders (or soldiers disguised as builders) employed by Dr Nicholas Barbon, the most notorious speculative builder of his day. The gentlemen were defeated, but inflicted considerable injuries.[53]

Apprentices, if anything, showed even greater solidarity and pugnacity. On Shrove Tuesday, 1670, a large group of Bristol apprentices assembled with staves and clubs, to fight; the mayor (with difficulty) dissuaded them.[54] In March 1664 there was an outcry when two London apprentices were sentenced to the pillory, and a whipping: some said it was for beating their master, others for using false weights. Their fellows pulled down the pillory (whereupon the lord mayor set up another) and attacked the master's house. That Sunday four or five thousand assembled in Moorfields, but were dispersed by the trained bands. Pepys heard that it was the first time that apprentices had been pilloried; they were reported to be gentlemen's sons and so above such plebeian forms of punishment.[55] On St George's day, 1670, London apprentices occupied the New Exchange in protest at their masters' refusal to give them the day off. In 1673 two hundred apprentices to coach- and harness-makers 'camped' for five days on Primrose Hill after being told that there would be no jobs for them. In 1676 apprentices gathered on several evenings on hearing that one of their number had been roasted on a spit by his master. In each case, when the trained bands arrived, they dispersed peacefully.[56]

It is clear that disorders, often violent, were common, but what were they about? Food riots were rare after the early 1660s, when there were several in south coast ports.[57] The population growth of the sixteenth and early seventeenth centuries had ended, food production was rising and prices were tending to fall. Together with the increasingly effective safety net provided by the poor laws – the amount dispensed in poor relief rose rapidly between 1662 and 1700 – the risk of starvation receded and with it the need to riot. The slackening of population pressure also removed much of the impetus for agrarian change. Although the struggle in the fens continued into the eighteenth century, elsewhere the pressure to convert arable to pasture slackened. Charles II, wary of provoking Parliament, gave no encouragement to predatory projectors and let the law run its course. This does not mean that there was no rural disorder. There were still localized protests against disafforestation. In 1670 there was a bitter conflict between the ranger of Kingswood Forest and local cottagers, who had been allowed to settle, clear the waste and open up mines and quarries. At least one local gentleman claimed that if anyone was behaving riotously it was the ranger's agents, some of whom had fought against the king; the justice who investigated the matter was told to ascertain the facts and stick to the law.[58] Lord Herbert (the future Duke of Beaufort) warned against allowing enclosures in the Forest of Dean, where the people were numerous, tough and lawless.[59] While there were some enclosure riots from this period,[60] more common were complaints about attacks on deer. Deer parks were widely seen as destructive of common rights and there had been a spate of attacks on them in the 1640s. In 1679 deer from Windsor Forest wrought havoc in cornfields around Staines. The local people assembled and for several days slaughtered deer, as many as sixty a day; it is unclear whether they confined themselves to the forest or went into private deer-parks as well. When a rioter was arrested, he was rescued by the local people, who refused to assist the sheriff in any way. There was also a report that deerstealers on the fringes of the New Forest had 'driven the woods', killing eighty to a hundred deer.[61] The renewed fashion for deer-parks, and the restriction of hunting rights under the game laws, created antagonism. The events at Staines could be seen as a response to a threat to the farmers' livelihood, but in 1677 it was reported that in Dorset gangs numbering over a thousand had gathered to destroy the Earl of Shaftesbury's deer. It was remarked that no-one knew who these people were, but they were clearly no friends to the earl. A few years earlier a much smaller band of people calling themselves Levellers, led by a man nicknamed Robin Hood, robbed and vandalized gentlemen's houses in Worcestershire.[62]

Illegal deer-hunting clearly caused concern to the landed elite. Parliament passed an Act against it in 1661; another, with more severe penalties, passed the Lords but not the Commons in 1678.[63] Equally, there was none of the panic which was to lead to the passing of the Black Act of 1723. Conflict in the countryside was probably more sporadic and less serious than under Charles I. It seems, indeed, that riot was now mainly an urban phenomenon. It was easier for crowds to gather in centres of population, especially on public occasions, such as elections. One source of urban riots was industrial disputes. We shall consider later the London weavers' riots of 1675. There were also weavers' riots, perhaps following London's lead, at Colchester and Exeter, while the Newcastle keelmen rioted in protest at low wages.[64] Another common reason for riot was perceived injustice. When fourteen-year-old Lord Gerard wounded a drunken porter who accosted him, a crowd hurried the boy to prison, broke his windows and smashed what was thought to be his mother's coach.[65] When a boy who tried to see a sideshow elephant without paying was stabbed by a soldier guarding the booth, youths pulled down the booth (twice). When some were arrested, a large crowd demanded their release and their captors were happy to let them go in return for money.[66] When some seamen were sent to gaol in 1666 for 'discontented words', several hundred of their fellows pulled down the gates and released them. In 1673 some seamen who asked for their arrears of pay at the Navy Office were pressed again. Others broke down the door, rescued them and threw the press-master out of the window. Although some were arrested, Secretary Coventry commented that the JPs had been able to 'appease' them.[67]

One important difference between England and France in the early seventeenth century was that French peasants and townsmen reacted bloodily to increases in taxation, whereas their English counterparts did not, because their tax burden (especially that of the poor) was very low. The 1640s saw a huge increase in the level of taxation and the introduction of the excise, which brought even the poorest within the tax system. The excise and hearth tax provoked bitter and violent opposition; several hearth tax collectors were killed. Often town magistrates were reluctant to assist the collectors, but even if they did their duty, people protested that they could not – or would not – pay and drove the collectors away with stones.[68] A three-year embargo on imports from France in 1678 led to an increase in smuggling and violent resistance to customs men.[69]

The revival of tax-riots offers one explanation for the apparently higher level of violence in post-Restoration riots: the relationship of taxpayer to tax collector could easily become adversarial. The pattern for riots associated with particular days is less clear. In those parts of Europe which practised carnival, Shrove Tuesday was the culmination of a period of indulgence and often 'licensed misrule' before the austerities of Lent.[70] Shrove Tuesday riots were common in London before the civil wars; usually they involved attacks on brothels or theatres. This continued under Charles II, in provincial towns as well as in London; the rioters now focused mainly on brothels. In Bristol in 1685 youths went to the house of a reputed bawd. She set her mastiffs on them, whereupon they burned the house to the ground. They then put her on a 'coal staff' and carried her around the city, visiting her daughter's house en route and smashing all the barrels in her cellar. She was eventually rescued by two constables and locked up in the Bridewell.[71] This case is unusual in that it involved a 'riding', the ritual humiliation of the woman; in locking her in the house of correction, the constables may have been concerned for her safety, but they were also meting out the punishment which the law prescribed for whores. To attack brothels was ostensibly not to challenge the authorities, but to assist in enforcing the law, albeit with a clear hint that they had been remiss. It could be seen as implying a continuing 'puritan' morality among young men. It could equally be that brothels were seen as a legitimate target for youthful violence: the Bristol apprentices had simply wanted a fight in 1670. We shall consider later the 1668 bawdy-house riots in London. There were other attacks on brothels in London in 1671 and 1679 (though neither on Shrove Tuesday)[72] and at Worcester in 1667.[73] At York an attempt on Shrove Tuesday 1673 to stop young people from making a noise near the minster led to a riot involving four or five hundred. A canon of the minster, who civilly (he said) asked them to be quiet was besieged in his house and had his windows broken. The lord mayor refused to intervene saying it was outside his jurisdiction. In this case the riot seems unlikely to have been planned, which shows how easily a crowd could assemble, particularly on a holiday.[74]

In the riots we have considered so far, there was generally a clear rationale: riots were not aimless, or random. Often that rationale rested on a sense of natural justice, in terms of the relations of master and apprentice, employer and employee, or the punishment of those seen as deviant. Although there was frequent violence against persons and property, there was rarely a direct trial of strength between the rioters and the military resources of the state – the militia and (less often) the army. This was partly because boys with stones stood little chance against men with guns, but also neither party wished it to come to that. In many ways riots continued to be demonstrations, which tried to jolt the authorities into action, but did not attempt to take over their responsibilities. The light punishments normally meted out could be a tacit recognition of this – or of the authorities' lack of power.[75] Many riots remained, like the food riots discussed by Keith Wrightston and John Walter, part of a process of bargaining and evidence of particular failures within a shared framework of values. They were not indicative of deep ideological division. The riots we have considered so far, while 'political' in the broader sense, cannot easily be seen as 'political' in the narrower sense. Consider, by contrast, events in 1641. In the provinces, the meeting of the Long Parliament was seen as presaging the righting of all wrongs. Aggrieved people paid off scores, confident that their actions would be approved by Parliament. Indeed, the Commons identified the targets for popular wrath: altar-rails, courtiers, papists. Only occasionally, as in the attack on Lady Rivers' house in the Stour valley, did the violence slide into indiscriminate destruction and looting.[76] In London, meanwhile, concerted crowd action forced Charles to sacrifice Strafford and dismiss Lunsford, kept the bishops out of the Lords and eventually drove the king out of his capital.

This popular action deepened political divisions and reflected the distrusts and hatreds which existed in 1641. In labelling papists, Arminians and courtiers as enemies of the people and of Protestantism, the Commons incited people to action based on the analysis of the nation's ills set out in the Grand Remonstrance. One can find, under Charles II, similar divisions and a similar analysis of the dangers England faced. In the winter of 1679–80 partisans of the Dukes of York and Monmouth urged passers-by to drink their health; when York's men chased some boys who cried out for Monmouth, some 'lusty fellows' broke their swords, wounded several and (it was said) killed one.[77] In November 1681 the queen's lacemaker provoked a riot by lighting a 'popish' bonfire to celebrate her birthday. In December bonfires were lit to celebrate the failure of the prosecution of Shaftesbury; those who tried to put them out were beaten up.[78] On 5 November 1682, after the usual bonfires, several hundred people marched through the London streets, crying 'a Monmouth, no York', breaking Tories' windows and attacking inns with names like the Mitre, the Cardinal's Head or the Duke's Head.[79]

There is no doubt that these riots expressed ideological divisions, but it should also be stressed that they were confined to the last years of the reign and that they were far smaller – and had far less impact on events – than the riots of 1641–42. But does it follow that riots for most of Charles II's reign were not 'political' in the narrower, ideological sense? They may appear that way to the historian, but that was not necessarily the way they appeared to the authorities at the time. Historians are aware that some Tudor rebellions – Wyatt's or the Northern Earls' – had hidden political agendas. Might that not also be the case of Restoration riots? Did their seemingly 'legitimate' aims conceal something deeper? To answer this, let us consider two sets of riots in London, which were undoubtedly seen as serious: the bawdy-house riots of 1668 and the weavers' riots of 1675.

The trouble in 1668 started on Easter Sunday when a mountebank put on a play satirizing tailors. Tailors' apprentices in the audience smashed the theatre and attacked the mountebank. A group of butchers came to his defence and a fight ensued which lasted three hours, after which those involved drifted off to the taverns. Next day about 4,000 people pillaged a brothel near the Tower. The guards, sent to disperse them, were reluctant to charge such an angry crowd and held back, although several soldiers were hurt by missiles. About twelve arrests were made. On the Tuesday they assembled in greater numbers, rescued their colleagues and pulled down several houses in Moorfields on the pretence that they were brothels. The soldiers were now ordered to charge; some dispersed quickly, others defended themselves resolutely. On the Wednesday they assembled again and were again dispersed by troops.[80] On the face of it, this was just another riot against brothels, starting on a public holiday. However, there were reports that there had been speeches to the crowd against the government: it was alleged that former New Model officers had incited the rioters and a spy claimed that the riots were part of a wider design.[81] The government certainly took them seriously: eight rioters were convicted of treason and four were executed. The riots also highlighted the problems of policing the fringes of the City, outside the direct, unambiguous sphere of authority of the lord mayor and the City trained bands.[82] Tim Harris concludes that there is no firm evidence of a design to overthrow the government, but argues that there are signs of nonconformist involvement.[83]

The weavers' riots worried the government still more, not least because they began at a time when the king and council were out of London. They were directed against new 'engine' looms for weaving ribbons, enabling one man to do the work of ten or twenty ordinary looms. There had been numerous petitions and protests against the looms, which were a French invention and widely believed to be illegal.[84] On 9 August 500 men and a similar number of women entered four houses and burned seven looms. The weavers petitioned that the king should order that the looms should not be used until the council had heard their case.[85] Next day much larger crowds attacked houses all around the eastern fringes of the City (especially Spitalfields) and across the river from Lambeth and Southwark as far as Greenwich. By 12 August there were estimated to be 30,000 rioters, some of whom presented a petition to the lord mayor; the Weavers' Company was also urged to petition the king, following the conventional pattern that appeals to authority continued in parallel with riot. At Newington Butts a Quaker, trying to defend his home, killed one man and wounded another. It was noted that the crowds were unarmed and that the JPs tried to be 'tender' towards them.[86] Thus far the rioters had kept out of the City, but on 11 August they made some forays near Newgate and Bishopsgate, only to be driven out by the militia. It was now reported that they talked of extending their attacks to the French in general and also to corn hoarders and salesmen (who sold ready-made clothes and so threatened the livelihood of the tailors, almost as numerous and poor as the weavers). It was claimed that they recognized one another by their green aprons and red ribbons in their hats.[87] The local authorities had hitherto stressed that violence and destruction had been limited; now they acted firmly, mobilizing the City and Tower Hamlets militias, and the disturbances petered out. Trying to excuse their earlier inaction, they pleaded lack of orders and blamed one another, or claimed that they did not have full legal power to act. The king's councillors feared some hidden agenda (although they could not see one) and were alarmed that the riots had exposed the government's weakness. It soon became clear that the riots started in the belly rather than the brain, driven by fear of hunger and unemployment, and that the rioters had been urged on by their wives.[88] The king, who had earlier wished to impose severe punishments, agreed in October to pardon the weavers, following a petition for clemency in which they declared that they were poor, ignorant and easily led.[89] Despite the government's anxieties, it is difficult to see these riots as driven by ideology, unlike those of 1641.

Elections

At one time historians assumed that, before the 1832 Reform Act, elections were controlled by great landowners, using their economic power and the patronage resources of the state. In the shires landlords marched their tenants to the polls and watched them vote; 'rotten' boroughs bowed to the will of their proprietors. More recently, while not denying the existence of rotten boroughs, historians have shown that elections in the shires and larger boroughs were hotly contested, even in the age of Walpole and Newcastle; rural voters often ignored their landlords' wishes.[90] Plumb, Hirst, Holmes and Speck have all argued that the electorate of Stuart England was much larger than used to be thought, reaching a peak of one quarter of adult males, or more, in 1715.[91] Such figures are, of course, conjectural and do not take into account inequities in the distribution of seats. The right to send burgesses (MPs) to Westminster had been granted to boroughs as a matter of historical accident. The last constituencies to be created before 1832 were Newark, County Durham and Durham City in 1672–73; major cities, like Birmingham, Manchester and Leeds were not represented in Parliament. A vote in a small borough, with a handful of electors, was worth far more than a vote in a large shire, with thousands. Moreover, in the counties many electors did not vote because they could not spare the time, or meet the cost of travelling to the town where the election would be held, especially as the poll could last for days. Although the county franchise had been standardized since 1422, at freehold land worth forty shillings (£2) a year, borough franchises varied enormously. At the widest it could embrace all resident adult male householders or all those paying local rates. At the narrowest it could be confined to the corporation or the owners of certain properties, usually known as burgages. In between came all sorts of variations, one of the commonest vesting the franchise in freemen of the town (which opened the possibility of creating non-resident 'freemen' to vote in elections). To confuse matters further, in many boroughs the extent of the franchise was uncertain. In 1679 Higham Ferrers claimed that since it had been granted representation in 1556, there had never been a contested election, so nobody knew what the franchise was.[92] In many boroughs, contests had been sufficiently infrequent or inconclusive for there to be scope for argument about the franchise. In the counties there were frequent complaints that the sheriff (as returning officer) allowed unqualified persons to vote.

If there were doubts about who could vote, electoral influence was not confined to those claiming to be voters. On one hand, peers (and peeresses) played a significant part in elections and the Commons committee of elections could overturn the electors' decision. Peers and non-resident gentlemen attended borough elections, ostensibly to see fair play, but also to influence the outcome. On the other hand, the unenfranchised poor could cheer, roar and throw missiles, to exhort or intimidate the voters. The increasing prevalence of treating – particularly the provision of free beer – reduced inhibitions and enflamed passions. The Commons repeatedly addressed the question of the influence of peers in elections and their use of inducements and threats, sometimes involving armed retainers or the militia.[93] They also complained of the growing cost of elections and the incidence of drunkenness and bribery.[94] Bills were brought in to regulate elections, but none passed, partly because some argued the need for 'civil hospitality' (such as a post-election dinner) or 'reasonable refreshment', especially in county elections, when many voters travelled considerable distances. When did a 'reasonable' level of treating become excessive?[95] The difficulty of defining 'corrupt' practices led an experienced MP to remark that such bills were seldom read a second time.[96]

Historians of the reigns of William III and Anne emphasize that elections were dominated by 'the rage of party', but had this always been the case? In seeking to answer this question, Mark Kishlansky offered a valuable framework for discussion.[97] He argued that the seventeenth century saw a transformation of the electoral process. Before 1640 'selections' were the norm. Candidates were preselected through processes of negotiation. Those for the shires were generally agreed in gentry meetings, often gatherings for county business, such as assizes or quarter sessions. In boroughs, there was a complex interplay between the town government, neighbouring peers and gentry and members of the central administration, in which the town sought burgesses who could advance or protect its interests, in the Commons and at court. The relationship between patron and borough was one of mutual advantage, rather than one of power on one side and dependency on the other.[98] This was an intensely **personal** process: people were chosen because of who they were, not because they represented any particular 'party', or set of principles. There was a preference for avoiding contests, which were divisive and expensive and brought dishonour on the loser. The fact that most constituencies had two members facilitated compromise. The few contests that occurred were the results of either misunderstanding or deep personal animosities, which led a candidate to stand despite all pressures to desist.

Kishlansky argued that this consensual approach to 'selection' was destroyed by the religious and political issues which burst forth in the two hotly contested elections of 1640 and divided the nation irrevocably in the civil wars. Issues became more important than personalities: to lose in a good cause was no disgrace.[99] Contests were accepted as normal. Would-be MPs set out to build 'interests' in boroughs, seeking to win support by gifts to the town and its inhabitants and promises of favours to be secured from the central government. Well aware that seats in the Commons were a valuable asset, the towns' rulers played one suitor against another, so that patronage relationships became more overtly reciprocal – and more competitive.[100] Although this might suggest that electoral politics were driven by material interests, Kishlansky sees these bids for the boroughs' favour as the product of ideological differences. Although there were attempts to go back to the old ways after the Restoration, the divisions opened up in the 1640s and 1650s were too deep to be covered over. Even if the boroughs were eager to cash in on their representation, they could do so only because the schisms within the landed elite ensured that contests, based on differences of principle, were now common.[101] The procedure for deciding contests became formalized. Whereas before 1640 simple acclamation (the 'shout') or a rough estimate of numerical strength (the 'view') had been seen as sufficient, now the poll became the norm, with voters giving their votes publicly on the hustings. Often, contestants agreed before the start how the poll would be taken and the books in which choices were noted became a public record. This was important because petitions against disputed returns became common. The aggrieved party would appeal to the Commons committee of elections, which since 1604 had the right to resolve disputes, and thus gain a second chance of success; many printed their 'case', to put it before the public.[102]

There is little doubt that the changes which Kishlansky analysed did indeed take place. The bitterly partisan elections of 1679–81, or of Anne's reign, were qualitatively different from the mostly uncontentious 'selections' of Elizabeth's reign. However, there is room for debate as to when the change occurred and how complete it was. Derek Hirst and Richard Cust have argued that there is strong evidence of ideological divisions in elections in the 1620s[103] and there are scattered examples even under Elizabeth.[104] From my point of view, the key question is how far were elections under Charles II dominated by ideology. Kishlansky's answer was more equivocal than the broad thrust of his book would suggest. The chapter dealing with 1640–60 was entitled 'the transition'. In it he declared that 'in all the sessions of the Revolution the process of selection was forged in the crucible of political crisis'.[105] Yet the next sentence stated that 'by the general election of 1678 [sic] the transformation was complete', which suggests that between 1660 and 1678 it was not. The logic of his argument suggested a continuous process over the half-century from the Petition of Right to the Exclusion Crisis, but the evidence proved frustratingly intractable, leading him to recognize that the old ideals of consensus continued in the 1650s and beyond.[106] Even in the Exclusion Crisis, he admitted, ideological factors were only part of the story.[107] If the process was not complete, nor was it continuous. He was well aware that the electoral process under the Protectorate was very different from that after the Restoration because so many were excluded for being Royalists or 'ungodly'; Royalists were also excluded (as least in theory) in 1660. Nevertheless, he suggested that a more systematic approach to building up an 'interest' developed in the 1650s[108] and he lumped together the three very different elections of 1659, 1660 and 1661. He also referred to the 'new meaning' of Parliament, which gave an added importance to membership.[109] This 'new meaning' presumably referred to the executive functions assumed by Parliament in the 1640s and 1650s – which it quietly abandoned after 1660.

It is my contention that ideology played only a limited part in elections between 1661 and 1678 and was by no means all-pervasive even in the Exclusion Crisis. If ideological divisions were to dominate the electoral process, elections had to be frequent, so that the issues raised in one election could be carried over into the next. Those running for re-election could be judged on their records, defeated candidates could plan for the next contest. This was the case in the 1620s, in 1640, in 1679–81 and under the Triennial Act of 1694. It was not the case between 1661 and 1678, when there was no general election. In an uncharacteristically confused passage, Kishlansky argued that this 'created a pent-up demand for seats . . . and allowed for the kind of planning on the part of candidates and government officials that had never before been possible'.[110] Later, however, he remarked that 'the frenzy of 1679 revived newsbooks and accounts of elections, both dormant since the Revolution', which hardly implied a vigorous electoral politics in the preceding years.[111] Underlying his whole argument was the assumption that the divisions of the civil war would inevitably determine the shape of politics under Charles II. I shall argue that they did for part of the reign, but by no means for all of it. Old-style electoral methods and ideals revived at the Restoration as part of the re-creation of the old constitutional and political order. And they remained vigorous even in the Exclusion Crisis.

As far as the shires were concerned, those ideals were stated by Lord Scudamore in March 1661. For over forty years, he said, the gentry of Herefordshire had met to agree on two gentlemen to propose to the freeholders. This practice had developed because the animosities from contested elections tended to spread into matters of justice and tax assessment – indeed, any in which an inferior had to deal with a superior of the opposing faction. As the main cause of contests had been dissension among the gentry, it was imperative that they should agree among themselves. This did not infringe the freedom of the freeholders, 'for the gentry is not to impose, but only to recommend unto the freeholders their judgment and opinion'. He went on that providence had ordained 'that inferiors are to receive from the superiors that participation of knowledge and light by which their resolutions and actions are to be guided', so he was sure that the freeholders would be glad to know the views of the gentry 'that they may be thereby enlightened what choice to make'.[112] While one may doubt the eagerness of the freeholders to embrace the advice of the gentry, a candidate who did not enjoy considerable gentry support was unlikely to be chosen a knight of the shire. Gentlemen canvassed their tenants and the neighbouring freeholders; many arranged to transport them to the county town for the election and paid for their food and lodgings (and sometimes compensated them for lost earnings as well).[113] This is not to suggest that the gentry invariably delivered bodies of compliant voters, although this often happened,[114] nor that freeholders never defied the wishes of the gentry: the cutlers of Sheffield reneged on their undertaking to vote for Reresby's chosen candidate in 1679.[115] However, freeholders were likely to show such defiance only if a contest raised real issues of principle which split the gentry. If the gentry remained united, they stood a reasonable chance of avoiding a contest, as Herefordshire did in every general election between 1661 and 1689 (although there was a contested by-election in 1668).[116] Agreement was easier to achieve if a balance was struck between different parts of the county[117] or between two parties, as in Dorset and Staffordshire, which avoided contests throughout the Exclusion Crisis.[118] At times, the meeting also allocated seats in the county's boroughs, although there was no guarantee that the boroughs would accept their nomination.[119]

Pre-selection was intended to avoid divisive contests and to keep down the cost of election.[120] Sometimes, there was an attempt to agree an orderly rotation of membership, with each leading gentleman having his turn.[121] There were complaints in some counties if individuals insisted on standing again and again,[122] or if, once the gentry had reached their decision, someone insisted on standing against the agreed candidates.[123] Conversely, the unanimous decision of the meeting could persuade a reluctant candidate to stand.[124] In the boroughs, however, almost the opposite considerations applied. While borough elections could involve ideological divisions, corporations and voters had every incentive to encourage contests. When Sir Francis North was chosen at King's Lynn, he gave the townsmen a treat which cost £100, but they would have preferred a contest 'to make the money fly'.[125] North, in fact, had been invited to stand and it was not uncommon for even substantial boroughs (like Yarmouth and Gloucester) to seek out members who could serve them well.[126] The small Kentish borough of Queenborough responded to an overture from the governor of Sheerness by inviting him 'to come and prove my credit among them, which cannot be done without some trouble and considerable expense'.[127] The thirteen burgesses of Buckingham had no need to seek out would-be members. They (and their wives) were wined and dined by a succession of aspirants for election, who promised benefits for the town. Lord Latimer, son of Lord Treasurer Danby, undertook to secure the summer assizes. Sir Richard Temple of Stowe promised in 1661 to give a load of well seasoned timber and a sum of money to build a new town hall, the old one having burned down, but neither materialized. Temple repeated the offer in 1677, this time producing the timber but not the cash and earning the sobriquet 'Sir Timber Temple'.[128] Even the smallest of boroughs could prove unreliable or demanding: Westbury was described as 'perfidious' in 1660[129] while at Queenborough the 'fickle people' complained in 1679 that James Herbert had not performed what he had promised when elected in 1677.[130] When Newark secured the right to choose MPs, the inhabitants were incensed by a Commons vote limiting election expenses to £10 and paraded an effigy of a 'ten pound burgess' around the town. Henry Savile, standing for election, placated them by drinking good ale and bad sack with them for four days, at considerable risk to his health.[131]

Many boroughs cannily exploited the demand for seats, but aristocratic patronage remained a potent force. In 1661 Henry Howard secured the return of both MPs for Castle Rising and one each at Aldeburgh and Thetford; an aspiring candidate was advised to seek a seat in 'one of Mr Howard's boroughs'.[132] At Christchurch the lords of the manor – Lord Baltimore, who (like Howard) was a Catholic, then the second Earl of Clarendon – assumed a proprietorial right to nominate at least one member.[133] At Appleby the Dowager Countess of Pembroke was all-powerful. She insisted in 1668 that the vacant seat should go to one of her grandsons, declaring that if none would accept it she would stand herself. In the event one was returned unopposed.[134] The Countess was one of several formidable matriarchs who influenced borough elections. In 1662 Lady Rochester demanded the writ for Malmesbury 'as belonging to my grandchildren', but she had to contend with the Earl and Countess of Berkshire, who secured the seat for one of their sons.[135] At East Grinstead the Dowager Countess of Dorset promoted the interest of Henry Powle, whom she was shortly to marry; her son favoured his cousin Edward Sackville. Sackville was returned, but Powle unseated him on petition.[136] Other ladies at odds with their kin were the Marchioness of Hertford at Great Bedwin in 1660 and 'Madame Danby' (no relation to the lord treasurer) at Malton, who assured William Leveson Gower in 1672 that if he did not keep his promises 'I will be as troublesome as a waking spirit'.[137] Along with frequent references to the need to entertain voters' wives, even in small boroughs like Aldborough, Yorkshire,[138] these examples show that electoral politics, like court politics, was by no means exclusively a male domain.

We thus have two opposite images of the behaviour of small boroughs: robust independence and supine dependence. Many fell between the two and the growing divisions in the latter part of the reign offered even the meekest borough the possibility of choice. The limits to Henry Howard's influence became clearer and clearer. In 1669, when he promoted Pepys's candidacy at Aldeburgh, he was told that he had the nomination of only one seat and it was the other which was vacant. Despite Howard's best efforts, and those of the Duke of York, Pepys was rejected. It was claimed that York's letter of recommendation was a forgery and that Pepys was a Papist.[139] Howard eventually secured Pepys a seat at Castle Rising in 1673, but Howard's Catholicism offered a pretext to challenge the return and Pepys was lucky to keep the seat. Howard's residual influence was destroyed by the Popish Plot: in 1679 he refused to endorse anyone, claiming that it would be counter-productive.[140] Pepys's difficulties were matched by those of Williamson, who was rejected at one borough after another. Morpeth chose Lord Morpeth, son of the Earl of Carlisle, on the pretext that he had done the town a great honour by taking its name, but it was reported that the townsmen said that (after having Sir George Downing as their MP) they would not choose another courtier or stranger.[141] Rebuffed at Dartmouth and Preston, and powerless to carry Appleby against Lady Pembroke, Williamson at last found a seat at the factious and impoverished town of Thetford, assisted by Howard and Arlington.[142]

The experience of Pepys and Williamson suggests that even small towns had several strategies to avoid having unwanted outsiders foisted on them. They could express a preference for one of their own, or at least someone not wholly a stranger.[143] They could plead that they were 'pre-engaged' to another, which was seen as an acceptable excuse, but encouraged contenders to build an 'interest' as early as possible.[144] The Exclusion Crisis offered a greater choice of patrons, some with power rooted at court, others (such as Buckingham, Grey and increasingly Monmouth) in their standing with the Commons and the people.[145] This in itself reflected the growing importance of ideology, which from 1679 was clearly a significant factor in elections: even Christchurch was contested in 1681. This would seem to support Kishlansky's view, but to test it further we need to assess the importance of political and religious divisions in elections before 1679.

The election of March–April 1660 was peculiar in that political circumstances discouraged discussion of the most important issue of the moment. Both Presbyterians and Royalists favoured the restoration of the monarchy in some form, but neither thought it safe to discuss the matter while the New

Model (which had repeatedly made clear its hostility) remained in being. Its commander in chief, General Monk, was purging the officer corps of republicans, but the process was incomplete and, publicly at least, Monk opposed the restoration of the monarchy. In another sense past political divisions lay at the centre of the campaign. Before dissolving itself on 16 March, the Long Parliament laid down qualifications for both candidates and voters, designed to secure a Presbyterian House of Commons, which would require the king to agree to limitations on his powers and a comprehensive national church. These excluded on one hand Catholics and those who had been in arms against Parliament or who had compounded for their 'delinquency', unless they had since shown good affection towards Parliament; on the other, those opposed to magistracy and ministry.[146] These qualifications caused confusion. People were uncertain whether the restrictions referred to the sons of active Royalists. In Staffordshire the general opinion was that they did, so two less active men of Royalist sympathies were chosen. In Somerset, John Ashburnham thought his son-in-law Hugh Smyth was disqualified because his father had been a Royalist, but others thought his recent service as a JP and grand juryman could be seen as evidence of 'good affection'. Ashburnham advised him not to stand for fear of an 'affront', but added if his friends thought otherwise he would bow to their better judgement. Smyth stood and was elected.[147] The king gave no lead to the old Cavaliers, making it known that he would not be averse to the election of the Presbyterian Edward Harley in Herefordshire; Harley was chosen.[148]

The qualifications focused attention on past conflicts, but some also looked to the future. In Cambridgeshire the freeholders chose an obscure gentleman after two more distinguished candidates rejected his challenge to declare for the restoration of king and church.[149] More remarkable was a speech drafted by Lord Scudamore, later the apostle of gentry consensus in Herefordshire; we do not know if it was given. Scudamore was deeply committed to the Church of Charles I and Laud. He declared that any settlement must include the Church, 'the spouse of our saviour'. Since 1640, the sacraments had been laid aside and the Lord's Prayer slighted; it was vital to re-establish the civil power in order to preserve the ecclesiastical. If active Royalists were to be excluded, the same should apply to active Parliamentarians. Those who had fought for neither side – honest gentlemen, lovers of their country – would be best able to heal its divisions.[150] One suspects that he was being disingenuous, as he was trying to prevent Harley's election; others alleged that Harley's opponents were Papists or favourers of Popery.[151] In general, however, the focus was on the past. Radicals and republicans fared worst. In Buckinghamshire, Cromwell's lord chancellor Bulstrode Whitelocke thought his recommendation would do more harm than good. At Leicester, two hundred of the gentry told the corporation that if they chose Sir Arthur Heselrig they would never again hold sessions or spend their money in the town; Heselrig failed to find a seat. The gentry of Northamptonshire resolved not to choose any member of the Long Parliament.[152] Elsewhere it was alleged that MPs 'secluded' in Pride's Purge were as bad as the Rumpers.[153] Attempts by the military, the Council of State or local radicals to frustrate the popular will proved unavailing. At Gloucester, Colonel Massey, once the city's Parliamentarian governor but now reconciled to the king, was returned despite Monk's order to have him arrested.[154] In Derbyshire, the 'Anabaptists' threatened the life of Lord Mansfield, son of the Marquis of Newcastle, Charles I's general in the North; Mansfield raised a troop of horse, rode to Derby and was elected.[155]

The elections of Harley and Massey offer a reminder that the popular tide was running in favour of Presbyterians as well as Royalists. In Norfolk, the freeholders rejected two who had sat in Cromwellian Parliaments (Sir John Hobart and Sir William Doyley) in favour of a third, Sir Horatio Townshend, who was chosen with Lord Richardson, the son of a Royalist. Both Hobart and Townshend had been too young to take part in the civil war, but Hobart had shown greater commitment to the Protectorate, having been created a member of Cromwell's 'Other House' in 1657. Doyley had been an active Parliamentarian and had assured Townshend as late as 9 March that he could not approve of a king. Thus of the three candidates active in the 1650s, the one least obnoxious to Royalists was chosen.[156] By contrast, powerful members of the current government proved relatively unsuccessful. Edward Montagu, general at sea, managed to secure his own election (along with a former active Royalist) at Dover, which frankly admitted it needed an MP with influence in high places, given the poor state of the port.[157] But he failed to find a seat for his cousin and namesake at Hythe, Sandwich or Hastings.[158] The fact that Montagu, perhaps (after Monk) the most powerful man in the country, but identified with the Protectorate, had so little electoral influence showed how strong was the desire for the restoration of monarchy. What sort of monarchy remained to be seen.

In the general election of 1661 there were no political 'qualifications' on either candidates or voters. The election of four religious radicals for London caused consternation among the old Cavaliers. Letters were sent into the provinces, urging voters to follow London's example, but few did.[159] In Southwark, two 'honest' candidates were chosen, despite the opposition of 'Presbyters, Independents, Anabaptists and Quakers'; one of the defeated candidates had been in the Rump.[160] In Yorkshire two Royalists joined against Lord Fairfax. Fairfax, the former commander of the New Model, had facilitated Monk's march into England and had been elected unopposed in 1660. Now, denounced as a 'black presbyter', he did not force a contest.[161] In Nottinghamshire, William Pierrepoint, a leading figure in the 1640s and 1650s, who had been returned unopposed in 1660, was defeated by a 'private gentleman'.[162] In Northamptonshire, Sir Justinian Isham (a sequestered Royalist) would have preferred that another should stand who had not been involved in the 'late unhappy differences'. However, the gentry insisted that he should stand, in opposition to Richard Knightley, who had the support of a handful of gentry, together with the Presbyterian clergy, the Baptists, Quakers and (it was alleged) the Papists. Isham and his partner carried it by three to one.[163] In Herefordshire Harley, chosen in 1660, realized he stood no chance against Scudamore and the Royalists and was returned for Radnorshire instead.[164]

In these cases, religious and political issues were clearly important, but they were not all-pervasive. In many small boroughs, like Christchurch, traditional aristocratic control quietly resumed. Henry Howard nominated four very different members. Sir Robert Paston was the son of a Royalist, but had served as a JP in 1659. Robert Steward, the other member for Castle Rising, had apparently been neutral in the civil war but sat in the 1659 Parliament. William Gawdy, chosen at Thetford, had apparently taken no part in the civil wars, although his father had sat in the Long Parliament until Pride's Purge, as had Sir John Holland (Aldeburgh), who had been elected to the council of state early in 1660.[165] In some constituencies ideological concerns were mixed with practical considerations. The corporation of Sandwich later proved reluctant to enforce the laws against Dissent, so might be expected to favour candidates of a puritan bent. Sir Edward Partherich, who had sat for the town in the Long Parliament, offered himself again. He proclaimed his support for a settlement of the Church as it had been under Edward VI and Elizabeth, with a liturgy according to the Word of God. He was not chosen, the town preferring one of its former members, John Thurbarne, and Edward Montagu, a more valuable asset now that his cousin, the admiral, enjoyed the king's favour.[166]

Still more confused was the case of Northallerton. With the return of episcopal lands, John Cosin, Bishop of Durham, became lord of the manor in place of the Lascelles family, one of whom had been involved in Charles I's trial. Cosin put forward Sir Paul Neile, seen as a friend of the Church, but some 'perverse spirits' sought a candidate who would oppose the bishop and secure a charter, to give the town greater autonomy.[167] The 'boroughmen' were willing to choose Cosin's son-in-law, Sir Gilbert Gerard, who had served as an official of the Duchy of Lancaster through most of the 1640s and 1650s, but claimed that they could not support Neile as they were pre-engaged to Major Roger Talbot, an old Cavalier. An agent reported that 'the Royalists' were willing to choose Neile, but the 'other party' was for Gerard and Talbot; it was alleged that Talbot had been pressed to stand by Lascelles's party and was supported by some of the bishop's tenants. The agent told the boroughmen 'how necessary it was to obey your lordship's desire in regard your honour had promised them good and would study and had great interest to favour them in any favour whatsoever'. They replied that the bishop's letter had come too late and that they were committed to Talbot. The agent added that the town expected Gerard to spend money there.[168] This advice was taken, but the townsmen remained opposed to Neile and there were fears that Lascelles's brother-in-law might stand; the bishop was assured that if Lascelles himself came into the county, the lord lieutenant would arrest him. Gerard and Talbot were returned without a contest.[169]

Religious issues and civil war allegiances both played some part in this election, but there were other issues, including the bishop's attempt to use his power as lord of the manor and the desire of some townsmen to escape from his tutelage. Lascelles's support for Talbot may have been tactical: the 'Presbyterian' faction at Northampton set up one old Cavalier against another in a by-election in 1663.[170] Nevertheless, it is clear that even in 1661 ideological differences were by no means all-pervasive. It will be argued in Chapter 11 that for the remainder of the Cavalier Parliament, political and religious issues played a limited part in electoral politics, not least because divisions within the court and the inconsistencies of royal policy blurred the divisions apparent in 1660–61. Only after 1673 did something akin to partisan divisions re-emerge and battle-lines were fully drawn only in the two general elections of 1679. Even then, the process of choosing MPs contained elements of both 'selection' and 'election'.

Notes

1 See R. Scribner, 'Is a History of Popular Culture Possible?', *HEI*, X, 1989, pp. 175–91; B. Reay, *Popular Cultures in England 1550–1750*, London, 1998, *passim*.
2 See Underdown, *Revel*; Stoyle, *Loyalty*; T. Harris, 'The Parties and the People' in L.K.J. Glassey (ed.), *The Reigns of Charles II and James VII and II*, London, 1997, ch. 6, especially pp. 124–6, 147–8; T. Harris, 'The Problem of "Popular Political Culture" in Seventeenth-century London', *HEI*, X, 1989, pp. 43–58, especially p. 44.
3 Seminar paper entitled 'Whose prerogative?' given to the seventeenth-century British history seminar, Institute of Historical Research, 27 May 1999.
4 Comber, *Autobiographies*, I.xix, 3. See also N.E. Key, 'The Political Culture and Political Rhetoric of County Feasts and Feast Sermons, 1654–1714', *JBS*, XXXIII, 1994, pp. 233–4, 240–6.
5 Key, 'Feasts', pp. 230–1, 236–7, 242.
6 Key, 'Feasts', pp. 232–3, 246–7; Browne, I.243, 254.
7 *CSPD 1661–62*, pp. 86, 196–7.
8 *CSPD 1673*, p. 417, *1675–76*, p. 179; *Williamson*, I.82.
9 *CSPD 1673*, p. 598 [quoted], *1673–75*, pp. 97, 139; *Williamson*, II.60, 129.
10 Pforz, Coleman to Bulstrode, 6 and 13 October 1676; BT 134, Courtin to Louis, 2 November 1676 NS; Egerton MS 3330, fo. 5.
11 Pepys Lib., MS 2875, fos 465–7, 474–5.
12 *HMC Ormond*, NS IV.514; Pepys Lib., MS 2875, fos 474, 478.
13 *HMC Ormond*, NS IV.561; *CSPD 1679–80*, p. 296.
14 BL, Add MS 28930, fo. 203; D. Allen, 'Political Clubs in Restoration London', *HJ*, XIX, 1976, pp. 571–3.
15 *CSPD July–September 1683*, pp. 61, 165–6, 250, 263, 296, 303; D.A. Scott, 'Politics, Dissent and Quakerism in York, 1640–1700', unpublished D. Phil. thesis, York, 1990, p. 326.
16 Ailesbury, I.64–5; Reresby, p. 244; Carte MS 232, fo. 99; Key, 'Feasts', pp. 236–7, 248–51. Allen, 'Clubs', pp. 574–8 refers to a 'Tory' club which met at Fuller's Rents from 1679; the presence of Sir Thomas Meres, who voted for exclusion, casts doubt on whether it was really 'Tory' – or indeed political.
17 See D. Cressy, *Bonfires and Bells: National Memory and the Protestant Calendar in Elizabethan and Stuart England*, London, 1989; P. Borsay, '"All the town's a stage": urban ritual and ceremony 1660–1800' in P. Clark (ed.), *The Transformation of English Provincial Towns*, London, 1984, ch. 7.
18 Coventry MS 83, fo. 3; BL, Add MS 25117, fo. 92.

19 *CSPD 1673*, pp. 37, 41, 49; Newcome, *Autobiography*, II.204.
20 *CSPD 1664–65*, p. 422, *1666–67*, p. 18; *HMC le Fleming*, p. 37.
21 *CSPD 1666–67*, pp. 2–3.
22 *CSPD 1667*, pp. 72, 141–2, 144.
23 *CSPD 1667*, p. 134, *1668–69*, p. 297.
24 *CSPD 1664–65*, p. 188. See also Josselin, p. 486.
25 Pepys, IV.163, VII.136; *CSPD 1671*, p. 282; Pforz, ? to Bulstrode, n.d., entered before 12 December 1679.
26 Wood, III.16; Evelyn, IV.204.
27 PC 2/68, p. 473.
28 PC 2/59, pp. 491–2; *CSPD 1667*, p. 272.
29 PC 2/60, p. 312; *CSPD 1671*, pp. 309–10; R. Clifton, *The Last Popular Rebellion: The Western Rising of 1685*, London, 1984, pp. 27–31, 38–40, 43–5.
30 *CSPD 1671*, p. 420.
31 Tanner MS 42, fo. 96.
32 Schellinks, p. 172; Newcome, *Diary*, p. 137; Pepys, VII.358; Hull RO, BRB 5, p. 76; Henry, p. 232.
33 *Williamson*, II.67; Evelyn, IV.26; BL, Add MS 25122, fo. 165.
34 CPA 108, Croissy to Pomponne, 20 November 1673 NS; *Williamson*, II.71 (quoted); *CSPD 1673–75*, pp. 40, 44.
35 BL, Add MSS 25117, fo. 144, 25122, fo. 165.
36 Carte MS 79, fo. 140; *CSPD 1677–78*, p. 446.
37 Schellinks, p. 172; Pforz, Coleman to Bulstrode, 20 November 1676; BL, Add MS 29556, fo. 272; *Hatton*, I.157. See also Neale, *Essays in Elizabethan History*, pp. 9–13.
38 BL, Add MS 25124, fo. 167 (quoted); CSPV (cont), Sarotti, 18 November 1678 NS.
39 *HMC 7th Report*, p. 477; Carte MS 232, fo. 61; Pepys Lib., MS 2875, fo. 484; Miller, *Popery*, pp. 184–8.
40 BT 147, Barrillon to Louis, 28 November and 2 December 1680 NS; Browning, *Danby*, II.379–80.
41 M636/36, John Verney to Edmund and Sir Ralph, 10 April 1682; Oates's Plot, ? to ?, 13 April 1682; Carte MS 216, fo. 29; T. Harris, *London Crowds in the Reign of Charles II*, Cambridge, 1987, pp. 168–72.
42 *CSPD Jan–June 1683*, pp. 250, 278, 286–7.
43 Stone, *Crisis*, ch. 5, especially pp. 223–34; James, *Society, Politics and Culture*, ch. 8. For Pembroke, see Herbert, William in *DNB*.
44 K. Wrightson and J. Walter, 'Dearth and the Social Order in early modern England', *P & P*, no. 71, 1976, pp. 22–42; J. Walter, 'Grain Riots and Popular Attitudes to the Law: Maldon and the Crisis of 1629' in Brewer and Styles (eds), *Ungovernable*, pp. 47–84; P. Clark, 'Popular protest and disturbance in Kent, 1558–1640', *EconHR*, XXIX, 1976, pp. 365–81.
45 See K.J. Lindley, *Fenland Riots and the English Revolution*, London, 1982, pp. 57–8 and *passim*; B. Sharp, *In Defiance of all Authority: Rural Artisans and Riot in the West of England, 1586–1660*, Berkeley, 1980.
46 C.S.L. Davies, 'Peasant revolts in France and England: a Comparison', *Agricultural History Review*, XXI, 1973, pp. 122–34.
47 K.J. Lindley, 'Riot Prevention and Control in early Stuart London', *TRHS* 5th series XXXIII, 1983, pp. 109–15.
48 Schellinks, p. 75.

49 BT 109, D'Estrades to Lionne, 10 and 17 October 1661 NS [D'Estrades was trying to justify himself to a very angry Louis XIV]; *CSPV 1661–64*, p. 55.
50 BT 109, D'Estrades to Brienne, 6 October 1661 NS; CPA 85, Cominges to Lionne, 22 June 1665 NS.
51 Pepys, V.222–3; PC 2/57, p. 95; *CSPD 1667–68*, p. 348.
52 *CSPD 1666–67*, p. 61.
53 *Williamson*, I.52; Morrice, pp. 439–40; *HMC 7th Report*, p. 481. For other disturbances involving the Inns, see Lindley, 'Riot prevention', pp. 113–14; Newdigate, pp. 228–32.
54 *CSPD 1670*, p. 76.
55 *HMC 7th Report*, p. 575; Pepys, V.99, 101; BT 113, Cominges to Lionne, 7 April 1664 NS; Whitelocke, pp. 680–1.
56 *HMC le Fleming*, p. 70; *Williamson*, I.172; Pforz, Coleman to Bulstrode 4 August 1676.
57 *CSPD 1661–62*, p. 602, *1663–64*, pp. 130–1; PC 2/56, fo. 163; Southampton RO, SC 2/1/8, fo. 192; A. Charlesworth (ed.), *An Atlas of Rural Protest in Britain, 1548–1900*, London, 1983, p. 80.
58 *CSPD 1670*, pp. 433, 435–6, 443–4, *1671*, pp. 248–9; Charlesworth, *Atlas*, pp. 42–3.
59 *CCSP*, V.490.
60 *CSPD 1668–69*, p. 594.
61 Charlesworth, *Atlas*, pp. 56–8; *HMC 7th Report*, pp. 472–3; M636/32, Sir Ralph to John Verney, 26 June, John to Sir Ralph, 30 June 1679; *CSPD 1679–80*, p. 186. For similar incidents in 1659, see A. Thomson, 'Hertfordshire communities and central-local relations, c. 1625–c. 1665', unpublished Ph.D. thesis, London, 1988, p. 435.
62 Carte MS 79, fo. 117; *CSPD 1670*, pp. 590–1, *1671*, pp. 18–19; *HMC le Fleming*, p. 74.
63 *LJ*, XI.330; *HMC 9th Report, appendix II*, pp. 119–20.
64 PC 2/65, pp. 6, 17; *CSPD 1675–76*, pp. 513–4; *HMC le Fleming*, p. 79.
65 *HMC 7th Report*, p. 469.
66 M636/32, John Verney to Sir Ralph, 31 August and 5 September 1678.
67 *HMC Portland*, III.303; Pepys, VII.415; M636/27, Sir Ralph to Edmund Verney, 11 December 1673; Coventry MS 83, fo. 202.
68 *CSPD 1667–68*, p. 224, *1666–67*, pp. 330–1.
69 Coleby, *Hampshire*, p. 192.
70 See P. Burke, *Popular Culture in Early Modern Europe*, London, 1978, ch. 7.
71 BCL, MS 10163, Annals of Bristol, under 17 February 1685.
72 Bradfer, S. Henshaw to Sir Robert Paston, 13 May 1671; CUL, Add MS 4878, fo. 612.
73 *CSPD 1666–67*, p. 560. See also *CSPD 1671*, p. 124.
74 *CSPD 1672–73*, pp. 546–7, *1673*, p. 36.
75 Lindley, 'Riot prevention', pp. 118, 121, 124–6.
76 See B. Manning, *The English People and the English Revolution*, London, 1976, chs 2–4; R. Clifton, 'The Popular Fear of Catholics in the English Revolution', *P & P*, no. 52, 1971, pp. 23–55; Morrill, *Nature*, ch. 4.
77 BL, Add MSS 25359, fo. 202, 29557, fo. 403; *Hatton*, I.204; Newdigate, pp. 69–70.
78 Oates Plot, John Litcot to ?, 17 November 1681; *CSPD 1681*, pp. 571–2, 583–4; Harris, *Crowds*, pp. 181–2.

79 *CSPD 1682*, p. 528; *HMC le Fleming*, p. 190; Harris, *Crowds*, pp. 186–7; Cressy, *Bonfires*, pp. 182–3.
80 BT 118, Ruvigny to Lionne, 5 April 1668 NS; Egerton MS 2539, fo. 180.
81 BT 118, Ruvigny to Lionne, 5 April 1668 NS; Egerton MS 2539, fo. 182; *CSPD 1667–68*, p. 310.
82 Egerton MS 2539, fos 182, 194; BL, Add MS 36916, fo. 89.
83 Harris, 'Bawdy', pp. 550–2, 554.
84 Harris, *Crowds*, pp. 195, 198–202.
85 *Hatton*, I.120; Coventry MS 16, fos 34, 40, 42.
86 *HMC 7th Report*, pp. 465–6; Coventry MS 16, fos 51, 60–4.
87 Coventry MS 16, fos 64, 74, 102–3.
88 Coventry MS 16, fo. 72; *HMC 7th Report*, pp. 465–6.
89 BL, Add MS 25124, fos 42–3, 50–1; PC 2/65, fo. 20.
90 For the fullest recent study, see F. O'Gorman, *Voters, patrons and parties: The unreformed electorate of Hanoverian England, 1734–1832*, Oxford, 1989.
91 J.H. Plumb, 'The growth of the electorate in England from 1600–1715', *P & P*, no. 45, 1969, p. 111; D. Hirst, *The representative of the people? Voters and voting under the early Stuarts*, Cambridge, 1975, pp. 104–5; G. Holmes, *The electorate and the national will in the first age of party*, Lancaster, 1975, pp. 23–4; W.A. Speck, *Tory and Whig: The struggle in the constituencies 1701–15*, London, 1970, p. 16.
92 *CSPD 1679–80*, p. 104.
93 BL, Add MS 34132, fo. 10; *HMC Kenyon*, p. 97; Coventry MS 6, fo. 27; M636/32, Edmund Verney to Sir Ralph, 20 March, 22 May 1679.
94 CJ, IX.374, 411, 517; *HMC 5th Report*, p. 197; *HMC 7th Report*, p. 471; Lawrence, pp. 11–12; *Norths*, I.121.
95 Grey, II.334, IV.1, 96–7.
96 Finch MS PP 42, p. 21.
97 M. Kishlansky, *Parliamentary Selection: Social and Political Choice in Early Modern England*, Cambridge, 1986.
98 *Ibid.*, pp. 31–41, especially pp. 37–8.
99 *Ibid.*, pp. 20–1, 113.
100 *Ibid.*, pp. 19–20, 115, 124–5, 149–51, 157.
101 *Ibid.*, pp. 106–7, 122–3, 138–9, 171–2, 228.
102 *Ibid.*, pp. 116–9, 181–3, 190–1.
103 Hirst, *Representative*, pp. 137–53; R. Cust, 'Politics and the Electorate in the 1620s' in Cust and A. Hughes (eds), *Conflict in Stuart England*, London, 1989, ch. 5. See also the reviews of Kishlansky by Hirst, *Albion*, XIX, 1987, pp. 428–34 and Cust, *PH*, VII, 1988, pp. 346–50.
104 A. Hassell Smith, *County and Court: Government and Politics in Norfolk, 1558–1603*, Oxford, 1974, pp. 325–30; P. Collinson, 'Puritans, Men of Business and Elizabethan Parliaments', *PH*, VII, 1988, pp. 205–6, 211 n.97.
105 Kishlansky, *Selection*, p. 107 and ch. 5.
106 *Ibid.*, pp. 106–7, 122–3, 126–7, 134, 138.
107 *Ibid.*, pp. 171–2.
108 *Ibid.*, pp. 112–21.
109 *Ibid.*, p. 107.
110 *Ibid.*, p. 19.
111 *Ibid.*, p. 137.

112 BL, Add MS 11044, fo. 253. See also P.R. Brindle, 'Politics and Society in Northamptonshire, 1649–1714', unpublished Ph.D. thesis, Leicester, 1983, p. 210.
113 BL, Add MS 27447, fo. 403; M636/32, Sir Ralph Verney to William Coleman, Edmund Verney to Sir Ralph, 2 February 1679; Bodl, Fairfax MS 33, fo. 51.
114 It was said that Sir Christopher Musgrave's tenants 'dare not deny him': *HMC le Fleming*, p. 135.
115 Reresby, pp. 186–7.
116 *HP*, I.261–2. Kishlansky, *Selection*, pp. 129–30 alludes to the 1668 contest, but not to the five uncontested elections which followed.
117 BL, Add MS 33923, fo. 464; M636/17, William Smith to Sir Ralph Verney 13 March 1660 (endorsed 6 November 1660); *HP*, I.433; FSL, MS X d 375(3).
118 *HP*, I.212, 381–3.
119 *HMC le Fleming*, p. 155; Dorset RO, D124, Box 233, Col. T. Strangways, letters to Weymouth and Bridport, 29 January 1679.
120 Worcs RO, BA 4739/2 (xiii)3; Leics RO, DE 730/4, Abel Barker to Sir T H[artop?], 23 December 1660; BL, Add MS 11051, fos 233–4; Clar MS 78, fo. 65; *HMC Kenyon*, pp. 110–11.
121 *HMC le Fleming*, p. 130.
122 Raynham, Holland, Holland to Townshend, 28 March 1681; *The Speech of the Honourable Henry Booth*, 1681, p. 2; Dering, *Papers*, pp. 116, 130. However, Sir Edward Harley urged Lord Scudamore to stand for a fifth time in 1681: PRO, C115/N10, no. 8898.
123 BL, Add MS 27447, fo. 342; *CSPD 1679–80*, p. 395.
124 *HMC Frankland-Russell-Astley*, pp. 38–40; Bodl, Fairfax MS 33, fo. 51; WYAL, MX/R 12/18.
125 *Norths*, I.111–12.
126 Althorp MS C5, Sir Thomas Thynne to Halifax, 1 February 1679 and 13 August 1681; Gloucs RO, GBR B3/3, pp. 780, 792.
127 BL, Add MS 29577, fos 390–1.
128 M636/29, Edmund Verney to Sir Ralph, 12 June 1676, M636/30, same to same, 19 February, Sir Ralph to Edmund Verney, 22 February 1677; *HP*, I.140.
129 M636/17, Thomas Baxter to John Carey, 28 March, Thomas Yates to Sir Ralph Verney 29 March, Carey to Verney, 4 April 1660.
130 Egerton MS 3331, fo. 99.
131 *Savile*, pp. 44–6.
132 Robbins, 'Correspondence', *passim*; Egerton MS 2717, fo. 191; *HP*, I.333.
133 Dorset RO, D10/C2/4; Christchurch Civic Offices, volume of 'Letters' on elections etc., p. 49; *HP*, I.247–8.
134 *CSPD 1667–68*, pp. 171–3, 176–7, 190–1, 219, 223.
135 M636/18, Lady Rochester to Sir Ralph Verney, 27 January, John Carey to Sir Ralph, 5 February 1662; *HP*, I.452.
136 CKS, U269/C98/17; *HP*, I.422.
137 M636/17, John Carey to Sir Ralph Verney, 4 April, Dr Denton to Sir Ralph, 9 April 1660; M636/22, same to same, 15 October 1668; Staffs RO, D868/8, fos 32–4.
138 WYAL, MX/R, 12/90.
139 Pepys, *Further*, pp. 247, 249, 256–7, 258–9.
140 *HP*, I.323; All Souls MS 171, fo. 12; Badminton, MS FmE 4/4/1.

141 *CSPD 1666–67*, pp. 163, 196, 198, *1660–85 (Addenda)*, p. 163.
142 Pepys, *Further*, pp. 257–8; *CSPD 1668–69*, pp. 490, 494, 535, 607.
143 *HP*, I.489–90; Stocks, *Leicester*, pp. 470–1; *CSPD 1672–73*, pp. 488–9.
144 Bodl, MS Eng Letters c. 210, p. 83; *CSPD 1672–73*, pp. 488–9.
145 BL, Add MS 28087, fo. 1; *HMC 7th Report*, p. 474; M636/33, Sir Ralph to John Verney, 11 September 1679; Tanner MS 38, fo. 126; Carte MS 222, fo. 248.
146 *CJ*, VII.873–4.
147 Staffs RO, D868/8, fo. 11 (partly printed *HMC 5th Report*, p. 195); BRO, AC/C74/11; *HMC Leybourne-Popham*, p. 173; *HP*, I.368–9, 381. For Smyth's father and the siege of Sherborne, see D. Underdown, *Somerset in the Civil War and Interregnum*, Newton Abbot, 1973, pp. 41–3.
148 BL, Add MS 11051, fos 229, 231; *HP*, I.261–2.
149 *CCSP*, IV.657.
150 BL, Add MS 11044, fos 251–2; *HP*, I.261–2.
151 *HMC Portland*, III.220.
152 Whitelocke, p. 578; M. Coate, 'William Morrice and the Restoration of Charles II', *EHR*, XXXIII, 1918, p. 376.
153 M636/17, Dr Thomas Hyde to Edmund Verney, 8 April 1660.
154 M636/17, William Denton to Sir Ralph Verney, 29 March 1660; *HMC Leybourne-Popham*, p. 229; *CCSP*, IV.643–4, 656, 657, 661; Rugg, pp. 68–9; *HP*, I.241.
155 Clar MS 72, fo. 102; *HP*, I.187.
156 *CCSP*, IV.640; *HP*, I.319–20, II.230, 552. For Doyley's opposition to the king, see NRO, MC 1601/19.
157 Carte MS 73, fos 357, 382; *HP*, I.493–4.
158 Carte MSS 73, fos 372, 393, 223, fo. 200; *HP*, I.491, 501.
159 Pepys, II.57; *CSPD 1660–61*, pp. 535–43; *HMC 5th Report*, pp. 159, 170.
160 *HMC 5th Report*, p. 181; *HP*, I.414–15.
161 *HP*, I.468; DUL, Mickleton-Spearman MS 46, fo. 139.
162 *HMC 5th Report*, p. 160; *HP*, I.349–50, III.243–4.
163 Isham, pp. 12–13; *HP*, I.335.
164 *HP*, I.261–2.
165 *HP*, II.381, III.210, 485–6; J. Miller, 'A Moderate in the first Age of Party: The Dilemmas of Sir John Holland, 1675–85', *EHR*, CXIV, 1999, pp. 851–3.
166 CKS, Sa/C4, no. 22; Carte MS 73, fos 347, 353; *HP*, I.501.
167 DUL, Mickleton-Spearman MS 46, fo. 135.
168 DUL, Mickleton-Spearman MSS 31, fo. 12, 46, fo. 151; *HP*, II.239.
169 DUL, Mickleton-Spearman MS 46, fos 139, 165.
170 Kishlansky, *Selection*, pp. 174–80; Brindle, 'Northants', pp. 221–34; *HP*, I.339–40.

Chapter six

Parliament

Representatives and represented

The relationship between MPs and the people was ambivalent. On one hand, Parliament derived its place in the constitution from its representative nature: the peers spoke for themselves, the Commons for the commons of England – all subjects other than peers. Members were elected (or selected) by, or in the name of, the voters of a constituency, to whom they were presumably answerable in some way. In 1661 it was recorded that the 'mayor, bailiffs and commonalty [of Winchester] have empowered and authorised [their two burgesses], for themselves and for the said city, to act, consent and do in the same Parliament those things which for the public good and by his Majesty's council in the same Parliament shall happen to be ordained'.[1] On the other hand, debates in the Commons were regarded as confidential. It was alleged that MPs could not speak or vote freely if their conduct could be discussed and censured by the general public. Lord Chancellor Clarendon told the Commons in 1661 that the English chose the 'learnedest, wealthiest and wisest' of the land to represent them.[2] Representatives were innately superior to represented; they pooled their wisdom through the process of debate and were additionally informed by the privy councillors in the House. It would be inappropriate for less able and less informed people to instruct MPs how to vote or to criticize their resolutions. Publicizing their proceedings could be seen as not merely informing the people but inviting them to express their views on Parliament's conduct, perhaps forcibly. This argument was given added weight by the experience of the civil wars. Having based its right to resist the king on its representative nature, Parliament was pressed to pay more heed to the wishes of those it claimed to represent. The Levellers turned Parliament's rhetoric against itself and demanded that it should base the nation's constitution on the 'agreement of the people'.

Conservative Parliamentarians, therefore, tried to separate the process of selection from the later functioning of Parliament: once chosen, they said, MPs were free agents. To reinforce this claim, they argued that MPs did not individually represent their constituents, however few or many, but collectively represented all the commons of England. This argument might be tenable in theory, but not in practice. An MP who wished to be re-elected needed to keep his constituents informed and to show that he was looking after their interests. Many were conscientious and maintained friendly relations with their townspeople: John Trenchard talked of 'my Tauntonians'.[3] But many were not. There were frequent complaints of absenteeism, giving rise to proposals that the names of persistent absentees should be printed or that they should pay double and be named (and shamed) in the subsidy bill. These proposals were rejected as an 'appeal to the people', but it was agreed that the Speaker should write to their corporations.[4] Many also fell far short of Clarendon's ideal of 'wealthiest, learnedest and wisest'. In 1669 it was reported that one was in the Fleet prison for debt, another had taken sanctuary in Gray's Inn to escape his creditors and another had sold his ancestral home and most of his estate. Others were in similar straits.[5] Others were laid low by old age or sickness, especially in the long Cavalier Parliament of 1661–79. The majority were country gentlemen, who had sought election for the local prestige it brought and did not wish to spend their time drudging in committees when London had so many delights to offer. The king's parliamentary managers had to scour the playhouses, eating-houses and brothels to bring in errant MPs.[6] The first exclusion bill received its first reading in a thin House because there was dog racing at Hampton Court and horse racing on Banstead downs.[7] Long sessions made members restive and with the approach of summer they longed to be in the country.[8] While some were articulate and persuasive speakers, many seem never to have spoken at all and some who ventured to speak subsided into incoherence. Proceedings were often confused, as members shouted one another down or wrangled about procedure.[9] At times half an hour or more passed in which nothing was said.[10]

Apart from attending the House MPs were expected to act as agents and lobbyists, seeking favours and looking after their town's interests. It was remarked that the previous members for Callington (Devon) had neither secured new fairs for the town nor prevented local rivals from securing them instead. A bevy of Cornish MPs presented a petition to transfer the assizes from Launceston to Bodmin.[11] Competition to host the Buckinghamshire assizes involved several peers, the lord chief baron, the two MPs for Buckingham and the Verneys' barber.[12] Sir Thomas Osborne, as MP for York, helped secure payment of £50 a year to the poor, promised by the Duke of York, and claimed to have reconciled the cathedral clergy and the corporation after the Shrove Tuesday riot in 1673.[13] Thomas Flint, MP for Coventry, discussed a draft petition from the city with Clarendon, received his advice on how to present it and secured his promise to be present when the king considered it.[14] The members for Chester promoted the city's cause in a long-running taxation dispute with the county, putting its case to the treasury commission and later seeking to broker an acceptable compromise.[15] Harwich's members complained to the Dutch ambassador about the number of Dutchmen begging in the town.[16] One of the members for Leicester lobbied in support of the mayor, summoned before the privy council to explain his rulings in recent excise cases. The mayor was found to have been in the wrong, but was pardoned on confessing his fault.[17]

Few members were as diligent as Andrew Marvell, MP for Hull. He sent detailed information about the Commons' proceedings (especially those relating to taxation), promoted bills, waited on ministers and officials and offered practical advice. Although at odds with his fellow-member, Colonel Gilbey, the two worked together in the town's interests.[18] Marvell urged the town to choose a high steward who was a privy councillor, who would be 'ready to represent your carriage here above and patronise the justice of your actions'. When the town chose its governor, Lord Bellasis, popular locally despite being a Catholic, Marvell enlisted his support for petitions from the corporation.[19] Marvell was perhaps exceptional in that he acted as agent for the town even when he was not a member,[20] but he was not unique. Given the numerous stages in the making of grants and decisions and the 'culture of reciprocity', towns, like individuals, needed the assistance of well-connected men with friends in high places. They might be peers, like Lord Townshend,[21] but they might also be MPs. The prospect of such assistance was an important factor in their selection and the fact that they were MPs would make the government more inclined to give them satisfaction. In some cases, the member approached might not sit for that town. The men of Daventry, which was not represented in Parliament, approached Daniel Finch, MP for Great Bedwin, but the son of their lord of the manor. Weymouth secured the assistance of Sir Humphrey Weld, MP for Christchurch; Weld was asked not to tell Colonel Reymes, member for Weymouth, of his assistance, for fear that Reymes might be offended.[22] The relationship between town and members worked best if courtesy and trust were maintained on both sides. Sir John Shaw was furious when the Duke of Albemarle superseded him as recorder of Colchester. He was awarded £500 damages against the town for the loss of his place (although there is no record that this was paid) and then sued for unpaid wages. Technically, MPs were entitled to wages, but with a few exceptions (such as Marvell) waived their right. Several other members now threatened to demand wages, unless they were chosen again. Sir Harbottle Grimston, the other MP for Colchester, brought in a bill to repeal the ancient statute under which the wages were due. Opinions were divided. Some thought the bill would prevent unscrupulous members threatening poor boroughs; others argued that it would deprive members of the opportunity to make a generous gesture and that it would cast aspersions on their honour. The bill did not pass; Shaw received his arrears and did not stand again.[23]

The business of Parliament

At the end of 1660, Lord Chancellor Hyde declared that MPs came up as the people's 'deputies' to the king and went home as the king's 'plenipotentiaries' to his people. 'You are now returning to your countries' he told them 'to receive the thanks and acknowledgements of your friends and neighbours for the great things you have done and to make the burdens you have laid upon them easy by convincing them of the inevitable necessity of their submitting to them'. Marvell had made a similar point to Hull corporation: another assessment was a price well worth paying to be rid of the New Model.[24] Nowhere should the culture of reciprocity have been more apparent than in Parliament, where king and people came together to transact measures for their common good. Opening and closing speeches were filled with the rhetoric of harmony and mutual affection. Such rhetoric may seem strange in the aftermath of civil war, but perhaps experience of civil war made it seem doubly necessary. It went deeper than that, however. 'Revisionist' historians of Elizabethan and early Stuart Parliaments have argued that it is misleading to see monarchy and Commons as set on a collision course. There were arguments, but these could be about means rather than ends and arguments offered a way of reconciling conflicting views and interests: disagreement can be evidence that a political system is working. It could be argued that under Elizabeth many disputes stemmed from her refusal to allow discussion of the most important issues of the day: the succession, Mary Queen of Scots and religious reform. From the 1590s to the 1620s there was increasingly bitter contention about corruption in high places and the crown's growing reliance on non-parliamentary taxation, which raised fears for the future of Parliament. Meanwhile, James I and Charles I became convinced that a section of the Commons wished to strip them of their legitimate powers and take over the direction of government.

Recent debates about Elizabethan and early Stuart Parliaments have discredited some aspects of the traditional 'Whig' historiography, notably the assertion that the Commons set out to wrest supreme power from the king.[25] There is general agreement that one cannot analyse parliamentary politics in isolation: what happened in Parliament was part of a wider political world, embracing also the royal court and the localities.[26] It is also generally acknowledged that to focus exclusively on conflict, or on what historians choose to see as 'important' constitutional or political issues, is misleading. Parliament was a place where much prosaic, but necessary, business was done. In late twentieth-century Britain, most legislation is government legislation, pushed through the Commons using the government's parliamentary majority, marshalled by the whips, within an adversarial political culture. For much of the sixteenth and seventeenth centuries there was nothing resembling parties in the Commons and the government felt little need to legislate. True, the Tudors needed extensive legislation to break with Rome and to transform the official religion, but that process was largely complete by 1571; James I wanted a union between England and Scotland. That apart, the only legislation they wanted concerned taxation, so the initiative for legislation – much of it local and private – generally came from backbenchers. Even great 'national' legislation, like the poor laws of 1598 and 1601, reflected an aggregation of local experience and drew on the methods used by local authorities to deal with poverty. Closer analysis of the business of Parliament also reveals that the **process** of legislation was designed to foster consensus.[27] All bills had to be approved by both Commons and Lords before being presented to the king and within the Houses there was a preference for talking their way to agreement, avoiding 'divisions' (votes) whereby the majority imposed its will on the minority.[28] Far from seeing the Commons as the mouthpiece of the 'country' against the 'court', Geoffrey Elton (like Hyde) saw them as a link, a 'point of contact'. Privy councillors explained the crown's needs (especially for money) to a significant cross-section of the landed elite, many of them involved in local government. MPs gave councillors their assessment of the mood of the provinces and the benefit of their experience of local problems and suggested how best to tackle them. Far from being storm-centres of political conflict, sessions of Parliament were essential to the effective running of government.[29]

Historians of Restoration Parliaments have perhaps been slow to apply the insights offered by their early Stuart colleagues. It could perhaps be argued – or assumed – that those insights are irrelevant as the mid-century upheavals irrevocably changed England's political landscape, a view seemingly confirmed by the partisan battles of the Exclusion Crisis. This argument – or assumption – risks repeating the cardinal 'Whig' error of focusing on conflict and treating it as the norm. Looking at the actual business of the Commons suggests a different picture. We have seen how active many MPs were **outside** the House, a reminder that it was not a closed political world. I should like now to consider the nature and content of legislation.

In 1667, Pepys's cousin Roger, MP for Cambridge, complained that in the Commons 'there is nothing done but by passion and faction and private interest'.[30] In 1678 the House debated corruption, condemning those who accepted pensions and other rewards from the king's ministers, but recognizing that the malaise was more widespread. Some accepted gifts from foreign ambassadors,[31] others were paid for their work as counsel for bills before the House, or as chairmen of committees, or for their votes. Others offered lavish hospitality in an effort to sway their colleagues. After some debate, the House resolved not to appoint a committee to investigate the matter.[32] Some Acts clearly reflected the material interests of MPs and their constituents. The Act banning imports of Irish cattle was pushed through by members from the pastoral regions of the North and West.[33] When discussing tax bills, MPs supported the system of assessment most beneficial to their locality.[34] Clarendon complained that MPs gave private bills priority over public, knowing the latter would pass anyway, and spun out the session to pass as many private bills as possible. Often, he claimed, those with a weak legal case tried to achieve their ends through a private bill and used treating or bribery to push it through.[35] An agent of the Countess of Rutland wined and dined all forty-six members of the committee on a private bill, after which it was approved without amendment. Cynics remarked that it was hardly surprising that men who bought their way into Parliament sold their votes.[36]

As at court, so in Parliament, slow and tortuous processes and a multiplicity of competing interests made success contingent partly on hard work and the right contacts, partly on luck. Each bill received two readings in each House, the first mainly for information, the second to give a chance to debate its principle and substance. If it passed the second reading, it was referred to a committee for detailed scrutiny and amendment. The committee reported any changes to the House, which could either approve them, or refer the bill back to the committee. If the House was satisfied, the bill then needed to pass a third reading, before being sent to the other House, which could reject the bill, quietly forget about it or suggest amendments. If these amendments were not acceptable to the House where the bill originated, the Houses might hold a formal conference in which representatives of each put their case and took the other's arguments back to their own House. Often they compromised, sometimes they did not. There were thus many hazards in the way of private bills, to which should be added sudden prorogations (which kept the Parliament in being, but aborted all uncompleted bills) and dissolutions; there was also the possibility that the king might use his veto, although he rarely did.

For any private bill, the support of the king was valuable. Without it, Sir Robert Paston's bill to develop Southtown would not have passed in the face of determined opposition from Great Yarmouth.[37] Seemingly uncontentious measures might also encounter difficulties. Hull corporation had long wished to secure an Act to make the town church, Holy Trinity, technically a chapel attached to nearby Hessle, a parish church in its own right. In 1661 a bill was brought in, which ran into problems on the issues of the minister's maintenance and the patronage of the living. Marvell had stressed the need to secure the consent, in writing, of those who were to contribute to the minister's stipend, as the Commons were reluctant to agree to any bill imposing payment on the people without their consent. In the event, the House's scruples were overcome and the bill passed.[38] Marvell was less successful in his efforts, in conjunction with Trinity House at Hull, to secure a lighthouse on Spurn Head. They initially sought a grant from the king, but found themselves opposed by Colonel Frowd, who claimed he already had one. Marvell suggested an Act of Parliament, which would cost about the same, but stressed that any payments made by shipowners towards the lighthouse would have to be voluntary; the king's law officers agreed. There was always, he added, an element of chance: he cited Yarmouth's failure to defeat Paston's bill, despite the fact that one of its MPs was Sir William Coventry, then a leading figure in the government. In the event there was stalemate, with Frowd able to prevent Trinity House receiving a grant from the king and Marvell and other members for East Coast ports able to prevent Frowd from securing an Act of Parliament.[39]

Restoration MPs did not spend all their time on local and material issues. The Houses repeatedly considered the sort of measures associated with 'puritans' before the civil wars. In 1664 they passed an Act against disorderly and excessive gaming and in 1677 an Act for the better observance of the Lord's Day. This laid down that people were to devote their Sundays to works of piety and to abstain from work or business.[40] The Commons deplored the prevalence of swearing, blasphemy and atheism and brought in bills to prevent them.[41] The Houses also addressed the problem of poverty, expressing concern about the disorderly poor and the cost of poor relief.[42] The main legislative achievement of the reign in this area was the Act of Settlement of 1662, which for the first time formally laid down the principle that every pauper should be assigned a parish responsible for their maintenance. The aim of the

Act was to facilitate the removal of unwanted incomers, but it had the effect of creating a sense of entitlement among those responsible for the poor and the amount spent on poor relief rose substantially.[43] The Act effectively completed the system of poor relief established at the end of Elizabeth's reign, a system abolished in 1834 because it was too expensive and too generous. Like so much legislation, it was the product of MPs' experience of local administration, not of government initiative.

King and Parliament

'We do not take ourselves to be part of the government' declared Sir William Coventry in 1677 'for then the government is no monarchy. We are only a part of the legislature.'[44] Having taken on executive functions in the 1640s, Parliament laid them down at the Restoration and reverted to its traditional role of passing bills. However, while accepting the 'revisionist' emphasis on legislation, it should be stressed that Parliament was never a purely legislative body. It relayed to the monarch the grievances of the subject, who could petition Parliament as well as the king. It claimed the right to advise the monarch on matters of public interest, which were often not fit subjects for legislation: foreign policy or royal marriages, for example. In presenting grievances or advice, there was scope for conflict which ran counter to the rhetoric of consensus. Usually such conflict was contained within limits by good sense on the king's side and good manners on Parliament's. Decorum decreed that the king should not be criticized directly. When Sir Thomas Littleton talked in 1668 of 'compelling the king' there was uproar in the House, which was allayed only when he claimed that he had really said 'compelling the thing'.[45] However, MPs felt few qualms about criticizing the king's ministers and servants or, if sufficiently aroused, calling them to account. The rhetoric of mutuality required responsibility and flexibility on both sides. The Commons expected Charles II to govern, but to govern responsibly – and responsibility lay in the eye of the beholder. The relationship between Charles I and Parliament broke down in 1641–42 because many members believed that he could not be trusted to abide by any concession that he had made and feared (correctly) that he wished to re-establish his power by armed force. Charles II's regime often appeared sordid, corrupt and inept, but it rarely seemed as threatening as his father's. As a result, although his relationship with Parliament was often strained, it rarely appeared in danger of breaking down altogether; there was never a real danger that he would make war on his opponents.

Charles II's struggles with Parliament were fought out in the political arena, rather than on the battlefield. His greatest asset was his control of the machinery of government, which his father had lost when he left London in 1642. His position was strengthened by memories of civil war: a king who misused his powers a little was a lesser evil than the 'world turned upside-down'. Parliament's greatest asset was the Commons' power to grant or refuse money: unlike his father, Charles II never tried to raise money from his subjects without Parliament's consent: ''Twas the old and good way of parliaments for the crown to give relief and pardon and to receive subsidies and it is our happiness that the king delights in those paths.'[46] The Commons were well aware of the leverage this gave them and were careful not to be too generous: ''tis good to leave something to give hereafter and not to endanger the people's goodwill by taking their benevolence' remarked Marvell.[47] Even when the Commons did not link redress of grievances to supply, they made it clear that they could have done so.[48] After voting him a series of revenues for life, the Commons preferred temporary to perpetual grants, as the king remarked.[49] However, he wished to avoid the impression that he called Parliaments only to ask for money – he did not do so in February 1664[50] – while the Commons often delayed the money bill in committee while they passed other measures, without making the link explicit.[51] As distrust grew, opposition MPs demanded redress without mentioning supply, arguing that the king had to regain the Commons' trust and goodwill before they could even consider giving money; the king's spokesmen argued that redress implied supply.[52] By the mid 1670s, however, the king's revenue, woefully inadequate in the 1660s, had increased markedly and he was able to get by (just about) without additional grants from Parliament. After the last such grant, early in 1679, to pay off the army raised in 1678, Charles survived on his own resources for the remainder of the reign.

We shall consider the changing relationship of king and Parliament in detail in Part II. I shall suggest that distrust of the king survived the errors and misgovernment of the 1660s but became acute as a result of repeated evidence of bad faith in 1672–73, which provoked fears of 'popery and arbitrary government'. It is hard to detect clear evidence of 'party' divisions before the mid 1670s, not least because the king lacked consistent policies and refused to play the part of a party leader. His ministers' attempts at parliamentary management were initially informal and amateur and the Commons strongly resisted attempts by 'undertakers' to direct their proceedings.[53] Only after 1673 did a minister try systematically to discipline and direct supporters of the 'court'. Danby's methods added to fears of 'arbitrary government' and extended the process of polarization, but there were still those who resisted the descent into partisanship and, like Reresby, Sir Edward Dering or Thomas Thynne, tried to reconcile their loyalties to 'court' and 'country'.[54] Between 1679 and 1681 the difficulty of trusting the king (or his brother) seemed to be leading to a political breakdown like that of 1641–42. Many of the same arguments were used, but no civil war ensued, partly because the political breakdown was less complete than it seemed and the forces of obedience or inertia were much stronger. Civil war was not a natural or inevitable condition in seventeenth-century England.

Notes

1 Hants RO, W/B1/5, fo. 164.
2 *LJ*, XI.248.

3 Dorset RO, D60/F56, John to Henry Trenchard, 2 October 1680. See also Isham, p. 145.
4 Dering, *Diary*, pp. 22, 40–1, 79–80; Dering, *Papers*, p. 90; Marvell, II.158.
5 BL, Add MS 28053, fo. 24; *CSPD 1665–66*, p. 163, *1671*, p. 402, *1671–72*, p. 53.
6 Pepys, VII.399; *Lauderdale*, III.142.
7 *HMC Ormond*, NS V.102.
8 Marvell, II.240.
9 *Norths*, III.186; Milward, pp. 11, 70; Pepys, VII.416. The Lords were apparently as bad: *LJ*, XII.413.
10 Bulstrode, I.315; *HMC Portland*, VIII.15.
11 *CSPD 1664–65*, pp. 257, 179.
12 M636/27, correspondence between Edmund Verney and Sir Ralph between 29 June and 23 July 1674.
13 BL, Add MS 28053, fo. 26; Browning, *Danby*, II.42–3.
14 Coventry RO, A79/244.
15 *HMC 8th Report, Appendix 1*, pp. 388–90.
16 *CSPD 1675–76*, pp. 158–9.
17 *CSPD 1673–75*, pp. 541, 548, 559–60.
18 Marvell, II.27.
19 Marvell, II.108–9 (quoted), 124.
20 Marvell, II.16, 18–19.
21 *HMC Townshend*, pp. 28–9.
22 *HMC Finch*, II.23; *CSPD 1663–64*, p. 427.
23 *HMC 7th Report*, p. 468; Marvell, II.183–4; Finch MS PP 42, p. 23; Grey, IV.177–9, 237–40; *HP*, III.429; T.C. Glines, 'Politics and Government in the Borough of Colchester, 1660–93', (unpublished Ph.D. thesis, Wisconsin, 1974), pp. 146–8, 164–5. See *HP*, II.685–6, for another MP suing for wages.
24 *LJ*, XI.238; Marvell, II.1–2.
25 M. Kishlansky, 'Tyranny denied: Charles I, Attorney General Heath and the Five Knights' Case', *HJ*, LXII, 1999, pp. 53–83 attempts to revitalize this view, but the argument rests very much on Charles I's perception of his critics.
26 See especially C. Russell, *Parliaments and English Politics, 1621–29*, Oxford, 1979, ch. 1.
27 R. L'Estrange (?), *A Plea for a Limited Monarchy*, 1660, p. 6.
28 See C. Robbins, 'Sir John Holland in the Convention of 1660', *BIHR*, XXIX, 1956, p. 248.
29 G.R. Elton, 'Tudor Government, the Points of Contact: I: Parliament', *TRHS*, 5th series, XXIV, 1974, pp. 183–200.
30 Pepys, VIII.512.
31 This claim is amply confirmed by the dispatches of the French ambassadors, especially Barrillon.
32 *CJ*, IX.500–1; Grey, VI.104–5. For earlier complaints, see *CJ*, IX.365.
33 *Norths*, III.181; HMC *Ormond*, NS III.58; Marvell, II.192; Carte MS 217, fo. 336.
34 Bowman, fos 110, 119–20; Robbins, 'Holland in the Convention', pp. 246–50.
35 Clarendon, II.152–5.
36 *HMC Rutland*, II.8; Lawrence, p. 11; *HMC Finch*, I.512.
37 Gauci, *Yarmouth*, pp. 113–16.
38 Marvell, II.8–9, 24–7, 29–32; *CJ*, VIII.304, 307, 336; Hull RO, BRB4, pp. 336–7, BRL 652–3, 655–6.

39 Marvell, II.258–9, 266–9.
40 *SR*, V.523, 848.
41 *CJ*, IX.440, 592, 687; *HMC 9th Report, Appendix II*, p. 98; *LJ*, XIII.715, 722.
42 See for example *CJ*, IX.374, 390, 439, 463, 607, 646–7.
43 See P. Slack, *Poverty and Policy in Tudor and Stuart England*, London, 1988, pp. 173–95.
44 Grey, IV.169.
45 Milward, pp. 189–90. In 1681 Henry Booth came close to criticizing the king directly: Grey, VIII.260–1; *HMC Beaufort*, p. 109.
46 Carte MS 73, fo. 543.
47 Marvell, II.13.
48 *CJ*, VIII.104, 107; *LJ*, XI.109–10; Newton, *House of Lyme*, p. 213.
49 Marvell, II.4; *CJ*, VIII.500–1.
50 Clarendon, II.285, 288; Carte MS 47, fo. 84.
51 Tanner MS 43, fo. 184. This makes the threat to refuse supply if the uniformity bill did not pass all the more noteworthy: *Rawdon*, p. 137; DUL, Cosin Letter Book 2, no. 70.
52 Miller, 'Parliaments', pp. 15–16.
53 Clarendon, I.361–2, II.195–7, 204–11; Carte MS 32, fos 597–8; Mapperton, Appendix to the Earl of Sandwich's Papers, fo. 153.
54 Reresby, pp. 110–11; Dering, *Papers*, pp. 74, 83–4; Althorp MS C5, Thynne to Halifax, 12 July 1679.

Part two

POLITICAL DIVISION AND CONFLICT

Chapter seven

The issues:
I. Popery and arbitrary government

The ancient constitution

In considering the working of politics and government, I have stressed the elements of participation and negotiation. In a society where individuals differed greatly in wealth and power, some participated and negotiated more effectively than others, so those with limited influence sought the support of the more powerful. The habit of resolving disputes and achieving goals through political or legal channels helped create an internalized and ingrained respect for law, which explains the relatively low level of disorder, despite the state's limited means of coercion. We have seen the pervasive concern for consensus and conciliation – in the processes of parliamentary legislation, in decisions about criminal prosecutions, in the rhetoric about the relationship between king and Parliament, king and people. But could this survive the fratricidal divisions of civil war? Would the political and religious issues of the 1640s divide the nation to a point where a return to the old ways was impossible? Kishlansky is one of many who have argued that this was indeed the case. In the second part of this book, we shall consider the process and extent of political division under Charles II. First, however, it is necessary to look at the ideological legacy of the civil wars, in terms first of politics and then of religion.

Much discussion about the English constitution took place within a historical framework. It was widely claimed that the monarchy, Parliament and the common law had evolved over many centuries, their origins lost in the mists of time, before written records. Each supported and fed off the others, to create an 'ancient' constitution in which the powers of the crown and the rights of the people complemented and reinforced one another.[1] The king defended his realm from attack and, through his law courts, maintained order, protected property and resolved disputes. His prerogatives – for example his power to command the armed forces – were necessary for the safety of the people and the proper conduct of government. The people assisted in governing the realm and, through their representatives in Parliament, created the framework of laws within which government operated and provided the money to pay for it. Throughout, the emphasis was on mutuality, participation, cooperation, consensus – which in many ways mirrored the workings of Elizabethan or Jacobean government. The most familiar images of kingly power repeated these emphases. When the king was compared to the head of the body politic or the father of a family, it implied that he possessed innate authority superior to any of his subjects. It also implied that he was morally obliged to rule in his subjects' best interests: for the head to damage any part of the body or for the father to harm his child was an affront to the law of nature and of God.

While stressing the benefits of cooperation, it was often necessary to resolve clashes of principle or interest by recourse to the law. Common law placed great reliance on precedent, but sometimes precedents offered little guidance. The concept of the ancient constitution allowed for ordered constitutional evolution. As John Pym put it in 1628: 'those commonwealths have been most durable and perpetual which have often reformed and recomposed themselves according to their first institution and ordinance; for by this means they repair the breaches and counterwork the ordinary and natural effects of time.'[2] This implied that, over and above specific precedents, there were within the ancient constitution certain 'fundamental' laws 'issuing from the first frame and constitution of the kingdom'.[3] The concept of 'the fundamental laws' played a key part in the trial of Strafford in 1641. Existing laws defined treason in terms of an overt act against the king. Strafford was accused of leading the king into illegality and injustice and so threatening to dissolve the union of 'protection and allegiance' between king and people. In other words, Strafford was accused of treason 'against the being of the law'.[4] In developing this argument, the majority in the Commons were moving away from the certainties of statute and precedent into the broader principles of mutuality which were assumed to underlie them. It was an intellectual shift which did not go unchallenged. Edmund Waller MP asked what the fundamental laws were; he was told that if he did not know, he should not be sitting in the House.[5] And yet the concept was already present in Pym's speech in 1628. Alan Cromartie has argued that the early seventeenth century saw a 'constitutionalist revolution', driven mainly by common lawyers, in which the law was seen as deriving its authority from the common weal, the public good.[6] The development of a concept of the public good largely separate from the person of the monarch owed much to a sense that it was not secure under kings who seemed bent on undermining their subjects' legal rights, especially through non-parliamentary taxation. The decades before 1640 saw an increasing articulation and refinement of the principles seen as implicit in the ancient constitution. The king's coronation oath (in which he promised to uphold the laws) and the subject's oath of allegiance could be seen as a tacit contract, a concept familiar to landowners and businessmen. James I referred to the laws as constituting a 'paction' between king and people and declared (in a passage later quoted by Locke) that a king who failed to rule according to his laws 'degenerates into a tyrant'.[7] The idea that the laws were the guardians of the **public** good could be seen as a response to James's references to **his** laws, 'which are properly made by the king only, but at the rogation of the people'.[8]

Cromartie's argument may offer an answer to a question which has long exercised historians of the 1640s: why was Parliament so slow to invoke a right of resistance? Surely Parliament's constitutional position cast it naturally in the role of the 'inferior magistrate' who (according to Calvinist political theorists) was entitled to resist a tyrant, although for ordinary people to resist would lead to anarchy. However, many Parliamentarians claimed to take up arms by the king's authority against his person, arguing that he was so misled by evil counsellors as to be 'deranged'; they were surprisingly reticent about referring to him as a tyrant.[9] They were rather more ready to invoke the law of nature, in particular the right of self-preservation, while frequent references to the maxim *salus populi suprema lex est* (the safety of the people is the supreme law) could be seen as a more limited statement of the concept of the public good.[10] Cromartie suggests that Parliament did not need to make use of French resistance theory: there was a developing English view of the public good of which Parliament was the natural custodian. As the Calvinists had realised, to invoke a right of resistance by virtue of Parliament's representing the people opened the way for the people to demand to dictate to Parliament. Later in the decade the Levellers argued that no form of government was ordained by God or prescription and none was sacrosanct. Government was an artificial construct, created for the people's good; it should be obeyed only as long as the people judged that it was serving its purpose, fulfilling its trust. The people should set out what they expected of their rulers in an 'original contract', an agreement of the people. Experience showed that Parliaments, like kings, were corrupted by power: both needed to be curbed. The Levellers therefore argued that there should be certain 'laws paramount' – fundamental laws which no Parliament could alter.

Historians have debated whether the Levellers were as 'democratic' as they seemed, but the very 'modernity' which now makes their ideas so accessible marginalized them in their own time: 'levelling' was a synonym for anarchy. It is worth remembering that the Putney debates of 1647 were private discussions within the army and the Levellers were rarely referred to in the second half of the century.[11] Similarly, while there was a lively strand of republican political writing in the 1650s, it could not be said to have won widespread popular acceptance.[12] On the other hand, Hobbes's attempt to construct a theoretical model of government from the basic principle of submission in return for protection was so 'atheistical' and bleak, leaving subjects with virtually no 'rights' against their ruler, that it won few supporters. The ferment of new ideas in the 1640s and 1650s is of great interest to historians of political thought, but it does not follow that these ideas changed the way most Englishmen thought about politics and the constitution. During the first civil war many, probably the great majority, on both sides, subscribed to competing visions of the 'ancient constitution'. After 1646, and still more after Pride's Purge, the political running was made by people with very different views, who had little time for the ancient constitution and claimed that it perpetuated tyranny and injustice.[13] The more dominant the army and its radical allies became, the more the moderates on both sides, members of the old political establishment, yearned to restore the traditional constitution. For it should be stressed that Cromartie's 'constitutionalist revolution' sought to clarify relationships **within** that constitution, to strengthen Parliament and the common law and so preserve the balance threatened by the early Stuarts. Although the emphasis changed, the basic principle of mutuality remained. Experience since 1642 confirmed the warning in the king's Answer to the Nineteen Propositions that any attempt to alter the balance of 'this splendid and excellently distinguished form of government' by appealing to the people would 'end in a dark equal chaos of confusion'.[14] The 'constitutionalist revolution' tipped the balance within the ancient constitution towards Parliament. Subsequent experience created a perceived need to tip it back towards the king, as members of the old elites came to see revolution from below as a greater threat than the possible misuse of royal power.

From the foregoing it should be apparent that when Hyde or the Speaker of the Commons used the rhetoric of harmony and cooperation in 1660,[15] they were not being hopelessly anachronistic. A Welsh writer had commented in 1644 'the deep stains these wars will leave behind, I fear all the water of the Severn, Trent or Thames cannot wash away.'[16] Since then, common resentment of political and religious change had driven old foes together. Not all was forgiven or forgotten, but there was more cooperation, a 'regrouping of elites' in the 1650s.[17] They agreed on the need to restore effective government, to repress Quakers, Baptists and other radicals. They accepted that the restoration of monarchy was an essential precondition for the restoration of gentry rule and the 'ancient constitution'. Within that constitution there seemed every reason to give Charles II the benefit of the doubt. The Parliamentarians' quarrel had always been with Charles I (misled by evil counsellors) rather than with the monarchy; many Royalists had shared their resentment of evil counsel. Laud and Strafford were long dead and it could be assumed that Charles II, chastened by exile, would rule more wisely than his father. Moreover, perceptions of Charles I had changed radically by 1660. In 1646–48 his defeat and imprisonment created sympathy; his restoration on almost any terms seemed to many a lesser evil than 'parliamentary tyranny'. Parliament rejected his requests to come to London because it feared demonstrations in his favour.[18] The transformation in his image to that of martyr for monarchy and church was completed by his dignity at his trial and execution and by his alleged prison writings, *Eikon Basilike*. This work went through many editions, its tone set by the frontispiece in which Charles, on his knees, exchanged a crown of thorns for a heavenly crown (see jacket).

Charles I's execution placed Parliamentarians and Whigs at a grave debating disadvantage after 1660. While Royalists often referred to the blood of the royal martyr, Parliamentarians were reduced to claiming (often correctly) that they had abhorred his execution; Royalists riposted that their using force against him had paved the way for his 'murder'. Similarly, Parliamentarians who had been wary of invoking a right of resistance in the 1640s became doubly so after 1660. In the Exclusion Crisis, the Whigs in Parliament largely avoided speculating on the origins of government, preferring to urge the king to heed the fates of Edward II, Richard II or Richard III and rule as his people (as represented in Parliament) advised.[19] By contrast, Royalists often invoked the divine right of kings, claiming that both the powers of the crown and the hereditary succession were determined by God. Kings were not as other men, having about them an element of the divine, emphasized by the anointing in the coronation and by the mystical healing powers displayed when the king's touch cured people of 'the king's evil' (scrofula). Active resistance to the Lord's anointed was a crime against God. While accepting that kings could err, Royalists stressed that they would be restrained by their conscience and by the need to answer to God for their conduct. Moreover, the occasional misuse of royal power was a far lesser evil than the confusion unleashed by active resistance. If the king commanded something against the law of God, his subjects, like the early Christians, should refuse to obey and meekly submit to punishment.

It should be stressed that emphasis on divine right was quite compatible with belief in the ancient constitution, itself a part of God's creation. Most Royalists and Tories believed firmly in the common law and expected the king to respect it.[20] They differed from Parliamentarians and Whigs in seeing the main threat to the constitution and the law as coming from revolution from below, rather than from the crown. The 'constitutionalist revolution' was born of the perception that, within the ancient constitution, the crown was becoming too strong; the Royalists and Tories believed that it had become too weak. With hindsight we know that the ancient constitution came under severe strain in the Exclusion Crisis and collapsed under James II, but that knowledge was not available to those involved in politics in the 1660s and early 1670s. Those who made the Restoration had every reason to restore the ancient constitution, not just because it was ancient, but because it offered a tried and tested means of providing effective, ordered government while securing the liberties of the people. It could be argued that in 1642 the ancient constitution had shown itself incapable of reconciling the king's powers and the subjects' rights when mutual trust had broken down. However, that breakdown could be seen as the product of exceptional circumstances: the very fact that it had happened made it less likely to happen again. Faced with the deliverance of the Restoration it would have seemed unduly pessimistic, indeed improper, to suggest that the revived cooperation of king and Parliament, king and people, would not last. In the absence of any expectation of a breakdown, why take steps to prevent it, steps which would be bound to evoke unpleasant memories, but also might, by manifesting distrust, bring about the very condition that they were designed to prevent? It was surely better to restore the old order and to trust to the good sense of men and the goodness of God, who had brought back the Stuarts and would surely now watch over His chosen people.

Anti-popery

Historians in the Whig tradition faced difficulties in addressing anti-popery. On one hand, Roman Catholic emancipation (1829) could be seen as a triumph of British liberal democracy. On the other, the Whig interpretation of earlier centuries rested on the premise that Catholicism was morally, intellectually and politically inferior to Protestantism, which was as inseparable from political and religious freedom as Catholicism was inseparable from tyranny and subjection. Nevertheless, Macaulay claimed that Catholic emancipation, along with many other 'good laws', had its roots in the Revolution of 1688–89.[21] However, the Revolution was designed to exclude Catholics from the English throne and restore the Protestant ascendancy in Ireland; it led to new penal laws against Catholics on both sides of the Irish Sea. During the eighteenth century, the Catholics and the French constituted a large part of the 'other', the rejection of which helped create a 'British' identity.[22] This was nothing new: in Elizabethan England the identity had been English, not British, and was defined in terms of enmity to Spain, which then seemed the main aspirant to 'universal monarchy'. The Reformation brought a change from a Catholic calendar to one which celebrated England's distinctive Protestantism. Foxe's 'book of martyrs' proclaimed the unique destiny of England and of Elizabeth in fulfilling God's plans for humankind, culminating in the overthrow of the papal Antichrist.[23]

While Victorian liberals celebrated the defeat of the Spanish Armada and condemned the Marian persecution, they found it hard to appreciate the millenarianism which provided the chronological framework (or frameworks[24]) of Foxe's book. Men who saw history in terms of political and intellectual progress found difficulty in coming to terms with a mindset predicated on the imminent end of the world or with the bigoted hatred shown towards Catholics and Catholicism. At best they could be quietly passed over, as unfortunate features of a more primitive age. And yet anti-popery was such an essential feature of seventeenth-century English politics that it requires serious analysis. Aspects of past ages which now seem irrational or embarrassing (like the persecution of witches) still happened and one cannot understand those times without trying to explain them.

For Protestant writers, Catholicism was too absurd to be taken seriously as a religion. 'Were it either open Judaism, or plain Turkery or honest paganism' wrote Marvell 'there is yet a certain *bona fides* in the most extravagant belief and the sincerity of an erroneous profession may render it pardonable; but this is a compound of all that is most ridiculous and impious in them, incorporated with more particular absurdities of its own'.[25] The source of these absurdities lay in the lust for power of popes and priests. Whereas Protestantism encouraged the laity to read and think about the Bible, Catholicism depended on ignorance: priests denied the people access to the Bible in their own language and 'amused' them with superstitions and rituals 'so unbeseeming in a Christian office that it represents rather the pranks and ceremonies of jugglers and conjurers'. The people were encouraged to worship images, relics, saints and the Virgin Mary – anything but the Father or the Son. By instilling belief in transubstantiation, the priests made the people believe that Christ's body, though in heaven, 'is sold again and crucified daily'. 'Thus by a new and antiscriptural belief, compiled of terrors to the fancy, contradictions to sense and impositions on the understanding, their laity have turned tenants for their souls and in consequence tributary for their estates to a more than omnipotent priesthood.'[26] English travellers to France commented frequently on the credulity and subservience of the peasantry and mocked their veneration of relics and belief in miracles.[27]

At the apex of this edifice of tyranny and corruption was the Pope, who in past centuries had tried to impose on kings a yoke similar to that which the priests imposed on laypeople. Rulers who failed to bow the knee were excommunicated and declared deposed. This had happened even before the Reformation, but with the coming of Protestantism popes and priests – above all the Jesuits – had set out to destroy those who exposed the falsehoods and corruptions at the heart of popery. Catholic monarchs were subjected to constant pressure to root out Protestantism with 'fire and faggot': Foxe depicted Mary Tudor not as wilfully 'bloody', but as driven by bigoted bishops to persecute Protestants. When Catholic kings, such as Henry III and IV of France, failed to proceed as savagely as the Pope or Jesuits demanded, they were murdered. Calvinist resistance theory was mirrored by Catholic writings on tyrannicide, which justified not only resistance but assassination – until the papacy backtracked in the face of the outcry at Henry IV's murder in 1610. The Pope had excommunicated Elizabeth in 1570 and had absolved her people from their allegiance; although he added that he did not wish his sentence to be carried out at once, this offered scant reassurance to her Protestant subjects. Until her execution in 1587, Mary Stuart had the strongest claim to succeed Elizabeth and the prospect of a second Catholic Queen Mary, and the renewed burning of heretics, sparked what Patrick Collinson has called the 'first exclusion crisis'. In 1584 many Protestants subscribed an Association, to defend the queen's person against possible assassins and to wreak revenge upon anyone who profited from her death. In 1585 an Act of Parliament legalized this Association, as well as providing for a tribunal, in the event of the queen's violent death, to prosecute those responsible.[28]

Under Elizabeth and James I it was believed that 'papists', when in power, persecuted with implacable cruelty: Foxe and his lesser imitators etched on the Protestant memory a picture of godly Protestants 'flaming in Smithfield'. In Protestant states, papists had no choice but to plot to overthrow their rulers, as evidenced by the plots against Elizabeth and the Gunpowder Plot. Because Protestantism differed from popery as day from night, or good from evil, there was no prospect that the two could coexist peacefully within the same state. Early in Elizabeth's reign, there was some prospect that Catholicism might wither away, but that disappeared with the excommunication and the coming of a new generation of priests, trained in English seminaries on the continent. At first the government sought only to persuade Catholics to attend church, by fining them for 'recusancy' (staying away); now they were subjected to a battery of laws which extended to every aspect of a Catholic life, including the possession of Catholic books or rosary beads. Punishments became much more severe – recusancy fines were increased from a shilling a week to £20 a month – and many offences (for example, harbouring a priest) carried the death penalty. It became treason for a priest to enter England or to convert someone to Catholicism.[29] Some 300 priests were executed under Elizabeth, mostly for refusing to deny the Pope's deposing power (which became a central feature of a new oath of allegiance in 1606). The government denied that they were executed for their religion, neglecting to mention that they would not have been asked about the Pope's deposing power if they had not been Catholic priests.

The intention of the legislation against Catholics was ostensibly to eradicate English Catholicism. It did not do so, but it succeeded in containing it, so that it survived mainly in some of the more remote upland areas, little enclaves around the homes of Catholic landowners and the western suburbs of London – in their own way as much a 'dark corner of the land' as the Yorkshire dales. Catholicism survived partly because of the ineffectiveness of the means of law enforcement, especially in remote areas, but also because the government did not try to extirpate it. It always proceeded more gently against the laity than against the clergy, realising (especially after the Armada crisis) that the great majority were loyal to the crown. It needed to avoid alienating friendly Catholic powers, notably France, but it also hoped to reach an understanding with the more moderate Catholic clergy. Under the early Stuarts – except during the ascendancy of Laud – the penal laws were enforced less vigorously than under Elizabeth. Catholics remained numerous among the peers and gentry – they comprised at least a tenth of the peerage in 1640 – but their numbers tended to fall and by the reign of Charles II Catholics probably made up little more than one per cent of the population.[30] Most Catholic landowners lived quietly on their estates, on good terms with their Protestant neighbours. While it was still possible, during the Thirty Years War (1618–48) or Louis XIV's bursts of aggression, between 1667 and 1684, to see Catholicism as a malign, aggressive international force, it was difficult to see the English Catholics, few and scattered, as posing much of a threat. To explain why 'popery' still seemed dangerous, we need to broaden the discussion and explain why 'popery' came to mean something wider than Catholicism.

Popery and arbitrary government

In an important essay, Peter Lake saw the Protestant view of popery as based on a series of polar opposites, through which the evils of popery highlighted the virtues of Protestantism. We have already noted the contrast between Protestant reliance on Scripture and the Catholic clergy's attempts to give invented superstitions the force of dogma and between Protestantism's supposed emphasis on free enquiry and Catholicism's reliance on authority and ignorance. In addition, whereas Protestantism encouraged self-discipline, urging lay-people to internalize and apply the moral precepts of the Bible, the Catholic church, through its cycle of confession, penance and absolution, effectively licensed sin. The story that the papacy derived revenue from Roman brothels was often repeated, as was the claim that celibacy was unnatural and that priests, monks and nuns found the vow of chastity impossible to sustain.[31]

The supple moral theology espoused by some of the Jesuits, with its tolerance of equivocation and 'permissible opinions', gave support to claims that Catholics were allowed to lie and break all the laws of God or man for the good of the church, in stark contrast to the moral rigour shown by Protestants.

The development of such antitheses was necessarily divisive, but it might simply differentiate the godly Protestant English from ungodly Catholic peoples on the continent (or in Ireland). More serious problems arose when notional Protestants exhibited 'popish' features. One example was a revived emphasis, among some of the clergy, on clerical authority over the laity and ceremonies, making holy communion, rather than the sermon, the centrepiece of the Sunday service. These developments were apparent from at least the 1590s, but became more prominent in the 1620s, when they were strongly supported by Charles I; their promoters came to be labelled 'Arminians'. Godly Protestants had complained under Elizabeth that the Prayer Book contained too many 'rags of Rome'; now more 'popish' elements were being added. To make matters worse, these changes in the church were seen as connected to changes in the state: the growing use of non-parliamentary taxation and the growing perception that laws, liberties and parliaments were under threat.[32] As Protestantism was identified in the English mind with the ancient constitution, so the perceived threat of absolute monarchy was linked to popery. There were structural similarities – the reliance on force, repression and on keeping the people ignorant. The most conspicuous continental monarchies, Spain and France, were seen by the English as absolute (and tyrannous). The identification was reinforced by Charles I's marriage to a demonstratively Catholic French princess, the relaxation of the persecution of Catholics and the strongly monarchist views expressed by some Arminians. Meanwhile, neither James nor Charles I offered any real leadership to the 'Protestant' cause in the Thirty Years War.

It might seem contradictory that popery should be associated both with absolute monarchy and with conspiracies against monarchs – even those of France. The contradiction can be resolved by remembering that 'popery' was a protean term, defined by association with certain moral characteristics, which changed over time. In 1605 popish plotters had allegedly tried to blow up the king **with** his Parliament. By 1640 popish plotters were seen as trying to turn the king against Parliament. Caroline Hibberd showed how pervasive was the belief in a 'popish plot' and how strong was its basis in fact.[33] The fact that so much of the case against Charles I's misgovernment was couched in terms of anti-popery was in itself deeply divisive. The polar opposites intrinsic to the mentality of anti-popery were utterly incompatible with the ideals of consensus and compromise inherent in the ancient constitution and the instincts of early seventeenth-century MPs.[34] In the winter of 1641–42, many recoiled at Pym's insistence on presenting the Commons with a stark choice between alternatives, one of which he labelled 'popish'. Faced with the prospect of being stigmatized as 'favourers of popery', many withdrew, strengthening the hand of the militants. Much of Parliament's appeal for popular support, in the Protestation and the Grand Remonstrance, was couched in terms of the threat from popery. Anti-popery played a substantial part in the crowd violence of 1640–42,[35] while the king's association with Catholics, especially Irish Catholics, figured prominently in Parliamentarian propaganda. This led Parliament in 1661 to make it an offence to call the king a Papist. As Halifax later remarked, Charles I was seen as 'leaning towards popery, without which handle it was morally impossible that the ill-affected part of the nation could ever have seduced the rest into a rebellion'.[36]

This is not to suggest that 'popery' was now identified exclusively with royal absolutism (in which would be subsumed an 'Arminian' regime in the Church). Lake identified a rival conspiracy theory dating from the 1620s, based on a Presbyterian rather than a popish plot to overthrow monarchy and episcopacy.[37] Initially confined to a relatively narrow circle consisting mainly of Arminians and Catholics, the idea of a 'presbyterian plot' gained added credence from the events of 1641 and after: the intervention of the Scots in English affairs, the attempt to abolish bishops and the perceived threat to the social and political order from radical rabble-rousing. Many Royalists came to see anti-popery as a smokescreen behind which the 'scheming presbyters' and their Scottish allies had advanced to seize power. Cavaliers remained suspicious of 'popery', but realized that 'presbytery' could be equally subversive. Writing in 1680, with the nation again concerned with popish plots, L'Estrange reminded his readers of 1641, warning of 'a plot upon a perpetual plot', to 'keep the nation so long in awe of the Popish Plot till the faction may execute another plot of their own'.[38] A broadside of 1681 had the Presbyterians declare: 'And we must root up monarchy/To stop the growth of Popery/And undermining church and state/Rome's practices we'll antedate; /The better to prevent the Plot/Ourselves will do what they could not.'[39]

The 'presbyterian plot' can be seen as an alternative to the 'popish plot', but there was also a tendency to conflate the two. This owed something to the Presbyterian response to the emergence of the New Model, Pride's Purge and the regicide: William Prynne, who had a history of anti-popish paranoia, became convinced that the army had been infiltrated by the Jesuits, who now put their maxims of king-killing into grisly practice. Prynne also claimed that the Jesuits were responsible for the rise of the Quakers, a claim which Royalist writers extended to all the sects. It was typical of the scheming Papists, they argued, that they should work underhand to create divisions within Protestantism and so hasten its overthrow.[40] This remained a minor theme in Anglican polemic after the Restoration and was used in arguments against toleration: rather than accelerating the fragmentation of Protestantism, the best way to oppose popery was to force froward nonconformists to return to the Church.[41] Titus Oates's depositions, which triggered the Popish Plot of 1678, included claims that the Jesuits had been responsible for Charles I's death and had tried to make Cromwell king; more recently, disguised as presbyterians, they had tried to provoke a rebellion in Scotland.[42]

If Anglican-Royalists made some polemical use of anti-popery under Charles II, they did so much less than Whigs and nonconformists, partly because they had a plausible alternative in the idea of a 'presbyterian' (or 'fanatic') plot, partly because the political circumstances of the 1670s made anti-popery a natural weapon for those opposed to the court. On one hand, the court was identified with Catholicism. Charles's mother and queen were Catholics, as were two leading mistresses, Castlemaine and Portsmouth. Several Catholics were prominent or active at court, such as the queen's almoner (Henry Howard's brother, Philip), Father Patrick McGinn and Richard Talbot, self-styled spokesman for the dispossessed Catholics of Ireland. The king allowed frequent and informal access to successive French ambassadors who, with the exception of the two Marquis de Ruvigny, father and son, were Catholics. In 1673 it became apparent that both the lord treasurer, Clifford, and the king's brother, James, Duke of York, had converted to Catholicism. Clifford died soon after, but York was heir presumptive to the throne so long as the king had no legitimate children. Some hoped that Charles might divorce his childless queen, others that he might legitimate his oldest illegitimate son, the Duke of Monmouth, but although he toyed with both expedients, he decided against them. Thus from 1673 until the end of the reign, the English faced the prospect of their first Catholic monarch since Mary. York's remarriage, to a Catholic, in 1673, created the prospect of an ongoing Catholic dynasty.

With the fear of popery went fear of absolutism. In 1672 Charles, in alliance with Louis XIV, made war against the Dutch. Louis was seen as the most 'absolute' king ever to have ruled France. Having crushed resistance within his kingdom, he now set out to assert himself internationally and establish a 'universal monarchy'. The English found it hard to understand why Charles should have joined with such a dangerous ally: one possibility, perhaps, was that he hoped that Louis would help him to impose popery and absolutism at home. One of Louis's demands was that the Dutch allow freedom of worship for Catholics. After declaring war Charles issued a declaration, in which he claimed a right to suspend the laws against religious nonconformity and allowed Catholics to worship in their own homes. In the declaration he claimed an 'arbitrary' power to override laws – for the benefit of the Papists. He also raised a substantial army, which contained a sprinkling of Catholic officers.

Given the court's association with popery and the perceived threat of absolutism, it is not surprising that the language of anti-popery was used mainly by its opponents, although little found its way into print.[43] The end of the war and Danby's attempt to reconstitute the old 'Cavalier' interest temporarily shifted public attention away from popery. Shaftesbury accused Danby of pandering to the bigotry of the bishops, who, he claimed, were far more hostile to Dissent than to Popery.[44] However, Shaftesbury was eager to enlist the Catholic peers as allies against Danby and made some not uncomplimentary remarks about them.[45] He was answered by the veteran journalist, Marchamont Nedham, who berated the nonconformists and accused Shaftesbury of 'a conspiracy of such a magnitude that none ever exceeded it but the Powder treason', a conspiracy he identified not with popery but with 'presbytery'.[46] Marvell, in *An Account of the Growth of Popery*, attacked Danby's regime as a conspiracy, by men who were neither Papists nor Cavaliers, to bring in 'arbitrary government' by undermining the independence of the institutions best able to guard against the misuse of royal power – the judiciary and Parliament.[47]

The raising of a massive army for a possible war against France in 1678 revived the rhetoric of anti-popery: many feared that it might be used to establish absolutism at home. Already in April some MPs suggested that there was a 'Protestant' and a 'popish' point of view on a particular question. Lord Chancellor Nottingham riposted that such language had served as a 'handle for sedition' in 1641.[48] With the outbreak of the Popish Plot (and the army not yet disbanded) anti-popery became more forceful and strident. One MP referred to 'the aspersion of this being a state plot'. Essex's brother blamed the civil war on 'the hand of popery' and went on: 'Since the king's restoration, popery has played in court in our negotiations of war and peace, of setting up ministers and taking them down.'[49] Despite the calls for firm measures against Catholics, some MPs made it clear that their real concern was the threat from absolutism, either now or under a 'popish successor'. 'Papists are enemies' declared Sir William Coventry 'not because they are erroneous in religion but because their principles are destructive to the government'.[50] 'Popery in a great measure is set up for arbitrary power's sake,' exclaimed another MP. 'They are not so forward for religion.'[51] The longer the crisis went on, the more the labels of 'papist' or 'favourer of popery' were applied to non-Catholics.[52]

Anti-popery in 1679–81 focused on York, partly because it was easier to attack the heir-presumptive rather than the king, partly because York was undoubtedly a Catholic – Charles was at most sympathetic towards Catholics – and was seen as more authoritarian and ruthless than his brother. In the campaign to exclude York from the succession, anti-popery played a central role. As king he could be expected to combine regal tyranny and savage persecution. Whatever he might promise now – and a papist's promises were worthless – if he became king he would behave like an amalgam of 'Queen Mary in breeches'[53] and Louis XIV (now stepping up the persecution of the Huguenots).[54] One pamphlet of 1679 asked its readers to imagine 'troops of Papists ravishing your wives and daughters . . . plundering your houses and cutting your own throats by the name of heretic dogs'. As the cannon from the Tower battered their houses, 'casting your eye towards Smithfield [imagine] you see your father or your mother . . . tied to a stake in the midst of flames'. If the papists were prepared to murder 'a prince so indulgent to them' they would 'hardly be less cruel towards his Protestant subjects'. Any attempt to impose legislative restrictions on a future Catholic king would be futile, 'for when he (as all other popish kings do) governs by an army, what will all your laws signify? You will not have Parliaments to appeal to; he and his council will levy his arbitrary taxes and his army shall gather them for him'.[55]

As we shall see in Chapter 12, many contemporaries saw the Exclusion Crisis as a re-run of 1641–42. The reversion to the ancient constitution at the Restoration could be seen as the product of instinct rather than inertia, of well-meaning optimism rather than moral cowardice. No-one could then have foreseen the extent to which the king would forfeit his subjects' trust, still less the conversion of his brother. Together these developments undermined the trust on which the Restoration Settlement has rested and again raised the unresolved question at the heart of the ancient constitution: if the king's rights and powers seemed incompatible with the safety of the subject, which was to take precedence? Who was to judge between the partners in a failed relationship? This was in many ways a more prosaic question than that of the location of sovereign power within the state and it was to be resolved more by power than by right, although the Tories undoubtedly believed that right as well as power was on the king's side. As in the 1620s, so in 1679–81, the Commons' leaders found that without effective financial leverage they lacked the power to impose their will on the king,[56] unless they were prepared to rebel – which they were not. That was to change only with the 'financial settlement' of 1689–90, which permanently transformed the balance of power between king and Commons.[57]

Notes

1 See especially, J.G.A. Pocock, *The Ancient Constitution and the Feudal Law*, Cambridge, 1987; G. Burgess, *The Politics of the Ancient Constitution*, London, 1992.
2 Kenyon, *Constitution*, 2nd edn., p. 15.
3 *Ibid.*
4 *Ibid.*, p. 192.
5 S.R. Gardiner, *History of England, 1603–42*, 10 vols, London, 1883–4, IX.336.
6 A. Cromartie, 'The Constitutionalist Revolution: The Transformation of Political Culture in early Stuart England', *P & P*, no. 163, 1999, pp. 76–120.
7 Kenyon, *Constitution*, 2nd edn., p. 12; J. Locke, *Second Treatise of Government*, para. 200.
8 Kenyon, *Constitution*, p. 12.
9 Morrill, *Nature*, ch. 15.
10 See for instance M.A. Judson, *The Crisis of the Constitution 1603–45*, New Brunswick, NJ, 1949; A. Sharp, *Political Ideas of the English Civil Wars*, London, 1986.
11 B. Worden, 'The Levellers in History and Memory', paper given at the Putney Conference in November 1997 and (in a revised version) to the Seventeenth-Century British History Seminar at the IHR May 1999.
12 J. Scott in J.S. Morrill (ed.), *Revolution and Restoration*, London, 1992, ch. 2.
13 See C. Hill, *Puritanism and Revolution*, London, 1958, ch. 3 (The Norman Yoke).
14 Kenyon, *Constitution*, 2nd edn., p. 20.
15 *OPH*, XXII.242; *CJ*, VIII.172–3; *LJ*, XI.238–9.
16 G.H. Jenkins, *The Foundations of Modern Wales 1642–1780*, Oxford, 1993, p. 30.
17 See D. Underdown, 'Settlement in the Counties, 1653–58' in G.E. Aylmer (ed.), *The Interregnum: the Quest for Settlement 1646–60*, London, 1972, ch. 7; G.E. Aylmer, 'Crisis and Regrouping in the Political Elites: England from the 1630s to the 1660s' in J.G.A. Pocock, *Three British Revolutions, 1641, 1688, 1776*, Princeton, 1980, pp. 147–60; A. Hughes, *Politics, Society and Civil War in Warwickshire, 1620–60*, Cambridge, 1987, pp. 300–2, 333–4, 336–7, 342–3.
18 See R. Ashton, 'From Cavalier to Roundhead Tyranny' in Morrill (ed.), *Reactions to the English Civil War*, ch. 8; I. Gentles, 'The Struggle for London in the Second Civil War', *HJ*, XXVI, 1983, pp. 277–305.

19 See B. Behrens, 'The Whig Theory of the Constitution in the Reign of Charles II', *CHJ*, VII, 1941, pp. 42–71; Miller, ' Parliaments', pp. 21–3.
20 See T. Harris, 'The Tories and the Rule of Law in the Reign of Charles II', *Seventeenth Century*, VIII, 1993, pp. 9–27.
21 T.B. Macaulay, *History of England from the Accession of James II*, initially 2 vols, 5th ed., London, 1849, II.662.
22 L. Colley, *Britons: Forging the Nation 1707–1837*, New Haven, 1992, ch. 1.
23 See W. Haller, *Foxe's Book of Martyrs and the Elect Nation*, London, 1963.
24 Miller, *Popery*, p. 72 and note 16.
25 A. Marvell, *An account of the Growth of Popery and Arbitrary Government*, 'Amsterdam', 1678, p. 5. This was reprinted in *State Tracts*, vol. I.
26 *Ibid.*, pp. 6–7.
27 See for example, J. Locke, *Travels in France 1675–79*, (ed.) J. Lough, Cambridge, 1953, pp. 85, 138, 223; J. Lough, *France Observed in the Seventeenth Century by British Travellers*, London, 1984, pp. 221–9.
28 Elton, *Tudor Constitution*, pp. 76–80; P. Collinson, 'The Monarchical Republic of Elizabeth I', *Bulletin of the John Rylands Library*, LXIX, 1986–87, pp. 394–424.
29 Miller, *Popery*, pp. 52–5.
30 *Ibid.*, pp. 9–12.
31 P. Lake, 'Anti-popery: the Structure of a Prejudice' in R. Cust and A. Hughes (eds), *Conflict in Early Stuart England*, London, 1989, ch. 3, especially pp. 74–6.
32 See Cust, 'News and Politics', pp. 73–5, 81–4; R. Cust, 'Charles I, the Privy Council and the Forced Loan', *JBS*, XXIV, 1985, pp. 208–35.
33 C. Hibberd, *Charles I and the Popish Plot*, Chapel Hill, 1983.
34 Lake, 'Anti-popery', p. 81.
35 Clifton, ' Fear', *passim.*
36 Halifax, *Works*, p. 78.
37 Lake, 'Anti-popery', pp. 84–92.
38 R. L'Estrange, *L'Estrange's Narrative of the Plot*, 1680, pp. 25–6.
39 *The Presbyterian Pater Noster*, 1681. For the date, February 1681, see Luttrell, I.68.
40 Miller, *Popery*, pp. 85–6.
41 See for example *England Bought and Sold, or a Discovery*, 1681, especially pp. 5, 11.
42 *State Trials*, VI.1430–1, 1442, 1472.
43 An exception is 'A Relation of the Most Material Matters Handled in Parliament', 1673, *State Tracts*, I.26–36, especially p. 29, 35.
44 Shaftesbury, 'A Letter from a Person of Quality', 1675 in *State Tracts*, I.43–4.
45 *Ibid.*, pp. 50, 55.
46 M. Nedham, *A Pacquet of Advices . . . to the Men of Shaftesbury*, 1676, pp. 55–6, 62.
47 Marvell, *Growth*, pp. 14–16, 66–7, 74–81. Marvell avoided direct criticism of the Duke of York: pp. 40, 47, 49.
48 Grey, V.282–3, 286; *HMC Ormond*, NS IV.422; *LJ*, XIII.222.
49 Grey, VI.190, 248.
50 Grey, VI.330. See also *HMC Finch*, II.30–1.
51 Grey, VIII.158. See also H. Booth, *A Collection of Speeches*, 1681, p. 11.
52 Grey, VI.151, 195, 250, 266, VII.53, 450, VIII.49, 163–5; *HMC Ormond*, NS V.7–8; Carte MS 39, fo. 21; *CSPD 1680–81*, pp. 146–7.

53 'Vox Populi, Vox Dei', 1681, *Somers Tracts*, VIII.302.
54 See *A Brief Relation of the Persecution and Sufferings of the Reformed Churches of France*, 1668; *Popery and Tyranny or the Present State of France*, 1679.
55 [C. Blount], 'An Appeal from the Country to the City', (1679), *State Tracts*, I.401–2.
56 C. Russell, 'Parliamentary History in Perspective, 1604–29', *History*, LXI, 1976, pp. 5–12.
57 C. Roberts, 'The Constitutional Significance of the Financial Settlement of 1690', *HJ*, XX, 1977, pp. 59–76.

Chapter eight

The issues: II. Church and Dissent

Before the Restoration

For a century before the Restoration there had been fierce debates about the nature and priorities of the Church of England. As established under Elizabeth, it embraced a theology generally seen as Calvinist while largely retaining the pre-Reformation system of church government. The Book of Common Prayer followed the Catholic Church in adhering to set liturgies, while reducing (but not eliminating) the elements of ritual. The people were officially required to kneel to receive communion, while the clergy were expected to wear a distinguishing gown, the surplice, and to make the sign of the cross over the baby's head during baptism. Committed Protestants urged that the English Church be brought into line with the 'Reformed' (Calvinist) churches on the continent and in Scotland. Their initial concerns were to eliminate 'popish' ceremonies and to remove the restrictions which Elizabeth imposed on preaching: only if the Gospel was preached freely could England be converted to Bible-based Protestantism. Later in the reign, as the bishops sought to impose fuller conformity, these 'hotter' Protestants extended their criticisms to episcopacy (government by bishops); the 1590s saw a significant attempt to build from below a presbyterian system akin to those established in the Scottish and French Reformed churches. Whereas in the Church of England power flowed down, from the monarch through the bishops, in a presbyterian system power flowed up from below, at least ostensibly, as parishes sent representatives to local synods (or **classes**), which in turn sent representatives to regional synods and ultimately a national assembly. The attempt to create such a system in England challenged the crown's control over the church and the nation's religious life; once discovered it was suppressed.

It might seem that the Church was already following the middle way (*via media*) between Catholic and Reformed, which was later to be seen as its distinguishing feature. Some argued exactly that, notably Richard Hooker, later depicted as the archetypal 'Anglican' of the time. Recently, however, scholars have argued that Hooker was a marginal rather than a typical figure[1] and that those who called for further reform, the 'puritans', were both numerous and influential. In opposing calls, from Parliament and the privy council, for further reform and for more preaching, Elizabeth was often in a minority of one: she even suspended her Archbishop of Canterbury, Edmund Grindal, for disobedience. Patrick Collinson has shown the extent to which puritan (or nonconformist) clergy operated **within** the church. Presented to parishes, and protected, by puritan laymen, many avoided wearing the surplice and omitted elements of the official liturgy which they disliked; the bishops either made little effort to make them conform or were frustrated by sympathetic churchwardens, magistrates and privy councillors.[2]

This view of the Elizabethan Church has not gone unchallenged. Christopher Haigh depicted 'puritans' as an unpopular minority, striving to impose their high standards of piety on an apathetic or hostile populace, which believed that people achieved salvation by living good lives and was content with the undemanding, repetitive piety of the Prayer Book. Such people saw worship as a social obligation and were unconcerned about its precise form or the theology behind it.[3] The rival models of Collinson and Haigh highlight the tension within the Elizabethan and Jacobean Church, between 'parish anglicanism' and evangelism. The former is the more difficult to analyse. Much of our evidence comes from puritans disillusioned by the lack of response to their preaching.[4] Parish anglicans rarely fell foul of the church courts or made their views known (unless provoked by an aggressively puritan minister), until the Long Parliament's assault on the church in 1641 provoked petitions, which reveal a positive commitment to the Prayer Book liturgy, with its emphasis on decency and its capacity to inspire awe and to bind communities together.[5] They also stated a view of the Church's ecclesiology, which stressed its continuity with both the Marian martyrs and the pre-Reformation Church.[6] Against this parish-based ideal was ranged the 'puritan' emphasis on conversion, from external conformity to internalized commitment: in Eamon Duffy's words, bringing the tepid to the boil. As many parishes lacked a preaching minister, this could be achieved only extra-parochially, by market-day lectures, itinerant preachers or worshippers 'gadding' to sermons in other parishes.[7] Only through sermons could laypeople address the issue of salvation: the official Prayer Book catechism discussed it only in terms of duties towards God and one's neighbours and did not mention faith.[8]

These two trends coexisted within the Church until the 1620s. Rather than representing opposed 'parties', they occupied parts of a broad spectrum of opinion from the most uncomprehending conformity to a principled commitment to a radically reformed liturgy and the abolition of episcopacy. 'Puritans' differed considerably among themselves, but agreed in wanting some further reform of the Church and in their zeal: they were 'the hotter sort of Protestants'. The diverse elements were able to coexist because Calvinist theology was rarely challenged – 'parish anglicans' were concerned with worship rather than theology[9] – and because some official requirements were widely ignored. Although parishes were supposed to move the communion table from the body of the church to the east end whenever communion was celebrated, few did so. Most congregations received communion sitting rather than kneeling, which suggested a position on the eucharist closer to the broadly commemorative view of Zurich and Geneva than to the Catholic doctrine of transubstantiation. In short, the Church was more 'Reformed' in practice than in theory and contained a significant measure of semi-conformity. From the 1590s, however, a new element emerged which saw the continuities with the pre-Reformation Church as a source of pride rather than embarrassment. Whereas Bishop Jewel had defended episcopacy as a useful means of governing the Church, neither good nor bad in itself, some argued that it was a defining mark of a true church. Against the Catholic claim to authority, based on a continuous line of popes going back to St Peter, some argued that the Church of England enjoyed a similar authority, based on a continuous succession of bishops. Established in the first century, it had been subordinated to Rome, and corrupted, but was now, thanks to the Reformation, the only pure church which could trace its origins back to Christ Himself.[10] Similarly, some clergymen defended ceremonies not just as *adiaphora*, practices indifferent in themselves which should be used because they were required by authority, but as essential aids to devotion. They sought to shift the focus of the service from the sermon to holy communion, for which they expected the people to kneel. They developed a theology of the eucharist which emphasized the mystical rather than the commemorative and claimed that consecration brought about a qualitative change, spiritual or even physical, in the bread and wine.[11] This highlighted the sacerdotal attributes of the priesthood, in the act of consecration, challenging the claim of the Reformed churches that clergy and laity were spiritually equal and that pastors were distinguished only by their training and vocation to preach.

Under Elizabeth this claim that the Reformation had gone too far was espoused by only a small minority. Under James I it grew stronger, but James extended his patronage to all shades of opinion and did not place too much pressure on the puritan clergy to conform. The 'high church' element gained ground among both bishops and parish clergy, but most puritans felt able to remain within the Church, especially as James did not share Elizabeth's suspicion of preaching.[12] Moreover, attempts to reinstate ritual and sacerdotal authority were not yet linked to an attack on the central Calvinist doctrine of predestination, whereby God had determined who was to be saved and who damned (thus removing any possibility of salvation through human action). In 1618 James sent a delegation to the Synod of Dort, which condemned the claim of the Dutch theologian Arminius that people could accept or reject the grace which God offered them. By contrast, Charles I openly favoured 'Arminian' clergymen, who attacked Calvinism and articulated an authoritarian, indeed absolutist, view of monarchy. In the eleven years without Parliament between 1629 and 1640 the Arminians, led by William Laud, Archbishop of Canterbury from 1633, sought to impose their brand of worship. Parish officials were ordered to move the communion table to the east end of the church, to set it up 'altar-wise' and to rail it off, which would save it from the unwelcome attentions of the more unruly parishioners (and their dogs) and make more visible the priest's role in the eucharist. They were to keep the church and churchyard in good repair and ensure that the parish possessed its full complement of furnishings and vestments: baptising babies in buckets or dispensing communion wine in alehouse tankards was just not good enough.[13]

It has been argued that there was nothing new in this, that Laud and Charles I were simply enforcing more rigorously what had always been the Church's official practice, refusing to compromise any longer with peasant boorishness.[14] Laud and his allies offended powerful interests. Pews which interrupted the congregation's view of the altar were cut down to size, removing an important indicator of status. The cost of meeting Laudian standards was borne by the parishioners. But there was more to the litany of complaint against the Laudians than resentment of cost, or of clerical bossiness. Even where the requirements imposed by Laud dated back to Elizabeth's reign, they had been enforced spasmodically, if at all, so they **seemed** novel and were criticized by 'parish anglicans' as well as by puritans.[15] They were also identified with 'popery', not only because of the greater emphasis on ceremony and communion, but also because of a reduced emphasis on – and sometimes outright hostility to – preaching. Some Laudian clergy never preached, concentrating on the homilies and on catechizing.[16] For people with no first-hand knowledge of 'popery', this seemed a large step back towards the days before the Reformation. Such fears may have been exaggerated, but they provoked hundreds of petitions to Parliament in 1640–41.[17]

Many saw these changes as a 'counter-reformation' within the Church: a small, mainly clerical minority trying to destroy the broad Church of James I and create a new brand of 'Anglicanism', further from Geneva and closer to Rome. This process was halted by the civil wars, but ensured that there would be several different visions of the restored Church of England, including those which could be crudely labelled 'Laudian', 'church-puritan' and 'parish anglican'. If the Laudian model threatened to sweep away the church-puritan in the 1630s, the roles were reversed in the 1640s. Even before the king left London, the Commons encouraged the removal of altars and altar-rails and condoned failure to use the Prayer Book.[18] The church courts were suppressed and the bishops excluded from the Lords. In the following years, Laudian clergymen were removed from their parishes by the Committee for Scandalous Ministers. Following the signing of the Solemn League and Covenant with the Scots in 1643, episcopacy was abolished and a new service-book, the Scottish Directory, replaced Common Prayer, the use of which was now forbidden (as was the celebration of 'popish' festivals). There is much evidence of hostility to these changes and some outright opposition, especially to the suppression of Christmas.[19] The net effect was to allow greater autonomy to individual parishes and patrons of livings (except for Royalists). The abolition of church courts and episcopacy meant that there was effectively no church government above the parish level. (This is why it is impossible accurately to assess the response to these changes: there were no mechanisms in place for enforcing conformity or gathering information.) Parliament set up the Westminster Assembly of Divines to devise a new system of church government, but it found it hard to satisfy both the puritan clergy and Parliament. Many of the clergy wanted a presbyterian system similar to that recently re-established in Scotland, which had given the parish clergy extensive powers to discipline errant parishioners and created a national assembly which claimed considerable influence over the state. Parliament, however, was wary of entrusting too much power to clergymen and the scheme which emerged in 1648 failed to establish a workable system of local classes (let alone a national one), making it impossible to create an effective system of discipline.[20]

When the army seized power in December 1648, it would not allow any coercive system, episcopalian or presbyterian. Since 1640 English puritanism had fragmented irretrievably. Free to preach at last, the puritan clergy expected God to bring about moral and spiritual regeneration. But no new godly order emerged and the godly fell out among themselves. For half a century they had emphasized their distinctness. If they could not find godly preaching in their own parish, they would 'gad' to hear a sermon in another, repeating and discussing it later. While notionally remaining members of the Church, they distanced themselves from their fellow parishioners and proclaimed their solidarity with puritans from other parishes, a solidarity emphasized by distinctiveness of dress and behaviour and (it seems) a growing determination to keep contacts with the ungodly to a minimum.[21] Where puritans were in positions of power, they used it to suppress drunkenness, swearing and sabbath-breaking. The cultural divisions between puritans and the rest had important implications for popular allegiance in the civil war,[22] but these habits of separation (which for the period before 1640 have been labelled 'non-separating congregationalism') became much more marked thereafter. A combination of heady millenarian excitement and the collapse of ecclesiastical authority encouraged those who saw themselves as the elect to dissociate themselves from the ungodly multitude and join with like-minded people to worship in their own way and await the millennium. An exercise of choice within the Church (supplemented by informal activity outside it) evolved into full-blown separatism. This was not what most of the puritan clergy had wanted, but they were powerless to prevent it. Nor could they prevent the proliferation of groups who challenged everything that they stood for: Calvinist theology, a university-trained ordained ministry, even the supreme authority of Scripture. At times the parochial system, and the tithes upon which it depended, came under threat. Oliver Cromwell maintained a basic provision of instruction, funded by tithe, at the parish level, but refused to prescribe what should be taught and thought it sufficient to require that parish ministers should match up to certain moral and educational standards. Those who wished to worship outside the parish system, other than Papists or 'prelatists' (adherents of the bishops) could do so.[23]

The religious legacy of the civil wars was complex. The Laudians were expelled from their parishes. Some ministered clandestinely, others found refuge abroad, or as chaplains to Royalist families, or scratched a living as schoolmasters. The king's execution was a fearsome psychological blow to men for whom the Church was closely identified with the monarchy. Some responded by placing greater emphasis on episcopacy as **the** distinguishing mark of the Church of England, but with the old bishops dying off and Charles II seemingly unwilling to appoint new ones, this argument appeared to have only a limited future.[24] While there was evidence of continued popular attachment to the Prayer Book, that should probably be seen as evidence of support less for 'Laudianism' than for 'parish anglicanism'.

For 'church puritans' things were, on the face of it, better. They were generally labelled 'presbyterians', although most (especially among the laity) had little fondness for Scottish-style presbyterianism; among the clergy, many had no doctrinaire hostility towards episcopacy and distinguished between the moderation of many bishops under Elizabeth and James and the haughty 'prelacy' of Laud and his cronies. With the Laudians driven into the wilderness, Presbyterians occupied most parochial livings, carrying on their ministry free of the restraints they had suffered in the 1630s. The 1650s saw a sustained campaign of evangelism,[25] but they lacked the disciplinary powers needed to make their ministry fully effective. Moral discipline was integral to Calvinism, but was ineffective without the mechanisms to identify, interrogate and punish errant members. The requirement of compulsory church attendance in the 1559 Act of Uniformity was a dead letter before it was abolished in 1650. The Presbyterians established what discipline they could, with the help of their leading parishioners, but it proved fully effective only for those willing voluntarily to accept it. Many parishes became divided, in a mirror-image of the 1630s, into an 'inner ring', on whom the minister focused his attention and who accepted his discipline, and the rest, excluded from communion, who came to services if they chose but were effectively 'unchurched'.[26] For the Presbyterians, frustrated by their lack of power and appalled by the excesses of Ranters and Quakers, the return of the monarchy offered the prospect of creating – at last – a truly effective puritan national church.[27] Others, after the tribulations of the 1650s, would welcome any effective national church, and the one system of church government proved to be effective was episcopacy.[28]

For the separatist sects, the 1640s and 1650s offered an intoxicating freedom which in time became overlaid by frustration. In the 1640s congregations formed, split and amalgamated in a bewildering kaleidoscope; lost souls, deprived of the certainties offered by a single church, wandered in search of truth. In time, most coalesced into a handful of substantial denominations. Of these, the Independents were closest to traditional puritanism. Calvinist in theology, they accepted the pre-eminent authority of Scripture. They differed from the Presbyterians partly in their willingness to countenance lay preaching, but more in their insistence that the godly must separate from the ungodly: the only true church was a voluntary association of 'visible saints'. While most had no objection to the maintenance of a parish system, they insisted that the state could not force people to attend its services.[29] The Baptists, who had established some churches before 1640, split into two major groups: Particular, wedded to Calvinism, and General, who followed Arminius in arguing for a substantial measure of free will. Both agreed that, as only adults were capable of making a reasoned decision to enter a church, entry should be marked by adult baptism (or re-baptism): they could find no evidence for infant baptism in Scripture. They noted that those who preached and prophesied in the Bible were mostly not trained priests and argued that the gift of preaching came from God. It owed nothing to a formal education and was likely to be inhibited by it. They expected their preachers to support themselves by practising a trade, denouncing university-trained ministers as 'hirelings', who preached for lucre; they were deeply hostile to tithes. The Quakers took this a stage further, seeing in the 'inner light' a continuous revelation of God's will, while the Bible set out His will only at a particular moment in time. Even more hostile than the Baptists to 'hireling priests', the Quakers argued that God could confer the gift of prophecy on anyone – even women – and used confrontation and shock tactics to draw attention to their message. While professing respect for the secular authorities, the Quakers made it clear that they expected them to follow God's guidance, as expressed through their 'light'. Their refusal of 'hat honour' affronted expectations of deference, their refusal to swear oaths threatened to undermine the legal process and dissolve the bonds of society, which depended heavily on people making – and keeping – promises.

By the 1650s Independents and Baptists had lost much of their earlier enthusiasm: the former joined locally with Presbyterians to counter the threat from the Quakers. While enjoying their freedom, they were disillusioned by their failure to win more support or to establish a new godly order. Trust in God's providence and His special mission for England, sustained by the conquest of Scotland and Ireland, came under strain in the later 1650s. Only the Quakers were still gathering momentum. For all of them the return of the monarchy posed huge problems: how had God allowed this to happen? For the regicide Edmund Ludlow, it was His punishment for their sins: he went off to Switzerland, to take his turn in the wilderness.[30] Others, who did not have the option of flight, sought to make their peace with the new regime. Baptists and Quakers, many of whom had done what they could to prevent the Restoration, now sought to persuade Charles II that they were harmless.

The Restoration settlement

Two distinct, yet related, questions faced the restored monarchy. There was general agreement, among both Royalists and moderate Parliamentarians, that a national church should be re-established, more uniform than that of the 1650s. But should it follow the Laudian model imposed so briefly and contentiously under Charles I? Or one closer to the church of James I, which would accommodate parish anglicans and most church puritans, or even move further in a puritan direction? The second question had scarcely applied in 1640: what was to be done about the determined minority who did not want to be part of **any** established church? Were they to be allowed to worship in peace, so long as they posed no threat to the state? Or would there be an attempt to force them into conformity? To use terms used at the time, the points at issue were 'comprehension' and 'indulgence'[31] and the Parliament elected in 1661 was hostile to both. The Act of Uniformity of 1662 reimposed the Prayer Book, slightly modified, and required the clergy to declare their approval of everything it contained: church puritans were given the choice of compromising their principles or leaving the church. A series of Acts was passed, designed to discriminate against and harass all, whether sectaries or presbyterians, who refused to conform to the Church of England.

In assessing the religious divisions of the 1660s, we need to remember that there were several overlapping visions of church-order – Laudian, parish anglican, church puritan, sectarian – so that a simple distinction between Church and Dissent is far too simplistic. In terms of committed adherents, all these groups (except perhaps the parish anglicans – but how 'committed' were they?) probably constituted smallish minorities of the population. In the sixteenth and seventeenth centuries the majority of laypeople and clergy complied with whatever religious system Parliament imposed. Only a minority of the clergy, albeit a large one, was removed in the 1640s[32] and a large majority conformed in 1662, even though most had also served in the 1650s. Of those outside the Church, the Compton census of 1676 suggested that full nonconformists comprised less than 5 per cent of the population, while the 'Evans list' of the 1710s (using figures supplied by nonconformist churches) suggested that they accounted for just over 6 per cent, half of whom were Presbyterians, the lineal descendants of the church puritans.[33]

The terms of the Act of Uniformity suggest the church settlement was firmly 'Anglican': R.S. Bosher described it as 'the triumph of the Laudians'. The process of re-establishment will be discussed in the next chapter. For the moment, my main concern is to analyse the nature of the restored 'Anglican' Church (although the term 'Anglican' was not normally used at this time). If we understand 'Anglican' as referring to the Church as it had been before 1640, there were several visions of 'Anglicanism' – and it is far from clear that the 'Laudian' was the strongest. By 1646 the Laudians had lost their parishes and their control of the universities, which trained most of the clergy. The clergy in place when Charles II returned included some ordained by bishops and many ordained by presbyters. Those who had held parishes in the 1640s should have taken the Covenant; those who held parishes in the 1650s should, in theory, have subscribed the Engagement. They had accepted posts in a church without bishops and they were required to use the Directory, although some had also used the Prayer Book.[34] The committed Laudians of the 1630s would by 1660 have been a dwindling minority, headed by an ageing group of bishops, who failed to show the leadership expected of them. A church settlement could have been reached which restored episcopacy and the Prayer Book (the touchstone of 'parish anglicanism'), while allowing sufficient flexibility in its use to accommodate most church puritans. Given the balance of forces in 1660, a 'triumph of the Laudians' seems the least likely of outcomes.

But Bosher's use of 'Laudian' was idiosyncratic: his 'Laudians' articulated an ecclesiology which emphasized the distinctiveness of the Church of England in opposition to the Roman Church on one side and the Reformed churches on the other. But he did not accord them a distinctive theological or liturgical position. Laud, he claimed, was tolerant of theological divisions and allowed 'divergence of opinion on secondary matters': 'the indispensable safeguard of the Church's unity was a prescribed common worship and a minimum standard of ceremonial'.[35] This was (as he rightly said) in line with 'Elizabethan tradition', as expressed by Whitgift, or James I. But the Laudianism of the 1630s had surely been more prescriptive and intolerant than that. Moreover, if Laud did not actively encourage the preaching of Arminian theology, his liturgical demands had significant theological implications. 'Laudian', in the sense I have used in this chapter, implies a view of the liturgy which emphasizes the sacrament of the altar and a spirituality which embraces the senses – the beauty of holiness, perhaps rich church music. This view of the liturgy and this spirituality had started to develop in the 1630s, but their development had then been brutally interrupted. Their development resumed during Charles II's reign and they became important strands of what is now understood as 'Anglicanism'. But they made no significant contribution to the Restoration settlement, nor was there initially any attempt to foster them at the parish level. Among the bishops, Laud's great ally Matthew Wren was passed over for promotion and of the new bishops only John Cosin could be described as a 'high churchman'. Peter Heylyn, Laud's chaplain and confidant, was not offered a bishopric; three 'church puritans', Baxter, Calamy and Reynolds, were.[36] As will be shown below, the bishops' aims were noticeably less ambitious than Laud's had been – to ensure a basic level of 'decency' in the parishes and to see that the clergy and their flocks were 'indifferent conformable'.[37] They did not try to drive 'church puritans' out of the Church: on the contrary, most tried hard to persuade them to remain in. Their arguments for their remaining were couched primarily in terms of obedience to authority, rather than theology or ecclesiology.

In this, the bishops were implementing legislation shaped by others. The Act of Uniformity was designed to make it as difficult as possible for church-puritan ministers to conform. They were required to declare their 'unfeigned assent and consent' to everything in the Prayer Book, to undertake to use all rites and ceremonies prescribed by the Church and to renounce the Covenant and any attempt to alter the government in church or state. They were required to subscribe all of the Thirty-nine Articles, whereas under an Act of 1571 they had had to subscribe only those relating to doctrine, omitting Articles 34 to 36, which dealt with the Church's right to impose ceremonies not required by Scripture, the use of homilies and episcopal ordination. Ministers who had not received episcopal ordination, and who refused to be reordained, were now to be excluded, although before 1640 ordinations in the Scottish church or the Reformed churches on the continent had been accepted as valid.[38] These requirements were extended to lecturers (ordained clergymen who preached market-day sermons or in chapels but did not hold a benefice) and schoolmasters. This last provision was one of several which were spiteful, designed to prevent ejected ministers from earning their living by taking pupils. Others included the denial of any maintenance[39] – those ejected in the 1640s had in theory been allowed one-fifth of their stipends[40] – and the requirement that they should declare their conformity by St Bartholomew's Day (24 August 1662), shortly before Michaelmas (29 September) the traditional day for the year's tithe payments.[41]

It should be stressed that these stringent requirements for conformity were imposed not by the bishops but by the Commons and that the Act of Uniformity was directed against the church-puritan **clergy**. Apart from the Act condemning the Solemn League and Covenant, the only measures passed against nonconformists in 1661–62 were the Corporation Act and the Quakers Act. The former was designed to exclude those regarded as 'disaffected' from town governments and can be seen as a measure of discrimination rather than of persecution. On the other hand, Parliament was slow to pass a new Act against nonconformist meetings to replace that of 1593, a draconian measure passed when separatist numbers had been very small.[42] In May 1661 the Commons resolved to bring in a bill against Quakers, 'Anabaptists' and other 'schismatics', who refused to swear oaths and held unlawful meetings.[43] The Act which eventually passed was clumsily drafted. It laid down penalties for those who went under the names of Quakers 'and other names of separation' who refused oaths and for Quakers (only) who held unauthorized meetings of five persons or more, apart from the immediate family. It referred to 'the great endangering of the public peace and safety' which oath refusal and unlawful meetings brought about – but banned no meetings other than those of the Quakers.[44] Not until 1664 was a measure passed which condemned all meetings 'on pretence of tender consciences' outside the Church of England. Passed in the aftermath of the Derwentdale Plot, the first Conventicle Act continued the Quaker Act's definition of a conventicle. In contrast to the laws against Catholics, which imposed penalties for all aspects of Catholic worship, the Act explicitly allowed family worship, but treated larger meetings as a threat to the state. It was to be temporary: the Commons presumably hoped that nonconformists would see the error of their ways and return to the Church.[45] The Five Mile Act of 1665 forbade the clergy ejected in 1662 to come to any corporate town or any parish which they had once held, unless they would swear not to attempt to change the government of church or state. This reflected the fear that the ministers were in league with the Dutch, with whom England was at war.[46]

It would seem that initially the Cavalier House of Commons was hostile to Presbyterians and sectaries primarily because it feared religious nonconformity could lead to political disaffection. The Acts it passed fell comparatively lightly on lay Dissenters (apart from Quakers). Those who suffered most were clergymen ejected from what they saw as **their** Church. The bishop of Exeter might remark that they had ejected themselves,[47] but the Commons were determined to make conformity difficult and many were harassed by Royalist magistrates. I shall suggest in Chapter 10 that the Commons became more hostile to Dissent as the 1660s wore on: the 1670 Conventicle Act was not only more 'arbitrary'[48] than that of 1664 – it was also permanent.

Church and people

The bishops were slow to establish effective leadership over the church. In most dioceses episcopal administration was not functioning fully until 1662 or 1663.[49] The clergy's role in legislation was limited to the Lords, where the bishops resumed their places only in November 1661. While some (notably Cosin) vigorously supported moves to enhance the level of conformity required, others were persuaded by Clarendon to support a proviso to allow the king to dispense individuals from the requirements of the uniformity bill.[50] Convocation met at the same time as Parliament. In late 1661 it rejected proposals to reform the Prayer Book in a 'Laudian' direction, but made changes which responded (in part) to objections raised by the Presbyterians in the recent Savoy conference.[51] Convocation's other major task was to revise the controversial canons of 1640, but nothing was agreed and in 1664 it went into abeyance after Archbishop Sheldon agreed that the clergy should give up their right to tax themselves. It was to handle no more substantive business until 1689.[52] In 1662, Sheldon thwarted an attempt to persuade the king to allow some presbyterian ministers not to conform fully, but even Sheldon supported Clarendon's proviso and granted Richard Baxter a licence to preach, without enquiring into his beliefs.[53] However, early in 1663, when Charles again pressed the Houses to grant him a power of dispensation, the bishops were said to have urged members to oppose it.[54]

It is hard to tell whether the bishops' moderation should be put down to principle, pragmatism, lack of confidence or lack of power. Some, like Reynolds, were undoubtedly moderate and many tried to persuade their clergy to conform and to make compliance easy.[55] As for the clergy, some would no doubt have subscribed anything to keep their livings.[56] Others had qualms about abandoning their flocks to inadequate pastors or saw the continuation of their ministry as more important than the precise form of service. The bishops were in no position to be too fussy: well qualified, espiscopally ordained, committed conformists were in short supply[57] and the bishops lacked the power to impose full conformity. The church courts were restored in 1661, but proved less effective without the backing of Star Chamber and high commission.[58] The bishops had been thrust into what was, for most, an unfamiliar role, using powers and institutions which had not functioned for almost twenty years. The parish clergy were a mixed bag. Baxter divided them into three groups: Presbyterians, persuaded to subscribe by their bishop; younger 'Latitudinarians', who disliked the imposition of 'little things', but thought them too unimportant to quibble over; and 'hearty conformists', some of them bigoted, or driven by ambition.[59] A survey of Canterbury diocese in late 1663 reveals a few 'Presbyterians',[60] or suspected Presbyterians.[61] One minister was 'a covetous fat Presbyterian conformist', another was 'an intruder, but now a convert and conformable': he had a surplice, and his church was in good repair, with 'all things decent'.[62] Such 'converts' were not necessarily insincere: they may have found the rituals of the restored Church more satisfying than the plainer worship of the 1650s. At least 171 who refused in 1662 later subscribed.[63] It is impossible to assess the extent of 'puritan' nonconformity among the clergy. Ralph Josselin was perhaps exceptional in almost never wearing a surplice in the two decades after 1662, but when William Lloyd came to the small diocese of Peterborough in 1679, he found that thirty-three of his clergy did not wear one.[64]

With the clergy so mixed, and the bishops so uncertain, the level of conformity required was limited. In Canterbury diocese in 1663, the visitation enquired whether parish churches possessed the king's arms, a Prayer Book and a surplice – many did not – and whether the church, chancel and parsonage were in good repair. The fact that Farningham church was mentioned as having rails around the communion table suggests that this was unusual.[65] In all dioceses, the bishops were faced with the effects of neglect and wanton damage. Exeter cathedral had been partitioned, with one half used by Presbyterians and the other by Independents. In the north-east, the Scots had left a trail of devastation. One of the main churches in Newcastle had holes in the roof and the congregation huddled to escape the rain and snow.[66] Elsewhere the problem was poverty. In two Gloucestershire villages, communion was said rarely, if at all, and the church plate consisted of a small silver cup, kept in a Quaker's house. At Geddington, Northamptonshire, there had been no communion and no settled minister for fifty years.[67] Towns often had too many parishes, all too poor to support a preacher. An Act of 1665 allowed for the joining of small parishes,[68] but often their income was too small even when joined together.[69] All Saints', Sudbury, was said in 1670 to be unable to support a minister, so that the church was used by nonconformists[70] and there are other examples of churches (or chapels in large parishes) being taken over by Dissenters.[71] In one Essex parish the Commonwealth's arms had still not been taken down in 1681 and the churchwardens resisted orders to put the king's arms up instead.[72]

The clergy's limited power and self-confidence made it imperative that they secure the support of the gentry. The survey of Canterbury noted the abodes of the leading gentry, although there was only a limited correlation between a resident squire and a well-maintained church or satisfactory level of conformity. One of the leading Royalists and persecutors of Dissenters in Kent, Sir Thomas Peyton, was lord of the manor of Tilmanstone and lived close by and yet the church had no surplice and was 'much out of order'. Northbourne, the abode of Sir Thomas Sandys, JP, was full of Baptists and Quakers. At Murston, with no resident gentry, there were many sectaries and few communicants and yet the people came 'orderly' to the church which was in good repair, with a surplice and Prayer Book.[73] The clergy needed the backing of the secular magistrate and the gentry were eager to reassert their power over the church. Royalist squires recovered advowsons and impropriations taken from them in the 1640s; bishops and deans and chapters leased land to friendly gentlemen on advantageous terms.[74] The priorities of patrons were not always those of bishops. One remarked that he wanted a parson who was good humoured and sang well; one minister apologized for missing a meeting called by his archdeacon because the gentry and churchwardens of his parish had sent him to lobby the JPs about a bridge.[75] Denis Granville, Dean of Durham, complained that his clergy were too willing to change service times to accommodate horse-races.[76] The church courts had many enemies and not just common lawyers. There were complaints about exorbitant fees and the misuse of excommunication.[77] Sheldon sometimes found the courts more of a hindrance than a help in disciplining errant clergy.[78] For much of the reign the bishops could not be confident that they had the backing of the king, which made that of the local peers and gentry all the more crucial. Sheldon upbraided one of his clergy for offending Sir Henry Yelverton, a good friend of the church.[79] At Exeter first Ward then Sparrow took pains to win over the county JPs[80] and city fathers.[81] In 1683 Lamplugh, their successor, now confident of royal and gentry support, was able to bring the Carews, hitherto 'far from the church', to receive communion and confirmation.[82]

By the early 1680s, helped by the Tory gentry and the crown, the bishops claimed to have achieved order and regularity. The hostility to the clergy and the bishops, apparent in the 1660s,[83] appears to have become more muted. In 1668 they found many defenders in the Commons and in 1676 Baxter complained that Londoners believed that prelacy was the best means to prevent schism.[84] They still had their enemies, but they had more and firmer friends and were increasingly self-confident. By the start of 1685 most Dissenting meetings had been suppressed and the bishops claimed that the churches were much fuller than before.[85] How far they had won over hearts and minds is a matter for conjecture. Evidence of popular resentment of the cost of building or refurbishing churches[86] can be balanced by cases where people were seemingly willing and eager to contribute.[87] In the early 1660s, some found the spectacle of bishops in their robes and Prayer Book rituals unfamiliar or distasteful.[88] Although the latter had acquired the force of habit since 1559, a whole generation of people was unused to them and even in 1683 Lloyd found the people of his diocese 'strangely averse to the liturgy'.[89] The restoration of the Prayer Book seems nevertheless to have been widely welcomed,[90] and thousands came to be confirmed.[91] Most people seem to have attended church at least once on a Sunday, less often on other days; some attended dissenting meetings as well. There are signs that they preferred the sermon to the formal services; some complained that their priest read them badly.[92] While there clearly was much principled hostility to the Church's liturgy, sometimes lack of conformity was due to 'a rude clownishness' rather than 'any factious or peevish opposition'.[93]

To some extent attendance at church was a social duty or habit, an expression of community: even active Dissenters might come to church for marriages or burials, as well as serving as churchwardens, or in other parish offices.[94] The clergy met most resistance in persuading the laity to take communion regularly. At Smarden, Kent, of 1,000 inhabitants barely 200 came to church and only eight had received communion at Easter. Elsewhere, many who attended church were reluctant to take communion, because they were out of charity with their neighbours, or did not have suitable clothes, or (most often) simply did not wish to. Communion had fallen into disuse in many parishes in the 1650s; Baxter claimed in 1670 that the three 'settled ministers' at Acton allowed only a handful of parishioners to receive.[95] Whereas some, like Sir Ralph Verney and Lord Yarmouth, took care to prepare,[96] Pepys remarked in 1662 that he had received communion only one or twice in his life and he could see little difference between the Anglican and Catholic eucharists. When Josselin received in 1665, it was the first time in over twenty years.[97] There were frequent comments on how few people received, despite the best endeavours of the clergy: Sheldon urged his clergy to celebrate communion weekly. Communion tables were increasingly replaced with altars, not always without opposition. At Deptford the order in 1662 to set up an altar was obeyed only in 1678. In one village the vicar repeatedly ordered the table to be moved to a more conspicuous position, only for the squire's sister to order that it be moved back.[98] The bishops and some of the clergy placed an increasingly 'Laudian' emphasis on communion as the reign went on, but they appear not to have carried their lay-people with them. Indeed it has been argued that nonconformist churches, many of which celebrated communion monthly, may have enjoyed a fuller and richer sacramental life than the Church of England.[99]

The added emphasis on communion might seem to imply a distrust of preaching. Duffy suggests that in 1662 the Church opted for parish anglicanism and the concern for conversion became the preserve of the nonconformists.[100] There were indeed those like the Earl of Sandwich who argued that there was too much preaching, but in general the bishops and clergy accepted that preaching was a necessary part of religious life. Evelyn thought the Church of England preachers of his day the most 'profitable' since the time of the apostles. In Hertfordshire the clergy held at least two conferences in 1679 where they discussed which style of preaching would most effectively instruct the people. In Bristol, Anglicans and nonconformists were equally diligent in preaching, especially in the suburbs. In the North, where parishes were large, Catholicism strong and the population sparse, bishops encouraged additional preaching, until it fell foul of the Tory gentry in the early 1680s.[101] In general, sermons were shorter and simpler than before the civil wars, eschewing controversy and focusing on living a good life.[102] Nevertheless, Sheldon placed increasing emphasis on catechising, which (he said) achieved more than sermons. He was supported by his bishops and by Parliament, which twice considered, but did not pass, bills requiring the clergy to catechise regularly.[103] Increasingly, Sunday afternoon sermons were replaced by catechising,[104] which had fallen into disuse during the Interregnum.[105]

During the reign there was a perceptible shift of emphasis in church services, away from the church-puritan concentration on the sermon, towards a more 'Laudian' (or parish anglican) stress on communion, ritual and catechism.[106] This reflected a concern to ensure that the people were properly instructed in their duties, especially that of obedience to lawful authority. More recondite or controversial preaching, it was thought, confused and divided the people and should be avoided.[107] But many argued that ceremonies were an essential part of worship. Sir William Coventry, often a thoughtful and articulate critic of royal policies, declared in 1675 that the Church of England had preserved more decency of ceremonies than any other.[108] Others, like Sir Thomas Littleton, deplored what they saw as a second Laudian counter-reformation, weakening English Protestantism by driving good Christians out of the Church. They accused many of the clergy of veering towards Arminian theology and claimed that many practices imposed by the Church were warranted neither by Scripture nor by any law.[109] How far some enthusiastic Laudians renounced their Elizabethan inheritance was shown when the mayor of Bridgewater denounced one of the inhabitants as a 'Grindalising presbyter'.[110] And yet, despite the protests, the 'Laudians' gained ground in the Church. Their success has been ascribed to their finding positions as chaplains after their ejection in the 1640s, which gave them an opportunity to indoctrinate a new generation of Royalist gentlemen,[111] but that in itself would not have transformed the character of the parish clergy. The crucial point was that after 1660 the 'Laudians' again established a firm, but never exclusive, hold on the universities, particularly Cambridge, where Arminian theology became dominant.[112] As the surviving semi-conformists died out and the universities produced ordinands fully committed to the Church as re-established in 1662, so the nature of the parochial clergy changed. Many went beyond mere 'parish anglicanism', adopting practices which were distinctively 'Laudian', especially in relation to communion. They also, as they saw their Church coming under threat, became more militant and politically active.

Did the eclipse of the church-puritan element change the character of the clergy? When in 1671 Sheldon set out his priorities for episcopal visitations, his first concern – ahead of precise observance of the liturgy and regular catechising – was the life and manners of the clergy. It was widely recognized that the Dissenters' outward piety won them much support, while people were repelled by the 'loose living' of many of the clergy.[113] For the nonconformists, who prided themselves on their 'sober' living, the beneficed clergy were notorious for 'drunkenness', although what some saw as drunkenness might seem to others harmless good fellowship. A Dutch visitor in 1662 was shocked to see clergymen smoking and drinking. The ecclesiastical authorities did indeed find some drunkards among their clergy – but not very many.[114] Some blamed this 'drunkenness' on clergymen mixing too much with the looser sort of gentry,[115] but it did not necessarily lose them the support of their parishioners. The people of Dymchurch were unanimous in wishing to keep their curate, 'an honest drunken fellow'.[116] Church-puritans felt that they were fighting a losing battle to maintain moral standards. Lay-people found rope-dancers and mountebanks more appealing than sermons and believed wedding celebrations were enhanced by fiddles and dancing.[117] The pre-civil war battles between the old festive culture and the puritan concern for godliness, between the proponents and opponents of the Book of Sports, were fought out again. On 1 May 1661, a group of 'profane youths and doting fools' set up a maypole in Adam Martindale's parish. His wife and three godly women cut it down, whereupon they set up another.[118] Even some church-puritan ministers succumbed at times to temptation. Henry Newcome denounced cockfights, with their attendant swearing and gambling, but watched mountebanks, played bowls and billiards, drank wine and took tobacco. When

Charles married his queen, Newcome confessed to drinking her health on his knees and wishing the king joy of his bridal bed – 'but it was after prayers'.[119]

It would be misleading to suggest that the established church was uniformly tolerant of popular recreations. Many of the clergy preached doggedly against sin and unbelief. However, despite the bishops' best efforts, many of their clergy were identified with the health-drinking, anti-puritan Tory gentry, who patronized raucous sports and provided free drink and entertainment. One should not assume that Dissent was inherently more attractive or popular than the established church. Historians are coming to accept the existence of a genuinely popular Royalism in the civil war. The half-century after 1660 saw the development of a formidably powerful popular 'Anglicanism', which by the reign of Anne was labelled 'High Church'.[120] This process has been relatively little studied in Charles II's reign, but by the early 1680s it was clearly well under way. And it is a major contention of this book that the newly militant Anglican clergy contributed substantially to the political polarization of the 1670s.

The nature of Dissent: Presbyterians

Historians like neat labels and categories, which make for ease of analysis. One major difficulty in studying religion in the seventeenth century is that some terms (such as 'Anglican') were not used at the time, some (like 'puritan') were initially terms of abuse, while others in common use were disowned by many to whom they were applied. 'Presbyterian' is one of these, but before tackling the problems which the term poses, it is worth remarking that English puritanism emphasized the spirit rather than outward forms, which for Cromwell (quoting St Paul) were 'dross and dung in comparison of Christ'.[121] Niceties of theology and church organization, so important to denominational historians, mattered less to those who simply sought a good sermon or an uplifting spiritual experience. The return of conventicles in Oxford diocese in 1669 revealed three described as a mixture of Presbyterians, Baptists and others and one of 'Presbyterians, Independents, Quakers and Baptists mixed'.[122] In one parish in 1682 the only Dissenters were five women: three Quakers and one Independent attended no meetings – 'their only pretext is the viciousness of others' – while one occasionally attended Baptist meetings. Several of the Quakers' children had been baptised in church.[123] Lest it should seem that such defiance of categorization was confined to the ill-educated, let us consider Bulstrode Whitelocke. For fifteen years after the Restoration he attended his parish church, when his health and the weather allowed, and occasionally received communion. On one occasion, when he was ill, the curate repeated at his house the sermon he had given in the morning.[124] But he also heard private sermons and attended conventicles,[125] where he heard the Independents John Owen, John Hodges and George Cokain; in 1675 the Quaker William Penn preached in his study.[126] He also preached at home, to audiences of up to a hundred.[127] Some years he celebrated Christmas, others he did not.[128]

Whitelocke's seeming inconsistency offers a reminder that, even after the fragmentation of puritanism, there remained a sense of common ground which embraced conformists in the 'church-puritan' tradition, Presbyterians, Independents and at times even Baptists and Quakers. Those who belonged to this mainstream puritan tradition shared a commitment to an essentially active piety, hearing the Word and seeking spiritual edification, and to a 'sober' personal morality.[129] They might differ on questions of theology and church government, and on the permissibility of conforming to the restored Church of England, but they were united by a similar world-view and way of life: in this sense even Quakers were part of a broad 'godly' tradition. They also shared a sense of Protestant identity, English and international, in the face of the threat from 'popery', at home and abroad. 'Laudians' and 'parish anglicans' distanced themselves from both this 'godly' tradition and foreign Reformed churches, instead emphasizing the Church's singularity as both reformed and episcopal.

Whether or not church puritan ministers remained within the church in 1662 depended largely on personal choice and whether the gentry and ecclesiastical authorities were eager to eject them.[130] There was much common ground between many who conformed and those who did not. Presbyterians (and Independents) claimed to have no quarrel with the doctrine of the Church. Presbyterians also accepted the need for a set liturgy and a properly endowed parochial ministry; many had no quarrel with episcopacy as such. Baxter disliked being labelled a 'presbyterian', claiming that the term misrepresented those who favoured a 'spiritual, serious way of worship'.[131] These refused to use 'unscriptural' (or 'popish') ceremonies and denied that bishops had the right to impose them. A significant group of MPs argued that the gulf between nonconformists and the more 'sober' conformists was narrow and could be bridged if the bishops showed a little flexibility. Ejected ministers often remained on good terms with their successors.[132] Most attended their parish churches if they could. Adam Martindale repeated his successor's sermons in the evening at his home but, like Oliver Heywood, he was careful not to draw people away from the church.[133] Both preached in churches, if invited by the minister or churchwardens, and (discreetly) at home, often to groups of four, to avoid falling foul of the Conventicle Act.[134] In time, they became bolder, especially after the Act lapsed. They preached to larger groups and travelled widely: Heywood covered much of West Yorkshire and Lancashire, recreating the itinerancy which had been an important part of puritan ministry before the civil wars.[135] A short period of persecution in 1670, after which Martindale became Lord Delamere's domestic chaplain,[136] was followed by the Declaration of Indulgence in 1672. Martindale doubted its legality and disliked the granting of toleration to Papists, Quakers and 'all other wicked sects'. Philip Henry remarked 'the danger is lest the allowing of separate places help to overthrow our parish order . . . and beget divisions and animosities amongst us'.[137] Nevertheless both accepted licences and resumed preaching, although Henry wished the minister of the parish had been consulted first. Newcome had no such qualms; nor had Heywood, who opened a meeting house at

Northowram and later welcomed part of an Independent congregation whose preacher had died.[138] After the licences were withdrawn, Henry gave up preaching for a while, but was arrested in 1681 preaching to 143 people. Martindale concentrated on his duties in the Delamere household, troubled that he ministered to so few people.[139] Newcome held only private meetings after 1673 and attended his parish church even in the 1680s, despite the minister's frequent diatribes against nonconformists.[140]

The varied experiences of these ejected ministers illustrate their dilemmas. Heywood eventually accepted that the logical consequence of ejection was to found his own congregation and that the presbyterians, like it or not, had become a sect: indeed, they had tacitly recognized this when they took out licences.[141] Many younger presbyterians either gave up hope of comprehension or decided that they did not want to be part of such a 'corrupt' body: presbyterian ordinations, suspended after 1662, resumed in 1672, although there is evidence of one at Exeter in 1666.[142] In 1672 some presbyterians, who had earlier sought to complement church services, began to compete instead, meeting at the same time, but few seem to have taken on the full attributes of 'churches', providing communion and drawing up lists of members.[143] Others continued to hope for comprehension. For Henry, the bond between pastor and people remained strong. He had felt obliged to witness against 'corruption' such as the use of the sign of the cross in baptism, 'but not therefore to separate from God's public worship'.[144] He found little 'sweetness and delight' in secret worship: unlike Josselin, he yearned to take communion at Easter, but his conscience would not allow him to kneel.[145] He believed that a 'church of Christ' should be governed by its pastors and that 'prelates' had no right to impose their wishes on the ministers, but rejected separation. The Independents, he wrote, 'unchurch the nation. . . . pluck up the hedge of parish order . . . [and] throw the ministry common and allow persons to preach who are unordained'. (However, he admired their discipline and solidarity.)[146] His ideal was of cooperation, with sober conformists allowing sober nonconformists to preach occasionally in the churches, removing misunderstandings and uniting them against the common enemy, the papists. His ideal was shared by some MPs, notably Birch, who argued that nonconformists should be allowed to preach in chapels and churches in which there was no preaching. He found little support in the Commons.[147] Henry remained torn between his refusal to conform and his refusal to separate. As Newcome put it, in 1662: 'The Royalists throw us among the fanatics because of piety. The fanatics throw us to them because of our loyalty. These two extremes harden one another and hate us, but God knows us and will own us.' To which Henry would have added 'amen'.[148]

Few agonised more about these matters than Richard Baxter. He normally attended his parish church, which had a learned preaching minister, and he was ready to preach, pray or take communion with Presbyterians, Independents or 'honest Anabaptists'.[149] He thought it lawful to kneel for communion and wear a surplice, although he would not willingly do so himself; he did not think it lawful to make the sign of the cross in baptism.[150] He disliked lay elders – his ideal form of church polity was 'limited episcopacy' – but disliked authoritarian 'prelates' who had driven godly ministers out of the Church, usurped those powers of moral discipline which should have belonged to the parish clergy and used them ineffectually.[151] On the other hand, the separatists had corrupted Cromwell's army, overturned all government and brought forth 'Quakers, Seekers, Ranters and Infidels'.[152] He accused them of both 'people-pleasing' and unchurching the greater part of the people, leaving them with nothing but 'public preaching'.[153] His own ministry was designed to supplement that of the established church: even when he took out a licence in 1672, he would not preach at the time of Anglican services.[154] After the licences were withdrawn, the presbyterians' exiguous synodical organization disintegrated; younger preachers, the 'Ducklings', under pressure from their followers, began to form 'gathered churches'.[155] But Baxter was always closer to 'sober conformists', or 'pious conformable men' than he was to the Independents.[156] Theologically he moved away from the 'Ducklings' towards a Calvinism tempered by Arminianism.[157] As the older 'Dons', who shared his 'church nostalgia', died off, he became an isolated and embittered figure. By 1680 few of the presbyterian clergy were really interested in comprehension; most accepted that they were Dissenters, along with the Independents, Baptists and Quakers.

Presbyterian laypeople sustained the ambivalence for much longer. They were not required to subscribe fully to the Prayer Book and had the option of partial or occasional conformity. (Henry stressed that he attended church as a private person, not as a minister.)[158] Many came only for the sermon and still more failed to take communion, except when they needed to qualify for office: 'it is a madness to lose an office for a bit of bread and a cup of wine'.[159] Of the 'puritan' peers and gentry, virtually all made at least some show of conformity to the church, although many also attended conventicles or kept nonconformist chaplains. Lord Wharton was several times found at a conventicle, but escaped punishment, thanks to his privilege as a peer.[160] The Earl of Anglesey, who consistently promoted the interests of nonconformists on the privy council, regularly went to Anglican sermons and mixed socially with bishops (and Catholics), but John Owen preached at his home.[161] As patrons of churches, heads of families, magistrates, MPs, peers and even privy councillors, puritan landowners were able to soften the rigours of conformity and protect pastors and people against the penalties of the law. In towns semi-conformist magistrates showed little eagerness to punish Dissent. As one Oxfordshire parson complained, Presbyterians were 'like the borderers betwixt two kingdoms, one can't tell what prince they are subject to'.[162] This frontier position enabled them to cushion the impact of persecution for most of the reign.

The nature of Dissent: Independents, Baptists and Quakers

If the frontiers between Churchmen and Presbyterians were blurred, there was no such ambivalence about their relations with the sects. Independents and Baptists had welcomed (or at least condoned) the regicide; Baptists and Quakers had actively opposed the Restoration. There was never any prospect of their being incorporated into the national church, because their conception of a church was exclusive rather than inclusive. For Baptists and Independents, a church was a voluntary association of 'visible saints', prepared to subscribe to the church's confession of faith and to submit to its discipline. For the Quakers, admission to 'membership' was for the moment more informal, but to stay the course those who attended meetings had to give evidence of their 'light' and submit to the admonition of fellow Friends.

By 1659, Independents and Baptists had become introverted and defensive: toleration was all they asked. The Independents' emphasis on congregational autonomy militated against the creation of a coherent national network, although they had cooperated with Presbyterians in the later 1650s against the Quaker threat. This cooperation was renewed in the Merchants' lectures at Pinners' Hall, started in 1672, but divisions soon appeared, especially after Baxter preached against the 'unwarrantable narrowing of Christ's church'.[163] The most prominent Independent, John Owen, tried to use his moral authority to resolve disputes in other churches, but he sought the endorsement of other ministers and his advice was not necessarily taken.[164] The Baptists had organized earlier and more fully. The Particular Baptists published a confession of faith in 1644 and had set up a national association; the General Baptists followed suit, but remained less tightly organized. Despite the Baptists' reputation as 'the fount of all heresies', their reasons for organizing were primarily defensive, to distance themselves from the excesses of the Anabaptists of Münster in the 1530s. This defensiveness became more marked as the Quakers made inroads into their membership. Many took up arms in defence of the republic in 1659, fearing that the restoration of monarchy would mean an end to religious liberty. When the king returned, both Independents and Baptists hastened to assure him that they were peaceable and harmless.[165]

The Quakers were far from defensive in the 1650s. As they swept down from the North, fighting the 'Lamb's War', even Baptists denounced their sensationalism and attacks on the authority of Scripture. From an early stage George Fox had struggled to establish control over the movement he had unleashed. Parliament's furious reaction to James Nayler's 'blasphemous' entry into Bristol in 1656 made it imperative to curb its wilder elements and sanitize its public image. This became all the more necessary after the Quakers' very visible efforts had failed to prevent the Restoration[166] and after Venner's rising of January 1661 showed that radical sectarians were prepared to rebel. Fox responded with his 'peace testimony', committing Friends to pacifism: henceforth they refused to serve in the militia (or to pay the militia rate). He also set out to repackage Quakerism as non-violent and innocuous. In the process, he and his aides and successors, such as William Penn, George Keith and Robert Barclay, sought to stamp the authority of the London meetings on those in the provinces. A system of internal censorship was set up,[167] missives were sent out and agents from 'head office' were sent to compose disputes, or secure compliance, in local meetings. The London leadership wished to end the shock tactics of the 'Lamb's War' and, through the press and skilled political lobbying,[168] to minimize or explain away the theological and other differences between Quakers and other Dissenters. Its ultimate triumphs came with the inclusion of Quakers in the 1689 Toleration Act and the Affirmation Act of 1696, which allowed Quakers to 'affirm' rather than swear in civil cases.[169]

There has been some debate how far Quakerism changed at the local level. Nicholas Morgan argued that there was considerable resistance from provincial Quakers, especially in the North, to what was seen as the betrayal of the principles of the movement (including a reduced role for women). Lancashire Quakers continued to refuse to swear oaths or pay tithes well into the eighteenth century.[170] David Scott argued that York Quakers had never shown much enthusiasm for the Lamb's War. They were well integrated into civic life and were concerned to maintain a good reputation 'amongst all sober people of other persuasions'.[171] These conflicting views highlight the paradoxes of Restoration Quakerism. A movement built on the 'inner light' of individuals developed much the most coherent and all-pervasive sectarian organization. Quakers cited Scripture to support their claim that its authority was inferior to that of the 'inner light'. While refusing to recognize the legitimacy of 'carnal' law, they exploited legal technicalities and loopholes in order to escape punishment.[172] Although Quakers were apparently well-integrated economically and socially into their communities, they maintained their singularity of speech, dress and behaviour – a singularity more marked than that of other sects or pre-civil war puritans.[173] And, while stressing their new-found pacifism and scaling down the Lamb's War, they retained their confrontational approach, even if the urge to shock now gave way to bloody-minded defiance. Quakers occasionally still went naked for a sign[174] and resorted to physical violence.[175] They caused offence by opening their shops on Christmas Day or 30 January and continued to issue challenges to the Anglican clergy.[176] When their meeting houses were closed, they refused to give security not to meet and met in the street or on the beach.[177]

It is often said that the experience of persecution fused the disparate sects – and eventually the Presbyterians as well – into a single phenomenon called 'Dissent' (or 'Nonconformity'). The fact that the relationship between Church and Dissent was a major political issue from the 1670s to the reign of Anne should not blind us to the fact that there were deep fissures within 'Dissent'. Presbyterians, Independents, Baptists and Quakers engaged in fierce polemics against one another, in print and in the meeting house.[178] Baxter saw some nonconformists as more 'tolerable' than others and was alarmed by the emergence of 'Seekers and I know not what' in Middlesex in 1670. The old radical Vavasour Powell complained of the havoc wrought by the Quakers.[179] But Baxter conceded that in 1664 the Quakers, by insisting on meeting publicly at stated times, drew most of the burden of persecution upon themselves and many others felt a grudging, if exasperated, admiration for their fortitude. In Suffolk in 1671, a group of Quakers refused to obey a summons by a constable, who was eventually reduced to stacking them in a cart and unloading them at the magistrate's door.[180] Although their defiance, oath refusal and careful record-keeping made them seem dangerous to the state – a proposal to include them in the 1672 Declaration of Indulgence was dropped[181] – it was also acknowledged that they led good lives and that their sufferings aroused compassion. Williamson wrote in 1671 that they 'have no pitiers so long as they are not beaten', but they often were: it has been estimated that as many as 15,000 were fined, imprisoned or transported under Charles II and 450 died.[182] Despite their singularity and the gulf between their theology and that of other nonconformists, their courage and determination in the face of persecution made them standard-bearers for nonconformity as a whole. Moreover, respect for their moral integrity, not least in business – an integrity which did not depend on observing oaths – reintegrated them into the broad spectrum of puritan values. Once seen as threatening to destroy English puritanism, the Quakers provided a catalyst for its transformation into Dissent.

Persecution

Of all manifestations of conflict, religious persecution was perhaps the most widespread and emotive. 1681–85 saw the most vigorous persecution of the century, but such vigour was the exception rather than the rule. The chronology of persecution will be considered in the chapters that follow. My aim here is to ask more general questions.

The history of persecution tends to favour its victims and is usually written by them: Quakers gathered and published evidence of sufferings to win sympathy for their cause, much as Foxe had done for early English Protestants. Liberal-minded historians find it hard to empathize with persecutors but there was a rationale to persecution. Religious nonconformity was seen as a threat to the state. It was divisive: 'the running into parties by multitudes . . . is a great disturbance both to our church and state'.[183] Private opinions were not dangerous: large gatherings of religious dissidents were. It was noted that Dissenters made a point of emphasizing their large numbers, as if to intimidate king and Parliament.[184] It should be stressed that whereas, before the civil wars, puritans had been harassed by church courts and the crown, using powers that were open to question, the persecution of dissent under Charles II rested squarely on the authority of Parliament. Against the authority of the body which articulated the collective will of the nation, appeals to individual 'conscience' counted for nothing. Refusal to submit to lawful authority was evidence of spiritual pride and probably seditious intent. The claim to be guided by conscience, like the Quaker claim to an 'inner light', could be used to justify anything, including popery and the most abhorrent heresies.[185] The king had promised liberty to tender consciences in the Declaration of Breda, but (as was often pointed out) he had added the qualifications that liberty should be granted only to such as 'do not disturb the peace of the kingdom' – which (for many) the Dissenters did – and that any indulgence would be granted by Parliament, which instead passed the Act of Uniformity and other measures against Dissent.[186] The identification of religious dissent with political sedition was supported by reference to the civil wars. 'Pretended conscience' had 'murdered the king, dissolved the parliament and enslaved the liberty of the nation'. 'A puritan' declared one MP 'was ever a rebel'. Many preachers, declared another, had Charles I's blood on their hands. When debating a proposal to bring some of the presbyterian clergy into the church, Henry Coventry declared 'I will never receive the blood of my saviour from that hand which stinks with the blood of my great master'.[187] Given what the Royalists had suffered at the hands of the 'fanatics', any punishment that they now received was not only deserved but mild.[188]

Such arguments show the hatreds aroused by civil war, but also insecurity and fear. Nonconformist sources depict their meetings as peaceful religious gatherings and those present as innocent victims. Others' perceptions were different. Defiance of authority escalated into wantonly offensive behaviour and outright violence. The years immediately following the Act of Uniformity saw a series of insults to the Prayer Book, communion vessels and the conforming clergy.[189] Large meetings refused to disperse and those who attended them used violence against the king's officers and rescued those whom they had arrested.[190] Not only did they insist on meeting at the time of divine service in Anglican churches but they posted guards who were allegedly armed (even the Quakers).[191] Magistrates and officers charged with suppressing the meetings were threatened.[192] Informers were stoned by 'boys', beaten up and even killed.[193] Even if they were not threatened with physical violence, informers or magistrates who tried to enforce the laws might face vexatious lawsuits.[194] An Anglican minister who tried to preach in a Quaker meeting house in 1670 was set upon by a mob.[195] At times the authorities in substantial towns like Coventry and Newcastle seemed to have lost control and the same seemed possible in London in 1670.[196] Small wonder that clergymen and officials feared for their safety.[197]

There were also religious arguments for persecution, resting partly on the authority of king and Parliament – once commanded, 'things indifferent' ceased to be so[198] – partly on Anglican ecclesiology. Most Christians assumed that God's truth was one and indivisible, but opinions differed as to how mere mortals could come to that truth. Some argued that individuals could do so, through Bible reading or the inner light, others that there must be one body which could state that truth with certainty, a body to which Christ had transmitted his own authority. For Catholics, that body was the church of Rome; for many of its members, it was the Church of England. The years without monarchy had seen a greater emphasis on the episcopal element of the church's authority at the expense of the crown's. Moreover, the growing emphasis on the sacerdotal, as opposed to the evangelical, aspect of the priesthood created a belief that the salvation of the laity required a submission to the clergy's spiritual direction akin to that demanded by the Roman church. To plead individual conscience against the institutional wisdom and Christ-given authority of the church was presumptuous. It was the duty of the clergy to guide their flocks and to subject them, where necessary, to wholesome and necessary reproof: it was better that they should suffer physical or pecuniary punishments in this world than suffer eternal torments in the next. It was also vital to preserve England from the sin of schism.[199]

This view of the church may seem deeply patronizing towards the laity, but it offered a rationale, indeed created an imperative, for persecution which convinced an increasing number of both clergy and laymen. Against such claims were deployed a variety of arguments for comprehension and toleration. Some rested on lay resentment of 'priestcraft': it was alleged that the clergy tried to establish dominion over the laity and sought to give the church dominion over the state, effectively depriving the king of his powers. Thus we find advocates of religious liberty arguing that the king could use his prerogative to grant toleration, while Cavalier Churchmen insisted that he was bound by Act of Parliament.[200] Those who favoured comprehension called for a relaxation of the rigorous conformity required of the parish clergy, stressed the theological common ground between conformists and presbyterians and looked back longingly to the Church of James I. There were calls to bring more people into the Church, to strengthen it against the papists and perhaps also against the sectaries.[201] Arguments about the need for Protestant unity were also invoked by advocates of toleration, but they used other arguments as well. Some were essentially religious. How could it be wrong, it was asked, to preach the pure Word of God or to follow one's conscience? Should one not obey God rather than man? Those who were now being harassed were, like the primitive Christians under the Roman Empire and the Protestants under Mary Tudor, true worshippers of God.[202] The Independents argued that they professed the fundamentals of Protestant belief on which all the Reformed churches agreed and, in 1660, Independents and Baptists claimed that, God's providence having restored the king, he should now do God's work by granting liberty to tender consciences, as promised at Breda. They also claimed that toleration would bring peace and stability. Sir Thomas Littleton claimed that restraint of conscience had caused the civil war.[203]

Another set of arguments rested on the economic benefits of toleration. In the 1660s there was much debate about the fall in food prices and decay of rents in England and the spectacular commercial success of the Dutch. There was a growing conviction that England was under-populated and suffering a shortage of skilled workers. It was argued that more people were needed to consume England's food surplus and that earlier immigrants had brought economic and technological benefits.[204] Persecution discouraged immigration and provoked emigration: there were claims that craftsmen were about to leave the country in their thousands or had already left,[205] although others argued that few or none had actually gone.[206] It was pointed out that the crown had earlier encouraged immigrants from the Low Countries and France and had allowed them their own churches, exempt from the requirements of the Act of Uniformity. Some argued that it was illogical to allow such freedom of worship to 'Dutch' and French immigrants but not to native English; others claimed that the prosperity of Holland and France was based on toleration.[207] It may seem strange, in view of the pressure on the Huguenots, that France should be cited as a model of tolerance, but Protestants enjoyed a statutory right to freedom of worship there which Dissenters did not have in England; some suggested that the French practice of allowing limited public worship and no private meetings could be followed in England.[208] The issue of toleration played a prominent part in the debates on bills for a general naturalization of immigrants brought in in 1667 and 1673: some argued that this would allow in sectaries of all kinds and so bring in toleration by the back door.[209] Further bills were brought in in 1678 and 1680, but in the early 1680s the French and Dutch churches were criticized by Tories for encouraging nonconformity.[210]

Moving from the debate about persecution to the reality, two points should be emphasized. First, not only local officials but also policy-makers, judges and legislators were often uncertain which laws were in force and how they were to be interpreted. In the early 1660s the only statute in force against conventicles was that of 1593 (although some were unsure whether it **was** still in force) and lords lieutenant were uncertain about the legal powers of the militia (and the attendant voluntary troops of horse).[211] Orders to suppress conventicles desribed them as riotous and unlawful or seditious, without referring to specific Acts.[212] The 1664 Conventicle Act clarified the position, but some of its penalties proved too severe to be realistic: poor Nonconformists simply could not pay the fines it laid down, which led some magistrates to release them and others to proceed under other laws with lesser penalties.[213] When it lapsed in 1668 (or 1669 – opinions differed) there was another period of uncertainty; in 1669 the council asked the judges which laws could be used against conventicles.[214] The Conventicle Act of 1670 again clarified the matter and was followed by a fierce but brief surge of persecution. Its enforcement was suspended by the 1672 Declaration of Indulgence. The Declaration was cancelled in 1673 but the licences issued under it were not formally withdrawn until 1675.[215]

After 1675 the legal position was in theory clear, but the laws were still enforced only spasmodically until the early 1680s, because local officials were uncertain whether the central government **wanted** them to be enforced. From about 1668 most judges took a firm line against Dissent, but earlier they often used their influence to secure acquittals.[216] The greatest uncertainty surrounded the attitude of the king. From the Declaration of Breda to the Declaration of Indulgence and beyond, Charles indicated that he inclined towards comprehension and/or toleration. His repeated changes of direction allowed Dissenters to convince themselves that even when he ordered the laws to be enforced, he did not really mean it. Those in the provinces noted the access he allowed to leading Dissenters and the fact that their brethren in the capital generally went unmolested.[217] Frequent rumours emanating from London that the king would grant indulgence encouraged provincial Dissenters to meet.[218] Great men at court gave out that the king did not want a severe execution of the laws; it was well known that privy councillors like Anglesey and Carlisle strongly opposed persecution, which suggested that orders to enforce the laws could soon be rescinded.[219] Such uncertainty discouraged those magistrates who were eager to enforce the laws, who feared they would be disavowed or reprimanded.[220] For this reason, they continually sought approval from 'above'.[221] In 1679–80 the king came under considerable political pressure not to enforce the laws, but even after the Oxford Parliament local Tories complained that they were still not receiving the endorsement they expected.[222]

Requests to king and council for explicit orders to act against conventicles often reflected a desire for reassurance, but there were other possible motives. For those less than eager to proceed they offered a means of delay or of shifting the responsibility for persecution. It was a tactic which often worked: the king could prove very reluctant to send an explicit letter of command, preferring seemingly unforced compliance.[223] Many magistrates were reluctant to convict nonconformists, even if they disliked their principles. Thomas Pepys declared that he would not serve as a JP because 'he is not free to exercise punishment according to the Act against Quakers and other people, for religion'. Sir John Busby was careful not to be at home when informations were brought against conventicles. Sir Ralph Verney disliked informers and thought the papists more dangerous than the 'foolish fanatics'.[224] The Earl of Carlisle wrote that he intended to keep the peace with a minimum of 'oppression'.[225] Lord Townshend, who was eager to suppress conventicles in 1663 was later much more reluctant.[226] Considerations of simple humanity[227] could be reinforced by neighbourhood and kinship. In Cornwall, where the JPs seemed reluctant to prosecute Prebyterians, Bishop Ward thought that they 'are most of them that way inclined, or else by kindred or debts or wives or some other mischief brought to a connivance.'[228] Such ties were even stronger in towns. Members of municipal elites were not only more likely than the county gentry to intermarry, but they were also bound together by a sense of corporate solidarity, contiguity, common economic interests and the simple need to do business with one another. A sheriff of London told a group of bishops in 1675 that he could not trade with his neighbours one day and send them to gaol the next.[229] In the 1680s, the bishops and other local Tories devoted considerable effort to ensuring that the laws against Dissent were enforced in the towns.[230] Reluctance to enforce the laws was not confined to the magistrates. Churchwardens were loath to make presentments, constables and other officials expressed doubts whether they could legally break down doors or proved unable to recognize those present at meetings. When goods were distrained in lieu of fines, few could be found to buy them.[231] Juries often refused to convict, in defiance of both the evidence and the judge. The Recorder of London allegedly said in 1676 that 'he knew not where to pick a jury out in the City to convict a nonconformist'.[232] The mayor of Taunton, who conducted a one-man crusade against meetings, remarked in 1683 that he had given up his shop as nobody would buy from him.[233]

In the last four years of the reign, local opposition to enforcing the laws was broken down, thanks to the determined efforts of the more militant clergy and Tories, endorsed more hesitantly by the central government. Before then, persecution was intermittent, concentrated at times when the king, for whatever reason, gave it his active support. There were numerous acts of cruelty and injustice, especially against Quakers: these were vulnerable people and there were always some ready to exploit their vulnerability.[234] Normally, however, persecution was spasmodic and localized and rarely amounted to a sustained campaign that could seriously divide the nation. Consider the experience of the Welsh Quaker Richard Davies. In theory he spent most of the 1660s in prison, but his 'prison' consisted of a house separate from the main gaol in Welshpool from which he could come and go as he pleased. He held meetings there and travelled to South Wales, Bristol and London.[235] He found the magistrates of Pembrokeshire, Cardiganshire and Carmarthenshire very civil: some even came to his meetings.[236] The 'priest' of the town, whom Davies had challenged in his own church, proved a good neighbour, asking him for less in tithe than he was entitled to.[237] In 1670 an informer planned to bring charges against Davies, for a share of the fine, but found himself ostracized and lost his livelihood. He went to Lord Herbert of Cherbury for a warrant to disrupt the meeting; Herbert refused, saying the Quakers were harmless. Later, when Colonel Price of Rhiwlas, 'put on by some peevish clergymen', persecuted his Quaker tenants and neighbours, Davies approached his 'particular friends', Lord and Lady Powis (both Catholics) to ask the Marquis of Worcester to send Price a letter, which he did, strongly advising him to desist.[238] Davies was fortunate to have friends in high places: even in the 1680s Penn persuaded Lord Hyde, generally regarded as a strong Churchman, to write to the Bishop of Llandaff on his behalf.[239] This is not to suggest that Davies did not have his tribulations – he did. But I would argue that there is only limited evidence of sustained persecution or extensive sectarian bigotry for much of the reign and that when religious divisions began to bite deeply, from the mid-1670s, they did so in conjunction with a growing **political** polarization.

Notes

1 See N. Tyacke, 'Anglican Attitudes: Some recent writings on English Religious History from the Reformation to the Civil War', *JBS*, XXXV, 1996, pp. 139–67, especially p. 150.

2 See above all Collinson's *The Elizabethan Puritan Movement*, London, 1967, and *The Religion of Protestants: the Church in English Society 1559–1625*, Oxford, 1982.

3 C. Haigh, 'Church, Catholics and the People' in C. Haigh (ed.), *The Reign of Elizabeth I*, London, 1984, ch. 8, especially pp. 213–14; C. Haigh, 'Puritan evangelism in the reign of Elizabeth I', *EHR*, XCII, 1977, pp. 30–58.

4 C. Haigh, *English Reformations*, Oxford, 1993, pp. 290–1, where he explains the term 'parish anglican'.

5 J. Maltby, *Prayer Book and People in Elizabethan and Early Stuart England*, Cambridge, 1998, ch. 3, especially pp. 113–21.

6 *Ibid.*, pp. 100–6, 115–16.

7 E. Duffy, 'The Long Reformation: Catholicism, Protestantism and the Multitude' in N. Tyacke (ed.), *England's Long Reformation*, London, 1998, pp. 38–42.

8 *Ibid.*, p. 43.

9 P. Lake, 'Calvinism and the English Church, 1570–1635', *P & P*, no. 114, 1987, pp. 32–76; Maltby, *Prayer Book*, pp. 105–6, 131.

10 Evelyn, III.333; Bosher, pp. 64–5. By 1641 this view was accepted by many parish anglicans too: Maltby, *Prayer Book*, pp. 100–4.
11 See K. Fincham (ed.), *The Early Stuart Church 1603–42*, London, 1993, chs 2, 4, 7.
12 Collinson, *Religion of Protestants*, pp. 48–51; Fincham (ed.), *Early Stuart Church*, pp. 23–36 and ch. 4.
13 N. Tyacke, 'Puritanism, Arminianism and Counter-Revolution' in C. Russell (ed.), *Origins of the English Civil War*, London, 1973; N. Tyacke, *Anti-Calvinists*, Oxford, 1987; A. Fletcher, *A County Community in Peace and War: Sussex 1600–60*, London, 1975, ch. 4; Fincham (ed.), *Early Stuart Church*, chs 1, 2, 7.
14 See K. Sharpe, *The Personal Rule of Charles I*, New Haven, 1992, ch. 6; Tyacke, 'Anglican Attitudes', pp. 162–7.
15 Maltby, *Prayer Book*, pp. 108–10.
16 See P. Lake, 'The Laudian Style' in Fincham (ed.), *Early Stuart Church*, ch. 7 especially pp. 168–71.
17 A. Fletcher, *The Outbreak of the English Civil War*, London, 1981, especially ch. 3.
18 Morrill, *Nature*, ch. 4.
19 See Morrill, *Nature*, ch. 7; I.M. Green, 'The Persecution of "Scandalous" and "Malignant" Clergy during the English Civil War' *EHR*, XCIV, 1979, pp. 507–31; Jenkins, *Wales*, pp. 81–2. For Christmas, see A. Everitt, *The Community of Kent and the Great Rebellion*, Leicester, 1966, pp. 231–4.
20 C.G. Bolam, J. Goring, H.L. Short and R. Thomas, *The English Presbyterians*, London, 1968, pp. 43–4.
21 C. Durston and J. Eales (eds), *The Culture of English Puritanism 1560–1700*, London, 1996, chs 1, 5; P. Collinson, 'The Cohabitation of the Godly and the Ungodly' in N. Tyacke, J. Israel and O. Grell (eds), *From Persecution to Toleration*, Oxford, 1991, ch. 3; P. Collinson, 'The English Conventicle' in W.J. Sheils and D. Wood (eds), *Voluntary Religion*, Oxford, 1986, pp. 223–59.
22 See Underdown, *Revel*; Stoyle, *Loyalty*.
23 See especially B. Worden, 'Cromwell and Toleration' in W.J. Sheils (ed.), *Persecution and Toleration*, Oxford, 1984, pp. 199–233; W.M. Lamont, *Godly Rule: Politics and Religion, 1603–60*, London, 1969, ch. 6.
24 R. Beddard, 'The Restoration Church' in J.R. Jones (ed.), *The Restored Monarchy, 1660–88*, London, 1979, pp. 156–9; J. Spurr, *The Restoration Church of England*, New Haven, 1991, chs 1, 3; Bosher, pp. 72–3, 91–100; Green, pp. 81–2.
25 Duffy, 'Long Reformation', pp. 45–52.
26 D. Hirst, 'The Failure of Godly Rule in the English Republic', *P & P*, no. 132, 1991, pp. 33–66; A. Hughes, 'The Frustrations of the Godly' in J. Morrill (ed.), *Revolution and Restoration*, London, 1992, pp. 70–90; R. Clark, 'Why was the Re-establishment of the Church of England in 1662 Possible? Derbyshire: A Provincial Perspective', *Midland History* VIII, 1983, pp. 87–90.
27 See W.M. Lamont, *Richard Baxter and the Millennium*, London, 1979.
28 Clark, 'Derbyshire', pp. 86–95; Spurr, *Church*, pp. 36–7.
29 See G.F. Nuttall, *Visible Saints: The Congregational Way*, London, 1948; M. Tolmie, *The Triumph of the Saints: The Separate Churches of London 1614–49*, Cambridge, 1977.
30 E. Ludlow, *A Voyce from the Watch Tower*, B. Worden (ed.), Camden Soc., 1978, pp. 149–50.

31 See R. Thomas, 'Comprehension and Indulgence' in *From Unif.*; J. Spurr, 'The Church of England, Comprehension and the Toleration Act of 1689', *EHR*, CIV, 1989, 927–46.
32 Bosher, pp. 5, 27–8.
33 A. Whiteman, *The Compton Census of 1676*, London, 1986, prints the returns and discusses their accuracy. For the Evans figures, see M. Watts, *The Dissenters from the Reformation to the French Revolution*, Oxford, 1978, pp. 267–89, especially p. 270.
34 Bosher, pp. 16–18, 28–9; Whiteman, 'The Restoration of the Church of England' in *From Unif.*, p. 36–7.
35 Bosher, p. 271.
36 Green, pp. 22–4, 90–2; N. Sykes, *From Sheldon to Secker*, Cambridge, 1959, pp. 6–8.
37 See LPL, MS 1126, passim.
38 Sykes, *Sheldon*, p. 5.
39 The Lords had added a proviso that ejected clergymen should receive 20% of their stipends, but the Commons rejected it: *CJ*, VIII.414; *LJ*, XI.449.
40 Bosher, p. 241.
41 Browning, *Docts.*, pp. 377–82. For the Commons' insistence on 24 August, see *CJ*, VIII.409.
42 Watts, *Dissenters*, pp. 39–40. Some doubted whether the Act was still in force: *SR*, V.516.
43 *CJ*, VIII.252; Egerton MS 2043, fo. 7.
44 *SR*, V.350–1.
45 *SR*, V.516–20.
46 Browning, *Docts.*, pp. 382–4; Seaward, pp. 192–3.
47 Tanner MS 48, fo. 45.
48 Marvell, II.314.
49 Green, p. 142; A. Whiteman, 'The re-establishment of the Church of England, 1660–3', *TRHS* 5th series V, 1955, pp. 111–31.
50 A. Swatland, *The House of Lords in the Reign of Charles II*, Cambridge, 1996, pp. 165–72; *Rawdon*, p. 138.
51 Bosher, pp. 245–7.
52 Sykes, *Sheldon*, pp. 36–44.
53 Carte MSS 31, fo. 602, 32, fo. 3, 47, fo. 359; Pepys, III.186; Martindale, p. 167; Newcome, *Diary*, p. 101; *RB*, II.302.
54 *CSPD 1663–64*, p. 64; *Mather*, p. 207; Seaward, pp. 181–6.
55 J.J. Jeremiah, 'Edward Reynolds, 1599–1676: "Pride of the Presbyterian Party"', unpublished Ph.D. thesis, George Washington, 1992, pp. 330–2; Bosher, pp. 271–3.
56 Clar MS 77, fo. 157; Clarendon, II.252.
57 *CSPD 1660–61*, p. 546; Green, ch. 8.
58 Clar MS 77, fo. 157; Bodl, MS Add c. 308, fo. 29; Grey, I.121; Whiteman, 'Re-establishment', pp. 117–20.
59 *RB* II.386–7.
60 LPL, MS 1126, fos 2, 10, 11, 16, 54.
61 *Ibid.*, fos 20, 24, 26, 36.
62 *Ibid.*, fos 51, 26.
63 J. Spurr 'Religion in Restoration England' in Glassey (ed.), *Reigns*, p. 92; Spurr, *Church*, pp. 42–7.

64 Josselin, *passim*; Rawl MS D1163, fo. 11.
65 LPL, MS 1126, fo. 56 and *passim*.
66 Bosher, p. 232; *Cosin*, II.ix; DCLD, Hunter MSS 9, nos 165, 269, 137, p. 4; DUL, Cosin Letter Book 1B, no. 182.
67 *HMC 9th Report, Appendix II*, p. 460; Tanner MS 37, fo. 139. For similar problems in Devon, see Bodl, MS Add c. 305, fo. 142.
68 *SR*, V.576–7.
69 Bodl, MS Add c. 305, fo. 175; Scott, 'York', pp. 102–3, 148.
70 *CSPD 1670*, p. 303.
71 *CCSP*, V.146–7; *CSPD 1664–65*, pp. 458–9, *1670*, p. 401; D.L. Wykes, 'The bishop of Gloucester and nonconformity in the late 1660s', *Southern History*, 1995, p. 35.
72 *CSPD 1680–81*, p. 423.
73 LPL MS 1126, fos 18, 17, 47.
74 Green, pp. 196–9; but see also Seaward, pp. 58–9.
75 CKS, U269/K2/124A; DCLD, Hunter MS 9, no. 269.
76 Granville, II.23–4.
77 Bodl, MS Add c. 308, fos 29, 114; Egerton MS 2539, fo. 168; Milward, p. 191. For fees, see Clar MS 92, fo. 95; *HMC le Fleming*, p. 183. For excommunication, see M636/31, Edmund to John Verney, 6 and 27 May, 27 June, 4 July, Sir Ralph to Edmund, 17 June 1678.
78 Bodl, MS Add c. 308, fos 70–1, 110, 114, 119.
79 *Ibid.*, fo. 139. Yelverton was against turning the Worcester House Declaration into a bill: Bodl, MS Eng Letters c. 210, p. 49. See also *RB*, II.380.
80 Aubrey, *Lives*, p. 473; Bodl, MS Add c. 305, fo. 227. See also *CSPD 1671–72*, p. 74; Coventry MS 7, fos 66, 72, 92.
81 Bodl, MS Add c. 305, fo. 232.
82 Tanner MS 34, fo. 174.
83 Pepys, II.167; BL, Add MS 10116, fo. 237; *Cosin*, II.101; Burnet, *Hist*, I.320.
84 Milward, pp. 230–1; *RB*, III.181.
85 Rawl MS D1163, fos 12–13; Tanner MSS 35, fos 9, 36, fo. 235.
86 DCLD, Hunter MS 9, no. 165; *Cosin*, II.ix; J. Pruett, *The Parish Clergy under the later Stuarts: the Leicestershire Experience*, Urbana, 1978, pp. 118–9.
87 PC 2/57, fos 8, 49, 56; *CSPD 1667–68*, p. 427, *1670*, p. 626.
88 Pepys, I.259; Heywood, I.180; *HMC 5th Report*, pp. 199–200.
89 Rawl MS D1163, fo. 16.
90 It was reported that the Presbyterian Thomas Manton was forced by his parishioners to use the Prayer Book: Rugg, p. 154.
91 *HMC 5th Report*, p. 199; DCLD, Hunter MS 7, fo. 38; *CCSP*, V.53; Schellinks, p. 140; Clar MS 73, fos 216–7; Tanner MS 45, fo. 13; Bodl, MS Add c. 305, fos 156, 231; Rawl MS D1163, fo. 21; *CSPD 1671*, p. 427, *1671–72*, p. 104, *1677–78*, p. 400.
92 Leicester, *Charges*, p. 47; *CSPD 1667*, p. 30; D.A. Spaeth, 'Common Prayer? Popular observance of the Anglican liturgy in Restoration Wiltshire' in S.J. Wright (ed.), *Parish, Church and People*, London, 1988, pp. 139–44; Spurr, *Church*, p. 354; Pruett, *Clergy*, p. 125.
93 LPL MS 1126, fo. 6.
94 Spaeth, in Wright (ed.), *Parish*, p. 145; W. Stevenson, 'The social integration of post-Restoration Dissenters' in M. Spufford, (ed.), *The World of Rural Dissenters 1525–1725*, Cambridge, 1995, ch. 9, especially pp. 368–72.

95 LPL, MS 1126, fo. 38; Rawl MS D1163, fos 16–17; Spaeth in Wright (ed.), *Parish*, pp. 130–9; Hirst, 'Failure', p. 47; Hughes, 'Frustrations', p. 81; *RB*, III.26; *Bax. Corr.*, II.70.
96 BL, M636/28, Sir Ralph to Edmund Verney, 24 December 1674, M636/33, same to same, 29 December 1679; Bradfer, Lord to Lady Yarmouth, 31 March and 3 April 1676.
97 Pepys, III.54, VII.99; Josselin, p. 516.
98 DUL, Cosin Letter Book IB, no. 179; Granville, I.172, 174–80, II.23–4, 42–3, 48–54; *CSPD 1683–84*, p. 88; Evelyn, III.317, IV.132+n; Tanner MS 47, fo. 203. See also *CSPD 1679–80*, p. 565.
99 A. Hunt, 'The Lord's supper in early modern England', *P & P*, no. 161, 1998, pp. 81–2; Spurr in Glassey (ed.), *Reigns*, pp. 113–4.
100 Duffy, 'Long Reformation', pp. 52–6.
101 Pepys, I.271; BL, Add MS 63057B, fo. 35; Jeremiah, 'Reynolds', pp. 325–7; Evelyn, IV.330; Rawl MS C983, fos 22, 38–9; J. Barry, 'Bristol as a Reformation City' in Tyacke (ed.), *Long Reformation*, pp. 268–9; *CSPD 1663–64*, pp. 62, 222, *1675–76*, p. 176; Harl MS 7377, fo. 41; Tanner MS 34, fo. 27.
102 Pruett, *Clergy*, pp. 121–5; Spurr, *Church*, ch. 6
103 *CJ*, IX.259, 429, 441.
104 Harl MS 7377, fos 22, 41–2; BL, Add MS 29571, fo. 192; *CSPD 1671*, p. 427; *CJ*, IX.259; Grey, II.73; Carte MS 79, fo. 72. Sparrow found some of his clergy opposed to additional catechizing: Bodl, MS Add c. 305, fo. 227.
105 Henry, p. 79; Bodl, MS Add c. 305, fo. 205.
106 Barry in Wright (ed.), *Parish*, p. 165; Spurr in Glassey (ed.), *Reigns*, p. 107; N. Tyacke, 'Introduction' in Tyacke (ed.), *Long Reformation*, p. 24.
107 *CSPD 1661–62*, p. 517; Evelyn, III.543; DUL, Cosin Letter Book 1A, no. 83; Strong, p. 183.
108 Grey, III.16; Strong, p. 189.
109 Pepys, V.147; Grey, I.104, 228, 441–2, II.69–70 For Littleton, see Grey, I.112–3, 115–6, IV.294–5; Finch MS PP42, p. 8; Milward, pp. 218–9.
110 *CSPD 1685*, no. 172.
111 Beddard, 'Restoration', pp. 156–8; Seaward, p. 63.
112 See Wood, III.7; J.T. Cliffe, *The Puritan Gentry Besieged, 1650–1700*, London, 1993, pp. 152–6; N. Tyacke, 'Arminianism and the Theology of the Restoration Church' in S. Groenveld and M. Wintle (eds), *The Exchange of Ideas*, Britain and the Netherlands, XI, Zutphen, 1994, pp. 68–83.
113 Harl MS 7377, fo. 22; Milward, pp. 215, 217; Grey, I.420.
114 Martindale, pp. 170, 196; Lawrence, p. 48; Heywood, II.290–1; Davies, p. 79; Schellinks, pp. 127–8; Aubrey, *Lives*, p. 103; DCLD, Hunter MSS 9, nos 166–7, 137, p. 11; *CSPD 1667–68*, pp. 492–3; Bodl, MS Add c. 305, fos 231, 245. There is only one mention of a drunkard in LPL, MS 1126 (fo. 40) and Rawl MS D1163 (fo. 27). See also Pruett, *Clergy*, pp. 128–30.
115 Tanner MS 34, fo. 117.
116 CKS, U269/K2/124A.
117 Coventry MS 7, fo.18; Heywood, II.238, 252–3, 257; Newcome, *Diary*, pp. 56, 66, 74; Josselin, pp. 467, 476, 477, 509.
118 Martindale, *Life*, pp. 156–8. Col Birch blamed the Book of Sports for the outbreak of the Civil War: Grey, I.422.
119 Newcome, *Diary*, pp. 56, 66, 74, 75, 77, 82, 88, 91, 93, 96–7n.

120 See for example G. Holmes, *The Trial of Dr Sacheverell*, London, 1973, ch. 2 and G.V. Bennett, *The Tory Crisis in Church and State*, Oxford, 1975, ch. 1.
121 A.S.P. Woodhouse, *Puritanism and Liberty*, London, 1938, p. 97.
122 M. Clapinson (ed.), *Bishop Fell and Nonconformity*, Oxfordshire Record Society, LII, 1980, pp. 40–2. See also *CSPD 1670*, p. 313.
123 Clapinson, *Fell*, p. 32.
124 Whitelocke, pp. 696–7, 716–7, 770 and *passim*.
125 *Ibid.*, pp. 666, 689.
126 *Ibid.*, pp. 711–6, 718, 726, 817, 825.
127 *Ibid.*, pp. 798, 815.
128 *Ibid.*, pp. 678, 726.
129 See Pepys, IX.31, 45; *HMC Hastings*, II.374; *RB*, III. 24–5; Tanner MS 43, fo. 179; C. Robbins, 'The Oxford session of the Long Parliament of Charles II', *BIHR* XXI, 1946–48, pp. 222–3.
130 *RB*, II.386–7; Carte MS 32, fo. 35; Henry, p. 153.
131 *RB*, II.173, 278 (quoted).
132 Henry, pp. 99–101; Martindale, pp. 173–4, 199; Heywood, I.192.
133 Henry, p. 232; Martindale, pp. 192–3; Heywood, I.192.
134 Heywood, I.184–6, 188, 189, 255, 269, 271; Martindale, p. 176. See also *HMC le Fleming*, p. 71; *CSPD 1670*, p. 321.
135 Heywood, I.190–1, 194–6, 201–2, 223–5, 255; Martindale, pp. 193–4. See also Duffy, 'Long Reformation', pp. 38–40; LPL, MS 1126, fos 35–6; J.D. Ramsbottom, 'Presbyterians and "Partial Conformity" in the Restoration Church', *JEH*, XLIII, 1992, pp. 254, 263; Clifton, *Rebellion*, p. 49.
136 Heywood, I.270–1; Martindale, p. 197.
137 Martindale, p. 198; Henry, p. 250.
138 Martindale, pp. 198–9; Henry, pp. 250–3, 256; Newcome, *Autobiography*, I.199–200; Heywood, I.176, 289, II.17–37; for the Sowerby congregation see *ibid.*, II.31–2.
139 Henry, p. 299; Martindale, pp. 202–3.
140 Newcome, *Autobiography*, II.205–6, 232, 237, 244, 252, 257.
141 Bolam *et al.*, *Presbyterians*, pp. 89–90. Some realized this as early as 1662: Lawrence, p. 48.
142 *CSPD 1671*, p. 496; Bolam *et al.*, *Presbyterians*, p. 86.
143 Ramsbottom, 'Partial', pp. 257–63.
144 Henry, pp. 99 (quoted), 102–3, 127, 232, 259.
145 *Ibid.*, pp. 84, 133, 134, 145 (quoted), 177–9, 254; Josselin, p. 516.
146 Henry, pp. 184–5, 277.
147 *Ibid.*, p. 250; Grey, II.40, 89–90; *HMC Kenyon*, p. 84; Bodl, MS Rawl Letters 50, fo. 254.
148 Henry, p. 250; Newcome, *Diary*, p. 95.
149 *RB*, II.437; *Bax. Corr.*, II.73.
150 *Bax. Corr.*, II.73, 156.
151 *Bax. Corr.*, II.156; *RB*, II.217, 262, 396–407.
152 *Bax. Corr.*, II.92.
153 *Bax. Corr.*, II.93, 118, 69–71.
154 *Bax. Corr.*, II.167, 188–9; *RB*, III.46–7, 51–6.
155 *RB*, III.42–3, 73–4; *Bax. Corr.*, II.118.
156 *Bax. Corr.*, II.117–8; *RB*, III.62; Bolam *et al.*, *Presbyterians*, p. 97.

157 Bolam *et al.*, *Presbyterians*, pp. 95, 103–5.
158 Henry, p. 277.
159 Leicester, *Charges*, p. 47; *CSPD 1667*, p. 30, *1676–77*, p. 232 (quoted); Browning, *Docts*, p. 416; Morrice, p. 396.
160 BL, Add MS 36916, fo. 173; *CSPV 1669–70*, p. 174; DUL, Cosin Letter Book 5A, no. 69; Coventry MS 4, fo. 256; *HMC Buccleuch (Montagu House)*, I.321; M636/28, Sir Ralph to Edmund Verney, 1 March 1675.
161 BL, Add MS 40860, fos 6, 66, 91 and *passim*; Cliffe, *Gentry*, chs 7–10.
162 Clapinson, *Fell*, p. 2.
163 *RB*, III.103
164 J. Owen, *Correspondence*, P. Toon (ed.), Cambridge, 1970, pp. 147–8; *Bax. Corr.*, II.112.
165 Clar MS 73, fo. 314; M636/17, Engagement of the Baptists, 22 January 1661.
166 See the declaration of November 1660: *CSPD 1660–61*, p. 361.
167 See T. O'Malley, 'Defying the Powers and Tempering the Spirit: a review of Quaker Control over their Publications, 1672–89', *JEH*, XXXIII, 1982, pp. 72–88.
168 This had already started in 1661: *CSPD 1660–61*, p. 481; *HMC 5th Report*, p. 151; *HMC 7th Report*, p. 144; *LJ*, XI.268–9, 268–9, 273.
169 See in general H.L. Ingle, *First among Friends: George Fox and the Creation of Quakerism*, New York, 1994; C. Leachman, 'From an "unruly" sect' to a society of "strict unity": the development of Quakerism, c. 1650–89', unpublished Ph.D. thesis, University College, London, 1997.
170 N. Morgan, *Lancashire Quakers and the Establishment 1660–1730*, Halifax, 1993. See also the work on Quakers in Beverly Adams's forthcoming London thesis on Hertford.
171 Scott, 'York', pp. 23–5, 83–9 (quotation from p. 85), 112–3.
172 See C.W. Horle, *The Quakers and the English Legal System, 1660–88*, Philadelphia, 1988.
173 Stevenson in Spufford (ed.), *Dissenters*, pp. 361–3, 382–7.
174 *CSPD 1660–61*, p. 472; *HMC Hastings*, II.154.
175 BL, Add MS 32324, fo. 141; *CSPD 1670*, p. 314.
176 Stevenson in Spufford (ed.), *Dissenters*, pp. 365–7; *CSPD 1675–76*, p. 536, *1678*, p. 442, *1680–81*, pp. 541–2; Tanner MS 37, fo. 119; Davies, pp. 103–8.
177 *CSPD 1660–61*, p. 514, *1663–64*, pp. 435–6, *1670*, pp. 321, 361.
178 *CSPD 1678*, p. 417; *RB*, III.103, 174; *Bax. Corr.*, II.179–80; Heywood, II.240–3; Beverly Adams's forthcoming thesis.
179 *RB*, II.387; *Bax. Corr.*, II.87–8; Davies, p. 81.
180 *RB*, II.436; *CSPD 1671*, p. 419.
181 For records, see *CSPD 1660–61*, p. 481, *1670*, pp. 361, 542–3. For the indulgence, see SP 104/177, fo. 16.
182 *CSPD 1660–61*, p. 466, *1670*, p. 361, *1671–72*, p. 28 (quoted); Watts, *Dissenters*, p. 236.
183 Leicester, *Charges*, p. 79.
184 *Ibid.*, p. 78; Finch MS PP 20; Grey, I.418.
185 Grey, I.221; Milward, pp. 249–50.
186 Browning, *Docts*, p. 58; *CJ*, VIII.442–3; *LJ*, XI.449; Milward, p. 214.
187 Milward, p. 217; Grey, II.133–4; Newton, *House of Lyme*, p. 253.

188 Finch MS PP20; Grey, I.133, 221; Robbins, 'Oxford session', pp. 223–4.
189 *CSPD 1663–64*, p. 395, *1665–66*, p. 225; *HMC le Fleming*, p. 29; Carte MSS 80, fo. 878, 222 fos 4–5, 34; BL, Add MS 32324, fo. 143; PC 2/62, pp. 145–6.
190 *CSPD 1660–61*, pp. 127, 130, *1667*, p. 16, *1668–69*, p. 342, *1678*, pp. 415, 419–20, 447, *January–June 1683*, p. 53; Grey, I.295–6, 305; BL, Add MS 4182, fos 29, 43.
191 *CSPD 1678*, p. 442, *1680–81*, pp. 568–9, 640, *1682*, pp. 36–7; Coventry MS 7, fos 66, 82–3
192 *CSPD 1670*, pp. 226, 256, 259, *1671*, p. 114.
193 *CSPD 1663–64*, p. 603, *1670*, p. 376, *1673–75*, p. 396, *January–June 1683*, p. 75; Corie, *Correspondence*, pp. 36–7.
194 *CSPD 1671*, pp. 20–1; PC 2/63, fo. 31; *CJ*, IX.167–9.
195 *CSPD 1670*, p. 314. See DUL, Cosin Letter Book 5A, no. 79.
196 *CSPD 1668–69*, pp. 77–8, 342, 458, 655, *1670*, pp. 226–48 *passim*; Grey, I.295–6, 305.
197 *CSPD 1667*, pp. 428, 454–5, *1668–69*, pp. 77–8.
198 *LJ*, XI.449; Grey, I.422, II.172.
199 See especially M. Goldie 'The theory of Religious Intolerance in Restoration England' in O.P. Grell, J. Israel and N. Tyacke (eds), *From Persecution to Toleration*, Oxford, 1991, ch. 13. Also J. Spurr, 'Schism and the Restoration Church', *JEH*, XLI, 1990, pp. 408–24.
200 M. Goldie, 'Priestcraft and the birth of Whiggism' in N. Phillipson and Q. Skinner (eds), *Political Discourse in early modern England*, Cambridge, 1993, pp. 220–2, 226–30.
201 Grey, I.111–2, 422–3.
202 *CSPD 1680–81*, pp. 613, 626; Milward, p. 216.
203 Clar MS 73, fos 69, 314; *HMC 7th Report*, p. 148; Milward, pp. 216, 249; Grey, II.135.
204 Grey, I.56, II.12, 156–7.
205 Pepys, IV.5; W.D. Christie, *Life of Shaftesbury*, 2 vols, London, 1971, II.appendix, p. vii; *HMC Hastings*, II.374; Grey, I.103–4, II.118, 133; Milward, p. 216; BT 122, Croissy to Lionne, 25 July 1669 NS; PRO, SP 104/176, fo. 181. The king used this argument in 1663: *LJ*, XI.478–9.
206 Bodl, MS Add c. 304a, fos 187–8; Grey, I.127.
207 Milward, p. 216; Grey, I.222; *CSPD 1680–81*, p. 626. For the Act of Uniformity see Browning, *Docts*, p. 381, clause xi.
208 DUL, Cosin Letter Book, 5A, no. 27; Grey, I.221, 423; M. Goldie, 'The Huguenot Experience and the Problem of Toleration in Restoration England', in C.E.J. Caldicott, H. Gough and J.-P. Pittion (eds), *The Huguenots in Ireland: Anatomy of an Emigration*, Dublin, 1987, pp. 178–84.
209 Milward, pp. 152–3; Grey, I.56, II.154–7.
210 *HMC 9th Report, Appendix II*, p. 120; *HMC House of Lords 1678–88*, pp. 259–60; *CSPD January–June 1683*, p. 103.
211 *SR*, V.516; *CSPD 1660–61*, p. 466. The privy council seemed equally uncertain: PC 2/56, fo. 125. There were certainly some attempts to apply the 1593 Act: Carte MS 222, fos 12, 32, 64; Dunn, *Journal*, p. 37; Cooper, *Annals*, III.511–12; *HMC Kenyon*, p. 86; *HMC le Fleming*, pp. 109–10; Morrice, p. 353; Reresby, p. 323; *CSPD 1682*, p. 601.

212 PC 2/55, fo. 48; Bodl, MS Eng Hist b 212, fo. 5.
213 *HMC Kenyon*, p. 160; *CSPD 1666–67*, pp. 114, 124, *1660–85 (addenda)*, p. 151.
214 *CSPD 1668–69*, p. 398; Tanner MS 44, fo. 120; SP 104/176, fos 139–40, 176.
215 See the discussion in April 1674 about how best to proceed: *HMC le Fleming*, pp. 109–10.
216 Henry, pp. 83, 183; *CSPD 1663–64*, p. 457, *1664–65*, pp. 20, 207; Bodl, MS Eng Hist b 212, fo. 16, MS Add c. 305, fo. 156.
217 Pepys, IX.45–6; BL, Add MS 36916, fo. 119; *RB*, III.36–7; *CSPD 1670*, p. 226.
218 *CSPD 1667*, pp. 457, 484, 552; BL, Add MS 32324, fos 107–8.
219 CPA 118, Ruvigny to Pomponne 9 April 1676 NS; *CSPD 1680–81*, pp. 45–6; Bodl, MS Eng Letters c. 210, pp. 113–4; *CSPV 1673–75*, pp. 357–8; M636/28, Sir Ralph to Edmund Verney, 4 and 18 February 1675.
220 *HMC le Fleming*, p. 58 etc. In 1682 the constables of Middlesex said they feared to be punished for carrying out the JPs' commands: Morrice, p. 328.
221 *CSPD 1670*, pp. 59–60; Tanner MS 37, fo. 17.
222 219. Tanner MSS 35, fos 9, 36, 36, fos 196, 235; *CSPD 1680–81*, pp. 400, 409, 420, 433, 652, *1682*, pp. 97–8, *July–September 1683*, p. 408.
223 See the case of the town clerk of Oxford: *CSPD 1680–81*, pp. 384–5, 481–2, 610, 617; Bodl, MS Eng Letters d 40, fos 146–9. The mayor of Plymouth claimed to be unsure what his powers were as late as December 1681: *CSPD 1680–81*, p. 626.
224 Pepys, VII.114; M636/23, Sir Ralph to Edmund Verney, 26 May 1670, M636/29, Sir Ralph to John Verney, 6 March and 10 April 1676.
225 *CSPD 1665–66*, p. 588.
226 Bodl, MS Eng Hist b 212, fo. 12; *CSPD 1666–67*, pp. 114, 124; FSL, MS V b 305, nos 24–5.
227 See, for example, *CSPD 1664–65*, p. 165; Grey, I.128, 412, II.132.
228 Bodl, MS Add c. 305, fo. 154.
229 *RB*, III.172. See also Carte MS 70, fo 447; *CSPD 1666–67*, p. 12, *1667–68*, p. 97, *1675–76*, p. 1, *1680–81*, p. 696; Gauci, *Yarmouth*, pp. 73–4, 103–4, 123, 135–8; Scott, 'York', pp. 61–2, 173–4, 178–82.
230 Tanner MS 36, fo. 235; *CSPD 1682*, p. 36.
231 *CSPD 1670*, pp. 243, 270, 417; Reresby, p. 204; Luttrell, I.232; *CSPD 1680–81*, pp. 505–6, 630, *January–June 1683*, p. 219, *July–September 1683*, p. 204.
232 Scott, 'York', p. 59; WSL, SMS 454, no. 23.
233 *CSPD July–September 1683*, p. 358.
234 Rugg, p. 142; *CSPD 1660–61*, p. 475, *1682*, pp. 519–20.
235 Davies, pp. 79–80, 114–5, 135, 141. See also *RB*, III.50–1.
236 Davies, pp. 126–9, 132, 137–8. See also Scott, 'York', p. 76.
237 Davies, pp. 103–8, 111.
238 *Ibid.*, pp. 141–6, 148–50. See also *ibid.*, pp. 163–5.
239 *Ibid.*, pp. 172–85.

Chapter nine

The frustrations of the Cavaliers, 1660–64

The liquidation of the past

In many ways the Restoration was remarkably bloodless. Charles II was brought back by his own people, rather than by force of arms. Although there were official reprisals against his father's enemies, few were executed. And although there was some local paying off of scores, it was far from amounting to a 'white terror'. If the Restoration settlement left a legacy of bitterness, this was not because Parliamentarians thought it had been too severe but because Royalists thought it had not been severe enough. This chapter will examine the settlement and will try to explain why Charles failed to satisfy 'his own party'.[1] The aim is not to give a comprehensive account of the politics of the period, which can be found elsewhere,[2] but rather to examine those aspects which created political divisions.

The problems faced by the king in April 1660 were addressed in his Declaration of Breda. He was very conscious that the improvement in his prospects owed far less to his own efforts than to the surge of feeling in his favour since the collapse of military rule in December 1659. This had brought about the readmission in February of the MPs excluded in Pride's Purge and the dissolution of the Long Parliament on 16 March. It had also persuaded General Monk that the return of the monarchy was not only feasible but quite possibly unavoidable; he gradually purged the army of those officers most likely to oppose it. It was, however, far from certain that the king would return without preconditions. The Presbyterians who dominated the restored Long Parliament hoped to impose on him restrictions similar to those proposed in 1648, with Parliament gaining considerable influence over his choice of ministers and control of the armed forces and the king having to accept some form of presbyterianism in the Church. Monk appears to have favoured a settlement of this type; as the only man who could prevent the army from opposing the king's return he possessed great bargaining power, which he also used to demand favours for himself and his numerous friends and relations. The Declaration of Breda was designed to calm the fears of the army in particular and former Parliamentarians in general. Legally those who had fought against Charles I could be charged with treason; those who had purchased crown or church lands feared that they might be taken back without compensation; and both presbyterians and sectaries feared the re-establishment of a narrow, persecuting episcopal church.

The Declaration addressed each of these issues. The king promised to assent to a general pardon, 'excepting only such persons as shall hereafter be excepted by Parliament'. He wished 'that henceforward all notes of discord, separation and difference of parties be utterly abolished' and invited his subjects to unite and settle 'our just rights and theirs in a free Parliament, by which, upon the word of a king, we will be advised'. He likewise referred the question of crown and church lands, and those confiscated from Royalists, to Parliament. As for religion, 'we do declare a liberty to tender consciences, and that no man shall be disquieted or called in question for differences of opinion in matter of religion which do not disturb the peace of the kingdom'. He would be ready to assent to an Act of Parliament 'for the full granting that indulgence'. Finally, he was prepared to take the officers and men of the New Model into his service, on the same pay and conditions as they currently enjoyed.[3]

These issues were all addressed by the Convention, which met on 25 April (a month before the king returned) and was dissolved at the end of the year. Initially it comprised only the Commons, but soon the Lords began to meet as well. The Commons seem to have been divided fairly evenly between men of Parliamentarian and Royalist antecedents; had the outgoing Long Parliament not declared ex-Royalists ineligible for election, Royalists would probably have been comfortably in the majority. The relatively even balance meant that the Royalists were able to thwart attempts to lay down preconditions for the king's return. It meant too that the Convention was unlikely to sanction highly partisan measures: what emerged represented a lowest common denominator, measures broadly acceptable to both sides. This does not imply an absence of contention. There were bitter disputes on several issues, which resulted either in the matter being shelved or in a compromise, sometimes under considerable pressure from the king.

On his arrival the king assented to a bill declaring the Convention a lawful Parliament, despite the fact that it had not been summoned by a king, and confirming judicial proceedings since 1642: without this, unsuccessful litigants could have tried to unravel eighteen years of verdicts and agreements and the courts would have ground to a halt. The 'Act of free and general pardon, indemnity and oblivion', which received the royal assent on 29 August, was a complex document. It offered a blanket pardon for most categories of offence – murder unconnected with the wars, rape and witchcraft were among those excluded – since 1638. It excluded from pardon those regicides who were dead or who had absconded, who were deemed to be guilty of treason. Those who had surrendered themselves when summoned by the king to do so, if tried and convicted of treason, were to be executed only if an Act of Parliament was passed to that effect. These and some others, not directly involved in the king's death, were excluded from office and were to be tried for treason only if Parliament specifically requested it. Those responsible for handling a wide range of public moneys were to be required to account for them.[4] The question of crown, church and Royalist lands proved so complex that the Commons confessed that it was too difficult for them and handed the matter back to the king. In the event, the issue was resolved with little lasting acrimony. Many who had purchased crown and church lands were excepted out of the Act of Indemnity, or were former tenants who negotiated new (and often favourable) leases; the king set up a commission of sales which awarded purchasers compensation, where appropriate, on an *ad hoc* basis. Royalists and Catholics had often compounded for their confiscated lands well before 1660, helped by various intermediaries: even Cromwell's second-in-command, John Lambert, had helped his Catholic relatives recover their lands. As a result, the only landowners who really lost out were Royalists who had been forced to sell land to pay debts or fines or to raise the money they needed to compound.[5] The problem of the New Model was also resolved, but not in the way envisaged by the Declaration. By the end of the year most regiments had been paid off. Whereas in 1647 the soldiers had been denied their full arrears and a full indemnity, now they received both; those who had been apprentices were allowed by law to start practising their trades without completing their time. Although a few, especially among the officers, remained disgruntled, most seem to have been reabsorbed into civilian life with a minimum of disruption.

Of the issues raised by the Declaration, only that of religion (which we shall consider later) had not been effectively resolved by the end of the Convention. By that time, the king's government was well on the way to being re-established along traditional lines. His right to choose his ministers, a major source of contention between king and Parliament in the 1640s, was now uncontested, as was his control over the direction of government; after eighteen years in which Parliament had performed many executive functions, its last significant task was to pay off the army. In addition, the Commons had taken the unprecedented step of assessing the cost of the king's government and had agreed to vote the king – for life or forever – revenues sufficient to meet that cost: the king was once more to 'live of his own'. Moreover, his 'own' would now consist of taxes voted by Parliament (both fiscally efficient and incontrovertibly legal) rather than Charles I's motley collection of feudal, personal and prerogative sources (fiscally inefficient and politically contentious). Some remaining uncertainties were removed by the Cavalier Parliament which assembled on 8 May 1661. The first Act it passed (besides declaring that no person was bound by the Covenant) declared that the two Houses could not legislate without the king, so that all legislation since 1641, which had not received the royal assent, was null and void.[6] Another Act of 1661 resolved another bone of contention from the 1640s by declaring that sole command of the armed forces and the militia was vested in the king. Other Acts tried to guard against the threat of popular revolt by condemning 'tumultuous' petitions and removing 'disaffected' people from offices in municipal corporations (of which more later). The Licensing Act of 1662 was the first to give a statutory basis to pre-publication press censorship.

Although in many respects the Restoration saw a return to traditional ways, the legislation of 1641, to which Charles I **had** assented, swept away the prerogative courts (which were not revived) and the fiscal devices misused by Charles I; his son would have to raise money in ways approved by Parliament. Although the Convention had agreed to vote him revenues sufficient to meet the costs of government, its estimates of tax yields proved over-optimistic. As his revenue failed to match his expenditure, the king fell further and further into debt. Although he had in theory regained most of the powers exercised by his father, his ability to use them in practice depended on his ability to get on with the Cavalier Parliament.[7]

The resentments of the Cavaliers

Aside from religion, the Cavaliers' resentment focused on the related issues of the indemnity and the distribution of rewards. In their view, the king was far too ready to forgive his enemies and forget his friends. Within days of his return there were complaints that he seemed more concerned to reward Presbyterians and Cromwellians than old Cavaliers.[8] Those appointed to the privy council between 27 May and 2 June included some zealous Royalists – Lindsey, Norwich, Southampton and Hertford – together with the Queen Mother's favourite, St Alban's. The rest included Monk and his brother-in-law Morrice (appointed secretary of state), Anthony Ashley Cooper (who had served in every Parliament of the 1640s and 1650s) and a group of Presbyterians: Manchester, Robartes, Annesley, Leicester, Charles Howard and Denzil Holles, one of the five members whom Charles I had tried to arrest in 1642. Two peers formerly regarded as Independents were also admitted. The Earl of Northumberland perhaps owed his appointment to his having been governor to the younger royal children, but it is hard to explain why Lord Saye and Sele, now nearly eighty, was appointed (presumably with no pun intended) lord privy seal.[9] Other councillors had been appointed in exile – Lord Chancellor Hyde (created Earl of Clarendon in 1661), Ormond and Nicholas (the other secretary) for example – but for those Royalists who had remained at home it seemed that the king preferred old Parliamentarians' counsel to theirs.[10] Resentment of the king's favour to his father's enemies gave an added venom to their attempts to exclude as many as possible from pardon.

Why did Charles seemingly go out of his way to slight his father's friends? It may have made administrative sense to employ some councillors with recent experience of government, but such an argument was unlikely to impress the Cavaliers; nor did they like the way the Presbyterians claimed credit for the Restoration. Hyde blamed Monk for using his position of power to recommend innumerable Parliamentarians.[11] He also acknowledged that the Presbyterians included many able and prudent men, who were willing to serve the king and had extensive support in the army and the City. He claimed that the king was 'nauseated' by the importunities of the Royalists, many of whom were drunken or inept.[12] To understand the king's attitude, we need to consider his perception of his position. He was only too aware that he owed his restoration to an apparently sudden change in the public mood. His cynical view of human nature had been reinforced by the tribulations of exile and he feared that another such swing could see him on his travels again. While he no doubt sympathized with the Royalists, and knew that the Presbyterians had sought to impose preconditions for his return, he appreciated that some, like Monk and Sandwich, had played a vital role in events. More cynically, he calculated that the Presbyterians were far more likely than the Royalists to harm him, especially if they made common cause with the sects. The Declaration of Breda committed him to an indemnity and implied that it would be extensive.[13] Last but not least, a wide indemnity would create a broad base of acceptance for his regime – and he did not believe that the army would disband until it had passed.[14]

In April and May 1660 the Royalists of several counties publicly renounced all thoughts of revenge.[15] When one MP exclaimed on 12 May that those who had fought against the king were as great offenders as those who cut off his head, he narrowly avoided being sent to the Tower.[16] This apparently conciliatory mood soon vanished. After the Commons decreed that twenty besides the regicides should be excluded from pardon but not suffer the death penalty, there were a series of debates in which Parliamentarians like William Prynne and Colonel King were as vengeful as the most extreme Royalists.[17] Some wanted the exclusions to be so wide as to render the pardon meaningless. Job Charlton 'moved against those that had petitioned against the king, or sat in Parliament between 48 or 49 and the High Court of Justice men and the contrivers of the Instrument [of Government] and the imposers of taxes under Oliver and major generals and decimators'. He concluded, somewhat surprisingly, that 'though he never pressed for the death of any, yet to secure the future peace of the kingdom he could not be silent'.[18] The Lords showed a particular concern to punish those who had sat in the high courts of justice which had sentenced to death their fellow-peers Capel, Holland, Hamilton, Derby and Cambridge; at the very least, they should be debarred from holding office forever.[19] They also wished all the regicides to lose their lives and estates.[20]

Against the cacophony of cries for vengeance and punishment there were those, like Sir Thomas Littleton and Sir Thomas Clarges, who argued that rigour would alienate the victims whereas mercy would convert them. The strongest argument for mercy, however, was that the king wished it.[21] Whatever his private feelings, publicly Charles exhorted the Houses to complete the bill and to exclude as few as possible.[22] The nearest he came to urging severity was when he made it known that by those who were obstinate and dangerous he had meant Heselrig, Vane, Lambert and Axtell. The Commons agreed to exclude Axtell, Lambert and Vane from pardon, but asked the king to spare the lives of the last two.[23] Once the bill had passed, however, Charles stressed that he would now be severe against any who refused to acquiesce or threatened the peace.[24] In the panic after Venner's rising in January 1661, the privy council ordered lords lieutenant to proceed against those who were notoriously ill-principled (as well as those who had disturbed the peace since the Act of Indemnity).[25] If the king paid lip-service to the principle of burying the past, his chancellor thought otherwise. On 31 March 1661 he wrote of the need to 'pull up those bitter roots from which rebellion might henceforth spring'. He added, somewhat disingenuously, that as the past had been forgotten, the memory of it should not be revived by countenancing anything that had stimulated rebellion; the new Parliament should declare its abhorrence of the Covenant.[26] But many MPs (and clergymen) believed that, as they had solemnly sworn to observe the Covenant, they could not denounce it; to require them to do so would rake up the past rather than bury it. Similarly, the king told the Houses on 8 May that he wished them to confirm the indemnity, but to be severe against new offenders acting on old principles.[27]

Subsequent events were to show that the king was determined to preserve the indemnity intact, but MPs could be forgiven for seeing in his speech an invitation to revise its terms. The House quickly ordered that the Covenant should be burned by the common hangman and that all members should take communion as laid down in the Prayer Book. The debates were ill-tempered: Royalists were furious at claims that those who had taken the Covenant had served the king as well as those who had refused it.[28] The Commons had already instructed the committee for the bill to confirm the Acts of the Convention to see whether the contents of certain Acts (including that of Indemnity) matched their titles. On 21 May a bill was read to give indemnity to the king's faithful subjects and to restore estates that had been taken from them, which stood the principle of indemnity on its head. As Clarendon remarked, the Cavaliers did not mind the king forgiving trespasses against himself, but resented his forgiving those against them; they hoped that property forfeited by those earlier granted indemnity would be used to compensate them.[29] A week later, it was resolved that the Indemnity Act should be one of three removed from the general bill to confirm the Acts of the Convention and made the subject of a separate bill.[30] In June an attempt to insert a proviso that would have altered the terms of the indemnity won much support in the Commons, but was dropped after the king declared that he regarded anyone who tampered with the Act as no friend of his. He insisted that he was honour bound to confirm the indemnity; the House promptly complied.[31] Still supporters of indemnity remained anxious. Roger Pepys feared that its nails would be pared until the blood ran, by private bills, like that to restore the estates of the Earl of Derby, which passed both Houses but was vetoed by the king.[32] Some private bills were rejected because they infringed the Act of Indemnity.[33] The Commons pursued a number of individuals, including James Phillips, MP, accused of sitting on a high court of justice and sought to inflict further punishment on those regicides and others, excluded from pardon by the original Act, who were still in custody.[34] Their cases were discussed one by one and some were again saved from execution, but the Commons' mood remained as vindictive as that of the Dean of Windsor, who in January 1662 blamed the wet weather on the failure to execute the remaining regicides.[35] In the end the Commons' only victim was Sir Henry Vane. The king complied with their request that he be brought to trial and he was convicted of treason. 'He is too dangerous a man to let live, if we can honestly put him out of the way', the king told Clarendon. He was executed in June 1662, the last victim of the reprisals of the Restoration.[36]

If the Commons gave up trying to overturn the Act of Indemnity, Cavalier resentment of the king's favour to former Parliamentarians continued. At the end of June 1660 one remarked sarcastically 'His Majesty, having not hitherto found enough in honours or offices to satisfy his enemies, expects his loyal friends to stay until he be more able'. When the Commons agreed to bring in a bill to compensate Sir John Pakington for his losses, Sir Thomas Fanshawe remarked that this was the first time he had seen any kindness shown to a Cavalier.[37] Many blamed Monk or Hyde for the failure of their petitions, but the simple truth was that the king could never have made good the enormous losses suffered by his father's supporters or paid back more than a tiny fraction of the moneys that they had spent. The volume of patronage at his disposal was limited and he could not give rewards which would upset Parliament or breach the Act of Indemnity. One form of reward which combined profit and revenge consisted of commissions to recover arrears of taxes and other public moneys from the 1640s and 1650s. Such commissions were issued to individuals as late as 1664, but Southampton preferred more 'public' methods, notably the regular machinery of the Exchequer.[38] In these as in other cases, a few lucky Cavaliers with the right connections achieved success, but most lacked the contacts or the cash and so came off worse than 'the gaining presbyter or saving neuter'.[39] Occasionally the Cavaliers protested against the favour shown to a former enemy. Many of the Cheshire gentry, led by the Earl of Derby, complained bitterly when Thomas Stanley was made a baronet, but the grant was confirmed after a small committee, including Holles, had heard both sides.[40] Similar charges were made against Colonel Robert Werden. The scars left by civil strife were perhaps more raw in Cheshire than elsewhere, thanks to the reprisals after Booth's rising: Booth testifed on Werden's behalf.[41] On the other hand, there appear to have been no complaints when the king not only pardoned Robert Reynolds, solicitor general under the Rump, but knighted him as well.[42]

Although the Cavaliers grumbled, Parliament at first did little to ease their plight, apart from voting £60,000 at the end of 1661 for loyal and suffering subjects, particularly former army officers; attempts as late as 1671 to ascertain what had become of the money suggest that they received limited benefit.[43] Meanwhile, complaints arose that the postmaster general, Colonel Bishop, was employing disaffected men as postmasters. These offices were not only items of patronage, valued by the gentry as rewards for clients; postmasters were also expected to disseminate the news from the secretaries' offices and intercept the mail of suspicious persons. So sensitive could the position become that in January 1662 there were two rival letter carriers at Wakefield: the postmaster, a Parliamentarian, who carried them for 'his own friends' and a Royalist who carried letters for 'good subjects'.[44] In May 1663 the king replaced Bishop with Daniel O'Neale, with orders to remove postmasters who had been notoriously opposed to his father and himself; he did not explain how this was compatible with the Act of Indemnity. O'Neale removed fifty and remarked that he could have dismissed many more. The king also issued a proclamation requiring all postmasters to bring in a certificate of conformity to the Church of England, on pain of dismissal.[45]

Charles dismissed Bishop in response to an explosion of anger from the Commons, who had resolved to bring in a bill to restrict offices to men who were loyal and conformable to the Church and to exclude all who had served against Charles I, with a few exceptions (such as Albemarle and Sandwich).[46] There were complaints that the king's revenues were mismanaged and that government and court were riddled with corruption. Bills were brought in to prohibit the sale of offices and to recall all grants made since the Restoration. It was also reported that all office-holders were to be required to renounce the Covenant.[47] There was more than one motive behind these measures. Nicholas, recently removed from his secretaryship, complained that the king's recent declaration in favour of relaxing the Act of Uniformity and the laws against Catholics had emboldened both Papists and 'fanatics', to the annoyance of the Church of England men. O'Neale blamed factional disputes at court which the king, abandoned to his lusts, seemed unable to control, but the feuding courtiers found little difficulty in rousing the Cavaliers to fury. Whatever the reasons, all agreed that the Cavaliers had lost their reverence for the king and had become bitterly critical of his government.[48] In the event none of the bills passed, but Royalist resentment continued. Pepys referred in 1665 to 'the discontented Cavaliers that thinks [sic] their loyalty is not considered'. In the Oxford Parliament of that year there was a bill to impose on all office-holders an oath not to attempt any alteration of the government in church or state. It was narrowly rejected, but a separate measure (the Five Mile Act) imposed the oath on all clergymen ejected in 1662.[49]

As we shall see, not until the mid 1670s did Charles systematically favour his father's supporters and their sons. Until then, former Parliamentarians enjoyed a degree of favour that seemed unmerited to the old Cavaliers. It should be stressed, however, that their resentments focused on offices which either were paid or gave access to the king and to royal patronage. Unpaid offices in the localities, in the commissions of the peace and the militia, were granted predominantly to old Cavaliers, except in a few counties where the lord lieutenant was a former Parliamentarian.[50] The same was even more true of the commissioners appointed to implement the Corporation Act: the very moderate Parliamentarian, Sir John Holland, was appointed a JP and deputy lieutenant for Norfolk but not (to his chagrin) a Corporation Act commissioner. His more radical colleague, Sir John Hobart, was removed from the lieutenancy in 1660 and did not reappear until 1668.[51] Much of the machinery of law enforcement and coercion was therefore in Cavalier hands and could be used for partisan vengeance. It is to the refurbishment of that machinery that we now turn.

The machinery of coercion

After the 'secluded members' had been restored to the Commons in 1660, the Presbyterian majority set out to secure its position. On one hand, it needed to disarm the Quakers and 'sectaries' recruited as militia-men in 1659 and to establish a force to counter the New Model. On the other, it did not wish to arm Royalists, for fear that they might bring the king back without conditions. The Commons passed a militia bill which required all officers and deputy lieutenants to declare that magistracy and ministry were ordinances of God (to exclude sectaries) and that the war against the king had been lawful (to exclude Royalists); in addition, no-one was to be allowed to serve who had been in arms against Parliament. MPs brought in lists of commissioners who would settle the militia of each county and ensure that officers were 'well-affected'.[52] Meanwhile, the City of London regained control of its trained bands; it remodelled the lieutenancy and raised 6,000 auxiliaries, including many gentlemen volunteers. As early as 2 March Pepys thought that Monk would be unable to do anything against the City's forces; at the end of April some 18,000 men mustered in Hyde Park.[53] The army was deeply unhappy with these developments, but Monk acquiesced and insisted that it should do likewise.[54] After the Long Parliament had dissolved itself, the Council of State tried to ensure that the qualifications it had laid down were enforced, but in some counties the commissioners appointed Royalists as well; when the Council rejected the list of officers from Yorkshire, the county's commissioners sent back the same list.[55] Although opinions differed as to the political affiliations of those appointed, it was agreed that (unlike the Quakers and sectaries) they were mostly gentlemen.[56] Alongside the militia the gentry raised volunteer troops of horse, sometimes with the permission of Monk and the Council of State, as in Dorset, where the gentry complained that the militia was in 'unfit' hands and that they needed to be able to defend their homes.[57] Elsewhere, the militia disarmed sectaries and others described as 'disaffected' to a point where adherents of the 'good old cause' feared it would cut their throats.[58] Some soldiers complained, but apart from Lambert offered little opposition. Some units were disarmed by the militia, at Monk's command or with his approval, and military governors of towns were ordered to hand them over.[59]

Although the Speaker of the outgoing Parliament advised the king to cede control of the militia, he showed no inclination to do so and Monk made little effort to persuade him.[60] When the Convention met, the Presbyterian peers in the Lords invited the Commons to form a joint committee to settle the militia, but the Commons refused.[61] Meanwhile, Royalists raised volunteer troops of horse, some of which met the king on his arrival.[62] Within days of coming to London, he ordered the attorney general to prepare commissions and instructions for lords lieutenant and deputies.[63] It was alleged that many of the new officers were given to drinking, swearing, whoring and 'maypoling'; Secretary Nicholas stressed that officers should be 'well affected'. He added that lords lieutenant were to encourage volunteers and to muster them separately from the militia, which became normal practice.[64] The volunteers continued to play a significant role alongside the militia for several years. Late in 1663 Sir Philip Musgrave wrote that he relied on his volunteer horse more than the militia, who in Cumberland and Westmorland were thin on the ground. The volunteers were also more mobile and horsemen were more effective than footsoldiers in striking fear into civilians.[65] The king asked for the names of volunteers, so that he could know who his friends were.[66]

Royalist gentlemen served the king at their own expense[67] because they were genuinely anxious about the threat from the 'disaffected'. It took time to appoint deputies and to get the militia's creaking administrative and financial machinery working again. Old records had been lost, much land had changed hands.[68] Some officials and ratepayers questioned the legality of the deputies' demands: it was only in 1661 that Parliament made it clear that the Long Parliament's militia ordinance was null and void and the militia had lacked a **statutory** basis since 1604. Claims that it rested on the Act of 1558 were questionable.[69] Some deputies were uncertain whether they possessed the power to raise money and feared being sued if they did so.[70] In the Convention, members expressed outrage at reports that militia-men, especially in Lancashire, had forced their way into the houses of 'Roundheads'; others denied the reports.[71] The Commons had brought in a bill to regulate the militia, but some MPs – even Royalists like Sir Heneage Finch – complained that it sanctioned martial law. Marvell, who initially favoured the bill, changed his mind, but it was still being considered in committee when the session ended.[72] The government argued that, as Parliament had yet to resolve the matter, the militia should continue to be organized in the old way, but hoped that the new Parliament would settle matters once and for all.[73] But the Cavalier House of Commons was preoccupied with other matters and the militia bill proceeded slowly; in some counties musters were suspended until it passed. As a stopgap, Parliament passed the bill stating that the sole command over the militia lay in the king.[74] Although he professed himself satisfied, he tried to persuade the Commons to agree to a standing army, which would be more permanent and proficient, but the Commons preferred to put the militia on a more stable footing and allowed the king to raise up to £70,000 a year for three years to deal with the current unrest. The new Act required all officers to swear an oath renouncing resistance to the king on any pretext whatsoever, which former Parliamentarians would not find easy to take.[75]

The Militia Act passed in May 1662, but in some counties it took time for the militia to become fully operational. There were complaints of a lack of direction from the centre and anxious deputies worried that they might be called to account for exceeding their powers.[76] In Cheshire its mobilization was hampered by Derby's refusal to cooperate with Lord Brereton, his co-lord lieutenant. In Lancashire the Earl complained that the king refused to accept three of his nominees as deputies and insisted that Alexander Rigby, Richard Kirkby and Sir Roger Bradshaigh should be appointed instead. Rigby was married to Colonel Birch's daughter and had been accused of encouraging constables to oppose the collection of the militia rate. Kirkby was seen as too sympathetic to Dissent and opposed Derby's wish for a drastic purge of

Lancaster corporation. Bradshaigh sought to protect Catholics from persecution.[77] As the new militia was gradually established, some volunteer companies were dismissed. The £70,000 was raised to pay the militia guards, which were now to be on foot for much of the year.[78] Opinions varied as to the militia's effectiveness. The Devon deputies assured their lord lieutenant that they would keep a constant guard at Exeter, Plymouth and Barnstaple and that the militia was now 'useful'.[79] The governor of Scarborough thought that the recent changes had weakened the militia, while in Cumberland and Westmorland the total number of soldiers was six hundred, so a guard of one twentieth would be too small to serve any useful purpose.[80] The council's plan was to have one twentieth of the militia on duty for fourteen days, to provide year-round cover, except in the depths of winter, but the Oxfordshire deputies pleaded that the 'seasons of seed-time and harvest' should be kept free of musters, except in dire emergencies.[81] Whatever its deficiencies, the militia was adequate to deal with the threat of rebellion from a population that was increasingly demilitarized, thanks to the government's growing control over the manufacture and transportation of firearms and repeated searches for weapons.[82] Much of the state's near-monopoly of weaponry was in the hands of the lords lieutenant and their deputies, the majority of them old Cavaliers. Moreover, the statutory basis of the militia was now beyond dispute, which removed any legal pretext to resist it.[83]

The Corporation Act

In seeking to root out the spirit of rebellion, the old Cavaliers were particularly anxious about the towns. The substantial autonomy which many of them enjoyed, the stubborn support for Parliament shown by the likes of Taunton and Gloucester and the continuance in municipal office of many who had served under the republic all gave cause for concern. Many corporations were equally anxious, especially those which had received new charters in the 1650s. They rushed to demonstrate their support for the new regime, with loyal addresses and gifts of money. The king, unsure of his position, approached the towns warily. A royal warrant of 7 May 1661 stated that in future charters the king should reserve the right to nominate the first set of aldermen and future recorders and town clerks. In addition, it was proposed, by charter, to reduce the parliamentary electorate in all boroughs to the 'common council', although such a move would have been politically very contentious.[84] A corporation bill was brought into the Commons on 19 June: its promoters included Sir Thomas Fanshawe, a vigorous persecutor of Dissenters. It required those holding municipal office to take a variety of political tests, including the oaths of allegiance and supremacy. The taking of these tests was to be supervised by commissioners nominated by Parliament, who would presumably mostly be Royalists. The bill passed the Commons easily – the vote on the final reading was 182 to 77 – and was sent up to the Lords on 5 July.[85]

For once the Lords were almost equally quick. On 24 July the bill was returned, but with amendments which transformed it beyond recognition. All corporations were to renew their charters within a year. Under the new charters the king would have the power to appoint recorders and town clerks and to select the mayor from a shortlist of six drawn up by the corporation; county JPs were to be empowered to act as magistrates in all towns in their county, except those that were counties in themselves, where the king, not the town, would choose the JPs. The Commons rejected these amendments without a division. They complained that the aim of their bill was to ensure 'present safety' by purging corporations of all 'disaffected' members, not just mayors, town clerks and recorders; after that they should be free to run their own affairs. The Lords' amendments allowed for permanent intervention in municipal affairs by both the king and the county JPs. It seems probable that the Lords' amendments reflected the desire of the king's advisers drastically to reduce the towns' autonomy. The provision concerning mayors and recorders echoed the warrant drawn up earlier and although the Lords' amendments made no mention of the franchise, the Commons suspected a hidden electoral agenda: 'so total an alteration of the government may have an ill influence upon the free elections'. The fact that four-fifths of the members sat for borough constituencies redoubled their concern. What the Commons wanted was a one-off, targeted act of revenge, by Cavalier peers and gentry.[86]

The conference between the Houses on the Lords' amendments was put off until after the summer recess. The Lords were then persuaded to recommit the bill and to abandon their amendments. The bill passed in December was similar to the Commons' original bill, although the commissioners were now to be nominated by the king and their powers were to last only until 25 March 1663. It required all members of corporations to take the oaths of allegiance and supremacy and the oath (later included in the Militia Act) that it was not lawful to take up arms against the king on any pretext whatsoever. They were also to renounce the Covenant and to have taken communion according to the rites of the Church of England within the twelve months before they were admitted to office. The commissioners were empowered to reinstate former members of the corporation who had been unlawfully removed and to remove persons who had complied with all the requirements of the Act if they 'shall deem it expedient for the public safety'.[87]

In choosing the commissioners to implement the Act, the king drew on the advice of his lords lieutenant, who were mostly Royalists. The commission was usually chaired either by the lord lieutenant (as with the Earl of Derby in Lancashire or Lord Townshend in Norfolk) or a leading local Royalist (such as Sir Thomas Peyton in Kent or Sir William Compton in Cambridgeshire).[88] Most commissioners were JPs or deputy lieutenants, plus the mayors or recorders of larger towns. At Bristol, which enjoyed county status, the mayor nominated the commissioners, but was strongly advised to act in conjunction with the 'country gentlemen'.[89] In most counties, the commissioners confined themselves to removing those who refused the oaths or the renunciation of the Covenant. In Lancashire Derby failed to persuade his colleagues to expel all who had opposed the king in the civil wars.[90] In some counties they went further, however. At Bath and Canterbury some were removed for refusing the oaths and declaration, others 'for good causes and reasons'. At Canterbury, although the Act referred only to aldermen, common council men, magistrates, officials and those holding places of trust, the commissioners removed and disfranchised 121 freemen 'for divers good causes and reasons . . . for the public peace and safety of the kingdom'; the same happened at Maidstone and Dover.[91] In the three Kent boroughs and at Cambridge, those removed from the corporation were declared disfranchised; elsewhere (for example at Norwich) there was no mention of disfranchisement.[92] At Northampton it was assumed that only the privy council could debar those removed from voting in a forthcoming by-election.[93] At Winchester and Cambridge some were removed for religious nonconformity.[94] Many were removed because they failed to appear, although the commissioners sometimes ascertained the reason for their non-appearance before removing them.[95] In addition, some regarded as particularly disaffected were required to give sureties for good behaviour.[96]

Taken in conjunction with piecemeal removals and voluntary withdrawals since 1660, the changes carried out by the commissioners were the most sweeping of the century so far. Although some corporations saw few changes – only two aldermen appear to have been removed at Hull[97] – others lost almost all their members. At Arundel, all but one refused to take the oaths, although the lord lieutenant later persuaded two more to comply. At Chard all the aldermen quit; the mayor complained that he could not carry on the government on his own.[98] Although the militia was occasionally used to enforce the commissioners' orders,[99] most removals were carried through peacefully, despite the fact that many occurred in August and September 1662,[100] when ministers were being ejected for failing to comply with the Act of Uniformity. The removal of so many 'disaffected' persons without resistance could be seen as a triumph for the Cavaliers, but in March 1663, before the commissioners' powers expired, the Commons appointed a committee to consider whether the Act had been defective in any way. One problem it identified was that the 'better sort' could avoid 'chargeable' offices by refusing the oaths and declarations; another was that those displaced might be reinstated by King's Bench on writs of *mandamus*. The committee recommended that the commissioners' powers be extended for twelve months and a new bill was brought in. In July the House voted (but by only 84 to 69) to give it a second reading.[101] In April 1664 an additional corporation bill was brought in; it was committed on 30 April, but again failed to pass through all its stages in the Commons.[102] This may have been the bill, a copy of which survives in the state papers, which would have continued the commissioners' powers for the king's lifetime. It noted that many ill-affected persons had taken the oaths and declarations or had refused them but later crept back into office. It proposed that nobody should be a member of any corporation who was known to have been of factious principles, or had acted with factious persons, or had been involved with sequestration or the purchase of crown lands, unless they had been constantly loyal since the passing of the 1661 Act. Where there were too few loyal persons in a town, the commissioners could (with the king's approval) draft in loyal gentlemen from the county.[103]

Given the extreme nature of its provisions, it is possible that this is not the bill that came before the Commons. Even so, it reflects an awareness that the Corporation Act had not achieved its objective of clearing out the disaffected once and for all. In many towns the pool of those suitable and willing to serve was small, while there were many family and business links between those who refused the oaths and those who did not; there was also nothing to stop those who had been ejected despite having qualified for office from serving after the commissioners' powers had expired. In Yarmouth, as Richard Bower repeated *ad nauseam*, those sympathetic to nonconformity regained control of the government in 1666 and ensured that the laws against Dissent were not enforced.[104] Significantly, however, successive lords lieutenant of Norfolk judged it politic to work with the ruling elements in the town.[105] In 1668 Ormond, lord lieutenant of Somerset, passed on to his deputies an order from the council to check that those holding municipal offices were properly qualified. Two of the deputies wrote on the letter that if their colleagues inspected the corporations within their divisions they would do the same, but no-one took up their offer.[106] Such episodes suggest that by the late 1660s the Cavalier gentry no longer saw the towns and their rulers as constituting a problem. The general elections of 1679–81 would change their minds.

The church settlement

Among interpretations of the church settlement, two deserve special attention. Bosher saw it as the 'triumph of the Laudians', whom he defined as a small group of clergy, closely associated with Hyde, who wanted the full restoration of episcopacy and the old church order (although he assumed that Laud's 'church order' was the same as Elizabeth's). In explaining how such a small group managed this, he saw the role of Charles and Hyde as crucial. Determined to secure a rigidly episcopal and Anglican settlement, but aware of the lack of support for such a settlement in the Convention, they strung the Presbyterians along with hopes of comprehension, while gradually re-establishing episcopacy. With the election of the Cavalier House of Commons, they were finally able to achieve their aims. In this Bosher to some extent followed Baxter, who doubted that deceit was intended from the start, as nobody could have foreseen the results of the 1661 election, but blamed the machinations of the 'prelates' for the failure of comprehension and the rigour of the Act of Uniformity.[107] We have seen that the bishops did far less to shape the settlement than Baxter claimed. Moreover, although Bosher's book is in many ways scholarly and perceptive, its central argument is fatally flawed. There is overwhelming evidence that Charles did **not** want a narrowly Anglican settlement and fought the Commons' attempts to impose one every step of the way. (Clarendon's position was more ambivalent.)[108] This led Ian Green and others to argue that the Commons expressed a strong gentry 'Anglicanism', a longing to get back to the days before the banning of the Prayer Book.[109]

There can be no doubt that many saw the restoration of an effective and uniform church as vital for the stability of the political and social order. Identifying a religious imperative behind the settlement is more difficult, however. Paul Seaward's careful researches suggest that only a smallish minority of MPs show evidence of strong 'Anglican' commitment, but argues that their zeal and determination carried along other less committed members.[110] I shall suggest a rather different explanation, which involves the frustrations of the Cavaliers, fear of revolt and the gentry's concern to regain control over the parish clergy. In developing this explanation, two points should be borne in mind. First, the sources for the parliamentary history of 1661–65 are very limited: there is only one terse parliamentary diary, so that one has to try to deduce the Houses' intentions mainly from the official record, the journals.[111] Second, one should not assume that the form in which the Act of Uniformity eventually passed had been sought from the outset by either king or Commons: the Act passed in May 1662 was significantly different from the bill discussed by the Commons in the summer of 1661.

At Breda Charles had promised to assent to any bill of indulgence passed by Parliament, but no such bill emerged from the Convention, whose members, whether Presbyterian or Royalist, were mostly against toleration. In July the Commons debated the Church. The Royalists argued that the old church order had never been legally abolished; the Presbyterians argued against reintroducing unscriptural and unnecessary ceremonies and over-powerful prelates. As the arguments became heated, it was agreed to postpone debate for three months and to ask the king to summon an assembly of divines to discuss the future of the church. This was seen as a victory for the Royalists: the Presbyterians had wanted Parliament to settle the matter.[112] In the interim the king began to appoint new bishops, which did not totally prejudge the form the Church would take. Many 'Presbyterians' were prepared to serve in a church with bishops, so long as their powers were limited and they did not impose unacceptable ceremonies. Moreover, the king's discussions with leading Presbyterians produced the Worcester House Declaration of 25 October. This laid down that the bishops should exercise some of their functions with the advice and consent of the 'presbyters' and made the most contentious ceremonies optional. Baxter was pleasantly surprised by its contents,[113] but was bitterly disappointed that a bill to give it the force of law failed to pass the Commons.

In retrospect, the failure to pass the bill marked the end of hopes of comprehension. It was claimed that the king did not want it to pass: Secretary Morrice, usually regarded as a Presbyterian but presumably acting on orders, favoured laying it aside.[114] Although it was rejected by only 183 votes to 157, it was rejected on the first reading, which was unusual: it was alleged that some of the 'commonwealth party' joined with the Cavaliers to defeat the bill.[115] Clarendon claimed later that the Declaration had been intended only as a temporary measure, pending fuller discussion in a synod. It should be remembered that in July the House had agreed this, so the move to confirm the Declaration could be seen as sharp practice.[116] Nicholas claimed that the bill had been destroyed by the violence of its supporters; he had earlier remarked that the king had taken the contentious business of church government into his own hands – which implies that he would not have been pleased that Parliament tried to regain control of it.[117] The heated debates in July showed the strength of Cavalier feeling against the Presbyterians.[118] Their ill-temper had since been increased by the passage of a bill to secure ministers in their livings. Attempts to impose doctrinal tests on incumbents or to eject those who had not been ordained by a bishop had failed: only those who rejected infant baptism or who had pressed for Charles I's death or actively opposed the Restoration were removed. About 700 ministers were ejected, mostly on the grounds that their predecessors had been removed illegally, but the Act confirmed in post several thousand, many of whom the Cavaliers regarded as politically and religiously unacceptable. The king openly supported the bill, but Hyde told the Houses that some unsuitable ministers might have been left in.[119]

The king supported the bill for the reason that he promoted the bill of indemnity: he gave a higher priority to appeasing his father's enemies than to rewarding his friends. His episcopal appointments in 1660 favoured moderates and even 'Presbyterians' rather than 'Laudians'.[120] Even after the rejection of the bill to confirm the Worcester House Declaration, he was prepared to countenance change. In May 1661 he instructed the attorney general to omit from the summons to Convocation the usual proviso that nothing was to be resolved contrary to the established liturgy, practice and doctrine of the Church.[121] By contrast the commission to the promised conference of divines, which met at the Savoy, instructed them to make only such changes in the liturgy as were truly necessary, because the people were used to the old forms. This led the bishops to insist that it was up to the Presbyterians to make a case for change. Together with Baxter's prolixity and intransigence, this tactic ensured that the conference ended with the bishops making only minor concessions, although there are signs that they were prepared to concede a little more.[122]

When Parliament met, on 8 May, Hyde warned the Houses of the need to protect the king against seditious preachers and plotters, but did not mention the form of the church, offering only exhortations not to be too rigid or rigorous in matters of conscience. The Commons ordered the burning of the Covenant and required all members to take communion according to the Anglican rite.[123] On 15 May the House resolved to bring in the bill against Quakers and other schismatics; four days earlier, the king had ordered the release from gaol of Quakers imprisoned only for scruples of conscience (such as not taking oaths). It also expressed reservations about confirming the Act of Indemnity.[124] It was not until 25 June that the Commons appointed a committee to consider what bills were necessary to confirm the liturgy of the Church and ensure effective conformity: the Savoy Conference was already discussing the liturgy and Convocation had convened. The committee was instructed to seek out the Prayer Book of 1552 – more acceptable to church puritans than those of 1549 and 1559 and so a more plausible basis for comprehension.[125] In the event, the original of the 1552 liturgy could not be found and the Commons opted for that of 1559, eventually settling for that book as revised by Convocation during the winter of 1661–62. The House did not seem unduly concerned **which** version of the Prayer Book was used – it could not be, as the matter was still under discussion, so there was a possibility that amendments could be made to accommodate church puritans. On the other hand, it was quick to insist that all incumbents and lecturers should declare their unfeigned assent and consent to everything in the Prayer Book. The fact of conformity was thus more important than the form of the liturgy: conformity was a matter more of obedience to authority than of theological principle.[126]

The Commons became more rigid and vindictive towards the church-puritan clergy as the uniformity bill progressed. Two reasons can be offered. First, they were irritated by the efforts of the king (through the Lords) to tone down the bill and to secure a right to dispense some of the clergy from complying fully with its requirements. At one point, some MPs threatened to delay the completion of the financial settlement unless the king allowed the bill to pass.[127] Nicholas and Clarendon claimed that the Cavaliers were angered by the Presbyterians' bragging of their access to the king.[128] Second, the Royalist gentry were determined to regain control over their parishes. By the early seventeenth century, many advowsons (giving the right to nominate incumbents) had passed into lay hands. Also, in many parishes, the tithes were impropriated – paid to someone other than the incumbent, most often a lay patron. In the 1640s Royalist patrons had lost these advowsons and impropriated tithes; the latter had often been used to augment the stipends of the parish clergy.[129] Now they wanted them back. In the debates on the bill for the confirmation of ministers in 1660, Royalists complained that many had been installed against the wishes of the patrons. Presbyterians argued that the impropriations belonging to bishops, deans and chapters should be used to increase the stipends of poor vicars, an argument which the king seemed to support.[130] When the Cavalier House of Commons was asked to confirm this Act, along with others passed by the Convention, it effectively overturned it by adding a series of amendments requiring (among other things) renunciation of the Covenant and the exclusion of those who had not been episcopally inducted and ordained. Those who had replaced ejected ministers should pay the full arrears of the 'fifths' due to their predecessors. The bill also included a clause that those whose patronage rights had been overridden in the 1640s and 1650s (and who had had ministers 'intruded' into their parishes) should be able to exercise them freely for six months. The bill did not require those presented to use the Prayer Book, although those 'illegally' presented who had used it since July 1660 were not to be removed. The Prayer Book was in fact still being revised when the ministers' bill was debated in December and did not go to the privy council until February 1662. The bill's main emphasis was on legal procedures and political loyalty, but its effect would be to drive out most church-puritan clergy. The Lords proposed various amendments, which angered the Commons, who were mollified only when the more draconian provisions were transferred to the uniformity bill, making it more severe than it had originally been.[131]

There is considerable evidence that the old Cavaliers were concerned more to regain their patronage rights than to impose any particular brand of conformity. Adam Martindale had been 'called' to the parish of Rotherston, Cheshire, in 1647 against the wishes of the patron, Peter Venables. In 1661 Venables and other Cheshire Royalists pressed presbyterian incumbents to use the Prayer Book.[132] By August 1662 Martindale was convinced that Venables would have him out whether he conformed or not, as he wanted the living for his chaplain.[133] Similarly, Philip Henry was indicted in March 1661 for not using Common Prayer and had his annuity withheld by the patron of the living. Accused of allowing strangers and 'fanatics' to attend his church, he was deprived by the Bishop of Chester in October 1661.[134] Baxter found his efforts to recover his cure of souls at Kidderminster opposed by the patron of the living, despite a letter from Hyde in his favour.[135]

The Royalist gentry were equally eager to recover their impropriated tithes, which they could do only at the expense of the parish clergy. In May 1661 a Shropshire gentleman remarked that parsons would not be able to 'vie purses' with gentlemen in litigation in Chancery and that the new Parliament was far more likely than the last to restore impropriations to their former owners.[136] A bill to restore advowsons and rectories taken from 'loyal subjects' in the 1640s was brought into the Commons on 4 July and had passed through all its stages by 13 July. The Lords feared that it might contravene the Acts of indemnity and judicial proceedings, but the judges decided it did not and it eventually passed.[137] The Lords' suggestion that one-third of the value of every impropriation should go to the parish was dropped after opposition from the Commons.[138] This is not to suggest that the Commons were unconcerned about the parishes. Bills were brought in to allow churchwardens to raise money to repair churches and to provide adequate payment for a curate (by the incumbent) where the latter was non-resident, but neither passed and neither would have affected the power or purses of the gentry.[139] The Marquis of Newcastle wished all clergymen to have adequate stipends – but not at the expense of the laity.[140]

The Lords passed the advowsons bill on 17 May 1662, ten months after the Commons sent it up. They proved similarly dilatory in considering the uniformity bill. Also sent up in July, it was first read in the Lords on 14 January 1662, by which time the ministers bill had also been sent up. The Lords had the excuse that the council had not yet considered the revised Prayer Book – why the two months' delay? – but the Commons were becoming frustrated by what they saw as the Lords' (and the king's) obstructiveness. The Lords referred the Book to the committee on the uniformity bill (which contained eight bishops), which accepted it as it stood and added to the Commons' bill the clauses from the ministers bill requiring episcopal ordination and renunciation of the covenant. The ministers bill was now essentially a bill of confirmation, but the uniformity bill was now more severe than when the Commons had sent it up and the form of liturgy to which the clergy were expected to conform was now known.[141] Having 'saved' the ministers bill, the Lords now hoped to soften the rigour of the uniformity bill by a series of amendments to the draft agreed in committee. These included changing the deadline for conformity from St Bartholomew's day to Michaelmas, stating that refusal to use the surplice or the sign of the cross was not grounds for removal and allowing ejected ministers one-fifth of the income of those who supplanted them. The Commons bitterly resented these proposals. They urged the Lords to complete the advowsons bill and threatened to pass no more important bills (including money bills) until the uniformity bill had passed.[142] In a conference on 7 May the Commons insisted that to allow divergence of practice would lead to schism and that the church had to have the authority to command obedience in 'things indifferent'. They also insisted on the requirement to promise not to endeavour any alteration of government in church or state and that all the requirements of the bill should extend to schoolmasters. Education of the young was too important to be entrusted to any but the truly loyal; many members of the Long Parliament had derived their principles from 'fanatic' teachers.[143] The Lords accepted the Commons' amendments the following day.

There is no doubt that the Lords' amendments reflected the king's wishes. On 17 March Clarendon had commended to the Lords, by the king's command, a proviso allowing him to dispense ministers from complying with the terms of the uniformity bill. After a furious debate, the Lords agreed to add it to the bill, but the Commons rejected it, along with a later proviso allowing the king to dispense with the requirement to renounce the Covenant.[144] These were the first of several attempts to allow the king some discretion or flexibility in the enforcement of the Act.[145] A proposal in council in August that he should dispense some ministers from the penalties of the Act was thwarted by the vigorous opposition of Sheldon.[146] On 26 December he issued a declaration stating that he hoped that, now the Church had been fully re-established, Parliament would allow him to dispense peaceable individuals whose tender (if misguided) consciences would not allow them to comply fully with the Act. He believed that he already possessed such a dispensing power, but a new Act would enable him to exercise it 'with a more universal satisfaction'. He also hoped that the Catholics could be included in such an Act, in view of their loyalty in the civil wars.[147] At the opening of the new session in February 1663, Charles told the Houses that the church's liturgy should be left pure and uncontaminated, but that he wished that he had the power to indulge peaceable dissenters. This suggested, first, that he did **not** think he possessed a dispensing power and, second, he was now resigned to church puritans leaving the church and wished to allow a measure of toleration to at least some dissenters. The Commons resolved to thank the king for his promise to maintain the Act of Uniformity and then voted (but only by 161 to 119) to advise him to give no indulgence to dissenters.[148] Later in the session they passed bills against conventicles and papists; both, to their annoyance, failed to pass the Lords. Roger Pepys described the conventicle bill as 'devilish', but a proposal to exempt from its provisions occasional conformists – those who went to meetings but also attended church and took communion – failed by only five votes. It was also agreed that the bill should be temporary.[149] This would suggest that the Commons were still not as overwhelmingly 'Anglican' as historians have assumed. However, at the end of the session, the Speaker asked the king to order that the laws against both sectaries and papists be fully enforced.[150]

Resentment of the king's attempts to undermine the Act of Uniformity contributed to the Commons ill-temper in the 1663 session. They saw his conduct as an affront to Parliament and a threat to the public peace.[151] They resented the favourable references to Catholics and the continued evidence that the king cared more about his father's enemies than about his friends. The impulse behind the conventicle bill was essentially the same as that behind the bill to remove non-Royalists and non-Anglicans from office. Moreover, whereas earlier legislation had targeted particular groups – municipal office-holders, Quakers and other more radical sectaries – the conventicle bill was directed against **all** types of Protestant nonconformity. The Commons had initially been aroused by reports of meetings of Anabaptists, Quakers and the like, but they instructed a committee to investigate the Act of 35 Elizabeth (1593) and to consider what needed to be done against 'sectaries', which some saw as including presbyterians.[152] Just as the barriers placed in the way of other measures (such as the ministers and advowson bills) had made the Commons more vindictive towards the church-puritan clergy, so the king's attempts to allow some indulgence to those driven out of the Church provoked the Commons to extend persecution. It may be that the motivation of many was political rather than religious: a concern to maintain the authority of Parliament in the face of widespread defiance and a backsliding king. The arguments against indulgence drawn up by the Commons on 27 February 1663 were almost exclusively legal and political. There was no justification of ceremonies as aids to devotion and the nearest there was to a religious argument was the claim that indulgence would establish schism by law.[153]

In response to the speaker's request to enforce the laws against 'sectaries' the king issued a proclamation to enforce the statutes for church attendance and against unlawful meetings. This followed shortly after an order to keep part of the militia on foot through most of the year.[154] This suggests that the government was coming to accept the need to punish conventicles, either because it saw them as a threat to public order, or because the Commons expected it.[155] In August Anglesey wrote that he favoured extending liberty to peaceable nonconformists and that he thought Clarendon agreed. In December he was warned that the king and Duke of York thought him too favourable to nonconformists and that he was almost alone in holding that view, apart from 'such as have been notedly of the party'.[156] This change of heart at court can be explained by the discovery of the Derwentdale conspiracy in October 1663.[157] In the next session, although the king's opening speech made no reference to conventicles, the government offered little real opposition to the Commons' conventicle bill, which passed into law (although again it was to be only temporary).[158]

The old Cavaliers' commitment to upholding the Act of Uniformity, which required a fuller undertaking to use ceremonies and the surplice than had been demanded under Elizabeth and James I, identified them with a 'Laudian' vision of the church which probably only a minority held, in terms of an internalized, conscious conviction. This made possible the creation of a more 'Laudian' Church of England, as young gentlemen and clergymen were imbued with 'Laudian' values at the universities. For the moment, however, true 'Laudians' were only a minority among the clergy and the bishops had contributed comparatively little to the church settlement: if anything they had been a force for moderation. The main components of that Act had come from two different sources of unequal importance: the role of the clergy in Convocation, which had agreed to only minor changes to the Prayer Book, had been far outweighed by that of the Cavaliers in the Commons, who had decided in the summer of 1661 to insist on complete conformity to a liturgy whose eventual content had yet to be determined. (A third component comprised the requirements of episcopal ordination and renunciation of the Covenant, which had originally been part of the ministers bill.) Having committed themselves to such a conformity they felt obliged to stick to it, not least because those who sought to change it seemed to threaten the stability of a still vulnerable regime. The king shared their view that Dissent posed a threat, but believed it would be dealt with better by conciliation than by repression. This difference of perception and policy had serious repercussions for the king's relationship with this most Royalist of Parliaments. It might seem praiseworthy that Charles set out to be the king of the whole nation and not of a party.[159] But the old Cavaliers regarded him as **their** king and were deeply frustrated by his refusal to behave in that way. In assenting to the 1664 Conventicle Act Charles suggested that he had at last learned this lesson.

The Cavaliers' revenge?

There was an element of revenge in both the Corporation Act and the Act of Uniformity, but how far was ill-will towards former enemies translated into acts of vindictiveness at the local level? Some exploited the vulnerability of prominent Cromwellians. Whitelocke, who feared exclusion from pardon, had to pay heavily to appease friend and foe alike.[160] Even after securing his pardon, he remained at a disadvantage in legal disputes and he was regarded as suspect by the authorities.[161] His daughter and son-in-law were turned out of their house and plundered by soldiers.[162] We have already seen that Parliamentarians were purged from the postal service. Claims that such people should be removed from offices and 'loyal' men put in their places remained commonplace for over a decade.[163] Loyalty in the civil wars could be cited as a reason for granting a Cambridge MA, a lease of church lands or a pardon.[164] When in 1667 the Commons voted to fine an attorney £1,000 for arresting one of their members, it was stressed that he had been a 'rebel' and purchased crown lands.[165] Accusations of having opposed the king, or the Restoration, were easy to make and sometimes hard to disprove.[166] Even such a conspicuous

Royalist as Sir John Pakington found that his petition to the Committee for Compounding in 1646 could be used as evidence of disloyalty.[167]

The malice was not all on one side: the Countess of Derby pleaded for the life of a 'loyalist' convicted of murder by a jury of 'sequestrators' and condemned to death despite the pleas of all the gentlemen present.[168] Nevertheless, the old Cavaliers occupied most positions of power and there were complaints that power had been abused. The most striking case occurred in the Isle of Man. William Christian had captured the island for the republic in 1651. The Earl of Derby, who was Lord of Man, also blamed Christian for the death of his father and had him sentenced to death and shot; an order from the privy council to spare his life arrived too late. Derby claimed that the Act of Indemnity did not apply on the Isle of Man, but the council was unconvinced and Christian's death added to the Earl's disfavour at court. The council printed its order condemning Derby's conduct, to show that the king was determined to maintain the Act of Indemnity.[169] Derby was a vindictive man. He was accused in 1660 of using the militia to harass Parliamentarians and nonconformists and in 1662 he tried in vain to have all former Parliamentarians expelled from Lancashire corporations. He had the purchaser of one of his estates arrested by 'my militia'; Lord Brereton had one of those who had condemned the Earl's father to death gaoled on the pretext that he held an office contrary to law.[170] The traditional power of the Stanleys in Lancashire and Cheshire, and the current Earl's standing as the son of a Royalist 'martyr', made him virtually irremoveable (although the king vetoed the private bill to enable him to recover his lands). Lesser men had to tread more carefully. Deputies who exceeded their authority, by removing the mayor of Wallingford, or nine burgesses of Christchurch, or by imprisoning nine members of Bath corporation, were reprimanded by the council.[171]

The fact that there were relatively few cases of this type, and that they were dealt with promptly, suggests that the **unauthorized** use of force or power was rare, but the orders given to the militia may still have allowed much paying off of scores. However, both the central government and the deputies repeatedly expressed concern that they should act according to law and, as we have seen, respect for the law and for due process ran deep. By law, nobody could be arrested except on a warrant signed by two deputies; when searching for arms they were to be accompanied by the appropriate civil officer; the 1662 Militia Act forbade searches or arrests at night, except in towns and then only when the warrant specifically required it.[172] Those accused of sedition were often summoned before the council or one of the secretaries, which took them out of the reach of local enmities. If no substance was found in the charges against them, they were released.[173] But perhaps the strongest factor against unfettered revenge was that for much of the time local rulers were unsure what the law was. The king's power to order the militia was questionable before the 1661 Militia Act and the detailed powers of lords lieutenant and deputies were laid down only in the Acts of 1662 and 1663; the legal position of the volunteers was even more doubtful.[174] The first orders to proceed against conventicles stated only that they were unlawful, but the council's resolution to issue the order referred to the laws against riot.[175] The first new law against dissenting meetings applied only to Quakers and was passed only in May 1662; the previous September Nicholas had complained that the Presbyterians preached very boldly 'and yet there is no law to punish them'. In November he told a Wiltshire deputy to refrain from issuing warrants against meetings until the uniformity bill had passed. In December 1662, when the Duke of Newcastle asked if he could re-commit sectaries who had not re-offended, the council left it up to him.[176] The 1593 Act against conventicles seems to have been used little, if at all, before 1663, and then not widely. Only with the Conventicle Act of 1664 could those who wished to disperse meetings be totally confident that they were acting according to law.

We have seen that after the Indemnity Act passed the king stressed the need to beware of new offenders acting on old principles.[177] This might seem disingenuous, paying lip-service to the Act of Indemnity while urging action against former Parliamentarians. Equally, Charles may have been torn between concern to uphold the Indemnity and fear of sedition. In practice, such commands were bound to encourage deputies and JPs to focus attention on those who had held those 'old principles'. From the summer of 1660 lords lieutenant were repeatedly instructed to secure vagrants and to watch and disarm the disaffected, leaving it to them and to their deputies to decide what constituted 'disaffection'.[178] Although some deputies stressed the need to act courteously, others seized the opportunity for recriminations about the past.[179] On 2 January 1661 the council ordered the drawing up of a proclamation against meetings of 'sectaries', which could serve as a cover for conspiracy. Nobody was to go to any religious exercise in another parish; those who attended such meetings were to be prosecuted under the laws against riotous and unlawful assembly. Two days later the council ordered the disarming of the disaffected.[180] These orders were sent out a few days later, by which time Venner's rising, on the night of 6 January, had given them a more intense relevance. They required lords lieutenant to proceed against those who had shown disaffection or disturbed the peace since the Act of Indemnity – or who were notoriously 'ill-principled'. Such people were to be tendered the oaths of allegiance and supremacy and required (if necessary) to give sureties for good behaviour.[181] The proclamation against conventicles, ordered earlier, was issued on 10 January: it referred to secret meetings of Anabaptists, Quakers and Fifth Monarchists and ordered that religious worship was to be allowed only in churches, chapels and private houses (for members of the household only).[182]

It is not surprising that lords lieutenant and deputies should have seen these instructions as a signal to suppress conventicles. Apart from a few cases in Wales, the state papers offer little evidence of action against dissenting meetings before January 1661.[183] Moderate Puritans feared that Venner's folly would bring down persecution on all their heads, but for the moment the authorities focused on the sectaries. The Hampshire deputies described these assemblies 'under pretence of worshipping God' in terms of deliberate defiance of authority; they were made up of those 'calling themselves' Quakers, Anabaptists and Fifth Monarchists 'as a mark of distinction and separation'.[184]

Volunteers were raised in several counties and proceeded so vigorously that the king issued a proclamation against arresting people and searching houses without a warrant. In London, soldiers searching the houses of Quakers, Anabaptists and Fifth Monarchists for arms 'robbed them, sorely wounded others and dragged some to prison and all this done without orders'.[185] At Brecon, the lord lieutenant ordered that all those with complaints against the soldiers should appear before him, with witnesses.[186] In March the lords lieutenant were ordered to release those arrested only on suspicion, especially Quakers, but in August the council warned them to watch for meetings of persons of 'an unreclaimable mutinous spirit', many of whom had been active under the 'usurpation' and now seemed more confident and busy than usual.[187] Some Wiltshire deputies understood this as an instruction to suppress meetings of Quakers, Baptists and the like, but some of their colleagues were unsure how they should proceed against those taken at meetings. Should they seek an order from the council to confirm the commitments? Should they be tried by a commission of *oyer and terminer*? Did tumultuous meetings fall within the law of treason? Their brethren in Hampshire were similarly unsure how to proceed against a leading Quaker.[188] In Somerset two prominent Parliamentarians, John Pyne and William Strode, were arrested and imprisoned in September for failing to meet their militia obligations and refusing to conform to the church. The following July, amid renewed fears of insurrection, Pyne was summoned before the council to answer charges of seditious words. John Ashburnham wrote that if the charges could be proved by two witnesses, Pyne would be hanged; he urged the deputies to be diligent 'as far as the law allows'.[189] In Hertfordshire Sir Thomas Fanshawe went rather further than the law allowed, prosecuting nonconformists and Parliamentarians on a variety of charges and having those from Hertford tried at the county rather than the borough sessions, where he feared juries would be more sympathetic.[190] In Kent, Sir Edward Hales, acting on the council's 'general order', arrested some of the 'creatures' of Sir Michael Livesey, a regicide and a leading figure in the county during the Interregnum, and searched their houses. He admitted that he had no special warrant or recent charges against them but, knowing that their principles had not changed, he had judged it wise to be 'beforehand'.[191] Sir John Pakington was equally active in Worcestershire, making many arrests.[192] However, the deputies of Hampshire and Derbyshire found little cause for alarm. In Wiltshire, apart from their doubts about the way to proceed against conventicles, some refused a request of the Bishop of Salisbury to arrest a factious preacher.[193]

It is clear from their correspondence that the likes of Pakington were convinced that there was a real danger of insurrection. The government arrested old Cromwellians and gave out that there had been a great plot; a proclamation ordered Parliamentarian soldiers to leave London. Pepys was sceptical, but added 'it is but justice that they should be served as they served the poor Cavaliers'.[194] The increased military weakness of the crown during the transition between the old and new militias heightened ministers' trepidation. In late June 1662 the council ordered that the walls of Coventry, Northampton,

Gloucester and Taunton should be slighted. Small garrisons were installed at Shrewsbury and Chester.[195] In July it again ordered lords lieutenant to be vigilant, to secure vagrants and those of republican principles and to mobilize volunteers.[196] At Northampton, the lord lieutenant, finding the corporation unwilling to assist him, hired labourers from the county to dismantle the walls, under the supervision of four troops of militia horse, some bodies of volunteers and many of the county gentry.[197] From the Somerset deputies came reports of plans for a rising. As many as a thousand horse and foot were sent to occupy Taunton while the fortifications were demolished; it was alleged that the factious there were refusing to pay taxes or rates. Ormond doubted the need to demolish the walls, but Clarendon and Nicholas assured him that it was vital, adding that there were further reports of sinister designs from Lancashire and Cheshire.[198] In Staffordshire and at Chepstow, lists were drawn up of those who had been in arms against Charles I or under Cromwell. The officers of the volunteer horse in Hampshire were ordered to arrest and disarm those who had been in arms against the king.[199] In London, soldiers broke up 'private meetings' and arrested those present.[200]

By the end of 1662, despite news of yet another plot in London, as a result of which five or six 'fanatics' were executed, the council appeared more confident. The new militia was largely settled and the first £70,000 was being raised to enable it to stay on duty for most of the year. The ejections of the church-puritan clergy had passed off without serious disorders, but the king still thought it necessary to try to allow a measure of indulgence to nonconformists. In January 1663 he ordered the release of Quakers held only on a charge of meeting unlawfully.[201] In the first half of 1663 the deputies of Cornwall tendered the oath in the Militia Act (against taking up arms by the king's authority against his person) to those they suspected of disaffection, telling them that they were not obliged to take it, but that doing so would free them from suspicion. They also tendered the oath of supremacy, to laymen as well as clergy. From Staffordshire Sir Brian Broughton sent details of 866 former Parliamentarians living within five miles of the major towns, adding that the militia was so scattered that it would be hard pressed to suppress a rising.[202] On the other hand the lord lieutenant of the North Riding of Yorkshire saw no cause for alarm.[203] The council issued no new instructions to lords lieutenant until 5 August, when it ordered them to keep one twentieth of the militia on guard at all times, preferably in a fortified town or towns. They were to rely on the infantry, keeping the horse in reserve for emergencies, unless they were needed to suppress conventicles.[204] On 22 August the king issued a proclamation to enforce the laws requiring church attendance and against unlawful assemblies. The indefatigable Sir Philip Musgrave exercised his men, made a number of arrests and expressed anxiety that the disaffected might seize one of the Countess of Pembroke's recently repaired castles. By contrast the Oxfordshire deputies, exhorted by Clarendon to act vigorously against 'sectaries', asked if musters could be delayed until after the harvest.[205]

In the weeks that followed there were reports from Chichester and Somerset that the sectaries were unusually bold. Early in October Lord Herbert of

Raglan doubled the guard at Gloucester, mobilized a troop of horse and warned the volunteers to be ready. As rumours of a rising intensified, the trained bands were raised in the West Riding of Yorkshire, but not in the other two ridings, to avoid undue alarm. Sir Thomas Gower, another vigilant deputy, preferred to rely on a couple of troops of horse and set some trusty gentlemen to watch the highways (and their neighbours).[206] By the time a small bedraggled body of men appeared in arms at Kaber Rigg, in Westmorland, on 12 October, Derby had raised three regiments of the Lancashire militia and Lords Conyers and Bellasis had each raised 300 volunteer horse in Yorkshire, as well as the militia; four troops of volunteer horse were raised in the North Riding. In Wiltshire, companies of foot were stationed in Malmesbury and other towns, while 'flying' troops of horse were to secure dangerous persons.[207] In Westmorland, Musgrave, conscious of the militia's weakness, raised fifty volunteers and asked that Carlisle garrison be reinforced with dragoons. Daniel Fleming made twenty arrests – former army officers, ejected ministers and Quakers; Musgrave reported that the Quakers were deeply implicated in the plot.[208] Early in January 1664 the 'loyal party' at Oxford were reported to be fearful following the discovery of some sinister letters. They were not reassured by short-lived guards of militia and asked that a troop of horse be stationed permanently in the city.[209] In County Durham, where the militia was said to be too scattered to be of much use, there was a voluntary agreement of 'loyal subjects' to appear with horses, arms and as many neighbours as possible, on the summons of the lord lieutenant (the bishop) and his deputies, to suppress the 'insurrections' of Quakers, Baptists and other disaffected persons and to disperse seditious conventicles.[210] A month later the bishop enquired secretly of his clergy how many of their parishioners had served against the king and how many could be relied on to defend him against his enemies.[211] In March the council ordered the dismantling of the fortifications of Poole (another factious town) and a proclamation again ordered all who had served in the 'rebel' armies to leave London.[212]

From the foregoing it would appear that, far from using their power to harass their former enemies, the 'king's party' felt beleaguered and vulnerable and believed that the militia was too weak and unreliable to protect them.[213] Lords lieutenant and deputies who acted vigorously had to contend with the sloth, absence or obstruction of their colleagues. In Northumberland the militia was still being settled in March 1664.[214] Frightened men may lash out and deputies like Fleming and Musgrave reacted to rumours of plots by rounding up the usual suspects, but most were quickly released on giving sureties for good behaviour.[215] A few of those accused of plotting languished in gaol for years, but that was the exception rather than the rule. Similarly, nonconformist meetings were rarely harassed, except in the immediate aftermath of Venner's rising[216] or at other times when the authorities were particularly edgy. Those whose meetings were disturbed were Baptists and above all Quakers; Presbyterians and Independents were generally left alone, which suggests that, while the Cavaliers were jealous of the king's favour to Presbyterians, they saw the radical sects as the major threat to the regime.[217] JPs and deputies were restrained by uncertainty as to the legal position and how far their actions would be approved 'above'; their uncertainty was compounded by attempts by some judges to soften the rigour of persecution.[218] Although the king's government upheld the Act of Indemnity less in practice than in theory, the mixed signals which it sent out undermined the confidence of even its most diligent servants in the provinces.[219] The king's Declaration of 26 December 1662 was said to have increased the confidence and boldness of the Quakers and others. On the other hand, the Commons' bill against conventicles in 1663 seems to have encouraged magistrates and deputies to start enforcing the Act of 1593, at least against the most recalcitrant.[220] Although there were instances of violence being used in dispersing meetings (especially those of the Quakers),[221] and although a few deputies seem to have gloried in persecution,[222] the abiding impression from the correspondence of the most active old Cavaliers is of impotence and frustration. However much they may have wanted to wreak revenge, they lacked either the power or the backing from 'above' to do so effectively. Further legislation, starting with the 1664 Conventicle Act, was to give them more power, but they were not to receive the king's wholehearted backing until the last years of the reign.

Notes

1 The phrase is Henry Coventry's: Carte MS 47, fo. 397.
2 See for example, Miller, *Charles II*, chs 2–4; Seaward; R. Hutton, *The Restoration*, Oxford, 1985.
3 Browning, *Docts*, pp. 57–8.
4 Kenyon, *Constitution*, 2nd edn. pp. 339–44; *SR*, V.231–4.
5 H.J. Habakkuk, 'The Land Settlement and the Restoration of Charles II', *TRHS*, 5th series, XXVIII, 1978, pp. 201–22; J. Thirsk, 'The Restoration Land Settlement', *Journal of Modern History*, XXVI, 1954, pp. 315–28. The information on Lambert comes from Dr David Farr.
6 Browning, *Docts*, pp. 63–5.
7 I have discussed the Restoration settlement at greater length in *The Restoration and the England of Charles II*, 2nd edn., Harlow, 1997, chs 2–3.
8 *CSP*, III.736; *HMC 5th Report*, p. 184; Staffs RO, D868/4, fo. 86.
9 PC 2/54, under dates given.
10 *HMC 5th Report*, p. 194.
11 Clarendon, I.323–6. See also *HMC 5th Report*, p. 184.
12 Clarendon, I.321–2, 328–31, 353–4.
13 Clarendon, I.472. For one Presbyterian's contribution to the king's return, see Thomson, 'Herts.', pp. 420–3.
14 Clarendon, I.471.
15 Rugg, pp. 70–1, 75–6; H. Townshend, *Diary*, ed. J.W. Willis Bund, 2 vols, Worcs. Hist. Soc., 1920, I.37–8; *CCSP*, IV.670–2.
16 *CJ*, VIII.24; Dering, *Papers*, pp. 41–2; *CSPD 1659–60*, p. 438.
17 Clarendon, I.467–70; *OPH*, XXII.367, 369; Bowman, fo. 70.
18 Bowman, fo. 41 (printed with rather different wording in *OPH*, XXII.366).
19 *LJ*, XI.84–5, 119, 121.
20 *LJ*, XI.126; Bowman, fos 144, 150.

21 *OPH*, XXII.369, 366; *HMC 5th Report*, p. 184.
22 *CJ*, VIII.67; *LJ*, XI.108–9.
23 *LJ*, XI.108–9; *HMC 5th Report*, p. 155; *CJ*, VIII.135.
24 *LJ*, XI.148.
25 Carte MS 130, fo. 274; BL, Add MS 21922, fo. 244; M636/17, Council to Bridgewater, 8 January 1661.
26 Clar MS 74, fo. 297.
27 *LJ*, XI.240–1.
28 *CJ*, VIII.245, 254; *HMC 5th Report*, p. 160.
29 *CJ*, VIII.249, 256; Clarendon, II.3, 98.
30 Egerton MS 2043, fo. 11; *CJ*, VIII.260.
31 BL, Add MS 11314, fo. 27x; *HMC Finch*, I.130; *CJ*, VIII.278; Seaward, p. 199.
32 Tanner MS 49, fo. 101; *LJ*, XI.281, 379; Seaward, pp. 201–3.
33 Clarendon, II.154–5; Carte MS 73, fo. 543.
34 *CJ*, VIII.281–2, 286–7, 298.
35 *CJ*, VIII.349, 351; Evelyn, III.311–2.
36 Hutton, *Restoration*, pp. 162–3; *Letters of Charles II*, ed. A. Bryant, London, 1935, p. 128.
37 *HMC 5th Report*, p. 205; Egerton MS 2043, fos 7–8.
38 S.K. Roberts, 'Public or Private? Revenge and Recovery in the Restoration of Charles II', *BIHR*, LIX, 1986, pp. 174–84.
39 *HMC 5th Report*, pp. 203–4 (quoted); *CSPV 1659–61*, p. 159; Burnet, *Suppl*, pp. 55–6; Burnet, *Hist*, I.280–2; *CSPD 1660–61*, pp. viii–ix; BL, Add MS 10116, fo. 237; Evelyn, III.493.
40 *CSPD 1660–61*, pp. 132–3, 364–5, 409–10; Clar MS 74, fo. 11 (another copy, Egerton MS 2549, fo. 110).
41 Clar MS 73, fo. 210. See J.S. Morrill, *Cheshire 1630–60*, Oxford, 1974, pp. 312, 328.
42 *CSPD 1660–61*, pp. 3, 106; B. Worden, *The Rump Parliament*, Cambridge, 1974, pp. 30, 61, 65 and *passim*.
43 *CJ*, VIII.376, IX.105, 113, 198, 199; Seaward, pp. 210–11.
44 *CSPD 1661–62*, p. 250. See also *ibid.*, pp. 38, 92, 305, 557, 560.
45 Carte MS 32, fo. 405; *CSPD 1663–64*, pp. 149, 156–7.
46 *CSPD 1663–64*, p. 132; *CJ*, VIII.476; *HMC 4th Report*, p. 329; Pepys, IV.125, 136.
47 Pepys, IV.169–70; Tanner MS 47, fo. 31; Carte MSS 32, fos 405, 597, 77, fo. 645.
48 Carte MS 32, fos 405, 516, 566, 597.
49 Pepys, VI.303; *CJ*, VIII.622; Seaward, pp. 192–3, 212–13.
50 Hutton, *Restoration*, pp. 129; Stater, *Noble*, pp. 71–8, 85–6; Brindle, 'Northants.', pp. 191–6; S. Roberts, *Recovery and Restoration in an English County: Devon Local Administration 1646–70*, Exeter, 1985, pp. 148–9, 151–3. Cheshire was an exception: P.J. Challinor, 'The Structure of Politics in Cheshire 1660–1715', unpublished Ph.D. thesis, Wolverhampton, 1983, pp. 20–3.
51 BL, Add MS 41656, fo. 17; Egerton MS 2717, fos 225–6; Dunn, *Journal*, pp. 8, 26–7, 106.
52 *CJ*, VII.849, 860, 862–5, 871; Rugg, p. 53; *HMC 7th Report*, p. 462.
53 *HMC Ormond*, NS I.334; Rugg, p. 51; *CCSP*, IV.630; Clar MSS 71, fos 99, 72, fo. 59; *CSPV 1659–61*, p. 141; Pepys, I.74; Carte MS 30, fo. 576.

54 *CJ*, VII.880; *HMC 7th Report*, pp. 463, 484; Ludlow, *Voyce*, p. 98; *CCSP*, IV.591, 605; BL, Add MS 15750, fo. 55; BT 106, Bordeaux to Brienne, 22 March, to Mazarin and to Brienne, 29 March 1660 NS; Clar MS 71, fo. 99.
55 Clar MS 71, fo. 110; *CCSP*, IV.629–30, 640, 670; *CSP*, III.721; BT 107, Bordeaux to Brienne, 3 May 1660 NS; Morrill, *Cheshire*, p. 326; Brindle, 'Northants.', pp. 174–8.
56 *CSP*, III.697; *HMC 7th Report*, p. 483; *CCSP*, IV.603, 615, 628; *HMC Portland*, III.219–20; *HMC Ormond*, NS I.335–6: Hughes, *Warwicks.*, pp. 333–4.
57 *CCSP*, IV.649, 656; Rugg, p. 85.
58 *CSP*, III.702; *HMC Leybourne Popham*, p. 172; BT 106, Bordeaux to Mazarin, 19 April 1660 NS; *CSPD 1659–60*, p. 414: Hughes, *Warwicks.*, pp. 334–5.
59 *CSP*, III.702; *CCSP*, IV.629–30; Clar MS 71, fo. 156; Stowe MS 185, fo. 153; *HMC Leybourne Popham*, p. 181; BRO, AC/C64/71.
60 *CSP*, III.713. The list of proposals sent by Monk made no explicit reference to the militia: Lister, III.500–3. Nor did the suggestions by Morrice that the king should come in on conditions specify what those conditions might be: Clar MS 72, fos 4, 222.
61 *LJ*, XI.10; *CCSP*, V.12; HLRO, Main Papers 2 April–14 May 1660, fos 194–200, 207.
62 BT 107, Bordeaux to Brienne, 3 June 1660 NS; Malcolm, 'Reconstruction', p. 312 claims that the creation of the volunteer troops was the king's idea, but they were already in being when he returned.
63 PC 2/54, fo. 33; *HMC 5th Report*, p. 153; Townshend, *Diary*, I.47.
64 Carte MS 73, fo. 472; *CSPD 1660–61*, p. 150; BL Add MSS 21922, fos 239–40, 32324, fo. 64.
65 *CSPD 1663–64*, pp. 258, 287, 332.
66 PC 2/56, fos 32–3 (summarized *CSPD 1661–62*, p. 442); Bodl, MS Eng Hist b 212, fos 2–3.
67 A proposal that they should be paid was rejected: *HMC Finch*, I.81.
68 SP 29/11, no. 52; *HMC 5th Report*, p. 195; BL, Add MS 21922, fo. 247.
69 *CSPD 1660–61*, pp. 462, 582, 592–3, *1661–62*, pp. 156, 181; PC 2/55, fo. 37; BL, Add MS 21922, fo. 244; Fletcher, *Reform*, pp. 318–20.
70 *CSPD 1660–61*, pp. 582, 592–3; Norrey, 'Regime', p. 793.
71 *OPH*, XXIII.51–3; *HMC 5th Report*, p. 200.
72 *OPH*, XXIII.14–15, 22–4; Marvell, II.2, 7–8; *HMC 5th Report*, p. 196; BL, Add MS 11043, fo. 109.
73 *LJ*, XI.237; *CSPD 1660–61*, p. 459; Marvell, II.22.
74 *HMC 5th Report*, p.160; BL, Add MSS 22919, fos 159, 36989, fo. 528; *HMC Beaufort*, p. 50; *LJ*, XI.331.
75 *LJ*, XI.331; Egerton MS 2043, fos 23, 24, 37; *CJ*, VIII.326; Pepys, III.15; *Rawdon*, pp. 140–1; Seaward, pp. 142–51.
76 *CSPD 1661–62*, p. 80; BL, Add MSS 21922, fo. 247, 32324, fo. 143; M636/18, letter to Bridgewater, dated 17 July, endorsed as received 30 August; BRO, AC/02/13, AC/C64/74; Norrey, 'Regime', pp. 789–94.
77 *CSPD 1661–62*, pp. 156, 463, 483, 495, 509, 517, 524–5, 552; *CCSP*, V.260, 270; PC 2/56, fo. 102; Coward, *Stanleys*, pp. 181–2.
78 Egerton MS 2538, fo. 184; *CSPD 1661–62*, p. 568; PC 2/56, fo. 124.
79 *CSPD 1661–62*, p. 538, *1663–64*, p. 252.
80 *CSPD 1661–62*, p. 551, *1663–64*, pp. 231, 258.

81 PC 2/56, fos 253–4 (summarized *CSPD 1663–64*, p. 231); Bodl, MS Eng Hist b 212, fo. 7.
82 Malcolm, 'Reconstruction', pp. 319–22; P.R. Seddon, 'A Restoration Militia and the Defence of the Shire: the Nottinghamshire Militia, 1660–c.1670', *The Historian*, no. 57, 1995, pp. 23–5.
83 Coleby, *Hants.*, pp. 108–9, 113.
84 SP 29/35, no. 18; J. Miller, 'The Crown and the Borough Charters in the Reign of Charles II', *EHR* C, 1985, pp. 57–9.
85 *CJ*, VIII.285, 287, 288; Hull RO, BRL 659; Miller, 'Charters', p. 59; Seaward, pp. 152–3.
86 *CJ*, VIII.310–12; Clar MS 75, fo. 48; *LJ*, XI.321–2; Miller, 'Charters', pp. 59–61.
87 Browning, *Docts*, pp. 375–6.
88 *CSPD 1661–62*, p. 517; NRO, Case 17d, City Revenues and Letters, fo. 90; CKS, Md/ACm1/3, fo. 122; W.M. Palmer, 'The Reformation of the Corporation of Cambridge, July 1662', *Proceedings of the Cambridge Antiquarian Soc.* XVII, 1913, p. 105.
89 BRO, AC/C74/18, 35.
90 *CSPD 1661–62*, p. 517; W.A.H. Schilling, 'The central government and the municipal corporations in England, 1642–63', unpublished Ph.D. thesis, Vanderbilt, 1970, ch. 6.
91 Bath RO, P.R. James, 'Documents of the City of Bath' (typescript), II.557–9, Corporation Book II (1649–84), pp. 271, 275; Canterbury Archives, AC5, fos 56–7, 59–62; CKS, Md/ACm1/3, fos 122–3, 126–7; CKS, Dover Corporation Minutes, James I to Charles II, rear of volume, fos 214–15. See also N. Marlowe, 'Government and Politics in West Country Incorporated Boroughs, 1642–62', unpublished Ph.D. thesis, Cambridge, 1985, pp. 276–89.
92 Palmer, 'Reformation', p. 108; NRO, Case 17d, fos 90–3.
93 BL, Add MS 29551, fo. 9.
94 Hants RO, W/F2/5, fos 141–2; Palmer, 'Reformation', pp. 105, 106.
95 Palmer, 'Reformation', pp. 105–6; Hants RO, 27M74/DBC 283.
96 PC 2/56, fo. 80; Palmer, 'Reformation', p. 108; *CSPD 1661–62*, pp. 419, 539.
97 Hull RO, BRB4, pp. 457–8.
98 PC 2/56, fo. 80; Egerton MS 2538, fo. 168; *CSPD 1661–62*, p. 539.
99 Egerton MS 2538, fo. 168.
100 This was true of Arundel, Canterbury, Winchester, Maidstone, Dover, Hull and Cambridge for which references have been given earlier. Also Portsmouth (R. East, *Extracts from the Records of Portsmouth*, [Portsmouth, 1891], pp. 168–9; *HMC 9th Report, Appendix 1*, p. 284; Portsmouth RO, CE 1/8, fo. 1).
101 *CJ*, VIII.445, 446, 517.
102 *CJ*, VIII.551, 553–4.
103 SP 29/440, no. 93.
104 *CSPD 1668–69*, pp. 99–100, 111, *1670*, pp. 512–3, 519, *1671*, pp. 46–8, *1676–77*, pp. 221–2; Gauci, *Yarmouth*, pp. 90–1, 103–9, 122–3, 127–8.
105 Gauci, *Yarmouth*, pp. 122, 127–8, 135–9.
106 BRO, AC/02/23b, 23a.
107 *RB*, II.287–8, III.40, 84–5.
108 See Green, ch. 1; Seaward, chs. 2–3, 7.
109 Green, *passim*.
110 Seaward, pp. 56–7, 61–7.

111 The diary is that of Bullen Reymes: Egerton MS 2043. The difficulties of the sources make Seaward's analysis of the legislation of these years all the more impressive.
112 Bowman, fos 62–6, 77–85 (*OPH*, XXII.374–6, 385–8); *HMC 5th Report*, pp. 155, 204; *CJ*, VIII.95.
113 *RB*, II.278–9.
114 BT 108, Bartet to Mazarin, 10 December 1660 NS; Staffs RO, D8684, fo. 55; *OPH*, XXIII.27–30 (Morrice appears on p. 29).
115 *HMC 5th Report*, p. 196.
116 Clarendon, I.480–1.
117 *CSPD 1660–61*, p. 404; also *ibid.*, p. 350.
118 Bowman, fo. 83. See also Bodl, MS Eng Letters c 210, fo. 49.
119 Harl MS 3784, fo. 2; *CJ*, VIII.106, 173; Bowman, fo. 96; Green, pp. 37–51; *LJ*, XI.176; Bosher, pp. 171–9.
120 Green, ch. 4.
121 PC 2/55, fo. 118.
122 *RB*, II.304; Burnet, *Hist*, I.308–11; *Cosin*, II.x–xi, 36; BL, Add MS 28053, fos 1–2; Bosher, pp. 228–30.
123 *LJ*, XI.240–4; *CJ*, VIII.247, 254.
124 *CJ*, VIII.249, 252; Egerton MS 2043, fo. 7; *CSPD 1660–61*, p. 587.
125 *CJ*, VIII.279; Bosher, p. 223.
126 Seaward, pp. 166–7, 174; *CJ*, VIII.377.
127 *Rawdon*, p. 138; DUL, Cosin Letter Book 2, no. 70. For a similar (alleged) threat in 1663, see Carte MS 221, fo. 52.
128 Clar MS 75, fo. 191; Clarendon, II.123–5. See also Clar MS 74, fo. 297; BL, Add MS 41656, fo. 21; M636/18, Lady Rochester to Sir Ralph Verney, 27 January 1662.
129 C. Hill, *Economic Problems of the Church from Whitgift to Laud*, Oxford, 1956; R. O'Day and A. Hughes, 'Augmentation and amalgamation: was there a systematic approach to the reform of parochial finance, 1640–60?', in R. O'Day and F. Heal (eds), *Princes and Paupers in the English Church, 1500–1800*, Leicester, 1981, pp. 167–94.
130 Bowman, fos 105, 121–2, 124; *CJ*, VIII.113–14.
131 *CJ*, VIII.325–6; Egerton MS 2043, fo. 7; Bosher, pp. 240–1; Seaward, pp. 172–4.
132 Martindale, pp. 77–8, 143, 158–61; *CSPD 1660–61*, p. 515.
133 Martindale, pp. 163–4.
134 Henry, pp. 82, 88, 95–8.
135 *RB*, II.298–300.
136 Staffs RO, D868/3, fo. 38.
137 *CJ*, VIII.290, 293, 300; *LJ*, XI.314, 364, 423, 441–2, 465.
138 *LJ*, XI.465; *HMC 7th Report*, pp. 166–7.
139 *CJ*, VIII.254, 273, 292, 308, 312; *HMC 7th Report*, pp. 149, 153.
140 Strong, p. 187.
141 *LJ*, XI.465; Seaward, pp. 174–5.
142 *CJ*, VIII.409, 413, 414, 423; DUL, Cosin Letter Book 2, no. 70.
143 *LJ*, XI.447–9.
144 *Rawdon*, pp. 141–3; *HMC 7th Report*, pp. 162–3; Seaward, pp. 175–8.
145 See Lister, III.198–201.
146 Carte MSS 31, fos 602, 32, fos 3, 47, fo. 359: Pepys, III.186.

147 Browning, *Docts*, pp. 371–4 (especially p. 373).
148 *LJ*, XI.478–9; *CJ*, VIII.440.
149 Carte MS 32, fo. 732; *CJ*, VIII.473, 513–14; Pepys, IV.90, 159–60; Seaward, pp. 186–8.
150 *CJ*, VIII.578.
151 *CJ*, VIII.442–3.
152 *CJ*, VIII.473; Seaward, pp. 186–7. The Commons answer to the Lords' proposal that the Quakers Act should apply only to Quakers stressed the difficulty of defining a Quaker, but implied that the Act should extend only to Anabaptists and other sectaries: *LJ*, XI.389.
153 *CJ*, VIII.442–3.
154 *CSPD 1663–64*, pp. 231, 249–50.
155 Carte MS 221, fo. 52.
156 *HMC Ormond*, NS III.71, 131–2.
157 For the conspiracy, see Marshall, *Intelligence*, pp. 108–112.
158 *LJ*, XI.582–3; Seaward, pp. 190–2.
159 *Mather*, p. 209.
160 Whitelocke, pp. 590–8, 600–1, 608, 628.
161 Whitelocke, pp. 641, 656–7, 623–4.
162 Whitelocke, pp. 616–17, 621.
163 *CSPD 1661–62*, pp. 323, 347, *1663–64*, p. 202, *1667*, p. 386, *1671–72*, p. 52, *1672–73*, p. 232.
164 *CSPD 1661–62*, pp. 199, 495–6, *1672–73*, pp. 250, 275.
165 Milward, pp. 78–9.
166 *CSPD 1660–61*, p. 122, 132–3, *1661–62*, p. 49, 323; Clar MSS 73, fos 210, 74, fo. 11.
167 Clar MS 81, fo. 238.
168 *CSPD 1664–65*, pp. 354–5, 368, 430.
169 *CSPD 1663–64*, pp. 238–9, 274, *1670*, pp. 687–8; BL Add MS 32324, fo. 166; Coward, *Stanleys*, pp. 104–5, 179–81.
170 *OPH*, XXIII.51–3; *HMC 5th Report*, p. 200; *CSPD 1661–62*, p. 517, *1663–64*, pp. 294, 335.
171 *CSPD 1660–61*, p. 550; PC 2/55, fos 74, 89; Bath RO, Corporation Book II (1649–84), pp. 266, 271, 275–6.
172 *CSPD 1661–62*, pp. 248, 439; BL, Add MS 21922, fo. 249; *SR*, V.360.
173 *CSPD 1661–62*, pp. 177, 181, 239, 244.
174 *CSPD 1660–61*, p. 466.
175 *CSPD 1660–61*, p. 470; Steele, *Proclamations*, no. 3278; PC 2/55, fo. 48.
176 Clar MS 75, fo. 191; *CSPD 1661–62*, pp. 153, 155, 160; PC 2/56, fo. 125; Norrey, 'Regime', p. 804.
177 *LJ*, XI.240–1.
178 *CSPD 1660–61*, p. 150; BL, Add MSS 21922, fos 239–40, 32324, fo. 64.
179 BL, Add MS 21922, fo. 244; *HMC 3rd Report*, pp. 244–5; *RB*, II.300–1.
180 PC 2/55, fos 48–50.
181 Carte MS 130, fo. 274; M636/17, Council to Bridgewater, 8 January 1661; BL, Add MS 21922, fo. 244.
182 *CSPD 1660–61*, p. 470; Steele, *Proclamations*, no. 3278.
183 For the incidents in Wales, see *CSPD 1660–61*, pp. 123, 127, 130; Jenkins, *Wales*, p. 135. See also Coleby, *Hants.*, pp. 134–5.
184 Josselin, p. 474; Henry, p. 75; BL, Add MS 21922, fo. 245.

185 *HMC 3rd Report*, p. 259; M636/17, Circular dated 12 January 1661; *CSPD 1660–61*, p. 478; PC 2/55, fo. 56; Rugg, p. 142 (quoted).
186 *CSPD 1660–61*, p. 511.
187 PC 2/55, fos 81, 174; Carte MS 130, fo. 278; BL, Add MSS 21048, fo. 5, 21922, fo. 246, 32324, fo. 91.
188 BL, Ad MSS 32324, fos 115, 108–9, 21922, fo. 250. See also *CSPD 1660–61*, p. 466.
189 BRO, AC/02/13, AC/C74/19; *CSPD 1661–62*, pp. 145, 437–8; Carte MS 47, fo. 340.
190 Thomson, 'Herts.', pp. 443–7.
191 *CSPD 1661–62*, p. 127.
192 *CSPD 1661–62*, p. 143.
193 BL, Add MSS 21922, fo. 247, 32324, fos 108–9; *CSPD 1661–62*, pp. 113, 155–6.
194 PC 2/55, fo. 244; Pepys, II.204, 225.
195 Lister, III.98–101; *CSPD 1661–62*, pp. 421, 423–4, 441; *HMC Finch*, I.206.
196 PC 2/56, fos 32–3; Egerton MS 2543, fos 91–3; BL, Add MS 21048, fos 7–8.
197 Clar MS 77, fo. 66a.
198 Lister, III.208; Carte MS 47, fos 336, 340; *CSPD 1661–62*, pp. 434, 437–8, 455, 505, 511; Schellinks, pp. 110–11.
199 *CSPD 1661–62*, pp. 420, 466; BL, Add MS 21922, fos 250–1, 254.
200 Whitelocke, p. 655.
201 Carte MS 47, fo. 385; PC 2/56, fo. 124; *CSPD 1663–64*, pp. 31, 50.
202 *CSPD 1663–64*, pp. 57, 155.
203 *CSPD 1663–64*, p. 26.
204 PC 2/56, fos 253–4 (summarized *CSPD 1663–64*, p. 231). A similar order to Lord Herbert of Raglan was dated 1 August: Carte MS 130, fo. 280.
205 *CSPD 1663–64*, pp. 249–50; *HMC le Fleming*, p. 31; *CSPD 1670*, p. 683; Bodl, MS Eng Hist b 212, fos 5–7.
206 *CSPD 1663–64*, pp. 277, 287, 293, 294.
207 *CSPD 1663–64*, pp. 295, 299, 301.
208 *CSPD 1663–64*, pp. 332, 340, 372.
209 Clar MS 81, fo. 32.
210 *CSPD 1663–64*, pp. 380–1; DUL, Mickleton Spearman MS 31, fos 77–9.
211 *CSPD 1663–64*, p. 646; *Cosin*, II.108; DCLD, Hunter MS 10, no. 86.
212 PC 2/57, fos 24, 29.
213 In addition to references given earlier, see also *CSPD 1663–64*, pp. 310, 403, 492, 496.
214 *CSPD 1663–64*, pp. 454, 504.
215 *CSPD 1663–64*, p. 340.
216 Rugg, p. 142; *CSPD 1660–61*, pp. 470, 471, 473–5, 477–8, 481, 483.
217 CPA 77, D'Estrades to Louis, 6 November 1662 NS; *CSPD 1660–61*, p. 471, *1663–64*, p. 298; Josselin, p. 504; Harl MS 3784, fo. 55; Carte MS 222, fo. 6; *CCSP*, V.391.
218 Clar MS 75, fo. 191; *CSPD 1660–61*, pp. 466, 570, *1663–64*, pp. 325, 457, 523; Bodl, MS Eng Hist b 212, fo. 16.
219 *CSPD 1663–64*, p. 444.
220 *HMC le Fleming*, p. 30; Carte MS 222, fos 12, 32, 64; Cooper, *Annals*, III.511–12; Dunn, *Journal*, p. 37; Bodl MS Eng Hist b 212, fo. 12. (In the last, Townshend interprets the proclamation of 22 August 1663 as a command to

enforce the 1593 Act, but the proclamation does not mention it, although it mentions several other Acts as well as the laws enforcing church attendance and forbidding unlawful assemblies: Steele, *Proclamations*, no. 3383.)

221 PC 2/55, fo. 203; Carte MS 222, fo. 6.

222 BL, Add MS 63081, fo. 164.

Chapter ten

Politics in flux, 1664–73

The second Dutch war and its aftermath

Early in 1664, William Legge, MP and former active Royalist, wrote that the king's wisest course would be to rely on 'the old royal party', who were more numerous than their opponents. Former Parliamentarians now in office, with a few exceptions, favoured their former allies, who were still contriving mischief.[1] Again and again during the next decade, old Cavaliers denounced the 'Presbyterians', or the 'old Parliament gang',[2] or those 'of the old stamp of the late times' who could be bound by neither favours nor oaths.[3] They favoured nonconformists, they were 'anti-Church'.[4] References abound to individuals having been in the Parliamentarian army or the New Model.[5] Men still quarrelled about the past[6] and at Hertford sessions a man accused of being at a conventicle objected to the foreman of the jury on the grounds that he had been for the king.[7] Old Cavaliers like Musgrave felt threatened by the presence of some of 'the opposing party' in county offices and still more in the corporations.[8] They urged the king to rely on his 'own party' – even Arlington used the term in opposition to 'the discontented party' and the 'suspected party' – or 'the loyal party' or 'the Cavaliers'.[9] Less often, the Cavaliers called themselves 'the moderate party'.[10] Several accepted that this 'loyal party' included many Catholics or remarked that Presbyterians' principles were more dangerous than papists' or claimed that Presbyterians were again using antipopery to achieve their malevolent ends.[11] A decade after the Restoration, the wounds of civil war, for many, had not healed. John Milward remarked in 1668 that he would not be 'an informer' against negligent JPs, but he would happily give the Commons the names of those who had been county committee men and decimators if the House would put them out of commission. In 1670 three hundred horsemen attended the Duke of Ormond near Burton on Trent, with 'not a Roundhead among them'.[12] Cases where old Cavaliers testified that individuals who had fought for Parliament posed no threat to the government were far less common.[13]

The fact that the Cavaliers talked in such terms showed that they still felt frustrated and betrayed. However, in 1664 the king dropped his opposition to a bill against conventicles and the following year he gave his assent to the Five Mile Act. The rapprochement between king and Cavaliers was reinforced by a surge of patriotic enthusiasm in the run-up to the Second Dutch War. In December 1664, on the motion of Sir Robert Paston, the Commons agreed to vote £2,500,000 for the war – considerably more than twice the king's current annual revenue and about six times the largest parliamentary grant in the 1620s. In the early stages of the war every hint of naval success was celebrated and the Duke of York's victory at Lowestoft was greeted with euphoria: letters from the fleet were passed eagerly from hand to hand. The Earl of Orrery wrote a play reinventing Agincourt as a naval battle.[14] But the victory at Lowestoft was not followed up, merchant shipping suffered heavy losses and there were many complaints that the cargoes of Dutch prize ships were being embezzled. As plague raged, morale crumbled and the public mood changed to anger: the inconclusive Four Days' Battle in June 1666 was widely seen as a defeat. The Great Fire added to the sense of despondency and paranoia: rumours spread that it had been started by the French or the papists. The burning of the City exacerbated the decay of trade and of the king's revenue. Despite a further substantial grant from Parliament, the king fell further and further into debt, to a point where it was decided that he could not afford to send out the fleet in 1667.[15]

By the winter of 1666–67 there was a new vocabulary to describe the divisions in Parliament: on one hand 'the courtiers' or 'the court party';[16] on the other, the 'country gentlemen' or 'the patriots'.[17] These terms dated back at least to the 1620s, but they indicated a different axis of division from that implied by terms such as 'the old Parliament gang', or 'the Royal party', which appeared less often.[18] Debates were notably more heated than in the recent past: those on the Irish cattle bill were compared with the clashes of 1641.[19] Pepys blamed the deterioration in the Commons' mood partly on incompetence among the king's spokesmen, who could not agree on strategy or tactics.[20] But there was more to it than that. As the war effort foundered and the public mood became angrier, the Cavaliers asked who was responsible and denounced those who profited from the war while unpaid seamen starved. Councillors and courtiers sought to divert the Commons' wrath towards others and in their frantic efforts to escape censure became ever more ruthless. Observers agreed that the storms in Parliament 'had their birth in the king's own house'.[21] Sheldon thought 'the king never had, nor never is likely to have, persons more willing to comply with his desires than the present House of Commons, nor would be, were they treated as they might be, for all the disorders have arisen from the king's family and servants'.[22] The ferocity of faction-fighting was increased considerably by the emergence of the Duke of Buckingham as an oppositionist figure late in 1666, after a quarrel with Lady Castlemaine. Buckingham was notoriously mercurial, but he possessed a persuasive tongue, a forceful personality and a capacity for hatred without equal. He was among the promoters of the Irish cattle bill, which was designed to pander to anti-Irish prejudice, as well as the self-interest of MPs from the North and West. It was hoped that Ormond, the lord lieutenant, would oppose the bill, which would lead the Commons to demand his dismissal. Charles openly opposed the bill, which made the Commons angrier and their sense of discontent spilled over into other issues, notably a demand for accounts for the money voted for the war.[23]

Some of those who promoted the Irish cattle bill – for example Ashley and Lauderdale – were far from being Royalists, but the grievances on which they played were shared by many old Cavaliers. This was not surprising given the latter's perception that the king had given too many jobs to old Parliamentarians: in 1667 it was noted with displeasure that he had granted military commissions to Fairfax and Manchester.[24] But the Commons' resentment was also directed against Royalist councillors, especially as the war went from bad to worse. In June, a Dutch fleet sailed up the Medway and captured or burned many of the king's finest ships. Amid fears of invasion, there were calls for heads to roll. When the king briefly recalled Parliament in July, a 'sequestered Cavalier', Sir Thomas Tompkins, complained that the nation's taxes had been diverted into private pockets and expressed fears that the newly raised forces might become the foundation of an absolute monarchy. He was seconded by other old Cavaliers, who all cried out against the courtiers.[25] Pepys doubted whether the king had any such intention, but remarked that many now compared the restored monarchy unfavourably with the Protectorate.[26] Meanwhile, Buckingham had been restored to favour. He claimed that his time as self-styled champion of the people had given him a deep understanding of Parliament and warned the king that the Commons would demand scapegoats. Given that many of their complaints were of financial mismanagement, Southampton, the elderly and ineffectual lord treasurer, might have seemed a possible candidate, but he was saved from censure by death and, anyway, Buckingham had his sights set on Ormond and Clarendon. Ormond, away in Ireland, could hardly be blamed for the mishandling of the war, so Buckingham and his allies focused their attack on Clarendon. The king was persuaded to dismiss him and then, when he was impeached, to urge the Lords to find him guilty and condemn him to death, in the belief that nothing less would satisfy the Commons. Realizing that the king wanted him dead, Clarendon fled abroad, dying in Montpellier in 1674.[27]

The proceedings against Clarendon produced what might seem strange alignments, in view of Clarendon's Royalist past. The charges were brought in by Sir Thomas Littleton, a former Royalist. Sir Charles Wheeler, very active for the king in the civil war, claimed that Clarendon had obstructed the settlement of the government in church and state, had favoured nonconformists and hindered the preferment of old Cavaliers. Similar arguments were used by Sir Richard Temple, a former Parliamentarian, while Wheeler's claim that Hyde had corresponded with Cromwell was echoed by the Royalist, Sir Robert Howard.[28] By contrast, a number of Presbyterians – Swynfen, Hampden, Maynard, Marvell, Prynne – argued that the charge of corresponding with Cromwell was inadmissable, because of the Act of Oblivion, and that Clarendon should be given a fair hearing: they rebutted the claim that treason was whatever the Commons declared it to be.[29] In the Lords the ex-chancellor was supported by most of the bishops (although Sheldon remarked privately that the Church had little reason to be grateful to him) and defended by Anglesey and Ashley; it was noted that many of his enemies in the Lords were 'of the royal party'.[30] Part of the apparent confusion can be resolved by noting that a number of leading promoters of the impeachment – Temple, Edward Seymour, Sir Thomas Osborne – were closely associated with Buckingham. Burnet later wrote that 'the court party' pressed to have Clarendon imprisoned pending trial, but in view of the divisions at court it is not entirely clear what the 'court party' was.[31] In general, however, it appears that Clarendon's fall owed much to a widespread sense among Cavaliers that he had betrayed them.

The Cabal

If the Cavaliers expected that Clarendon's removal would lead to a more acceptable ministry, they were in for a rude shock. The Commons had appointed a committee to nominate what became known as the Brooke House Committee, which was to investigate the accounts for the Dutch War and was to include no member of either House. When the committee brought in its list, on 12 December, the Commons were outraged that it included 'many villains and enemies to the late king', including the pugnacious Colonel King and the former Leveller John Wildman, now closely associated with Buckingham. The committee was instructed to bring in a new list, but for the old Cavaliers the signs were ominous.[32] Worse was to come. The prime movers in Clarendon's downfall had been Buckingham and Arlington, ambitious men who agreed on the need to remove the chancellor, if on little else. To guard against any possibility that Clarendon might return to power, they told the king that he would never recover the Commons' goodwill until he had removed Clarendon's followers (the 'Clarendonians') from office and replaced them with their own, allegedly more acceptable to the House. Their priorities were different. Arlington believed Clarendon had been incompetent, as an administrator and a parliamentary manager. His strategy of relying on a few old Cavalier cronies to persuade the House had failed. A more systematic approach was needed: spokesmen should be thoroughly briefed, court supporters and those who abandoned opposition should be rewarded. Buckingham's aims were more extravagant and less coherent. His faith in his own abilities was unlimited and he presumed upon his special relationship with the king: following his father's assassination in 1628, Charles I had the young duke brought up with his own children. Buckingham wanted power, but had few consistent objectives, apart from pursuing feuds with personal enemies (and the Church of England clergy) and securing greater freedom for nonconformists.[33] At times he advocated something akin to absolute monarchy, at times he supported measures which would weaken the crown: confident of his ability to control Parliament, he encouraged it to strip the king of his prerogatives in order to assume quasi-regal power himself. His personal following included both former republicans and Cromwellians (like Wildman) and disgruntled ex-Royalists (like Seymour and Osborne). His huge personal influence over the king (based on his encouraging Charles's frenetic pursuit of pleasure and on sheer force of personality) and his fundamental lack of direction made for political instability. He quickly became locked in a power struggle with the more pragmatic and competent Arlington. Buckingham persuaded the king that a group of his clients, the 'undertakers', headed by Sir Richard Temple, could manage the Commons. These undertakers insisted that the Commons would demand a tough investigation into the mismanagement of the Dutch War, which many old Cavaliers wanted, and steps to restrict the prerogative and indulge Dissenters, which they did not. Buckingham pressed the king to give the old Cavaliers policies which they disliked, and to make appointments which they liked even less, and endorsed Arlington's methods of parliamentary management, which provoked 'country' sensibilities among both old Cavaliers and independently-minded Presbyterians, like Marvell. Faced with the Commons' resentment, Buckingham urged the king to dissolve Parliament, with promises that a new House of Commons would prove more amenable. The king was torn between his own common sense and his susceptibility to Buckingham's charisma. His policies vacillated and the divisions within Parliament varied according to the issue involved: at times, the old Cavaliers urged the king to rely on his old friends, at others, they were swept up in 'country' resentment against those who currently comprised 'the court' and their attempts to manipulate the Houses.[34]

In January 1668 Anglesey noted that mutual trust at court had been destroyed by recent events.[35] Under pressure from Buckingham and to a lesser extent Arlington, the Clarendonians were replaced in office by a mixture of 'opposition men', such as Seymour, Osborne, Littleton, Temple and Sir Robert Howard, and those the Duke of York labelled 'Cromwellians' – Robartes, Orrery, Anglesey and Sir John Trevor, who became secretary of state. Former republicans were released from gaol.[36] New legal appointments also included 'Cromwellians', although Sir Ralph Verney remarked on the dearth of able lawyers among the Cavaliers. Sir Orlando Bridgeman, who had shown moderation towards Dissenters, succeeded Clarendon, in the lesser office of lord keeper.[37] The Duke of York, the natural leader of the Cavaliers at court, was obliged to keep a low profile because of his close association with Clarendon (his father-in-law) and claims that he wished to set up a reversionary interest in opposition to his brother.[38] The fall of Clarendon and its aftermath had seriously weakened the Cavalier interest, to a point where non-Royalists (or anti-Royalists) had gained a greater share of power than at any time since the Restoration. Confusion and recrimination reigned. In the Commons, the 'country gentlemen' talked of squeezing the 'sponges' who had absorbed so much public money and saw no reason to vote money for the fleet: the last time they had done so, no fleet had been sent out. However, the old Cavaliers reacted with hostility to the undertakers' attempt to reduce the king's freedom to summon and dismiss Parliaments at will by, in effect, re-enacting the 1641 Triennial Act.[39] The 'royal party' also resented the attempts of Sir Robert Brooke, Colonel Birch 'and others of that gang' to delay the discussion of supply until grievances had been more fully investigated.[40] When the House agreed to vote money, Howard and Seymour proposed that it should be appropriated for the fleet, but the House rejected this because 'it did seem to put a distrust in the king': the old Cavaliers seemed more concerned about the king's prerogative and interest than those who claimed to enjoy his favour – and indeed the king himself.[41] And, as we shall see, the king seemed disconcertingly inclined to favour comprehension and indulgence.

The old Cavaliers watched the behaviour of the king and his ministers with a mixture of anger and bewilderment: the ascendancy which Charles allowed Buckingham defied rational analysis. In 1669 the Duke finally had Ormond removed from the lord lieutenancy of Ireland; he was replaced by Robartes.[42] This brought Ormond back to England, giving the Cavaliers a leader at court less vulnerable than York, but contemporaries remained confused about the balance of political forces. Ruvigny, who was much better informed about English politics than most French ambassadors, discerned three parties in the Commons in 1668: the 'Presbyterians', who wished to have the Cavalier Parliament dissolved; the 'Clarendonians' who wanted revenge on those in power; and the 'Royalists', who opposed the court because they felt insufficiently rewarded for their loyalty. Of these the Royalists were the strongest, but the Commons as a whole were angry at reports that Buckingham had told the king that he could control them.[43] Temple divided the House into Clarendonians, anti-Clarendonians, Presbyterians and the 'country gentlemen': he seemingly did not see the Cavaliers as a distinct group. He argued that now the Clarendonians had been crushed, it should be possible to weld the other three groups into a coherent alliance, on the basis of the punishment of past misdeeds, the restriction of the royal prerogative and comprehension and indulgence.[44] A year or so later Sandwich distinguished two parties. Buckingham's derived its main strength from the Brooke House Committee, which he hoped to use to ruin his enemies. This party was strong only when it could win the support of the Presbyterians and the country gentlemen on issues such as accounts, trade or liberty of conscience. Ormond's party drew its support from the friends of the Church and the Duke of York, the Clarendonians and the old Royalists. In other words, this was a 'Church and Cavalier party', concerned to defend the Church and Ormond (who faced the prospect of impeachment). It intended to impose political and religious tests on those appointed to offices and elected to Parliament.[45]

Of these analyses, Sandwich's most closely mirrored the behaviour of the Commons, but those in power at court had no wish to recognise that the Cavaliers were a potent force, nor that 'country' sentiment could be turned against the undertakers as well as against those who had mismanaged the Dutch war.[46] Moreover, both choices of strategy which now faced the king – of relying on the old Cavaliers or on their opponents – were from 1668 being undermined by a major, but as yet secret, new initiative in foreign policy. Charles had long sought an alliance with France against the Dutch. Early in 1668 he signed the Triple Alliance, with the Dutch Republic and Sweden, which was designed in part to limit French expansion into the Spanish Netherlands. He soon resumed overtures to France, in which proposals for an alliance became linked to a promise to declare himself a Catholic; he asked Louis XIV to promise help if this declaration provoked a revolt among his subjects.

The end product was the Secret Treaty of Dover, signed on 22 May 1670, which included (in a secret clause) the promise to announce his conversion.

In the absence of conclusive evidence, Charles's motives remain a matter for speculation: they need not concern us here.[47] What does concern us is that Charles committed himself to a French alliance against the Dutch, at a time when both Cavaliers and Parliamentarians were coming to see the French as a much more potent threat than the Dutch, in geopolitical, commercial and colonial terms. Louis XIV seemed to be aiming to establish a 'universal monarchy'.[48] His identification with militant Catholicism and absolute monarchy would raise doubts about Charles II's motives in allying with him: did he plan to follow his French cousin's example? It should be stressed, however, that the alliance remained secret until the commencement of hostilities in the spring of 1672 and the 'Catholic clause' remained secret for the rest of the reign. Among the king's ministers, some knew more than others. Arlington was involved from the start in negotiations concerning both the alliance and the promise of conversion. Sir Thomas Clifford, Arlington's right-hand man in the Commons, became a privy councillor in 1666 and was made lord treasurer and Baron Clifford in 1672. Although he appears to have converted to Catholicism only in 1671 or 1672, he too was involved from the outset in the discussions about the king's religion. The king's other leading ministers were aware only of the negotiations about the alliance. Buckingham embraced the idea with enthusiasm, perhaps judging that the war and Louis's friendship would make it possible to strengthen the monarchy, which would enhance his own power and enable the king to defy the Commons and allow greater freedom for Dissenters. Ashley saw the war as in England's economic interests, a chance to break the commercial dominance of the Dutch. In addition, he argued that it would be necessary to allow greater liberty to Dissenters, to avoid the risk of disorder at home while England fought another Protestant power. This view appears to have been shared by the Duke of Lauderdale, the leading figure in the king's government in Scotland: although his main interest lay north of the Border, he needed to maintain his favour at court and supported the foreign policy that the king clearly wanted.

The fact that some ministers knew more than others made it necessary to go through the charade of additional negotiations for a treaty of alliance, so that Buckingham, in particular, could see it as his own work. Despite their rivalries, the five came to be seen as a distinct and rather sinister group, whose initials happened to form the word 'cabal'. Meanwhile, the Commons remained blissfully unaware of these momentous developments. The brief parliamentary session late in 1669 heightened the Cavaliers' annoyance at the king's perverse refusal to place his trust in the natural supporters of the monarchy and the Church, but in early 1670 there were hopes that he would now rely on 'his own party'[49] and it was made known that he would agree to a new bill against conventicles. When Parliament reconvened in February the king declared that he had questioned the Brooke House Committee and was satisfied that all the money received had been spent on the war. The Commons resolved to debate supply before grievances. The king proposed to erase from the journals all reference to the recent jurisdictional dispute between the Houses. The Commons resolved to wait on the king as a body and spent the rest of the day drinking the king's health on their knees in the royal cellars. For the Cavaliers, it was an occasion of unalloyed joy.[50] For Marvell it was a disaster. He blamed 'some undertakers of the meanest of our House' for agreeing to abandon the investigation of accounts. The conventicle bill was 'the price of money'. Thanks to this most compliant of Parliaments, the king was more powerful than any of his predecessors since 1066.[51] The final form of the Conventicle Act and the grant of an additional duty on wines merely added to his gloom. He denounced most of his fellow-members as 'venal cowards', a judgment confirmed when Howard, Seymour, Temple and others abandoned their 'former party' and came over to the court. Other oppositionist figures, like Richard Hampden, stayed away. In 1671, Marvell fulminated that these 'apostate patriots' had been bought off with rewards worth as much as £15,000 a year, but the Commons remained more cooperative than at any time since the Restoration.[52]

It seems that the divisions between Cavalier and Parliamentarian, Churchman and Dissenter, slurred over first by common enthusiasm for the Dutch War and then by common anger at its mismanagement, had been sharpened once more by the changes in personnel and policies which followed Clarendon's fall – or at least those policies that were known. In 1668–69 the prevailing tone among the Cavaliers was of anxiety or frustration.[53] In 1670–71, the Cavaliers became more confident of support from 'above', to a point where the coffee-man Richard Bower denounced Lord Townshend for allegedly favouring only those of 'the old stamp', while Sir Thomas Medowes upbraided him openly for placing his greatest trust in those who had been in arms against Charles I.[54] Such renewed confidence did not last long. In November 1671 Williamson remarked that 'even the Cavaliers dread a war and abominate ill', adding that they were 'still unrewarded for their sufferings'. In February 1672 Daniel Fleming, congratulating Guy Carleton on his appointment as bishop of Bristol, remarked that it was good to see an old Cavalier in such a post, with the clear implication that this was not happening often enough.[55] By the end of 1672 their recently revived faith in the king's kindness had been damaged beyond repair. Part of the explanation lies in the revelation of the French alliance just over a year after the king had asked for money to guard against the danger from France. However, the Cavaliers were equally incensed by the duplicity revealed by the king's contorted religious policy: having granted them what they wanted, he snatched it away and left them worse off than before.

Church and Dissent

The 1664 Conventicle Act was enforced unevenly. There were numerous complaints that juries of 'fanatics' refused to find against fellow-Dissenters.[56] At Exeter a group of Quakers were acquitted because the jury found no evidence of seditious intent. Judges Hyde and Kelyng browbeat six of the jurymen into changing their minds, but the other six were bound over to appear before King's Bench. Other Quakers were sentenced without even being asked if they wished to plead. A Middlesex jury was told that at the last sessions jurors had been heavily fined for bringing in a verdict of not guilty against Quakers; the jury duly brought in verdicts of guilty.[57] Judge Rainsford declared that one witness and the notoriety of the fact were sufficient to prove a conventicle.[58] In 1667 Kelyng was summoned before the Commons for maltreating juries. In one case, the jurors had claimed that 'they had not full proof that there was not [sic] any religious worship performed' even though the Quakers admitted that they had come to 'seek God in the spirit'. Kelyng had fined the jurors and sent them to gaol until the fines were paid. The House accepted that his intentions had been good.[59] In the case of Penn and Meade in 1670, the mayor and recorder of London refused to accept a verdict of not guilty, kept the jurors without food or drink for three days and fined and imprisoned some who refused to change their minds. One of the jurors, Edward Bushell, obtained a writ of *habeas corpus*. The case eventually came before King's Bench, where Mr Justice Vaughan ruled that the fining and imprisoning of jurors was illegal.[60]

These examples suggest that judges habitually bullied juries into finding verdicts against their consciences. However, in 1664–65 several judges encouraged jurors to acquit those accused under the Conventicle Act: Hale told a jury at Exeter that he could see no evidence of sedition. Bishop Ward complained that the judges had discouraged JPs from acting against meetings, but with Kelyng's help he persuaded most of them to be more diligent.[61] The mixed signals sent by the judges undermined the government's orders to enforce the laws. Bridgeman defined a conventicle as a meeting to plot against the state, so that purely religious meetings were not conventicles, and claimed that the oath in the Five Mile Act related only to attempts to change the government by force or sedition.[62] Most magistrates and lords lieutenant proved reluctant to enforce the laws rigorously; those taken at meetings were often imprisoned for a short time and then released, or let off with small fines. In 1666 the JPs of Cumberland and Westmorland agreed to use the recusancy laws, with the fine of a shilling a week, rather than trying to enforce the Conventicle Act: the fines were more realistic and could be levied on Catholics as well as Dissenters.[63] Philip Henry later remarked that, while the Act had made life more difficult for Dissenters, few had suffered much under it.[64]

At first the king seemed committed to enforcing the Acts passed by Parliament, but from late 1667 there were signs of change. Clarendon's fall brought into power men hostile or indifferent to the Church. Most of the bishops had opposed the measures against Clarendon, which the king would not forgive: Sheldon fell so completely out of favour that he was not asked to preach the Christmas sermon at court.[65] Those now in favour vilified the clergy and talked of solving the king's financial problems by confiscating the lands of the deans and chapters.[66] They claimed that Dissenters were superior to conformists in numbers and wealth and that attempts at coercion were likely to provoke them to revolt. But Charles also feared that the Dissenters might revolt if allowed liberty to meet in greater numbers, a fear encouraged by advocates of persecution like Ormond, York and (later) the bishops. Fearful and uncertain, the king oscillated uncomfortably between repression and conciliation, apparently plumping for the former in 1670 only to switch to the latter in 1672. Meanwhile, the emphasis of the strategy of conciliation changed, reflecting the division among the Presbyterians, between the 'Dons', who still hoped for comprehension, and the 'Ducklings', who were coming to accept sectarian status. This can be traced back to the 'Oxford oath' of 1665. Encouraged by Bridgeman's statement that it referred only to changing church government by force (and urged on by some of the bishops) a significant number of Presbyterians, mostly 'Dons', took the oath.[67] In 1667–68 both Bridgeman and Dr John Wilkins (soon to be raised to the episcopate) discussed terms for a possible comprehension with Baxter, Thomas Manton and other 'Dons'. Manton blamed the failure of the negotiations on John Owen's rival scheme, for toleration. The creation of a broader church would weaken the case for toleration, but it was significant that Owen was supported by Samuel Annesley, a leading 'Duckling'.[68] The divisions were widened by the younger Presbyterians' eagerness to hold conventicles after the 1664 Act lapsed, which alarmed the king and made him more receptive to arguments for repression.

In retrospect, Baxter saw the king's abandonment of comprehension in favour of indulgence as part of a covert design to allow toleration to Catholics, which dated back to the proposal to include 'others' in the Worcester House Declaration in 1660.[69] He suspected that the king agreed to the 1670 Conventicle Act to show Dissenters that they depended on his protection and to make them willing to embrace the Declaration of Indulgence, even though it also allowed liberty to Catholics.[70] There is no hard evidence to confirm (or disprove) this view. It was suggestive that Owen told Manton in 1668 that 'comprehension would neither do the king's business nor ours'.[71] In addition, the indulgence proposed by Bridgeman in 1668 was to last for only three years, but this may just have reflected fears that the Dissenters might abuse it.[72] Baxter's hypothesis would depend on the king's being fully aware that a growing number of Presbyterians now favoured toleration rather than comprehension. Owen emphasized the divisions among the Presbyterians in 1668, but the king probably fully grasped the differences between 'Dons' and 'Ducklings' only when Williamson engaged in extensive discussions with London Dissenters late in 1671.[73] It is equally possible that Charles was simply suffering from his usual inability to choose between rival policies.

There were rumours in the winter of 1667–68 that toleration would be allowed to Dissenters, and even to Quakers; in anticipation, they began to meet in larger numbers.[74] There was a flurry of pamphlets against the coercion of conscience: some claimed that freedom of worship was a fundamental right of Englishmen, which even Parliament could not take away – hardly an argument that would appeal to the Commons.[75] The king's new advisers were confident, however, that when Parliament met it would agree to the proposals of Bridgeman and Wilkins concerning comprehension and indulgence. Instead, the Commons, hearing of swarms of conventicles in the provinces, voted to petition the king to issue a proclamation 'to restrain the disorderly and tumultuous meeting of dissenters from the Act of Uniformity and from the government of the Church'.[76] This vote passed just before the king came to give his speech, in which he urged 'that you would seriously think of some course to beget a better union and composure in the minds of my Protestant subjects in matters of religion'. When he showed no inclination to order the enforcement of the laws, the Commons again debated the 'insolence of sectaries' and on 4 March resolved to wait on the king 'in a body' to ask him to issue a proclamation.[77] This time he complied, but it was couched in 'gentle' terms and included a statement that he was seeking ways to unite Protestants.[78] Next day the Commons debated the king's speech. The arguments for and against comprehension and indulgence were fully aired, but the opponents of change had the better of the debate and Secretary Morrice (as in 1660) moved to adjourn it; the House agreed.[79]

The king's new advisers had seriously misread the mood of the House. Birch had a comprehension bill ready, but dared not bring it in.[80] The adjournment of the debate on comprehension ensured the Commons did not condemn it, but they were now aroused by reports of seditious meetings and parsons being pulled from their pulpits. On 13 March they resolved, by 'a multitude of voices', to bring in a bill to renew the Conventicle Act for seven years. 'The king, if he pleases,' wrote one MP 'may take a right measure of our temper by this and leave off crediting the undertakers.'[81] The bill passed the Commons and went up to the Lords on 28 April, but the peers were in no hurry and the bill made little progress before the king adjourned Parliament on 9 May.[82]

Why had the king so misjudged the Commons? Perhaps he saw the hostility to Clarendon, which he himself had done so much to foment, as evidence of hostility to the Church, or he may simply have been misled by his new advisers. It is also possible that the Commons had changed. On two occasions debates were initiated by reports from the provinces of the boldness of Dissenters. These reports were carefully prepared, although at least one was untrue. The opponents of Dissent were also directly, but covertly, encouraged by Sheldon.[83] This would suggest that experience of Dissenters' defiance of the law, indeed of the authority of Parliament, and the disorders that they caused, convinced MPs of the need to renew the Conventicle Act. The old Cavaliers disliked the king's new advisers, who made no secret of their hostility towards the Church, as shown by appointments such as that of Wilkins, scientist, philosopher and supporter of comprehension, as bishop of Chester. Milward noted that the bishops had many defenders in the Commons, especially when Sir Thomas Littleton attacked them in a speech in which he also defended Buckingham, who had recently killed his mistress's husband in a duel.[84] For whatever reason, the Commons seem to have become **more** hostile to Dissent and more attached to the Church in the later 1660s; the Cavaliers were coming to see a strong Church as vital for a return to a 'Cavalier' regime.

For the moment, however, Parliament was not sitting and there was little they could do. The Conventicle Act had been in force for three years from

May 1664 and then to the end of the next session of Parliament. The king had adjourned Parliament in May and finally prorogued it on 1 March 1669.[85] Some believed that the Act lapsed in August 1668 which, together with the king's declared support for a relaxation of the laws, encouraged Dissenters to meet more freely than ever. Bishop Sparrow was relieved when Judge Vaughan assured the JPs of Devon that the Act was still in force.[86] The king, perturbed by reports of meetings, ordered the mayor and aldermen of Newcastle to enforce the Conventicle Act. When some London ministers thanked him for conniving at meetings, he tried to persuade them to meet more discreetly and in smaller numbers.[87] When there was no longer any doubt that the Act had lapsed, the king vacillated. At times he seemed 'hot . . . against conventicles' or complained that they multiplied too fast; at other times he seemed inclined to leave them alone.[88] Prompted by complaints from lords lieutenant, the committee for foreign affairs considered the matter on 15 April 1669. Bridgeman, Trevor and Arlington argued that the Dissenters were not seditious and should be left alone, while Buckingham declared that they were the trading part of the nation. Ormond declared that men of such principles had kept the king out of his kingdom. Caught in the middle, Charles complained that they claimed that he wished them to be indulged and suggested that meetings should be suppressed in London. In the end, the committee asked the lords lieutenant to investigate whether numbers were in fact increasing and whether the Five Mile Act was being enforced: a marginal note suggested uncertainty as to whether it was still in force.[89]

By June the proponents of firmness were gaining ground. Orders had been issued to suppress meetings but little had been done, partly because those who were eager to act were unsure how best to do so.[90] Sheldon sent a circular to his bishops, assuring them that there was no truth in claims that the king favoured meetings and that they would receive the full support of the secular authorities in suppressing them. The bishops were to send in details of the meetings, including the names of the preachers and leading members. He added in a postcript that they were to enquire whether some people went to several meetings, which would make Dissenters seem more numerous than they were, and to consider how easy it would be to suppress them: he had heard that many consisted of 'women, children and inconsiderable persons'.[91] The wording suggests that Sheldon wrote the letter (but probably not the postscript) with the king's approval, or even at his command; the king wanted to know whether conventicles were really becoming larger and more numerous. One newsletter stated that the council had ordered the bishops to draw up an account of meetings in their dioceses.[92] Sheldon had been rebuilding his influence at court since December; some letters complaining of conventicles passed through him and he may well have solicited others. His return to favour, followed by the bishops of Rochester and Winchester, showed a shift in the balance of power at court.[93] On 30 June the council asked the judges which laws were in force against Dissent. They suggested several: the Act of 1593 and the Quakers Act of 1662 dealt with conventicles; the Five Mile Act could be used against ejected ministers; it was possible to use the recusancy laws and the Act of 1606 imposing penalties for refusing the oath of allegiance; and any assemblies which disturbed the peace were punishable under common law.[94]

A week later, the council set up a committee on conventicles. On 16 July the king issued a proclamation ordering JPs to enforce the laws against them and complaining that they had become more numerous; orders were sent to the governors of a number of garrison towns to disperse conventicles there. Sheldon was disappointed that the proclamation focused on the Five Mile Act and did not mention the recusancy laws, but it had some effect: there were reports that Dissenters had ceased to meet. In Cumberland the JPs ordered that absentees from church be fined a shilling a week.[95] The grand juries of Cambridgeshire, Suffolk, Northamptonshire and Lincolnshire thanked the king for his proclamation, but by the end of the year its impact was wearing off and meetings began again.[96] Sheldon was well aware that the battle was far from won. The promoters of toleration organized petitions from artisans threatening to take their skills abroad if their meetings were molested.[97] Too many bishops had failed to respond diligently to his circular – sometimes because vicars and churchwardens refused to provide the necessary information – and those who were active against meetings found some magistrates unhelpful. This was understandable: just after the proclamation was issued, the assiduous Sir Philip Musgrave was troubled to hear that Charles had met a group of London Baptists. What, he asked, was the king's real intention?[98] Lacking a law specifically directed against meetings and a clear lead from the king, those of the bishops and the gentry who really wanted to suppress conventicles were fighting a losing battle against inertia, apathy and distaste for persecution.

The situation was soon to change. When the Commons reconvened in October 1669 they made it clear that their attitude towards Dissent had not softened, thanking the king for his proclamation and bringing in another bill to renew the Conventicle Act. Following reports that Jesuits and former New Model officers had been seen at meetings, a committee was appointed to investigate seditious meetings, especially around Westminster, and the House resolved to defend the present government in church and state against its enemies.[99] The bill was committed on 10 November and the report from the committee was debated on 18 November. In the debates, some complained that the nonconformists and their allies had misled the king, suggesting that they were both powerful and numerous. There were reports that the Commons wished to make the Act more severe and to prevent the king from remitting his share of the fines. In the end, however, the Commons became bogged down in a long-running dispute with the Lords and the measure was lost.[100] By the time Parliament reconvened in February 1670, the king had changed his strategy. On 17 February, three days after the session began, the House resolved to bring in a bill against conventicles. It was committed on 2 March and received its third reading on 9 March, when it passed by 138 votes to 78.[101] The king let it be known that he favoured the bill. When Sir Gilbert Talbot told the House that 'one Fox' had said in a conventicle that he acknowledged no king, he stressed that he passed on this information with the king's permission.[102] When the bill went up to the Lords the king made it clear that he wished it to pass; on 21 March, he attended the debate in person, claiming that his predecessors had often done so. The bill completed its progress through the Lords on 26 March.[103] The form in which it emerged did not please the Commons. The Lords wished to increase the minimum size of a 'conventicle' from five to ten, over and above the immediate family, to reduce many of the penalties and to make the Act only temporary. Most controversial of all was a proviso that nothing in the Act should undermine or destroy the king's ecclesiastical supremacy or 'any of His Majesty's rights, powers or prerogatives belonging to the imperial crown of this realm or at any time exercised or enjoyed, or which might have been exercised or enjoyed' by any previous monarch.[104] The Commons reacted with horror. Sir Heneage Finch, Sir Thomas Clifford and Sir John Maynard all declared that the proviso would give the king the power to sweep away Magna Carta and all the nation's liberties. Only Secretary Trevor, Sir Richard Temple and Sir Robert Howard, all supporters of comprehension and indulgence, defended the proviso; the two last argued that the king needed such powers to protect the Stranger churches. The House was not convinced, but agreed to a proviso safeguarding the king's supremacy in ecclesiastical affairs only. The Lords abandoned most of their other provisos and the bill passed largely in the form laid down by the Commons.[105] It targeted preachers and those who allowed their houses to be used for meetings and it provided for payments to informers and fines on magistrates who refused to act. It also contained a clause that in case of doubt it should always be construed in such a way as to secure a conviction. Baxter thought that this clause referred to recent proceedings against himself, but it was probably provoked by the Quakers' success in exploiting legal technicalities in order to avoid conviction.[106]

Why, having seemed so determined to improve the lot of Dissenters, did the king not only assent to the bill but encourage the Houses to pass it? Andrew Marvell offered one answer – it was 'the price of money' – but, like Baxter, he suspected that the real reason lay deeper. He saw in the Lords' proviso concerning the prerogative a plan to give the king the power to dispense with the law, which would enable him to relieve Dissenters and make them wholly dependent on his favour.[107] This interpretation was given added plausibility by what followed. The council ordered that the Act should be rigorously enforced: meeting houses (especially in London) were to be shut, soldiers were to prevent people entering them and those with no known owner were to have their seats and other fittings removed.[108] Sheldon ordered his clergy to inform their local magistrates about conventicles and to give the names of preachers.[109] Dissenters flocked to London in a bid to make the new Act unenforceable: if it could not be enforced in the capital, it would not be enforced elsewhere. Those taken at conventicles refused to pay fines; guards and soldiers were threatened. The military responded with gratuitous violence and in the latter part of May the city seemed on the verge of civil war.[110] By the middle of June, with the help of the trained bands and the Honourable Artillery Company (which contained not a single 'fanatic'), the authorities had gained the upper hand. Even the largest meetings had been broken up; the seats had been ripped out of some meeting houses and conformist ministers had been sent to preach in others.[111] The success of persecution in London gave heart to those in the provinces who had hitherto been uncertain whether firm action would be approved of 'above'; the Dissenters ceased to meet, or else met secretly or in smaller numbers. The persecution continued into the autumn and winter.[112]

The experience of 1670 suggested that persecution worked. Meetings were suppressed without provoking rebellion; Sparrow reported that 'the churches fill apace'.[113] The king was not convinced: he told the French ambassador that England would never be quiet until the Dissenters enjoyed liberty of conscience and he encouraged preachers to approach him for relief.[114] He may have wished to establish a general liberty from which Catholics could benefit, but he also did not want to go to war with the Dutch with the nonconformists resentful and perhaps rebellious.[115] By the summer of 1671 the persecution had ended and nonconformists met freely in London.[116] A new conventicle bill had passed the Commons in the spring, which (among other provisions) would have allowed constables, with a magistrate's warrant, to break open doors. It was also proposed to declare conventicles riots and to give indemnity to officials who had been over-zealous, but both proposals were rejected. Some thought that the bill was ill-considered and perhaps unnecessary; the Commons did not seem unduly distressed when it did not pass. Perhaps they now felt that the laws against Dissent were now sufficient.[117]

There is no evidence that Charles encouraged the passing of this bill. Instead he resumed his contacts with the London preachers through Williamson, who urged them to meet discreetly and suggested that the king might use his 'supreme power in ecclesiastics' to grant them relief. Privately he noted that it was better for the king to give a limited relief of his own volition than to be forced later to grant a more extensive liberty. Above all, the king had to have some 'moral security' that they would 'live peaceably'.[118] The negotiations led to the Declaration of Indulgence, issued on 15 March 1672, shortly after the start of the Dutch War. It declared that all penal laws in matters of religion were suspended. Dissenters were to be free to worship, but only in venues approved by the king, as proposed by Bridgeman in 1668; unauthorized conventicles remained illegal. Catholics could worship only in their own homes. Preachers were not to teach sedition or to attack the Church of England, which was to 'be preserved and remain entire in its doctrine, discipline and government'. The Declaration was based on 'that supreme power in ecclesiastical matters which is not only inherent in us but hath been declared and recognised to be so by several statutes and Acts of Parliament'.[119]

The confident tone of the Declaration only partially concealed the profound anxieties which led the king to issue it. The minutes of the committee of foreign affairs show that he and his ministers were unsure whether he had the power to suspend the laws: in 1663 he had declared that he **wished he had** the power to relieve peaceable Dissenters.[120] While Buckingham and Ashley genuinely wanted toleration for Dissenters, the king wanted to control them: hence his insistence on approving preachers and meeting-places.[121] It was agreed that the various sects should thank the king separately: 'by that means they will be still kept from having an understanding'. 'Comprehension presbyterians' and 'high presbyterians' were to thank the king together 'and so the design of the presbyterian comprehension will be lost'.[122] Thus the 'Dons' would remain excluded from the Church, leaving it narrow and weak, and adding to the number of nonconformist sects, which could be played off against each other. All would be dependent on the king's favour. The concern for control was apparent also in the way licences were issued. They were freely granted to individual preachers and for private houses or barns, but not for halls or other public buildings: holding meetings in a town hall could lead to disruptive disputes, while meetings in private houses were likely to be smaller.[123] On the other hand, the king had no qualms about issuing licences to a considerable number of specifically designated meeting-houses.[124]

Of those granted licences, most were Presbyterians or Independents, together with some Baptists and one who described himself as an 'antinomian'.[125] No Quaker applied for a licence and the government clearly regarded them as more subversive than the other sects. It had originally been agreed to include in the Declaration a statement that they should be allowed to open meeting houses but should be left to the law 'as to the point of not swearing and the putting off their hats, &c.' This was later omitted, and the council made it clear that any Quakers in gaol for other than purely religious offences were to remain there.[126] However, the king granted licences to excommunicates and men active against his father in the civil wars.[127]

Reactions to the Declaration were mixed. Reports suggested that nonconformist numbers grew rapidly, especially Presbyterians and Quakers.[128] Some, especially Presbyterians, had reservations about its legality, or resented the liberty granted to Catholics, or feared that it was intended to divide the Dissenters and prevent comprehension, but most embraced the liberty which the king offered.[129] The conformists, by contrast, were demoralized. Initially, some magistrates and judges challenged the legality of the licences, on the grounds that the Declaration had not passed the Great Seal: it was affixed only in December, after Bridgeman (who had refused) had been replaced by Ashley, now raised to the earldom of Shaftesbury.[130] More common were reports that magistrates refused to meddle even with unlicensed preachers – it was often difficult to tell who was licensed and who was not – or that Dissenters were meeting at the time of church services or taking over chapels belonging to the established church; one preacher had his licence revoked for doing so.[131] The Anglican clergy saw their congregations dwindling: Sparrow, despite the support of the gentry and the judges, admitted that the churches were less full than before.[132] There were a few cases of outright defiance – notably at Oxford, where undergraduates disrupted meetings using a combination of mockery and an enormous dog[133] – and some of the clergy preached hard against popery, at which the king was not amused.[134] Most Anglican clergy and laymen reacted with shocked disbelief to what they saw as a betrayal and an act of egregious folly: as Evelyn remarked, it was most unwise to let go the reins of discipline thinking one could pick them up again later. It was also foolish to inflict serious damage on the Church without winning the Dissenters' gratitude.[135] Both Morley and Sheldon feared that the king planned to use his newly-raised army to destroy the whole fabric of church and state.[136]

It was not, however, in the Churchmen's nature openly to resist their king. Like their aggrieved forebears in the 1630s, they looked to Parliament for redress: the king's cancellation of the Declaration in March 1673 was greeted with widespread rejoicing. But religious life in the provinces did not return to normal. The council resolved neither to confirm nor to withdraw the licences and many JPs were reluctant to act against meetings in case this displeased the king.[137] Some who broke up conventicles found themselves complained of 'above', where the Dissenters had a powerful patron in Anglesey. Usually the king let them off with a reprimand, but there were reports that some had been dismissed.[138] These uncertainties continued through most of 1674: although some meetings were disturbed, very many were not and meeting-houses continued to open.[139] For the Anglican clergy, the experience of having to compete for the people's allegiance was a bruising one, which left lasting animosities, especially where meetings continued and church attendance remained low. Dissenting preachers had sought confrontation and tried to take over Anglican chapels. They were quick to complain 'above' of magistrates who tried to disturb their meetings. Old Cavaliers were summoned before the council at the behest of those they regarded as 'disaffected', reviving unpleasant memories of the 1640s and 1650s. Moreover, the Declaration had directly challenged the very being of the established church. Having been made brutally aware that they could not trust the king to protect their interests, those who loved the Church realised that they had to stand up and fight, in the political arena and using the machinery of government and law. The Declaration, far from calming religious animosities, had enflamed them.

Notes

1 Carte MS 232, fo. 20.
2 BL, Add MS 27447, fo. 308; *CSPD 1666–67*, p. 268, *1667*, p. 224; Milward, p. 16.
3 *CSPD 1671*, p. 517, *1668–69*, p. 625.
4 Milward, p. 100; Bodl, MS Eng Letters c 210, p. 110.
5 Mapperton, Sandwich Journal, I.251; *HMC le Fleming*, pp. 63, 68; *CSPD 1666–67*, pp. 166–7, pp. 91, 182.
6 *HMC 3rd Report*, p. 93; *CSPD 1664–65*, p. 539, *1668–69*, pp. 465–6, *1677–78*, p. 618; Carte MS 217, fo. 354.
7 Rawl C719, fo. 3.
8 *CSPD 1667–68*, p. 143. See also *CSPD 1663–64*, pp. 491, 496.
9 H. Bennet, Earl of Arlington, *Letters* (ed.) T. Bebington (2 vols, London, 1701) II.193; *Cosin*, II.216; *CSPD 1667–68*, pp. 418, 464.

10 NRO, MC 1601/20; Mapperton, Appendix to the Earl of Sandwich's papers, fo. 153.
11 E. Suffolk RO, HD 36/2672/138; *CSPD 1664–65*, p. 353, *1665–66*, p. 546, *1666–67*, p. 268; BL, Add MS 27447, fo. 308.
12 Milward, p. 238; *HMC Ormond*, NS III.306.
13 *CSPD 1670*, p. 223, *1673*, p. 92. (The second, interestingly, is a certificate from Sir Philip Musgrave.)
14 Warwicks RO, CR136/B534A; B. Mertens, 'Restoration Drama and the Art of Political Disguise', unpublished M.Litt thesis, Cambridge, 1999, pp. 33–4.
15 For an excellent account of the change in the public and parliamentary mood, see Seaward, ch. 10.
16 Milward, pp. 21, 25; Pepys, VII.356, 402.
17 Pepys, VII.356; Carte MS 35, fos 246, 305.
18 Milward, pp. 16, 25.
19 Carte MS 34, fos 459–60.
20 Pepys, VII.380–1, 387–8, 402, 416.
21 Clarendon, III.144.
22 Carte MS 45, fo. 212.
23 Miller, *Charles II*, p. 123–7; Seaward, pp. 252–4, 266–70 and ch. 10 *passim*.
24 Carte MS 35, fos 120, 126; *CSPD 1667*, p. 199
25 Carte MS 35, fo. 649; Milward, p. 83.
26 Pepys, VIII.332, 355–6, 378, 390.
27 C. Roberts, 'The Impeachment of the Earl of Clarendon', *CHJ*, XIII, 1957, pp. 1–18; Miller, *Charles II*, pp. 135–7.
28 Milward, pp. 99–100, 111–16; Grey, I. 23, 28; *Proceedings of the House of Commons touching the Impeachment of Edward, late Earl of Clarendon*, London, 1700, pp. 23–4.
29 *Proceedings*, pp. 23–4; Grey, I.14, 65.
30 *LJ*, XII.142, 143; Carte MS 45, fos. 222, 228, 232; Milward, p. 134; BL, Add MS 63057A, fo. 167.
31 BL, Add MS 63057A, fos 165, 167; Pepys, VIII.355–6, 512.
32 *CJ*, IX.36–7; Milward, p. 164; M636/22, Sir Ralph to Edmund Verney, 18 December 1667.
33 For a more sceptical view of his commitment to toleration, see B. Yardley, 'George Villiers, second Duke of Buckingham and the Politics of Toleration', *HLQ*, LV, 1992, pp. 317–37.
34 Mapperton, Appendix to the Earl of Sandwich's Papers, fo. 153; Miller, *Charles II*, pp. 137–41; D.T. Witcombe, *Charles II and the Cavalier House of Commons 1663–74*, Manchester, 1966, ch. 7; Roberts, 'Sir Richard Temple, the "Pickthank Undertaker"', *HLQ*, XLI, 1977–8, pp. 137–55.
35 Carte MS 217, fo. 433. See also BT 118, Ruvigny to Louis, 26 March 1668 NS.
36 Clarke, I.434–5.
37 M636/22, Sir Ralph to Edmund Verney, 5 May 1668.
38 J. Miller, *James II:A Study in Kingship*, London, 1989, pp. 54–7.
39 Carte MS 36, fos 167, 199; Egerton MS 2539, fos. 155, 157; Milward, pp. 189–90; Witcombe, *Commons*, p. 81.
40 Milward, pp. 198, 239–40.
41 Grey, I.148–50; Milward, pp. 285–6.
42 See Miller, *Charles II*, pp. 150–3.
43 BT118, Ruvigny to Lionne, 23 [*recte* 27?] February and 5 March 1668 NS.

44 C. Roberts, 'Sir Richard Temple's Discourse on the Parliament of 1667–8', *HLQ*, XX, 1956–7, pp. 137–44. I find it difficult to share Witcombe's view (*Commons*, p. 81n) that this analysis 'tallies closely with' Ruvigny's.
45 F.R. Harris, *Life of Edward Montagu, first Earl of Sandwich*, 2 vols., London, 1912, II.311–2, dated 11 December 1669, 313–5 (undated, but probably from much the same time).
46 *Norths*, I.120; Mapperton, Appendix to the Earl of Sandwich's Papers, fo. 153; Browning, *Docts*, pp. 233–6. See also *POAS*, I.107–15 for Marvell's view of 'court' and 'country' in 1666–7.
47 Miller, *Charles II*, ch. 7.
48 See S. Pincus, 'From Butterboxes to Wooden Shoes: the Shift in English Popular Sentiment from anti-Dutch to anti-French in the 1670s', *HJ*, XXXVIII, 1995, pp. 333–61.
49 *CSPD 1668–69*, p. 625; *Cosin*, II.226.
50 *CJ*, IX.121, 124, 126; Marvell, II.314; BL Add MS 36916, fos 166–7; Newton, *House of Lyme*, pp. 242–3; Bodl, MS Eng Letters c 210, p. 133
51 Marvell, II.314–15.
52 Marvell, II.317, 318, 324–5; Bodl, MS Eng Letters c 210, p. 150; *HMC 7th Report*, p. 488; Witcombe, *Commons*, ch. 9.
53 Carte MS 215, fo. 417; *CSPD 1667–68*, pp. 143, 418, 464, *1670*, p. 13; *HMC le Fleming*, p. 63; Bodl, MS Add c 305, fo. 263.
54 *HMC Ormond*, NS III.306; BL, Add MS 29571, fo. 117; Bodl, MS Add c 305, fo. 225. For Townshend, see *CSPD 1670*, p. 512, *1671*, pp. 46–8, 517.
55 *CSPD 1671*, p. 563; *HMC le Fleming*, p. 88.
56 *CSPD 1664–65*, p. 80, *1665–66*, p. 15, 42, *1668–69*, p. 159.
57 *CSPD 1664–65*, pp. 20, 39; BL, Add MS 4182, fo. 21. For a similar case at Norwich just before the Act passed, see Carte MS 222, fo. 64.
58 DCLD, Hunter MS 137, 'Acta secularia', p. 5.
59 Milward, pp. 159–60, 166–7, 170; Grey, I.67–8; M636/22, Sir Ralph to Edmund Verney, 12 December 1667.
60 *Cosin*, II.252; Marvell, II.318; *CSPD 1671*, pp. 385–6; Kenyon, *Constitution*, 2nd edn., pp. 399–400. Vaughan was generally seen as no friend to Dissenters: *RB*, III.59.
61 *CSPD 1663–64*, pp. 457, 523, *1664–65*, pp. 20, 207; Bodl, MS Eng Hist b 212, fo. 16, MS Add c 305, fos 154, 156; *RB*, III.59. Apart from Hale, those mentioned as lenient towards conventicles were Twysden, Turner, Tyrrell and Archer.
62 PC 2/57, fo. 95; *CSPD 1664–65*, pp. 373, 476; Henry, p. 183.
63 *CSPD 1664–65*, p. 478, *1665–66*, p. 588, *1666–67*, pp. 114, 124, 127–8, *1660–85 (Addenda)*, p. 151.
64 Henry, pp. 212–13.
65 Pepys, VIII.585, 596; BL, Add MS 36916, fo. 56.
66 Pepys, VIII.596, IX.347, 360; BL, Add MS 36916, fo. 58; *RB* III.22–3 [check].
67 *RB*, III.13–15; *Bax. Corr.*, II.48–9; Newcome, *Autobiography*, I.154–5; Bodl, MS Add c 305, fos 168–9, 175; Thomas in *From Unif.*, p. 210.
68 *RB*, III.22–5; *Bax. Corr.*, II.65; Thomas in *From Unif.*, pp. 204–5.
69 *RB*, II.277, III. '36'[*recte* 26], 36.
70 *RB*, III.87–8, 99.
71 *Bax. Corr.*, II.65.
72 *RB*, III.25.

73 *Bax. Corr.*, II.65; Thomas in *From Unif.*, pp. 204–5, 207–9.
74 Pepys, VIII.584–5; Carte MS 36, fo. 41; BL, Add MS 36916, fo. 37; *CSPD 1667*, pp. 454–5, 457, 550.
75 G. De Krey, 'Rethinking the Restoration: Dissenting Cases of Conscience 1667–72', *HJ*, XXXVIII, 1995, pp. 53–83, especially pp. 70–1. I am sceptical how far a few pamphlets, however radical, can be seen as constituting a 'crisis', unless one ascribes enormous power to ideas and the printed word. The parliamentary politics of 1670–71 were the most harmonious of the reign and the struggle to enforce the Conventicle Act in London was both short-lived and successful.
76 *CSPD 1667*, p. 447; Pepys, IX.31, 45–6; Carte MS 36, fo. 155; Milward, p. 180 (quoted).
77 Milward, pp. 201, 206; *LJ*, XII.181; Grey, I.103–6; *CJ*, IX.60; Egerton MS 2539, fo. 162.
78 *CSPD 1667–68*, pp. 276, 300; Egerton MS 2539, fo. 167; BL, Add MS 36916, fo. 86.
79 Grey, I.110–14; Milward, pp. 214–22.
80 Carte MS 36, fo. 153; Bodl, B.14.15.Linc., p. 4; Egerton MS 2539, fo. 155.
81 Egerton MS 2539, fos. 162, 170 (quoted); *CJ*, IX.66; Milward, p. 225.
82 *CJ*, IX.90, 93; Egerton MS 2539, fo. 215; BL, Add MS 36916, fo. 95; *HMC 3rd Report*, p. 95.
83 Milward, p. 206; Carte MS 36, fo. 155; M636/32, Margaret Elmes to Sir Ralph Verney, 5 March 1668; Egerton MS 2539, fo. 162; Tanner MS 45, fo. 78. For the false report, see Henry, p. 209.
84 Milward, pp. 230–1.
85 *SR*, V.520; *CJ*, IX.97. The very brief session of July 1667 was not counted as a 'session', presumably because no legislation was passed. The House had been adjourned after the autumn session. *CJ*, VIII.692, IX.43.
86 Pepys, IX.277–8; *Cosin*, II.198–201; Hodgson, p. 188; *CSPD 1668–69*, pp. 77–8, 94–5; Bodl, MS Add c 305, fo. 205. Henry, p. 212 thought the Act expired on 1 March 1669.
87 *CSPD 1668–69*, pp. 77–8; *Cosin*, II.198–201; Hodgson, p. 188; BL, Add MS 36916, fo. 119; *RB*, III.36–7.
88 Pepys, IX.502; M636/23, Margaret Elmes to Sir Ralph Verney, 31 March and 7 April 1669.
89 SP 104/176, fos 130, 139–40; *CSPD 1668–69*, pp. 294, 297.
90 BL, Add 36916, fo. 134; Tanner MS 44, fo. 101; *HMC 3rd Report*, p. 245; *CSPD 1668–69*, pp. 350, 354, 373, 394.
91 The postcript appears in only some of the surviving copies of the letter. Those with the postscript include BL, Add MS 19399, fo. 107; Coventry MS 7, fo. 227; W. Wynne, *Life of Sir Leoline Jenkins*, 2 vols., London, 1724, II.660. Those without include DUL, Cosin Letter Book 1B, no. 180; E. Suffolk RO, HD36/2672/12.
92 BL, Add MS 36916, fo. 137.
93 Egerton 2539, fo. 292; BL, Add MS 36916, fo. 121; SP 104/176, fo. 145; *HMC le Fleming*, p. 66.
94 *CSPD 1668–69*, p. 398. This refers to an Act of 13 Eliz.; another copy (Tanner MS 44, fo. 120) has 35 Eliz. (1593) which is surely correct.
95 BL, Add MS 36916, fo. 139; *CSPD 1668–69*, pp. 412, 430, 438, 463, 466; Steele, *Proclamations*, no. 3529; Harl MS 7377, fo. 4. The order to garrisons

(undated) is in *CSPD 1668–69*, p. 655, but there is an order for Plymouth dated 13 July: *ibid.*, p. 408.

96 SP 104/176, fo. 221; *CSPD 1668–69*, pp. 449, 564, 623, *1670*, pp. 25, 59–60; *HMC le Fleming*, pp. 68–9.

97 SP 104/176, fo. 181; BT 122, Croissy to Lionne, 25 July, Croissy to Louis, 29 July 1669 NS; *CSPV 1669–70*, pp. 84–5.

98 Harl MS 7377, fo. 6; DCLD, Hunter MS 137, pp. 11–12; Tanner MS 44, fos 140, 151; *CSPD 1668–9*, pp. 419–20.

99 PRO, C115/N3/8568; *CJ*, IX.101–2, 108–9.

100 Grey, I.160–3, 174–5; BT 123, Croissy to Louis, 17 November 1669 NS.

101 *CJ*, IX.123, 130, 138.

102 Grey, I.222–3; Marvell, II.100–1.

103 Bodl, MS Eng Letters c 210, p. 141; DUL, Cosin Letter Book 5A, no. 69; *LJ*, XII.318, 325–6.

104 *HMC 8th Report*, pp. 142–3; *CJ*, IX.148 (quoted).

105 Grey, I.246–50; Kenyon, *Constitution*, 2nd edn., p. 359; *SR*, V.651.

106 *RB*, III.74; Horle, *Quakers*, passim.

107 Marvell, II.315, 104; *RB*, III.74, 87–8. See also M636/23, Dr Denton to Sir Ralph Verney, 14 April 1670: 'I cannot yet unriddle why the presbyterians should promote it' (the Lords' proviso).

108 PC 2/62, pp. 214, 219, 226, 233, 295–6; SP 104/176, fos 239, 241; NLI, MS 4728, fo. 22.

109 BL, Add MS 19399, fos. 113–14; Wynne, *Jenkins*, II.660–1; *CSPD 1671*, p. 424; Davies, p. 149; Bodl, MS Add c 305, fos 215, 225.

110 *CSPD 1670*, pp. 226, 229, 233–4, 236, 239, 240; BL, Add MS 36916, fo. 181; *Cosin*, II.243; *Hatton*, I.58; NLI, MS 4728, fo. 22.

111 *CSPD 1670*, pp. 243, 248, 276, 283.

112 *CSPD 1670*, pp. 261, 321, 327, 366, 401, 431, *1671*, pp. 75–6; *HMC le Fleming*, p. 71; Norrey, 'Regime', pp. 806–8.

113 Bodl, MS Add c. 305, fo. 213.

114 BT 125, Croissy to Louis, 4 August and 29 September 1670 NS; *RB*, III.87–8.

115 *RB*, III.88; *CSPD 1671–72*, p. 63; Miller, *Charles II*, pp. 188–9.

116 *CSPD 1671*, p. 368; Norrey, 'Regime', p. 808. Baxter wrote that the hot persecution lasted six months: *RB*, III.74.

117 *HMC 9th Report, Appendix II*, p. 9; BL, Add MS 36916, fos 216, 218; Marvell, II.137–8; Grey, I.420–1.

118 *CSPD 1671*, pp. 562–3, 568–9, *1671–72*, pp. 28, 63; SP 104/176, fo. 319.

119 Browning, *Docts*, pp. 387–8. For the 1668 proposals, see *RB*, III.25.

120 SP 104/177, fos 12, 14; *LJ*, XI.478–9.

121 SP 104/177, fo. 12; Browning, *Docts*, p. 388.

122 SP 104/177, fo. 19.

123 For refusals of licences for public buildings see *CSPD 1671–72*, pp. 313–4, 333, 343, 376, 387, 409, 410, 446–8. For more general comments, see *ibid.*, pp. 372, 381–2.

124 *CSPD 1671–72*, pp. 552–3, 558, 590, *1672*, pp. 352, 475, 578–80, 679–80, *1672–73*, pp. 178, 260–1, 309, 514.

125 *CSPD 1672*, pp. 10, 99.

126 SP 104/177, fo. 16; *CSPD 1671–72*, pp. 489–90.

127 *CSPD 1671–72*, p. 328, *1672*, pp. 63, 271.

128 Tanner MS 43, fo. 25; *CSPD 1672*, pp. 450, 543, 589, *1672–73*, p. 300.
129 Tanner MS 43, fo. 14; *RB*, III.99; Henry, p. 250.
130 *HMC 7th Report*, p. 490; SP 104/177, fo. 115; PC 2/63, p. 353; *CSPD 1671–72*, pp. 396–7. Fleming wrote that the judges were not at liberty to discuss the legality of the Declaration: *HMC le Fleming*, p. 90.
131 *CSPD 1672*, pp. 457, 543, 589, *1672–73*, pp. 300, 484, 504–5; PC 2/63, p. 396; *Bax. Corr.*, II.143–4.
132 *CSPD 1672*, p. 589, *1672–73*, p. 300; Bodl, MS Add c 305, fo. 242.
133 BL, Add MS 29571, fo. 151.
134 Burnet, *Hist*, I.537; *HMC Fitzherbert*, p. 271.
135 Evelyn, III.607–8; Grey, II.102; Reresby, pp. 84–5; *CSPD 1671–72*, p. 215.
136 Tanner MS 43, fo. 31.
137 *CSPD 1672–73*, p. 613, *1673*, p. 37; Tanner MS 42, fo. 7; BL, Add MS 28051, fo. 12.
138 Bodl, MS Rawl Letters 104, fo. 92; *CSPD 1673*, p. 369, *1673–75*, p. 152; *Williamson*, I.33–4, 93, 134, 151; SP 104/177, fo. 158; PC 2/64, pp. 14, 27, 40; *HMC 6th Report*, p. 454.
139 Tanner MS 42, fo. 112; *CSPD 1673–75*, pp. 424, 581; Granville, II.13–14; *HMC le Fleming*, pp. 109–10; DCLD, Hunter MS 7, no. 114; Bodl, MS Rawl Letters 51, fo. 39.

Chapter eleven

The rebirth of party, 1673–78

Danby and the direction of policy

Sir Thomas Osborne, created Viscount Latimer in 1673 and Earl of Danby in 1674, was a Yorkshireman of modest fortune. Before his appointment as lord treasurer, following Clifford's resignation in 1673, he had held no office more senior than treasurer of the navy; he had been a privy councillor only since 1672. He owed his rise to prominence to the patronage of Buckingham and survived his patron's fall from favour. Despite frequent ill-health he established a growing mastery over the treasury and the royal finances, which gave him greater control over patronage than any of Charles's previous ministers. It also provided him with a battery of financial arguments to use when trying to persuade the king to follow his preferred policy options. In seeking to establish a degree of control over policy-making that none of his predecessors had enjoyed, he was helped by the fact that when he came to power the government was in disarray. 'The king calls a cabinet council for the purpose of not listening to it', wrote the Venetian envoy in December 1673 'and the ministers hold forth in it so as not to be understood.'[1] Ministers rushed to accuse one another and to exculpate themselves before Parliament. Of the Cabal, by early 1674 Clifford was dead, Ashley (now Earl of Shaftesbury) had been dismissed from the lord chancellorship, Buckingham was in disgrace and Arlington had moved from the secretaryship to the comparatively apolitical post of lord chamberlain: although he hoped to recover his influence, he never did. Lauderdale had to defend himself against attacks from both the English Parliament and the Scottish nobility, but remained sufficiently influential for Danby to take him into a somewhat uneasy partnership.[2] The Duke of York was also on the defensive because of the revelation of his conversion and the suggestion, early in 1674, that he should be excluded from the succession. Danby's determination to pursue policies of hostility to France and to Catholicism inevitably brought him into conflict with York, who was drawn into an unlikely collaboration with oppositionist peers like Shaftesbury and Holles.[3]

The willingness of Parliament and the political nation to trust the king had been damaged, perhaps beyond repair. He cancelled the Declaration of Indulgence and extricated himself from the Dutch War, but could not dispel the suspicion that these had been part of a design to impose 'popery and arbitrary government'. He had misled the Commons in 1671, asking for money to defend the realm against the French only to reveal that he had secretly allied with them. The Stop of the Exchequer of 1672 freed ready cash for the war, but destroyed the credit apparatus built up since 1665. Small wonder that Sir Robert Southwell wrote in February 1674, 'nothing is to be trusted to good nature in the future'.[4]

From the outset Danby realised that, while it was vital to bring order to the royal finances, the problems facing him were as much political as financial, because the debts incurred during the war made it imperative to secure money from Parliament. In the Commons the old Cavaliers were those most inclined by temperament to support the king's measures, but they felt betrayed by the changes in policy since the euphoric days of the 'going into the cellar' and by the favours which (in their eyes) continued to be heaped on to the 'disloyal'.[5] In November 1673 there was an unprecedented unity in opposition to the court. The Cavaliers' feelings were summed up by Sir Richard Wiseman, who was to become one of Danby's agents in the Commons:

> the spirits of men are almost invincibly alarmed at and set against the counsels that have hitherto taken place . . . I find it a great evil under the sun that the king's conscientious good friends are (as they have always been) little regarded, both in themselves and in the principles they own. It is an ill omen of the fall of a state where such as serve the public out of a good conscience have no other reward for so doing but the satisfaction of their good conscience . . . I assure you it sticks in a great many men's stomachs and undoubtedly if such men and their principles were but at this day regarded, all would speedily do well.[6]

Danby had reached a similar conclusion. He bluntly spelled out the options open to the king, arguing that he had to win back the trust of the present House of Commons – a new one would be less amenable – and that he could do this only by 'executing the laws both against popery and nonconformity and withdrawing apparently from the French interest'.[7] Charles proved more resistant to the latter suggestion than the former. Although he bowed to the inevitable and made peace with the Dutch, he was very reluctant to break with Louis XIV, whose friendship he wished to retain in case he had to face a rebellion at home. Not until the end of 1677 did he enter into a serious collaboration with William III and the Dutch, as a result of which he found himself, reluctantly, preparing to make war on France in 1678.[8] On the question of religion, he proved more amenable. Despite his personal sympathy for the Catholics, he had issued a series of orders to enforce the laws against them and further proclamations appeared in November 1673 and January 1674. A number of priests, Irish Catholics and Catholic peers (including the Earl Marshal) prepared to leave the country.[9] Early in 1674 there were proposals in the Lords to ensure that all children of the royal family should be raised as Protestants and that none should marry a Catholic.[10]

The proposals failed, but in 1677 Danby brought in a similar measure, hoping to defuse the Commons' fears of a popish successor. The bill would also transfer ecclesiastical appointments, under a Catholic, from the king to the bishops, which prompted scathing comments on the ambitions of the episcopate. It was rejected, as was another bill designed to make it easier to identify and convict papists, prompting the comment that some MPs did not **want** to reduce the fear of popery.[11]

The question of Protestant nonconformity was more complex. Danby was sure that the Commons were against indulgence for Quakers and Baptists, but their position on comprehension was unclear. When in February 1673 they drew up an address against the Indulgence, they also brought in a bill to give ease to Protestant Dissenters, to show the king 'that we did not dislike the matter of his declaration, but the manner'.[12] It contained elements of both comprehension and indulgence. The House agreed to drop the requirement in the Act of Uniformity that the clergy declare 'assent and consent', but resolved to retain the renunciation of the Covenant, thanks in part to Henry Coventry's emotive reference to the blood of his dead master.[13] As for indulgence, the House seemed inclined to allow it to those prepared to subscribe the thirty-six doctrinal articles and to take the oaths of supremacy and allegiance (which would exclude Baptists and Quakers), and who worshipped in existing licensed meeting houses, provided that these were regulated and supervised by JPs. Any such relief would be temporary.[14] An attempt by the Lords to allow the king to relax the laws by proclamation was firmly resisted by the Commons, who made it clear that the indulgence was to extend only to those who differed from the Church in some 'circumstances' or 'ceremonial parts'.[15]

The Houses failed to agree, to the annoyance of the king, who delayed ending the session in the hope that the bill would pass.[16] Others were relieved. Bishop Morley wrote that he would have accepted a limited comprehension, dropping 'assent and consent' to everything in the Prayer Book and the renunciation of the Covenant, but insisting on subscription to all the articles and canons; this (he claimed) would make it possible to separate the Presbyterians from the sectaries. Ceremonies were not 'indifferent': allowing different practices would lead to schism. In other words, for Morley, 'comprehension' meant coming into the Church on terms laid down by the bishops.[17] Even before the Lords' amendments, Sir Edward Dering had little enthusiasm for the bill, seeing it as damaging the Church; he was sure that many felt the same, but 'we had gone so far, both in the observation of the world, and in our engagement to the king . . . that something seemed necessary to be done'.[18] We cannot tell how widely Dering's views were shared. Some in the Commons – Henry Coventry, Sir Heneage Finch, Sir John Duncombe, Sir Giles Strangways – fought the bill every step of the way. The debates were confused, as MPs wrestled with the complex inter-relationship between comprehension and indulgence. Danby, then Sir Thomas Osborne, declared that they should bring as many Dissenters as possible into the Church, but that he was against encouraging them in their wickedness by taking off 'assent and consent'; anyone who believed himself to be bound by the Covenant was 'no good man'.[19] Like Morley, he seems to have expected presbyterians to re-enter a Church whose liturgy remained virtually unchanged. The suggestion that the Commons had little real enthusiasm for comprehension or indulgence is given credence by the fact that it brought in no other bill to that effect during the remainder of the Cavalier Parliament. A comprehension bill was introduced into the Lords in February 1674, apparently by Morley. It would have removed the requirements of 'assent and consent' and abjuration of the Covenant, while keeping the liturgy unchanged. It was committed, but died with the prorogation.[20]

Recent experience, then, offered Danby little guidance as to whether the Commons would support a limited comprehension or indulgence. The king's preferences were clear. Although he had cancelled the Declaration, he took no steps to withdraw the licences, claiming that Parliament had the matter under consideration.[21] This uncertainty continued through much of 1674[22] and there were renewed rumours of comprehension and indulgence. In October Danby told Morley that the king wished the bishops and some of the council to consult before Parliament next met about the best means to unite and pacify the people.[23] It seemed likely that there would be further moves in favour of the Dissenters, who had powerful friends at court, notably Anglesey, Holles and Orrery, who were supported by the Duke of York, eager to prevent new severities against Catholics.[24]

For several months the bishops were under sustained pressure to make concessions, but refused. Danby, Lauderdale and the two secretaries (Coventry and Williamson) urged Sheldon to agree to comprehension, but found him as obstinate as a mule.[25] Led by Morley and Ward, the bishops stressed the need to enforce the laws against Catholics, but added that it was also necessary to withdraw the licences and suppress meetings held during the time of divine service. If this brought hardship upon the Dissenters ''tis the law is severe and that's the rule'.[26] It had been proposed that, when the licences were withdrawn, some 'door of hope' should be given the Dissenters that they should be indulged if Parliament advised it.[27] The bishops demanded that that door should be closed. The council agreed on 3 February that the king should issue a proclamation against popery, which would also order the enforcement of the laws against conventicles and state that the licences had long since been recalled.[28] A bitter struggle ensued over the wording of the proclamation. Amid many rumours, a proclamation was issued which referred only to Catholics and then another in which the order to suppress conventicles appeared in a modified form. Small wonder that observers in the provinces found it hard to assess the king's real intentions.[29] To confuse matters further, Danby and Lauderdale continued to hold out to the Presbyterians the prospect of comprehension and persuaded the bishops to draw up proposals to that effect. However, the bishops firmly opposed any change to the liturgy, which some thought rendered any negotiations futile.[30] When Danby wrote in late January that the king was determined to take firm measures against popery, he made no mention of conventicles; small wonder that the bishops were reluctant to trust him.[31]

It seems that Danby's commitment to an anti-nonconformist religious policy was the product less of conviction than of the stubbornness of the bishops; the treasurer's hostility to York, who now set up as an advocate of toleration, may have been another factor.[32] Danby became further identified with the bishops when he tried to persuade Parliament to extend the 'Oxford oath' (not to attempt to change the government in church or state) from ejected ministers, as required by the Five Mile Act, to all office-holders; the French ambassador claimed that 'Danby's test' had been drawn up by the treasurer, Morley and Ward. The bill was introduced in the Lords; it was supported by most of the bishops, who were bitterly attacked by the likes of Anglesey and Buckingham, but the Catholic peers also opposed the bill. It did not complete its passage through the House and so was never presented to the Commons.[33] As the test would effectively have confined office-holding to firm Anglicans, it was denounced as reopening the divisions of the civil wars. In supporting the test, and persuading the king to renew the persecution of conventicles, the bishops played a more active, sustained and conspicuous role in policy-making than at any time since the Restoration. In so doing, they rendered themselves open to attack, as partisan figures, but they had the prospect of more active support from the secular authorities in their efforts to impose conformity.[34]

During 1675 there were attempts to suppress conventicles in London[35] and in 1676 the judges instructed JPs to enforce the laws against Dissenters, particularly Baptists and Quakers, but the king's ministers still had to rebut claims that the king did not really wish meetings to be disturbed.[36] Sheldon and Morley still had to contend with the king's belief that nonconformists and Catholics together outnumbered conformists. Sheldon had already organized a rough census of conventicles in 1669. Now, encouraged by Danby, he promoted what became known as the Compton census. It aimed to show that Dissenters were so few that their meetings could be suppressed and they could be forced to attend church without the risk of either rebellion or mass emigration. This was not made explicit in the instructions to the clergy, who were simply asked how many of their parishioners wholly stayed away from church; this ensured that semi- or occasional conformists were not returned as nonconformists, but there is no evidence that the figures were systematically distorted to 'prove' the bishops' point.[37] The census indicated that full nonconformists made up less than 5 per cent of the population and seems to have convinced the king that he need have no qualms about having the laws enforced, although he wished to avoid undue severity[38] and judged it politic to move the combative Carleton from Bristol to the more lucrative but politically less sensitive see of Chichester.[39] There were still occasional rumours of comprehension,[40] and the laws were often laxly enforced, but many Quakers were fined for recusancy. They complained to the Commons but, despite winning the sympathy of some MPs, others denounced them for holding themselves 'absolved from all ties of government' and for refusing to fulfil their obligations as citizens. Sir Charles Wheeler refused to describe them as Protestants, Williamson denied that they were Christians and the House resolved not to bring in a bill to distinguish between popish and Protestant recusants.[41] As no bill to relax the laws against Dissent had been brought in since 1673, it could be argued that Danby's policy of exclusive and intolerant Anglicanism might be divisive, but assisted in the management of Parliament.

Danby and the patronage system

However unfair the distribution of rewards may have been in the 1660s, it was never dominated by a single minister or exploited for the benefit of one 'party'. This was hardly surprising given the range of people who enjoyed the king's favour, from Albemarle to Clarendon, from Buckingham to Ormond, from Ashley to Arlington. This, and the king's inconsistencies of policy, meant that few groups were wholly excluded from the hope of enjoying the king's bounty. Danby's efforts to impose a greater consistency on policy inevitably affected the distribution of patronage. He urged the king to remove the disaffected or those who had served under the Commonwealth and Protectorate from local and judicial office and to give preference in local appointments to 'those within the said counties who have actually been in arms or sufferers for your Majesty or royal father, and to the sons of such.'[42] He was not deterred by the shortage of men of talent, especially lawyers, among the old Cavaliers.[43] Not only were favours concentrated on his followers, but those who defied him were likely to be dismissed and denied rewards. The practice of 'taking off' vocal critics of the crown ceased: Edward Coleman remarked, when a number of 'Country' MPs lost their offices in June 1675 and Sir Giles Strangways was made a privy councillor, that it was a change for the king to reward those who served well and punish those who served badly.[44] Duncombe lost his place as chancellor of the exchequer because he 'interfered' with the treasurer. The king told him he would not have his treasurer made uneasy. Duncombe kept his pension, but this was seen as conditional on good behaviour.[45]

By 1678 Danby was 'as absolute as ever the Lord Clarendon was',[46] but in several respects his power was greater. Clarendon never mastered his rivals and his position at court was often precarious; he survived because he was a useful workhorse, little more. Danby was fortunate to find something of a power vacuum at court and, unlike Clarendon, he had no qualms about working with the king's mistresses, embarking on a mutually advantageous collaboration with Portsmouth. Still more important, Danby appreciated (as Clarendon had not) that the treasurer, not the chancellor, was the key officer. The stringency and retrenchment which followed the Third Dutch War strengthened his position. With less patronage available, and a serious shortage of ready cash,[47] what remained became all the more valuable. He told the king that his financial situation left him no option but to follow policies acceptable to Parliament (as formulated by Danby).[48] Having convinced Charles that he alone could save him from financial ruin, he gained an exceptional degree of control over the king's patronage, which he used to build up a coherent 'court party' in Parliament and to some extent in the provinces. This encouraged the development of a more cohesive 'country party'.

On becoming lord treasurer, he extended his authority throughout the central revenue administration.[49] Duncombe was removed from the chancellorship of the exchequer and Sir Stephen Fox lost his place as paymaster of the forces. It seems that Danby saw Fox as a possible rival for the treasurership and persuaded himself that the large sums Fox handled as paymaster provided the basis for his unrivalled credit in the City.[50] His ostensible replacement, Sir Henry Puckering, an 'old Cavalier' (and MP) was merely a front man: he was to receive a pension and the duties of the office were to be performed by a deputy named by the king, but nominated by the treasurer.[51] Danby also tried first to bypass Sir Robert Howard, the auditor of the receipt in the Exchequer,[52] who held his office for life, and then to have him dismissed on charges of malpractice, which he was unable to prove.[53] The reversion of Howard's place had been granted in 1675 to Danby's younger son, Lord Dunblane. The grant was later renewed in favour of Dunblane's older brother, Lord Latimer, but as he was only 23 in 1677, there was little doubt who would really have controlled the office.[54] Danby was more successful in establishing control over the revenue (and patronage) of Ireland. In 1675 he secured the king's consent to the principle that all orders relating to money or land in Ireland required his approval.[55] This deeply offended Secretary Coventry, who nominally dealt with Irish matters, but found himself rubber-stamping Danby's orders.[56] It also infuriated the lord lieutenant, Essex, whose recommendations were repeatedly overruled.[57] When Essex was recalled in 1677, he found grave difficulty securing payment of £13,000 promised him by the king out of the Irish revenue.[58] Essex suspected payment was held up because he did not sufficiently 'acknowledge the gift' from Danby, but thought it wrong for thanks for the king's bounty to be addressed primarily to a minister. He suspected that he would receive his money only when he submitted to Danby's will.[59]

Essex's experience was typical. Danby was an implacable enemy, adept at making others dependent on him and persuading them that he would assist them, but often not delivering what he promised. When Reresby, who saw Danby as his patron, secured the governorship of Bridlington, he discovered that York, not Danby was responsible.[60] The young Sir Thomas Osborne had been a close friend of Evelyn's father-in-law, but when he became lord treasurer Evelyn found him less obliging than his predecessor, Clifford.[61] Lord Yarmouth, whose mother was Lady Danby's aunt, looked to the treasurer to mend his fortunes. He failed to secure the favourable treatment he expected and instead found himself plunged into Norfolk politics as Danby's agent. When Williamson – one of the two principal secretaries of state – sought reimbursement of his expenses at the Cologne peace conference, the obsequious tone in which he addressed Charles Bertie, Danby's brother-in-law and secretary to the treasury, told its own story.[62]

A key element of Danby's political strategy involved installing members of his family in positions of power. With a modest estate, encumbered by debt, he had every incentive to use his position to build up his fortune. His son (thanks to Portsmouth) was made a gentleman of the bedchamber and he made good marriages for his daughters.[63] As his two sons were too young for high office – the elder was born in 1654 – his major allies were his wife's brothers (notably Robert Bertie, third earl of Lindsey, another gentleman of the bedchamber, and Charles Bertie, secretary to the treasury); one other brother and a half-brother served as MPs during Danby's treasurership and his brother-in-law, Lord Norreys, sat in the Lords.[64] Another brother-in-law, Vere Bertie, was made a judge in 1675, despite general agreement that his legal ability was 'undiscernable'.[65] Danby also began to create a provincial power-base by installing his kinsmen as lords lieutenant: himself in the West Riding, Lindsey in Lincolnshire, Norreys in Oxfordshire, Yarmouth in Norfolk and other, more distant kin in Rutland, Hampshire, Wiltshire and Cornwall. Other lieutenancies were held by political allies such as the Duke of Newcastle and the Earl of Northampton and it seems that he planned to fill all the lieutenancies with his kinsmen and allies.[66] Edmund Verney remarked, in 1676, that 'the Lindseys' and their allies would soon monopolize the best places in the kingdom.[67] In 1678, one MP exclaimed that Osbornes and Berties would get all the places that fell vacant.[68]

To maintain and extend his power, Danby had to manage Parliament and above all to extract supply. At first he seems to have assumed that it would be sufficient to encourage his supporters to attend regularly and to give the Commons the policies that they wanted, but there was one key policy which the king would not let him deliver – a breach with France – and both sessions in 1675 were bedevilled by an acrimonious jurisdictional dispute between the Houses.[69] After the autumn session, Danby decided that more systematic organization was needed, to bind together those whose inclinations or interests led them to favour the court and to impose greater discipline on them.[70] Before both sessions in 1675 he had arranged for letters to be sent to those regarded as favourable to the court, asking them to come up promptly; this led to questions in the Commons as to why some MPs had been singled out.[71] After the autumn session, with the aid of Sir Richard Wiseman,[72] he assessed systematically the number of MPs who supported the court and identified others who might be persuaded.[73] This information provided the basis for the systematic use of rewards and punishments, already prefigured by the dismissals in June. Following Fox's dismissal in January 1676 the 'secret service' fund, for which Fox had been largely responsible, was transferred to Charles Bertie. As payments were made on the king's personal order and were not subject to audit in the Exchequer, this provided a means of making secret payments to MPs. Questioned by the Commons in 1679, Bertie refused to testify, pleading the king's positive command.[74]

Danby also sought to create new forms of patronage. He planned to enforce the recusancy laws far more rigorously, with the fines used to pay salaries to JPs, sheriffs and militia officers 'by which they may be made offices of benefit as well as trust'.[75] He seriously considered a proposal that the new excise farm to be awarded in 1677 should be assigned to groups of 'country gentlemen', as rewards for the court's supporters in the Commons. Robert Brent, a treasury official, assured the ever-hopeful Yarmouth that he had secured the farm of seven counties for his partners and himself. Danby asked Reresby if he was interested in becoming involved, only three weeks before it was due to come into effect. In the end, however, financial and perhaps political wisdom prevailed and the farm was let to a syndicate similar to the last.[76] More successful was his use of the so-called excise pensions. Parliament had wished to encourage country gentlemen to farm the excise, but they had been squeezed out by City financiers. When Clifford farmed out the excise en bloc in 1673, he insisted that the farmers should provide money to compensate those who had earlier lost the farm. The king paid these pensions, as part of the secret service money, including one or two to men who had never been associated with the excise; fourteen of the original nineteen recipients were MPs. Danby substantially increased the number of such pensions. Because of Bertie's obduracy we cannot tell by how much, but the very secrecy of the payments led the court's opponents to suspect the worst and encouraged allegations of bribery.[77] However, when the Commons investigated in 1679, it was agreed that some 'pensioners' had a reasonable claim to compensation.[78] Danby also exploited his discretion in paying moneys owed by the crown. So many people were owed (or had lost) so much that the king could never repay it all,[79] but Danby was the first to make payments dependent on following the correct political line, as we have seen in the cases of Duncombe and Essex. To strengthen the crown's control over office-holders, from 1675 they were increasingly appointed 'during pleasure' rather than 'for life'.[80] Judges were appointed 'at the king's pleasure' rather than 'as long as they behave well', while some appointed under the older form of tenure were dismissed.[81] Danby – and his wife[82] – were widely blamed for these changes.[83]

Danby sought to impose coherence on royal policy and to use the crown's patronage to create a coherent 'court party'. Those already in office were required to follow Danby's party line or risk dismissal.[84] By linking reward to obedience in the Commons, he created a situation where 'our measues now at court are so taken that it is essential to a man's succeeding there to be of the Parliament.'[85] He could never eliminate all rivals and suffered occasional defeats, as when York secured the appointment of William Sancroft, rather than Danby's candidate (Compton), as archbishop of Canterbury.[86] Some officials, like Sir Robert Howard and Sir Robert Carr, held their places for life.[87] Some areas of patronage remained outside Danby's control, such as the queen's household.[88] But Danby established an ascendancy unmatched by any of Charles's other ministers by using the crown's patronage resources exclusively and systematically, whereas they had previously been used inclusively, according to the random interplay of the diverse forces at court. By confining rewards to 'the court', he imparted greater coherence to 'the country'. The threat which his patronage system seemed to pose to the independence and integrity of Parliament revitalized fears of 'arbitrary government' as he tried to damp down fears of 'popery'. There had earlier been attacks on sales of office or the 'corrupt' use of crown patronage, but these had been driven mainly by resentment that Parliamentarians had been rewarded at the expense of Cavaliers.[89] Now, however, fears were expressed that Danby was reducing Parliament to a mere rubber-stamp for the king's will.[90] Fears for the survival of the ancient constitution gave added depth to the divisions created by Danby's abrasive and adversarial approach to politics.

Partisan divisions: Parliament

There had been many references to 'party' in accounts of parliamentary debates in the 1660s. While many talked of 'the royal party' or 'the presbyterian party', disgust at the court's moral depravity and incompetence cut across divisions between Cavalier and Parliamentarian, leading to a revival of the terms 'court' and 'country'. These were used occasionally in the 1660s, but far more widely from 1673. According to Reresby, the 'Country' claimed 'to protect the country from being overburdened in their estates, in their privileges and liberties . . . and to stand by the religion and government as established by law'. The 'Court' 'declared for that too, but at the same time for the king to have a sufficient revenue and power for the exercise of his regal authority': if he became too weak, there was a danger of another civil war.[91] Both claimed to stand for the ancient constitution and expected competent, honest and frugal government and respect for the rule of law – ideals which were almost universally shared. But the old Cavaliers also had more partisan expectations. They looked to the king to reward his old friends and protect the Church against popery and Dissent. Danby set out to create a partisan 'court', by appealing to the old Cavaliers' political and religious prejudices and material interests. His methods created unease among moderate Cavaliers like Reresby, because they were morally questionable (many would have said 'corrupt') and divisive: the selective letters of summons to MPs led to references to 'the unsummoned party'.[92] Both Danby and his opponents drew up lists, dividing the Houses into those for and against them. In March 1677 the names of the 88 MPs opposed to the bill to empower the bishops to make ecclesiastical appointments under a Catholic king were 'posted'. Early in 1678 a highly contentious 'blacklist' was published, perhaps by Marvell, listing 'court' supporters and the rewards which they had allegedly received for their votes.[93]

In terms of parliamentary parties, the sessions of 1673–74 appear a time of flux. As late as June 1673 it was still possible to assess the strength of the 'old honest party' in the 'cabinet'.[94] In the autumn there was unanimous opposition to the Duke of York's marriage; the 'moderate party' (a term used, of themselves, by Cavaliers) was said to be willing to vote supply, but wished to be 'secured in religion and freed from other apprehensions'. In a debate on the peace terms proposed by the Dutch, Sir William Temple identified no fewer than four 'parties' in the Commons.[95] But there were already references to like-minded men sitting together in the 'south-east corner' of the Commons; these references became more frequent in 1674.[96] There were also frequent references, in debate and in diaries, to 'sides' of the House, although the term was routinely denounced as unparliamentary.[97] There was deep resentment of any implication that one 'side' was more loyal than the other, or that it was impossible for office-holders to serve both king and people; courtiers claimed that 'country' members were after their places,[98] but some office-holders complained of being compelled to vote against their judgment.[99] When Lord Hatton wished to promote a private bill in 1677, his son warned that the Lords were so divided that it was impossible to avoid disobliging one party or the other.[100] By 1678 every division was seen as an indicator of party strength and shifts in the party balance were closely noted.[101]

The last five years of the Cavalier Parliament saw a polarization between 'court' and 'country', but some issues cut across 'party' lines: Arlington's impeachment,[102] for example, or the confirmation of the ban on Irish cattle imports.[103] 'Danby's test' created an alliance in the Lords between Presbyterians and Catholics, while jurisdictional disputes set Commons against Lords and 'strangely mingled' the parties.[104] Perhaps the most important factor blurring divisions between 'court' and 'country' was that many of the former still clung to a consensual view of Parliamentary politics – or could not fully trust the king. Reresby, who became identified with the 'court', thought in 1675 that the 'country party had great reason in their debates'. Later, when interviewed by Danby, he said that he would follow his own reason and conscience, seeing his duty as 'to be moderate and healing between the two extremes and to have a due regard to the king's prerogative as well as the liberty of the subject'.[105] Moreover, Danby was unable to commit Charles to a fully anti-French foreign policy or to conjure away the fears of popery created by York's conversion. Even the king acknowledged that some honest gentlemen were genuinely afraid of France.[106] Despite the alarmist claims of its opponents, the 'court' party never constituted an unassailable majority in the Commons, nor was Danby's control over it ever complete, because there was still no complete congruence between the king's policies and those which the old Cavaliers wanted. That congruence was much closer by 1678 than in the 1660s, however, which helps explain the increasingly sharp 'party' divisions not only within Parliament,[107] but also in the localities.

Partisan divisions: the localities

In February 1673 the gentry and freeholders of Suffolk gathered at Ipswich to elect a knight of the shire. The candidates were Lord Huntingtower, a young man of a distinguished local family (and Lauderdale's son-in-law), and Sir Samuel Barnardiston, whose father had sided with Parliament and who was well-known for his Dissenting sympathies. As the competitors were carried around the market place, neither would yield, so a poll was held in which there were many accusations of sharp practice by Huntingtower's supporters and violence and intimidation by Barnardiston's. At one stage the latter began to demolish Barnardiston's booth (by mistake) and the situation became so ugly that the sheriff's wife fainted and some of the gentry feared for their lives. Huntingtower claimed to have the support of most of the nobility and gentry, while Barnardiston's supporters were alleged to consist of Dissenters and 'the meaner sort of trades out of the clothing and great towns, besides a strange rabble of poor common seamen'. Many were allegedly not qualified to vote, but they were 'all armed with clubs and great staves'. On the other side it was alleged that the gentry brought in voters who were not resident in the county and subjected the freeholders to all kinds of threats and entreaties.

When the poll ended, showing Barnardiston with 2,280 votes and Huntingtower with 2,202, the sheriff decided that discretion was the better part of valour and made a double return. The Commons decided that Barnardiston had been elected.[108]

The Suffolk election attracted considerable attention, not least because the social and religious differences between the two sides seemed to presage another civil war.[109] It was all the more striking in that it took place in a county which had been exceptionally untouched by the civil wars and seems to support Kishlansky's argument that ideology now played a determining role in elections. And it was not unique: there was an equally divisive by-election in Norfolk in 1675, albeit one in which the configuration of 'parties' was very different. The surviving documentation is sufficiently rich to enable us to trace further the process of division within a county's landed elite.

In Norfolk, as in Suffolk, the civil wars left few lasting animosities. There had been little fighting and the few Royalists in the county had mostly suffered only modest losses. Historically, the greatest landed family was the Howards, whose *de facto* head became Earl Marshal in 1672 and sixth Duke of Norfolk in 1677. An influential figure, he was debarred by his Catholicism from holding public office and before 1675 used his influence in a largely non-partisan manner. The diocese of Norwich (which included Norfolk and Suffolk) was blessed before 1676 with one of the most eirenic of bishops, Edward Reynolds. From 1661 the lord lieutenant was Horatio, Lord Townshend, who had been too young to to take sides in the wars. Although his deputies were mostly Royalists, they included former Parliamentarians like Sir John Holland and Sir John Hobart. In April 1673 Townshend congratulated his deputies: 'we have been so happy to appear united in all our consultations and actions relating either to our civil or military capacities and employments in our king and country's service'.[110] In February Hobart had been returned unopposed as knight of the shire; there had been rumours that Howard's Protestant son would stand against him, but no challenger appeared.[111]

In May 1674 the other knight of the shire died. Townshend quickly proposed Sir Robert Kemp. A man of firmly Anglican Royalist antecedents and principles,[112] he must have seemed a statesmanlike choice, a natural complement to Hobart, especially as he came from the opposite end of the county.[113] There was no sign of opposition among the gentry until December, when Sir Francis North, member for King's Lynn, was appointed a judge. Danby quickly advanced the claim of his son-in-law, Robert Coke of Holkham, for the vacant seat. A member of a leading north-west Norfolk family, Coke would seem an appropriate candidate, but he was vigorously opposed by Simon Taylor, a merchant of the town, who was supported by Townshend and Hobart. After an acrimonious contest, with much treating, Coke emerged victorious, having allegedly spent £7,000.[114]

At first it seems strange that Townshend should have intervened so actively at Lynn. Although his house, Raynham Hall, was not far away, and he was chosen high steward in 1664, he possessed little electoral influence there.[115] He had been a loyal and diligent lord lieutenant. He had admittedly complained at times that the government undervalued his services and that he was losing money heavily on his farm of the customs on coals, as a result of the Dutch War,[116] but by the end of 1674 the coaling trade was back to normal; soon after, the king and Duke of York agreed to stand godfathers to his latest child.[117] It seems likely that Townshend resented Danby's interference in his 'country'. He allegedly threatened to take Danby's 'letter' to the Commons' committee of elections if Coke were chosen.[118] He complained that Lynn corporation slighted him by preferring Coke's (and Danby's) interest to his; he described Coke as 'this purse-proud young man, otherwise as insignificant and incapable of your service, who knows less of himself and the world than he is known to you by his meat and drink'. This could be read as a denunciation of electoral corruption or a sour acknowledgement that, in financial terms, he could not compete.[119]

Whether or not Danby saw Townshend's comments, his opposition to Coke identified him 'above' as hostile to Danby and within the county as an enemy of the Church. In the latter process, a key role was played by Dr Owen Hughes, who (thanks to the Earl Marshal) had been made commissary of Norfolk, judge of the vice-admiralty court and a county JP. Hughes fell foul of Townshend and Hobart, who he claimed were opposed to the enforcement of the Conventicle Act; he extended the charge to include Kemp and claimed that Simon Taylor was 'suspected' of Presbyterianism, because he expressed fears of popery.[120] In fact, Townshend had, in the early 1660s, been very active against conventicles. Although he became less severe with time, a paper, possibly from 1672, refers to the dual threat from papists and Presbyterians. And in late 1674, when Hughes first made his accusations, the licences issued under the Indulgence had not yet been withdrawn and even committed enemies of Dissent like Daniel Fleming were uncertain whether the Conventicle Act was in force.[121] Kemp had a record of persecuting conventicles and congratulated Sancroft on becoming archbishop. He bitterly rebutted claims that he favoured comprehension and complained of being misrepresented by 'the black coats, the high fliers I mean', who accused him of being a presbyterian.[122] Sir John Holland, who was said, with Townshend and Hobart, to form a 'triumvirate' running Kemp's campaign, was a conventional conformist, who disliked attempts by the clergy to dictate to the laity. Even Hobart, whose sympathy for Dissenters was more open, denied that he had ever attended a conventicle and claimed to find great satisfaction within the Church of England.[123] Nevertheless, the accusations stuck and Kemp's opponents mobilized, given added confidence by Coke's victory at Lynn. Sir Neville Catelyne, who had promised that he would not stand against Kemp, changed his mind.[124] The campaign became bitter, charges and counter-charges flew thick and fast. Townshend and his allies were accused of threatening Catelyne's supporters, of using the militia to overawe voters and of sharp practice on election day. Kemp was declared elected, but it was claimed that Catelyne had as many as 1,700 supporters.[125]

The charge that Kemp was hostile to the Church turned a fairly routine 'selection' into a bitterly contested 'election'. But where did the impetus come from? While Danby's hand was apparent at Lynn, I can find no evidence of his intervening in the county. Reynolds recommended his clergy to vote for Kemp[126] but most supported Catelyne. A much publicized letter from Holland described the clergy as the chief promoters of opposition to Kemp and warned them of 'the ill effects of a contested election, which our neighbour county feels and complains of'; they would be wise not to risk the wrath of their lay patrons and should not take it upon themselves to question the collective wisdom of 'the lord lieutenant, most of the deputy lieutenants, most of the justices of the peace, most of the gentlemen and persons of the greatest interest and quality in the county'.[127] Kemp and his supporters were accused of denouncing their opponents as 'drunken clergy' or 'high Church of England men'. This allegation was one of many in a paper of 'queries', which Hughes confessed to circulating among his clerical friends and in coffee-houses and taverns, but denied writing. One witness declared that Hughes had allowed copies to be taken and had stressed to the clergy that on this occasion their normal duty to obey their bishop did not apply. The paper also denounced the machinations of the 'moderate sort of men' – 'moderate', for ultra-Royalists, had become a term of abuse. Kemp was accused of seeking the support of 'stubborn fanatics' and those who had signed a petition to bring Charles I to justice and of using electoral tactics – including invocation of the fear of popery – similar to those used in 1640. It also claimed that it was improper for a peer to seek to 'awe and influence' voters in an election to the Commons.[128]

It is clear that the emergence of this 'church party' owed little to elite support. Some expressed surprise that it could stand against the chief men of the county and remarked that if it could find a leader it would be formidable.[129] Again and again, commentators stressed the role of the clergy, who were described at times as an indispensable component of the electorate; one account denounced Townshend's setting Kemp up in 'opposition to the commonalty of the county as well as the clergy and their ancient birthrights'.[130] In Suffolk 'popular' opposition to gentry attempts to determine the outcome of the election was identified with Dissent; in Norfolk it was driven by support for the Church and orchestrated by the clergy. They called for a rigorous enforcement within the Church of the 'Laudian' brand of Anglicanism and for the effective suppression of Dissent; and they claimed for the clergy an active and authoritative role in church and state. By contrast Townshend, Holland and Kemp inclined towards a broader, more inclusive vision of the Church and a more relaxed attitude towards those who remained outside it. They also assumed that the clergy should remain subordinate to the laity. Holland's letter remarked that the gentry were increasingly making the clergy enter into bonds of resignation, whereby they could be required to resign if they displeased their patrons. A bill to outlaw this practice was introduced in the Commons in 1677; it was thrown out on the first reading by 147 votes to 62.[131]

The sudden eruption of the Norfolk clergy into electoral politics defies simple explanation. Mark Goldie has argued that in the 1670s many of the younger clergy were showing a militancy and political extremism which was sharpened by the surge in nonconformist activity following the Indulgence.[132] Only since 1664 had the clergy been eligible to vote in parliamentary elections and they were exceptionally numerous in Norfolk, a county of over 700 parishes. Dissent was significant in some of the towns, notably Norwich and Yarmouth; the Compton census revealed that in the diocese of Norwich nonconformists made up between 4 and 5 per cent of the population, close to the national average; relatively few meeting-houses were licensed in 1672. Nevertheless, the reluctance of the authorities to persecute Dissent bred frustration among the clergy, which was increased by the lack of leadership from Reynolds,[133] at a time when his fellow-bishops were finally persuading the king to take a firm line against Dissent.

One person who seemingly played no part in the politicization of the clergy was the man who from 1676 emerged as the leader of the 'church party' in Norfolk. Because Lord Yarmouth superseded Townshend as lord lieutenant, it is easy to assume that he set out to supplant him, but there is no evidence that he did so. He seems to have been selected by Danby to head the county's 'church party'; his financial problems (which only Danby could resolve) left him in no position to refuse: 'whosoever were now in his place and under his circumstances must obey in what they are commanded'.[134] Yarmouth's modest income and heavy debts had compelled him to spend most of his time in London, soliciting favours. He played little part in county affairs – he attended only eight meetings of deputy lieutenants in fifteen years. He was on friendly terms with Townshend, Hobart, Holland and Kemp, but his standing in the county was limited: 'my lord hath not the fortune to be known enough'.[135] His straitened means forced him to limit his hospitality when he became lord lieutenant.[136] He was pleasantly surprised by the large turnout of horsemen – and clergy – when he visited the county,[137] but remained very conscious that his limited 'interest' in Norfolk needed to be buttressed by those of Coke, Danby and the Earl Marshal.[138]

Yarmouth's correspondence, especially with his wife, does not suggest an innately partisan figure. His family was Royalist and his commitment to the Church was beyond question: Reynolds thought his little church at Oxnead as beautiful as any in the diocese.[139] He welcomed Sparrow's appointment as bishop of Norwich and reported that he 'carries himself like a bishop . . . to the satisfaction of the right clergy'.[140] He (and more particularly his wife) were associated with some of the most militant of the 'church party', notably Dr Hughes and Dr John Hildeyard; she was allegedly responsible for having Hildeyard made a JP.[141] Yarmouth described Hildeyard as his friend, but confessed that he could behave imprudently and remarked that parsons could be 'silly creatures'.[142] Yarmouth's letters make clear that his first priority was still to repair his tattered finances.[143] His instinct, on his appointment as lord lieutenant in February 1676, was to make as few enemies as possible and he often declared himself weary of fighting others' battles.[144] At times he was profoundly depressed: his health was poor, at times he could hardly walk, and his much-loved second daughter died in November 1676.[145]

Despite his reluctance, Yarmouth was drawn into partisan politics. In 1675 the 5 November sermon in Norwich cathedral emphasized the sin of regicide as much as popish treason: 'You see how thin the ashes are under which the embers of our late fire seem to be raked up', wrote Hobart's uncle.[146] A letter in the name of many of the gentry and clergy warned against the danger of leaving lords lieutenant in office too long and urged that Yarmouth should make an appearance in the county.[147] The subscription to meet the costs of the shrievalty, of which more shortly, in Norfolk took on a partisan character: subscribers had to be approved by Hobart, Holland and their allies and the list consisted mainly of future Whigs: the few future Tories had not played an active part in the county by-election.[148] The subscription enhanced the solidarity of Townshend's supporters: those who were deputy lieutenants – even Holland – refused to serve under Yarmouth. The lieutenancy was comprehensively reshaped, followed in due course by the commission of the peace. His efforts at bridge-building rebuffed, Yarmouth had little choice but to make himself the head of the 'church party', especially as he knew how much Danby and the king disapproved of Townshend, Hobart and Holland.[149] Yarmouth and his deputies waited on the judge separately from the sheriff and his fellow-subscribers, whom Yarmouth called 'blue boys', because the livery they provided for the sheriff's attendants was edged in blue. Yarmouth's retinue was much the larger and its trumpets were louder.[150] Opposition to the election of his son to a vacant seat at Norwich drew Yarmouth into the city's politics as well. Despite his occasional expressions of distaste for partisan divisions, Yarmouth felt affronted by the opposition of the 'fanatics' and exulted in the chance to show his 'strength' and to 'rout' his opponents.[151] His aggressive stance was encouraged by Hildeyard[152] and his confidence in the backing of Howard, now Duke of Norfolk, and Sparrow.[153] Yarmouth's metamorphosis illustrates how partisan divisions, once they reached a certain critical point, developed their own momentum.

How typical were Norfolk's divisions? In Suffolk the one account sympathetic to Dissent focuses on the alleged sharp practice of Huntingtower's supporters and does not mention the clergy.[154] The same was necessarily true of petitions to the Commons' committee of elections, which could take cognizance only of alleged irregularities. We therefore have to rely on the surviving comments of contemporaries, which suggest that religious divisions played a part in a limited number of elections. In Derbyshire in 1670 William Sacheverell, with nonconformist support, carried the day against the candidate supported by most of the gentry, but without the violence threatened in Suffolk.[155] In Devon, Ward and Sparrow had long complained that Albemarle used his influence to keep nonconformist sympathizers in the commission of the peace. When he died, his son moved to the Lords, leaving a vacancy for knight of the shire. The lord lieutenant, Albemarle's kinsman the Earl of Bath, wrote to his deputies in favour of his own kinsman, Robert Fortescue; two of them instructed high constables to pass on his recommendation to the freeholders. The Commons, while careful not to censure the earl, condemned the letters as a violation of the electors' freedom, on which Fortescue stood down. An attempt by another candidate with nonconformist sympathies to stand against the gentry's agreed candidate was said by Sparrow to show both the insolence and the weakness of 'the factious'.[156]

We are on firmer ground when considering the Dorset by-election of 1675. At first it seemed that Lord Digby, the son of the earl of Bristol, would carry it without opposition. Shaftesbury, a Dorset man, initially expressed no hostility to his candidature, but became perturbed when he learned of 'what we must expect from my Lord Digby and of the designs of some of our great men above and the correspondence which my lord had with them'. These great men presumably included Danby, as Digby was later noted as always voting against the 'country party'. A letter in which Digby was described in this way was widely circulated; Bristol denounced it as an affront to his son's honour and challenged Shaftesbury to disavow it. Shaftesbury, on the advice of some of the gentry, approached Thomas Moore, who agreed to stand against Digby. Next time they met, Digby accused Shaftesbury of turning against him and of being 'against the king and for a commonwealth'.[157] The choice of Moore, allegedly the greatest upholder of conventicles in the county, provoked Bishop Carleton to urge his clergy to vote for Digby, on the grounds that Moore was an enemy of the Church. In the event, Digby won by a majority of more than three to one, much to the disappointment of the 'nonconformist party'.[158] In County Durham Thomas Vane emerged victorious, allegedly with nonconformist support, against the bulk of the gentry. However, Vane died just after the election and his brother Christopher was returned unopposed in his place, having reportedly won over the bishop and the gentry. Durham was, however, a special case: this was the first election held for the county and Thomas Vane had been chosen with Sir Ralph Cole, generally seen as a supporter of the court. The gentry may have wished to avoid the disruption of a second contest or judged it less divisive to return a balanced ticket.[159]

There is scattered evidence of partisanship in borough elections. In 1666 Williamson and Baptist May were rejected by Morpeth and Winchelsea respectively as 'courtiers'; at Winchelsea it was alleged that six of the nine who voted against May and four of the seven who voted for him never came to church, which does not suggest a division on religious lines.[160] At Dover, the Dissenting vote was thrown behind first Lord Hinchingbrooke and then Thomas Papillon, but one of Papillon's opponents in 1673 was a fellow Huguenot. It was also stressed that Hinchingbrooke's father, the Earl of Sandwich, and Papillon, a commissioner for trade, were well placed to help the town. Papillon was defeated, but the result was overturned when it was shown that his opponents had had fifty freemen created specifically to vote in the election.[161] There were also references to the extent of the Dissenting vote in Bristol and at Berwick, where the rector, Richard Stote, acted as agent for Danby's son, Dunblane. Stote claimed that the Dissenters whom he had had excommunicated were ineligible to vote, 'though perhaps such things have been rarely if ever practised'.[162] Lord Wharton was assured that at Abingdon, if his son-in-law chose to stand, 'he would not fail of any one vote among all the nonconforming party, whether Presbyterian, Independent or Anabaptist and that many of the sober persons of the other party might also be made for him'. In the event, however, the son of the previous member was elected.[163]

Despite such examples, and evidence of growing political and religious divisions in the localities,[164] it is striking how many by-elections between 1673 and 1678 do not seem to have been fought on party lines. Two-thirds of the populace of Chester were said to be of the 'royal party', while the other third were 'fanatics'. In a by-election in 1673, the candidate favoured by the Dissenters stood down and the two candidates of the 'royal party' fought a gruelling contest in the course of which nine people were crushed to death as a crowd surged down the town hall steps.[165] The hotly fought election at Stamford in 1677 was essentially a contest between the Earls of Exeter and Lindsey. Lindsey, the lord lieutenant and Danby's brother-in-law, joined his interest with that of the presbyterian Hatcher family. As both sides treated the electors furiously, issues of principle were conspicuous by their absence.[166] At Grantham there was a similar power struggle between Lindsey and Sir Robert Carr, chancellor of the duchy of Lancaster and Arlington's brother-in-law. After an orgy of treating in the run-up to the election, Lindsey mustered the militia in the town on the day of the poll and his candidate, Sir Robert Markham, was declared elected. Carr's candidate – Sir William Ellis, the nephew of the recently dismissed Judge Ellis – petitioned against the return, stressing the misuse of the militia. The committee of elections narrowly rejected the petition, after the king canvassed members to keep Markham in. Carr was removed from the privy council.[167] A similar mixture of heavy treating and aristocratic intervention secured a seat at Northampton for the initially unpopular Ralph Montagu. It was claimed at first that Montagu's father had a great interest with the parsons, but when that proved insufficient he relied on strong liquor; Danby's attempts to prevent Montagu's election proved unsuccessful.[168]

From the foregoing no clear pattern emerges. Contests fought on religious or political lines appear the exception rather than the rule and I can find no other county contest before 1679 in which the clergy played as prominent a role as they did in Norfolk. A number of shire by-elections were decided without a contest. This does not necessarily imply an absence of conflict. It could show that one side lacked the confidence or the commitment to challenge the other: this appears to have been the case in Norfolk in 1673 and (initially) in Dorset in 1675; it also may explain the uncontested return of a well-know patron of Dissent, Sir Francis Rolle, for Hampshire in 1675. However, in Northamptonshire, where there had been no contest in 1675, there was another by-election in 1678 which was warmly contested but in which issues of principle appear to have played little part.[169] While local disputes between Church and Dissent were common, and the Dissenting vote might sometimes be significant, it was only one variable among many in a multifaceted process. Treating remained important, as did aristocratic power. At Newark, the electors, having finally secured parliamentary representation, were determined to enjoy it. Henry Savile treated lavishly and asked his brother, Lord Halifax, to make the aldermen welcome at Rufford and to give his custom to a cooper and a pewterer who were working on his behalf. At Leicester Lord Roos asked all who had any dependence on his father or himself, in the militia or otherwise, to vote for his uncle, John Grey.[170] Patrons and candidates continued to stress the material benefits they could bring. Abuse of power might provoke complaints: we have noted the resentment at Lindsey's misuse of the militia and of the attempts by Danby and his kinsmen to add to the Osborne-Bertie caucus in Parliament, especially when their candidates were under-age. Often it is hard to distinguish between factional or personal and ideological divisions. In Kent sixteen justices protested against the lord lieutenant's support for the businessman Sir John Banks (Hugh Peter's 'cloakbag carrier') at Winchelsea. He had also been a county committee man and a member of Cromwell's Parliaments. The lord lieutenant complained to the king of their public affront to Banks, and himself, at Maidstone sessions and five justices, three of them MPs, were put out of commission.[171] It is hard to see clear partisan divisions here. Despite his past political affiliations, Banks was supported by the Royalist lord lieutenant, Winchilsea, and the Duke of York, but the gentry may still have disliked him as an outsider – Kent was a notoriously introverted county – and because of his record in the Interregnum.[172] In the winter of 1675–76, there were reports from Herefordshire that the enemies of the Church, expecting a dissolution, had drawn up a slate of candidates for the shire and boroughs and that their opponents were responding in kind. One cannot tell whether these projects reached even the planning stage, but the reports are plausible in that Herefordshire was a county with a tradition of seeking consensus, while in Westmorland it was remarked in 1676 that Sir John Lowther 'is to have the next vacancy'.[173] A study of the electoral process in 1673–78 suggests that 'selections' were only occasionally superseded by 'elections' and that piecemeal local divisions had not yet developed into a polarization along party lines.

The politicization of the legal system

Before Danby's rise to power there had occasionally been a 'political' dimension to law enforcement, most notably in the 'Cavalier revenge' of the early 1660s and the sporadic use of arbitrary imprisonment against those deemed dangerous to the state: refusal to take the oaths of allegiance and supremacy provided a plausible pretext. The Commons occasionally complained of the misuse of royal power – for example the imprisonment of John Harrington for refusing to answer questions before the privy council. It is noteworthy that the Commons merely sought assurances that the council's powers would not be abused in future.[174] They felt on stronger ground when complaining that the council was too apt to summon JPs and others and to commit people for 'slight' causes, notably relating to the excise.[175] When the Commons brought in a bill in 1674 to ensure that judges served during good behaviour rather than at pleasure, while some complained about the judges' 'arbitrary' conduct, the main concern was to prevent a 'popish successor' removing the existing judges.[176] Complaints in 1677 by the firebrand William Sacheverell of royal interference with the judiciary won only limited support.[177] The king continued to declare that he would abide by the law and would be advised by his judges[178] but the appointment of judges was becoming influenced by politics. This was the consequence not so much of a change in government policy as of partisan divisions, and especially in elections, and the willingness of those who felt aggrieved to seek redress in the courts.

As we have seen, the Suffolk by-election of February 1673 was exceptionally contentious. The sheriff, Sir Stephen Soame, made a double return which the Commons decided in favour of Barnardiston. Barnardiston sued Soame for a false return and the jury in King's Bench awarded him damages of £800. Soame appealed against the verdict and in June 1676 six out of eight judges found in his favour. Of the two who did not, Ellis was quickly dismissed: it was reported that 'the fanatics' were crestfallen. The other, Atkins, survived for the moment.[179] Ellis's replacement, Sir William Scroggs, purveyed a strident Royalism akin to that of the most militant Anglican clergy – and he was seen as Danby's man.[180] His appointment triggered a ferocious battle at court to influence judicial appointments, for reasons which were as much personal as political: even the much respected Henry Coventry tried to pay off a score against Atkins.[181] Lord Chancellor Finch struggled to prevent Danby and his wife from undermining the integrity of the judiciary,[182] while public opinion ascribed the changes either to corruption – places on the bench were to be sold to the highest bidder – or a wish to make the judges politically compliant.[183]

The second dispute with lasting legal repercussions originated in the Dorset by-election of 1675. Shaftesbury sued Digby for damages under the fourteenth-century statute of *scandalum magnatum*, under which commoners (Digby's was a courtesy title) could be punished for defaming a peer. A Wiltshire jury awarded £1,000 damages (upon which they were lavishly treated). An attempt to overturn the verdict on a technicality was unsuccessful, but Digby's supporters among the Dorset gentry clubbed together and raised well over £1,000 to meet his expenses.[184] Shaftesbury's success encouraged other peers to seek similar revenge, to a point where Coleman remarked that it would increase the demand for peerages; Shaftesbury was said to be planning actions against Scroggs, the Bishop of Bath and Wells and two others.[185] In Norfolk, Townshend's action against Hughes attracted wide interest. Hughes claimed that he had fallen foul of Townshend for upholding the interests of the Church.[186] He begged the Earl Marshal to ensure that his case was not heard by Ellis, whom he regarded as biased towards 'the faction'.[187] Ellis was removed before he could go on circuit and the case was heard by Chief Baron Montagu, whom the 'church party' regarded as more friendly, but despite all that the earl could say on Hughes's behalf, the jury awarded Townshend £4,000 in damages.[188]

One reason why Hughes lost was that the sheriff for 1676, John Pell, had been appointed by the king despite Townshend's plea to have him exempted. In most counties the office of sheriff was burdensome and unpopular and so appointment to the shrievalty could be seen as a punishment. As partisan divisions became more serious, the gentry of a number of counties joined to protect themselves. The Gloucestershire gentry agreed in November 1675 to subscribe to a fund to cover some of the costs of the newly-nominated sheriff, notably providing liveries for his attendants and hospitality and presents for the judges.[189] The practice spread to other counties, including Bedfordshire and Oxfordshire. By the time Sir Ralph and Edmund Verney discussed the proposals for Buckinghamshire, there were several papers, printed and handwritten, circulating on the subject.[190]

The agreement for Norfolk in January 1676 might seem no more than a form of collective insurance against the cost of being sheriff. Hughes, however, saw it as reinforcing the power which Townshend and his allies enjoyed through control of the militia: now they would also ensure that juries were selected from among the subscribers, so that their opponents would get no justice.[191] Hughes was far from an impartial observer, and he ignored the fact that sheriffs were appointed by the king, but his claims were not wholly implausible, as the outcome of his trial was to show. The Norfolk subscription made no mention of juries, but it had been proposed in Bedfordshire that juries should be composed entirely of subscribers; subscribers featured prominently, but not overwhelmingly, on Norfolk juries in 1676.[192] Moreover, admittance to the panel of subscribers was effectively controlled by Townshend's allies. By contrast, those who subscribed in Northamptonshire – a county apparently not yet split on party lines – were almost equally divided between future Whigs and future Tories.[193]

The promoters of the subscription were probably concerned less to create a 'party organization' than to avoid victimization by Danby and to prevent good men avoiding an office whose duties included that of county returning officer. Nevertheless, the subscription showed how far the by-elections of 1675 had divided the county. Yarmouth tried to identify the subscribers and urged that the subscription be condemned by the council or the judges and that no 'subscriber' should be made sheriff.[194] On the latter point he need not have worried. Except in 1681, when the king was wrongly advised, all Norfolk sheriffs were chosen from the 'loyal party'.[195] The selection of both sheriffs and juries was increasingly influenced by partisanship. In July 1676 Secretary Coventry complained about a case at Worcester assizes, in which the jury had insisted on returning a verdict different from that recommended by the judge and JPs. He suspected 'partiality' on the part of the under-sheriff who had drawn up the panel. It was all the more worrying that this was a county reputed to be 'loyal'.[196] Appointing partisan sheriffs made juries more partisan. When in 1677 Hobart appeared before Dr Hughes in the vice-admiralty court, in a case about a wreck, Hobart lost; one of Yarmouth's agents wrote 'the jury were very honest and such as we informed ourselves of their inclinations'.[197] When partisan differences affected the selection of jurors for the Norfolk vice-admiralty court, the politicization of the legal process had advanced to a point where justice took second place to party advantage and revenge. As in the patronage system, the advent of party divisions ensured that distortions ceased to be occasional and personal, the result of the interplay of individual rivalries, and became systematic and all-pervasive, so that by the early 1680s the law had become just another weapon in the fighting of party battles.

Notes

1 *CSPV 1673–75*, p. 187. See also *Williamson*, II.62.
2 Carte MS 72, fo. 253.
3 See Browning, *Danby*, I, chs 7–12; Haley, *Shaftesbury*, chs 17–20; Miller, *Charles II*, ch. 9.
4 *Williamson*, II.142. See also (for the perception of 1672–73 as a watershed) Burnet, *Hist*, II.1; Dering, *Papers*, pp. 125–6. Also Miller, *Charles II*, ch. 8.
5 Newton, *House of Lyme*, p. 252; *Williamson*, I.85, 89, 100.
6 *Williamson*, II.55, 78 (quoted).
7 Browning, *Danby*, II.63–4. See also *ibid.*, p. 70.
8 Miller, *Charles II*, chs 9–10.
9 *CSPD 1673–75*, pp. 27, 57, 102; *Williamson*, II.27, 30, 80–1, 99.
10 BT 130, Ruvigny to Louis, 5 February 1674 NS; *HMC 9th Report, Appendix II*, p. 42; Macpherson, I.71–2.
11 BT 135, Courtin to Louis, 8 and 22 March NS; Finch MS PP 42, pp. 3–9, 13 (comment on p. 9); Grey, IV.284–96; Miller, *Popery*, pp. 144–7.
12 Dering, *Diary*, pp. 119–20; Newton, *House of Lyme*, p. 252.
13 Dering, *Diary*, pp. 122–6, 137–8; Grey, II.38–48, 101–6; Newton, *House of Lyme*, p. 253.
14 Grey, II.39–40, 69–74; BL, Add MS 29571, fo. 192; Carte MS 79, fo. 72.
15 Grey, II.163–9, 177–80; *CJ*, IX.280–1; *LJ*, XII.579–80; Stowe MS 201, fo. 309. It seems that the bill as sent up by the Commons is as in Tanner MS 43, fos 191–4, and as amended by the Lords in *ibid.*, fos 189–90. Sancroft's date of March 1673 is therefore correct: see Spurr, 'Toleration Act', p. 936n. (The final short paragraph, quoted by Spurr on p. 936, does refer to the bill of February 1674.)
16 CPA 106, Croissy to Pomponne, 10 April 1673 NS.
17 Tanner MS 42, fo. 7.
18 Dering, *Diary*, p. 145.
19 Grey, II.45–7. See also Aungier's comment on the bill, Stowe MS 201, fo. 188 and Duncombe's distinction between 'indulgence' and 'toleration': Grey, II.142.
20 *LJ*, XII.644; *HMC 9th Report, Appendix II*, p. 44; BL, Add MS 23136, fo. 98; BT 130, Ruvigny to Pomponne, 5 March 1674 NS. Spurr, following *RB*, III.140, states that this was a response to a bill introduced in the Commons, but no trace of one survives in the *Journals*: Spurr, 'Toleration Act', pp. 935–6.
21 PC 2/64, pp. 6, 14, 27, 40; *CSPD 1673*, pp. 367–9; *Williamson*, I.34, 42; *HMC 6th Report*, p. 454; *HMC le Fleming*, p. 101.
22 *HMC le Fleming*, pp. 109–10; Tanner MS 42, fo. 14; DCLD, Hunter MS 7, no. 114.
23 Carte MS 72, fo. 229.
24 *Williamson*, I.33; *RB*, III.109; *CSPV 1673–75*, pp. 307–8, 324, 331; BL, Add MS 63057B, fo. 30; Macpherson, I.75.
25 *CSPV 1673–75*, pp. 310–12; Stowe MS 206, fos 161, 180; Carte MSS 38, fo. 232, 72, fo. 253; WYAL, MX/R 8/5.
26 *CSPV 1673–75*, p. 357; Finch MS Ecc 2, paper 3. (Papers 1 and 2 are calendared in *CSPD 1673–75*, pp. 548–50.)
27 *CSPD 1673–75*, p. 551.

28 PC 2/64, pp. 365, 372–3; Finch MS Ecc 2, papers 4–5.
29 BL, M636/28, Sir Ralph to Edmund Verney, 4 and 18 February 1675; *CSPV 1673–75*, pp. 357–8; PC 2/64, pp. 365, 372–3; *CSPD 1673–75*, pp. 578, 590, 594. The order that all priests were to leave was dated 5 February, but it seems likely that the proclamation ordering the enforcement of the order in council of 3 February was not issued until the 12th: Steele, *Proclamations*, nos 3608–10.
30 *CSPV 1673–75*, pp. 363–4, 376, 390; *HMC Portland*, III.349.
31 Browning, *Danby*, II.55; Marvell, II.338.
32 Stowe MS 208, fo. 61; *HMC Portland*, III.348.
33 *HMC 7th Report*, p. 492; Marvell, II.343. See also Browning, *Danby*, I, ch. 9; Haley, *Shaftesbury*, ch. 18; Swatland, *Lords*, pp. 213–15.
34 See Goldie, 'Danby, the Bishops and the Whigs', in *Pol of Rel*, pp. 81–3.
35 *HMC 2nd Report*, p. 22; *HMC Buccleuch (Montagu House)*, I.321.
36 PC 2/65, p. 123; Browning, *Danby*, II.45; Coventry MS 7, fo. 78; Pforz, Coleman to Bulstrode,14 July 1676; WSL, SMS 454, no. 23; *CSPD 1676–77*, pp. 56, 132; CPA 118, Ruvigny to Pomponne, 9 April 1676 NS.
37 Whiteman, *Census*, pp. xxiv–xxix; *HMC Leeds*, p. 14. Note the reference (Whiteman, p. xxviii) to a person close to the king.
38 BL, Add MS 25124, fos 66–7, 130; Pforz, Coleman to Bulstrode, 4 December 1676, 8 January 1677.
39 *HMC 7th Report*, p. 465; Dorset RO, D124, box 233, bundle labelled Col. T. Strangways, Bishop to Strangways, 10 and 24 February, Strangways to Bishop, 1 March 1675; Coventry MS 7, fos 98, 100, 126; *CSPD 1677–78*, pp. 320, 351–4, 382–3.
40 CPA 122, Courtin to Pomponne 25 January 1677 NS; *Essex*, II.63; Finch MS PP 44, p. 4.
41 *CJ*, IX.455–6, 506; Grey, V.250–5, 283, 286.
42 Browning, *Danby*, II.66. Although this paper was ostensibly drawn up by a group of peers, it is in Danby's handwriting and clearly reflects his views.
43 North, *Examen*, p. 528; M636/22, Sir Ralph to Edmund Verney, 5 May 1668.
44 Bulstrode, I.302–3. See also M636/28, Sir Ralph to John Verney, 3 May 1675 and earlier comments: *CSPV 1673–75*, pp. 176–7; BT 128, Croissy to Louis, 5 March 1673 NS.
45 *Hatton*, I.122; BL, Add MS 29555, fo. 421.
46 BL, Add MS 29572, fo. 17.
47 See for example *Savile*, p. 40; CPA 116, Ruvigny to Pomponne, 1 August 1675 NS; *Essex*, I.293.
48 Browning, *Danby*, II.63–72.
49 Coventry MS 83, fo. 91; BL, Add MS 29572, fo. 17; Comber, *Autobiography*, II.10.
50 Evelyn, IV.267; Dorset RO, D124, box 235, bundle 1, part 1, 'Narrative how Earl of Danby . . .'; C. Clay, *Public Finance and Private Wealth: The Career of Sir Stephen Fox*, Oxford, 1978, pp. 104–5.
51 M636/29, Sir Ralph to Edmund Verney, 10 February, Edmund to Sir Ralph, 14 February 1676; *HP*, III.300.
52 *HMC 7th Report*, p. 492.
53 PC 2/66, pp. 109, 120; *HMC Ormond*, NS IV.383–4; A. Browning, 'Parties and Party Organisation in the Reign of Charles II', *TRHS*, 4th series XXX, 1948, p. 27.

54 M636/28, Sir Ralph to Edmund Verney, 8 January 1675; BL, Add MS 32095, fo. 40; Browning, *Danby*, I.137–8 and 138n.2.
55 Stowe MS 207, fos 21, 332.
56 Stowe MS 207, fo. 21; Carte 72, fo. 257; Finch MS PP 37, fo. 18.
57 Stowe MSS 215, fo. 97, 217, fos 62–3.
58 Stowe MS 212, fos 179–80, 307.
59 Stowe MS 217, fos 227–8.
60 Burnet, *Hist*, II.12; Reresby, pp. 130, 131, 133.
61 Evelyn, IV.14, 20.
62 *CSPD 1675–76*, p. 574.
63 *HP*, III.185; *Essex*, I.258–60.
64 *HP*, I.639–47.
65 *Essex*, II.19–20; M636/28, Sir Ralph to Edmund Verney, 27 May 1675.
66 Browning, 'Parties', p. 33; Browning, *Danby*, II.65–6; BL, Add MS 28088, fo. 3 – list of lords lieutenant, some marked with a cross, including Townshend and Winchester, both removed in February 1676.
67 M636/29, Edmund Verney to Sir Ralph, 28 December 1676. See also *Williamson*, II.14; BL, Add MS 29571, fo. 323.
68 *HMC Ormond*, NS IV.434.
69 Browning, *Danby*, I, ch. 9; Haley, *Shaftesbury*, ch. 18.
70 *Lauderdale*, III.142.
71 BL, Add MS 25124, fos 25–9, 61; *CSPD 1675–76*, pp. 302, 304; Browning, *Danby*, I.171–2; Grey, III.367–8.
72 See *HP*, III.749–50. Wiseman was noted to be visiting Danby frequently in February 1675: M636/28, Sir Ralph to Edmund Verney, 8 February 1675.
73 Browning, *Danby*, I.191–3 and 193n.3, III.86–93.
74 Browning, *Danby*, I.195–6; *HP*, I.641–2.
75 Browning, *Danby*, II.66.
76 Pforz, Coleman to Bulstrode, 2 June 1676; *HMC 6th Report*, p. 379; Reresby, p. 125; Browning, *Danby*, I.210 and n.1, III.4–6; Chandaman, *Revenue*, pp. 66–7. The other sources suggest that Danby took the project more seriously than Browning thought; the Yorkshire excise had been farmed separately: Chandaman, *Revenue*, p. 65.
77 Browning, *Danby*, I.168–71; Browning, 'Parties', pp. 34–6.
78 Grey, VII.329–31; *HMC Ormond*, NS IV.518.
79 Browning, *Danby*, I.168; Browning, 'Parties', pp. 24–5.
80 BL, Add MSS 25124, fo. 48, 25125, fo. 4.
81 Havighurst, 'Judiciary', pp. 230–1; Marvell, *Growth*, pp. 66–7.
82 Reresby, p. 172.
83 *Hatton*, I.132–3; BL, Add MS 29571, fos 304, 310, 323–4; FSL, MS X.d.529(117).
84 *Essex*, II.4.
85 *Savile*, p. 45.
86 E. Lake, 'Diary', (ed.) G.P. Elliott, pp. 11, 19–20 in *Camden Miscellany*, I (1847); E. Campana di Cavelli, *Les Derniers Stuart à Saint Germain en Laye* (2 vols, London, 1871), I.207.
87 *Hatton*, I.166; BL, Add MS 29571, fo. 494.
88 M636/28, Sir Ralph to John Verney, 3 May 1675; CPA 128, Barrillon to Pomponne, 17 March 1678 NS, CPA 130, same to same, 4 August 1678 NS.

89 *CJ*, VIII.475; Pepys, IV.125, 136; Evelyn, III.493.
90 Marvell, *Growth*, pp. 74–81; *HMC 7th Report*, p. 492.
91 Reresby, p. 90.
92 Tanner MS 42, fo. 183.
93 Browning, *Danby*, III.44–151; K.H.D. Haley, 'Shaftesbury's Lists of the Lay Peers and Members of the Commons, 1677–8', *BIHR*, XLIII, 1970, pp. 86–105; Finch MS PP 42, p. 9; Browning, *Docts*, pp. 237–49.
94 *Williamson*, I.77.
95 *Williamson*, II.55–6, 94; *Essex*, I.131–2 ('William Coventry's brother' should read 'Henry Coventry's brother'). Their opponents called the old Cavaliers 'the violent party': Tanner MS 42, fo. 145.
96 *Williamson*, II.51–2, 59, 127, 156–7; *CSPD 1675–76*, p. 563.
97 Grey, II.52, V.314–5; Dering, *Diary*, p. 140; *CJ*, IX.474–5; *HMC Ormond*, NS IV.398.
98 Grey, II.9, III.[71], V.314–15; Finch MS PP 37, fos 21–2. See also Reresby, pp. 111, 112.
99 *Essex*, II.4.
100 BL, Add MS 29571, fos 374–5. See also Reresby, p. 97.
101 Pforz, Coleman to Bulstrode, 31 May 1678; M636/31, Sir Ralph to Edmund Verney, 25 March 1678.
102 Stowe MS 204, fo. 116; M636/27, Sir Ralph to Edmund Verney, 22 January 1674.
103 Stowe MS 211, fo. 265; *HMC 7th Report*, p. 468.
104 Grey, IV.49.
105 Reresby, pp. 97, 110–11. For his identification with the 'Court' in 1678, see Browning, *Docts*, p. 248; Pforz, Coleman to Bulstrode, 31 May 1678.
106 BL, Add MS 63057B, fos 32–3; Burnet, *Hist*, II.117; *CSPD 1678*, pp. 168, 182; Temple, *Works*, I.450, 458.
107 See Swatland, *Lords*, ch. 11.
108 *HP*, I.393; CKS, U951/F15 (under 24 February 1673); *CSPD 1672–73*, pp, 597, 608, 613; K. Doughty, *The Betts of Wortham in Suffolk*, London, 1912, pp. 110–14 (this last account not used by *HP*). Skippon gives 2,278 votes for Barnardiston, Doughty's account 2,280, *CSPD 1672–73*, p. 613 a majority of 78.
109 Doughty, *Betts*, p. 113. It is significant that many years later Roger North included an account of the election in *Examen*, pp. 516–17.
110 NRO, WKC 7/6/44.
111 *CSPD 1672–73*, p. 572; *HP*, I.320.
112 Dunn, *Journal*, pp. 16, 155; BL, Add MS 63081, fo. 164.
113 Blickling is north of Norwich, Gissing close to the Suffolk border.
114 *HP*, I.328.
115 J.M. Rosenheim, *The Townshends of Raynham*, Middletown, CT, 1989, pp. 30–1; *HP*, I. 327–8.
116 Rosenheim, *Townshends*, pp. 36–7; BL, Add MS 41654, fo. 63; Coventry MS 4, fos 61, 67.
117 Tanner MS 42, fo. 146.
118 FSL, MS V b 305, nos 24–6; Raynham, Corr., Townshend to Arlington, 28 January 1675.
119 NRO, MC 1601/74. Also MC 1601/18, in which this is presumably the letter referred to.

120 Rosenheim, *Townshends*, pp. 47–8; FSL, MS V b 305, nos 24–6, 28, 34.
121 Bodl, MS Eng Hist b 212, fo. 12; *CSPD 1665–66*, p. 130, *1666–67*, pp. 114, 124; *HMC le Fleming*, pp. 109–10. The reference to papists and Presbyterians is in BL, Add MS 41654, fo. 63, which is undated, but the reference to a lord chancellor places it in 1660–67 or (more likely) 1672–73.
122 Tanner MS 40, fo. 155; BL, Add MS 63081, fo. 164; NRO, MC 1601/35; Raynham, Corr., Hobart to Townshend, 19 March 1675, Kemp to Townshend, 'Sunday 30 May' (quoted) and 2 May 1681.
123 Miller, 'Holland', pp. 856–7; NRO, WKC 7/6/49.
124 Raynham, Corr., Hobart to Townshend, 19 March 1675; *HMC 6th Report*, p. 371.
125 Bradfer, John Gough to Lady Yarmouth, John Hurton to Lord Yarmouth, 7 May 1675; BL, Add MS 27447, fos 344–5; 350–2 (extensive summary, *HMC 6th Report*, pp. 371–2); Tanner MS 42, fo. 148; FSL, MS V b 305, nos 34–5.
126 FSL, MS V b 305, nos 31, 33; Tanner MS 42, fo. 148.
127 Bradfer, William de Grey to the gentlemen and freeholders of Thompson and Tottington, 1 May 1675, Holland to Mr Barnard, 1 April 1675. There is another copy of the latter in BL, Add MS 27447, fo. 342. It is not certain that Holland wrote it, but he never denied authorship and there is other evidence of his antipathy to clerical power: Miller, 'Holland', pp. 856–7.
128 The 'queries' can be found, along with an account of Hughes having them read to the clergy, in NRO, MC 1601/73. See also *CSPD 1675–76*, p. 54; Tanner MS 42, fo. 148; FSL, V b 305, nos 36–7.
129 Bradfer, Gough to Lady Yarmouth, Hurton to Lord Yarmouth, 7 May 1675.
130 NRO, MC 1601/73; BL, Add MS 27447, fo. 345 (printed *HMC 6th Report*, p. 372). For other references to the clergy, see *CSPD 1675–76*, p. 54; *HMC 6th Report*, p. 371; FSL, MS V b 305, no. 31; Bradfer, Gough to Lord Yarmouth, Hurton to Lady Yarmouth, 7 May.
131 BL, Add MS 27447, fo. 342; *CJ*, IX.389.
132 See M. Goldie, 'John Locke and Anglican Royalism', *Political Studies*, XXI, 1983, pp. 61–85; Goldie, 'Priestcraft', pp. 212–13.
133 *HMC 6th Report*, p. 375; *CSPD 1677–78*, p. 400; Whiteman, *Census*, pp. 101, 103.
134 Miller, 'Holland', pp. 863–5; Raynham, 'Holland', Holland to Townshend, 6 August 1676.
135 Dunn, *Journal*, p. 155. The quotation is from BL, Add MS 27448, fo. 212 (undated, but the content suggests a date of September/October 1675). For his friendships, see BL, Add MS 27447, fos 318, 327, 329; Bradfer, Townshend to Paston, 12 August 1672 and 10 August 1673, Kemp to Paston, 22 August 1673.
136 *HMC 6th Report*, p. 377–8, 379.
137 *Ibid.*, pp. 373–4, 375; Bradfer, Yarmouth to wife, 29 September 1675, John Gough to Lady Yarmouth, 31 March 1676; BL, Add MS 27447, fo. 366.
138 BL, Add MSS 27447, fos 360, 362, 36988, fos 117, 119; Bradfer, Yarmouth to wife, 30 April 1676.
139 *HMC 6th Report*, p. 383; Bradfer, Yarmouth to wife, 31 March 1676, 20 May 1678; Tanner MS 135, fo. 182.
140 BL, Add MS 27447, fo. 370; Bradfer, Yarmouth to wife, 26 October 1677.
141 Bradfer, Hildeyard to Lord Yarmouth, 28 August 1675, Hughes to Lady Yarmouth, 17 January 1676; R.H. Mason, *History of Norfolk* (London, 1884) p. 368.
142 Bradfer, Yarmouth to wife, 12 May 1676.

143 BL, Add MS 27447, fos 329, 368, 431; *HMC 6th Report*, pp. 364, 379; Bradfer, Paston to wife, 12 June 1666.
144 *HMC 6th Report*, pp. 376–9, 390; Bradfer, Yarmouth to wife, 17 May 1676, 22 and 25 March, 14 April 1678.
145 Bradfer, Yarmouth to wife, 31 March 1676; R. Wenley, 'Robert Paston and "the Yarmouth collection"', *Norf Arch*, XLI, 1993, pp. 123–4. For his health, see *HMC 6th Report*, p. 378; Bradfer, Yarmouth to wife, 8 April, 20 May 1678.
146 Tanner MS 42, fo. 96.
147 BL, Add MS 27447, fo. 353: copy of an unsigned letter, perhaps from Sir Henry Bedingfield senior, who was an active but (as a Catholic) covert supporter of Yarmouth and the 'church party': Bradfer, Hildeyard to Yarmouth, 29 August 1675.
148 *HMC Lothian*, pp. 122–4; J.M. Rosenheim, 'Party organisation at the local level: the Norfolk sheriff's subscription of 1676', *HJ*, XXIX, 1986, 717–18.
149 Raynham, 'Holland', Holland to Townshend, 27 March, 6 August 1676; BL, Add MS 41656, fo. 54; *HMC Finch*, II.42.
150 BL, Add MSS 27447, fos 364, 366, 36988, fos 113, 115.
151 Bradfer, Yarmouth to wife, 7 and 14 January, 14 April 1678.
152 Bradfer, Yarmouth to wife, 21 January, 15 March 1678.
153 BL, Add MS 28621, fos 34–5; Bradfer, Yarmouth to wife, 28 December 1677, 21 January, 25 March 1678; *HMC 6th Report*, p. 385–6.
154 CKS, U951/F15, under 21 February 1673.
155 *HP*, I.187–8.
156 Grey, I.353–5; Dering, *Diary*, pp. 52–6; *HP*, I. 190–1; Bodl, MS Add c. 305, fo. 225.
157 BL, Add MS 41568, fo. 3 (quoted); PRO, PRO 30/24/5, fos 270–1 (another copy), 372–3; *HMC Somerset/Ailesbury*, pp. 177–8; Coventry MS 2, fo. 71.
158 *CSPD 1675–76*, pp. 245, 355; Tanner MS 42, fo. 176 (another copy PRO, PRO 30/24/5, fo. 272); *HP*, I.211.
159 *CSPD 1675–76*, pp. 184–5, 288, 362; *HP*, I.226, II.104–5.
160 Pepys, VII.337; Milward, p. 60.
161 *CSPD 1670*, pp. 288, 506, *1672–73*, pp. 510, 522; CKS, U1015, O 20/1; *The Case of Thomas Papillon*, 1673 (copy in BL, Add MS 34152, fo. 10); Coventry MS 4, fos 121–2; *HP*, I.494–5; Kishlansky, *Selection*, pp. 163–71.
162 *CSPD 1677–78*, pp. 423–6; *HP*, I.129, 345; Kishlansky, *Selection*, p. 188.
163 Bodl, MS Rawl Letters 51, fo. 132.
164 Challinor, 'Cheshire', pp. 61–2, 66–8; Coleby, *Hants.*, pp. 149–55.
165 *CSPD 1672–73*, pp. 505–6, 559, 587, *1675–76*, pp. 124–5; *HP*, I.153. The 1674 Cambridgeshire by-election also turned into a contest between two 'loyalist' candidates: *HP*, I.146.
166 *HMC 7th Report*, p. 493; M636/30, Sir Ralph to Edmund Verney, 29 January 1677; Bucks RO, D135/A1/3/28; Egerton MS 3330, fo. 77; *HP*, I.306–7.
167 *HMC Buccleuch (Montagu House)*, I.328; *HMC Rutland*, II.44; *HMC Ormond*, NS IV.429, 431, 433–4; *Hatton*, I.166; Coventry MS 5, fo. 300; *HP*, I.300–1.
168 M636/32, Sir Ralph to Edmund Verney, 26 and 30 September 1678; Carte MS 103, fo. 236; Egerton MS 3331, fo. 63; Finch MS PP 57(i), p. 11; *HP*, I.340–1.
169 Coleby, *Hants.*, p. 149; Brindle, 'Northants.', pp. 247, 260–5.
170 *Savile*, pp. 44–6, 48, 54–5; *HMC Rutland*, II.35.
171 CKS, Sa/ZB 3/1; M636/31, John Verney to Sir Ralph, 18 April, Sir Ralph to John Verney, 29 April 1678; *HMC Finch*, II.42, 44; *HP*, I.590–1.

172 *HP*, I.503–4.
173 *CSPD 1675–76*, pp. 460–1; Egerton MS 3329, fo. 64; BL, Add MSS 11044, fos 253–4, 11051, fos 233–4; *HMC le Fleming*, p. 130.
174 Grey, IV.263–4, 266–7, 269–72, 281–3; Haley, *Shaftesbury*, pp. 424–6.
175 Grey, II.366–7, III.436, 445; *CJ*, IX.372.
176 Grey, II.415–20; *Williamson*, II.147–8.
177 Grey, IV.140–1; Finch MS P.P.42, pp. 25–6.
178 See, for example, *CSPD 1676–77*, p. 232.
179 BL, Add MS 29571, fo. 310; *Hatton*, I.132–3; *HMC 7th Report*, p. 467; *HP*, I.596. Atkins survived initially because he had gone out on circuit and later made his peace at court: M636/29, John Verney to Sir Ralph, 29 June 1676; *Clar Corr*, I.3. There were still complaints about his conduct as recorder of Bristol: Coventry MS 7, fo. 78.
180 BL, Add MS 29571, fos 323–4; *Hatton*, I.132 For Scroggs's political views, see *Clar Corr*, I.2; *HMC 7th Report*, p. 679.
181 M636/29, John Verney to Sir Ralph, 17 November 1676; M636/30, Sir Ralph to John Verney, 20 and 27 November 1676; *HMC 7th Report*, p. 467; BL, Add MS 29571, fo. 304, *Clar Corr*, I.3.
182 BL, Add 29571, fos 304, 429; Burnet, *Hist*, II.200.
183 *HMC 7th Report*, pp. 468, 494; BL, Add MS 29571, fos 425–6, 429. One of those who wrote of selling places, William Fall, worked in the lord chancellor's office.
184 Haley, *Shaftesbury*, pp. 387–8, 407–8; *Hatton*, I.123–4, 126; M636/29, Sir Ralph to Edmund Verney, 28 April, 5 and 8 June 1676.
185 *Hatton*, I.124; Pforz, Coleman to Bulstrode, 16 June 1676.
186 FSL, MS V.b.305, nos 24–6, 34; Bradfer, Hughes to Lady Yarmouth, 17 January 1676.
187 FSL, MS V.b.305, no. 34; Arundel Castle, Autograph Letters 1632–1723, no. 412.
188 BL, Add MS 36988, fo. 117.
189 Rosenheim, 'Organization', p. 717; *HMC 7th Report*, p. 493.
190 M636/29, Sir Ralph to Edmund Verney, 6, 13 and 30 December 1675, 6 and 20 January 1676, Edmund to Sir Ralph, 9 and 16 December 1675, Sir Roger Burgoyne to Sir Ralph, 20 December 1675 and 3 January 1676.
191 Bradfer, Hughes to Lady Yarmouth, 17 January 1676.
192 M636/29, Burgoyne to Sir Ralph, 20 December 1675; Rosenheim, 'Organization', p. 718.
193 Brindle, 'Northants', pp. 257–8.
194 *HMC 6th Report*, pp. 380–1, 385.
195 Rosenheim, 'Organization', p. 721.
196 BL, Add MS 25124, fo. 80.
197 NRO, Bradfer, Thomas Doughty to Lady Yarmouth and John Gough to Lady Yarmouth, 14 December 1677.

Chapter twelve

'Guelphs and Ghibellines', 1679–81

A county divided

In April 1679 news arrived in Norwich that, following Sir John Hobart's petition against the return for the county election in February, the Commons had ordered a fresh election. The peaceable Sir Thomas Browne wrote sadly: 'There is like to be very great endeavouring for the places, which will keep open divisions which were too wide before and make it a country of Guelphs and Ghibellines.'[1] In comparing Norfolk's divisions with the bloody faction-fighting of medieval Italy, he was not being unduly melodramatic. The 1675 by-election had polarized the county and that polarization had been extended by Lord Yarmouth's appointment as lord lieutenant. In 1678 Norwich had threatened to become similarly divided. The corporation had been purged in 1662, but there had since been little evidence of contention; the Corporation Act was laxly enforced.[2] There was little effort to suppress nonconformity and relations between corporation and cathedral were generally good. Townshend's disgrace and Reynolds's death threatened to change the situation, but the corporation (whose financial problems did not allow it the luxury of making enemies) was quick to wait on both Yarmouth and Sparrow.[3]

When Christopher Jay, one of the city's MPs, died on 21 August 1677, Yarmouth sought the seat for his son William, Lord Paston. He saw the city as divided between 'the right party' and 'the fanatics', but hoped he could win the support of both:[4] despite his position as leader of the 'church party' in the county, at Great Yarmouth he cooperated with elements in the corporation which were tolerant towards Dissent. The mayor and the majority of Norwich's aldermen were not willing to have Paston imposed on them, either because they disliked his father's identification with aggressive Anglicanism, or because they traditionally chose inhabitants of the city. Yarmouth was confident, however, that the generality of citizens favoured his son and ascribed the opposition he faced to the machinations of Townshend and Hobart.[5] Initially the aldermen hoped that their popular and moderate colleague, Augustine Briggs, could be persuaded to stand, but he was frightened off when Yarmouth sent word that he regarded him as 'juggling and white-livered'.[6] The mayor was made of sterner stuff. He created over three hundred freemen to vote in the election, which suggests that Paston did have extensive popular support, and ignored a command from the new Duke of Norfolk to assist Paston's candidacy.[7]

The mayor's defiance enraged Yarmouth, who sought help 'above'. He claimed that if a few factious rogues were removed, Norwich would be as loyal as any city in the kingdom. He added that, once the election was over, he and the bishop would root out the city's conventicles.[8] Hildeyard apparently sent the mayor a threatening letter and was active in the election.[9] Yarmouth's opponents had great difficulty finding a candidate. Hobart's venerable uncle declined to stand, as did the timid William Windham, who saw no point in losing face by standing against a popular lieutenant 'who in all likelihood will be encouraged from above'.[10] Alderman Cockey, who was half Dutch, was eventually persuaded to appear, but he was cruelly mocked by Paston's supporters, who paraded a cheese on a pole, and was defeated by 2,163 votes to 672 (the latter presumably including some of the mayor's new freemen).[11]

Having gained victory, Yarmouth sought revenge against the mayor and his 'venerable companions'. Now was the time, he told Danby, to 'purge the bench': it was vital that the king should support those who stood up for his interests.[12] But Danby had other things on his mind, as the king prepared reluctantly to make war on France and tried to coax supply from a suspicious House of Commons. Danby praised Yarmouth's prudence and the people's good affections and asked exactly what he meant by 'purging the bench'.[13] Yarmouth replied that many aldermen were not legally qualified as they had not subscribed the declaration against the Covenant, a claim confirmed by their rushing to do so. Confident of the king's backing, he complied with the freemen's desire to elect new aldermen in their places. The mayor refused to swear them, leaving the corporation inquorate and unable to function.[14] The king ordered the mayor to swear them; he refused and was summoned before the privy council.[15] The council decided that the old aldermen had been legally unqualified, but also, after taking the judges' advice, that the recent elections had been irregular and that fresh ones should be held.[16] Some of the 'fanatic' aldermen lost their seats, but others (including Cockey) were re-elected. Yarmouth's leading ally on the corporation estimated initially that nineteen of the twenty-four were 'well-affected', but this was probably over-optimistic. Experience showed that the aldermen were fairly evenly divided, although the 'church party' was the stronger in the more 'popular' common council.[17]

Yarmouth had become embroiled in Norwich politics, not to promote the interests of the 'church party' but to secure the seat for Paston. When his son's candidacy was opposed, he set out to drive the 'fanatics' out of the corporation, for the good of church and king. The limited backing he received 'above' made him tread more warily. When the city's other MP died, Yarmouth and his allies decided that Briggs would certainly be chosen if he stood and sought a reconciliation. Briggs assured him privately that he would be right for the king's interest and, when he was returned unopposed, publicly declared his respect for the Paston family. His election marked a compromise between the church interest and a broad spectrum of opinion within the city, more tolerant of Dissent. Paston and Briggs were returned in the next three general elections.[18]

If partisan politics did not fully triumph in Norwich, it was a different story in the county. The dominance of the 'church party' was severely weakened by the Popish Plot, which drove the Duke of Norfolk into exile and destroyed his electoral influence,[19] and by Danby's fall from power. In the general election of February 1679, the 'church party' candidates, Sir Neville Catelyne and Sir Christopher Calthorpe, were returned, despite determined opposition from Hobart. Hobart's petition against the return cited irregularities on the part of the sheriff and under-sheriff and a letter from the bishop to Hildeyard, urging his friends to support candidates who would heal the divisions in church and state (which Hildeyard interpreted as meaning Calthorpe and Catelyne).[20] Yarmouth and his allies bleated that the election had been fair and that the result reflected the wishes of the 'gentry and clergy' – a change from the position in 1675.[21] Moreover, Yarmouth (like Townshend in 1675) was accused of misusing his power as lord lieutenant. He had urged his militia officers and his friends to vote for Catelyne and Calthorpe[22] and Hildeyard had circulated a letter in which Yarmouth deplored that anyone should presume to stand for the shire without informing him. 'You may inform any of my friends how ill I resent such proceedings and that I will have it known what office it is I bear.'[23]

Hobart compared the style of Yarmouth's letter to that of a Turkish vizir or bashaw; Yarmouth protested that in producing it before the Commons Hobart undermined his authority as lord lieutenant and that for Hobart not to tell him of his intention to stand had been a breach of common courtesy.[24] The Commons expressed concern about Hobart's allegations and instructed the committee of elections to report on 'all undue practices, letters, promises, threats or oppressions in any elections'.[25] As the weeks went by, and the Commons angrily pursued his former patron, Danby, Yarmouth realized that Hobart's petition was likely to succeed and both sides prepared for another contest. On 21 April, the Commons resolved that Calthorpe and Catelyne had not been duly elected, but also (by a narrow margin) that Hobart had not been elected either.[26] As Hobart and his running-partner Windham appealed for support, Catelyne denounced the annulling of what he claimed had been the fairest election ever held in Norfolk and proclaimed his determination to stand up for the county's liberties. Sparrow claimed that the Commons' decision had disheartened the gentry and clergy and encouraged the 'disaffected populacy'.[27] The new election, held on 5 May, was vigorously contested. With over 6,000 votes cast, Windham in fourth place received a little over 400 fewer than Hobart, who headed the poll and was returned along with Catelyne. Sir Thomas Browne thought that the election had been conducted fairly, but Hobart complained of sharp practice by the sheriff and Sir Thomas Hare and others of the 'church party' complained to the Commons of Hobart's undue and illegal practices: 'by reason of the printing and publishing of the resolves and orders of this House, the freeholders of the said county were affrighted and terrified'.[28]

Norfolk was clearly divided into two parties. When the dissolution of Parliament brought another general election, each party had its own selection process. Townshend called a meeting at Raynham to discuss who would partner Hobart, while 'the gentlemen' who described themselves as true to king and church unanimously endorsed Catelyne and Calthorpe. Both parties, as in other counties, launched subscriptions to meet the cost of the election.[29] Hobart and Sir Peter Gleane were returned after another hard-fought contest; their opponents complained that they had been denigrated as 'popishly affected' and deterred from voting by fears that the Commons would void any election favouring the 'church party'.[30] Each party had a recognized headquarters in Norwich. The 'church party' had for some time claimed the 'King's Head'; now their opponents foregathered at the 'White Horse'.[31] The 1681 general election was again fought on party lines and, following the dissolution of the Oxford Parliament, the two party machines swung into action again. A suggestion in January 1682 that they might agree on two compromise candidates was 'utterly rejected and despised' by 'the White Horse blades'.[32]

The descent into partisanship was widely deplored. The annual county feast was cancelled in 1679 and in 1684 Norwich corporation referred sadly to the loss of 'the comfort of converse, hospitality and good neighbourhood'.[33] The leading protagonists in county politics went through the motions of maintaining normal social relations, but their efforts had a hollow ring.[34] And yet most at some stage expressed sadness at the wounds which disfigured Norfolk's body politic. Holland, by instinct a moderate, repeatedly sought compromise and reconciliation, in which he was supported intermittently by the prickly and inconstant Townshend. Windham, unhappy at having been drawn into taking sides, responded warmly to Holland's proposals.[35] Gleane wrote in 1681 that he hoped Hobart would not stand again.[36] Similar regrets were expressed by those widely seen as the party leaders. Yarmouth's commitment to Church and king was undoubted and he was quick to respond to slights, real or imagined, but he became weary of a role which he had not sought and was sometimes profoundly depressed.[37] Even Hobart, whom Holland accused of seeking to become 'perpetual dictator' in Norfolk,[38] expressed distaste at the excessive partisanship shown by the Commons. At first he decided not to stand in February 1679, because 'our country was broken a-pieces' by Kemp's election in 1675 and he feared that a contest would exacerbate the 'feuds' within the county.[39]

Despite the regrets, and in some cases the yearning for compromise, the county's leading figures remained aligned with one party or the other until at least 1682. Holland, Townshend and Windham were bound by 'engagements' which they might with hindsight regret but which they could not with honour abandon. Holland promised to support Hobart and Windham in 1679 and to be bound by the unanimous decision of the gentlemen at the White Horse in 1681. He had, moreover, given his word in writing: 'I know it is kept carefully upon record, to be made use of as occasion shall serve.'[40] Townshend compared himself to a slave, unable to use his vote freely. Windham was attracted to Holland's proposals for compromise, but was bound by his promises to Hobart.[41] For others compromise was impossible. 'How can any man that is upon our principles be an instrument to send a man of another principle to the House of Commons?' asked Kemp. To sue for peace would be an admission of weakness. Hobart told Windham that it was easy to gain the name of a 'lover of peace' by abject surrender: 'he who in conscience, honour and by his own promise is engaged has left himself no room for retreat'. He had no intention of laying himself open to 'the asperity of a factious violent sort of people'; he had a call and a duty to serve a good cause and good friends.[42]

The political issues: an exclusion crisis?

The divisions within Norfolk were by no means unique. In Warwickshire Sir Richard Newdigate fell foul of the Earl of Denbigh, first by standing for the county against the wishes of most of the gentry, then by giving the Earl 'rough and uncivil words' at the hustings and finally by opposing the election of Denbigh's son at Coventry, 'where he had nothing to do'. Newdigate found himself accused of favouring fanatics and of fomenting a riot. Although he was exonerated on the latter charge, he was removed from the commission of the peace and was clearly regarded 'above' as seditious, suffering the humiliation of having his house searched for arms in 1683. Lady Denbigh wrote to Lady Newdigate of her sorrow that 'these things [should] force a separation between you and I', but Newdigate saw no reason to apologize for standing for Parliament and was bitter at being misrepresented to the king.[43] All over the country, neighbour turned against neighbour and friend against friend, recalling the divisions on the eve of the civil war. If some thought that fears of civil war were exaggerated,[44] others (including Halifax, one of the king's leading ministers) did not.[45]

What were the issues which so divided the nation? What 'principles' made up the 'cause' for which Kemp and Hobart stood and which the likes of Yarmouth opposed? By 1678 the Commons were generally seen as divided between 'court' and 'country'. Danby had embraced a policy of support for the Church and hostility to Dissent and had concentrated patronage on those he judged loyal to the court. This alienated those opposed to the persecution of Dissent and created fears that he might undermine the independence and integrity of Parliament and facilitate the establishment of 'arbitrary government'. The situation was complicated by the prospect of a Catholic successor and by the dilemmas created by fears of France. The Commons pressed the king to act decisively to prevent Louis XIV from overrunning the remainder of the Spanish Netherlands. However, when Charles finally sent Louis an ultimatum (which he rejected), 'country' MPs feared that this was a pretext to raise an army which would be used to establish absolutism at home. Over 25,000 additional officers and men were raised[46] – a far larger force than had been present in England in the 1650s. Given the fears that had festered since 1672–73 of Charles and James's absolutist intentions, the raising of a substantial army added greatly to political tension.

The tension was further increased in the autumn of 1678 by the revelation of a 'Popish Plot' to murder the king and (presumably) set his Catholic brother on the throne. A number of Catholics were executed for treason and a new Test Act was passed, excluding Catholics from both Houses of Parliament and from the king's court and presence. Although it removed the Catholic peers from the Lords, its main purpose was to prevent the Duke of York from influencing his brother; its promoters were bitterly disappointed when the Commons approved by two votes a proviso exempting York from its provisions.[47] Its passage showed the continuing strength of the court and of Danby, for whom the Plot offered a welcome distraction from complaints about corruption, but not for long. In December Ralph Montagu, recently ambassador to Paris, revealed to a horrified Commons letters he had received from Danby (countersigned by the king) instructing him to ask Louis XIV for money to make peace at the same time as he was asking them for money to make war. Danby's erstwhile supporters deserted him and the king finally brought the Cavalier Parliament to an end and called the first general election since 1661.

As late as 10 December 1678, Secretary Coventry thought that there were so many divisions and subdivisions within Parliament that they might end up without any clearly defined parties.[48] He soon realized that this was wishful thinking, as the elections showed massive popular hostility to the court: Josselin thought that all courtiers were either implicated in the Plot or knew about it.[49] Much of this hostility focused on Danby and the 'corruption' with which he was identified. More generally, as Southwell shrewdly remarked, 'all the mismanagements and evil maxims of the government since the Restoration are ripped up and exposed'. Everyone agreed that much needed to be amended: the only question was how far Parliament would go.[50] A few weeks later, he reconsidered the situation. By now Danby had been impeached, but Southwell judged that it would take more than a change of personnel to regain the Commons' trust: they viewed members of the new privy council with suspicion because they were now identified with the court.[51] This meant that 'till there is a resignation to the public sense there is no likelihood of satisfaction'. Among proposals that had been mooted were 'prefixed times of Parliament'; provisions against the threat from a popish successor; a broader Church; greater reliance on the militia as against the army; greater accountability for the running of the navy; public moneys to be appropriated for particular purposes (and in particular the customs for the navy); and the reduction of the size of the council, so that there would be no need for a 'cabinet'.[52]

It should be stressed that these proposals did not form part of any particular 'programme', but had come to the attention of one well-informed individual. Most had been aired earlier, as the Commons sought greater accountability for decisions taken in council and the management of public money and the navy; the concern for 'prefixed times of Parliament' reflected frustration that debates and investigations had often been interrupted by adjournments and prorogations. Most reflected a concern to investigate mismanagement and corruption and to punish those responsible. There was also, however, concern at York's influence and the threat posed to religion and liberty by his possible succession to the throne. This can be seen in the call to investigate the navy (York had been lord admiral and still exercised covert influence over naval matters) and the suggestion that the crown's power over the militia should last only for Charles's lifetime. And there was the clear suggestion that James's religion, and the style of government with which his religion was associated, made it necessary to exclude him from the succession.[53]

The period 1679–81 has long been known as the 'exclusion crisis', but recently that term has been called in question. Jonathan Scott has argued that exclusion was a minor issue compared to the Commons' concern to guard against the threat that Charles might establish 'arbitrary government'. He stressed the similarities between 1679–81 and 1640–42, with debates about the extent of the royal prerogative, the need to ensure regular meetings of Parliament (for Scott control over the calling of Parliaments was perhaps the key issue), the nature of the established Church and the threat from 'popery'.[54] Mark Knights has argued that these years saw a series of inter-related crises, of which one of the most important concerned the succession; this raised wider questions about the nature of England's government and the relationship between ruler and ruled.[55] The Parliament of 1679 first met on 6 March, but it was not until 27 April that the Commons squarely addressed the question of the Catholic successor. A number of expedients were proposed and the king responded with others of his own. The first exclusion bill was introduced on 15 May and was still at the committee stage when the king prorogued Parliament on 27 May.[56]

For most of the session the Commons were more concerned with investigating the Plot and allegations of 'corruption', with paying off the army and with the prosecution of Danby than with exclusion. But this does not mean exclusion was unimportant. Parliament was concerned partly with present dangers (from popish plotters and the army) and partly with rooting corruption out of the body politic: the prosecution and punishment of Danby would serve as a warning to future ministers.[57] By the time of the prorogation, the recently-raised forces had been disbanded and a number of Catholics had been executed. Danby had not been convicted, but he had been removed from office and sent to the Tower. Attention shifted from present danger and revenge for past wrongs to the future. In 1641 the Commons leaders had moved from seeking redress for things past to demanding novel restrictions on the king's prerogative, because they did not believe that Charles I could be trusted to abide by the concessions he had made; they feared that he would seek to reassert himself by force and to wreak revenge on those who had brought Strafford to the block. After the prorogation in 1679, those who had sat in Parliament feared that Charles – and James – might seek revenge for the humiliations they had suffered. Although the newly-raised forces had been disbanded, Charles still had his guards and garrisons, together with substantial forces in Ireland and in Tangier; the Scots Parliament had passed an Act in 1663 allowing the Scottish militia to be used outside Scotland. It was widely believed that many officers in the army and navy owed their positions to the Duke of York, while the bulk of JPs, lords lieutenant and deputies were old Cavaliers and their sons. There were calls to remove James's 'creatures' from the army, navy and militia, but under the Act of 1661 military and naval appointments and the deployment of the armed forces were a matter for the king alone. Charles watched vigilantly for attempts to impinge on his prerogative, in 1678 vetoing a public bill for the only time: it was designed to allow the militia to serve longer than the statutory period, to guard against the threat from the papists, but Charles feared that it would deprive him of the power to dismiss the militia when he judged fit.[58]

Fear of royal revenge led to attempts not so much to deny the king's military prerogative as to argue that he should use it only as Parliament (or rather the Commons) should advise. Similarly, the Commons argued that Charles should not have pardoned Danby for all offences committed while in office, even though he unquestionably possessed the power of pardon. The exclusion bill raised a different question, but one still central to the English monarchy: the hereditary transmission of the crown. The debates on the dangers from a popish successor showed that fear of future tyranny and retribution led logically to the demand for exclusion; but having threatened James's birthright, the threat of retribution became greater. Having embarked on exclusion, it became a matter of self-preservation to go through with it. As early as June 1679,[59] attitudes to (and voting records on) exclusion were seen as an indicator of political allegiance, a tendency which became more marked with time. In the Parliament which sat from October 1680 to January 1681, exclusion played a far more prominent part: Daniel Finch (a shrewd observer) described it as the thread which ran through the session.[60]

When the king dissolved the 1679 Parliament and called a general election, corruption and suspicion of the court remained the dominant issues. A blacklist was published of those alleged to have received rewards (headed by Sir 'Timber' Temple), with extracts from the Commons journals relating to pensioners.[61] The election produced a House of Commons similar to that elected earlier in the year and Charles decided to delay summoning it. The leaders of the opposition to the court promoted petitions (of which more later) that the king should summon Parliament and allow it to sit until it had remedied the nation's grievances. But calling and dismissing Parliament was another fundamental royal prerogative, which he was now urged to use at the behest not so much of his Parliament as of his people. Few challenged the king's right to these prerogatives, but the demands of the petitions and the Commons would have severely reduced his ability to use them in practice. The demands were justified by claims, strongly reminiscent of 1641–42, that the king was so misled by evil advisers that he was, in effect, deranged; his stated wishes did not represent his true feelings and could be ignored. As Sir John Trevor, a lawyer, told the House in April 1679:

> The king's eyes are closed; he knows nothing of the danger we are in and the Commons have always the liberty to tell the king that persons near him, that are entrusted by him, are false to him and traitors; and how should the king know it else? I therefore move that the officers of the navy and militia, etc. may be by the king told in Parliament, that they may advise and inform him whether they be faithful and fit to be trusted, or not.[62]

The debates over Danby, exclusion and the issues which they raised exposed, as in 1640–42, the fundamental flaw in the ancient constitution. It assumed that the interests of king and people were complementary and provided no mechanism for judging between them if their interests appeared to be incompatible. The logic of the arguments of the supporters of exclusion was that the people's interests mattered more than those of the king, or royal family. The king had a moral duty to do what was best for his people. If he failed to recognise that duty, it must be because he was misled by evil counsel. But the effect of that argument was to deny the king the autonomous use of his prerogatives. He should choose only such ministers and other servants and follow only such policies as were recommended by Parliament, which had the right and duty to make such recommendations because it represented the people. To impose its will effectively, however, Parliament had to have the right to use force, so Parliament in the 1640s claimed a right to resist the king (in the name of the people), in order to safeguard the people's liberties and to free him from evil counsellors. But if Parliament could resist the king, what was to prevent the people from resisting those who claimed to represent them? Having advanced the principle of a right of resistance, it was difficult to limit it. Tampering with the balance of the constitution had led to civil war, Pride's Purge and the king's execution. Many believed that exclusion was legally and morally wrong. It would deprive the Duke of York of his birthright without due process of law, condemning him unheard for actions which his religion might lead him to commit, if he ever became king. Many believed too that the succession was determined by God, who decided who was to be born and die, so that it was not in Parliament's power to change it. Equally there was a widespread belief that exclusion and anti-popery were merely pretexts used by politically-motivated men, to foment another civil war and establish another republic.

Opponents of exclusion continually harked back to the civil wars because there were strong structural similarities between the situation in 1679–81 and in 1640–42. In 1679, as in 1640, there was widespread revulsion at the past misdeeds of the king and his ministers and widespread concern about popish plots, in which many suspected (at least privately) that the king and his family might be implicated. Charles II was not as isolated politically as his father had been in 1640, but (as Southwell conceded) much needed to be amended; his brother was a serious political liability. Once steps were taken (or proposed) to right past wrongs, divisions began to appear, as the remedies appeared to many more dangerous than the disease. Not only did the king's opponents challenge his central prerogatives and threaten to reduce him to a figurehead, but they appealed to the people in an effort to overcome the opposition of the Lords and king to measures which they claimed were vital for the public safety. In 1641 the Commons disseminated the Protestation, printed their 'votes' and published the Grand Remonstrance in the hope of overcoming opposition to Strafford's attainder and the militia bill. In 1679–81 the Commons printed their 'votes', including resolutions that were highly tendentious and polemical, together with Coleman's letters and other documents relating to the Popish Plot, in the hope of arousing a massive popular demand for exclusion. One can argue with hindsight that the popular support mobilized by the exclusionists was much less substantial and threatening than it seemed, that the thousands who turned out to watch pope-burnings were good-natured and harmless compared to those who bayed for Strafford's blood or demanded Lunsford's removal from the Tower. Indeed, the political crisis of 1679–81 provoked remarkably little violence.[63] But contemporaries did not have the benefit of hindsight: their perceptions were coloured by memories of civil war, when ideological divisions had led to pressure on individuals to declare themselves and ultimately to bloodshed. There seemed every possibility that this would happen again.

Church and Dissent

Before considering the process of political division in 1679–81, it is necessary to discuss the religious dimension to the political crisis, which also raised echoes of 1640–42. There was relatively little debate about the nature of the Church. There was some discussion of comprehension and a bill for that purpose was brought in (by a moderate Anglican, Daniel Finch). It aroused relatively little interest among the Presbyterians, to whom it was designed to appeal, because most had come to accept sectarian status: those who favoured comprehension also wanted indulgence, but not vice versa.[64] As a result, arguments about the need for Protestants to unite against the threat of popery focused more on the ending of persecution. Finch also brought in a bill for a limited indulgence which, with some modifications, served as a model for the Toleration Act of 1689. Like the comprehension bill, it failed to pass. The measure that came closest to becoming law was a bill to repeal the conventicle Act of 1593, which passed both Houses, but failed to receive the royal assent because the king told the clerk not to present it. In general, the Commons were concerned less to repeal existing legislation than to ensure that it was not enforced. In 1678 and 1680 the Commons resolved that the Elizabethan and Jacobean laws against recusancy, designed against Catholics, should not be used against Protestants, but no bill passed to that effect.[65]

If the Parliaments of 1679–81 showed only a limited concern to improve the lot of Dissenters, they showed considerable animus against the Anglican clergy. In the 1670s 'country' leaders, like Shaftesbury and Buckingham, had responded to the political activism of bishops and clergy by denouncing 'priestcraft', accusing them of trying to establish a dominion over the laity akin to that of priests over lay Catholics. The vocal opposition of many of the clergy to exclusion, their defence of the hereditary succession and their condemnation of resistance provoked vehement claims that the 'high-fliers' were 'Papists in masquerade'.[66] The bishops were attacked with particular venom, because of their role in the Lords. During the impeachment proceedings against Danby, controversy arose as to whether they should be present. Some argued that as men of God they should not participate in proceedings which might end in the shedding of blood, but the obvious subtext was the calculation that most of them would support Danby. This raised echoes of the Act of 1642 expelling the bishops from the Lords, as well as their forcible exclusion from the House by an angry crowd in December 1641. As time went on the bishops were blamed for a variety of evils, including the prorogation of Parliament in 1679 and the Lords' rejection of the second exclusion bill in November 1680, despite the fact that a majority of temporal peers had also been against the bill.[67]

Apart from their exertions in the press and in the pulpit,[68] the clergy were very active in elections. We have seen the conspicuous role of the clergy in Norfolk. The bishops of London and Bath and Wells used what interest they could. Sparrow, at Norwich, was more equivocal, or wary, but there was little doubt where his sympathies lay.[69] In the shires, the clergy formed a conspicuous bloc of voters. In the second Essex election of 1679, the 200 or so clergy present were met with cries of 'no black coat' and were denounced as dumb dogs or Jesuits. Some were punched and had dirt thrown at them, others had their gowns torn, which they bore (according to a sympathetic account) with the patience of the primitive Christians. At the Somerset election, which was uncontested, the clergy suffered similar affronts; one was attacked by a leading exclusionist, George Speke, and had to be rescued by some of the gentry.[70] Not all of the parish clergy opposed exclusion – Josselin was active on behalf of Colonel Mildmay in Essex[71] – but the great majority did, leading Henry Booth to advise them to preach more and meddle less, although that was not the way to become known as a true son of the Church.[72]

Despite claims that the clergy were striving to bring the laity to blind obedience,[73] they felt beleaguered and harped on the theme of non-resistance because resistance seemed all too likely. They received little backing from the king, who feared that firm measures in favour of the Church would provoke the Commons. In March 1679 the privy council instructed the judges to charge juries to enforce the Five Mile Act and ordered the bishops to tender the test in the 1678 Act to Quakers. But then the king remodelled his council and the order to the bishops was rescinded.[74] In July 1680 the judges were told to use the recusancy laws only against Catholics, unless others who stayed away from church disturbed the peace. This was generally seen as implying that the laws should be enforced severely against Catholics and mildly against others, but some of the judges declared that Dissenters should be prosecuted too. At Norwich the gentry applauded this interpretation, saying that they had never heard a better charge, to which the judge replied that he had never seen a better jury.[75] Meanwhile, the king's ministers tried to dissuade nonconformist preachers from promoting petitions, hinting that the connivance they currently enjoyed might come to an end.[76] Privately, however, Secretary of State Sir Leoline Jenkins conceded that the time to suppress the sectaries had passed: the government was now on the defensive. The Earl of Anglesey, always a champion of Dissent, rebuked the mayor of Gloucester for imprisoning a minister under the Five Mile Act.[77] Early in 1681, the king was still reluctant to give his full backing to the enforcement of the laws against Dissent which the bulk of county JPs now wanted,[78] but in the years that followed the clergy and their lay allies were to enjoy ample revenge for the indignities they had suffered.

The process of political division

Most historians of the 'exclusion crisis'[79] have discussed political divisions mainly in terms of opposed sets of ideas rather than of the way in which, and the extent to which, people took sides. In many ways the process of 'taking sides' replicated that of 1642: while a minority in the provinces sided decisively with king or Parliament, most reacted to the political breakdown at Westminster with incomprehension and hoped that some compromise could be found to save England from a fratricidal civil war. However, once the king sent out commissions of array and Parliament sent out commissions in the militia, the leading figures in the provinces were forced to declare themselves. As hostilities spread, neutrality became less and less of an option, even for less prominent people. Moreover, the propaganda battle carried the issues well beyond the traditional political nation; humble men (and women) tried to influence the actions of their social superiors. Similarly, the flood of propaganda which followed the lapsing of the Licensing Act in May 1679, and the exclusionists' capture of the London shrievalty shortly thereafter, meant that those involved in politics came under pressure from both above and below: from the king or the Commons or the political leaders of their shires on one hand, from a vociferous and partisan populace on the other. As Holland and Windham discovered in Norfolk, once a man had committed himself, it was difficult if not impossible to change his mind: he was 'labelled' in the eyes of both allies and enemies. In Norfolk this process was under way before 1678, notably in the subscription to meet the expenses of the shrievalty. From 1679 it was taken much further.

In taking sides in 1642, men used to seeking compromise and consensus had been forced to choose between stark alternatives. Much the same happened in 1679–81, in the face of the need to decide how to vote, in Parliament or in elections, and whether to sign petitions and abhorrences. I shall deal separately with the most important modes of 'labelling' – elections and petitions. But there were others. There were at least two printed 'blacklists' of 'courtiers' and 'pensioners'.[80] Even before 1678 Danby and his opponents had drawn up lists of friends and foes in Parliament. Division lists, especially for the exclusion bills, now circulated widely in manuscript and the way in which MPs 'carried themselves' in the Commons became public knowledge.[81] There were other ways in which people could proclaim their allegiances. In the autumn of 1679 Charles resolved to banish both York and his Protestant rival for the succession, the Duke of Monmouth. Each left London accompanied by a retinue of peers and gentry, although it was claimed that York's, which included eighteen peers, was the more distinguished. Such competition was by not new: rival retinues, of the lord lieutenant and the sheriff, welcomed the chief baron to Norfolk in 1676.[82] Note was taken of the peers and gentry who waited on York on his way to Scotland and of those, like the Earl of Salisbury, who took care to be away from home.[83] When York attended the annual feast of the Honourable Artillery Company, a placard was attached to the door that the names of those who attended would be taken, so that the nation could be informed that they were 'Yorkists' or 'Papists in masquerade'. In December it was alleged that the names of those refusing to sign petitions would be noted.[84] One way and another, more and more people became identified, through their own actions or those of others, with one of the political parties.

The result of this process of choosing and labelling, as Knights has shown, was that opinion became polarized. Reresby had earlier thought that both 'court' and 'country' had some right on their side; now he had to plump for one or the other.[85] But how did these 'sides' describe themselves? 'Courtier' was used largely as a term of abuse. I have used the term 'exclusionist' because I see attitudes to exclusion as a major touchstone of party allegiance, but it was rarely if ever used at the time. By 1680 the terms 'Yorkist' and 'anti-Yorkist' were being used: the Bishop of Bath and Wells saw no disgrace in being known as a 'Yorkist'.[86] More often the labels used were either religious – 'the church party' on one side, the 'presbyterians' or 'fanatics' on the other – or referred back to the civil wars – the 'Cavaliers' or the 'loyal party' (or the 'moderate party') against the 'factious' or, more emotively, 'such who have been eminently dipped in the blood of His Majesty's most loyal subjects'.[87] Memories of the civil wars were naturally invoked mainly by those in the Cavalier-Anglican tradition. Their opponents described themselves as good Protestants or 'patriots' and denounced the Churchmen as courtiers, papists or favourers of popery and caricatured them savagely in pamphlets and ballads, prints and pope-burnings. In 1680, exclusionist petitions were met with anti-exclusionist 'abhorrences', which gave rise to the terms 'petitioner' and 'abhorrer', corrupted into 'Whig' and 'Tory', respectively Scots Presbyterians and Irish Catholic bandits. These were initially terms of abuse and took time to enter the mainstream of political language. They rarely appear before 1681: a set of 'annals' of Bristol noted (under 13 June 1681) 'the names of Wig [sic] and Tory were now much used by way of distinction, as pretended to know the loyal from the disloyal party'.[88] By the time the two terms were being widely used, the phenomena which they were coined to describe, in terms of both bodies of ideas and groups of people, were an established fact.

Elections

After eighteen years without a general election, there were two in 1679 and another early in 1681. The animosities aroused in one election had little time to cool before the next. Conflicts within Parliament were transmitted to the provinces by the press and the other news media and by MPs themselves.[89] Those standing for re-election were judged on their record in Parliament.[90] In the first election of 1679, there were great efforts to dissuade voters from choosing those associated with the court. Some were accused of being papists, having Catholic wives, or denying that there had been a Popish Plot.[91] In Norfolk, William Cooke complained of 'the old 41 stratagems of calumniating the gentlemen of the Church of England with the name of Papists'.[92] Those associated with Danby and York were especially likely to be rejected. At Oxford Lord Norreys (Danby's brother-in-law) was hooted out of town when he tried to propose a candidate and it was said that his neighbours and tenants would vote against him.[93] At Christchurch, a pocket borough if ever there was one, the Earl of Clarendon (the lord of the manor – and York's brother-in-law) reminded the mayor that the corporation had promised to choose whoever he recommended and stressed his power to serve the town. But he also stressed that his nominees had shown themselves good 'patriots' and Protestants in the last Parliament. They were elected unopposed.[94] Other aristocratic patrons could also claim success: the nominees of Monmouth – not yet a Protestant icon – were chosen at Hull and Stafford, but even small and normally biddable boroughs were becoming fractious: Pepys found himself rejected at Castle Rising following renewed rumours that he was a papist.[95] In one constituency after another, observers noted the independence of the electors, the strength of the Dissenting interest and the boisterousness, to say no more, of the proceedings.[96] Some who were associated with the court decided not to stand or to make recommendations.[97] Sir Ralph Verney welcomed the result as a victory for the 'Country': earlier he remarked (when discussing Buckinghamshire) that so long as honest men were chosen, it did not matter who they were. His son Edmund had mixed feelings about the election of his kinsman Sir Charles Gawdy at Eye, because he was associated with the court: he would have preferred 'some plain honest country gentleman'.[98] Ideology was coming to count for more than personalities or family.

In the second election of 1679, contested in July and August, the picture was similar, although some candidates lost out because they had opposed exclusion.[99] In a number of counties, the gentry of each party joined together both to select candidates and to meet the cost of lodging and feeding electors and compensating them for lost earnings.[100] The most striking feature of this election, however, was the heightened degree of animosity. At Eye, one young man, who was reluctant to vote, was driven to the hustings with a hayfork by his father, while another elector was kept a virtual prisoner. At Buckingham, where twelve of the burgesses were equally divided, the thirteenth absented himself, because he did not wish to offend either side.[101] Voting was a public act; although it was not yet common practice to print poll-books, they were already seen as a public record.[102] The pressures on voters were considerable. Peers and gentlemen attended borough elections with substantial bodies of servants, in their masters' liveries – ostensibly to see fair play, but also to intimidate voters.[103] Pressure on voters did not come only from the elite. At Abingdon, where the mayor was accused of declaring elected a candidate who had been heavily outvoted, women and children hissed him and called him a cheat and he was forced to hide all day in a nettle-bed.[104] At Great Marlow Sir Humphrey Winch was chosen after a violent contest in which a bargeman ducked him 'so under water that all cried to save him'.[105] The defeated candidate was bound over for caning 'an ordinary fellow' who called him a liar. The animosities continued after the elections finished. Edmund Verney remarked:

'There are vast feuds in our Chiltern as well as in our Vale, occasioned by elections and so 'tis, I suppose, all over England.'[106] Partisanship was becoming a permanent feature of political life.

Nowhere was this more apparent than in Buckinghamshire, where the normal round of social visits ceased.[107] Sir Richard Temple, now closely associated with the court, persuaded the sheriff to adjourn the county election from Aylesbury, where it was normally held, to Buckingham. He wished to ingratiate himself with Buckingham's thirteen electors, who had recently chosen him their MP, along with Danby's son, Latimer. This stratagem annoyed the gentry and freeholders, not least because Buckingham was at one end of the county, forcing some to travel thirty miles to vote. It was also claimed that they disapproved of the town's choice of members. They resolved that Buckingham should gain no profit from the election, so they rode (led by the Duke of Buckingham, who was active in a number of constituencies) to Winslow; wagons were provided to transport those without horses. Next morning they marched to a field outside Buckingham where they elected Thomas Wharton and Richard Hampden; when the sheriff's son called for a poll, he was hunted back into the town, like a hare. The freeholders and gentry then marched through the town, crying 'No Timber Temple, no traitor's son [Latimer], no pensioner, no papist, no betrayer of their country!'.[108] A printed account of the election triggered a pamphlet war. *An Answer to a letter from a Freeholder of Buckinghamshire*, written either by Temple or by one of his supporters, included a bitter attack on the Duke of Buckingham, not omitting his killing the Earl of Shrewsbury in a duel or his part in the breaking of the Triple Alliance. Readers were reminded that Hampden's father had been one of the Five Members whom Charles I had tried to arrest in 1642 and of the quasi-martial nature of the march from Aylesbury to Winslow, with more than a hint of rebellion. Buckingham (it said) had been condemned for choosing two loyal servants of the king, the sort who were routinely castigated as papists, pensioners and betrayers of their country. Meanwhile the county election was managed by John Wildman, while the Essex campaign had been managed by Henry Ireton. The pamphlet provoked at least four replies of varying degrees of scurrility, which were eagerly devoured by the Verneys. Apart from accusing Temple of making the bailiff's wife pregnant and raking up the story of the timber for the town hall, readers were reminded of Temple's record. He had served Cromwell, came over to the king in 1660, opposed the court and then supported it – once he had obtained office.[109] One pamphlet mocked the burgesses' threadbare gowns and idle ceremonies and denounced their drunkenness and their folly, in choosing Temple and Latimer. The town deserved to be boycotted and disfranchised.[110] The corporation, furious, sought redress at law, as did Temple against allegations that he had been seen at Mass; he took communion at Chesham and in London.[111]

When the king dissolved Parliament in January 1681, after a fraught and ill-tempered session, both parties prepared for another election. In Norfolk, Yarmouth called for a meeting of 'our friends' to agree on candidates to oppose Hobart 'that we may be unanimous for two, whosoever they are'.

Issues counted for more than personalities, a point acknowledged by Henry Booth who brushed aside complaints at his standing a fourth time in Cheshire, saying that the electors had shown themselves satisfied with his services.[112] Some clung to older values. Sir Ralph Verney, persuaded to stand at Buckingham, rebutted arguments that standing with Temple would harm his chances. 'He is my kinsman', he said 'and I told him I would join with him, therefore I cannot desert him. I would not be guilty of so ugly a thing to gain all the voices in the country'.[113] The election was complicated by controversy over the franchise: did it reside only in the thirteen burgesses or in all the freemen? Temple sought to gain a majority of both but Sir Ralph took his stand on the narrower franchise. He was influenced in part by financial considerations: it would cost more to treat the 'populacy' than to treat the burgesses and their wives. But he also thought it would be discourteous to court the 'populacy' after the burgesses had invited him to stand.[114] Verney's reluctance to treat was reinforced by his dislike of drunkenness, but the candidates' ambitions and the townspeople's appetites ensured that the taps ran freely in the alehouses.[115] Tempers frayed, fists flew: one candidate was thrown in the dirt and had his periwig knocked off. Verney was returned, with Temple, as elected by the burgesses, with eight votes each, but he derived little satisfaction from his victory: he remarked sadly that contests always ended in calumnies and censures.[116]

The election of 1681 was fought at least as fiercely as the previous one. Clarendon's candidates were challenged at Christchurch by two members of the Green Ribbon Club; the challenge was defeated, after an ill-tempered contest in which he was accused of being a papist.[117] Similar accusations were made elsewhere, especially against those who had opposed exclusion.[118] There were signs that the Tories were gaining popular support. At Bristol two Tories were returned after a hard-fought contest despite the best efforts of the Dissenters.[119] In Southwark, which had one of the widest franchises in the country, the Tories carried it despite the urgings of nonconformist preachers and the formidable presence of Grey and Buckingham.[120] In Cambridgeshire, the sitting MPs were returned having (it was claimed) behaved with loyalty, prudence and moderation to the general satisfaction of the people 'as became worthy patriots': the Whigs did not have a monopoly of patriotism. To create a pretext to challenge the return, the Dissenters began to 'bustle', threatening violence; they were hissed and hooted by the crowd and one of the Whig candidates was escorted from the fray by his opponent, for his own safety.[121] Not all elections were contested or dominated by ideology. In Staffordshire in all three elections of 1679–81, the gentry agreed on two candidates, one identified with the court and one with the country, who were returned without a contest. Candidates still presented themselves in terms of neighbourhood and ability to advance the town's interests, without mentioning issues.[122] Sir Ralph Verney's correspondence about Buckingham makes no mention of issues either, but the earlier pamphlets show that more was involved than personal rivalries and ambitions. The dissolution of the short-lived Oxford Parliament on 28 March 1681 triggered a fresh wave of electoral preparations.

In Norfolk, the King's Head and White Horse lined up their candidates and similar steps were taken in Worcestershire, Dorset, Herefordshire and elsewhere. These received little encouragement from the king: Jenkins wrote that he had no intention of calling Parliament.[123] In Buckinghamshire, Sir Thomas Lee sought to maintain his interest at Aylesbury by entertaining the townspeople in their hundreds, while Temple continued to feast the burgesses of Buckingham.[124] Such entertainments show the need for constant electoral preparedness in a politically divided society.

Petitions and addresses

On 7 December 1679 a petition, signed by seventeen peers, was presented to the king. It asked him to allow Parliament to meet in January and to sit until the nation's grievances had been redressed. It had been hoped that the lord mayor of London could be persuaded to summon the common council to endorse it, but he refused. The petition was intended to be the first of a campaign. Forms had been printed, to be sent into the shires and taken from parish to parish. There was more than one type of form; some referred to the king's coronation oath, his promise on 20 April 1679 to be advised by Parliament and the dangers to his person from the papists.[125] He received the peers' petition coldly, remarking that he wished others were as concerned as he was for the peace of the kingdom. He prorogued Parliament until the following November and issued a proclamation against petitions designed to incite sedition or rebellion.[126] Confident though the proclamation seemed, it was a moot point (as we shall see) whether the king had the power to forbid petitions which did not infringe the 1661 Act against tumultuous petitioning. As Edmund Verney remarked, it was not illegal to petition, provided it was done with decorum.[127] The promoters of petitions continued to gather signatures in the provinces and the king continued to receive them with obvious disapproval and pointed references to the civil wars.[128]

The level of organization shown by the petitioning campaign, and the fact that some were presented by 'fanatics' or old republicans,[129] provoked various responses from the 'church party'. Some stressed that the petitions had not been endorsed by the county's grand jury or leading gentry or claimed that they had been subscribed (often many times over) by Scots, gypsies and 'the rabble'.[130] The mayor of Chichester told Monmouth that the 'late rebellion' had started with petitions for Parliament to sit. In London a quarrel over subscribing ended with the petition being thrown in the fire, complaints to a magistrate and an indictment for riot.[131] At the Somerset assizes, some of the gentry drew up a paper expressing their dislike of the petition delivered in the name of the county and suchlike 'tumultuary' proceedings. In March the county's grand jury made a presentment disowning the petition and calling for the laws to be enforced against both Catholics and Dissenters.[132] It was later alleged that the Bishop of Bath and Wells was behind this paper: he was present at the assizes, to encourage the gentry in their good intentions.[133] The Somerset address was printed in the *Gazette*, an indication of royal approval and an encouragement to others to follow suit. The king became bolder in stating his determination to stand by his 'old friends'. In May 1679 his new privy councillors had persuaded him to reinstate a few JPs who had been removed earlier, including Hobart, Holland and Kemp in Norfolk. From November new commissions of the peace were issued which omitted those hostile to the court. JPs who subscribed petitions were dismissed.[134] In April, Yarmouth remarked that several counties had presented addresses abhorring the petitions and promising to stand by the king and the lawful succession. He suggested that Norfolk should do the same: it would 'separate the dross from the right metal in the king's memory'.[135] As the 'abhorrers' tightened their grip on county government, attempts to promote new petitions failed: Chief Justice North described petitioning as a 'failed strategem', defeated by the gentry and clergy.[136] Abhorrences and loyal addresses proliferated and were published in the *Gazette*, while petitions were printed (if at all) only in the oppositionist *Domestic Intelligence*.[137] Only in London and Middlesex did petitions for a Parliament continue to be presented, despite the manifest disapproval of the judges and the king.[138]

The petitioning campaign of 1679–80 had been not so much unsuccessful as counter-productive. It had failed to persuade Charles to summon Parliament quickly. It had alarmed and antagonized the 'abhorrers', who developed their arguments and became conscious of their strength. Taking the 'labelling' process one stage further had benefited abhorrers more than petitioners, because it had provoked the king to remove petitioners from office, increasing their opponents' power in the shires. Only in London (and other towns) did 'petitioners' remain powerful as magistrates. By the summer of 1680 it was becoming clearer that if the king used his authority to the full he could contain and crush his enemies, but as yet he lacked the confidence to do so. Despite his talk of standing by his old friends, fear of rebellion still inclined him to conciliate his enemies. The 'petitioners' still had one potential trump card, their majority in the Commons, which in the session of 1680–81 they used ruthlessly and, as we shall see, with questionable legality. Their proceedings were motivated in part by revenge, but they were also an expression of anger and impotence, following the rejection of the second exclusion bill. The attack on abhorrers was losing momentum before the end of the session: perhaps, as Daniel Finch suggested, MPs were growing weary and ashamed.[139]

The early weeks of 1681 saw petitions from London to prorogue the old Parliament and then, after it was dissolved, from a group of peers asking that the new one should meet at Westminster rather than Oxford.[140] As the elections got under way, petitions to the king were superseded by addresses or instructions to MPs, the former thanking them for their services in the last Parliament, the latter telling them how to conduct themselves in the next. For the Whigs, this was intended to show the degree of support which they enjoyed among the people and to remind the king of the danger of displeasing his subjects.[141] By now, however, the Tories had lost their inhibitions about 'popular' tactics: they were ready to take the Whigs on in the press, to open their own political clubs and to use addresses and instructions. While continuing to claim that Whig addresses were unrepresentative or obtained by surprise, Tories now claimed that they, not the Whigs, spoke for the people.[142] These addresses generated further conflict. It was alleged that the *Address of the Freeholders of Middlesex* was forged by Francis Smith. At Salisbury assizes, the grand jury presented the paper read at the Wiltshire election as seditious.[143] After the Oxford Parliament, London and Middlesex continued to petition the king, but elsewhere addresses became increasingly Tory and increasingly extreme, expressions of party orthodoxy, organized and scrutinized by party bosses.[144]

The law

Since 1676 judicial appointments and law enforcement had become influenced by politics. Between November 1678 and July 1679 the judges worked hard to secure the convictions of Coleman and others accused of complicity in the Plot. They were clearly acting on instructions from the king, who believed a few scapegoats were needed to reassure the public that the Plot was under control. In April 1679, following the appointment of the new privy council, four moderate and 'worthy' judges were appointed (including Ellis, who had been removed earlier); two were to be removed in 1680.[145] In the autumn, however, the king began to revise the commissions of the peace and looked to the judges to defend his authority. In October he issued a proclamation to seize libels against the government and arrest their authors and publishers. As the crown's control over the press had depended since 1662 on the Licensing Act, which had now lapsed, his power to issue such a proclamation was questionable. It seemed that he was again claiming that power over the press was part of his prerogative. The government brought several prosecutions against London pamphleteers and printers, but could do little to stem the flood of oppositionist literature.[146]

Equally questionable was the proclamation against petitions, issued on 12 December 1679, in response to the peers' petition. It denounced petitions 'for specious ends', which tended to provoke sedition or rebellion. The 1661 Act against 'tumultuous' petitions forbade the securing of more than twenty subscriptions to any petition, unless it had been approved by three county JPs or the majority of a grand jury; the petition could be presented by no more than ten persons. The peers' petition had been signed by seventeen and presented by nine, so complied with the letter of the Act. However, it was common knowledge that a campaign of mass petitioning was under way and the peers' petition was printed immediately.[147] The proclamation did not use the word 'tumultuous' or mention any particular law, but when the council discussed the petition on 10 December, reference was made to a judgment in Star Chamber in 1604, by the 'lords, judges &c', which denounced the puritan Millenary Petition as 'tending to the raising of sedition, rebellion and discontent' and as 'near treason'. At least two pamphlets were published explaining this judgment.[148] However, the attorney general later told the Commons that the council had told him to seek the judges' opinion and that they had all agreed that the judgment had been illegal. It was also claimed that the law report describing it was apocryphal.[149]

The exclusionists complained loud and long about the proclamations against 'libels' and petitions, but they showed equally scant regard for fair play or natural justice. They raised no objections to the rough justice meted out to those accused of complicity in the Plot, but protested stridently when the first acquittals came. However, their power to act unjustly or arbitrarily was limited. Their major strongholds were the Commons and the City of London. The Commons had the power, as advised by the committee of elections and privileges, to decide election disputes. Since at least the 1620s, its decisions had been coloured by politics: it generally preferred a wider to a narrower franchise, to reduce the possibility of royal interference.[150] Even Shaftesbury admitted that the committee's recommendations owed more to interest than to the merits of the case.[151] In 1679 the Commons extended the committee's powers. It could now examine and report on all undue practices and it was instructed to search for precedents to punish returning officers for false returns.[152] In the Parliaments of 1679 and 1680–81, the committee's decisions became so partisan that anti-exclusionists wondered if it was worth standing only to have their elections annulled.[153] Still more partisan was the House's treatment in 1680 of abhorrers. The House described discountenancing petitions as a betrayal of the liberties of the subject. Several members were expelled, but the House had no jurisdiction over anyone else, except in cases of breach of privilege. A number of people, including the foreman and other members of the Somerset grand jury which had produced the first abhorrence, were summoned on the pretext that abhorrences constituted breaches of privilege.[154] Those summoned had little option but to comply, answer questions and, if condemned, meekly receive the House's censures.[155] In the provinces, anti-exclusionists waited fearfully for a summons.[156] The House's arbitrary conduct towards abhorrers, and the almost frivolous alacrity with which it began impeachment proceedings, undermined its authority and dignity and provided valuable ammunition for loyalist propagandists.[157]

Over much of the country, the machinery of law enforcement was controlled by the king and used in an increasingly partisan manner. In 1680, the council told the judges to ensure that grand jurors were 'well-principled'[158] and the king chose the sort of sheriffs who would see that they would be. Grand juries subscribed abhorrences and loyal addresses and issued presentments or found true bills against Dissenters and Whigs. In Somerset, Thomas Dare, the promoter of the county petition, was prosecuted on a charge of encouraging rebellion. The instigators of the prosecution included the Bishop of Bath and Wells, who claimed that several of the witnesses were afraid of testifying at the assizes, which were to be held at Taunton; he suggested that a troop of the militia horse should be present, to reassure them. The grand jury, which included some of the leading county gentry, found a true bill. Seeing that the trial jury also consisted of gentlemen and the foreman was a leading Royalist, Dare pleaded guilty. He was sentenced to a £500 fine and to remain in gaol until it was paid. He was also bound to good behaviour for three years and turned off Taunton corporation; and he soon faced another prosecution for seditious words.[159]

If Tories ruled the roost in the shires, in London and Middlesex the sheriffs were elected annually in Common Hall, the assembly which also elected the City's MPs. In 1680 and 1681 strongly Whig sheriffs were elected. For two years they returned partisan juries, so that it was almost impossible to convict a Whig of a political offence in London or to enforce the laws against Dissent. In July 1680 a London jury found Henry Care guilty of publishing a libel, despite the vociferous disapproval of the people in the courtroom. In September, with the new sheriffs in office, a grand jury returned an *ignoramus* on two printers accused of press offences.[160] A similar picture can be found in many provincial towns. The effect of these developments on the legal process, and on royal policy towards the towns, will be examined in the next chapter. For the moment it need only be added that individuals were quick to have recourse to the law to seek redress for slights or other injuries arising from political conflict. In 1680 the Duke of Buckingham secured damages of £1,000 on an action of *scandalum magnatum* against Henry Hayward, or Howard, a barber, one of the burgesses of Buckingham. It was expected that Buckingham would waive the damages if Hayward submitted, which he was very willing to do; indeed, Buckingham had assured the jury (of which Sir Ralph Verney was foreman) that he would do so. Unfortunately, at the same time Sir Richard Temple secured £500 damages against a shoemaker called Barton who had alleged that he was a papist and Buckingham refused to discharge Hayward until Temple discharged Barton. As a result, Hayward remained in gaol until 1685.[161] Temple was not satisfied with his damages: Barton was found guilty of subornation of perjury and sentenced to the pillory.[162] Hayward and Barton were unfortunate in falling foul of powerful and vindictive men, but they were by no means unique. The legal system always to some extent favoured the well-connected; now its workings were further distorted by political partisanship. And, from the point of view of Whigs and Dissenters, worse was to come.

Notes

1 Browne, *Works*, I.238.
2 Statements that new aldermen had made the declaration against the Covenant were written in later: NRO, MCB 24, fos 25, 69. See also NRO, FAB 8, fos 36–8.
3 Evans, *Norwich*, pp. 243–51; Bradfer, John Gough to Lady Yarmouth, 31 March 1676; *HMC 6th Report*, p. 375; NRO, MCB 25, fo. 10.
4 *HMC 6th Report*, p. 383.
5 *HP*, I.329–30; *HMC 6th Report*, p. 384; Bradfer, Yarmouth to wife, 21 and 28 December 1677.
6 Bradfer, Yarmouth to wife, 21 and 28 December 1677.
7 NRO, MCB 25, fos 13–17; Bradfer, Yarmouth to wife, 21 January 1678.
8 *HMC 6th Report*, p. 385; *CSPD 1677–78*, pp. 634–5.
9 NRO, MCB 25, fo. 19; Bradfer, Yarmouth to wife, 21 January 1678.

10 *HMC 6th Report*, p. 385; Bradfer, Yarmouth to wife, 4 February 1678; NRO, WKC 7/6/8.
11 *HMC 6th Report*, p. 385; Bradfer, Yarmouth to Danby, 20 February 1678.
12 Bradfer, Yarmouth to wife, 7 January, Yarmouth to Danby, 20 February 1678; *HMC 6th Report*, p. 385.
13 BL, Add MS 36540, fo. 27.
14 BL, Add MS 28621, fo. 37; NRO, MCB 25, fos 20–2; *CSPD 1678*, p. 45; *HMC 6th Report*, p. 385; Bradfer, Yarmouth to wife, 25 March 1678.
15 *CSPD 1678*, pp. 76–7, 97.
16 *CSPD 1678*, pp. 108, 131–2.
17 Bradfer, Bendish to Lady Yarmouth, 1 May 1678; BL, Add MSS 27447, fos 387, 389, 27448, fo. 127; Evans, *Norwich*, pp. 262–7.
18 Bradfer, Yarmouth to wife, 8 April and 17 May 1678; *HP*, I.330–1.
19 *CSPD 1679–80*, p. 50; Browne, *Works*, I.261; Badminton House, MS FmE 4/4/1.
20 Tanner MS 39, fo. 200; Carte MS 81, fo. 604.
21 Tanner MS 39, fo. 179; *HMC 6th Report*, pp. 387, 390; NRO, Hare MS 6365/11 (copy NRO WKC 7/6/41).
22 *HMC 6th Report*, p. 389; BL Add MSS 27447, fos 399, 401, 36988, fo. 134; NRO, Bradfer, Yarmouth to ?, 31 January 1679.
23 Bradfer, letter dated 4 February 1679, not in Yarmouth's hand but with his signature; BL, Add MS 36988, fo. 135 ('a copy of my lord lieutenant of Norfolk's letter to Dr Hildeyard, which was sent throughout the county'). There are two copies in Lord Wharton's papers: Carte MS 81, fos 604, 611.
24 NRO, WKC 7/6/19; *HMC 6th Report*, p. 387.
25 *CJ*, IX.568, 571 (quoted).
26 *HMC 6th Report*, p. 387; Bradfer, Yarmouth to wife, 24 March 1679; NRO, WKC 7/6/19, 27; BL, Add MS 37911, fo. 7; Raynham, SP, Thomas Townshend to Lord Townshend, 5 April 1679; *CJ*, IX.599–600.
27 BL, Add MS 37911, fo. 9; NRO, Hare MS 6365/11 (copy WKC 7/6/41); Tanner MS 38, fo. 22.
28 *HP*, I.321; Browne, *Works*, I.240–1; Tanner MS 38, fo. 25; NRO, WKC 7/6/39; *CJ*, IX.631.
29 Tanner MS 38, fos 55, 58; BL, Add MS 36988, fos 143, 147.
30 BL, Add MS 36988, fo. 149; Tanner MS 314, fo. 34; *HP*, I.321–2.
31 *HP*, I.320–1; *HMC 6th Report*, p. 389; Raynham, SP, Thomas Townshend to Lord Townshend, 21 June 1680.
32 Raynham, SP, Thomas Townshend to Lord Townshend, 13 and 23 January 1682.
33 Browne, *Works*, I.243, 254; NRO, FAB 8, fo. 107.
34 *HMC 6th Report*, pp. 378–9; BL, Add MS 36988, fo. 119; NRO, WKC 7/6/61, 68–9.
35 Miller, 'Holland', pp. 867–70; NRO, WKC 7/6/59–60.
36 Raynham, Corr, Gleane to Townshend, 16 May 1681.
37 *HMC 6th Report*, pp. 377–8; Bradfer, Yarmouth to wife, 31 March and 17 May 1676, 22 and 25 March, 14 April 1678.
38 Raynham, Holland, Holland to Townshend, 28 March 1681.
39 NRO, WKC 7/6/14 (quoted), 47.
40 NRO, WKC 7/6/30, 31, 32, 34, 52; Raynham, Holland, Holland to Townshend, 19 February 1681; NRO, MC 1601/27(quoted).

41 NRO, MC 1601/25, WKC 7/6/59, 60, 75.
42 Raynham, Corr, Kemp to Townshend, 2 May 1681; NRO, WKC 7/6/60, 56; Tanner MS 38, fo. 4.
43 Newdigate, pp. 143, 144 (the first of these letters is dated 23 September 1680: Warwicks. RO, CR136/B87); *CSPD 1679–80*, pp. 280–1, 286, 288, 395, 405, 550, *1680–81*, pp. 43–4; Coventry MS 6, fos 149–50; *HP*, III.134.
44 Clarke, I.633; BL, Add MS 29577, fo. 213.
45 Reresby, pp. 205, 219n; *HMC 1st Report*, p. 51; Burnet, *History*, II.238.
46 *CJ*, IX.487.
47 Kenyon, *Constitution* (2nd edn.), pp. 386–7; Haley, *Shaftesbury*, pp. 480–2.
48 *HMC Ormond*, NS IV.269; Knights, *Opinion*, pp. 25–8.
49 Josselin, p. 620.
50 *HMC Ormond*, NS IV 317, 325, 500 (quoted).
51 *HMC Ormond*, NS IV.xviii, V.57; Reresby, pp. 177–8; BT 142, Barillon to Louis, 17 April 1679 NS; M636/32, Edmund Verney to Sir Ralph, 28 April 1679.
52 *HMC Ormond*, NS IV.xix–xx.
53 *Ibid.*, p. xix.
54 Scott, *Sidney*, pp. 17–21 and *passim*.
55 Knights, *Opinion*, *passim*.
56 Grey, VII.138–52; *HMC Ormond*, NS IV.506–8; *CJ*, IX.607–8, 623, 626.
57 NRO, Bradfer-Lawrence MS VIb(v), James Hoste MP to Thomas Stringer, 5 April 1679: this letter deals mainly with evil counsellors: it says little of the Popish Plot and does not mention the popish successor.
58 Miller, *Charles II*, pp. 296–8.
59 Coventry MS 6, fo. 76; WYAL, MX/R 14/75.
60 *HMC Finch*, II.96. Scott argues that the Commons spent little time on exclusion, but the bill passed quickly through the House and once it had been rejected by the Lords it could not be reintroduced that session, unless the king could be persuaded to wipe the slate clean by a prorogation. Some of the measures pursued by the Commons (such as the impeachments) could be seen as attempts to drive the king to prorogue, while others (notably the Association) attempted to achieve the same ends by other means, although Finch regarded it as totally unworkable: *HMC Finch*, II.97. See also Knights, *Opinion*, pp. 78–87.
61 *A List of one Unanimous Club of Voters in his Majesties Long Parliament*, 1679.
62 Grey, VII.148–9.
63 Browning, *Danby*, II.379–80; Miller, *Popery*, pp. 182–8.
64 Morrice, p. 288; Thomas in *From Unif*, pp. 222–31.
65 *CJ*, IX.506, 647; Grey, V.250–5.
66 *The Prospect of a Popish Successor*, 1681; WYAL, MX/R 14/75. See also Goldie, 'Priestcraft'.
67 Tanner MS 38, fo. 45; *POAS*, II.375–9; Goldie, in *Pol of Rel*, pp. 90–100.
68 See the comments on their preaching in Henry, p. 299; Newcome, *Autobiography*, II.232, 234, 237; Raynham, SP, Thomas Townshend to Lord Townshend, 29 December 1679.
69 M636/33, John Verney to Sir Ralph and Dr Denton to Sir Ralph, both 31 July 1679; Coventry MS 7, fos 148, 150. See also Carte MS 103, fo. 221. For Sparrow, see BL, Add. MSS 27447, fo. 423, 28621, fo. 39; Tanner MSS 38, fo. 22, 39, fo. 200, 314, fo. 34.
70 *A Faithful and Impartial Account of the Behaviour of a Party of the Essex Freeholders*, 1679, pp. 5–7; *Essex's Excellency*, 1679, pp. 3, 7; Coventry MS 7, fo. 164.

71 Josselin, p. 623. See also *A Letter from a Freeholder of Buckinghamshire*, 1679, p. 3.
72 Tanner MS 36, fo. 230; *The Speech of the Honourable Henry Booth, Esq.*, 1681, p. 2.
73 *Essex's Excellency*, p. 3.
74 PC 2/67, pp. 123, 131, 2/68, p. 20.
75 M636/34, John Stewkeley to Sir Ralph Verney, 1 July 1680; Morrice, p. 263; BT 146, Barrillon to Louis, 15 July 1680 NS; Burnet, 'Letters', p. 39; BL, Add MS 29572, fo. 247; Granville, II.51n; Tanner MS 37, fo. 114.
76 *HMC 7th Report*, p. 479; Morrice, p. 264.
77 *CSPD 1680–81*, pp. 45–6.
78 FSL, MS V.b.302, p. 4; *CSPD 1680–81*, p. 187; North, *Examen*, pp. 363–4.
79 Mark Knights is a distinguished exception.
80 Browning, *Docts*, pp. 237–9; *Unanimous Club*. Note the reference to the latter in *A Mild but Searching Expostulatory Letter to the Men of Buckingham*, 1679.
81 See for example M636/33, John Stewkeley to Sir Ralph Verney, 28 July and 11 August, John Verney to Sir Ralph, 4 August 1679; *The Manner of the Election of . . . Sir Harbottle Grimston . . . and Captain Reynolds*, 1681.
82 *HMC Ormond*, NS IV.537; above, p. 232.
83 *HMC Ormond*, NS V.234–5; Reresby, p. 191; Morrison, 1st series, III.171–2.
84 Newdigate, p. 67; *HMC Ormond*, NS IV.565.
85 Reresby, pp. 90, 110–11, 177–8.
86 Henry, p. 284; Carte MS 39, fo. 175; *CSPD 1679–80*, p. 405.
87 *CSPD 1678*, pp. 563–4, *1679–80*, p. 197; Morrison, 1st ser., III.171–2; *HMC Ormond*, NS V.157; *Hatton*, I.194; Carte MS 39, fo. 68; *HMC Kenyon*, pp. 113–4; Prinsterer, V.393, 422; Egerton MS 3331, fo. 101 (quoted).
88 BCL, MS B10166, unfoliated, 3rd 'calendar'. See R. Willman, 'The Origins of Whig and Tory in English Political Language', *HJ*, XVII, 1974, pp. 247–64.
89 *HMC Ormond*, NS IV.535–5; Tanner MS 38, fo. 45; Althorp MS C5, Sir Thomas Thynne to Halifax, 12 July 1679.
90 M636/32, Sir Ralph to Edmund Verney, 29 January 1679; BCL, MS 11151, Col Romsey to Southwell, 1 February 1679; *HMC Various*, II.166; Althorp MS C2, Hickman to Halifax, 15 August and 13 September 1679.
91 *HMC Ormond*, NS IV.317; Coventry MS 7, fo. 148; WYAL, MX/R 13/1; Aubrey, *Lives*, p. 186; Ailesbury, I.33–4; Carte MS 228, fo. 147; Coventry RO, A79/226; Badminton MS FmF 1/2/70; M636/32, Vere Gawdy to Sir Ralph Verney, 6 February 1679.
92 Tanner MS 39*, fo. 190.
93 M636/32, John Verney to Sir Ralph, 17 February, Sir Ralph to John, 17 February, Edmund to John, 20 February 1679.
94 Christchurch Civic Offices, volume of 'Letters' on elections, etc., p. 49; *HP*, I.247.
95 *CSPD 1679–80*, p. 96; Pepys, *Further*, pp. 331–2, 340–1.
96 Egerton MS 3331, fo. 101; BL, Add MS 61903, fos 9–10; M636/32, Sir Ralph to Edmund Verney, 21 February 1679; Browne, *Works*, I.231; *CSPD 1679–80*, p. 77; Newdigate, pp. 50–1; Heywood, II.259; *HP*, I.199.
97 WYAL, MX/R13/1; Badminton, FmF 1/2/71; BCL, MS B11152, Col. John Romsey to Southwell, 8 and 12 February 1679.
98 M636/32, Sir Ralph to Edmund Verney, 31 January, Edmund to Sir Ralph 3 March 1679.
99 Coventry MS 7, fo. 164; *HP*, I.368–9, III.442.

100 BL, Add MSS 29910, fo. 137, 172, 36988, fos 143–4, 149; *HMC 7th Report*, p. 495; Althorp MS C2, Sir William Hickman to Halifax, 9 and 15 August, 13 September 1679; M636/33, Sir Ralph to John Verney, 23 July 1679; *CSPD 1680–81*, p. 555.
101 E. Suffolk RO, EE2/04/1; *HP*, I.401–2: M636/33, Edmund to John Verney, 11 August 1679.
102 *CSPD 1679–80*, p. 395. Beaufort had his own copy of the 1685 poll-book for Gloucestershire: Badminton, MS FmG 3/1.
103 M636/35, Coleman to Sir Ralph Verney, 7 February 1681.
104 A.B., *A Letter from a friend in Abingdon to a Gentleman in London*, 1679, pp. 3–4.
105 Carte MS 103, fo. 221; *HMC 7th Report*, p. 495.
106 M636/33, Edmund to John Verney, 16 October 1679.
107 M636/33, same to same, 30 October 1679.
108 M636/32, Sir Ralph to John Verney, 18 August 1679 (entered under April); M636/33, William Grosvenor to John Verney, 20 and 21 August 1679; *A Letter from a Freeholder of Buckinghamshire to a Friend in London*, 1679.
109 *A Sale of Esau's Birthright*, 1679; *New news of a Strange Monster found in Stowe Woods*, 1679.
110 *The Answer of the Burgesses and other Inhabitants of. . . Buckingham*, 1679; *A Mild but Searching Expostulatory Letter . . . to the Men of Buckingham*, 1679.
111 BL, Add MS 52475A, fos 131, 144, 148; M636/33, Sir Ralph to John Verney, 25 September, Edmund to Sir John Verney, 25 September, 2 October, 12 November, Sir Richard Temple to Sir John Busby, 5 October, John to Edmund Verney, 27 October 1679.
112 BL, Add MS 27448, fo. 5; *The Speech of. . . Henry Booth*, p. 2.
113 M636/35, Sir Ralph to Alex Denton, 7 February 1681.
114 M636/35, Alex Denton to Sir Ralph, 4 February, Temple to Sir Ralph, 2 February, Sir Ralph to Temple , 4 and 11 February, Sir Ralph to Denton, 7 February 1681.
115 M636/35, Coleman to Sir Ralph, 4 February, Henry Lawley to Sir Ralph, 2 February, Sir Ralph to Temple, 7 February, Sir Ralph to Denton, 9 February 1681. See also M636/32, Sir Ralph to Edmund, 23 January 1679.
116 M636/35, Coleman to Sir Ralph, 7 February, Sir Ralph to Denton, 7 February, Sir Ralph to Vere Gawdy, 7 'February' (*recte* March).
117 *CSPD 1680–81*, p. 165; *HP*, I.247–8.
118 Carte MS 222, fo. 256; *The Manner of the Election of Grimston and Reynolds*; *HMC le Fleming*, p. 180.
119 *HP*, I.238–9.
120 *How and Rich: An Impartial account of the Proceedings of the . . . Election . . . for . . . Southwark*, 1681; WYAL, MX/R 18/44.
121 *A True Account of the Election at Cambridge*, 1681.
122 *HP*, I.381–2; CKS, Qb/C1/41–3.
123 Althorp MS C1, Windsor to Halifax, 16 April, 20 September and 10 October 1681; Dorset RO, D60/56, John to Henry Trenchard, 1 October 1681; *CSPD 1680–81*, pp. 521–2.
124 M636/36, Edmund Verney to Sir Ralph, 9, 12 and 16 January 1682.
125 BL, Add MS 29572, fo. 173; *HMC Ormond*, NS IV.565; *CSPD 1660–85 (Addenda)*, p. 478; *HMC 7th Report*, p. 496. For the content of petitions, see Knights, *Opinion*, pp. 227–37.

126 Morrice, pp. 241–2; BL, Add MS 29572, fo. 173; PC 2/68, p. 318; *London Gazette*, no, 1468, 11–15 December 1679.
127 M636/33, Edmund to John Verney, 18 December 1679.
128 *HMC le Fleming*, p. 165; *HMC Ormond*, NS IV.574; *Hatton*, I.215, 219; *CSPD 1679–80*, p. 377; BL, Add MS 29572, fo. 253; Pforz, ? to Bulstrode, 23 January 1680.
129 *HMC Ormond*, NS IV.576; *Hatton*, I.215; Morrice, p. 247; *Reasons Offered by a Well-wisher to the King and Kingdom*, [1680], p. 3; M636/34, John to Edmund Verney, 14 January 1680.
130 *Hatton*, I.219; Coventry MS 6, fo. 230; *POAS*, II.320–6.
131 *CSPD 1679–80*, pp. 364–5; Morrice, pp. 246, 250.
132 *HMC Ormond*, NS IV.576; BL, Add MS 29577, fo. 229; Pepys Lib, MS 2875, fo. 480; *CSPD 1679–80*, p. 425.
133 Grey, VII.371; Coventry MS 7, fo. 202.
134 *HMC Ormond*, NS IV.574, V.276; *CSPD 1679–80*, p. 535; Reresby, p. 202; Prinsterer, V.393; L.K.J. Glassey, *Politics and the Appointment of Justices of the Peace, 1675–1720*, Oxford, 1979, pp. 39–45.
135 BL, Add MS 36988, fo. 157 (quoted). For the address, see BL Add MS 41656, fo. 57. (There is a copy in the archives at Raynham.)
136 *CSPD 1679–80*, pp. 566–7, 607; UCL, MS 268, Godolphin to Bulstrode, 26 July, 13 August 1680; Reresby, pp. 198–9; Tanner MS 38, fo. 121; Prinsterer, V.393.
137 UCL, MS 268, Godolphin to Bulstrode, 13 August 1680; *CSPD 1679–80*, p. 307.
138 Luttrell, I.49; *HMC 7th Report*, p. 496; *HMC Ormond*, NS V.487; Morrice, p. 276; BT 147, Barrillon to Louis, 25 November 1680 NS; Knights, *Opinion*, pp. 268–75.
139 *HMC Finch*, II.103
140 Morrice, pp. 293–4, 295, 298; *HMC Ormond*, NS V.563–4, 579.
141 *The Speech of Henry Booth*, p. 3; see also Grey, VII.465.
142 *HMC Ormond*, NS V.599; Reresby, p. 219; Knights, *Opinion*, pp. 286–93, 298–303. For Tory addresses see *T.W., Strange and Wonderful News from Norwich*, 1681; *A True Account of the election at Cambridge*, 1681, p. 2; *The Southwark Address presented by several Inhabitants of Note*, 1681; *The Bristol Address to . . . Sir Richard Hart Kt and Thomas Earle*, 1681.
143 *A True Account of the Election at Cambridge*; *HMC Ormond*, NS V.599.
144 BL Add MS 36988, fo. 182.
145 Havighurst, 'Judiciary', pp. 232–5, 237.
146 *Ibid.*, pp. 235–6.
147 *London Gazette*, no. 1468, 11–15 December 1679; Browning, *Docts*, p. 66; *The Humble Address and Advice of Several of the Peers*, [1679]; *HMC Ormond*, NS IV.565; Morrice, p. 241.
148 PC 2/68, p. 313; *The Judgment or Resolution of all the Lords*, [1679]; *The Judges Opinions concerning Petitions to the King*, 1679.
149 Grey, VIII.61–2, 71.
150 M636/17, Sir Ralph Verney to John Carey, 6 April 1660, M636/33, John to Edmund Verney, 7 August 1679; Hirst, *Representative*, ch. 4 and *passim*.
151 Browning, *Docts*, p. 212.
152 *CJ*, IX.571, 609.

153 Reresby, p. 172; WYAL, MX/R 13/10; M636/35, Dr Denton to Sir Ralph and John Verney to Sir Ralph, 2 December 1680; BL, Add MSS 28053, fo. 228, 36988, fo. 149; CKS, Qb/C1/41; M636/34, Dr Denton to Sir Ralph Verney, 17 November 1680.
154 *CJ*, IX.653, 656, 658; Grey, VIII.32–4; Ailesbury, I.47–8.
155 Grey, VIII.52–3, 61–2; *CJ*, IX.658, 660–1, 676–8; Reresby, pp. 198–9, 202.
156 WYAL, MX/R 15/69, 16/14.
157 Knights, *Opinion*, pp. 307–12.
158 *HMC Ormond*, NS V.342.
159 Coventry MS 7, fo. 198; *CSPD 1679–80*, pp. 428–9; Dorset RO, D60/X9; Clifton, *Rebellion*, p. 61.
160 *HMC 7th Report*, p. 479; Morrice, pp. 265, 266; *CSPD 1680–81*, pp. 39, 44.
161 M636/34, Edmund to John Verney, 20 July, Sir Ralph to John Verney, 22 July 1680; M636/35, Temple to Sir Ralph, 17 and 29 July 1681, Sir Ralph to Hayward, 29 September 1681; M636/39, Sir Ralph to John Verney, 15 March 1685; *CSPD 1679–80*, pp. 575–6, *1682*, pp. 614–15.
162 BL, Add MS 52475A, fo. 145; M636/35, Temple to Sir Ralph, 13 September 1681, M636/36, Sir Ralph to John Verney, 27 July, M636/37, same to same, 20 November 1682.

Chapter thirteen

The triumph of the Tories, 1681–85

Tory and Whig

By the end of the Oxford Parliament England was as divided ideologically as in the civil wars. The Whigs were frustrated and angry. Their celebrations and demonstrations became more violent; their pamphlet attacks on the Tories became even more vituperative; some now embraced, at least privately, a contractual view of government which allowed the people an unlimited right of resistance. Others became embroiled in conspiracies, which involved armed insurrection and even the assassination of the king and his brother; these became public with the investigations into the Rye House Plot in 1683.[1] The Tories, led by the clergy, remorselessly proclaimed the divine origins of monarchy and the sanctity of the hereditary succession. Faced with the spectre of revolt, they argued that active resistance to lawful authority could never be justified. Some slid from this into an assertion that it was the subject's duty to obey whatever their king commanded. 'Non-resistance' and 'passive obedience' were distinct concepts: most of the clergy taught that if the king commanded something against the law of God, one should refuse to obey and then passively submit to punishment. However, it was easy to confuse the two: Whig polemicists and the bluff, straightforward Duke of York both assumed that one necessarily implied the other.[2] In their enthusiasm – or panic – some Tory apologists advanced quasi-absolutist views of royal authority. At Cambridge, Robert Brady's historical works undermined the concept of the ancient constitution, arguing that monarchy antedated either Parliaments or laws, with the implication that what kings had created they could take away.[3] The University of Oxford in 1683 condemned a whole series of opinions concerning the right of resistance and other rights of subjects and a series of works, including Baxter's *Holy Commonwealth*, almost all published before 1660.[4] Knowing how badly James II was to treat the Church and the Tories, this crying up royal authority and belittling subjects' rights might seem foolish. But since his first return from exile in 1679, York had assured the Tories that he would support the Church and the king's old friends. His vigorous endorsement of the episcopal church in Scotland suggested that he was sincere. Moreover, the most elementary calculation of self-interest would surely impel him to rely on the supporters of monarchy and the hereditary succession.

Meanwhile, the process of labelling continued relentlessly. Tory leaders promoted a series of loyal addresses: thanking the king for his declaration (to be read in every parish church) giving reasons for dissolving the Oxford Parliament; abhorring the 'Association' (allegedly a blueprint for rebellion) found in Shaftesbury's closet; and expressing horror at the Rye House Plot. The language of these addresses became steadily more extreme. In 1681 some focused on the king's assurance that he would call regular Parliaments in future, rather than on the misdeeds of the last two. By 1683 condemnation of factious and Dissenting principles was *de rigueur*, as were promises to stand by the king, his brother, the rightful succession and the Church. The address from Norfolk referred to 'the miscreants of 1642, who dyed these nations deep in blood'.[5] The names of those refusing to sign were noted – Lindsey thought refusers should be removed from office – and in some cases sent to the king.[6] There was much drawing up and scrutinizing of lists: of those who had voted for exclusion, of those who helped keep watch in Sussex during Monmouth's visit, of members of Yarmouth corporation for and against complying with an order in council.[7] Charges of Dissent, disloyalty and Whiggery were easy to make and difficult to disprove.[8]

The titles used by the two parties, of themselves and their opponents, remained diverse. Terms like the 'loyal', or 'Church party', or the 'fanatic' or 'disaffected party', were used interchangeably with 'Tory' and 'Whig'.[9] A newsletter of May 1681 explained: 'You must understand that as loyalists are called Tories by factious Presbyterians, so they again are called Whigs by loyalists.'[10] Narcissus Luttrell noted in September that the terms Whig and Tory were coming into common usage, but John Verney first used them only in April 1682 and his brother Edmund six months later.[11] Secretary Jenkins first referred to Tories in July 1682.[12] The parties were also distinguished by emblems. According to Roger North, the Exclusionists at the Oxford Parliament wore purple ribbons in their hats with the legend 'no popery, no slavery'. In July 1681 York's supporters were wearing red ribbons and Monmouth's blue.[13] In November Heywood learned that 'Tories' was the new word for those he called 'ranters' (drinkers and swearers) and that they wore red ribbons and their opponents violet.[14] It was said that these colours originated in Scotland, where Presbyterians wore 'true blue' and episcopalians red. What is clear is that the Whigs did not adopt the colours of the Green Ribbon Club.[15]

This process of labelling and division did not proceed without opposition or regret. In Norfolk Holland continued to seek a middle way.[16] In Cheshire the Earl of Derby (unlike his father) sought to distance himself from the high-fliers on either side.[17] The Duke of Newcastle asked to be relieved of his two lieutenancies on grounds of ill-health, complaining that he could not please everyone.[18] Others proceeded cautiously for reasons of self-interest: Reresby because he was aware of the jealousy aroused by his appointment as governor of York, the Earl of Burlington because he feared for his vast estates should the wrong party prevail.[19] The partisan conflict disrupted gentry social life.[20] It was claimed that Whigs no longer sent their sons to Oxford, for fear that they would end up Tories or papists. When Lord Wharton's son went to Tunbridge

Wells, his father was assured that he kept company only with 'true lovers of the Protestant profession'.[21] Party rancour led to blows and duels.[22] By 1683 whether or not one believed in the Rye House Plot was a matter of party allegiance.[23] Small wonder that instinctive moderates, like Gilbert Burnet, became weary.[24]

One reason for the ferocity of the passions aroused, and the unease of men like Reresby, was that it was far from clear how the faction-struggle would turn out. Fears of civil war remained strong, reinforced by awareness of the military limitations of the militia.[25] The Whigs' main strength was seen as lying in the 'populacy', which had ensured their success in elections, but which also suggested that, if it came to fighting, they would have numbers on their side. They also had the charismatic figure of Monmouth, widely believed to be the king's rightful heir, despite Charles's repeated public denials that he had married the Duke's mother and that proof of the marriage had been found in a 'black box'.[26] Many saw politics in terms of a contest between Monmouth and York and there was no doubt that the former was the more popular. Nowhere did the popular base of Whiggism seem more threatening than in London, by far the largest concentration of people, and the centre of government, politics, finance and the press. The highest level of the City's government, the aldermen (from whom the lord mayor was chosen), served for life and could block the election of newcomers whom they disliked; a comfortable majority were Tories. However, in January 1642 the lord mayor and aldermen had been overthrown by the common council, which was elected annually: could this happen again? Moreover, following the election of radical Whig sheriffs in 1680 and 1681, Whigs were routinely acquitted in political trials. The few Whigs who were sentenced to the pillory were protected by the people, whereas Tories were brutally treated. Threats and rowdyism against Tories went unpunished.[27] For the government and the Tories, there was a gaping hole in the machinery of law enforcement at its most sensitive point: what was to stop the Whigs taking to the streets, as in 1641–42, and driving the king from his capital?

Whig strength in the provinces was seen as resting on a variety of disaffected elements – ex-Roundheads, Dissenters and those who conformed to the Church just sufficiently to qualify for office. But these needed leaders, so the Tories were particularly wary of Whig aristocrats, especially where their influence was reinforced by the appeal of Monmouth. This was seen most strikingly in Cheshire in 1682, when the Tories' problems were compounded by a lord lieutenant, Derby, who was seen as dangerously ineffectual. Two of the county's major landowners were strong Whigs: the Earl of Macclesfield, a Royalist general, and Lord Delamere, a Parliamentarian, who (as Sir George Booth) had led the rising of 1659. Many of the Cheshire gentry were regarded as loyal, but their influence over the people was outweighed by Delamere's.[28] At Chester, the mayor, backed by the recorder (the former speaker William Williams), actively opposed loyal addresses and the persecution of Dissent.[29] In July it was noted that the Whig gentry were showing as much enthusiasm for race-meetings and cock-fights as the Royalists had under Cromwell. Tory gentlemen who gathered on 'our bowling day' suspected that they were plotting mischief.[30] On hearing Monmouth was coming to the county, the mayor and some of the aldermen invited him to Chester. The local Tories were fearful, especially because the castle was under the command of Derby, who had ordered the removal of the powder store to a house in the city some years before. Ormond advised Derby, his son-in-law, to avoid any contact with Monmouth because he was out of favour with the king.[31] Shortly afterwards the king agreed to re-appoint Sir Geoffrey Shakerley as governor of Chester, but he had not received his commission by the time Monmouth arrived. Ormond told his son to gather troops at Dublin in case of need.[32]

In late August Monmouth was reported to be meeting privately with Macclesfield, Delamere and others. On 9 September he came to Chester, accompanied by Macclesfield, his son and Colonel Roger Whitley. The people rang the church bells (except those of the cathedral and St Peter's, which were locked), bonfires were lit and Alderman Street provided several barrels of beer.[33] The Duke lodged with the mayor and stood godfather to his daughter.[34] On 12 September at least eighty gentlemen and 2,000 of 'the vulgar' met in Delamere Forest to hunt and hold horse and foot races; Monmouth and the Whigs had gathered for a similar purpose at Wallasey.[35] When the Tories returned to Chester that evening, they found the city ablaze with bonfires because Monmouth had won the plate at Wallasey; the mayor's wife had lit the first fire. The crowd broke the doors and windows of St Peter's to ring the bells. They sang ballads in the Duke's honour and cried out 'a Monmouth, a Monmouth!' outside Tories' doors. A crowd of 500 threw stones at Matthew Anderton's house and did not disperse till daybreak; the dean's windows were broken too. As the mayor was with Monmouth, the other magistrates were out of town and there was no deputy lieutenant within ten miles, there were only a few constables to maintain law and order. The helpless Tories reiterated that only a proper garrison could secure the city.[36]

The first attempt at redress came through the law. Sir George Jeffreys, chief justice of Chester, proposed a commission of *oyer and terminer*, which could try cases of treason (which the city's courts could not). Monmouth was arrested in Staffordshire and the commission was sent north, to try those accused of breaking the doors of St Peter's and the dean's windows.[37] The accused were gaoled, but were quickly bailed and feted by the citizens. The horse on which Monmouth had won his race was paraded through the streets, as the people chanted his name, lit bonfires and threatened to knock down any Tory they met.[38] The 'loyal' gentry again met in large numbers in Delamere Forest. Delamere was reported to be handing out hundreds of blue ribbons. It was claimed that 6,000 people gathered at Macclesfield's house to greet Monmouth – he was said to have ordered all his tenants to attend – and that the Earl rode abroad with an armed guard.[39] Meanwhile, there were repeated rumours that Derby had been seen talking with Monmouth and drinking his health.[40] Although the rumours were mostly found to be untrue, Derby's attitude appeared equivocal. His deputies accused him of refusing to call out the militia and complained of his allowing the powder to be moved from Chester Castle.[41]

The commission of *oyer and terminer* reached Chester by 25 September, in time to be produced at the assizes; Jeffreys was perturbed to find that the mayor and Street were included, but thought the majority were 'of our side'. The dean, James Arderne, whose brother was foreman of the grand jury, preached a 'sharp' sermon against popularity, for which Jeffreys thanked him. When the commission was read, Williams claimed that it infringed the city's charter. At the city's sessions the grand jury returned an *ignoramus* against those accused of riot, but Anderton brought the case before the commissioners and an 'honest' jury found a true bill and subscribed an address to the king dissociating themselves from the disorders. But the wheels of the law moved slowly, the mayor and recorder delayed as much as they could and the commission expired before the cases of the alleged rioters could be concluded.[42] Meanwhile, it was reported that, in his charge to the county quarter sessions, Delamere's firebrand son, Henry Booth, had declared that the laws against Protestant Dissenters should not be enforced, that the Presbyterians had brought back the king and that it was not treason to compass or imagine the death of the heir presumptive. Faced with such reports, the Tories planned to hunt again in Delamere Forest.[43] Jenkins was sure that some deep design had been discussed at Wallasey, but politely asked Derby about the reports of his moving the powder and ordered his deputies to take whatever steps they legally could, without the concurrence of the lord lieutenant, to put the militia in order.[44]

Tories elsewhere watched events in Cheshire with deep concern. With the militia paralysed by Derby's indecision, the Tories there were very much on their own in the face of a combination of Whig aristocratic power and Monmouth's popularity, reinforced by bonfires, bells and strong ale. They had learned that they could not rely on swift or decisive support from 'above'. The hereditary local standing of the Stanleys ensured that Derby was unlikely to be removed, provided he avoided open disobedience. The king and council showed themselves determined to hear all sides and to proceed according to law, whereas the Cheshire Tories wanted firm and ruthless action: a strong garrison in Chester and a radical shake-up in the city's government. But the government moved slowly. Whigs were increasingly removed from county office, but too slowly for hardline Tories, who alleged that many 'disaffected' JPs remained in commission (as Henry Booth did in Cheshire).[45] Although the Tories largely controlled the militia, Derby was by no means the only lord lieutenant regarded as a moderate.[46] Some of these became more actively partisan with time, especially after the Rye House Plot, harassing Dissenters and making shows of force to keep the people in awe. When the Duke of Beaufort, who was far from being a moderate, toured Wales in 1684, accompanied by a large entourage, he mustered the militia in one town after another and put the soldiers through their paces.[47]

But for the Tories, control over county government offered insufficient security. For a start, they did not control many of the towns, but there was also the prospect of conspiracy and rebellion. Force and the law were not enough: they also needed to win hearts and minds. Like Charles I in 1641–42, they saw no inconsistency in denouncing 'popularity' while seeking popular support.[48] The clergy sought to mobilize their flocks. L'Estrange discussed the issues of the day in lively, humorous and accessible prose. By the end of 1681, the Tories were getting the better of the propaganda battle.[49] If they had no-one to match Monmouth for charisma, they could provide drink and entertainment. Beaufort's 'progress' around Wales offered spectacle (in the shape of military exercises) and much feasting and drinking of loyal toasts. At Presteigne people occupied every possible vantage point to watch the militia drill, while a village near Haverfordwest insisted on laying on bonfires and fireworks although it was midday.[50] The hundreds of 'the vulgar' who came to Delamere Forest were regaled with food and drink as well as races. Despite Monmouth's triumph at Wallasey, racing, whether on horse or foot, was identified with the Tories rather than the Whigs, whose nonconformist supporters disapproved of the drinking, gambling and other disorders which normally accompanied it. In Lancashire and West Yorkshire, Heywood noted a veritable epidemic of races starting in 1678, some involving naked men or near-naked women.[51] This was accompanied by a revival of pagan customs, such as rushbearing or the celebration of May Day. On Easter Day 1681 great crowds played stoolball in the streets of Halifax, a dreadful profanation of the sabbath. 'Hell is broke loose', he wrote.[52] Along with all this went bawdy songs, promiscuity, swearing and, the root of it all, drunkenness.

The 'horrors' noted by Heywood could be seen simply as people having a good time, encouraged by brewers and alehousekeepers eager for profit.[53] Heywood, however, believed there was a political dimension. He noted the participation (and drunkenness) of many of the Anglican clergy,[54] explicitly identified drunken 'ranting' with the Tories[55] and reported that people at Ripon celebrated the dissolution of the Oxford Parliament with bonfires, bells and ale.[56] David Underdown and Mark Stoyle have argued that the divisions of the civil war were cultural as well as political and that a major component of popular Royalism was anti-puritanism, a resentment of attempts to suppress popular pastimes and self-indulgence. Similarly, nonconformists' austere and meddling morality was unpopular with a section of their neighbours and popular Toryism appears to have owed much to the Tory gentry's encouragement of drunken popular recreation.[57] The Tories' use of bonfires and bells was similar to the Whigs', but Tory celebrations were punctuated at regular intervals by healths or loyal toasts, which participants often drank on their knees. Some moderate Tories complained that those who 'ran about drinking and huzzaing' were a liability and had little aptitude for business,[58] but there is no doubt that their rough and exuberant sociability helped create a popular following for the Tory party.

Royal policy

In analysing Charles II's policies, we must remember that he could not know that the Exclusion Crisis was not to be followed by civil war. The similarities with 1640–42 made it seem all too likely and his lack of control over London and sporadic disturbances in the provinces gave added cause for concern. As in 1641–42 the radical tactics used by the king's opponents created a backlash, which was to be greatly intensified by the Rye House Plot. As in 1641–42 the king sought to exploit that backlash by taking his stand on the ancient constitution and the rule of law. Unlike his father, Charles II did not, despite York's urging, undermine this strategy by half-baked attempts to resort to force. Charles pursued this strategy because he, and most of his advisers, believed that it was the safest. His ministers knew that a major war on the continent or a rebellion in Scotland or Ireland would force him to call Parliament, so kept themselves as 'parliament-proof'[59] as possible. Some, like Jenkins, Lord Chancellor Nottingham and his successor Lord Keeper Guilford, believed on principle that the king should maintain the legal and moral high ground. Jenkins insisted that the king should never act after hearing just one side in an argument, still less on the basis of anonymous letters or unsubstantiated allegations.[60] He feared that if the king commanded something questionably legal, local office-holders or otherwise loyal subjects might refuse to obey. This concern for legality and fairness meant that convicted Dissenters, who appealed against their convictions, or who found a notable to speak for them, sometimes got off.[61] At a routine level, the courts remained surprisingly impartial. In the bitterly divided town of Rye, the Tories appealed to the privy council on political grounds, while the Whigs appealed to the King's Bench on legal grounds – and as late as 1683 the Whigs won.[62] Nevertheless, Charles was becoming more willing to play the part of a partisan king. His ministers still included a few moderates or mavericks like Halifax (called a 'trimmer', because of his dislike of extremism), or Anglesey. But they were outnumbered by firm Tories like Hyde (later Earl of Rochester), Ormond, Seymour and (for all his legalism) Jenkins. York, who returned from Scotland early in 1682, became the focus of a more extreme Tory element, which included the Earl of Sunderland and Jeffreys. The Rye House Plot led to more drastic measures, which included the disarming of anyone the deputies regarded as disaffected. By the end of 1684 York and his allies exercised a powerful influence over policy.[63]

In April 1681 the king issued a declaration condemning Parliament's recent illegal and arbitrary conduct, stressing that 'religion, liberty and property were all lost and gone when the monarchy was shaken off'. However, he had no intention of dispensing with parliaments and would summon them frequently, once 'a little time' had opened his subjects' eyes.[64] The tone was one of injured rectitude, designed to appeal to the middle ground. Initially, he did not welcome the addresses which it provoked, but he liked them better when they became more numerous.[65] He made it clear that he intended to rely on his 'old friends'. He expressed the view that 'there is no dallying now, and that there ought to be made a clean sweep of such kind of men whose principles are averse to the government . . . if he did not keep them under they would ruin him'.[66] Ormond, one of his shrewdest advisers, agreed: now was the time to take a stand, he wrote in May 1681. But the king remained hesitant and he was clearly alarmed by events in Cheshire: in late September 1682 he asked

Ormond to remain in England for the winter, in order to use his credit with 'the old loyal party'.[67] By January 1683 Ormond was more sanguine. He noted the presence at court of 'trimmers', who joined with the Whigs in their care for religion and property and with the Tories 'for monarchy and a just and legal prerogative'. Ormond did not see such a middle way as realistic. He found the trimmers' principles 'inscrutable', adding 'it is so easy to slip into either of the extremes from such a mediocrity'. However, 'if we have good luck we shall be all Tories; if we have bad luck we shall not be all Whigs.'[68]

Charles's move between 1681 and the end of 1684 from moderate to extreme Tory policies owed much to pressure from the provinces. Fearful, angry and eager for revenge, the Tories looked to the king. For much of the time central government simply reacted to information and requests for action, although the changing balance of power at court and the impact of events gradually convinced the king of the need to take more of an initiative. The ongoing defiance of London hardened his attitude and the destruction of its autonomy increased his confidence. Whig notables came forward, declaring that they had seen the error of their ways. The trickle became a flood after the Rye House Plot: the penitents included Delamere, Macclesfield and Buckingham.[69] Repentant 'sinners' continued to find forgiveness in 1684.[70] The plot seemed to offer conclusive proof of the longstanding Tory claim that the Whigs were traitors. There was clear evidence of some sort of conspiracy and that some had talked of assassinating the king. Moreover, the fact that some of those implicated were regarded as moderates (such as Essex and Russell) made it easy to assume that all the Whigs were involved.[71] The plot led to searches for arms and a more severe persecution of Dissenters. Now the greatest divisions were not between Whig and Tory but among the Tories. Jenkins urged that searches should be carried out with restraint and 'decency'.[72] Guilford stressed that it was vital for the king to retain his people's goodwill.[73] Lord Brooke wrote that although the people of Coventry had not always behaved as the king would wish (as in welcoming Monmouth), their faults were not so grave as to merit drastic action.[74] Such arguments cut little ice with Tory ultras like Jeffreys, for whom 'trimmer' was a term of abuse.[75] Late in 1684 York and his allies pushed, with some success, for a relaxation of the persecution of Catholics,[76] which would have been politically unthinkable a few years before and showed that Charles was confident that he and his Tory allies had vanquished the Whigs. How long that alliance would survive his death remained to be seen.

Church and Dissent

During the Exclusion Crisis the Church of England clergy had been on the defensive. From the spring of 1681, they went on to the attack. To ensure that preferment went to men who were both liturgically conformable and politically reliable, a commission for ecclesiastical promotions was set up in February 1681. Its membership, as finalized in August, included Archbishop Sancroft, Bishop Compton and four laymen: Hyde and Seymour, who were regarded as strong Churchmen, but also Halifax, whose religious views were a matter for conjecture, and the Earl of Radnor (formerly Lord Robartes) who had been regarded as a Presbyterian.[77] Some also doubted the depth of Compton's commitment to the eradication of Dissent.[78] If the membership of the commission did not suggest that the king was prepared to commit himself to the hardliners, it became clear that the key figures were Sancroft, Hyde and Hyde's brother, Clarendon,[79] all three closely associated with the Duke of York. The power of this connection was shown by the rapid rise to prominence of York's chaplain, Francis Turner, who became Bishop of Rochester in 1683 and Bishop of Ely in 1684.[80] By 1684 the commission was being outflanked by extreme Tories. In April Turner noted that no decision could be made about the new Bishop of Bristol until Beaufort came to town and in October it was reported that the majority of the commission (including Sancroft) had opposed the appointment of Beaufort's protégé, the firebrand Richard Thompson, as dean of Bristol.[81] In fact, the commission had been revoked the previous month; Bishop Fell of Oxford remarked that some of its recent appointments had been unwise.[82]

This is not to suggest that the Tory clergy were less militant than their lay counterparts. Humphrey Prideaux, who became a canon of Norwich in 1681, quickly identified John Hildeyard as the most disruptive man in the county.[83] Whereas clergymen had earlier tended to defer to laymen, now some upbraided them for leniency towards Dissent.[84] The few surviving semi-conformist clergy came under greater pressure to conform.[85] Bishop Barlow of Lincoln complained that he was accused of favouring nonconformists and suspected that his real crime was to have written so much against popery.[86] By contrast, Bishop Womock of St David's wrote that trimmers and timeservers posed as great a threat to the Church as papists and fanatics.[87] Zachary Cawdray, rector of Bartholmy, Cheshire, had in the 1660s helped establish weekday lectures at Tarvin, Nantwich and Knutsford. These (he claimed) had kept many in the Church who might otherwise have left for want of good preaching. In the recent elections, some who frequented the lectures had carried it against the Tory gentry; a Tory grand jury called for their suppression. Bishop Pearson complied, but later agreed to re-establish that at Tarvin, prompting Dean Arderne's 'sharp' sermon against 'popularity'. Pearson sympathized with Cawdray's wish to win over the Dissenters by peaceable means, but felt he could not contend with 'those of the gentry who have been more than ordinarily entrusted with the management of the affairs of the government'.[88] Cawdray was left denouncing clergymen who mixed with the looser sort of the gentry and condemned those who were soberer than themselves.[89]

The promoters of the drive for conformity which gathered pace from 1681 comprised both High Church clerics and Tory laymen, motivated by a mixture of Anglican commitment, fear of rebellion and revenge for humiliations suffered during the Exclusion Crisis: Jenkins told Richard Davies that he was not hostile to Quakers as such, but they 'gave their votes for the election of Parliament-men that were against the king's interest'.[90] Some bishops, like Lamplugh of Exeter or Gulston of Bristol, chivvied the gentry to act. Others, like Pearson or Barlow, were less than enthusiastic about persecution. Sparrow, who had been very active against Dissent first at Exeter then at Norwich, complained in 1682 that some who professed zeal for the Church denounced him for refusing to proceed 'beyond the rules of law'.[91] Elsewhere the lead was given by Tory peers, such as Beaufort, or gentlemen, like Captain Gregory Alford, who pursued a vendetta against the Dissenters at Lyme Regis and a JP who refused to act against them.[92] Tory magistrates secured presentments from carefully selected grand juries calling for tough measures against Dissent, which led to orders from the bench to enforce a wide range of laws. The language of these presentments and orders became more extreme with time and the measures they demanded became more severe.

However, for these calls to action to be effective their promoters needed backing from 'above'. In 1680 those wishing to enforce the laws against Dissent received no public encouragement from the king, who was still wary of upsetting Parliament.[93] For most of 1681 bishops and Tory activists were still denied unequivocal endorsement;[94] reluctant magistrates used the absence of explicit orders as an excuse not to act.[95] Dissenters were heartened by the freedom enjoyed by their brethren in London and by the belief that they had friends at court,[96] where Anglesey, Radnor and Halifax were still prominent. Dissenters still had access to ministers: Richard Davies waited on Hyde and Jenkins in 1682, the Presbyterian Sir John Baber spent an hour with Charles and James in 1683.[97] The first sign of greater toughness came in December 1681: the king launched his attack on London's charter and issued firm orders to enforce all the laws against nonconformity and to remove all Dissenters from offices in the navy and the revenue.[98] (An order of early November had referred only to 'active and turbulent Dissenters'.)[99] It took a while for this message to get through to some in the provinces, but others were quick off the mark. In January 1682 Devon quarter sessions issued orders for sweeping measures against Dissenters, including denying them poor relief.[100] Its example was followed in Middlesex, where the JPs had already pressed for a tougher approach. The JPs complained that they were not fully supported by the judges and that constables had qualms about obeying their orders.[101] Lamplugh wrote that Jenkins's approval of the Devon JPs' order encouraged them to produce another, but when there was no news that the king had approved it, their zeal slackened.[102] The king did agree to thank the mayor of Taunton for his zeal against conventicles,[103] but he also ordered that complaints of maltreatment in gaol, from Quakers and others, should be investigated.[104]

Despite the king's failure to satisfy the Tories' craving for approval, grand juries and JPs (especially in Middlesex) continued to call for more stringent measures against Dissent.[105] After the Rye House Plot, the Devon grand jury declared that conventicles were treasonable and that those refusing the Oxford oath should be deemed to be engaged in conspiracy. The JPs ordered churchwardens to return the names of those who did not attend church every Sunday, the crafty and perfidious occasional conformists; it was alleged that Lamplugh was behind this order.[106] Gulston ordered his clergy to read an earlier order from the Dorset JPs in their churches.[107] The Middlesex grand jury requested that the oath of allegiance should be tendered to all persons over eighteen and called for strict enforcement of the laws against vagrants and scolds.[108] In other dioceses, persecution was less brisk. At Chichester, Carleton, certainly no friend to Dissent, complained that the JPs showed no inclination to implement the laws.[109] Gulston complained that he found the Dorset JPs lacked the power to intervene in 'peculiars' (reserved jurisdictions). There and elsewhere constables and JPs (including Alford's *bête noire* Ellesdon) still doubted whether they had the legal authority to act.[110]

The weapons used against Dissent varied. Some rested squarely on statute. The Conventicle and Five Mile Acts had been the Cavalier Parliament's response to the perceived threat from Dissenting meetings, and these were vigorously enforced, but the Tories wished also to force the Dissenters into full conformity with the Church. To this end they used the recusancy laws, passed under Elizabeth to force Catholics to attend church. These were already used against Quakers: now Tory militants demanded that they be applied universally, at the full rate of £20 for each month's absence, to weed out occasional or partial conformists.[111] An increasing proportion of those convicted of recusancy were now Protestant Dissenters.[112] There were moves to enforce the Act of 1606 requiring everyone over sixteen to take Anglican communion at least once a year.[113] The oath of allegiance, designed for use against Catholics, was deployed against Dissenters.[114] A few were prosecuted under the draconian conventicle act of 1593.[115] The ecclesiastical law was used less extensively, because the church courts were slow and their penalties mild: excommunication held few terrors, especially for the poor. However, it was used to provide a pretext to debar Dissenters from voting, especially in London.[116] The threat of being denied burial in consecrated ground was another incentive to conform.[117] Other pressures rested on power rather than law. Revenue and naval officers were dismissed for nonconformity.[118] Poor relief was denied those who did not attend church.[119] There were moves to deny alehouse licences to those who did not attend church and take communion.[120] The laws against riot were invoked, especially against Quakers,[121] and Dissenters were threatened with action under other public order laws (such as the vagrancy laws) and sent to the house of correction. Even before the Rye House Plot, there were calls for Dissenters to be disarmed, as dangerous persons.[122] The wholesale disarming which followed the revelation of the plot led to the discovery of more conventicles, a greater willingness to break down doors and extensive damage and plunder.[123]

Although the persecution of Dissenters in 1681–85 varied in intensity, it was clearly by far the most severe of the reign. At first the Dissenters were defiant, meeting at the time of Anglican services and opening new meeting houses.[124] From early 1682 some bishops claimed that the churches were much fuller and that many conventicles had been suppressed,[125] but it was only in the summer of 1683 that the meeting-houses in Lyme, Bridport, Bridgewater and Taunton were closed. The suppression was brutal and the Tories exulted in their triumph. At Bridgewater, 'the gentlemen' built a bonfire fourteen feet high with the meeting-house fittings (with the pulpit cushion on top) and drank healths as it burned.[126] At Taunton, the mayor, Stephen Timewell, waged a lonely crusade against the Dissenters, in the face of massive hostility.[127] He was encouraged by the lord lieutenant, Lord Stawell, the Bishop of Bath and Wells and Jenkins.[128] Having faced a riot on 11 May, the anniversary of the lifting of the Royalist siege, Timewell made a point of celebrating the king's birthday on 29 May with bonfires, bells, drums, trumpets and the drinking of healths; the bonfire included posts from a recently demolished meeting house. The town had seen nothing like it since the Restoration, he said.[129] Following the Rye House Plot, he searched for arms and tendered the oath of allegiance to all over eighteen. He continued to pull down meeting houses, burning the doors and fittings until three in the morning, with the church bells pealing. The church, he added, was now full and informers began to come forward.[130] The Dissenters were reduced to meeting secretly. Elsewhere, where they were less numerous, they varied the times and places of their meetings to avoid detection.[131] Many were imprisoned, especially Quakers, always vulnerable because of their stubbornness and refusal to swear oaths. Baxter was saved from gaol only because the king took pity on his age and ill-health.[132] Persecution seemed to be working. The sincerity of those who now came to church may be doubted. Some Southwark magistrates thought that some were sincere and that others had attended conventicles mainly for business reasons. Of the rest, some could be brought at least to sullen neutrality, but the most hardened nonconformists had been forced to leave their trades and homes.[133] A significant minority went into exile. Others left their home towns: Samuel Jeake senior of Rye moved to London for five years to escape harassment by the local Tories.[134] If the struggles of 1681–85 saw no real battles, they produced many casualties.

The law

From the foregoing it would seem that the machinery of law was used and misused mainly against Dissenters, but we saw in the previous chapter that failures of justice were not only on one side. One anonymous contemporary saw the law as the battleground in a new civil war[135] and for a while it seemed far from inevitable that the Tories would win, especially in London. During 1681 one London grand jury presented the Tory instructions to Norwich's MPs as a libel; two claimed the right to examine witnesses in secret.[136] Of forty-nine jurors empanelled in October, all but two produced certificates that they had attended church, but Jenkins claimed only two did so regularly.[137] The king had already considered various expedients to get round the problem of biased juries.[138] Suggestions that the Middlesex JPs could change the panel, or that a Westminster jury could act instead, were firmly rebuffed; the king did not press the matter, saying he was determined to proceed according to law.[139] The conduct of the jury in Stephen College's trial elicited the comment that arbitrariness could be more in the people than in the king.[140] In November, Shaftesbury was accused of treason, partly on the basis of the 'Association'. The king's friends did not expect a conviction, but wanted the evidence to be made public. Monmouth, Essex and other Whig notables were conspicuously present; the prosecution witnesses were loudly hissed and had to have an armed escort when they left the court. The grand jury returned an *ignoramus*, amid wild popular rejoicing, prompting the chief justice to declare that the king could get no justice in London, even when his life was in danger.[141]

Shaftesbury's acquittal infuriated the king: he ordered a legal challenge to London's charter and the general enforcement of the laws against Dissent. London juries remained defiant: in February a grand jury refused to find a true bill against two Dissenters, but found several against Jenkins and others for illegal prosecutions and commitments.[142] But the king was fighting back: the Tories set out to build up popular support in London. The shrieval elections, full of controversy and sharp practice, were held in June, but not finally decided until September, when two Tories were declared elected. Shaftesbury, seeing that he was no longer safe, left for Holland, where he died the following year. The forfeiture of the City's charter in the summer of 1683 made permanent the Tories' control over London's machinery of law enforcement. In the shires the Tories had started to seize control earlier. In July 1681, after a London grand jury had found an *ignoramus* in the case of College, the council had him tried in Oxford and instructed the lord lieutenant of Oxfordshire to secure an 'honest substantial jury'; he was convicted. In February 1682 Lamplugh wrote that the Devon grand jury would consist mostly of baronets and others of great estates. The gentry had once disdained serving on grand juries: now they saw it as politically vital.[143] In June Luttrell wrote: 'If anything of Whig or Tory comes in question, it is ruled according to the interest of the party; if in the City of London, against the Tories; if in any of the counties, against the Whigs.'[144] This was an exaggeration: Tories continued to complain of unreliable grand juries.[145] Nevertheless, law enforcement and local government were distorted by partisanship. In Norfolk it was reported that 'in sessions they do not debate matters . . . but immediately cry "put it to the vote" and the cause is carried as the person concerned has an interest on the bench'.[146]

This law was used in a partisan fashion against Dissenters, but also for personal revenge. Several sought damages in 1681 after being called a papist in election disputes.[147] From 1682 there were a series of actions of *scandalum magnatum*: the Duke of York was awarded damages of £100,000 against both Pilkington, a former London sheriff, and Titus Oates. The Whigs tried to respond in kind. In 1684 Macclesfield brought an action against Sir Thomas Grosvenor, the foreman of a grand jury which had presented him as disaffected.[148] He stood little chance of success. His ally, Colonel Whitley, came to London to clear himself from accusations of disloyalty – it was alleged that he had knelt before Monmouth – and found himself accused of cheating the king of large sums in his employment in the Post Office. It was made very clear that his reputation for 'disloyalty' counted against him and that he would be well advised to 'compound' by making the king a 'present' of two or three thousand pounds.[149] Whitley was not, perhaps, as innocent as he seemed: those he met in London included Wildman, Pilkington and Sir Samuel Barnardiston, the foreman of Shaftesbury's grand jury, recently convicted of uttering seditious words.[150] Whitley's experience showed that Whigs could now be as vulnerable to predators as Whitelocke had been at the Restoration.

Traditionally the jury system was seen as a cornerstone of English liberties, but no longer: Sir Ralph Verney commented that even if all York's witnesses against Pilkington were dead 'a willing jury may supply the want of proof'.[151] The key to 'good' juries was to appoint Tory sheriffs, which now became the norm. In late 1683 it was reported that the freeholders' books, from which jury panels were chosen, were being 'revised'.[152] In seeking political revenge through the courts, few were as tenacious as a group of Northamptonshire Tories, who claimed that the instructions presented to the knights of the shire in 1681 constituted a summons to rebellion. In late 1681 or early 1682, and in July 1683, grand juries presented this paper as evidence of a sinister design, referring to meetings, clubs and cabals: the Whigs met weekly at the Swan at Northampton. The 1683 presentment called for many named persons to give security to keep the peace; it was printed with the title *A List of all the Conspirators*.[153] (Grand juries drew up similar lists in Cheshire and Sussex.)[154] In December 1683 a leading Tory, Sir Roger Norwich, brought the instructions to the king's attention; the king referred the matter to the attorney general, who did nothing, to the disappointment of 'the gentlemen'. At the March assizes the grand jury found an indictment against Richard Butler for presenting the instructions. Sir Roger asked that the case might be heard at King's Bench, to serve as a precedent for punishing those who had presented petitions and instructions. Presumably the attorney general did not agree, because in November 1684 Butler was convicted at Northampton assizes of delivering a seditious paper and fined £500.[155]

These events show that much of the impetus for the politicization of law enforcement came from the Tories, rather than the crown. However, Norwich remarked that the assize judges carried themselves very kindly towards the loyal party. Even in 1681 the judiciary was predominantly Tory and its partisan character was reinforced by changes in 1682–83.[156] The effect of this was seen in the trials after the Rye House Plot. In treason trials the judges were under pressure to secure a conviction, to protect the king's person and to emphasize the heinousness of the crime, a point underlined by the gruesome mode of execution. Lord Russell and Algernon Sidney were condemned on inadequate evidence: one 'witness' against Sidney was an unpublished republican tract found in his closet. The verdicts were not criticized by the Tories, very conscious that, had the roles been reversed, the Whigs would have treated them in a similar fashion: one need only consider their response to the Popish Plot trials. In a political world dominated by partisanship, racked by fears of conspiracy and civil war, justice was bound to suffer.

The towns[157]

From 1681 the king and the Tories together secured control over the machinery of law enforcement in the shires, but corporate towns retained a measure of jurisdictional autonomy: the problem created by London was replicated in many provincial towns. The Corporation Act had been designed to purge 'disaffected' members rather than challenge the corporations' autonomy. After the purge of 1662–63 the provisions of the Act were not rigorously observed and could not prevent the admission to office of occasional or unenthusiastic conformists. Some towns had become deeply divided by the mid 1670s, but many had not: Norwich, Cambridge and Hull, for example.[158] The elections of 1679 and 1681 divided many boroughs and highlighted the ineffectiveness of the Corporation Act. Many peers and gentry came to share the view of Sir Thomas Peyton, who had presided over the purge in Kent, that the petitioning campaign showed that the corporations were 'the seminaries of all separation in church and state'.[159] From 1681 Tories, both inside and outside the boroughs, appealed to the king for help in overcoming the Whigs. Sometimes local magnates did not need outside help. The Marquis of Worcester had been lord lieutenant of Bristol since 1673. He had been incensed when, in 1676, his nominee for the post of town clerk was not on the shortlist considered by the common council.[160] (Compare the alacrity with which Norwich had chosen Howard's nominee in 1664.) Stung by this defeat, Worcester developed his military power, reviving the Bristol Artillery Company and adding a youth branch, the Society of Loyal Young Men, whose members played a prominent part in elections during the Exclusion Crisis and later on grand juries.[161] In September 1682, now Duke of Beaufort, he ostentatiously mustered the militia on the day for the election of mayor and sheriffs: acceptable men were chosen.[162]

Aristocratic intervention in municipal affairs was rarely as crude as that, but it was common.[163] The Tories were by no means always the weaker element in towns: in Norwich they were the stronger, especially among the freemen, and even in Bristol they had been strong enough to return two Tories in 1681.[164] But even where the Tories were strong, it was possible that time would bring a change in fortunes. Where they were weak, they saw little prospect of power unless the rules of the political game were changed. In either case, the Tories would seek a new charter, which could either perpetuate their hold on power or bring them into power for the first time. The many new borough charters issued from 1682 usually named the first members of the corporation (which offered a means of easing out Whigs) and almost always allowed the king to remove any member of the corporation at any time. The latter provision would enable the king to influence corporate personnel continuously, something the Commons had been unwilling to contemplate in 1661. Now, however, they could trust the king to favour his 'old friends'. Moreover, experience had shown that such powers of royal intervention were vital for Tory electoral success. It should be stressed that, as with the persecution of Dissent, the initiative for the new charters usually came from the localities – from within the boroughs[165] or from their aristocratic neighbours. The king was angry at being denied justice, as he saw it, but (as elsewhere) he wished to be seen to be acting according to law and his ministers and law officers rejected some of the more extreme proposals from the localities and even urged reconciliation.[166]

The new charters sometimes granted the towns additional privileges and in fifteen to twenty cases altered the franchise, usually by making it narrower or vesting it in the freemen (which made it possible to draft in county gentry as electors)[167] In most cases, however, they left the boroughs' powers and privileges little changed.

Of the relatively few cases where the initiative for the challenge to charters came from the king, the most important by far was London. On 21 December 1681 the attorney general initiated an action of *quo warranto*, asking by what authority the corporation governed the City and alleging that it had abused its powers by levying tolls without the king's permission and by endorsing a 'seditious' petition presented in the name of the common council. The action raised complex legal issues concerning the nature of corporations. What sort of bodies were they? Could the privileges of the whole be forfeited for the misdeeds of a part? (Jenkins thought not.)[168] While the legal proceedings ground on, the king's supporters built up their electoral support in the City, sought to disqualify nonconformists from voting and carried through the contentious election of two Tory sheriffs, which led to riots and the arrest of Whig sheriffs and a Tory lord mayor. In June 1683 the judges declared the City's charter forfeit, but the judgment was not enrolled, giving the corporation the opportunity to surrender; after much debate, it refused. The judgment was entered and the king appointed twenty-six commissioners, including eighteen former aldermen, to govern the City and act as magistrates.[169] In terms of everyday government, this probably made little difference, but if the commissioners displeased the king they could be removed. Charles II had done what no previous monarch had done: he had brought London fully under royal control.

The proceedings against London's charter were followed avidly in the provinces, not only because of the legal issues, but also because if London could not defend its charter, lesser towns would certainly be unable to do so. Corporations were concerned that if they surrendered their charters they might cease to exist, if only momentarily, which might annul their title to corporation property; procedures had to be found to obviate this anxiety.[170] Debates about whether or not to surrender were often bitter: many Tories feared that to surrender would be a breach of their oath of office, in which they had sworn to preserve the town's privileges. This was the case at Norwich, where it took all Yarmouth's influence and perseverance to procure a surrender.[171] At Nottingham the dispute over surrender led to the election of two rival mayors in 1682 and to prosecutions for riot which ended only in 1684.[172] As Paul Halliday has emphasized, seeking to end divisions within a corporate body by expelling some of its members served only to perpetuate them.[173]

For the moment, however, the campaign against the borough charters succeeded. The king provided the authority, the legal procedures (such as *quo warranto*, although such pressure was not always necessary) and the law courts. The Tories provided the agents, the information and above all the determination in the localities to push the changes through. The motives of king and Tories were similar, but not identical. Both saw the towns as centres of disaffection which could prove dangerous in the event of civil war. Both were concerned that urban magistrates were remiss in punishing religious nonconformity. In each of these areas, there was a shared concern for present security. In addition, the Tories were concerned to improve their electoral performance, which in many boroughs had been inadequate in 1679–81. Moves to change the franchise seem invariably to have originated with the Tories, not the king, because Charles did not intend to call Parliament if he could possibly avoid it. In 1684 the pace of surrenders increased, with Jeffreys particularly active, but the content of charters did not change, nor was there any indication that Charles was planning to call an election.[174] For the moment, the differences in the priorities of the king and the Tories mattered far less than their shared aim of crushing Whiggery and Dissent. Only later would it be apparent that the sweeping powers granted to the crown by the new charters could also be used against the Tories.

The general election of 1685

The extent of the Tory triumph was seen in the election called by the new king early in 1685. In some ways, this appeared similar to earlier elections. Many of the same issues were raised – notably exclusion – but only by the Tories. In Nottinghamshire, a long pole was brought out with a black box on the end and a slogan 'no black box, no bill of exclusion, no Association'. When the election was over, it was burned in Newark market-place.[175] Secretary Sunderland wrote to many peers and other notables to use their best efforts to ensure that loyal men were chosen. In Norfolk, Surrey and Derbyshire, gentry meetings agreed on two candidates – by means of a ballot in Surrey.[176] Tory peers were very active: despite his infirmity, the Duke of Newcastle attended the election at Nottingham and was prepared to attend the county election if need be. In the event, Lord Kingston (whose relationship with Newcastle had not always been easy) was persuaded to order his tenants to support the Tories and there was no contest. Newcastle was given much of the credit for the Tories' good showing.[177] There was considerable evidence that the public mood had turned against the Whigs. In Nottinghamshire the whole county allegedly opposed Sir Scrope Howe, while at Nottingham the Whigs, to their surprise, found themselves heavily outvoted.[178] Colonel Birch was 'laid by' at Weobley, 'his own town, where he did believe no flesh living could receive any kindness, but by his permission'. In Essex, 'the principal nest of nonconformists', the Whigs were defeated by many votes.[179]

It would seem there was a genuine popular toryism, which was encouraged and exploited by peers, gentry and clergy. In Sussex Carleton ascribed the Whigs' decision to avoid a contest to 'my interest in this my diocese with the clergy and theirs upon my account with the freeholders of their parishes'. In County Durham Dean Granville sent word to the curates and leading men of his two parishes that he expected no opposition to his recommendations for knights of the shire. He was prepared to forgive their past defiance and ill usage 'provided they will do their duty and be governed by me . . . for the future'.[180] As usual, local interests were often important. Sometimes patrons clashed, as at Clitheroe or Mitchell.[181] Towns continued to bargain with would-be patrons. Hull was prepared to offer the Earl of Plymouth the nomination to one seat; Rye tried to prevent the Warden of the Cinque Ports from nominating to either.[182] But this election differed from others in the extent to which it was directed from the centre. It was normal for the king to encourage Tory notables to use their interests on behalf of 'loyal' candidates, or to try to find places for important royal servants, like Pepys and Solicitor General Finch.[183] But he also tried to ensure that unsuitable candidates did not stand. In Nottinghamshire Sir Scrope Howe may have enjoyed only limited support, but he was advised by the judges to desist. When Sunderland heard that his kinsman Edward Montagu was planning to stand for Northamptonshire with the factious Edward Harby, he intimated that it would be wise for Montagu to join with a loyal man (which he did, and was returned). Although Sunderland wrote on the advice of a Northamptonshire magnate, his warning was much more powerful because of his position as secretary of state.[184] Once someone was seen at court as sympathetic to the Whigs, it was difficult to dispel the impression.[185] Sir William Frankland was persuaded by his son and Lord Fauconberg not to stand again at Thirsk. His son told him bluntly that the king wished him to stand in his father's stead, adding that if he was not prepared to do as the king bade in Parliament, he would be better off not being there. Others with Whig records had come to court intending to stand, but changed their minds. The defiant few who insisted on standing were likely to suffer for it. It was also intimated that Frankland would be wise to visit his Catholic neighbours. Frankland replied that he would not try to justify his past conduct and would submit to the king's will.[186]

The king did not confine himself to discouraging Whigs from standing: he also actively encouraged the election of those he favoured and his 'recommendations' resembled commands.[187] At Winchester, a strongly Royalist city, the local Tories had agreed to put forward Sir John Clobery and Francis Morley, who had considerable support and the backing of the joint lords lieutenant, the Earl of Gainsborough and his son. The king insisted that two outsiders, Roger L'Estrange and Charles Hanses, should be chosen instead, for the good of his service. The assize judge was told to make this clear to all and sundry and Bernard Howard (Henry's brother and a Catholic, who had acted as an agent of the city since 1676) was sent to secure the election of L'Estrange and Hanses. He sent word to Gainsborough that, as he had earlier supported Clobery and Morley so actively, mere neutrality now was not enough: he should support the king's candidates publicly, to show that he was not being governed by his 'Whig' deputies. Clobery and Morley were persuaded to desist, the latter by the bishop, and L'Estrange and Hanses were returned, but with little enthusiasm.[188] This case was not unique: at Bedford Jeffreys effectively imposed the king's nominees on the town (despite their own unwillingness to be chosen). Small wonder that Colonel Ralph Widdrington felt impelled to justify his election at Berwick, contrary to the king's instructions, which he claimed were based on misinformation.[189] Jeffreys was similarly active in

Buckinghamshire where, despite his and the court's best (or worst) efforts, he was unable to prevent the election of Thomas Wharton.[190] Such cases of undue royal interference were not numerous and, as most worked to the Tories' advantage, they were not inclined to complain too much. Nevertheless they showed that the new king had a noticeably more authoritarian, even arbitrary, attitude to the electoral process which they would not relish if it were turned against themselves. Having exalted and unleashed the crown's power, the Tories had given more hostages to fortune than they yet realised. Triumphant in 1685, by 1687 they were staring disaster in the face.

Notes

1 The classic work of Whig political theory from this period is Locke's *Second Treatise of Government*. On Locke and conspiracy see R. Ashcraft, *Revolutionary Politics and Locke's 'Two Treatises of Government'*, Princeton, 1986. Ashcraft's interpretation has proved controversial; for a more balanced account of conspiracy in these years, see Greaves, *Secrets*, chs 1–5.
2 Burnet, *Hist.*, II.27.
3 Pocock, *Ancient Constitution*, ch. 8.
4 Kenyon, *Constitution*, 1966 edn., pp. 471–4.
5 BL, Add MS 41656, fo. 60.
6 BL Add MS 36988, fo. 182; *CSPD 1680–81*, p. 409, *1682*, p. 212.
7 *HMC Various*, II.173; Morrice, p. 396; *CSPD 1682*, p. 215, *Jan–June 1683*, pp. 46, 69.
8 H. Prideaux, *Letters to John Ellis*, (ed.) E.M. Thompson, Camden Soc., 1875, p. 94; *CSPD July–Sept 1683*, p. 232–3, 292; Warwicks RO, CR136/1307 F, A, D.
9 See the example of Lord Longford: *HMC Ormond*, NS VI.154; Carte MSS 232, fo. 122, 216, fo. 195.
10 'Oates Plot', newsletter 4 May 1681.
11 Luttrell, I.124; M636/36, John to Edmund Verney, 10 April, M636/37, Edmund to John, 9 October 1682.
12 *CSPD 1682*, p. 302.
13 North, *Examen*, pp. 101–2; Luttrell, I.110–11; Althorp MS C2, John Millington to Halifax, 27 July 1681.
14 Heywood, II.285.
15 Allen, 'Clubs', pp. 568–9.
16 Miller, 'Holland', pp. 868–71. See the comments of Lord Fauconberg, *HMC Frankland-Russell-Astley*, p. 48.
17 *HMC Kenyon*, p. 145; *HMC Ormond*, NS VII.59, 62–3.
18 *CSPD Jan–June 1683*, pp. 273, 300.
19 Reresby, pp. 278–9, 307, 312–13.
20 M636/37, Edmund to John Verney, 16 April, John to Edmund, 21 April 1683.
21 Wood, III.7; Bodl, MS Rawl Letters 104, fo. 37.
22 *CSPD 1680–81*, pp. 588–9; BL, Add MS 29559, fo. 333.
23 BL, Add MS 29560, fos 45, 59.
24 BL, Add MS 63057B, fo. 66. See also Warwicks RO, CR136/B1307A.
25 *CSPD July–Sept 1683*, pp. 9, 62; *Hatton*, II.30.
26 Clifton, *Rebellion*, pp. 121–4.

27 *CSPD 1680–81*, pp. 583–4, 588–9; *HMC Ormond*, NS VI.237; Harris, *Crowds*, pp. 180–4.
28 *CSPD 1682*, pp. 313, 343; *Hatton*, II.18.
29 *CSPD 1682*, pp. 92, 107, 120–1, 157–8.
30 *Ibid.*, pp. 313–4.
31 *Ibid.*, p. 342; Carte MS 50, fo. 293; *HMC Ormond*, NS VI.428, 453, 455.
32 *CSPD 1682*, pp. 387, 411; *HMC Ormond*, NS VI.436. The commission arrived on 11 September, two days after Monmouth, but Shakerley does not seem to have attempted to act upon it.
33 BL, Add MS 36988, fo. 199; *CSPD 1682*, pp. 383, 387–9.
34 *CSPD 1682*, p. 387; BL, Add MS 36988, fo. 201.
35 BL, Add MS 36988, fo. 201; *HMC Ormond*, NS VI.444; *CSPD 1682*, pp. 387, 390, 391. The Tories met a good 25 miles away from the Whigs – but close to Chester. Monmouth had left Chester for Wallasey on the 11th.
36 *HMC Ormond*, NS VI.444–5; *CSPD 1682*, pp. 393–4; BL, Add MS 36988, fo. 201 (the date of 11 September on this last letter is clearly wrong, although it may have been started then).
37 *CSPD 1682*, pp. 395, 411; Carte MS 216, fo. 181.
38 *CSPD 1682*, pp. 398, 402, 406.
39 *Ibid.*, pp. 398, 407–9, 416, 457.
40 BL, Add MS 36988, fos 199, 201; *CSPD 1682*, pp. 396–7, 406–7.
41 *CSPD 1682*, pp. 399, 409, 421, 422; *HMC Ormond*, NS VI.486–7.
42 *CSPD 1682*, pp. 426–7, 434, 438–9, 449, 475; *HMC Ormond*, NS VI.456.
43 *CSPD 1682*, pp. 456–8.
44 Newton, *House of Lyme*, pp. 302–3; *CSPD 1682*, pp. 431–2, 461.
45 *CSPD 1682*, p. 138, *Jan–June 1683*, p. 367; Glassey, *Justices*, pp. 52–5. Booth had been put into commission in January 1681, but virtually all Whigs had been removed by January 1683: PC 2/69, p. 207; Challinor, 'Cheshire', pp. 84–90.
46 Others included Dorset, Pembroke, Gainsborough, Newcastle and Burlington: Stater, *Noble*, pp. 153–4; Coleby, *Hants.*, pp. 162–3; letters of Newcastle in *CSPD*; Reresby, p. 307.
47 T. Dineley, *The Account of the Official Progress of the first Duke of Beaufort through Wales in 1684*, London, 1888, pp. 52–4, 92–3, 379; M.McClain, 'The Duke of Beaufort's Tory Progress through Wales, 1684', *Welsh History Review* XVIII, 1997, pp. 592–620.
48 Knights, *Opinion*, pp. 298–303, 306; Harris in Glassey (ed.), *Reigns*, pp. 143–7.
49 Knights, *Opinion*, pp. 343–7.
50 Dineley, *Progress*, pp. 176–7, 264, 278–9, 351; McClain, 'Progress', pp. 612–13. Fletcher, *Reform*, pp. 330–2 notes the importance of musters as theatre.
51 Heywood, II.246, 264, 271–2, 274, 279–80, 284, 293–5.
52 *Ibid.*, II.270–2, 279, 294.
53 *Ibid.*, II.246, 279–80, 287.
54 *Ibid.*, II.281–2, 284.
55 *Ibid.*, II.285, 288.
56 *Ibid.*, II.278.
57 *Ibid.*, II.271–2, 294–5.
58 *Norths*, I.237.
59 The phrase was Essex's: Stowe MS 214, fo. 154.
60 *CSPD July–Sept 1683*, pp. 199, 245, 416.

61 *CSPD 1682*, pp. 270–1, *July–Sept 1683*, p. 145; Morrice, pp. 305, 431; Coleby, *Hants.*, pp. 201, 203; C.E. Whiting, *Nathaniel Lord Crew, Bishop of Durham*, London, 1940, pp. 116–17.
62 Halliday, *Dismembering*, pp. 132–5.
63 See Miller, *Charles II*, chs 13–14; J.P. Kenyon, *Robert Spencer, Earl of Sunderland*, London, 1958, ch. 3.
64 Browning, *Docts*, pp. 185–8.
65 Reresby, pp. 246–7.
66 *HMC Ormond*, NS VI.143–4.
67 T. Carte, *Life of James, Duke of Ormond*, (6 vols) Oxford, 1851, V.161–3; Carte MSS 70, fo. 558, 219, fo. 381.
68 Carte MSS 70, fo. 564, 219, fo. 417.
69 *HMC Ormond*, NS VI.204; *CSPD 1682*, p. 356; Egerton MS 2540, fo. 45; *Hatton*, II.33–4; BT 155, Barrillon to Louis, 9 August 1683 NS.
70 Morrice, p. 436; Miller, 'Holland', p. 871.
71 Carte MSS 118, fos 210–11, 219, fo. 560; *HMC Dartmouth*, I.82. For a full discussion of the evidence, see Greaves, *Secrets*, chs 4–5.
72 *CSPD July–Sept 1683*, pp. 6, 68, 94.
73 *Norths*, I.319–20.
74 BL, Add MS 41803, fo. 53.
75 *Norths*, I.328; *CSPD 1684–85*, pp. 187–8.
76 Miller, *Charles II*, pp. 379–81.
77 FSL, MS V.b.302, pp. 4, 32; *CSPD 1680–81*, pp. 187, 364, 399. For Radnor, see Swatland, *Lords*, pp. 133, 163, 205. The presence of Radnor and Halifax makes it hard to accept Beddard's claim that the members 'without exception represented the *avant-garde* of the Tory reaction': R. Beddard, 'The Commission for Ecclesiastical Promotions, 1681–4: An Instrument of Tory Reaction', *HJ*, X, 1967, p. 17.
78 Burnet, *Hist.*, II.328; BL, Add MS 63057B, fo. 67; BL, Add MS 29559, fo. 387.
79 It is not clear that Clarendon was actually a member of the commission rather than just a political ally of Sancroft: see Beddard, 'Commission', pp. 35, 37–8; *HP*, II.626.
80 Beddard, 'Commission', p. 25–30.
81 Tanner MS 32, fo. 37; Morrice, p. 443. For Thompson, see Barry in *Pol of Rel*, p. 173.
82 *Hatton*, II.50; Carte MS 130, fo. 22; Tanner MS 32, fos 158–9.
83 Mason, *Norfolk*, pp. 367–8; Prideaux, *Letters*, pp. 123–4.
84 Warwicks RO, CR136/B413; *HMC le Fleming*, p. 183.
85 Tanner MSS 32, fo. 98, 34, fos 142, 276, 35, fos 39, 98.
86 Tanner MS 32, fo. 54.
87 Tanner MS 34, fo. 253.
88 Tanner MS 34, fos 26–7.
89 Tanner MS 35, fo. 117.
90 Davies, p. 184.
91 Tanner MS 36, fo. 228.
92 *CSPD 1680–81*, p. 652, *1682*, pp. 46, 60, 72, 80.
93 *HMC Ormond*, NS V.342; Burnet, Letters, p. 39; Morrice, p. 263; M636/34, John Stewkeley to Sir Ralph Verney, 1 July 1680.
94 Tanner MS 36, fos 11, 196; *CSPD 1680–81*, pp. 400, 409, 420, *1682*, pp. 97–8; PC 2/69, p. 425.

95 *CSPD 1680–81*, pp. 626, 652.
96 Tanner MSS 35, fo. 67, 36, fo. 62; *CSPD 1680–81*, p. 433.
97 Davies, pp. 183–5; Morrice, p. 351.
98 *HMC Ormond*, NS VI.264, 274; Morrice, pp. 318, 319; *CSPD 1680–81*, pp. 600, 606; *HMC le Fleming*, p. 183.
99 PC 2/69, p. 386.
100 Tanner MS 36*, fos 212–13; *CSPD 1682*, pp. 25–6.
101 *HMC Ormond*, NS VI.155; PC 2/69, p. 425; *CSPD 1682*, p. 59; Morrice, p. 328.
102 Tanner MSS 35, fos 9, 36, 36, fo. 235.
103 *CSPD 1682*, pp. 97–8, 113, 145.
104 *CSPD Jan–June 1683*, pp. 77–8, 111, 164–5; *HMC Kenyon*, pp. 159–60.
105 *CSPD 1682*, pp. 467–8, 534–5, 556–7, *Jan–June 1683*, p. 205.
106 *CSPD July–Sept 1683*, pp. 262–3; Dr Williams' Library, MS 31J, 1691, p. 2/1. See Lamplugh's letter, Tanner MS 34, fo. 174.
107 *CSPD Jan–June 1683*, p. 205.
108 *CSPD 1683–84*, p. 30–1; Morrice, p. 415.
109 *CSPD July–Sept 1683*, pp. 362, 380, *1684–5*, p. 433.
110 Tanner MS 34, fos 75, 123; *CSPD Jan–June 1683*, pp. 60, 291, *July–Sept 1683*, p. 408; *HMC Kenyon*, p. 172.
111 Tanner MS 36*, fos 212–13; *CSPD July–Sept 1683*, pp. 204, 362, *1683–84*, p. 31; Morrice, pp. 356, 358, 365, 396.
112 Miller, *Popery*, pp. 265–8.
113 Morrice, p. 362; *Mather*, p. 510; *CSPD 1682*, p. 205.
114 Morrice, p. 365; Tanner MS 36*, fo. 212; Althorp MS C1, Windsor to Halifax, 10 October 1681.
115 Morrice, p. 353; *CSPD 1682*, p. 601; Reresby, p. 323. See also Tanner MS 36*, fos 212–13.
116 Luttrell, I.242, 251.
117 Tanner MS 35, fo. 190.
118 Luttrell, I.171–2.
119 *HMC Ormond*, NS VI.155; Tanner MS 36*, fo. 213; *CSPD 1682*, p. 59.
120 *CSPD 1680–81*, pp. 511, 549–50, *1682*, p. 467, *Jan–June 1683*, p. 103.
121 *CSPD 1682*, p. 534; Morrice, p. 413.
122 Morrice, p. 423; *CSPD 1682*, pp. 534, 556–7; *HMC Egmont*, II.121.
123 *CSPD July–Sept 1683*, pp. 60, 204; Tanner MS 34, fo. 75; *HMC le Fleming*, p. 192.
124 *CSPD 1680–81*, pp. 352, 640, 695–6; Tanner MS 36, fo. 62.
125 Tanner MSS 35, fo. 9, 36, fos 235, 251.
126 Tanner MS 34, fo. 75; *CSPD July–Sept 1683*, pp. 60, 279.
127 *CSPD Jan–June 1683*, pp. 250, 258, *July–Sept 1683*, pp. 251, 358.
128 *CSPD Jan–June 1683*, pp.212, 257–8, 266, 272, 288, 322, *July–Sept 1683*, p. 9.
129 *CSPD Jan–June 1683*, pp. 250, 278, 286–7.
130 *CSPD July–Sept 1683*, pp. 9, 19, 130, 251, 278–9.
131 *Ibid.*, p. 358; Carte MS 222, fo. 322; Morrice, p. 362; *Mather*, p. 500.
132 Luttrell, I.230; Morrice, p. 340.
133 *CSPD 1683–84*, pp. 61–2.
134 S. Jeake, *An Astrological Diary of the Seventeenth Century*, (ed.) M. Hunter and A. Gregory, Oxford, 1987, pp. 156–9, 161.
135 *CSPD 1680–81*, p. 660.

136 Luttrell, I.91, 137; BL, Add MS 29558, fo. 276; Oates's Plot, 'Tuesday morning', 'M' to Mme Cellier, [17 May 1681].
137 *HMC Ormond*, NS VI.193, 199; *CSPD 1680–81*, pp. 496, 500.
138 Carte MS 222, fo. 313; *CSPD 1680–81*, pp. 305, 307, 321, 353, 370; *Strange News from Hicks's Hall*, 1681, pp. 1–3.
139 *CSPD 1680–81*, pp. 426, 507, 509–11, 517; Luttrell, I.119; *HMC Ormond*, NS VI.155, 212; M636/36, William Denton to Sir Ralph Verney, 7 and 10 November 1681.
140 BL, Add MS 29558, fo. 357.
141 *HMC Ormond*, NS VI.229, 236–7; *HMC Beaufort*, p. 87; BL, Add MS 29577, fo. 401; Morrice MS P, p. 318 Haley, *Shaftesbury*, pp. 675–83.
142 *CSPD 1682*, p. 82.
143 *CSPD 1680–81*, p. 353, *1682*, p. 347; Tanner MS 36, fo. 235.
144 Luttrell, I.199.
145 *CSPD 1680–81*, p. 670, *1682*, p. 321, *July–Sept 1683*, p. 204.
146 Mason, *Norfolk*, p. 367. See also the comment from Northumberland, *CSPD Jan–June 1683*, p. 72.
147 *CSPD 1680–81*, pp. 386, 422–3; BL, Add MS 29558, fo. 382.
148 *HMC Portland*, II.156, III.378.
149 Bodl, MS Eng Hist c 711, fos 5, 8, 9, 13, 18, 19, 22; *CSPD 1684–85*, p. 233.
150 Bodl, MS Eng Hist c 711, fos 5, 19.
151 M636/37, Sir Ralph to John Verney, 20 November, John to Sir Ralph, 27 November 1682.
152 *CSPD 1682*, p. 514; Morrice, p. 387.
153 *CSPD 1680–81*, p. 543; *A List of all the Conspirators*, 1683, copy in Egerton MS 2543, fo. 251. The reference in the first presentment to the Association suggests that the date given in *CSPD* (October 1681?) is a little early.
154 Morrice, p. 378.
155 *CSPD 1683–84*, pp. 200, 345, *1684–85*, p. 224; Brindle, 'Northants.', pp. 281–91.
156 *CSPD 1683–84*, p. 345; Havighurst, 'Judiciary', pp. 244–7.
157 Fuller accounts of the crown and the corporations can be found in Halliday, *Dismembering*, chs 4–6 and Miller, 'Charters', pp. 70–84.
158 Halliday, *Dismembering*, is based heavily on records of legal disputes and so inevitably emphasizes conflict rather than consensus.
159 Coventry MS 6, fo. 230. See also Tanner MSS 36, fo. 235, 36*, fo. 212.
160 BL, Add MS 25124, fos 71–2; Coventry MS 4, fos 408–9, 415–17; BRO, Common Council Proceedings 1670–87, fo. 79.
161 J. Latimer, *Annals of Bristol in the Seventeenth Century*, Bristol, 1900, pp. 383, 391–3; BCL, MS B10166, 'third calendar' under 25 April 1682; M. De L. Landon, 'The Bristol Artillery Company and the Tory Triumph in Bristol', *Proceedings of the American Philosophical Society*, CXIV, 1970, pp, 155–61; Barry in *Pol of Rel*, p. 178.
162 BCL, MS B10166, 'third calendar', under 11 September 1682; *CSPD 1682*, p. 392.
163 For examples, see C. Lee, '"Fanatic Magistrates": Religious and Political Conflict in three Kent Boroughs, 1680–4', *HJ*, XXXV, 1992, pp. 51–2; Scott, 'York', pp. 315–41.
164 Evans, *Norwich*, pp. 269–71; *HP*, I.238–9.
165 Lee, 'Magistrates', *passim*.

166 SP 44/68, p. 21; Lee, 'Magistrates', pp. 48, 59–60; Miller, 'Charters', pp. 80, 82 and *passim.*
167 Miller, 'Charters', pp. 81–4.
168 Wynne, *Jenkins,* II.684–5. For a valuable discussion of the legal issues, see Halliday, *Dismembering,* pp. 203–11.
169 See Miller, *Charles II,* pp. 368–72.
170 Halliday, *Dismembering,* pp. 212–20.
171 Evans, *Norwich,* pp. 281–96.
172 Halliday, *Dismembering,* pp. 224–7; Morrice MS P, pp. 435, 438–40.
173 Halliday, *Dismembering,* ch. 1 and *passim.*
174 Miller, 'Charters', pp. 69–84; Miller, *Charles II,* p. 372. Halliday sees the main 'policy' behind the new charters as a concern to improve urban justice: *Dismembering,* pp. 220–2.
175 Althorp MS C2, John Millington to Halifax, 23 March 1685; *CSPD 1685,* no. 149; *HMC Frankland-Russell-Astley,* p. 61; C. Hamilton, 'The Election of 1685 at Aylesbury', *PH,* XII (1993), p. 72.
176 *CSPD 1685,* nos 93–4; *HMC Leeds etc,* pp. 105–6; *HMC Rutland,* II.86–7.
177 Althorp MS C1, Newcastle to Halifax, 18 and 22 March, 13 and 20 April 1685; Althorp MS C2, John Millington to Halifax, 31 March and 21 April 1683, 18 and 23 March 1685.
178 Althorp MS C2, Millington to Halifax, 16 March, Althorp MS C1, Newcastle to Halifax, 18 March 1685.
179 *HMC Kenyon,* p. 179; Carte MS 50, fo. 357: *HP,* I.229–30.
180 Tanner MS 31, fo. 4; Granville, I.196.
181 *HMC Kenyon,* pp. 178–80; Arundell MSS, Box marked Bellings Letters, Sir John Arundell to Sir Richard Bellings, 9 March 1685.
182 Althorp MS C1, Plymouth to Halifax, 15 February 1685; *CSPD 1685,* no. 104.
183 *CSPD 1685,* nos 339, 410, 520.
184 Althorp MS C2, Millington to Halifax, 16 March 1685; *CSPD 1685,* nos 471, 475.
185 *HMC 5th Report,* p. 186; BL, Add MS 15949, fo. 2.
186 *HMC Frankland-Russell-Astley,* pp. 58–62.
187 Althorp MS C2, Millington to Halifax, 9 March 1685; *HMC 3rd Report,* p. 270.
188 *CSPD 1685,* nos 290, 366, 392; *HMC Dartmouth,* I.123; Rosen, 'Winchester', pp. 182–3; Coleby, *Hants.,* pp. 163, 218–19; *HP,* I.260.
189 Morrice, p. 457; *HMC Dartmouth,* I.124.
190 *Memoirs of the life of the . . . Marquess of Wharton,* 1715, pp. 28–30; *HMC Buccleuch (Montagu House),* I.341; *CSPD 1685,* nos 505, 510; *HP,* I.136–7.

Abbreviations

Ailesbury	T. Bruce, Earl of Ailesbury, *Memoirs*, (ed.) W.E. Buckley, 2 vols, Roxburgh Club, 1890
Althorp MSS	British Library, Althorp MSS
Arundell MSS	MSS of the Arundells of Wardour, in the possession of the Arundell family
Bax Corr	N. Keeble and G.F. Nuttall (eds), *Calendar of the Correspondence of Richard Baxter*, 2 vols, Oxford, 1991
BCL	Bristol Central Library, Reference Section
BIHR	*Bulletin of the Institute of Historical Research*
BL	British Library
Bodl	Bodleian Library
Bosher	R.S. Bosher, *The Making of the Restoration Settlement: The Influence of the Laudians 1649–62*, London, 1951
Bowman	Bodleian, MS Dep f 9 (Parliamentary diary of Seymour Bowman)
Bradfer	Norfolk Record Office, Bradfer-Lawrence MS Ic (Paston letters)
BRO	Bristol Record Office
Browne	Sir T. Browne, *Works*, (ed.) S. Wilkin, 4 vols, London, 1836
Browning, *Danby*	A. Browning, *Thomas Earl of Danby*, 3 vols, Glasgow, 1951
Browning, *Docts*	*English Historical Documents, 1660–1714*, (ed.) A. Browning, London, 1953
BT	Public Record Office, Baschet transcripts of French ambassadors' dispatches (PRO 31/3, cited by bundle and date)
Bulstrode	*Bulstrode Papers*, (ed.) E.W. Thibaudeau, London, 1897
Burnet, *Hist*	G. Burnet, *History of my own Time*, 6 vols, Oxford, 1823
Burnet, Letters	G. Burnet, 'Some Unpublished Letters', (ed.) H.C. Foxcroft, *Camden Miscellany*, XI, 1907
Burnet, *Suppl*	*Supplement to the History of my own time*, (ed.) H.C. Foxcroft, Oxford, 1902
Carte MSS	Bodleian Library, Carte MSS

CCSP	*Calendar of Clarendon State Papers*, 5 vols, Oxford, 1872–1970
CHJ	*Cambridge Historical Journal*
CJ	*Commons Journals*
CKS	Centre for Kentish Studies (formerly Kent Archives Office), Maidstone
Clar Corr	*Correspondence of Henry Hyde, Earl of Clarendon*, (ed.) S.W. Singer, 2 vols, London, 1828
Clar MSS	Bodleian Library, Clarendon MSS
Clarendon	E. Hyde, Earl of Clarendon, *Life*, 3 vols, Oxford, 1827
Clarke	J.S. Clarke (ed.), *Life of James II*, 2 vols, London, 1816
Cosin	*Cosin Correspondence*, (ed.) G. Ornsby, 2 vols, Surtees Soc., 1872
Coventry MSS	Longleat, Coventry MSS (consulted on microfilm)
CPA	Archives des Affaires Etrangères, Paris, Correspondance Politique, Angleterre (cited by volume and date)
CSP	*State Papers collected by Edward Earl of Clarendon*, 3 vols, Oxford, 1767–86
CSPD	*Calendar of State Papers Domestic*
CSPI	*Calendar of State Papers Ireland*
CSPV	*Calendar of State Papers Venetian* (typescript continuation for 1676–78, PRO, E/M/21/58)
CUL	Cambridge University Library
Davies	*An Account of the Convincement of Richard Davies*, London, 1771
DCLD	Dean and Chapter Library, Durham
Dering, *Diary*	Sir E. Dering, *Parliamentary Diary*, (ed.) B.D. Henning, New Haven, 1940
Dering, *Papers*	Sir E. Dering, *Diaries and Papers*, (ed.) M.F. Bond, London, 1976
DNB	*Dictionary of National Biography*
DUL	Durham University Library
Egerton MSS	British Library, Egerton MSS
EconHR	*Economic History Review*
EHR	*English Historical Review*
Essex	*Essex Papers*, vol. I, (ed.) O. Airy, vol. II, (ed.) C.E. Pike, Camden Soc., 1890, 1913
Evelyn	J. Evelyn, *Diary*, (ed.) E.S. de Beer, 6 vols, London, 1955
FAB	NRO, Case 16d, Norwich Folio Assembly Books
Finch MSS	Leicestershire Record Office, Finch MSS (DG 7)
FSL	Folger Shakespeare Library, Washington DC
From Unif	G. Nuttall and O. Chadwick (eds), *From Uniformity to Unity, 1662–1962*, London, 1962
Granville	D. Granville, *Remains*, (ed.) G. Ornsby, Surtees Soc., XXXVII (1861) and LXVII (1867) (Part I is included in *Miscellanea* I, but paginated separately)

Green I.M. Green, *The Re-establishment of the Church of England, 1660–3*, Oxford, 1978

Grey A. Grey, *Debates in the House of Commons, 1667–94*, 10 vols, London, 1769

Harl MSS British Library, Harleian MSS

Hatton *Hatton Correspondence*, (ed.) E.M. Thompson, 2 vols, Camden Soc., 1878

HEI *History of European Ideas*

Henry P. Henry, *Diaries and Letters*, (ed.) H.M Lee, London, 1882

Heywood O. Heywood, *Autobiographies, Diaries, Anecdotes and Event Books*, (ed.) J. Horsfall Turner, 4 vols, Brighouse, 1882–85

HJ *Historical Journal*

HLQ *Huntington Library Quarterly*

HLRO House of Lords Record Office

HMC *Historical Manuscripts Commission Reports*

Hodgson J.C. Hodgson (ed.), *Northumbrian Documents of the Seventeenth and Eighteenth Centuries*, Surtees Soc., 1918

HP *History of Parliament: The Commons 1660–90*, (ed.) B.D. Henning, 3 vols, London, 1983

Isham T. Isham, *Diary*, (ed.) G. Isham, Farnborough, 1971

JBS *Journal of British Studies*

JEH *Journal of Ecclesiastical History*

Josselin R. Josselin, *Diary*, (ed.) A. Macfarlane, Oxford, 1976

JRL John Rylands Library, Manchester

Lauderdale *Lauderdale Papers*, (ed.) O. Airy, 3 vols, Camden Soc., 1884–85

Lawrence W. Lawrence, *Diary*, (ed.) G.E. Aylmer, Beaminster, 1961

Lister T.H. Lister, *Life and Administration of Clarendon*, 3 vols, London, 1837–38

LJ *Lords Journals*

LPL Lambeth Palace Library

Luttrell N. Luttrell, *A Brief Historical Relation of State Affairs 1660–1714*, 6 vols, Oxford, 1857

M636 British Library, microfilms of Verney MSS

Macpherson J. Macpherson, *Original Papers containing the Secret History of Great Britain*, 2 vols, 1775

Mapperton Mapperton House, Dorset (Sandwich MSS)

Martindale *The Life of Adam Martindale, written by himself*, (ed.) R. Parkinson, Chetham Soc., IV, 1845

Marvell A. Marvell, *Poems and Letters*, (ed.) H.M. Margoliouth, rev. E. Duncan Jones, 3rd edn, 2 vols, Oxford, 1971

Mather *Mather Papers*, Collections of the Massachusetts Hist. Soc., 4th series, VIII, 1868

MCB	NRO, Case 16a, Norwich Mayor's Court Books
Milward	J. Milward, *Diary*, (ed.) C. Robbins, Cambridge, 1938
Morrice	Dr Williams' Library, MS 31P, Roger Morrice's Entering Book. vol. I
Morrill, *Nature*	J.S. Morrill, *The Nature of the English Revolution*, London, 1993
Morrison	*Autograph Letters in the Collection of Alfred Morrison*, (ed.), E.W. Thibaudeau, 1st series, 6 vols, 2nd series, 3 vols, London, 1883–96
Newdigate	Lady Newdigate-Newdegate, *Cavalier and Puritan in the Days of the Stuarts*, London, 1901
NLI	National Library of Ireland
Norf Arch	*Norfolk Archaeology*
Norths	R. North, *Lives of the Norths*, (ed.) A. Jessopp, 3 vols, London, 1890
NRO	Norfolk Record Office, Norwich
NRS	Norfolk Record Society
NS	New series or (of dates) New style
'Oates's Plot'	Warwicks RO, CR 1998, 'Large Carved Box', item 17, unfoliated volume entitled 'Titus Oates's Plot'
OPH	*Old Parliamentary History*, 23 vols, London, 1751–61
P & P	*Past and Present*
PC 2	Public Record Office, Privy Council Registers
Pepys	S. Pepys, *Diary*, (ed.) R.C. Latham and W. Matthews, 11 vols, London, 1971–83
Pepys, *Further*	S. Pepys, *Further Correspondence*, (ed.) J.R. Tanner, London, 1929
Pepys Lib	Magdalene College, Cambridge, Pepys Library
Pforz	University of Texas at Austin, Humanities Research Centre, Pforzheimer MS 103c, vol. IX (Bulstrode newsletters)
PH	*Parliamentary History*
POAS	*Poems on Affairs of State*, I (ed.) G. de F. Lord, II (ed.) L.F. Mengel, jnr, New Haven, 1963, 1965
Pol Of Rel	T. Harris, M. Goldie and P. Seaward (eds), *The Politics of Religion in Restoration England*, Oxford, 1990
Prinsterer	G. Groen van Prinsterer, *Archives de la Maison Orange Nassau*, 2nd series, 5 vols, The Hague, 1858–61
PRO	Public Record Office
Rawdon	*Rawdon Papers*, (ed.) E. Berwick, 1819
Rawl MSS	Bodleian Library, Rawlinson MSS
Raynham, Corr	Raynham Hall, Norfolk, Boxfile 'Horatio, 1st Viscount, Misc. Correspondence, etc. 1650s–1687'
Raynham, Holland	Raynham Hall, Boxfile '1st Viscount Townshend, T. Felton, etc', folder 'Correspondence with Sir John Holland'

Raynham, SP	Raynham Hall, Boxfile '1st Viscount Townshend, T. Felton etc', blue folder 'State Papers'
RB	*Reliquiae Baxterianae*, (ed.) M. Sylvester, London, 1696 (Book I, Part I, Book I, Part II and Part III cited as I, II and III respectively)
Reresby	Sir John Reresby, *Memoirs*, (ed.) A. Browning, revised by M.K. Geiter and W.A. Speck, London, 1991
RO	Record Office
Rugg	T. Rugg, *Diurnal*, (ed.) W.L. Sachse, Camden Soc., 1961
Savile	*Savile Correspondence*, (ed.) W.D. Cooper, Camden Soc., 1858
Schellinks	W. Schellinks, *Journal of Travels in England, 1661–3*, (ed.) M. Exwood and H.L. Lehmann, Camden Soc., 1993
Seaward	P. Seaward, *The Cavalier Parliament and the Reconstruction of the Old Regime, 1661–67*, Cambridge, 1989
Somers Tracts	*Somers Tracts*, (ed.) Sir W. Scott, 13 vols, London, 1809–15
SP	Public Record Office, State Papers
SR	*Statutes of the Realm*
State Tracts	*State Tracts*, 2 vols, 1689–92
State Trials	*State Trials*, (ed.) W. Cobbett and T.B. Howell, 33 vols, London, 1809–26
Stowe MSS	British Library, Stowe MSS
Strong	S.A. Strong, *A Catalogue of Letters and other Historical Documents at Welbeck*, London, 1903
Tanner MSS	Bodleian Library, Tanner MSS
THSLC	Transactions of the Historical Society of Lancashire and Cheshire
TRHS	*Transactions of the Royal Historical Society*
UCL	University of Chicago Library
Whitelocke	B. Whitelocke, *Diary*, (ed.) R. Spalding, Oxford, 1990
Williamson	*Letters addressed from London to Sir Joseph Williamson, 1673–74*, (ed.) W.D. Christie, 2 vols, Camden Soc., 1874
Wing	D. Wing *et al.*, *Short-title Catalogue, 1640–1700*, 3 vols
Wood	A. Wood, *Life and Times*, (ed.) A. Clark, 5 vols, Oxford Hist. Soc., 1891–1900
WSL	William Salt Library, Stafford
WYAL	West Yorkshire Archives, Leeds

Select bibliography

(*Not including items entered under 'Abbreviations'*)

Allen, D.F., 'Political clubs in Restoration London', *HJ*, XIX, 1976
Aubrey, J., *Brief Lives*, (ed.) O. Lawson Dick, Harmondsworth, 1962
Beddard, R., 'The Commission for Ecclesiastical Promotions, 1681–84: An Instrument of Tory Reaction', *HJ*, X, 1967
Beddard, R., 'The Restoration Church' in J.R. Jones (ed.), *The Restored Monarchy*, London, 1979
Blomefield, F., *An essay towards a topographical history of Norfolk*, 11 vols, London, 1805–10
Bolam, C.G., Goring, J., Short, H.L. and Thomas, R., *The English Presbyterians from Elizabethan Puritanism to Modern Unitarianism*, London, 1968
Borsay, P., *The English Urban Renaissance: Culture and society in the English town, 1660–1770*, Oxford 1989
Braddick, M.J., *The Nerves of State: Taxation and the Financing of the English State, 1558–1714*, Manchester, 1996
Braddick, M.J., *Parliamentary taxation in seventeenth-century England*, Woodbridge, 1994
Braddick, M.J., 'State formation and social change in early modern England', *Social History*, XVI, 1991
Bramston, Sir John, *Autobiography*, (ed.) Lord Braybrooke, Camden Soc., 1845
Brewer, J. and Styles, J. (eds), *An Ungovernable People? The English and their Law in the Seventeenth and Eighteenth Centuries*, London, 1980
Brindle, P.R., 'Politics and Society in Northamptonshire, 1649–1714', unpublished Ph.D. thesis, Leicester, 1983
Browning, A., 'Parties and Party Organisation in the Reign of Charles II', *TRHS* 4th series XXX, 1948
Carter, D.P., 'The Lancashire Militia, 1660–88', THSLC CXXXII, 1983 for 1982
Challinor, P.J., 'The structure of politics in Cheshire, 1660–1715', unpublished Ph.D. thesis, Wolverhampton, 1983
Chandaman, C.D., *The English Public Revenue, 1660–88*, Oxford, 1975
Childs, J., *The Army of Charles II*, London, 1976
Christie, W.D., *Life of Shaftesbury*, 2 vols, London, 1871
Clark, R., 'Why was the re-establishment of the Church of England possible? Derbyshire, a provincial perspective', *Midland History*, VIII, 1983
Clay, C., *Public finance and private wealth: the career of Sir Stephen Fox*, Oxford, 1978
Cliffe, J.T., *The Puritan Gentry Besieged, 1650–1700*, London, 1993
Clifton, R., *The Last Popular Rebellion: The Western Rising of 1685*, London, 1984

Clifton, R., 'The Popular Fear of Catholics in the English Revolution', *P & P*, no. 52, 1971
Coleby, A.M., *Central Government and the Localities: Hampshire 1649–89*, Cambridge, 1987
Comber, T., *Autobiography and Letters,* (ed.) C.E. Whiting, Surtees Soc., CLVI–CLVII, 1946–7
Cooper, C.H., *Annals of Cambridge,* 4 vols, Cambridge, 1842–52; fifth vol. by J.W. Cooper, 1908
Corie, T., *Correspondence,* (ed.) R.H. Hill, NRS, XXVII, 1956
Coward, B., 'The Social and political position of the Earls of Derby in later seventeenth-century Lancashire', *THSLC,* CXXXII, 1983 for 1982
Coward, B., *The Stanleys, Lords Stanley and Earls of Derby, 1385–1672,* Chetham Soc., 1983
Cozens-Hardy, B. (ed.), *Norfolk Lieutenancy Journal, 1676–1701,* NRS, XXX, 1961
Cressy, D., *Bonfires and Bells: National Memory and the Protestant Calendar in Elizabethan and Stuart England,* London, 1989
Crist, T.J., 'Francis Smith and the opposition press in England, 1660–88', unpublished Ph.D. thesis, Cambridge, 1977
Crist, T.J., 'Government control of the press after the expiration of the Printing Act in 1679', *Publishing History,* V, 1979
Cust, R., 'News and Politics in Early Seventeenth-century England', *P & P*, no. 112, 1986
Dineley, T., *The Account of the Official Progress of the First Duke of Beaufort through Wales in 1684,* London, 1888
Duffy, E., 'The Long Reformation: Catholicism, Protestantism and the Multitude' in N. Tyacke (ed.), *England's Long Reformation*, London, 1998
Dunn, R.M. (ed.), *Norfolk Lieutenancy Journal, 1660–76,* NRS, XLV, 1977
Evans, J.T., *Seventeenth-century Norwich: Politics, religion and government, 1620–90,* Oxford, 1979
Feiling, K.G., *History of the Tory Party, 1640–1714,* Oxford, 1924
Fincham, K. (ed.), *The Early Stuart Church, 1603–42,* London, 1993
Fletcher, A., *A county community in peace and war: Sussex 1600–60,* London, 1975
Fletcher, A., *Reform in the Provinces: The government of Stuart England,* New Haven, 1986
Forster, G.C.F., 'Government in provincial England under the later Stuarts', *TRHS,* 5th series, XXXIII, 1983
Fraser, P., *The Intelligence of the Secretaries of State and their Monopoly of Licensed News,* Cambridge, 1956
Gauci, P., *Politics and Society in Great Yarmouth, 1660–1722,* Oxford, 1996
Glassey, L.K.J., *Politics and the Appointment of Justices of the Peace, 1675–1720,* Oxford, 1979
Glassey, L.K.J. (ed.), *The Reigns of Charles II and James VII and II,* London, 1997
Glines, T., 'Politics and society in the borough of Colchester, 1660–93', unpublished Ph.D. thesis, Wisconsin, 1974
Goldie, M.A., 'John Locke and Anglican Royalism', *Political Studies,* XXXI, 1983
Goldie, M.A., 'Priestcraft and the birth of Whiggism' in N. Phillipson and Q. Skinner (eds), *Political Discourse in early modern England,* Cambridge, 1993
Goldie, M.A., 'The theory of religious intolerance in Restoration England' in O.P. Grell, J.I. Israel and N. Tyacke (eds), *From Persecution to Toleration: The Glorious Revolution and Religion in England,* Oxford, 1991

Greaves, R.L., *Secrets of the Kingdom: British Radicals from the Popish Plot to the Revolution of 1688–89*, Stanford, 1992
Griffiths, P., Fox, A. and Hindle, S. (eds), *The experience of authority in early modern England*, London, 1996
Haley, K.H.D, *The First Earl of Shaftesbury*, Oxford, 1968
Halifax, G. Savile, Marquis of, *Complete Works*, (ed.), J.P. Kenyon, Harmondsworth, 1969
Halliday, P.D., *Dismembering the Body Politic: Partisan politics in England's Towns, 1650–1730*, Cambridge, 1998
Hamburger, P., 'The development of the law of seditious libel and the control of the press', *Stanford Law Review*, XXXVII, Feb. 1985
Harris, F.R., *Life of Edward Montagu, first Earl of Sandwich*, 2 vols, London, 1912
Harris, T., 'The Bawdy-House Riots of 1668', *HJ*, XXIX, 1986
Harris, T., *London Crowds in the Reign of Charles II*, Cambridge, 1987
Harris, T., *Politics under the later Stuarts: Party conflict in a divided society, 1660–1714*, Harlow, 1993
Harris, T., 'The Tories and the rule of law in the reign of Charles II', *Seventeenth Century*, VIII, 1993
Harris, T., 'Was the Tory reaction popular? Attitudes of Londoners towards the prosecution of Dissent, 1681–6', *London Journal*, 1987–8
Hartmann, C.H., *Charles II and Madame*, London, 1934
Havighurst, A.F., 'The Judiciary and Politics in the Reign of Charles II', *Law Quarterly Review*, LXVI, 1950
Hirst, D., 'The Failure of Godly Rule in the English Republic', *P & P*, no. 132, 1991
Hirst, D., *The Representative of the People? Voters and Voting in England under the Early Stuarts*, Cambridge, 1975
Horle, C.W., *The Quakers and the English Legal System, 1660–88*, Philadelphia, 1988
Hughes, A., *Politics, society and Civil War in Warwickshire, 1620–60*, Cambridge, 1987
Hughes, A., 'The Frustrations of the Godly' in J.S. Morrill (ed.), *Revolution and Restoration*, London, 1992
Hutton, R., *The Restoration, 1658–67*, Oxford, 1985
James, M.E., *Society, Politics and Culture: Studies in early modern England*, Cambridge, 1986
Jenkins, G.H., *The Foundations of Modern Wales, 1642–1780*, Oxford, 1987
Jeremiah, J.J., 'Edward Reynolds, 1599–1676, "Pride of the Presbyterian Party"', unpublished Ph.D. thesis, George Washington University, 1992
Jones, J.R., *The First Whigs: The politics of the Exclusion Crisis, 1678–83*, Oxford, 1961
Kent, J., 'The centre and the localities: state formation and parish government, 1640–1740', *HJ*, XXXIX, 1996
Kenyon, J.P., *The Popish Plot*, 1972
Kenyon, J.P., *Robert Spencer, Earl of Sunderland*, London, 1958
Kenyon, J.P., *The Stuart Constitution*, 1st edn, Cambridge, 1966, 2nd edn, Cambridge, 1986
Ketton-Cremer, R.W., *Norfolk Portraits*, London, 1944
Key, N.E. 'Political Culture and Political Rhetoric in County Feasts and Feast Sermons, 1654–1714', *JBS*, XXXIII, 1994
Kishlansky, M.A., *Parliamentary Selection: Social and Political Choice in Early Modern England*, Cambridge, 1986

Knights, M., *Politics and Opinion in Crisis, 1678–81*, Cambridge, 1994
Landau, N., *The Justices of the Peace, 1679–1760*, Berkeley, 1984
Lee, C, '"Fanatic magistrates": Religious and political conflict in three Kent boroughs, 1680–4', *HJ*, XXXV, 1992
Leicester, Sir P., *Charges to the Grand Jury at Quarter Sessions, 1660–77*, (ed.) E.M. Halcrow, Chetham Soc., 1953
Ludlow, E., *A Voyce from the Watchtower*, (ed.) B. Worden, Camden Soc., 1978
Malcolm, J.L., 'Charles II and the reconstruction of royal power', *HJ*, XXXV, 1992
Marlowe, N., 'Government and politics in West Country incorporated boroughs, 1642–62', unpublished Ph.D. thesis, Cambridge, 1985
Marshall, A., *Intelligence and Espionage in the Reign of Charles II*, Cambridge, 1994
Marvell, A., *An Account of the Growth of Popery and Arbitrary Government*, London, 1678
Mason, R.H., *History of Norfolk*, London, 1884
McClain, M.A., '"I scorn to change or fear": Henry Somerset, first Duke of Beaufort and the survival of the nobility following the English Civil War', unpublished Ph.D. thesis, Yale, 1994
Miller, J., *Charles II*, London, 1991
Miller, J., 'Charles II and his Parliaments', *TRHS*, 5th Series, XXXII, 1982
Miller, J., 'The Crown and the Borough Charters in the Reign of Charles II', *EHR*, C, 1985
Miller, J., 'A Moderate in the first age of Party: The dilemmas of Sir John Holland, 1675–85', *EHR*, CXIV, 1999
Miller, J., *Popery and Politics in England, 1660–88*, London, 1973
Moore, J.S. and Smith, R. (eds), *The House of Lords*, London, 1994
Morrill, J.S., *Cheshire, 1630–60*, Oxford, 1974
Muddiman, J.G., *The King's Journalist*, London, 1923
Muldrew, C., 'The culture of reconciliation and the settlement of economic disputes in early modern England', *HJ*, XXXIX, 1996
Newcome, H., *Autobiography* (ed.), R. Parkinson, Chetham Soc., XXVI–XXVII, 1852
Newcome, H., *Diary 1661–63* (ed.), T. Heywood, Chetham Soc., XVIII, 1849
Newton, E., *The House of Lyme*, London, 1917
Norrey, P.J., 'The Restoration regime in action: The relationship between central and local government in Dorset, Somerset and Wiltshire', *HJ*, XXXI, 1988
North, R., *Examen*, London, 1740
Palmer, W.M., 'The Reformation of the Corporation of Cambridge, July 1662', *Proceedings of the Cambridge Antiquarian Society*, XVII, 1913
Pocock, J.G.A., *The Ancient Constitution and the Feudal Law*, Cambridge, 1987
Prideaux, H., *Letters to John Ellis*, (ed.) E.M. Thompson, Camden Soc., 1875
Pruett, J., *The Parish Clergy under the Later Stuarts: The Leicestershire Experience*, Urbana, 1978
Ramsbottom, J.D., 'Presbyterians and "Partial Conformity" in the Restoration Church', *JEH*, XLIII, 1992
Robbins, C., 'Electoral Correspondence of Sir John Holland, 1661', *Norf. Arch.*, XXX, 1947–52
Robbins, C., 'The Oxford session of the Long Parliament of Charles II, 9 to 31 October 1665', *BIHR*, XXI, 1946–8.
Roberts, S.K., 'Public or Private? Revenge and Recovery in the Restoration of Charles II', *BIHR*, LIX, 1986

Roberts, S.K., *Recovery and Restoration in an English County: Devon Local Administration, 1646–70*, Exeter, 1985
Robinson, J.M., *The Dukes of Norfolk*, Oxford, 1982
Rochester, J. Wilmot, Earl of, *Letters*, (ed.) J. Treglown, Oxford, 1980
Rosen, A., 'Winchester in Transition, 1580–1700' in P. Clark (ed.), *Country Towns in Pre-industrial England*, Leicester, 1981
Rosenheim, J.M., 'An examination of oligarchy: the gentry of Restoration Norfolk', unpublished Ph.D. thesis, Princeton, 1981
Rosenheim, J.M., *The Townshends of Raynham*, Middletown, CT, 1989
Roseveare, H., *The Treasury 1660–1870: The Foundations of Control*, London, 1973
Rye, W. (ed.), *Depositions before the Mayor and Aldermen of Norwich and Extracts from the Court Books*, Norfolk and Norwich Archaeological Society, 1905
Schilling, W.A.H., 'The central government and the municipal corporations in England, 1642–63', unpublished Ph.D. thesis, Vanderbilt, 1970
Scott, D.A., 'Politics, Dissent and Quakerism in York, 1640–1700', unpublished D.Phil. thesis, York, 1990
Scott, J., *Algernon Sidney and the Restoration Crisis, 1677–83*, Cambridge, 1991
Shoemaker, R.B., *Prosecution and Punishment: petty crime and the law in London and rural Middlesex, c 1660–1725*, Cambridge, 1991
Sommerville, C.J., *The News Revolution in England*, New York, 1996
Sorbière, S., *Relation d'un voyage en Angleterre*, (ed.) L. Roux, St Etienne, 1980
Spufford, M., *Small Books and Pleasant Histories: Popular Fiction and its Readership in Seventeenth-century England*, London, 1981
Spufford, M. (ed.), *The World of Rural Dissenters, 1520–1725*, Cambridge, 1995
Spurr, J., 'The Church of England, Comprehension and the Toleration Act of 1689', *EHR*, CIV, 1989
Spurr, J., *English Puritanism, 1603–89*, London, 1998
Spurr, J., 'Perjury, profanity and politics', *Seventeenth Century*, VIII, 1993
Spurr, J., *The Restoration Church of England, 1646–89*, New Haven, 1991
Spurr, J., 'Schism and the Restoration Church', *JEH*, XLI, 1990
Stater, V., *Noble Government: the Stuart lord lieutenancy and the transformation of English Politics*, Athens, GA, 1994
Steele, R., *Tudor and Stuart Proclamations I. England and Wales*, Bibliotheca Lindesiana, Oxford, 1910
Stocks, H. and Stevenson, W.H. (eds), *Records of the Borough of Leicester, IV. 1603–88*, Cambridge, 1923
Stone, L., *The Crisis of the Aristocracy, 1558–1641*, Oxford, 1965
Stoyle, M., *Loyalty and Locality: Popular Allegiance in Devon during the English Civil War*, Exeter, 1994
Swatland, A., *The House of Lords in the Reign of Charles II*, Cambridge, 1996
Sykes, N., *From Sheldon to Secker*, Cambridge, 1959
Temple, Sir W., *Works*, 2 vols, 1731
Thomson, A., 'Hertfordshire communities and central-local relations, c. 1625–c. 1665', unpublished Ph.D. thesis, London, 1988
Townshend, H., *Diary*, (ed.) J.W. Willis Bund, 2 vols, Worcestershire Hist. Soc., 1920
Tyacke, N. (ed.), *England's Long Reformation, 1500–1800*, London, 1998
Underdown, D., *A Freeborn People: Politics and the Nation in Seventeenth-century England*, Oxford, 1996

Underdown, D., *Revel, riot and rebellion: popular politics and culture in England, 1603–60*, Oxford, 1985
Watts, M.R., *The Dissenters, from the Reformation to the French Revolution*, Oxford, 1978
Whiteman, A. (ed.), *The Compton Census of 1676*, London, 1986
Witcombe, D.T., *Charles II and the Cavalier House of Commons, 1663–74*, Manchester, 1966
Wright, S.J. (ed.), *Parish, Church and People: Local studies in lay religion, 1350–1750*, London, 1988
Wynne, W., *Life of Sir Leoline Jenkins*, 2 vols, London, 1724

Glossary

(Where a word in the text is given in bold, it indicates that there is an entry under that word.)

Adjournment Procedure by which the king brought a parliamentary session to an end, without annulling proceedings on bills already under consideration [see also **prorogation**].

Advowson The right to nominate the clergymen of a parish, often owned by a layman.

Alderman In many towns (including London) the upper tier of the corporation, comprising its more senior members, from whom the mayor was usually chosen. Aldermen generally played a major role in the town's law courts and administration.

Arminian Strictly speaking, a follower of the Dutch theologian, Arminius, who challenged strict Calvinist views on predestination. Often (in England) extended to mean those who, like Laud, advocated a greater measure of ceremonial and visual beauty in worship.

Assizes The top law courts held in each county, which dealt with the more serious civil and criminal cases, with judges (or **serjeants**) from London presiding. The assizes were usually held in the county town, but other towns often competed to host them, because of the business they brought.

Benefice An ecclesiastical living, usually a parish, held by an ordained clergyman [see **ordination**].

Burgess This term has several meanings, all relating to boroughs: a member of Parliament for a borough constituency, or a member of a borough corporation, or an inhabitant of a borough possessing full political and trading rights (i.e., a freeman).

Chapter The governing body of a cathedral, who also administered its landed property, normally headed by a dean.

Charter A solemn legal document, usually granted by the crown, conferring on a town or other corporate body (such as a guild or charity) the right to function as a 'body politic', which could involve holding property, levying rates and making by-laws. Once granted, charters could normally be revoked only for failure to respect the conditions of the grant [see ***quo warranto***].

Churchwarden Parish officials, usually elected, who were responsible for the upkeep of the church and churchyard and answerable to episcopal **visitations**. They also 'presented' a wide range of offences to the church courts and sometimes had responsibility for poor relief.

Classis (plural classes) In a presbyterian system of church government, an assembly of the pastors and elders of the parishes of a district.

Commission of the peace The document through which the monarch conferred on the justices of the peace of a county the power to act as magistrates; by extension, the justices themselves.

Compounding The practice of paying less than the full amount for a fine or tax payment, usually following a process of negotiation.

Conventicle An unauthorized nonconformist religious meeting.

Covenant A national agreement in Scotland from 1638, whereby all adult male Protestants undertook to preserve the Scottish church without bishops. Under the terms of the Solemn League and Covenant of 1643, the Scots agreed to assist the English Parliament against the king and Parliament agreed to reform the English Church 'according to the Word of God and the example of the best Reformed Churches'. All office-holders and clergymen in England were required to subscribe the Covenant; at the Restoration, clergymen and many office-holders were required to renounce it.

Curate A clergymen who ministered to a parish on behalf of either another clergyman, who had another **benefice** elsewhere, or a layman who owned the right to collect the tithes [see **impropriation**].

Deputy lieutenants Commanded and organized the county militia, under the **lord lieutenant**. They were usually nominated by the lord lieutenant and received commissions from the king; Charles II reserved the right to reject nominations, but rarely did.

Dissolution The procedure by which a Parliament was brought to an end; a general election had to be held before another could be called.

Distraint/distress Confiscating goods or animals, for sale in lieu of unpaid fines.

Engagement Oath imposed in 1650, on all adult males, to be loyal to the government as established, without a king or House of Lords. It was required especially of office-holders and the parish clergy.

Eucharist That part of Christian services in which those present took bread and wine, as in the Last Supper. Also known as the Lord's supper and holy communion.

Farming (of taxes.) The practice of contracting out areas of tax collection to syndicates, who paid an agreed price to the crown and kept the net receipts above that figure as profit.

Grand juries At quarter sessions and assizes, these drew up 'presentments' of what they judged to be amiss in the county and also heard the evidence for the prosecution in criminal cases and decided whether there was a case to answer (*billa vera*) or not (***ignoramus***).

House of correction (or Bridewell) An institution in which 'loose, idle and disorderly' persons were to be punished, usually with a whipping and a spell of hard labour. Houses of correction were in theory distinguished from workhouses by the element of punishment; in practice, the distinction was often unclear.

Ignoramus See **grand juries**.

Impropriation The practice whereby the tithe of a parish was paid to someone other than the **incumbent**, often a layman. It had become common when monastic rights to tithe had been sold off under Henry VIII.

Incumbent The holder of an ecclesiastical **benefice**, usually a parish.

Justice of the peace Magistrate, who combined judicial and administrative functions: in the counties, chosen and commissioned by the crown. In many towns, certain officers (usually the mayor and some senior aldermen) had the right to act as magistrates, though not necessarily with the same powers as county justices, who could often (but not always) act within the borough to deal with certain types of case.

Knight of the shire Member of Parliament for a county.

Lecturer Unbeneficed, but ordained clergyman, who could be licensed to preach occasional sermons in town churches, or else to minister in a chapel in a large parish.

Lord chancellor (or lord keeper) Traditionally the most important office under the crown (the title varied, the duties did not: the former was the more prestigious). Its holder controlled the great seal, still used to authenticate charters, commissions, grants etc., but was also the crown's senior law officer and Speaker of the House of Lords and presided over the court of Chancery.

Lord lieutenant Acted on the king's behalf in a particular area. In the counties, he commanded the militia and more generally supervized county government. In Ireland, the lord lieutenant (or lord deputy) was the king's viceroy – commander-in-chief of the army and head of the government.

Mandamus Writ issued by the Court of King's Bench ordering some specific action, such as the reinstatement of a person removed from a borough corporation.

Ordination Admission of a clergyman to the ministry, after an examination of his suitability in terms of learning and character. In the Church of England, ministers were ordained by a bishop in a ceremony which included the laying on of hands. **Presbyterian** ordination followed examination of the ordinand by a group of 'presbyters' (fellow-pastors).

Overseer of the poor Parish officer, responsible for the raising of the poor rate and the payment of poor relief.

Oyer and terminer Commission to 'hear and determine' certain types of legal case. Issued routinely to judges going out 'on circuit' to county **assizes** and exceptionally to select groups in cases where it might be expected that the regular authorities might not administer effective justice.

Presbyterian Used in a political sense to describe moderate Parliamentarians, who had favoured a settlement with the king in 1648, deplored the regicide and favoured the restoration of monarchy in 1660. In a religious sense, it was used of those who favoured a puritan, parish-based national church, hostile to 'unscriptural' ceremonies and (if not wholly opposed to episcopacy) to 'prelates' who harassed nonconformist clergy and required the use of ceremonies. After 1662 the term was used to describe 'church-puritan' clergy who would not comply with the terms of the Act of Uniformity.

Prorogation Procedure by which a parliamentary session was brought to an end, leaving the Parliament in being, but aborting all bills and other proceedings currently under consideration in either House [see **adjournment**].

Quarter sessions Meetings of county justices of the peace, held four times a year, to deal with administrative business and (usually) less serious criminal cases than those heard at the **assizes**. In many counties, the sessions rotated between several towns in the course of the year.

Quo warranto A legal writ, demanding that a person or body show 'by what right' they exercised certain powers. Used especially in the 1680s to persuade boroughs' corporations to surrender their **charters**.

Recognizance Legal bond, required by a court or magistrate, to keep the peace, appear in court or fulfil some other obligation, on pain of forfeiting a specified sum of money.

Recorder A magistrate or judge in a borough, usually its chief legal officer; often a professional lawyer, but sometimes a local aristocrat, with a lawyer acting as his deputy.

Recusancy Refusal to attend church, which rendered a person liable to a fine. Used generally of Roman Catholics (popish recusants), but laws originally passed to force Catholics to attend Protestant services were sometimes used against Protestant Dissenters as well.

Sacerdotal Derived from the Latin for 'priest', the term implies a heavy emphasis on priestly characteristics: the spiritual authority said to derive from **ordination** and more particularly in the celebration of the **eucharist** [see also **transubstantiation**].

Sequestration Confiscation: used particularly of the lands of the Royalists, during and after the first Civil War. Many were later allowed to **compound** and regain their lands.

Serjeant (at law) Superior body of barristers, from whom judges were chosen.

Surplice A white gown, which Church of England clergymen were required to wear, much disliked by puritans.

Transubstantiation Belief that in the **eucharist** the bread and wine turned physically into the body and blood of Christ. Fully held by the Catholic church; many Protestants believed in some sort of spiritual change, but not a change of physical substance.

Vestry Ruling council of a parish, so called after the room where it usually met. Some were democratically elected, others were 'select', effectively filling vacancies by co-option.

Visitation Tour of a diocese (or part of it) by a bishop or his deputy, designed to check on the proper functioning of the parishes. **Churchwardens** were required to answer questions on a range of issues, ranging from the church fabric and the conduct of services to moral offences within the parish.

Index

advowsons, 177–8, 179, 180
Albemarle, Duke of, *see* Monk, George and Monk, Christopher
Alford, Captain Gregory, 281, 282
allegiance, oath of, 14, 118, 172, 207, 235, 282, 283
ancient constitution, 111–15, 119, 122–3, 225, 226, 253
Anderton, Matthew, 275, 276
Anglesey, Earl of, *see* Annesley, Arthur
Annesley, Arthur, Earl of Anglesey, 42, 144, 150, 164, 180, 197, 199, 211, 220, 221, 255, 278, 281
anti-popery, 75–6, 115–18, 123, 129, 210, 217–19, 227, 253
Arderne, James, 276, 280
Arlington, Earl of, *see* Bennet, Henry
'Arminians', *see* 'Laudians'
army, 26–8, 30, 81, 89–90, 102, 106, 113, 120, 161–2, 163, 169–70, 195, 249–52, 276
Ashburnham, John, 41, 46, 90, 184
Ashley Cooper, Anthony, Lord Ashley and Earl of Shaftesbury, 21, 42, 56, 73, 79, 82, 121, 196, 197, 201, 209, 210, 217, 222, 233, 236, 254, 264, 273, 283–5
'Association', 273, 283, 288

Baptists, 131–2, 142, 144–5, 146, 183–4, 186, 219
Barlow, William, 280, 281
Barnardiston, Sir Samuel, 42, 227–8, 236
Bath, Earl of, *see* Granville, John
Baxter, Richard, 134, 136, 138, 142, 143–4, 145, 146, 174, 175, 176, 178, 204, 208, 272, 283
Beaufort, Duke of, *see* Somerset, Henry
Bellasis, John Lord, 101, 186
Bellasis, Thomas, Viscount Fauconberg, 289
Bennet, (Sir) Henry, Earl of Arlington, 37, 40, 55, 61, 89, 195, 198, 199, 201, 206, 217, 222, 227, 234
Berkshire, Earl of, *see* Howard, Thomas
Bertie, Charles, 223–5
Bertie, James, Lord Norreys, 224, 258
Bertie, Robert, Earl of Lindsey, 30, 164, 223–4, 234, 235, 273
Birch, Colonel John, 28, 39, 143, 170, 199, 205
Bishop, Colonel Henry, 73, 167, 168
bishops, 121, 130, 133, 134, 135–6, 138, 142, 151, 175, 176, 203, 204, 205, 206, 220–1, 254–5, 279–82, 288–9
Booth, George, Lord Delamere, 36, 142, 143, 167, 274–6, 279
Booth, Henry, 255, 260, 276
Bower, Richard, 62, 174, 202
Boyle, Richard, Earl of Burlington, 273
Boyle, Roger, Earl of Orrery, 59, 196, 199, 220
Bradshaigh, Sir Roger, 170–1
Breda, Declaration of (1660), 1, 147, 149, 150, 161–2, 163, 165, 175
Brereton, William Lord, 170, 182
Bridgeman, Sir Orlando, 27, 199, 203, 204, 206, 209, 210
Briggs, Augustine, 245, 246
Bristol, Earl of, *see* Digby, George
Brooke House Committee, 198, 200, 201
Browne, Sir Thomas, 245, 247
Buckingham, Duke of, *see* Villiers, George

Buckinghamshire, 59, 60, 88, 90, 100, 258–61, 265, 289–90
Burlington, Earl of, *see* Boyle, Richard
Burnet, Gilbert, 197, 274
Busby, Sir John, 63, 151
Butler, James, Marquis and Duke of Ormond, 22, 39, 56, 59, 164, 174, 185, 195, 196, 197, 200, 204, 206, 222, 275, 278–9
Butler, Thomas, Earl of Ossory, 37

Calthorpe, Sir Christopher, 247, 248
Capel, Arthur, Earl of Essex, 22, 47, 59, 223, 225, 279
Care, Henry, 57, 73, 265
Carleton, Guy, Bishop, 28, 202, 221, 233, 282
Carlisle, Earl of, *see* Howard, Charles
Carr, Sir Robert, 225, 234
Castlemaine, Countess of, *see* Palmer, Barbara
Catelyne, Sir Neville, 229–30, 247, 248
Catherine of Braganza, Queen, 121, 225
Catholics, 82, 90, 115–18, 119, 121, 168, 179, 180, 204, 209, 218, 220, 221, 255, 261, 279, 282
Cavendish, William, Marquis and Duke of Newcastle, 42, 53, 54, 55, 91, 178, 183, 224, 273, 288
Charles I, 2, 20, 21, 22, 24, 77, 105, 114, 119–20, 129
Charles II, 1, 54, 57, 59, 65, 90, 105–6, 114, 229, 246, 249, 250–3
  kingship, 2, 19–23, 37–9
  policies, 2, 19–23, 27–30, 41–8, 79, 82–3, 130, 150–2, 161–8, 170–2, 174–87, 195, 197, 198–202, 203–11, 217–21, 255, 261–2, 277–9, 281–3, 287–8
church courts, 129, 136, 138, 147, 282
Church of England, 104, 126–41, 147–9, 174–81, 198, 200, 210–11, 218–21, 226, 230–1, 254–6, 261–2, 272, 277, 279–82, 288–9
Clarendon, Earl of, *see* Hyde, Edward and Hyde, Henry
Clifford, (Sir) Thomas, Lord Clifford, 27, 37, 46, 121, 201, 208, 217, 223, 225
Clubs, 64, 72–3, 76, 262
Coffee-houses, 60, 62, 64, 72
Coke, Robert, 228, 229, 231
Coleman, Edward, 60, 62–3, 222, 236, 253, 263
College, Stephen, 283, 284
Common Prayer, 126–7, 129, 130–1, 132, 134, 137, 138, 148, 174, 176–8, 181
communion, 127–9, 138–9, 144, 172, 176, 282
Compton, Henry, Bishop of London, 225, 255, 279–80
Compton, James, Earl of Northampton, 224
Compton Census (1676), 133, 221, 231
Conventicle Act (1593), 135, 150, 180, 183, 187, 194, 206, 254, 282
Conventicle Act (1664), 15, 135, 142, 150, 181, 183, 187, 195, 203, 204, 205–6
Conventicle Act (1670), 44, 135, 150, 201–2, 204, 207–8, 229, 282
Conventicle bills, 179–80, 187, 205, 207, 209
Convocation, 136, 176, 181
Corporation Act (1661), 135, 168, 171–4, 181, 286
Cosin, John, bishop of Durham, 92, 134, 136, 186
Covenant, 129, 133, 134, 163, 166, 168, 172, 176, 179, 181, 219, 220, 246
Coventry, Henry, 63, 65, 75, 80, 148, 219, 220, 223, 236, 237, 250
Coventry, Sir William, 104, 105, 122, 139

Danby, Earl of, *see* Osborne, Thomas
Dare, Thomas, 264–5
Davies, Richard, 152, 280, 281
Delamere, Lord, *see* Booth, George
Derby, Earl of *see* Stanley, Charles and Stanley, William
Dering, Sir Edward, 37, 53, 66, 106, 219

Derwentdale Plot (1663), 135, 180
Digby, George, Earl of Bristol, 37, 63, 233
Digby, John Lord, 233, 236
Dissenters, 1, 2,15, 28, 73, 137, 138, 139, 141–52, 171–4, 180–1, 181–7, 195, 198, 199, 201, 202–11, 219–21, 226, 227, 229, 231, 233–4, 249, 254–5, 258, 260, 261, 279, 281–2, 287–8
'Dons', 144, 204, 210 (*see also* Presbyterians [religious])
Dover, Secret Treaty of (1670), 201
Downing, Sir George, 47, 89
'Ducklings', 144, 204 (*see also* Presbyterians [religious])
Duncombe, Sir John, 219, 222, 225

elections, parliamentary, 35–6, 83–93, 172, 227–30, 232–5, 245–8, 255, 257–61, 280, 286, 288–9
Ellis, Sir William (judge), 234, 236, 263
Essex, Earl of, *see* Capel, Arthur
Evelyn, John, 37, 139, 211, 223
exclusion, 117, 250–5, 256–7, 262, 267, 273, 288

Fairfax, Thomas Lord, 91, 197
Fanshawe, Sir Thomas, 167, 171, 184
Fauconberg, Viscount, *see* Bellasis, Thomas
Fifth Monarchists, 183–4
Finch, Daniel, 101, 252, 254, 262, 267
Finch, Heneage, Lord Finch and Earl of Nottingham, 21, 122, 170, 208, 219, 236, 278
Finch, Heneage, Earl of Winchilsea, 37, 38, 50, 235
Finch, Heneage, 289
Five Mile Act (1665), 15, 135, 168, 195, 203, 206, 207, 221, 255, 282
Fleming, Daniel, 36–7, 42, 48, 52, 58, 62, 186, 202, 216, 229
Fox, Sir Stephen, 222, 223, 224

Gazette, London, 28, 54, 57, 61, 65, 261, 262
Gerard, Charles, Earl of Macclesfield, 274, 275, 279, 284
Granville, Denis, 137–8, 288
Granville, John, Earl of Bath, 42, 232
Green Ribbon Club, 73, 76, 260, 273
Grey of Wark, Ford, Lord, 46, 89, 260
Guilford, Lord, *see* North, Francis
Gulston, William, 280, 281, 282

Halifax, Earl and Marquis of, *see* Savile, George
Hampden, Richard, 197, 202, 259
Harley, Edward, 90, 91, 97
Hawley, Francis Lord, 28, 46
Hayward (or Howard), Henry, 100, 265
Henry, Philip, 75, 142, 143, 144, 178, 203
Herbert of Raglan, Lord *see* Somerset, Henry
Heselrig, Sir Arthur, 90, 165
Heywood, Oliver, 142–3, 273, 277
Hildeyard, Dr John, 231, 232, 246, 247, 280
Hobart, John, 232, 246
Hobart, Sir John, 91, 168, 228, 229, 231, 232, 237, 245, 247–9, 259, 262
Holland, Sir John, 36, 92, 168, 228–32, 248, 256, 262, 273
Holles, Denzil Lord, 42, 164, 167, 217, 220
Honourable Artillery Company, 73, 208, 257
Howard, Bernard, 289
Howard, Charles, Earl of Carlisle, 89, 150, 151, 164
Howard, Henry, Earl Marshal and 6th Duke of Norfolk, 35–6, 48, 88, 89, 92, 121, 218, 228, 229, 231, 232, 236, 245, 247, 286
Howard, James, Earl of Suffolk, 45
Howard, Sir Robert, 45, 197, 199, 202, 208, 223, 225
Howard, Thomas, Earl of Berkshire, 44–5, 88
Howe, Sir Scrope, 288, 289
Hughes, Dr Owen, 229, 230, 231, 236, 237
Huntingtower, Lord, *see* Tollemache, Lionel

Hyde, Edward, Earl of Clarendon, 20, 40–1, 42, 44, 45, 63, 99, 100, 101, 103, 136, 164, 166, 167, 174–80, 185, 197–8, 199, 202, 203, 205, 222
Hyde, Henry, 2nd Earl of Clarendon, 88, 258, 260, 280
Hyde, Lawrence, Lord Hyde and Earl of Rochester, 152, 278, 279, 280, 281

Indemnity, Act of (1660), 44, 45, 162–3, 164–7, 168, 176, 182, 183, 187
Independents, 131, 132, 143, 144–5, 146, 186, 210
Indulgence, Declaration of (1672), 74, 142, 143, 147, 150, 204, 209–11, 217, 219, 229, 231
  licences issued under, 144, 150, 210–11, 219, 220, 229
informers, 44, 148, 152, 283
Ireland, 20, 22, 38, 46–7, 59, 132, 196–7, 200, 223
Irish Cattle bill, 196–7, 227

James, Duke of York, James II, 2, 21, 22, 46, 75, 82, 89, 100, 121, 122, 123, 180, 196, 199, 200, 204, 217, 220, 223, 225, 226, 227, 235, 249–51, 253, 256–7, 258, 272, 273, 274, 279, 284, 285, 288–90
Jeffreys, (Sir) George, Lord, 46, 57, 275–6, 278, 279, 288, 289
Jenkins, Sir Leoline, 255, 273, 276, 278, 279, 280, 283, 284, 287
Josselin, Ralph, 136, 139, 143, 250, 255
judges, 11, 12, 13, 15, 16, 23, 26, 45, 56–7, 63, 122, 150, 187, 202–3, 206–7, 210, 216, 221, 224, 225, 235–6, 246, 255, 262, 263, 264, 276, 284–5, 287, 289
juries, 8, 10, 11, 13, 14–16, 23, 26, 63–4, 151, 202–3, 237, 264–5, 283–5
justices of the peace, 7, 10, 11–12, 23, 25, 30, 77, 168, 224, 262, 263, 283

Kelyng, Sir John, 15, 202–3
Kemp, Sir Robert, 228–31, 248, 249, 262
King, Colonel Edward, 165, 198
Kishlansky, Mark, 85–6

Lambert, John, 163, 165, 169
Lamplugh, Thomas, Bishop, 138, 280, 281, 284
Latimer, Lord, *see* Osborne, Edward
Lauderdale, Duke of, *see* Maitland, Thomas
'Laudians', 82, 119, 120, 128–9, 130–1, 133–4, 140, 142, 174–81
law enforcement, 9–16, 24–6, 44–6, 56–7, 64–5, 81–3, 150–2, 182–7, 235–7, 263–5, 278
L'Estrange, Sir Roger, 55, 56, 57–8, 61, 65, 120, 277, 289
Licensing Act (1662), 55, 56, 163, 256, 263
Lindsey, Earl of, *see* Bertie, Robert
Littleton, Sir Thomas, 105, 140, 149, 165, 197, 199, 205
Lloyd, William, Bishop, 136–7, 138
Luttrell, Narcissus, 273, 284

Macclesfield, Earl of, *see* Gerard, Charles
Maitland, Thomas, Duke of Lauderdale, 197, 201, 217, 220, 227
Manchester, Earl of, *see* Montagu, Edward
Marshal, Earl, *see* Howard, Henry
Martindale, Adam, 140, 142, 143, 178
Marvell, Andrew, 38, 56, 60, 101, 104, 116–17, 121–2, 170, 197, 199, 202, 208, 226
Maynard, Sir John, 197, 208
Meade, William, 15, 203
Mews, Peter, bishop of Bath and Wells, 255, 261, 264, 283
militia, 9, 26–30, 81–3, 84, 150, 163, 168, 169–71, 173, 180, 182–6, 208, 224, 229, 232, 235, 237, 247, 250, 252, 264, 274–6, 286
Milward, John, 195, 205
Ministers bills (1660, 1661–2), 176–80
Monk, Christopher, 2nd Duke of Albemarle, 101, 232

Monk, George, Duke of Albemarle, 42, 90, 91, 161, 164, 165, 167, 168, 169, 189, 222, 232
Monmouth, Duke of, *see* Scott, James
Montagu, Edward, Earl of Manchester, 164, 197
Montagu, Edward, Earl of Sandwich, 40, 46, 91, 92, 139, 165, 168, 200, 233
Montagu, Edward, 91, 92
Montagu, Edward, 289
Montagu, Ralph, 42, 60, 250
Morley, George, Bishop of Winchester, 211, 219, 220, 221
Morrice, Sir William, 61, 164, 175, 189, 205
Muddiman, Henry, 57, 58, 61–2
Musgrave, Sir Christopher, 97
Musgrave, Sir Philip, 170, 185, 186, 195, 207

Nedham, Marchamont, 57, 121
Newcastle, Marquis and Duke of, *see* Cavendish William
Newcome, Henry, 140–1, 142, 143
newsletters, 54–5, 61–3, 66
Nicholas, Sir Edward, 14, 61, 164, 168, 169, 175–6, 177, 183, 185
Nonconformists, *see* Dissenters
non-resistance, 115, 255, 272
Norfolk, 29–30, 35–6, 48, 62, 74, 75, 88, 89, 91, 104, 168, 172, 174, 202, 224, 228–32, 236, 237, 245–9, 257–8, 259, 262, 280, 286, 287
Norfolk, Duke of, *see* Howard, Henry
Norreys, Lord, *see* Bertie, James
North, (Sir) Francis, Lord Guilford, 56, 88, 228, 262, 278, 279
Northampton, Earl of, *see* Compton, James
Nottingham, Earl of, *see* Finch, Heneage

O'Neale, Daniel, 59, 168
Ormond, Duke of, *see* Butler, James
Orrery, Earl of, *see* Boyle, Roger
Osborne, Edward, Viscount Latimer, 60, 88, 223, 259
Osborne, Peregrine, Viscount Dunblane, 223, 233
Osborne, (Sir) Thomas, Earl of Danby, 13, 25–6, 38, 46, 60, 100, 106, 121, 198, 217–27, 228–9, 230, 231, 232, 233, 236–7, 246, 247, 249–52, 254, 258, 259
Ossory, Earl of, *see* Butler, Thomas
Owen, John, 141, 144, 145, 204

Pakington, Sir John, 167, 182, 184
Palmer, Barbara, Countess of Castlemaine, 22, 37, 46, 121, 196
parish, 7, 8, 9, 104, 126–31, 135–41
'parish anglicanism', 127, 129, 131, 132, 139–40, 142
Parliament, constitutional role, 19, 99–106
  legislation (*see* also under individual Acts), 14–15, 20
  proceedings in, 1, 14–15, 59–61, 161–70, 196–7, 204–5, 207–8, 218–21, 247, 264
Paston, Rebecca, Lady Paston, Viscountess and Countess of Yarmouth, 38, 231
Paston, (Sir) Robert, Viscount and Earl of Yarmouth, 29, 38, 46, 47, 92, 104, 139, 196, 223, 224, 231, 232, 237, 245–8, 249, 259, 262, 287
Paston, William Lord, 232, 245–6
Pearson, John, bishop of Chester, 280, 281
Pembroke, Dowager Countess of, 88, 89, 185
Penn, William, 15, 141, 145, 152, 203
Pepys, Roger, 103, 166, 179
Pepys, Samuel, 22, 37, 40, 46, 63, 74, 78, 89, 139, 168, 169, 184, 196, 197, 258, 289
petitions, 163, 252, 255, 256–7, 261–3, 264, 285
Peyton, Sir Thomas, 137, 172, 286
Pilkington, Thomas, 284, 285
Plymouth, Earl of, *see* Windsor, Thomas
poor, treatment of the, 7, 12, 13, 19, 20, 24, 25, 102, 104–5, 282
pope burnings, 75–6, 254
Portsmouth, Duchess of, *see* Quérouaille, Louise de

Post Office, 55, 58–9, 61, 167–8
Poulett, Amyas, 1, 2
Powle, Henry, 73, 88
Prayer Book, *see* Common Prayer
prerogative, royal, 111, 161–4, 170, 198–200, 250–3
presbyterianism, 126, 129–30
Presbyterians (political), 89–90, 161, 164–5, 169, 199
Presbyterians (religious), 131, 132–5, 136, 141–4, 174–81, 183, 186, 203–5, 210 (*see also* 'Dons' and 'Ducklings')
Prynne, William, 120, 165, 197
puritans, 126–7, 129–30, 142, 148

Quakers, 53, 56, 91, 120, 131, 132, 142, 144–7, 151–2, 169, 180, 183–7, 202–3, 208, 210, 219, 221, 255, 280, 281, 283
Quakers Act (1662), 135, 192, 206
Quérouaille, Louise de, Duchess of Portsmouth, 22, 37, 38, 121, 222, 223

Radnor, Earl of, *see* Robartes, John
recusancy laws, 117–18, 206, 221, 224, 254–5, 282
Reresby, Sir John, 23, 25–6, 37, 40, 48, 87, 106, 223, 224, 226, 227, 257, 273, 274
resistance, right of, 113, 114, 117, 253, 254, 272
revenue, 24–6, 38, 40, 45–8, 64, 80–1, 102, 105–6, 112, 119, 163–4, 168, 177, 179, 196, 224–5
Reynolds, Edward, bishop of Norwich, 26, 134, 136, 228, 230, 231, 245
Richmond, Duke of, *see* Stuart Charles
riots, 14, 24, 25, 76–83, 120, 283, 287
Robartes, John, Lord Robartes and Earl of Radnor, 164, 199, 200, 280, 281
Russell, William, Lord, 57, 279, 285
Ruvigny, Henri de Massue, marquis de, 121, 200

Sacheverell, William, 232, 235
Sancroft, William, Archbishop of Canterbury, 225, 229, 279, 280
Sandwich, Earl of, *see* Montagu, Edward
Savile, George, Earl and Marquis of Halifax, 21, 120, 234, 249, 278, 280, 281
Savile, Henry, 88, 234
Savoy Conference (1661), 136, 176
scandalum magnatum, 56, 236, 265, 284
Scotland, 20, 120, 129–30, 132, 201, 272
Scott, James, Duke of Monmouth, 46, 73, 82, 89, 121, 256, 258, 261, 273–5, 277, 279, 284
Scroggs, Sir William, 56, 57, 236
Scudamore, John Viscount, 87, 90, 91, 97
Seymour, Edward, 62, 198, 202, 278, 279
Shaftesbury, Earl of, *see* Ashley Cooper, Anthony
Sheldon, Gilbert, Archbishop of Canterbury, 136, 138, 139, 140, 179, 196, 197, 203, 205, 206, 207, 208, 211, 220, 221
sheriff, shrievalty, 8, 14, 15, 23, 29, 40, 57, 79, 224, 228, 232, 236–7, 256, 259, 264–5, 274, 284, 285, 287
Shrewsbury, Earl of, *see* Talbot, Francis
Sidney, Algernon, 285
Smith, Francis, 55, 263
Somerset, Henry, Lord Herbert of Raglan, Marquis of Worcester and Duke of Beaufort, 13, 42, 54, 58, 79, 152, 185–6, 276, 277, 280, 281, 286
Southampton, Earl of, *see* Wriothesley, Thomas
Southwell, Sir Robert, 218, 250, 253
Sparrow, Anthony, Bishop, 138, 206, 209, 210, 231, 232, 245, 246, 247, 255, 281
Spencer, Robert, Earl of Sunderland, 278, 288, 289
Stanley, Charles, Earl of Derby, 166, 167, 170–1, 172, 182
Stanley, William, Earl of Derby, 273, 274–6
Stationers Company, 55–7
Stop of the Exchequer (1672), 41, 218

Strangways, Sir Giles, 219, 222
Street, Alderman, of Chester, 275, 276
Stuart, Charles, Duke of Richmond, 29, 37, 38
Suffolk, Earl of, *see* Howard, James
Sunderland, Earl of, *see* Spencer, Robert

Talbot, Francis, Earl of Shrewsbury, 259
Taunton, 73, 75, 76, 100, 151, 171, 185, 283
taxation, *see* revenue
Taylor, Simon, 228, 229
Temple, Sir Richard, 88, 197, 198, 199, 200, 202, 208, 252, 259, 260, 261, 265
Temple, Sir William, 22, 226
tithes, 130, 177, 178
Toleration Act (1689), 146, 254
Tollemache, Lionel, Lord Huntingtower, 227–8, 232
towns, charters, 7, 171–2, 284, 286–8
  government and politics, 7–8, 64, 73–6, 80–1, 151–2, 171, 173–4, 184–6, 282–3, 285–8
  (*see also* Corporation Act)
Townshend, Horatio, Lord, 47, 91, 151, 172, 193–4, 202, 228–32, 236, 237, 245, 247, 248
treasury commission, 41, 46
Trenchard, John, 73, 100
Trevor, Sir John, secretary of state, 199, 206, 208
Trevor, Sir John, 252
Triple Alliance (1668), 200, 259

Uniformity, Act of (1559), 131
Uniformity, Act of (1662), 132–5, 136, 148, 149, 168, 173, 174–81, 219

Vane, Sir Henry, 165, 167
Vaughan, Sir John, 15, 203, 206
Venner's rising (1661), 165, 183, 186
Verney, Edmund, 14, 24, 27, 53, 224, 237, 258, 261, 273
Verney, John, 14, 53, 273
Verney, Sir Ralph, 13, 14, 53, 60, 63, 64, 66, 139, 151, 199, 237, 258, 260, 265, 285
Villiers, George, Duke of Buckingham, 13, 39, 63, 89, 196–201, 205, 206, 209, 217, 221, 222, 254, 259, 260, 265, 279
volunteers, 28, 169–71, 182, 184, 186, 189

Ward, Seth, Bishop, 138, 151, 184, 203, 220, 221, 232
Wharton, Philip, Lord, 144, 233, 259, 273
Wharton, Thomas, 289
Wheeler, Sir Charles, 197, 221
Whitelocke, Bulstrode, 44, 90, 141–2, 181, 285
Whitley, Colonel Roger, 275, 284–5
Wildman, John, 73, 198, 259, 284
Wilkins, John, Bishop, 204, 205
William III, Prince of Orange, 75, 218
Williams, William, 274, 276
Williamson, George, 47
Williamson, Sir Joseph, 21, 37, 39–40, 47, 57, 61–2, 89, 147, 202, 204, 209, 220, 221, 223, 233
Winchilsea, Earl of, *see* Finch, Heneage
Windham, William, 246, 247, 249, 256
Windsor, Thomas, Earl of Plymouth, 42, 289
Wiseman, Sir Richard, 218, 224
Worcester, Marquis of, *see* Somerset, Henry
Worcester House Declaration (1660), 175–6, 204
Wriothesley, Thomas, Earl of Southampton, 20, 37, 45, 50, 164, 167, 197

Yarmouth, Viscount and Earl of, *see* Paston, Robert
York, Duke of, *see* James